Civil Society and Fanaticism

Mestizo Spaces

Espaces Métissés

V. Y. Mudimbe
EDITOR

Bogumil Jewsiewicki
ASSOCIATE EDITOR

Civil Society and Fanaticism

Conjoined Histories

Dominique Colas

Translated from the French by Amy Jacobs

STANFORD UNIVERSITY PRESS

STANFORD, CALIFORNIA 1997

Stanford University Press
Stanford, California
© 1997 by the Board of Trustees of the
Leland Stanford Junior University
Printed in the United States of America

Assistance for the translation was provided by the
French Ministry of Culture.

Civil Society and Fanaticism: Conjoined Histories
was originally published in French as *Le Glaive et
le fléau: Généalogie du fanatisme et de la société
civile*, © 1992 Editions Grasset & Fasquelle.

CIP data appear at the end of the book

Acknowledgments

While researching and writing this book, I received valuable suggestions and encouragement from numerous friends and colleagues, especially Emmanuel Le Roy Ladurie, Jean-Philippe Genet, Jacques-Alain Miller, Judith Miller, Pierre Pellegrin, Evelyne Pisier, François George, Blandine Kriegel, Jean Piel, Ernest Gellner, and Michel Foucault. I would also like to thank the professors and students at the institutions where, in courses and seminars in the late 1980's, I had the opportunity to present my research at various stages: the Université de Paris-Dauphine, the Université de Paris Panthéon-Sorbonne, the Ecole des Hautes Etudes en Sciences sociales, and the Institut d'Etudes politiques de Paris. Thanks go as well to my editor at Grasset, Denis Bourgeois.

I first put forward certain of the book's hypotheses in a seminar at the Ecole des Hautes Etudes organized and taught with Jean-Loup Amselle and François Pouillon in 1988–89. It was in this context that I met my colleagues Valentin Y. Mudimbe and Bogumil Jewsiewicki, with whom I have had the pleasure of working on several occasions since. It is thanks to them that the American edition was made possible.

Both text and bibliography needed to be adapted for this edition—close work admirably done by my translator, Amy Jacobs. Her competence and vigilance, while producing an English text faithful to the original, have also enabled me to make a number of improvements, all toward greater clarity.

Contents

Illustrations

Preface to the English Edition

Civil society is a term widely used these days, by politicians and journalists as well as sociologists and specialists of political theory. But the notion–or rather notions–of civil society is hardly recent, and the expression has received rich and complex meanings that have varied with the political-philosophical systems of which it has been a part. In this book I seek, among other things, to elucidate those meanings and to show how they elucidate each other. I demonstrate namely that "civil society" and "fanaticism" have mutually defined each other since the beginning of the sixteenth century, the time of both Renaissance humanism and the Protestant Reformation; that if we want to understand civil society and fanaticism it is necessary to understand the relation between them; and that this relation sheds light on major political questions. My approach has been to reconstruct the long cycles in the history of political thought systems articulated around changes in the meaning of "civil society." Such a study, both genealogical and structural, of the denotations and connotations of "civil society" seems to me indispensable if we are to understand the widespread, even inflationist use of the term today, its relevance for Pope John Paul II as well as for ideological heirs to Hegel and Marx, and its presence in such varied texts as anthropologists' writings, journalism about the former Soviet Union, and political speeches, to give only a few examples.

It is to better understand present uses of "civil society" that the book goes far back in time–back to the Middle Ages and, because that period obliges us to think about the relations between church and state, back even further, to Augustine and Aristotle. While many recent works on civil society have either adopted or taken as their object of study the meanings and implications of the term that have come down to us from the eighteenth century or from the Hegelian-Marxist tradition–see for example Cohen and Arato's *Civil Society and Political Theory*, Charles Taylor's article "Invoking Civil Society," in his *Philosophical Arguments*, and the slightly older anthology of articles, *Civil Society and the State*, edited by John Keane–in this book, I've tried to go back to the beginning.

My research demonstrates that the opposition civil society/fanaticism is a philosopheme that has been widely accepted ever since the sixteenth century (see Appendix A) and brings to light a particular and constant feature of all definitions of fanaticism: its rejection of representation. The most elemental form of such rejection is iconoclasm in the literal sense of the word, the hatred and destruction of icons and images; and above and beyond my interest in the dualist oppositions that have defined civil society–family/civil society, civil society/City of God, state of nature/civil society, civil society/state–in Western political thought, this work is meant as a critique of critiques of representation, that is, figurative mediation and the mediating, "stand-in" role fulfilled by political institutions. Globally, consistently, if not always directly, my concern has been to call into question systems that in the name of the represented, seek to abolish the representative. In political terms, there will be no positive transformation of the former Soviet system until the people most directly concerned conceive of representative democracy as valid and effective (it was, moreover, the analysis by certain antitotalitarian thinkers of the old system in crisis which brought "civil society" into vogue in the 1970's and 1980's). Meanwhile, the values of representative democracy are being contested with increased vigor by fundamentalist religious groups within the Muslim world, groups qualified by their opponents as fanatics. The book is thus the culmination of what began as two distinct investigations in which I worked to reconstitute the lexical and conceptual histories of "civil society" on the one hand and "fanaticism" on the other so as to situate them in their historical and intellectual contexts in order better to delimit their meaning, in an undertaking which more closely resembles the analysis of thought systems developed by Michel Foucault than Jacques Derrida's deconstruction. But the two studies turned out to bear on the same object–the Western definition of the political–while leading me to reflect on representation in politics and painting.

One of the things that first motivated my research into the notion of civil society was my dissatisfaction with what seemed the imprecise dating of the first use of the term in French. Certain French authors somewhat naively referred to the indication given in Emile Littré's *Dictionnaire de la langue française*, a nineteenth-century lexicographical monument which cites as a first user of *société civile* Jacques Bénigne Bossuet, sermonist to the court of Louis XIV. Though renowned for his oratorical genius, Bossuet was neither a forger of concepts or a coiner of expressions, so the attribution as well as the date seemed dubious. I have been able to establish that *société civile* was first used not in the middle of the classical seventeenth century but a full century earlier, in 1546, in a French translation of a theological text by the great German humanist and Protestant Reformer, Philipp Melanchthon.

My research was also spurred by dissatisfaction with interpretations of Marx's political theory, interpretations which seemed to go hand in hand with, if not to be based on, unfounded French and English translations of his texts.[1] More exactly, it was clear to me that the notions of "civil society" and "bourgeois society" had been taken as interchangeable and needed to be distinguished from each other. Marx's theory of the state and civil society, though quite complex, obeys the same logic as his other analytic concepts: their validity is universal, but their emergence is historically determined. The starting point for Marx's whole analytical undertaking was his 1843 critique–today we may be tempted to say deconstruction–of Hegel's theory of "civil society," and he remained consistent on this point throughout his work.[2] Marx redefined civil society in opposition to Hegel, but the differences between Hegel and his predecessors are likewise highly significant– Hegel distinguished civil society from the state, whereas for Rousseau and Hobbes before him civil society was opposed to the state of nature–and following the conceptual contrasts backward through time I arrived at what I have, with others, taken for the first term: Aristotle's *koinonia politikè*.[3]

The hypothesis guiding my research was that *société civile*–and the same goes for "civil society"–was the vernacular translation of the Latin *societas civilis*, and that this was itself a translation of *koinonia politikè*. Through a systematic reading of Latin, French, Italian, English, and German translations of Aristotle's *Politics* and *Nicomachean Ethics* (see Appendix B), I discovered that *societas civilis* had indeed been used to translate the Greek, and this as early as the first quarter of the fifteenth century. Although the Latin term had been used in a commentary on Aristotle by the medieval theologian Giles of Rome, the decisive lexical choice was made by the great Florentine humanist Leonardo Bruni, a figure well known to historians of civic humanism and the republican tradition such as Hans Baron, Eugenio Garin, and J. G. A. Pocock,[4] though these authors had not picked up on this point, probably because when they were writing, the term "civil society" was not as widely used as it has been since the 1970's. Bruni's translations of Aristotle made their way from Florence into Northern Europe in the same vast movement of European cultural creation by which aesthetic models passed from Italy into Germany.[5] And it was Bruni's Latin translation of Aristotle's *Politics* (together with the original Greek) that was used by Melanchthon, close friend and fellow combatant of Martin Luther, as the basis for a Latin commentary on that text in the course of which Melanchthon made *societas civilis* his own. From there by way of translation, and at a moment when printing was revolutionizing the circulation of signifiers, the term passed into the vernacular languages.

But whereas Aristotle had defined civil society within a pagan civilization, Melanchthon was positioned at the heart of Christianity in a period of tremendous religious and political upheaval and conceptual and institutional restructuring. His definition of civil society, which he understood by opposition to the City of God, was at the same time a definition of fanaticism. In a text written in 1530 as an attack on the Anabaptists, among others, Melanchthon explained that fanatical men are those who do not accept the legitimacy of the "interval" between the City of God and civil society. The "fanatics" he was referring to were also in many cases iconoclasts, and as such they had already been reprehended by Luther and certain of his followers, among whom was another of Luther's remarkable friends, Albrecht Dürer.

It was from my thinking about one of Dürer's works that the French

title of the book emerged: *Le Glaive et le fléau,* "sword and flail."
Chapter 4, which forms the center of the book, proposes an analysis of
Dürer's painting *The Adoration of the Trinity,* in which we see side by
side a nobleman in armor with a sword at his hip and a peasant carrying
a wheat flail, symbols of power and labor, sovereignty and economy,
might and submission. Some years after painting this work–whose
composition I argue both exhibits and resolves, through representation, the political problems that would later shake the Reformation–
Dürer wrote and published a defense of the legitimacy of painting
which implied a vision of civil society that, like Luther's, was hostile
to the iconoclasts smashing paintings and sculptures in Catholic
churches in a hatred of representation that was also aimed at the political powers in place. Iconoclasm was a first effect of the Reformation;
the religious protest soon grew to include radical social protest. The
Peasants' War (1525), led by the rebel prophet Thomas Müntzer, the
insurgents armed only with apocalyptic discourse and the implements
of agricultural labor, was the flail's revolt–to be brutally crushed by
the sword. With the unconditional approval of many of those who had
propelled the anti-Catholic split (whom by analogy, if anachronistically, we might call moderates as opposed to radicals), civil society, the
political power, the state–synonymous terms at the time–rose up in
violent sovereignty to annihilate those who, in a fever of millenarian
hope, sought to smash it. The insurgent peasants were ready to sacrifice their lives to abolish the Earthly City, convinced that by so doing
they would ensure the advent of the kingdom of God on earth. This
dream–and because it was during this same period that Thomas More
wrote his celebrated work, let us call it a utopian dream–Luther denounced as the phantasm of dangerous madmen, "false prophets,"
"fanatics."

Nothing in Luther's denunciation of fanaticism protected him from
the same madness, the same systematic hatred, a hatred directed at
individuals or groups who are then treated as profaners who must be
purged or destroyed. Such was Luther's hatred of Jews as expressed in
certain late texts, texts written after the period studied here. With the
same vehemence he used to call for the destruction of the Catholic
Church in 1520 and to legitimate the bloody repression of the peasants
in 1525, Luther would, in 1543, appeal to German Christians to set
Jewish synagogues and schools on fire as houses of lies, "so that no

man will ever again see a stone or cinder of them." To do so would be proof that "we are Christians in the eyes of God."[6]

In 1850, a little more than three hundred years after the Peasant War in Germany and in a text bearing precisely that title, Friedrich Engels reversed the judgment in favor of political authority defended by Luther and his followers: he lauded the "fanatics" of 1525 as ancestors of the modern communist proletariat, which, with the Revolution of 1848, had just affirmed itself, in France, at least, as the iconoclast of the bourgeois state. Meanwhile the repression of insurrectionary workers in Paris in June 1848 by a French power based on a national parliamentary assembly definitively convinced Marx of the well-foundedness of his critique of the representative state. More generally, we may say that Marxist political theory developed as a radical rejection of political representation and a championing of fanaticism, where the end of capitalism figures as a joyous Apocalypse that will witness the famous "withering of the state" and the triumph of "civil society," classless, like a New Jerusalem.

While from Luther to Marx we may trace a long cycle in the history of Western thought systems which, in its Leninist prolongation, includes the imposition of a new, terroristic type of political regime in Russia, the political theory of the Reformers, Calvin as well as Luther, must itself be situated in another, even longer cycle. Luther's refusal to allow his desire to destroy the authority of the Catholic Church to bring about the destruction of *political* authority represents a specific moment in Christian political tradition, a moment to be understood in terms of the paradoxical-seeming medieval synthesis of Augustine and Aristotle, *The City of God* and *The Politics*. How these two traditions fit together—the one affirming the ontological and theological superiority of the City of God, the mystical and mysterious heavenly Jerusalem, the other the validity of civil society, a formula equivalent to the polis or state—was consistently an issue in medieval debates: in the conflict between the French king Philip the Fair and Pope Boniface VIII at the very beginning of the fourteenth century, for example. The life and works of Giles of Rome, who was both close counselor to Boniface VIII and familiar at the court of Philip the Fair, illustrate the complexity of medieval political theology. One seminal formulation of the church-versus-civil society dispute was the metaphor of the two swords, spiritual and temporal. Did the Church have a right to wield the temporal sword? Could the state–civil society–free itself of the spiritual sword's control? Subordination or separation–a whole range of institutional positions, from Caesaro-papism to the affirmation of the secular state, was opened up by the fundamental dualism of the authorities that defined and structured Western public and private space. If it is true that in the twentieth century the dispute between the two swords has taken forms quite different from those of Late Antiquity and the Middle Ages–the Catholic Church's intervention in the organization of education systems in Europe, for example, or the battle led by religious extremists in the United States and now Europe against the right to abortion–that dispute is by no means over. We need only think of how at certain moments–the 1995 International Women's Conference in Beijing, for example–the Vatican accepts being associated with religious fundamentalism of the sort the Iranian state applies in its citizens' lives.

This of course does not mean that in modern societies where Catholicism is the dominant religion, women's civic status and political rights are not recognized (though there are, for example, striking differences between women's rights in France and Ireland). Worldwide– and recognizing that this is greatly simplifying matters–we may distinguish two types of sociopolitical regime: those in which women are considered citizens endowed with the same rights as men, others where the access to the public sphere is either forbidden to women or strictly limited. In certain societies, as we know, women are defined by, shut away in, their family roles–daughter, sister, mother. To use Kant's terms, they cannot pass from the status of minor into their majority; they cannot enter civil society. Though this book does not directly discuss women's status in civil society, it provides certain elements for understanding how women were able to acquire political rights. The complexity that women's status assumes from the moment society is no longer simply a grouping based on kinship but is defined by *political* ties may be illustrated, for example, by Aristotle's political theory. For Aristotle, women were not necessarily excluded from citizenship, membership in the *politeia*–but by "citizenship" Aristotle meant something closer to what we call nationality. As we know, Athenian women did not possess civil rights; they could neither vote, nor serve as magistrates, nor perform any other public function. It was as if the consequence of their exclusion from military duty was political incapacity. But this did not mean that the female "citizen" was situated outside civil society. Aristotle explains that, though the relations man/woman in marriage, parent/child within the family, and master/slave in the household are all irreversible relations of inequality, adult Athenian women have quite a different status than slaves, male or female, children, or foreigners. What defined Athenian female citizenship was that the children born of an Athenian woman's marriage to a male citizen were also citizens; in this sense the Greek conception of citizenship may be considered more biological than political. The Athenian woman's political status was founded in her woman's body: barred from making war because this would endanger the reproduction of the polis, she could not have the same political rights as free men (who acquired their full rights by performing military service).[7] But as a potential mother of Athenian citizens, she enjoyed legal guarantees and protection denied any slave, child, or foreigner.[8]

And it is possible to detect in the Athenian example certain of the principles that have opened the way for women's acquiring full political rights. What for the Athenians represented the highest value was not, finally, the woman's body as mother of citizens or the man's body as soldier. Supreme legitimacy resided in the laws of the polis, the constitution (*politeia*). As soon as civil society is defined as a juridical-political sphere–Aristotle was among the first to define the law-governed state–political participation can be based on simple membership in a given society, and instead of women's citizenship referring to nationality, nationality becomes the necessary and sufficient condition for citizenship, as in contemporary democracies, where the fact that men and women are endowed with equal political rights makes any discrimination against women all the more apparent and at the same time furnishes means of combating such discrimination. Often, religious arguments are given to legitimate discrimination against women, their political marginalization or exclusion from certain activities or professions. It is often in the name of divine law, the divinely decreed order of things, that women's freedom of choice is attacked. This is a case of invoking the imperatives of the City of God to criticize, reject, or undermine the Earthly City. The refusal on religious grounds to accept the application of laws permitting abortion is fanaticism, iconoclasm directed against the law-governed state, whose legitimacy is thereby flouted and denied.

But the will of certain intolerant religious groups to impose a biblical order on the Earthly City runs up against the specificity of Western societies: they are indeed heirs to the Christian biblical tradition, but where the Bible may be *the* book, it has not been the only book. The Christian opposition between Heaven and Earth, City of God and Earthly City, was, as I have suggested, profoundly influenced, penetrated, by Greek and Roman civic tradition as constituted in the texts of Aristotle, the Stoics, and Cicero, a tradition according to which civil society is the place of justice. In fact, civil society was accorded positive, if only relative, value and a certain legitimacy in the Christian scheme of things. The distinction between the theological and political spheres has played a structuring role in the history of Western thought systems, while providing a kind of backdrop to all Western political institutions and issues. While theocracy may be a constant threat and temptation, it is one thwarted in the West by the fundamental duality between church and state. And it is this duality which allowed for the emergence of theories of tolerance, the quality which for Spinoza, Leibniz, and Locke in the seventeenth and early eighteenth centuries was the essential, defining virtue of civil society.

The dualism church/state is of course not the only opposition relevant to an understanding of the status of civil society in the West. Starting in the eighteenth century with the English political economists, theories of a new dualism were developed, that between civil society and the state. The development of political economy accompanied the great material transformation we know as the industrial revolution, and while the spectacular success of this type of economy explains its universal valorization, exporting the dualist *political* model historically tied to it has proved more difficult.

This tension is one of the factors explaining why, at the end of the twentieth century, "civil society" and "fanaticism" are enjoying such widespread use. "Fanaticism" is often used to describe and disqualify different forms of religious fundamentalism which have in common their refusal to accept duality between state and religious order. And while in the case of Khomeini's Iran or the Algerian Armed Islamic Group (the terrorist branch of the Islamic Salvation Front, whose actions have included murdering Algerian journalists and slitting the throats of adolescent girls who had gone to school unveiled) the accusation of fanaticism seems well founded, it is also true that in the

West an *essential* rather than accidental "fanaticism" is regularly imputed to the Arab-Muslim world taken abusively as a totality–as if the emergence of civil society were necessarily precluded in a culture where an autonomous public sphere seems an alien idea.

As for civil society, because it is a concept at the heart of the great philosophical systems, we find it as a signifier in Derrida's texts on political theory, especially Hegel's,[9] and in the writings of several French theorists of the modern state, Michel Foucault, for example, who used the term, though rarely, in *Surveiller et punir*,[10] and Jean-François Lyotard, who takes it from both Marx and Kant,[11] or Jean Baudrillard, who used it in his French translations of Marx and uses it regularly now in his essays on contemporary society. Civil society has become an analytic concept at the heart of investigations into the modern political world[12] and the great transformation represented by the collapse of the communist system, as for example in one of the late Ernest Gellner's last books, *Conditions of Liberty: Civil Society and Its Rivals*, in which he devotes a chapter to the conception of civil society proposed by the eighteenth-century Scottish political economist Adam Ferguson, whose *Essay on the History of Civil Society* (1767) stands as a bridge between the political, Aristotelian meaning of the term and the essentially economic meaning being affirmed in Ferguson's time by the development of industry and the market.[13]

If, however, I was particularly struck by the conjoined definitions of civil society and fanaticism at the time of the Protestant Reformation, this was because I was interested at the same time in the accusation of fanaticism directed at the end of the seventeenth century against a group of insurgent Protestants in the south of France, the Camisards of the Cévennes, a few years after Louis XIV revoked the nearly century-old Edict of Nantes, which had formalized tolerance of Protestants. The Camisards conducted a small but fierce guerrilla war, in which they were inspired and guided by their own, sudden capacity to prophesy. It was this collective madness that was qualified at the time as fanaticism–or hysteria, the latter term being taken up by present-day historians such as Emmanuel Le Roy Ladurie. My research on the Camisards had in turn been motivated by my study of Lenin's use–rare but consistent–of the term "hysteria." The Bolshevik leader stigmatized as "hysterics" those political adversaries who favored "words" over "force." In this he was appropriating the cliché–which Freud

would radically criticize–according to which hysterics, who vocifer-
ated, were simulators, malingerers, liars (as opposed to truly sick persons, epileptics, for example, who suffered from organic afflictions),
transposing it into the political domain, which he defined as the science of power relations, relations of force. Lenin's hatred of hysteria
went hand in hand with his hatred of political representation.

Collecting materials on the Camisards, I noticed that numerous
contemporary texts–administrative reports, pamphlets written by
Catholics, passages in memoirs written by the rebels themselves on
how they were treated–designated them as "fanatics," and, less frequently, "hysterics." This equivalence between fanaticism and hysteria
oriented my research into discourses denouncing fanaticism. Here I
encountered issues widely discussed in theorizing about the genesis of
psychoanalysis and its categories and the passage from theological
to medical discourse–a passage illustrated by the equating of "false
prophet" with "fanatic," for by the end of the seventeenth century
"fanatic" was being used as a psychiatric type classification. I was
unaware until the 1995 publication of *Dits et écrits*, the complete collection of his articles in four volumes, that in 1969 Michel Foucault had
been reading some of the seventeenth-century texts I refer to in this
book and that his conclusions anticipated mine in a particular area, the
relations between theological and psychiatric discourses.[14] There is
nothing surprising in this convergence, because I, like many others,
am greatly indebted to Michel Foucault and his *Histoire de la folie à
l'âge classique* for my interest in and understanding of psychiatric discourse. It is, moreover, possible that Foucault's interest in "fanatics"
was in part due to his French translation of Kant's *Anthropology from
a Pragmatic Point of View* (and the thesis, unfortunately never published, he devoted to that text), in which the German philosopher
developed a theory of "fanaticism" (*Schwärmerei*) as opposed to "enthusiasm." But Michel Foucault played a more direct role in the writing of this book when, after reading my article on Lenin's use of "hysteria," he encouraged me to pursue my research on the subject.

I was completing the French edition of this work just as the communist system in the U.S.S.R. imploded, between August and December
of 1991.[15] The collapse has often been presented as civil society's revenge on the party-state; but very quickly the economic, social, cultural, and political situation in Russia and other states comprising the

former Soviet Union led specialists to underline the fact that the decades of communist rule had involved something quite different than the building of a superstructure. In fact, Soviet communism was enjoying a kind of posthumous victory, for it had not been built above or outside civil society but had itself constructed a particular type of society, one deliberately antagonistic to the type founded on the existence of an economic sphere regulated by right and law. The metaphor according to which one had only to clear away the ruins of communism in order for civil society to reappear was rooted in an illusion. Those few groups who had combated communism in Russia, groups whose emblematic figure was Andrei Sakharov, were not, to use another metaphor, the visible summit of a dynamic, organized, and thriving society but rather constituted all by themselves what there was of civil society in Russia. The difficulty, among many others, which the country is having creating a legal system, implying as it does legal codes and their enforcement, lawyers, courts–more importantly a shared belief in the juridical order–is proof that the Leninist vision of law as a mere instrument of political power can never be without profound effects. Ten years after Gorbachev took over the position of general secretary of the Communist Party, trial by jury, for which provisions were made in the 1993 constitution, remains an exception in Russia, which is only slowly and chaotically moving to create a law-governed state. As I argue at the end of the book, one cannot speak of civil society where there is no such state, at least not if one situates oneself in that Hegelian tradition–toppled by Marx–according to which civil society cannot exist without legal regulation, not only because it would not be civil or civic, but also because without the rule of law there can be no political economy. While the tendency in the 1980's was to underline the effectiveness with which civil society was battling the party-state, particularly in Poland through Solidarnosc,[16] in the late 1990's we respond with anxiety and perhaps astonishment to the evident weakness of civil societies in countries undergoing post-totalitarian transitions.[17] What we seem to be witnessing is the rebirth of a kind of Hobbesian "state of nature," a "war of all against all," in the form of *sauvage* (unregulated) economic competition, and, more tragically still, in a form that evokes the civil wars of religion which Hobbes thought might be eradicated by combining the political sovereign and the religious authority into one–as nationalist war.

It is indeed the dramatic upsurge in ethnic nationalism in Eastern Europe and the states of the former Soviet Union, not the 1995 electoral successes of the neocommunists in Poland and Russia, which seems a continuation of totalitarianism by other means. Ethnic nationalism as fanatic desire to be purified of bad elements, culminating in the creation of a community welded together by the emotions of hatred of the other and guilt for crimes committed in common.[18] And it is remarkable that even in those formerly communist societies where transformations favoring political pluralism and institutionally guaranteed economic competition are the most advanced, citizenship seems to be a privilege based on belonging to a particular ethnic community, a privilege from which any others are excluded–one example being the case of the gypsies in the Czech Republic. Meanwhile, throughout the European Union of fifteen industrial and democratic countries, a kind of intolerance of otherness is developing, a defense of French, German, simply European "identity," which finds its alibi in the idea that only well-guarded borders can effectively protect the internal labor market.

It is obvious that the end of the communist regimes in Eastern Europe and Russia, which as we know is not the end of the communists, is likewise not the end of history. The absence of a civil society and a law-governed state–the two are in fact a single concrete reality, which constitutes democracy–leaves open a multitude of possibilities, and presents a fundamental impasse: there where the need for democracy is the keenest, it is the hardest to bring into being and to keep alive. The problem is not restricted to the former Soviet zone but concerns either directly or indirectly the entire world political system. As we know only too well, the end of communism alone in no way implies the end of violence between states or, to use Augustine's expression, the decline of the *libido dominandi*.

What reduces force, what restricts the use of violence is not the deployment of a counterforce but rather the capacity to bring to the fore modes of societal regulation based on the recognition of *symbolic efficacy* and the validity of political *representation*: law and elections.

The state has recently become the object of "postmodern" mistrust because of the place it occupies in the Big Narratives, the eschatological philosophy or science of history–a mistrust which in turn valorizes civil society. But in France at least there are other logics than postmodernism, other ideological currents which have worked, deliberately or not, to disseminate the notion of civil society, a dissemination itself made possible by the polysemy of the signifier, the accumulation of signifieds. The term was used as a weapon in the denunciation of the state as oppression long before postmodernism came into vogue, and in the various French apologies of civil society in the 1970's and 1980's we can find everything from a paean to *l'autogestion* (self-management, a society–not the state–which will take charge of its own purposes and projects) to a championing of the freest of free markets. Any number of thinkers and politicians might be cited, but I would like to focus for a moment on a particular issue of *Les Temps modernes*,[19] the review published by Jean-Paul Sartre and Simone de Beauvoir, because it clarifies one of the most influential theoretical bases for rejection of the representative state and highlights, by way of contrast, my own position.

The issue in question came out in January 1973, shortly before the French legislative elections of that year, the first since General de Gaulle resigned as President of the Republic in 1969, the first since 1968, when a majority very much to the right had been elected in reaction to the celebrated events of May. One of the articles in the review is titled "Institutions, appareils d'Etat et société civile dans la bataille électorale" (Institutions, state apparatuses, and civil society in the electoral battle). The author, André Grannou, while admitting the difficulty of defining civil society and referring the reader to Antonio Gramsci's use of the term, underlines how difficult it is for the French government to apply *any* policy given the complexity and unpredictability of "la société civile," how difficult for the state to resolve the crisis it finds itself in, which May 1968 had fully exposed. This text is framed, as it were, by an article by Sartre and another by Pierre Bourdieu which can be brought together regardless of significant differences in the political theories of their respective authors. Sartre, then very close to the Maoist extreme left, which at that time was at its apogee in France, titled his article "Elections pièges à cons" ("Elections: A Trap for Fools").[20] His argument is that elections are a "serial" mechanism in which individuals, separated from each other, no longer exist as specific beings but are treated and treat one another as merely identical equivalents. In an election there is neither man or woman, worker or boss, but a citizen–abstract and empty: indirect democracy is a mystification. Sartre thus returns to Marx's thesis, formulated most vehemently in *On The Jewish Question* (1843), denouncing the deceptiveness of the Rights of Man: they swept aside "real man." Without referring explicitly to Marx any more than Sartre does, Pierre Bourdieu in "L'Opinion publique n'existe pas" ("Public Opinion Does Not Exist") seeks to expose the mechanisms by which existing power relations are masked, denied, legitimated. In so doing he is in complete agreement with Sartre's critique of universal suffrage. Opinion polls, he explains, are artifacts that create public opinion by imposing one and the same questionnaire (something quite different from a scientifically constructed problem) on distinct individuals who in many cases have never asked themselves the questions they are being called upon to answer. We may therefore reproach the opinion poll with being, like universal suffrage, a universalizing process of abstraction that metamorphoses ethical questions into political ones, fabricating a reality that doesn't exist and which in turn legitimates the existing order, for is not what characterizes power relations the fact that they dissimulate themselves and is not this dissimulation precisely what gives them their "power" in the first place?[21] Some years earlier, in *Sociologie de l'Algérie*, Bourdieu had praised "lived democracy" among the Kabyles of North Africa and contrasted their society to ours, where people talk too much. In sum, Bourdieu's argument is analogous to Sartre's: authenticity is soiled by representation; mediation is a threat to truth.

In the slow elaboration of this book, one moment was particularly important: the academic year 1975–76, when I gave a course titled "Histoire et psychanalyse" in the department of psychoanalysis at the Université de Vincennes. I was working at the same time as a psychologist-in-training at the psychiatric hospital of Charenton, outside Paris, and had enrolled in training at the psychoanalytic clinic organized under the direction of Jacques Lacan. In preparing for my courses and in the clinical experience I was acquiring, in my interviews with patients and the thinking stimulated by Lacan's work, I was confronted with the experience of paranoia, which sheds much light on the workings of fanaticism. But the effect of Lacan's psychoanalytic understanding on the writing of this book is more thoroughgoing than may perhaps appear. His reconstruction of the Freudian theory of the unconscious in terms of the now celebrated three categories, the Imag-

inary, the Real, and the Symbolic, was crucial in enabling me to distance myself from doctrines, the prototype of which is Marx's conception of ideology, that affirm that the sphere of representation can only
be understood as the reflection or effect of a sphere of the "real"
assumed external to it; the idea that ideology can only mask or "legitimate," to borrow Max Weber's word, but changes nothing, neither
interest or power relations. Far from conceptualizing the symbolic as
an eclipsing of the real, the locus of a misrecognition which stabilizes
domination by obscuring it (the position of certain members of Bourdieu's school), Lacan's theories, following those of Lévi-Strauss and
Marcel Mauss,[22] posit the specific, inherent efficacy of the symbolic.
The symbolic possesses its own causal power–an idea nicely embodied
in the double meaning of the French verb *causer*: provoke an effect,
and talk, use symbolic signifiers. If "symbolic violence" has relevance,
it is not in Bourdieu's sense as a cultural legitimation of domination
which comes to reinforce "objective," "real" power relations, but
rather as a *failure of symbolization*, such as that which brings on a
proliferation of images in hallucination or opens the way to violent
"acting out." More generally, through its consideration of the connection between fanaticism and iconoclasm–either as "acting out" or a
refusal "on principle" to accept representation–this book invites its
reader to question the presuppositions of doctrines which conceive of
the political in terms of the opposition represented/representation
and representation as a distancing, forgetting, or masking of presence.
The politics of presence, the quest for authenticity in the form of an
immediate encounter with the real as truth, has taken quite varying
forms, but they all have in common a critique of political institutions
based on delegation, spokespersons, mandate-holders, representatives. The iconoclastic will to denounce political representation as imposture can no more found a politics than realism in painting can
found an aesthetics.[23] It can only give way to the same dangerous
disgust with the political that seizes the fanatic each time he thinks it
possible to bring forth, without delay, the kingdom of God on earth.

Civil Society and Fanaticism

Introduction

The Fanatic's Truth

A fanatic would burn this book, for although fanatics can love a book containing the words of their God, they hate images of God and those who love them. The fanatic wants to purify the world of idolatry, that intolerable obstacle to love for the pure and immediate divine presence. And it is from God that the fanatic claims to receive orders, inspiration, and the energy to destroy those who worship foreign deities or painted images.

Figure 1 shows an engraving of the Last Judgment done by an anonymous German artist at the end of the fifteenth century. Early on in the Reformation Martin Luther described and commented upon just such an image:

> Artists portray Christ seated on a rainbow, with a sword and twig proceeding out of his mouth, a conception based on Isaiah 11[:4], where he says, "He shall smite the earth with the rod of his mouth, and with the breath of his lips he shall slay the wicked." But the artists depict a twig in blossom; that is not right. It should be a rod or staff, and both rod and sword should be on the same side, extending only over the damned. Psalm 10[:15] says, "Break thou the arm of the ungodly; seek out his wickedness, and his godlessness will not remain."

Luther goes on to explain that this is in fact to be the fate of the Roman Church:

1. ANONYMOUS GERMAN. *The Last Judgment, in Presence of the Apostles*, woodcut, between 1480 and 1500. In W. L. Schreiber, *Manuel de la gravure sur bois et sur métal au XVè siècle*, 1, no. 599 (1891): 167 (photo: Photographitou, Paris).

From these texts we learn how the pope and his anti-Christian regime shall be destroyed. Through the word of Christ, which is the breath, the rod and the sword, of his mouth, the pope's villainy, deceit, rascality, tyranny, and beguilements shall be revealed and laid open to the world's derision.[1]

Here, in tones befitting an evocation of the Last Days, is a vehement, violent condemnation of the papacy, often represented in this period as the Babylonian whore of the Apocalypse, destined to be crushed to death. And yet, as the title of the 1522 text from which the passage is taken suggests—*A Sincere Admonition to All Christians to Guard Against Insurrection or Rebellion*—the Reformer is speaking out in it against "fanatics." The sword that is to annihilate the papacy is the "word of Christ": Luther thus rejects any move to violent action on the part of Rome's enemies themselves. Moreover, he expounds his lesson by means of a pictorial reference, thereby defending painting as a legitimate way of mediating God's Word. The positive value given to painting here is all the more clear and meaningful for readers of the time in that a year earlier Luther had had to do battle—with only temporary and limited success—against the iconoclasts, who had begun destroying statues and paintings in Wittenberg churches in what constituted a violent radicalization of the Reformation.

Wittenberg, which might be thought of as the Rome of the Reformation, was Martin Luther's city, and also that of the painter Lucas Cranach. Both spent the essential part of their lives there, and they developed a friendship whose energetic expression can be found in their correspondence and in the host of portraits that Luther's friend left of him, his wife, children, and parents. In fact, thanks to the Reformer and his defense, on theological grounds, of the legitimacy of painting, Cranach—like Dürer, another of Luther's admirers—was able to continue work. His production was prolific, and included many graceful, open-armed female nudes (Lucretia, for example, or Venus), an art clearly not limited to pious edification or the representing of sacred things. In a Wittenberg church, an altarpiece by Cranach of the Last Supper, with Luther figuring as one of the dinner guests, would come to replace a painting that had been destroyed by the image smashers, antipapal extremists whose other activities included throwing open the doors of monasteries and convents to incite the monks and nuns to marry and systematically eating meat on Fridays.

The iconoclast episode of 1521 was the first event in the long fight Luther led against a variety of extremists, "fanatic" iconoclasts all—Thomas Müntzer, the rebel peasants, the Anabaptists—in a polemic that repeatedly defended the legitimacy of the Earthly City, of civil society. When he wrote the *Sincere Admonition*, the movement he had begun in 1517 with his theses against papal indulgences was still in its ascendancy, reaching out to new territory, rallying new supporters, and undergoing doctrinal radicalization. Even though Luther clearly warned against disorganized violence, he was then still brandishing the threat that the common peasant—*Karsthans*, or "John Hoe"—could start rioting, that he would fall on the pope and papists "with his flail." But Luther would soon turn his invective against what had become looting bands of enraged peasants and justify the action of German princes who had unsheathed their swords to subdue the rebels. It was no longer a matter of *Karsthans* but of Mr. Everybody, *Herr Omnes*: the masses that must be put down by the sword.

This was a decisive turning point in Luther's thinking. If the king-dom of Christ was not of this world, then Christ's name could not be invoked in calls to destroy earthly kingdoms by the sword so that celes-tial Jerusalem might be built on the ruins of Babylon the whore. Luther further stigmatized those he called false prophets, prophets of death—visionaries who called for the overturning and abolition of images, all of them contemptuously rejecting the Earthly City, civil society—with the term *Schwärmer*, fanatic. This was not merely an insult (one quickly turned against Luther himself, as it happened) but a concept at the heart of his political theory, just as it would be central to many thinkers after him: Luther stigmatized fanaticism as a wrongheaded struggle to abolish civil society in the name of the Holy City. The term "civil society," inherited from ancient and medieval philosophy and political theology, thus took on a new meaning at the start of a new cycle of history and has provided a key to conceptualizing how that cycle evolved: it is to be found, for example, in the writings on the Reformation itself by Michelet and Marx. Considered in a still wider framework, the concept of civil society is, as we shall see, at the core of all modern definitions of the political.

In the tragic dawn of the German sixteenth century, Luther rescued Dürer and Cranach from the iconoclasts and legitimated the power of earthly princes. More than resolving the problem of idolatry, these positions evidenced a contradiction, a tension within the Reformation, between the struggle against the Roman Catholic Church and the defense of civil society, which had to be protected from the fanatic's fury.

*

The fanatic enjoys instead an immediate and unmediated kind of total fanatic has no need to construct or discover what is true, or to take the mystic's slow and solitary way through the dark night toward God. The fanatic enjoys instead an immediate and unmediated kind of total certitude which inhabits, possesses, and violently propels him.

Gathered together in the love of a Great Pronouncer of Pure Truth that is the foundation of their community, fanatics believe that his Word is absolute and that they are its only authorized interpreters. Proud to be its servants and instruments, they hate those who ignore or disdain it, and they desire to make the world comply with the commandments of their supreme rector: either an anthropomorphic God, who like a king, loves to command, or a Law, "all-powerful because true," as Lenin said of Marx's theory, that bends the universe to its necessity. That the world has until now slipped the grasp of the supreme injunctions of this ultimate power is an accident that must be corrected. Fanatics, fervent vehicles of the words of an order that surpasses and sustains them, are ready for sacrifice. They erase themselves as subjects, as loci of self-conscious subjectivity, to the point of considering of no account their pilgrimage on earth, of no account the lives of those who gather elsewhere than in the love of the master whose absolute authority they wish to impose. Their "egos" are swallowed up in the truth they love and by which they desire to be loved, while those who ignore, reject, or combat their just cause are necessarily doomed to annihilation.

Regardless of the principle that illuminates and animates them, whether their enthusiasm is excited by an omnipotent God or some absolute knowledge, fanatics move to attack the unbearable disorder of an imperfect, impure, inadequate world. They are, therefore, always sacrilegious or, to follow the etymology, the *fan*atic is always pro*fan*ing: attacking the temples, polluting the relics, defying the taboos, and cursing the gods of the "other"–shitting in the pope's tiara, a commonplace in anti-Catholic engravings of the Reformation period. Iconoclastic violation, and the intense pleasure they take in it, are their first and simplest forms of acting-out: they wallow in their filthy destruction of the other's sacred object.

*

Yet fanaticism can be something other than an absurd and monstrous pathology provoking only disgust. The moment that the government of a civil society is recognized as having the right to exercise political domination, the moment that civil society becomes the legitimate arena in which each person seeks the personally useful, fanaticism moves into absolute opposition to such society, mobilizing those faithful to a prince not of this world or who, oppressed, proclaim the prophecy of a just realm. For to promote civil society as a positive value is to promote both tolerance and "bourgeois" values, the free market as well as freedom of thought; and civil society's enemies are of at least two types – although both types may be found united in a single individual. Fanatics, who by definition reject mediation and representation and wish to establish a new world without delay and without institutions, may be disciplined militants marching lock-step at the command of a supreme sovereign or anarchists, iconoclasts revolted by the complacency of the guardians of the temple, whom they see as idol worshipers. They may be servants to an inflexible law or relentless utopians, activist assassins or asocial outcasts moved by impatient hopes.

The denunciation of fanaticism, in some instances its defense, and all definitions of its specific forms are to be inscribed not in the margins but at the very heart of modern conceptions of the political. The issue of fanaticism – the threat that the sky will crush the earth, but also the imagined possibility of a human community not regulated by the sum of individual selfishnesses, where the distribution of power would cease to be radically unequal – is hardly archaic or exotic but is rather to be found at the center of current political forms. The medieval Muslim sect of the Assassins in the service of the Old Man of the Mountain (see Chapter 2), or the Ayatollah Khomeini's calls in 1989 for the execution of Salman Rushdie, seem to qualify readily as expressions of fanaticism. But if we persist in thinking about and understanding fanaticism only from a distance, as something that characterizes the other, we may forget that it penetrates all modernity and can even be considered a virtue, as it was by Rousseau and certain Marxist thinkers.

After the Protestant Reformation, the conceptual pair fanaticism/

civil society would reappear, albeit with different valuations and connotations, in the writings of all thinkers seeking to conceptualize the
polity. Meanwhile, political forms would be developed that took as
their foundation the values associated with fanaticism on the one hand,
civil society on the other, and the institutions that incarnate those
values: tolerance as incarnated in the law-governed state, intolerance
as the principle of the single-party state.

The sometimes radical changes in the meaning of the term "civil
society" (the accumulated ambiguities of the expression, its polymor-
phism, have allowed for an inflationary use of it recently), together
with the oscillations of the term "fanaticism," invite us to identify the
essential moments and turning points of their conjoined histories. Any
exhaustive recapitulation is, of course, impossible, but we can trace
certain configurations, certain distinct topologies. The Lutheran Reformation and the clarifying of positions necessitated by the iconoclast
crisis represent a nodal point in that evolution.

1 Civil Society and Fanaticism

Conjoined Histories

Civil society and *fanatic* first appeared together in Latin as *societas civilis* and *fanaticus homo* in a commentary on Aristotle's *Politics* written in 1529 by Luther's loyal friend and supporter Philipp Melanchthon.[1] In it the author insists on the legitimacy, from a theological perspective, of social and political life and of political authorities. A few years later Melanchthon enlisted the aid of Aristotle in a pamphlet decrying the Anabaptists, written as they made their attempt to establish the kingdom of God at Münster (1535). He also opposed the terms in several later texts, most particularly the 1545 version of his main work, *Loci communes theologici* (Common topics in theology). It should be stressed that there is nothing fortuitous in this joint appearance of the notions; in Melanchthon's texts they are to be understood in terms of each other, and they were at the core of Reformation political debates and theorizing.

The 1545 version of Melanchthon's *Loci communes* was translated into French almost immediately (1546); an amplified translation was published in 1551, this time with a preface by the French Reformer Jean Calvin. It was therefore in 1546 that the conception of fanaticism as involving hostility to civil society was imported, together with its specific signifiers, into French, a language that was to be nearly as important as Latin in the dissemination of the two terms and their various denotations and connotations.

In the commentary he wrote in *Loci communes* on the seventh commandment, "Thou shalt not steal," Melanchthon denounced those who claimed that the Gospel forbade ownership of property, calling them "fanatical people." Clearly he was referring to the Anabaptists, whom he condemned throughout the work for rejecting civil society. The formula *societas civilis* is used as a synonym for "political society" or "political order"–that is, what we might define as a society endowed with a constitution.[2] His defense of civil society against the Anabaptists, who had wreaked havoc in Germany, found direct resonance in the thinking of Calvin, who although he did not know German, had fairly easy access to Melanchthon's texts in Latin as well as to Latin and French translations of Luther, which were available quite early on.[3] The influence of the German Reformers on Calvin is evident in book 4, chapter 20 of *Institutes of the Christian Religion*, "On Civil Government," where he denounces in Latin the *fanatici*, in French the *fantastiques* (the equivalent of Luther's *Schwärmer*), for their rejection of political authority.[4] It is thus with the propulsive force of Aristotelianism in the service of the Reformation that the pair fanaticism/civil society would come to assert itself in nearly all idioms of the political.

The two terms have received, as we have said, a multitude of meanings, and their history is all the more complex and iridescent in that it has involved the whole of Europe since antiquity. So it is that "fanaticism" once designated religious fervor and zealotry, was later distinguished from "enthusiasm," and thus came to encompass nihilistic or millenarian political violence. As for "civil society," that formula has been understood by opposition to a series of other notions–the family, the City of God, or the state of nature–in which it was identical to what modern political science calls the state, whereas later it would be distinguished from and opposed to the state. "Civil" may even now have for its antonym "savage" or "barbarian" and is thus intended to mean "civilized." Reconstructing the genealogy of the term seems an endless task, because in addition to this conceptual heterogeneity, one must take into account the metamorphoses due to translation and a chronology that is hardly linear. An imaginary reader in the middle of the nineteenth century confronted with original texts and translations of Aristotle, Hobbes, Vauban, Rousseau, Ferguson, Kant, Hegel, Bonald, Fichte, Tocqueville, Marx, and Pope Pius IX would have had to assimilate as many different meanings as authors. Supreme pontiffs used "civil society" as medieval authors did, to mean the state as op-posed to the Church, whereas in Fichte's evaluation of the French Revolution, civil society (*bürgerliche Gesellschaft*) is used as a synonym for "the state" in contradistinction to the "state of nature," the opposi-tion "civil society/the state" being established only later. For his part, Tocqueville gave the expression a specific meaning that differs from all the others.[5]

But in the polysemic history of the term there is one constant: the ever-present threat to civil society, the shadow cast upon it by the heavens, is fanaticism. We may even go so far as to say that the return of the coupled terms at the heart of political reflection–reflection that may be expressed in denunciatory or anxious tones, intensified and made urgent by the great upheavals that mark our particular present (the collapse of the Soviet system, the rise of Islamic fundamental-ism)–takes the form of a repeated question, a dilemma constitutive of the political in the modern age: either society is taken in its un-mediated existence as subsisting in and for itself–self-sufficient, self-instituted, and self-referential, the source of all value and meaning–or else civil society is taken to be insufficient, insignificant, unworthy in relation to an ideal society that transcends the senses and is history's end. The first of these positions gives violent rise to narcissistic fanati-cisms, in particular nationalisms; the second to millenarianisms ready to sacrifice self and other. The choice is quite an impossible one, in that to call for the establishment of the City of God against those believed to worship the Earthly City, for example, is to found a fanati-cism, while the desire to reject all suprasocial criteria of judgment leads to idolizing the world of the senses. In sum, any politics that is ethically demanding but at the same time distinguishes itself from theology necessarily finds itself confronted, in the form of either an internal threat or its own distorted double, with the very fantasy that totalitarian societies seek to realize, the fantasy of unity, unicity, the One. The problem might be posed in psychoanalytic terms: Can a politics posit the primacy of the Other without sinking into paranoia?

Appendix A lists important occurrences, either joint or separate, of "civil society" and "fanaticism" (the works mentioned are cited in full in the Bibliography). From it we can see that the notional pair "civil society/fanaticism" renders more aptly the conceptual richness of "civil society" than the standard opposition "civil society/the state."

The two terms appear, though not together, as early as Cicero, and it is clear from the names assembled in the table that the pair initially present in Melanchthon's work, far from being an oddity of the moment, is a characteristic feature of Western political ideologies. Among the authors who used both "civil society" and "fanaticism" or "fanatic," there were some who made no effort to relate the two (Cicero, Montaigne) and others, of course, who used them as related concepts. Certain authors have been included because of their contribution to the development of one of the terms (Aristotle, Adam Ferguson, Antonio Gramsci for "civil society"); certain names may seem surprising (Baudelaire for "fanaticism"), but the reason for their presence in the table, as well as that of little-known authors (Philippe Codurc and David de Brueys) will become clear. Conversely, certain important authors present in the table will not be discussed, even though their work is of great interest (Diderot's and d'Alembert's articles for the *Encyclopédie*, for example).

It would have been possible to draw up several distinct lists, one, for example, elucidating the long cycle of Aristotelian-influenced Christian thinking that stretches from antiquity and the Middle Ages to Pope John Paul II, including Thomas Aquinas and combining with the philosophical perspective first presented by Augustine. Another possible group would have been those authors for whom the opposition "state of nature/civil society" was critical: Spinoza, Locke, Samuel Pufendorf, Jacques Burlamaqui, Rousseau. Or again, I might have presented separately, as the very backbone of this history, the cycle with which the book opens, starting with Luther and culminating in Marx and his complete reversal of values. Whereas Luther affirmed, against the fanatics, the positive value of civil society, that is, the state, Marx advocated what may be called fanatic revolt by civil society against the state; in his thinking, as we shall see in Chapters 9 and 10, civil society took the place of the City of God against the state. The list presented in Appendix A, however, is meant simply to show the proximity of the two terms throughout intellectual history. A study of their lexical histories will begin to elucidate how and why they came to be intertwined.

"Fanatic": Insult and Concept

"Fanatic" comes from the Latin word *fanum*, meaning temple, holy place.[6] An alternative spelling, *phanatique* in French, the same or "phanatik" in English, may also be found in sixteenth-century texts, the difference resulting from the mistaken assumption that the word was of Greek origin. The error is in fact highly informative about the global meaning of the term, because, spelled "*ph*anatic," the word looks like a derivation of the Greek *phantasma*, meaning representation (from the Greek root *phos*, light), which would tie the word to the series *phantasme*, *phantôme*, *phantaisie* in sixteenth-century French spelling, "phantasm" and "phantom" in English, with their connotations of "vision" and more particularly "hallucination." It is indeed this lexical field that Calvin mobilized when he denounced the *phantaisies* of the Anabaptists, qualified as phantom-forging *phantastiques* (as we have said, the word is his French translation of the Latin *fanatici*): they were madmen, dangerous "heretics," "enemies of God and humankind."[7] Philipp Melanchthon's vehement denunciation of the Anabaptists and other sects likewise underlines the raving madness of such visionaries (designated alternatively in the French translation as *phantastiques* or *fanatiques*):

> The Anabaptists scorn both priests and their ordination and imagine it necessary to wait for new revelations and illuminations from God, which they seek to obtain by means of bodily macerations such as monks and other enthusiasts have invented. Their fanatic ravings should be abominated.[8]

In French the "Greek" spelling persisted. We find *phanatique* in Rabelais, although he used it as a synonym for "enthusiastic"—that is, following the Greek meaning, touched with poetic inspiration[9]—and late into the seventeenth century, in the writings of the Abbé de Rancé, reformer of the Trappist monks. The *ph-* spelling was also current in other languages: Luther and Melanchthon, writing in Latin, sometimes spelled the word *phanaticus*, and one of the first occurrences of the term in English (1533) takes a form already cited, "phanatik."[10] Jonathan Swift reproduced this spelling in *The Mechanical Operation of the Spirit* (1710), although in *Gulliver's Travels* we also find "fanatick."

We have seen that even before the appearance of *fanatique*, a pseudo-Greek double, *phantastique*, had been used by Calvin for the Anabaptists as the equivalent of the Latin *fanaticus*. There was in fact a kind of indistinct competition between the two French terms, *phantastique* (occurring first in the texts) and *fanatique*, and between the two spellings, *ph-* and *f-*, with the latter gradually taking over.[11] In the sixteenth century, however, no distinction was made, and against the

Anabaptists, who claimed that because we had already been "trans- lated" to the kingdom of God, it was "far beneath our excellence to be occupied with [such] profane and unclean cares" as the business of this world,[12] Calvin defended the "utility of the polity" (*police*), that is, of social and political organization, and he deemed it necessary to dis- tinguish between political "regime" and heavenly "realm." The pur- pose of the temporal regime was to enable us to "frame our lives to fellowship of men"–that is, to civil society–while on earth.[13] Political organization would be useless if the kingdom of God existed here and now, but since it did not and could not, except in the minds of mad- men, the political regime enabled humanity to protect itself from bar- barity and to protect the true religion.

While the spelling corresponding to the correct Latin etymology did come to replace that which followed the erroneous Greek one, the close phonetic resemblance between *fantasme* and *fanatisme* only en- couraged stronger semantic linkings of the two, culminating in the interpretation developed in the nineteenth century by Jacques Joseph Moreau de Tours in *Du Haschisch*. The author, a doctor who prepared the drug for meetings of the Club des Haschischins (whose visiting and more often than not partaking members included Baudelaire, Balzac, Dumas, and Théophile Gautier), associated in his orientalizing imagi- nation the phantasms brought on by consuming hashish with the figure of the Persian Old Man of the Mountain and his fanatic followers of the sect of Assassins. The link will be explained in the next chapter.

The fanatic, then, could be defined as one believed to receive a false light, be it a hallucination brought on by drugs or an illumination inspired by the devil. The idea that such illumination was not merely a vision, a kind of reverie, but also endowed those who experienced it with the terrible energy of sacred fury seems not to have become part of the term's meaning until the beginning of the Protestant Reforma- tion. And it is this meaning which is prevalent in writings from the period of the English revolution, where it was used to denounce sects in general and Puritan extremists in particular.

It was in connection with the English revolution, more specifically through reading accounts and commentaries on it in Théophraste Renaudot's *Gazette de France*, that Jacques Bénigne Bossuet, French bishop and celebrated sermonist to the court of Louis XIV, encoun- tered the term.[14] He used it against the Quakers in 1669 in his funeral oration for Henriette de France, widow of the beheaded English king Charles I. Describing the pullulation of sects in England at the time— responsible in his view for the revolution there—he named, along with the Socinians and Anabaptists, the Quakers (*les Trembleurs*), "fanatical people who believe that all their reveries are inspired in them [by God]."[15] Thirty years later he would use the word again, this time against the Quietists in what came to be known as *la querelle du pur amour*, the dispute about pure love, in which the celebrated prelate, teacher, and writer François Fénelon, also at the court of the Sun King, tried unsuccessfully to defend himself and the Quietist mystic Madame Guyon against the charge of fanaticism. In the meantime the term *fanatique* became current in Catholic France for any and all varieties of Protestant, whether Lutheran, Calvinist, or Anabaptist.[16]

For Catholics close to Bossuet who vehemently opposed the Calvinist prophets known as the Camisards and who sought to legitimate Louis XIV's violent repression of them,[17] fanaticism was synonymous with raging superstition. Whereas Luther had stigmatized the "false prophets," the "prophets of death," as being possessed by the devil, denunciation of the Camisards often involved explaining their prophesying and the supposedly divinely inspired visions and declamations in terms of bodily dysfunction. Their violent spirituality was reduced to an organic disorder, and when the term "fanatic" was applied to their convulsed prophets, it designated less a heresy than a pathology, in what one could call, albeit with a certain anachronism, a psychiatric interpretation of the phenomenon (see Chapter 6).

The turmoil of the English revolution had the effect of reintroducing the term "fanatic" into French in the seventeenth century, after its first importation from Germany via Latin more than a century earlier at the beginning of the Reformation. But the itinerary of the word is even more complex.

Following its English path we find a first occurrence in 1525 in a ballad about the celebrated outlaw of Sherwood Forest. He and two of his companions encounter a traveling nobleman, his *damselles*, and guards in the form of giants. They set to, and we know of course who will win. What is of particular interest are the insults they exchange before the fight: "Fool, *fanatick*, baboon!" cries the king (to which Robin Hood retorts with "Turk" and "Infidel").[18]

About 150 years later "fanatic" and also sometimes "enthusiast" had become terms used in England to designate and stigmatize religious visionaries. We also find evidence of a belief in the German origin of the English fanatics. In an anonymous text written in 1660, *Semper idem: Or a Parallel Between the Ancient and Modern Fanatiks*, it is asserted that the phenomenon dates back to one Walter Lollard, a German according to the author, who lived around 1315 and whose followers significantly increased in number thanks to a certain "Wickliff." The author likewise affirms that "fanatik" is the correct modern word for designating the disciples of the Swiss Reformer and contemporary of Luther, Huldrych Zwingli. And in an effort to establish some symmetry between the sixteenth-century fanatics and those of his own time, he includes a few lines on the two Cromwells, Thomas, chief adviser to Henry VIII, and Oliver, the Puritan dictator, both of whom are labeled fanatics. Many other examples exist to support the conclusion that "fanatic" or "fanatique" (the latter spelling occurred in English) was the English equivalent of *Schwärmer*, the term Luther had employed against Andreas Karlstadt, Thomas Müntzer, Zwingli, and all those he considered false prophets.[19] The word was, in any case, insulting enough to move John Locke to suggest in 1667, in one of his first texts on toleration, that the "opprobrious name" might best be "laid aside and forgotten."[20]

We see that the term "fanatic," arriving in France from Germany at the time of the Reformation, was also imported from Germany into England, whence it was reexported to France during the English revolution, this reinforcing its first French usage. But it was also to recross the Channel from France to England: when the Protestant Camisards, fleeing France after the War of the Cévennes, arrived in London, the epithet took on new life in English. The French prophets were in fact not much better liked in England than in their native country, although by crossing the Channel they did manage to escape violent persecution.

Nor did the English refrain, in the eighteenth century, from ridiculing their own, homegrown fanatics. The Quakers, and all those said to communicate with God by humming and nodding, were perfect objects for the caustic satire of Swift, among others. In *A Discourse Concerning the Mechanical Operation of the Spirit* he proposes a genealogy of fanaticism going back to the Egyptians, pointing out that it is wrong to accuse the initiates of the cult of Osiris—distant ancestors, in his

scheme, of the Lutheran enthusiasts–of having gotten drunk on wine:
one had only to open one's Herodotus to realize that in ancient Egypt
the natives drank only ale. As for a more recent brand of fanatic,
namely Luther's followers, they showed a fine understanding of the
meaning of life when they proclaimed that priests need no longer be
celibate, for "human life is a continual navigation . . . thro' the waves
and tempests of this fluctuating world," and the voyager, like the sailor
with his stock of dried beef, did well to set off with a good store of
flesh.[21] The pleasures of the flesh are also evoked by the name Swift
attributed to his Luther figure–Lustrog–in the first book of *Gulliver's
Travels* (the appellation may be seen as an anticipation of Max Weber's
sociology of religion: he made a point of contrasting skinny English
Calvinists and plump German Lutherans). The name Lustrog is also of
course an anagram for *Gros*(s) *Lut*(her).[22]

   "Fanatic" as employed by Luther (or Swift) thus meant "false
prophet," but it also came to mean "intolerant." This is a crucial part
of the meaning John Locke gave it and is one of the main connotations
the word has today. The two meanings are in conflict with each other, in
that he who denounces "false prophets" necessarily tends to believe
there are true ones. When he uses the abusive term "fanatic" to refer to
someone who does not share his beliefs, it may be that he shows his own
intolerance: condemning the other's fanaticism may well be a way of affirming one's own, and, as we have said, the fanatic necessarily tends to
become the profaner of what is sacred to the other. One hardly protects
oneself from this particular insult by being the one to use it; denouncing fanaticism can be the speaker's way of claiming to have exclusive
rights on truth, a truth he wants universally recognized for its unicity,
so that everyone will see but one true light. Luther, unremitting denouncer of false prophets, was himself portrayed as a *Schwärmer*: in a
German Catholic tract of 1529 he is drawn with seven heads, the face
of one resembling Barabbas, while another, bearing his features, is
topped with wildly disheveled hair around which bees *swarm*–an image of the word's literal meaning, with its connotation of a certain
crazed exaltation.

   Let it quickly be said that believers of differing faiths who at other
moments may sharply criticize one another can sometimes feel a certain solidarity when one of the groups is accused of fanaticism. A few
months after decrying the distribution of Martin Scorsese's film *The*

Last Temptation of Christ (1988), French bishops could be heard saying that they understood the fury that had inspired the Ayatollah Khomeini to issue a *fatwah* against Salman Rushdie for his *Satanic Verses* and legitimating, as did the Gaullist Jacques Chirac (then prime minister, now president), the anger of certain Muslims claiming to be hurt by the book. Different religious bureaucracies manage to find grounds for agreement in their corporatist defense of the very principle that sustains them—the sacred, unconditional respect they believe is their due. Such bureaucracies feel themselves directly threatened by indifference in religious matters.

But even if all religions, whether their love object be God or Caesar, Jesus or Stalin, may ultimately involve an explosive development of hatred and intolerance, fanaticism requires a rather particular casuistry. When the Roman Catholic Church defends its monopoly on the legitimate representation of a certain dogmatic content by condemning *The Last Temptation of Christ*, this is not the same thing as wanting to abolish figurative representation. The Catholic Church cannot be said to lean toward iconoclasm, given that it systematically uses images in its propaganda for the faith. As the temporal mediator of the sacred—participating in both the world of the senses and the world beyond and incarnating, embodying, the Holy Spirit, Rome could hardly endorse a religion from which representation had been eliminated; that would be the equivalent of self-condemnation. The Counter Reformation went so far as to discover in architecture and painting essential resources for the newly militant Church: the Council of Trent of 1545 approved and justified their use for religious ends, reaffirming the principles established by the Council of Nicaea, which, at the end of the long iconoclast crisis that had plagued and divided the Byzantine Empire from 730 to 843, authorized paintings of God and the worship of saints' images. Whereas Luther, and to an even greater degree Calvin and Zwingli, tended to reduce the role of priests and images in their theology of the immediacy of the Word, of the *logos* as person, privileging the believer's direct relation with God and interpreting communion as symbolic participation rather than actual ingestion, the Catholic Church relies on a corps of selected professionals, tested and authenticated by a specific sacrament and specially trained to accomplish within a rigid institutional framework certain performances that involve manipulating sacred objects whose substance has, it is believed, actually become divine. The Catholic Church's hostility toward what it sees as bad images is not then to be thought of as part of a general strategy rooted in a rejection of figurative representation as in all cases idolatrous, but rather as an occasional tactic. Although it can lead to moments of iconoclasm, to a fight—which may end up being quite destructive—against what it considers bad images and bad books, it in no way seeks to crush all image-inings of the sacred. The Incarnation is understood as a figurative representation, where the Cross is indeed a sign, pointing toward something other than itself, but not in such a way that it abolishes the reality of the human body it held: divinity may be painted with a human face. Following a similar logic, the Catholic Church in no way supports the destruction of civil society but rather would claim (or wish) to command or control it.

The move from the first meaning of *fanatic*, "false prophet," to the second, "one who is intolerant," reflects a developing recognition and acceptance of the principle of freedom of thought. Spinoza, with his critique of "superstitious fervor," represents a key moment in this development (see Chapter 5). Fanaticism came to seem less a deviation in the matter of religious faith and more a perversion in the activity of belief, a disturbance in one's relation to truth, whatever the content of that truth. Significantly, Leibniz could affirm at the beginning of the eighteenth century the existence of "atheist fanatics."[23] And could it not be argued that the decrease in religious fanaticism opened the way for political fanaticism?

The history of the term "fanatic" is further complicated by the distinction that came to be made in the course of the eighteenth century between an "enthusiast"—one who believed himself to receive God's light—and a "fanatic"—one who was ready to "act out" in the name of that illumination. This difference, sharp and clear in the writings of Voltaire, has quite other ramifications in those of Kant, who used the German abstract nouns, *Enthusiasmus* (enthusiasm) and *Schwärmerei* (fanaticism). He saw in *Schwärmerei* a kind of madness, a "deep-seated, brooding passion";[24] understanding his rejection of it is essential to grasping the construction of his critical system as a whole, with its insistence on the need for reason to set limits on itself. His rejection of fanaticism also had a political motive, however, namely, his belief that the political *community* could not be based on a claim to possess some *incommunicable* truth received through inspiration and illumination (see Chapter 8).

If *fanatique* was the French equivalent, via Latin, of the German *Schwärmer*, *fanatisme* would later pass from France to Germany in the form of *Fanatismus*. Use of the French word, extensive during the eighteenth century—this included Leibniz as well as Voltaire—became even more common with the advent of the French Revolution. Hegel, who used *Fanatismus*, went further than Kant in applying the word not only to religious but more particularly to political contexts and phenomena. He did not distinguish between *Enthusiasmus* and *Schwärmerei* but instead between two forms of *Fanatismus*, which he presented as two modalities of "the freedom of the void," and he denounced the Terror that succeeded the first stages of the French Revolution as reflecting a desire for such emptiness. In short, we may say that in Hegel's thinking civil society is an instance of the state that gives concrete, substantial content to freedom and thus prevents the desire for freedom from remaining abstract, for if it remained so it could only be actualized as the empty freedom of political fanaticism. Thus it is that Hegel can speak of the fanaticism of those who, during the French Revolution, themselves denounced the fanaticism of the aristocrats—and we see how the word has been secularized, referring no longer to zealous religious visionaries but to all thin-skinned partisans of a cause whose rightness seems so clear to them that they are moved to extreme actions to ensure its triumph. The move from the problematic issue in the Reformation of the legitimate place of God's citizen in the Earthly City to that of the Revolution of 1789, where the citizen was considered *only* in relation to the Earthly City, is symbolized by the substitution of *Fanatismus* for *Schwärmerei*, a substitution that would shortly thereafter be accompanied by a reversal of values.

Although not deliberately seeking to refute Hegel on this point, Engels arrived at an opposite position on fanaticism, which he viewed not as freedom without content but as an aspiration toward concrete freedom, a desire itself tied to the emergence of "modern civil society." In *Fanatismus* or *Schwärmerei*—Engels used the words interchangeably—he saw a positive means of political mobilization, an idea that Lenin would concretize to great effect, acting on *his* belief that the energy that galvanized masses in revolt was not hope, but hatred. We may say, then, that with Engels the word "fanatic" came full circle–but with a complete reversal in the way it was valued–becoming once again a political term for those who rebel against civil society. In this sense, totalitarianism may be understood as the modern version of the fanatic's hatred of civil society.

The Metamorphoses of "Civil Society"

While "fanaticism" and "civil society" are often found separately, they have also existed since their first appearance together in the sixteenth century like two stars in the same conceptual sky, close or distant, but in any case united by a kind of mutual attraction into one constellation, a common system wherein they are intelligible in terms of their reciprocal influences. This becomes apparent when we focus on the evolution of the term "civil society," which became part of the vocabulary of political science in the sixteenth century, although it did not come into common usage until the second half of the twentieth. In the last few decades its use in journalistic writing and talk has spread remarkably, so that, overflowing the specialized lexicons of theology, philosophy, and sociology, it has come to enrich, and confuse, the more ordinary vocabulary of political life.

In 1568, 22 years after the joint entrance into French of "civil society" and "fanaticism" by way of Melanchthon's *Loci communes*, Loys Le Roy, a professor of Greek, translated Aristotle's *Politics* into French and wrote a commentary on it in which he used the term *société civile*:

> Que justice soit politique, appartenant à la police de la cité, il appert parce que le droit est l'ordre de la société civile.

In 1598 his translation was in turn translated into English; and it is here that the term "civil society" occurs for the first time, to our knowledge, in this language:

> That iustice is fit for a Common-wealth and appertaining to the government of a Cittie, it appeareth by that, that law is the order of civill societie.[25]

A purely Aristotelian source may thus be added to the mixed Protestant and Aristotelian one. But the ultimate success of the expression may have more directly to do with the fact that it took on a variety of meanings. Montaigne, for example, when he wrote in one of the *Essais* that Plutarch had mild opinions, "accommodables à la société civile," was clearly using *civile* as the equivalent of "civilized," as opposed to barbarous, while in the "Apology for Raimond Sebond" we find the word *fanatique* used as an adjective with a meaning close to "raving."[26] Montaigne did not, however, link the two terms in any way, unlike the Protestant Reformers, and they would not be used with any frequency in French until somewhat later.

In fact, "civil society" had some difficulty establishing itself in French, as if the expression were too markedly Latin. Jean Bodin did not use it in the *République* (1576), whereas in his own Latin translation of the work he employed, if rarely, the term *societas civilis*.[27] But we do begin to find it a short time later in various writings in both Latin and French; it served both French Protestant and Catholic League authors in the period of the Counter Reformation. At the end of the sixteenth century, *societas civilis* and *société civile* had become standard elements of political vocabulary in France, more particularly of the polemics tied to the Wars of Religion about the autonomy of temporal in relation to ecclesiastical power and rulers in relation to the ruled.

While the Huguenot jurisconsult François Hotman retrospectively qualified Boniface VIII, pope from 1294 to 1303, as a fanatic, Catholic Leaguers were arguing that the primacy of civil society meant that the people had the right to choose its kings and that since the particular people of France was in its essence Catholic, an ex-Huguenot, in this case Henri de Navarre, could not possibly accede to the French throne. Conversely, the Gallican affirmation of the French monarchy's right to autonomy became part of the general argument for civil society's autonomy from the papacy. This was the argument developed to legitimate Henri de Navarre's accession to the French throne: he took it in that same year of 1589 in the name of the separation between spiritual and political powers, the irreducible difference between the Church and civil society. Thus it was that the defenders of the theory of the divine right of kings–those who affirmed, against the pope and the Jesuits, that kings were the sovereign rulers within their kingdoms, that the legitimacy of political power was not secondary, derived, precarious, but rather founded in God–also underlined, by these very arguments, the distance between the two worlds of the state and the City of God.

It was the idea of civil society that provided a foundation for the divine right of kings, whereas partisans of the primacy of the City of God also advocated the supremacy of the pope. We can understand why in 1610, the same year that Ravaillac assassinated Henri IV, the Parliament of Paris ordered the burning of the Jesuit Robert Bellarmin's book on papal power, in which he vigorously asserted the primacy of pontiffs over temporal rulers. In sum, the ambiguities of the term are not new, and it has served contrary political purposes. We find it used as part of a system for legitimating the autonomy of the secular sphere by authors, Protestant or Gallican, for whom popes seeking to impose their authority on sovereign rulers were fanatics, but also in the opposite political sense to support the right to tyrannicide in the name of the sovereignty of the people—by the Spanish Jesuit Juan de Mariana, for instance, for whom the young monk who killed Henri III represented "the eternal honor of Gaul."[28]

The very intensity of these disputes in connection with the French Wars of Religion ensured wide diffusion of the term *société civile*. It may be found, for example in a seventeenth-century French translation of Luther,[29] as well as in Hobbes's French version of *De cive* (The citizen), where he includes it in the full title—*Eléments philosophiques du citoyen, traicté politique où les fondemens de la société civile sont descouverts*[30]—and in writings by Bossuet.[31] The expression came to be quite widely used—it is present in the work of the military engineer Sébastien Le Prestre de Vauban (1633-1707), among others[32]—particularly as a replacement for *Cité*, a term whose meaning is approximate to "polity" but which could be confused with *cité*, a synonym for *ville*. For similar reasons, *Etat* was a potentially confusing translation of the Latin (whereas *Etat* refers to a political unit, *état* is the equivalent of "state" in such expressions as "state of mind" or "state of nature"),[33] and by the eighteenth century *société civile* had been adopted in France as the very object and matter of such sciences as *droit politique* (political right)[34] and political economy.

From this brief account of how the term developed in France we can now turn to a more global history and try to understand its various significations by considering the series of oppositions the notion has entered into. The following chart, although greatly simplified, can begin to give an idea of this variety. Let me clarify from the outset that in the thought of all the authors here named, "civil society" was opposed to "family."

OPPOSED TERM

	a people (*ethnos*)	(Aristotle)
civil society	City of God	(Augustine)
	state of nature	(Hobbes, Rousseau)
	state	(Hegel, Marx)

For Aristotle, "civil society" (*koinonia politikè*) was synonymous with "state" (*polis*) and designated the highest form of community or association, surpassing namely the "household" (*oikos*) and "peoples" (*ethne*), a people being defined negatively as a human grouping without political institutions. The passage from Greek to French and other vernacular languages, chiefly English, Italian, Spanish, and German, was effected through the intermediary of Latin: one of the possible Latin translations of *koinonia politikè* is *societas civilis*, and it could also be translated into French as *Cité* or *Etat*, and into English as "polity," "commonwealth," or "state." The conceptual and lexical identification of civil society with the state–which may seem surprising, given some of the ways the first term is being used these days–was standard all the way up through the nineteenth century. Meanwhile, the Aristotelian sense of the expression has dominated Catholic philosophical tradition by way of Thomism.

For Augustine, the polity (*civitas*) or earthly society (*societas terrestra*) was to be understood in opposition–non-Manichaean opposition–to the City of God: Babylon against Jerusalem. Medieval Christianity, at least in part, would identify the City of God with the Church, and the Earthly City with the state (see Chapter 2). It is in the framework of a reworked Augustinism that we may situate the Lutheran political moment, which attributed great positive value to civil society and, by making each believer a priest, forbade the identification of the Church with the City of God.

For all theorists of the classical period, the crucial opposition was between "civil society" and the "state of nature"; our term thus continued to be synonymous with "state" or "commonwealth." At the end of the civil wars of religion, "civil society" was the expression that enabled these thinkers, from Hobbes to Rousseau, from Spinoza to Fichte, to establish a distinction between an organized political community and the state of nature (this last often sharing many features with Augustine's Earthly City).[35] With the notable exception of Rousseau, who considered giving the title *De la société civile* to the first version of the work we know as *Du contrat social*, these authors valued civil society for giving men greater strength and ensuring their safety (see Chapters 5 and 7).

Following the English theorists, who had underlined the opposition civil/savage and insisted on the importance of the economy in the development of civilization, Hegel defined civil society (*bürgerliche Gesellschaft*) as the sphere regulated by law and the professional corporations in which men might satisfy their needs through work. For him civil society, far from being in antagonistic contradiction to the state as it would be for Marx, was closely related to it and could not exist without it (see Chapter 8).

For Marx, as for Hegel, "civil society" did not refer to the whole of an organized society; rather, the "political development" of society corresponded to a progressive differentiation of civil society from the state. Unlike Hegel, however, Marx defined civil society as a purely economic entity, one that included no political-juridical element; as such it was the first and founding substance of human history. And while Marx thus reversed Hegel by giving priority to civil society over the state, Engels reversed Luther in his reinterpretation of the Peasants' War in Germany (1525), where he praised the fanaticism of Thomas Müntzer, the prophet-leader of the insurrectionary peasants who perished with his followers. In the thinking of Marx and Engels, championing civil society meant justifying civil war, and it was of course civil war that would triumph with Lenin, with Leninist thinking and its paradoxical abolition of that same civil society. Clearly, then, the opposition between civil society and the state that has been present in the public mind since roughly the 1980's is nowhere to be found in Renaissance and classical philosophical thought, having been first sharply asserted only in the second half of the nineteenth century by Marx, who himself imposed distinct limitations on it.

The various meanings of the term as I have just briefly outlined them constitute particular semantic fields; to be able to comprehend and apprehend them, we need a map—a map in addition to a chronological sequence of development, because, although the meanings evolved successively, none completely disappeared from circulation. This causes a sort of confusion that has grown worse recently but is by no means itself new. Such heterogeneity of meaning hardly precludes the overlapping of different meanings, or rather the combining in a single theory of meanings that seem incompatible. There exist, for instance, several examples of systems that synthesize Aristotle's and Augustine's theories of the polity, the theory of a pagan Greek with that of a Roman Christian, and it can also be remarked that the place assigned to the state by those who at present vigorously distinguish it from civil society is analogous to that attributed to the Church by those who oppose *it* to civil society. In our time we may meet both pious supporters of the state, for whom civil society cannot hope to exist without it, and skeptics about the state, atheists as it were, for whom civil society can and must be autonomous.

The long history of the term, already complex at the level of philosophical theory, becomes even more so when we take into account the effects of translation and the fact that the various issues that came to the fore throughout European political history loaded the expression with such a plurality of values that they became mutually contradictory. The Greek word *polis*, often translated into Latin by *civitas*, contains the same ambiguities as the French pair *cité* (which can mean "city")/*Cité* (state). The Latin word *cives* can thus designate either a person who has civic and political rights or one who lives in a city, and Jean Bodin, writing in his native language, first used the word *bourgeois*, then translated it as *cives*. This lexical ambiguity exists in many languages; to consider only French, isn't a *bourgeois* an inhabitant of a *bourg* (town), *ville*, or *cité*? There is a tendency in Western political culture to assimilate "city," "society," "civilization," "state." Isn't civil society indeed "civilized" as opposed to savage or barbarian society, and isn't "civilized society"–civil, bourgeois society–*policée* in the archaic French sense of "civilized," and "policed" in the archaic English sense of "governed"?

The German case is of particular interest, because *bürgerliche Gesellschaft* can be translated either "bourgeois society" or "civil society," which was hardly unknown to Kant or Hegel, and Marx used the ambiguity to the full, not as a defect in the term but as a positive intellectual and epistemological resource: his theory of "civil-bourgeois society" is, in fact, the key to understanding his political theory as a whole, as we shall see in Chapter 9. But the ambiguity has nonetheless been the cause of a number of spectacularly erroneous translations of and commentaries on Marx in various languages, including French and English.

There are still other potential sources of confusion. In Latin but also in the French, English, and German vernaculars, *civilis, civil,* "civil," and *bürgerlich* can be understood by opposition to "religious" (witness the distinction we make between a "civil" ceremony and a "church" wedding), and civil society could refer to secular as opposed to clerical society, the state as opposed to the Church.[36] This is the oldest attested meaning in German, to be found in a Latin-German dictionary of 1480: the expression *bürgerliche Gesellschaft*, perhaps appearing for the first time, is there defined as "human society" (*societas humana*), that is, in this dictionary, secular as opposed to religious society.[37] And we may say that the secularization of the Western polity that characterized the end of the Middle Ages corresponds to civil society's development in this direction, a development that led Locke to call for toleration within such a society, which he duly distinguished from any religious community.

Although less frequently encountered, the opposition civil/military allows for a sociological distinction between civil and what may be called Pretorian societies.[38] In the middle of the 1980's this particular connotation fueled the irritation of Portuguese communists, who, confronted with an upsurge of interest in the "civil society" theme, interpreted it as a critique of the army, more specifically of the young captains who had been the heroes of the April 1974 revolution and of the president of the Republic at the time, General Eanes, whom they tended to favor. Though this is a marginal meaning of the expression "civil society," it only increases the possibility of confusion, for we see that "civil" can be understood as the opposite of "savage," "barbarian," "religious," "military," or even "political" (this last in that Marxists on the one hand, theorists of the free market on the other, taking their cue from the English political economists of the eighteenth century, affirm that *civil* society is the equivalent of the *economic* sphere of activity), and "society" may be understood as the opposite of "individual," "community," and "state."

If we are to grasp the numerous meanings of the term without risking too much vertigo and without having to recapitulate the whole of Western political thought, it is necessary to further our investigation into the semantic history of the expression, which seems not to have been the object of global systematic study. We have already established that "civil society" originated with Aristotle (in roughly 350 B.C.), but how did it pass from Greek into Latin and the vernacular languages? Because the first joint appearance of "fanatic" and "civil society" is to be found in a Lutheran text where the latter term was used in an Aristotelian sense, and because "civil society" is one of the possible translations of *koinonia politikè*, the term Aristotle used in both the *Nicomachean Ethics* and the *Politics*, research into when the expression began to appear in vernacular languages with the meaning "politically organized society" must involve a study of how Aristotle's political vocabulary was received by the thinkers that succeeded him. This approach enables us to follow the term's history very closely.

We should clarify from the outset that although Aristotle used *koinonia politikè* in the *Nicomachean Ethics* (once: book 8, chapter 9), our primary interest is in the *Politics*, where the expression has the status of a key term. As can be seen in Appendix B, the very first translation of the term I was able to discover occurs in Robert Grosseteste's 1246–47 Latin translation of the *Nicomachean Ethics*; the *Politics* was first translated into Latin in 1260, then into the vernacular languages early on in the Renaissance period, and frequently thereafter. Appendix B provides a chronological list of renderings of the terms *koinonia politikè* and *polis* to be found in translations of the first paragraph of the *Politics* and in commentaries on that text. (We have also indicated cases of particular interest where the translation in question is from the *Nicomachean Ethics*.) A version of the first paragraph of the *Politics* is forthwith quoted in its entirety; the source is the much appreciated 1946 translation by Ernest Barker (it may be noted that this particular translator rendered *koinonia politiké* as "political association"):

> Observation shows us, first, that every polis (or state) is a species of association, and, secondly, that all associations are instituted for the purpose of attaining some good–for all men do all their acts with a view to achieving something which is, in their view, a good. We may therefore hold [on the basis of what we actually observe] that all associations aim at some good; and we may also hold that the particular association which is the most sovereign of all, and includes all the rest, will pursue this aim most, and will thus be directed to the most sovereign of all goods. This most sovereign and inclusive association is the polis, as it is called, or the political association.[39]

In the first known translation of the *Politics*, William of Moerbeke, a Dominican monk and member of the erudite circle at the court of the

Holy Roman Emperor Frederick II, used *communicatio politica* and *civilis communitas* as translations of *koinonia politikè*, along with *civitas*, which was used to translate *polis*. Moerbeke's translation became the object of numerous long commentaries, most notably by Albert the Great, Thomas Aquinas (for the first three books, published with Peter of Auvergne's commentary on the remaining books), and Jean Buridan. It was not until the fifteenth century that Moerbeke's version was challenged, and roundly, in a new translation by the Florentine humanist Leonardo Bruni (1369-1444). Bruni used *societas civilis*, the term that would enter into all European languages.

The Latin expression had, in fact, been used once before to translate *koinonia politikè*, as early as 1279, in a "mirror" for princes written most immediately for the dauphin and soon-to-be French king Philip IV (known as Philip the Fair) by an Augustinian monk, Giles of Rome. In certain passages of this well-known text, which circulated up through the seventeenth century, the author combined an inexact translation of Aristotle's *Politics* with a commentary. But despite the work's celebrity and its wide dissemination, Giles's *societas civilis* was not adopted: in the numerous French, Spanish, and Castilian versions of the text, the Latin term was not translated word for word.[40] The first use of *societas civilis*–in 1279–thus largely preceded generalized acceptance of the term, which dates, according to our study, from Bruni's 1416 translation of the *Nicomachean Ethics* and, more spectacularly, his translation of the *Politics*, which appeared in about 1438.

How may we explain this lapse of well over a century? Obviously, *communicatio* and *societas* are not perfect synonyms, and it is possible that the first term was semantically more relevant to the medieval understanding of Aristotle. It should be noted that in his gloss of the *Politics*, Thomas Aquinas underlined the communal aspect of political groupings, particularly in his discussion of language. Language, Aristotle had affirmed and Aquinas here emphasized, was given to human beings by Nature, who did nothing in vain: people were meant to use language to communicate among themselves about what was useful or harmful, just or unjust. It followed that because communication concerning these points characterized the polity, human beings were by nature domestic and political animals.[41] Because they were by nature speaking animals, they were also naturally social, that is, political animals: the demonstration of the naturalness of political community, or, to translate word for word, "political communication," is based on the naturalness of communication through language. Human beings were political animals because they were, to use Jacques Lacan's term, *parlêtres*. The expression *communicatio politica*, clearly closer to the Greek, thus had the effect of evoking "communal" and "community" – which may well explain why it was preferred over *societas civilis* in the thirteenth century, a period whose thought was marked, as we have seen, by an organicist conception of political grouping.

When Leonardo Bruni of Arezzo, in his translations of the *Nicomachean Ethics* (1416) and later of the *Politics* (1438)–the second quickly benefited from the wide circulation made possible by the expanding use of printing–substituted *societas* for *communicatio*, his choice may be interpreted as a sign of the emergence of civic humanism in the Italian city-states, where the communal, with its emphasis on the biological tie of kinship, was giving way to the associative, that is, the voluntary ties men established between each other in guilds and other professional corporations.

Bruni wanted to produce a text whose style in Latin would be as perfect as Aristotle's in Greek; his choice of *societas civilis* expresses a deep concern for the elegant transmission of culture, this being for him a veritable civic imperative. *Societas* was a word often used by Cicero,[42] an author whom Bruni mentions in the preface to his translation of the *Politics*, and the translation itself is explicitly intended to replace Moerbeke's, which he judged barbarous in its borrowings from Greek, as well as enigmatic and capable of inducing interpretative folly. His rejection of Hellenisms (in many cases Moerbeke had not translated but merely transliterated Greek words into his otherwise Latin text)[43] is perfectly emblematic of that nascent Florentine humanism in the context of which Bruni worked, and his affirmation of the superiority of poets over the Scholastic philosophers is consistent with a much less naturalistic, organicist conception of the polity than that of his predecessors. Leonardo Bruni is exemplary of the original alliance between humanism and the sense of civic duty forged in quattrocento Florence. In an early work, written around 1400, where he expressed in a literary form that borrowed from classical models the Florentine reaction to the city's being subjugated by the Visconti dynasty of Milan, he presented the Tuscan city as a fully realized and accomplished *politeia* (a word which for Bruni in this context meant a city organized by a good constitution). Athens, the *koinonia politikè* par excellence, had thus reappeared in the *societas civilis* par excellence that was Florence. From this perspective, translating Aristotle's *Politics* into classical, normalized, Ciceronian Latin–the ideal, idealized language of his fellow citizens in civil society–represented to Leonardo Bruni a political duty.

Max Weber distinguished between the ancient Greek cities, where the integration of citizens was essentially political, and Renaissance Italian ones, where it was based on professional guilds,[44] but this opposition is not at all relevant to the way political theorists of Renaissance Italy conceived of their own situation. In an original synthesis, they fused the social reality of the city-states of their time with the Greek and Latin heritage. Leonardo Bruni, a prolific translator himself and the initiator of a vast project for translating works by Plato and Aristotle, wrote among other things a text in praise of wealth and, elsewhere, following the Roman model of political virtue, an apology for Caesar's murder as having freed Rome from tyranny.[45] In his *History of the Florentine People* he presented republican Florence as the legitimate heir of Athens and Rome and an ideal homeland for all men.[46] We may therefore say that both philologically and ideologically, the first civil society was that of fifteenth-century Florence as the humanists represented it to themselves at the time when Cosimo di Medici was settling into power.[47]

Symbolic of a new political culture, Bruni's translation of the *Politics* benefited, as we have said, from the technical developments of the late fifteenth century: the use of paper had reduced the weight and price of books and thus favored the development of a literally portable culture. Incunabula of his translation were quickly published throughout Europe, and with Gutenberg's invention of movable type, which made paper use more efficient and reduced fabrication costs while at the same time making it easier to manipulate books, the text was widely disseminated in the sixteenth century, when translations of it into the vernacular languages also began to be printed. Bruni's translation from the Greek dates from 1438; the first printed edition, an incunabulum, was published in 1475 at Strasbourg–which explains at least in part its influence on German culture–and in the following years it was printed in Barcelona, Paris, Salamanca, and Rome. Between 1501 and 1600 almost fifty different editions appeared throughout Europe from Basel to Leipzig.

A success due to the boom in book printing, the triumph of a more elegant Latin expression than the medieval William of Moerbeke's *communicatio politica*, considered barbarous in Medici Florence:[48] the victory of *societas civilis* is indeed that of Renaissance civilization, within which civic humanism circulated from southern to northern Europe in much the same way as the various motifs of recently exhumed classical statues–the Laocoön, to choose a well-known example, which from Athens reached Rome, later Mantua and Florence, and then Nuremberg by way of Dürer, in whose *Hercules Killing the Stymphalian Birds* its influence may be seen.[49]

We may therefore calculate that it took about two hundred years, from the circulation of Giles of Rome's manuscript to Leonardo Bruni's printed books, for *societas civilis* to impose itself, and even then it was not a total or definitive victory, either in later Latin or vernacular translations. Whether a translator into the vernacular chose his language's equivalent of "civil society" instead of "political community" or "political communication" depended on his conceptual choices and, in part, on the source of the translation: authors who worked more closely with the Greek text tended to use expressions of the second type, whereas those who were translating from Bruni's Latin version or were otherwise influenced by his thinking tended to use "civil society." As has been mentioned, Loys Le Roy arrived at a compromise: when translating into French directly from the Greek he used *communauté politique*, whereas in his commentary we find *societé civile*. But how are we to understand the fact that a technical expression originating in Aristotle's political vocabulary has now become so ordinary that since the 1970's it has regularly appeared in newspapers and news magazines, and in the case of France, invaded them?

"Civil Society": An Expression Much in Use These Days

Appendix A does not include many references to the most recent uses of "civil society," though this book was written in part in reaction to the present inflationary use of the term and the application of "fanaticism" to Muslim fundamentalism, for example. What is relevant to this study is that the meanings assigned to "civil society" these days are not in fact new but correspond closely to prior meanings of the term, a fact of which the user is often not conscious.

Unless of course the term is being used as mere ready-made thought, in which case its use can have the same effect as the Dadaist ready-mades, arising from the same causes—incongruous juxtapositions, semantic skids. Whereas the opposition between *societé civile* and *societé politique* (the latter being an expression currently used by French politicians and journalists to refer to the political elite or the political establishment in general) seems perfectly obvious to modern French journalists, even the least gifted etymology hound can immediately see that "civil" is the Latin equivalent of the Greek "political." How, then, could the two represent an opposition? It is no doubt true, as Emile Benveniste has shown, that the Greek *polis* and the Latin *civitas* do not mean quite the same thing in that a Roman citizen (*cives*) attained to that identity by means of his relation to other Roman citizens, the Roman polity being defined by the principle of co-citizenship, whereas the Greek polis existed independently of the ties linking individuals who were a part of it.[50] But this point is probably not what explains the present popular distinction between *société civile* and *société politique*. The very expression *société politique* might set one wondering: could not one just as logically say "social society," given that *politikon* in Greek can be understood, from a certain point of view, to mean "social"? The traits that for Aristotle defined "man" as a "political animal" (*zoon politikon*) are those connected with "sociability," namely the power of speech. And it is often forgotten that the distinction between civil society and the state, so widely and readily accepted since Hegel and Marx, was not always so evident, and that translated back into the idiom of Aristotle or that of Rousseau it would result in the "oppositions" state/state or civil society/civil society!

Without tracing the paths of all the streams, with their various rates of flow and the varying quality of their waters, that have gone to make up the vast river of "civil society" since the end of the 1980's, we can at least distinguish three of its sources: the use of the term by the Catholic Church, by critics of totalitarianism, and by sociologists studying the state. An examination of the three will explain at least in part why the term has been playing such an important role in political and journalistic discourse: it carries with it immense conceptual wealth (much greater than that of "democracy," for instance) and extreme diversity of meaning. It has been and is being used to put major phenomena and problems into focus: the Church's redefinition, in connection with Vatican II, of its relation to the secular world; the critique of totalitarianism and, more recently, analyses of the communist system's collapse in the former Soviet bloc; analysis of political development in Third World countries and questions about the role of the state in developed countries. These fields of investigative concern regularly overlap.

Although the Catholic Church has employed "civil society" for centuries, its use in opposition to "state" in the 1963 papal encyclical of John XXIII, *Pacem in terris*, stands as a key moment in the recent history of the term, even though in this text it occurs less frequently than its synonym, "political community," a term originating, as we have said, in the Latin of William of Moerbeke and Thomas Aquinas. By distinguishing civil society from the state, Pope John affirmed the priority of the first over the second. The state, the embodiment of authority, was destined to serve the common good of civil society; its positive role is not denied in this text, but its mission should, in the pope's view, be realized in the domain and at the scale of international regulation, not in those of domestic political and social order. His analysis of political life involves three essential elements—the Church, the person, and civil society (or the political community)—and the state is seen to be more of a threat or an obstacle to them than anything else. Almost thirty years later we find the same three terms in *Centesimus annus*, Pope John Paul II's encyclical written for May 1, 1991, in which he specifies the economic and social doctrine of the Church. During his trip to Poland that same year, he once again demanded that the Church play a directive role in relation to civil society. In this the Church seemed to want to succeed the old Communist Party in that country, both institutions denying, in their respective ways, civil society's autonomy.

It is, in fact, the Polish critique of totalitarianism that created one of the principal areas of the term's recent use: "civil society" was used in Poland, first in critical analysis by intellectuals wishing to turn Marx's own analysis against certain thinkers who claimed to be continuing it, and later as part of real political demands. In an important article written in 1973, the philosopher Leszek Kolakowski hypothesized a historical connection between the Marxian vision of a unified man and the fact that, in actuality, communism appeared only in totalitarian form, that is, with a tendency to replace all the associations and activities of civil society by the coercive mechanisms and institutions of the party-state.[51] Undeniably, this analysis has enjoyed great intellectual and political prosperity:[52] it took up a term already present in Marx and applied it to societies established in accordance with Marxist-Leninist doctrine, thus giving concrete conceptual definition to the intuition that what characterized the Soviet Union and Eastern bloc communist countries in general was nondifferentiation between state and society. As the political project of power apparatuses and more particularly of Leninist ideology, the internal logic of which required that it seek to actualize itself in the form of the single party, this fusion of state and society had in fact been vigorously and brilliantly criticized in the last, antitotalitarian sentences Trotsky penned of his *Stalin* before being assassinated on August 21, 1940.[53] Later, the critique of totalitarianism and the will to impose a distinction between state and civil society were incarnated in the conflict connected with the communist party-state in Poland, and then, spectacularly, in Solidarnosc. After the 1968 invasion of Czechoslovakia by Warsaw Pact troops and the vast anticultural pogrom in Poland that same year, the advent of Solidarnosc marked the exhaustion of attempts to revise Marxism: civil society seemed to have been reborn, thus manifesting its ability to survive, its unquenchable vitality, in a country still ruled for all intents and purposes by the Communist Party.[54] The expression "civil society" had that much more resonance in this context given that for a large fraction of the Poles, the combat against the Communist Party was fought explicitly in the name of civil rights. What we may call Polish civil society was thus animated by the will to affirm its political rights against the claims of the totalitarian state. Far from seeking to reject or put an end to the political in the name of the social, Polish civil society founded itself on the demand that *all* be able to exercise political rights. Put another way, civil society's assertion of itself in Poland against the Communist Party's political monopoly did not signify a demand for *less* politics in society or for more free market, but rather for the politicization of society and the free exercise of the rights of man and citizen (and this despite Solidarnosc's vehement denial–a condition of its survival–that it had any political intentions itself).[55]

It is an irony of history that, in the case of the concept of civil society, the thinking of Hegel and Marx has fueled reflection about Marxist societies and thereby revealed their grim purpose to those conducting what Marx himself would have called the "practical" critique of them. Moreover, during the 1970's and 1980's in the United States, England, Germany, and France there was a marked increase in Hegelian and Marxian studies of civil society,[56] although in France Marxian studies have either ignored Marx's version of the concept or else dealt with it quite unsatisfactorily.

During recent decades a great variety of "ways out" of totalitarianism have been imagined, together with a great number of ways of determining its etiology or genesis, and, after Gorbachev's taking power in the mid-1980's, of describing the process that is unfolding. Nevertheless, certain elements of the diagnoses seem to have been obvious to all whose work is to analyze former Soviet society's transition to a kind of democracy and free-market economy—the strange, uncertain, and troubling attempt that characterizes political life in Russia today. The birth of a civil society is the objective that Gorbachevians set themselves and that a large number of the new teams in power in the countries of Central and Eastern Europe are also aiming at in their transition from communism. But it is also in these terms that Alexander Solzhenitsyn, hardly to be accused of Hegelian or Marxist thinking, has come to conceive of Russian reality at the end of the czarist regime.[57] "Civil society" can thus facilitate an overall grasp of political realities in Central and Eastern Europe and analysis of the impasses and tragedies of a society of the "impossible citizen,"[58] while also designating a task and a goal for the forces struggling for their freedom there or the groups who, having undertaken first to renew and then to abolish the system of the party-state, are trying to create a civil society in countries where it has never before existed. Still an empty concept, a concept without referents, in the context of the Soviet bloc in the 1970's—civil society could not be found within it, either because it had never existed or because it had been absorbed by the party-state— "civil society" had become both an empirical notion and a governmental project by the end of the 1980's. The term was used by Soviets with an active role in the perestroika, is used by the new leaders, and is an element of the basic vocabulary of all commentators and analysts who claim to have a scientific approach.[59]

"Civil society" also enables us to reflect upon and conceptualize another major phenomenon of the modern world (though perhaps in a less immediately generalizable way than for the former Soviet bloc): namely, nation building or state building, the political construction of new nations in the Third World. It is a functioning concept in the work of Clifford Geertz–particularly in *Old Societies and New States*–Reinhard Bendix, and most especially Edward Shils, who began using the notion of civil society in 1960 to analyze what he saw as the absence of integration characterizing many new states, specifically in Africa, where the center, not as a geographic notion but as locus of power and source of values, has great difficulty exercising hegemony over the periphery.[60] (Given the weight of kinship and lineage in these states, recent anthropological use of "civil society" is reminiscent of Aristotle's insistence on its opposition to "family.")

Geertz, Bendix, and Shils had a significant influence on political sociology in France in the 1970's and 1980's.[61] The notion of civil society also got into the air by way of works by Antonio Gramsci, who, as a Marxist attributing to the term a different meaning than did Marx, provoked widespread and intense debate in both Italy and France.[62] Indeed, it is perhaps not without interest to recount briefly the recent history of the expression's use in France, where intellectual and political issues are intertwined in ways that might themselves be analyzed– to the benefit of the sociological study of ruling elites, and thereby of French civil society. Certain investigations of the state in France may be characterized as historical; they examine the specificity of national political models. The opposition between nations where the state is strong and civil society "weak" (France for example) and those where civil society is "strong" and the state weak (England and the United States) is crucial in the theory of European political development elaborated by the French political scientists Bertrand Badie and Pierre Birnbaum. In contrast, the political philosopher Blandine Barret-Kriegel–whose perspective is strongly influenced by the classical political philosophical tradition, that of Spinoza and Hegel, and by that first experiment in state-founding, namely Moses' leadership of the people of Israel–insists on the legal, juridical function of the state, the specificity of the state governed by law, and places the opposition "law-governed state/totalitarian state" at the core of her analysis.[63] The notions of "law-governed state" and "civil society" have also been rejected for epistemological reasons, but these criticisms have been largely without effect. Meanwhile "civil society" seems to have transcended even the barriers separating rival schools of thought, inasmuch as it is to be found in the review directed by the celebrated sociologist Pierre Bourdieu – although it would seem more representative of the thought of Alain Touraine, who is largely responsible for its dissemination in France and also in Latin America.[64] (The transition from Pinochet's regime toward democracy in Chile has been presented as a transformation of relations between civil society and the state.)

But the debate about civil society is not simply a key element of recent thought in the disciplines of political sociology and philosophy; it has also, indissociably, become a live issue in French politics. More specifically, it is the rallying call for all those who are suspicious of the state and believe it should leave more room for social movements, citizens' initiatives, or the free market. It was erected as a totem by the "second left" for the project of self-management they had devised for thwarting what they considered the paleo-Marxism in which the 1972 common platform of the united left was steeped. They needed to legitimate the faction of the left that, even though it had rallied to the policy of an alliance between the French Socialist and Communist Parties, wanted to maintain its specificity as well as its particular clientele: left-looking people often marked by Catholicism and identifying themselves with the humanist and liberal, rather than leftist and libertarian, ideas of May 1968. "Self-management" and "civil society" became somewhat all-purpose signifiers, giving rise to a semantic looseness that led some to attribute such vague objectives to civil society as society's liberation from what was deemed, following Marx, its "fetishism of commodities."[65] Thinkers rather weakly continuing the legacy of certain nineteenth-century utopians such as Etienne Cabet affirmed that civil society could facilitate the elaboration of new social projects outside the state: liberated as it was from the primacy of power relations, civil society in their vision made possible new models of love and new models of the family.[66] The formula received further promotion when certain segments of the French right whose opinions had previously been marked by Colbertist, Jacobin, and Gaullist traditions were converted to free market, antigovernment liberalism after the socialist François Mitterrand's victory over the center right's Valéry Giscard d'Estaing in May 1981.[67] Thus it was that "civil society," one of Marx's key terms, became for some the very symbol of the Smithian ideology of the "hidden hand."

The procession of users further lengthened when the habit developed of opposing "civil society" not to the state or the *société politique* but to the *classe politique*. This was an elegant way of denouncing politicians, or even of using Gramsci's communist terminology to spout the ideas of Charles Maurras, founder of the extreme right organization Action Française, notably his opposition between *pays légal* ("legal or official country") and *nation réelle* ("real or authentic nation").[68] The expression *classe politique* can be either neutral or demagogic, depending on whether it figures in the three-piece-suit style of articles in *Le Monde* or the suspenders-sporting, sneering, antiparliamentarian language of the extreme right Front National, the party of Jean-Marie Le Pen.

When, after the French legislative elections of 1988, at the same moment he chose Michel Rocard as his new prime minister with the task of forming the next government, the socialist president of the Republic François Mitterrand used the term "civil society"–a novelty for him, but part of the basic vocabulary of the intellectual current with which the new prime minister identified himself–it was obvious that the expression had arrived.[69] And Rocard brought with him an innovation, not in the meaning of the term, but in the way it was used by the French "second left": unlike certain of his close associates, he did not oppose civil society to the state but rather associated it with the law-governed state.[70] As we shall see in Chapter 8, this conception goes back to Hegel, for whom the state constituted civil society's condition of possibility. However, in the particular political situation in which France found itself at the time, the term gained polemical charge at the expense of clarity, especially given the confusion between the new prime minister's will to make "overtures" toward the political center and government's "opening up" to accommodate "civil society." Thus it was that Rocard appointed as ministers a certain number of individuals who, because they did not belong to any political party, were presented as not being political professionals, even though they might well be important personalities in public life and what one is tempted to call professionals when it comes to projecting their chosen image of themselves in the media.[71] Those among them who used the term "civil society" presented themselves–in the media, of course–as its promoters against either the state or the *société politique* or *classe politique*. The term alone came to stand for a whole political platform: Bernard Kouchner, a founder of Doctors without Borders, took it as the name of his new, and ephemeral, political organization in 1993. (Kouchner's presence as health minister in Edith Cresson's short-lived government, 1991–92, symbolized the continuation of the "opening-up-to-civil-society" policy–in the absence of its initiator, Michel Rocard, who was dismissed by Mitterrand.)

Devoid of context, no longer linked to a particular period or a precise doctrine, gushing out of everyone's mouth at once, "civil society" acceded at the end of the 1980's to a sort of empty universality. When the term is to be found gracing the columns of *Le Monde*, *The New York Times*, *Libération*, *Il Corriere della Sera*, *Le Nouvel Observateur*, *L'Express*, *Pravda*, and *Le Canard Enchaîné*, how can one not have the soothing feeling that politics has finally found its universal grammar? At last, a language common to Monseigneur Lustiger, cardinal and archbishop of Paris, for whom Christianity remains one of the fundamental resources of "our" civil society,[72] and Régis Debray, former admirer of Chè Guevara, who hates civil society;[73] to Daniel Cohn-Bendit, leader of the May 1968 student movement, who loves it; Yuri Afanassiev, former Soviet deputy and director of the Historical Archives Institute of Moscow, who also loves it; an editorialist for *Il Corriere della Sera*; Flora Lewis of the *New York Times*; Alexander Solzhenitsyn; former prime minister Michel Rocard; former president of the French Republic François Mitterrand; and various others, including Pope John Paul II. And what luck to have had a quasi-universal word at hand when the war in the Gulf broke out: Iraq's "civil society" immediately became a center of attention in France, where it was affirmed, on the one hand, that Saddam Hussein would be able to draw support from it, on the other, that he had destroyed it.[74]

The communion that the expression seems to have made possible has its source, as we have said, not in any systematic, logical political reflection but in its very ambiguities: it can only be used as a currency of exchange because its different values have been forgotten, its heavy heritage, rarely conceived of as such, of centuries-old traditions in which it represented precise concepts in carefully reasoned, structured systems and which in turn prevented its meaning from drifting too much in any given period. Now that it has become a label for all sorts of goods, and in certain cases even a mask for intellectual emptiness, "civil society" allows people to speak without knowing what they are saying, which in turn helps them to avoid arguing with each other. As for what we might call the historical unconscious, it takes its revenge, causes slips of the tongue; conceptual irony sometimes takes the form of involuntary witticism—as, for example, when the savant French financier Alain Minc, discussing a book by Pierre Bourdieu, called for the "subversion" of the state by "civil society," thereby identifying his opinion (if not in spirit at least to the letter) with that of Karl Marx when he applauded the Paris Commune as the first experiment in the dictatorship of the proletariat, civil society's revenge, as Marx conceived it, on the state.[75]

The staggering proliferation of the word, whether as the emblem of lukewarm consensus or the symbol of a new way of apprehending the political, could be seen as either an opportunity for further pedantic mockery or an incitement to look further for the reasons behind such infatuation, the sociological and intellectual factors involved in the expanding use of the term. But the sociology of public opinion in this case would quickly be reduced to opinions about opinion and would not teach us much, other than that Marx is dead and that he was more brilliant than his epigones and many of his critics, or that journalists don't read enough Hegel, even though it was Hegel who said that reading the daily newspaper was how modern man prayed. The decline of analysis in terms of social class, the advanced decrepitude of the "bourgeoisie/proletariat" pair, the valuing of the business corporation as the seminal place of human life, the defeat of even revised communism, have no doubt favored the (re-)emergence of the opposition "civil society/state," an opposition that tends to present political issues as problems of management rather than as conflicts between various powers and groups with divergent or antagonistic interests. Nonetheless, as we have seen, much of the dynamism of the formula "civil society" comes from its being instrumental in the critique of totalitarianism, and when we observe how the Hegelian system explaining the articulation of civil society with the rule of law and the law-governed state is being taken up again not only in Western Europe but also, in an utterly new way, in Central and Eastern Europe, and even in the Muslim world, it becomes clear that we cannot reduce present-day use of the term to a mere "new" way of dressing up free-market liberal thought, antistatism, or antipolitical demagogy. We would do better to see in it a symptom of the discontents that characterize modern political life, and also a sign that certain political objectives have become universal. Might we not discern–in a positive way this time–in the unbridled use of "civil society" the sign of an aspiration, more or less conscious, toward a society that does not have to be identical with itself, a will to leave the subject, the "I," some room to be different from the state, the City of God, or the Party?

Rather than denounce facile use of the term or flush out, reactively, conceptual deficits inherent in such use, we can try to put the notion of civil society back into determined contexts by analyzing its place in certain reasoned systems. Its link to fanaticism will enable us better to grasp the issues and problems raised by the expression, for if "fanatic" is an insult, we know that insults always partake of thought: they must be invented by the mind, just like concepts, and there is a logic behind stigmatization–for hatred must be socially and intellectually constructed.

We may begin by observing that, in order for "fanatic" to have become an insult, a certain philosophical separating out of civil society from the City of God needed to be accomplished. This process began in the Middle Ages, and its effect was to affirm the relevance and value of civil society.

2   Civil Society and the City of God

Among the men that Judas led up to the Mount of Olives to arrest Jesus was a high priest's servant named Malchus (John 18:10). Just after Judas's notorious kiss, the apostle Peter pulls Malchus aside and cuts his ear off with his sword. Jesus will later heal the ear miraculously, but immediately after Peter's act he makes a statement found in all four gospels that has fueled a multitude of interpretations, saying to his armed disciple, the one who will build his Church: "Put up again thy sword into his place: for all they that take the sword shall perish with the sword" (Matthew 26:52).[1] Interpretation is further complicated by an enigmatic verse in the Gospel according to Saint Luke that narrates an earlier moment in the story. Just before Jesus leaves to pray in solitude, where the angel will come to give him strength in his agony, his disciples present him with weapons for his defense: "And they said, Lord, behold, here are two swords. And he said unto them, It is enough" (Luke 22:38). These words, the problem of the "two swords," more than Saint Peter's excessive zeal, were to impel and animate Christian theopolitical reflection.

What are the two swords? Since the Middle Ages the allegorical exegesis according to which one represents temporal, the other spiritual power, has been almost universally accepted, and these two mysterious arms would be brandished in the incessant disputes about their respective powers between ecclesiastical and political authorities, church and state. Rather than structuring these debates into divergent ideologies, the swords were the enigmatic image that fired them. At issue was the nature of the temporal sword's subordination to the spiritual one, for in a Christian context it could not of course be denied that the latter had preeminence over the former, and in the question of their specific status concrete power interests were at stake, having to do with such things as who might manage religious professionals, levy taxes, and accede to the throne. There were numerous components to the dispute, and some of them carried a potentially enormous impact: the right of popes, for example, to recognize as legitimate the bastard sons of kings and thereby modify royal lineages. In each conflict, the legitimacy of a given political power, the prerogatives and boundaries of political power in general, were called into question, and with them the degree of autonomy—always relative in Christian eschatology—of civil society.

The accusation of fanaticism directed at the beginning of the Protestant Reformation against iconoclasts, Anabaptists—against *Schwärmer* in the name of civil society—was part of this long tradition of debate about the relation between the temporal and spiritual swords. Luther and Melanchthon proposed a solution to the conflict that was based on a combination of Aristotle's and Augustine's respective legacies. Is it possible to resolve the contradiction, seemingly absolute, between the Greek philosopher, apologist for civil society (and thus indirectly for the temporal sword) as the natural framework for the highest good, and the Christian saint, herald of the City of God, toward which, in his vision, God's pilgrims touched by his grace made their way during their time on earth? Actually, Melanchthon's synthesis of the two in the sixteenth century was not in itself new, although his application of it was unprecedented; the principle of a reconciliation between them was already well accepted, and one of the thinkers who had done the most to advance it has already been mentioned and will be considered in detail further on in this chapter: Giles of Rome. This complex figure, both monk and archbishop, responsible for the unification of the Augustinian orders in Paris, is, according to our research, the first to have used the term *societas civilis* in a translation of Aristotle. He also played an essential role in the conflict between the papacy and the monarchy, the Catholic Church and the king of France, who in this particular instance were incarnated by Pope Boniface VIII and Philip the Fair. Giles of Rome sided with the pope, which may seem surprising given that he is also believed to have been Philip IV's personal tutor. He served the pope unswervingly in a dispute that may be seen as an attempt by the monarchy to become autonomous in relation to the Church. The Church's claim to represent the City of God on earth and to dominate any and all temporal, that is political, powers in accordance with a sacred hierarchy had reduced the latter almost to the status of an instrument, and in this sense the French monarchy's protest against the Church's insistence on treating all human creatures as its "subjects"–the pope's word–was a demand for equal dignity.

In Pope Boniface VIII and his ideologue, Giles of Rome, we may see a specific form of fanaticism: not the reactive fanaticism of those who wish to destroy civil society, but rather that of a doctrine and an institution that claim to control human social life in the name of a certain *oneness*. Some kinds of ideology are fanatical in and of themselves, by virtue of their institutionalized logic, and only external constraints keep them from realizing their desires. When the Catholic Church in the nineteenth century claimed a right to exercise control over civil society, it was formulating a centuries-old demand that cannot be accounted for by any accidental circumstances of the historical moment. It is legitimate to ask whether, when it affirms the primacy of the spiritual sword over the temporal one, the Church fundamentally differs from those currents in Islam which deny that there can be an autonomous political sphere. Denunciations of Muslim fanaticism can be signs of its proximity and familiarity to the denouncer, as if the Catholic Church were projecting its own anxiety onto a terrifying Other.

Before we turn to Aristotle, let it also be said that certain authors used *his* thought to elaborate a fanaticism of the state which is just as threatening to the citizen as religious fanaticism.

Aristotle: Civil Society, a Natural Community

The expression in Aristotle's writing that became our "civil society" defined the polity by genre–it was a type of society (*koinonia*), that is, a community, association, grouping–and by what differentiated it from other societies: it was political (*politikè*). But who, according to Aristotle, might participate in civil society? Although he defined human beings as political animals, this did not mean that everyone lived in political communities, that they were all members of civil society, for "political" had both a looser meaning, according to which it was a synonym for "social," and a stricter one, for which the relevant synonym is more like "civic." A human being, while indeed a social animal, was not necessarily a civic one. Life in a group was obviously not reserved for people; there were other gregarious animals, among them some who, like human beings, were engaged in a common activity (*ergon*) and thus formed, in Aristotle's terms, a "society." In this respect people were the same as cranes or bees,[2] and in this sense all three of these animals could be called "political." The difference between humans and other "social" animals, however, was that only humans had the capacity to perceive good and bad, just and unjust: it was from the "community" of these perceptions that both the family and civil society came into being.[3] However, although the polity was the highest form of social organization and the possibility of its realization was what differentiated human beings from all other animals, not all human beings lived in civil societies. Put another way, if it was true that persons by nature lived in community with others of their kind, and if human nature was only fully realized in a superior version of that community called the polis, if political existence in the sense of life in civil society was the highest form of communal life to which people could accede, it was also true that their political nature was not necessarily—in all cases, for all persons—fully realized.

In order to live organized into a polity, human beings had to have certain qualities that not everyone could possess. As Aristotle explained it, this was because of how the climates in which they lived affected their character. Peoples (*ethne*) living in cold regions, especially in the western part of Europe (the Celts, the Gauls), were very brave but lacked intelligence and technical skill, while Asian peoples were intelligent and inventive but lacked courage. As for the Greeks, geographically situated halfway between Asia and Europe—the perfect mean—they were both brave and intelligent; they might therefore live in a community organized by political, constitutionally regulated institutions: a civil society. But the Hellenic nations were themselves diverse; certain of them possessed one quality to the detriment of the other, and this had the effect once again of making it impossible for them to organize themselves into polities.[4] On the other hand, certain member nations of the Hellenic family possessed both qualities in such

perfect–balanced–proportion that not only could they organize themselves into civil societies, they could also rally together all the various
Greeks and thereby govern the world. The polis capable of governing
the world was of course, in Aristotle's mind, first and foremost Athens.

Peoples differed from one another, as we have said, and Aristotle
affirmed that the particularities of each people must be taken into
account by the study or science of the political, as well as by political practitioners, that is, legislators.[5] Let us repeat, however, that although Aristotle considered civil society exceptional, he did not mean
that it was arbitrary, precarious, or *artificial*: human beings were only
fully human–they fully realized their *nature* and essence–in civil, civic
life, and civil society was a specific institution of civilization, as opposed to barbarity.

What features distinguished civil society from other types of association, a ship's crew, for example, or a company of soldiers, but also from
the family? Ties of friendship (*philia*) could only exist, for Aristotle?
within associations, but all such ties were not the same. He distinguished several different types of friendship ties: those that existed
between fellow citizens, between members of the same tribe or team,
between hosts and guests, and between members of the same family.
Blood ties are compared to those which link the different parts of the
body, whereas all the others are more a matter of agreements or contracts.[6] But civil society sharply distinguished itself from all these other
"societies," for the polity was a collectivity of *citizens* who, though they
differed from one another, had the same work: to collaborate for the
good of the polity in general.[7] The chief purpose of a political community was "the good life," but it could also be said that human beings
came together and formed and continued to maintain a political association so that life itself might continue.[8]

Civil, or political, society was thus superior to all other associations
in two ways: first, its purpose was higher, more general, in that it was
not aimed at "some advantage close at hand, but at advantage for the
whole of life";[9] second, it was itself the widest association because it
included all partial associations, encompassing ships' crews, military
troops, banquet associations, but also two other crucial forms of community, namely the family, itself made up of the community of husband
and wife, and the household or domain (*oikos*), where the master
wielded authority over his slaves. "All societies," Aristotle wrote,

"would seem to be parts of civil society [*koinonia politikè*]."[10] More particularly, he insisted on the distinct quality of the political tie in contrast to the relation of private dependence that characterized the family and the *oikos* (affirming once again that it was of greater value because in it humanity fully realized its nature). Between master and slave or within the family, relations were fundamentally asymmetrical and inegalitarian, whereas in the polity–and this was what was truly original in the political tie–all citizens were equal before the law: "Political rule is over free and equal persons."[11]

While the specific character of civil society was that it was made up of citizens equal to each other, these citizens were at the same time involved in other types of relations, ones involving noncitizens and taking the forms of the other diverse associations or societies mentioned. We may say then that civil society is composed of segments. Indeed, Aristotle's way of discussing the subdivisions within civil society evokes the segmentary model elaborated by anthropologists from Evans-Pritchard to Ernest Gellner. Without referring explicitly to either Aristotle's works on logic or his political treatises, Gellner has proposed an interpretation of segmentation in Aristotelian terms: "Distant ancestors are like abstract concepts, denoting more (people alive now) and connoting less; close ancestors are more concrete, 'denoting' fewer descendants and 'connoting' more intense relationships."[12] In a segmentary society, or more particularly a lineage-based one, individuals recognize each other as belonging to one and the same segment by virtue of their relation to a common ancestor: in a patrilineal system, for example, two male individuals might define themselves each as "X's great-grandson" and as such recognize a close tie between them. The intensity of their solidarity diminishes as the length of the lineage segment increases; that is, as X comes to represent a more distant ancestor, whose descendants are necessarily more numerous than those of a closer one. The more distant the ancestor whom the individuals in question consider as determining that they form a community, the weaker and the less frequently acted upon are the obligations that these linked individuals have to each other. The "denotation" and "connotation" of the ancestor, like those of the concept for Aristotle, are inversely proportional. It follows that individuals who recognize one another as having a common great-great grandfather are numerous (strong denotation), but their mutual ties and obligations are weak (weak connotation). This structural rule of segmentarity, which may be seen, to take a common example, in vendetta rules, where the obligation to take revenge diminishes in proportion to the distance of the relative in question, was in fact formulated by Aristotle when he said that the obligation to be just increases with friendship or, put negatively, that the offense committed is that much greater if the offender and the offended are close. It is worse to be disloyal to a companion than to a fellow citizen, worse to fail to help a brother than a stranger.[13] The logic of segmentary solidarity is clearly expressed in the following Berber proverb: "I and my brothers against our cousins; I, my brothers, and my cousins against our enemies."

Civil society, the polis, may be said to be exempt from the system of social obligation through *proximity* (of which kinship relations are the classic embodiment), because it is based on a system of obligation through *reciprocity*. (This is why the anthropologists of development we mentioned in Chapter 1 consider the establishment of civil society a necessary condition of political modernization.) As Aristotle explained it, in civil society each citizen might in turn be one of the governed and one of the governing: in a polity based on the equality of citizens and their perfect similitude, each had in theory the right to a turn at governing: "When the constitution of a state is constructed on the principle that its members are equals and peers, the citizens think it proper that they should hold office by turns."[14]

The polity was a society of equals whose purpose was to enable all who belonged to it to lead the best possible life. In this respect its superiority was that of the highest possible unit, the one within which segments (families, age groups, professional corporations) fissioned and fused. Significantly, it could not itself fuse with another set of segments, another civil society. The polity is defined as the ensemble of segments constituting a given grouping within which problems are resolved politically, not by war, for within the polity, justice (*dikè*) reigns: "Justice belongs to the polis; for, justice, which is the determination of what is just, is an ordering of the political association."[15] This is why, if we remember that "civil society," that is *koinonia politikè*, was synonymous with "polis," "the polity," or "state," and that *dikè*, justice, implied the ideas of law, we may affirm—the anachronism is deliberate—that by opposition to an *ethnos* (a society without a constitution), civil society was for Aristotle the equivalent of what we call today the law-governed state.

Criticizing Socrates' conception of the polis as expressed in Plato's *Republic*, namely, that "the greatest possible unity of the whole polis is the supreme good," Aristotle affirmed that the polis must have multiple components:

> It is obvious that a polis which goes on and on, and becomes more and more of a unit, will eventually cease to be a polis at all. A polis by its nature is some sort of aggregation: [i.e. it has the quality of including a large number of members]. If it becomes more of a unit, it will first become a household instead of a polis, and then an individual instead of a household.[16]

But although the polity is presented as grouping within itself communities of lower rank, groups produced and characterized by the division of labor—manual workers, warriors, philosophers—it is not in this feature that the fundamental principle of its multiplicity resides. The polity was composed of persons different from one another for precisely the same reason that they were similar; namely, their "reciprocal equality" as citizens, the fact that, at a given moment in time, some were magistrates while others were not, some ruled while others did not.[17] So it was that while civil society included segmentary, lineage-based elements, it followed a different kind of logic: for each member of civil society, the other was no longer a relative or companion but a fellow citizen, and the society that they formed, civil society, was based on justice, on law. And there could only be citizens (and therefore co-citizens) in a society organized by a *politeia*, that is by defined political institutions, a constitution.[18] Following Plato, Aristotle developed a theory of types of *politeia*, of political regimes and their transformations: changing a given constitution meant changing the polity, or civil society, governed by that constitution. Nevertheless, such a change did not modify the society more loosely defined. "Societies" or associations of lower status—families, businesses, the army, for example—were not necessarily affected by changes in the constitution. In short, the idea—the platitude even—that social life maintains a certain independence from political life is already present in Aristotle's work, just as it is to be found in that of most theorists of the political (who do not, however, make it the alpha and omega of their reflection, as do many political professionals today).

Civil society for Aristotle was superior not only as the outer limit of a given social body encompassing all other associations; it also enjoyed both moral and practical superiority.[19] Whereas other sciences (medicine, military strategy, economics) were practiced with particular ends in mind (health, victory, wealth), the science of the ultimate practical end, practiced for itself and not with some intermediate purpose, aimed at the supreme good. This sovereign science, dominating all specific, segmentary ones, this all-organizing, architectonic science, was the science of the polity, of civil society: *épistémè politikè*, political science. Even though the individual's good could be identified with that of the polity, it seemed to Aristotle much more important, much more in keeping with humanity's true ultimate purposes, to manage and safeguard the polity's good as a *whole*: the good of separate individuals was of course desirable, but good was more beautiful, more divine, when it concerned entire polities.[20] To each type of grouping, association, social segment, corresponded, according to Aristotle, a merely regional, particular science; it was political science that must legislate for all these lesser ones. Political science was the worthiest of all (with the exception of theoretical science, philosophy) not only because its object was universal, but also because it aimed at that good to which nothing was superior.

It is easy to see how these affirmations may be used in the service of a certain exalting of the state (since "state" is a justifiable translation of the Greek word *polis*). And it is possible to see in Aristotle's thought the origin of modern deification of the state. Hegel is often said to be at the root of the particular way the global state has been valued in Germany, but the nineteenth-century German theorists of the *Machtstaat* or power state claimed instead to be taking their cue from Aristotle. Leopold von Ranke and Heinrich von Treitschke, for example, cited the *Politics* as a source for their thinking and generally preferred to associate themselves with the Greek philosopher rather than the one from Berlin in their affirmation of the state as a superior ethical reality of natural origin. These authors of course distinguished themselves sharply from contractualist theorists, for whom humanity's first state was pre-political, namely the state of nature, and who therefore maintained that civil society or the state was not natural but artificial, thereby contingent, and, in a way, fragile.[21]

The would-be-Aristotelian legitimation of the power state in Germany makes clear the absurdity of imagining the term or theme of "civil society" as necessarily involving anti-authoritarian ideas (contrary to what its most recent uses may lead one to believe). The affirmation, no matter how vehement, of society's preeminence over political power can serve as a support for a variety of political attitudes. We have already pointed out that in the context of the sixteenth-century French Wars of Religion, certain Catholic League pamphleteers who refused on principle to accept that a Huguenot could take the French throne made use of theories that were themselves based on the Aristotelian naturalism of civil society. The anonymous author of one of the most violent works of this kind, for whom Calvinists were "dogs," "Jews," "Mohammedans," and finally worse than pagans, began his tract with the affirmation that "civil society" was not artificial, but rather corresponded to human nature, to humanity's needs and aspirations, and that it was based on the division of labor. Civil society, in this view, thus preceded any and all political regimes. But, the author continued, if Nature was one, how could we explain the diversity of political institutions and the fact that they varied from people to people? Why such variety—it could not be God's work—between Poland and England, for example? Why should France have a special law, the Salic Law, that excluded women from the royal succession? The author finally explains this multiplicity as expressing "the will of the [different] peoples": for the essentially Catholic people of France, Henri of Navarre could only be an illegitimate intruder. Furthermore, if the "republic"—a term the author uses as a synonym for "civil society"—should deem that a given sovereign was a heretic, it had a perfect right to kill him. In this way the author excuses the act of Jacques Clement, Henri III's assassin and a typically fanatical figure.[22]

Civil society as the people against the political class. Modern-day polemicists, namely, those who in various styles and tones play out the Maurrasian opposition *pays légal/pays réel* or who, worse yet, function within a system that opposes "the Catholic people" against the "Protestant establishment"—this last supported, moreover, by the Jewish lobby and playing into the hands of Muslim fundamentalists—are thus the unconscious heirs of this affirmation of the preeminence of the "social" over the "political," the natural over the artificial. To a radical rejection of foreigners they add the belief that in order to be a true member of the French Republic one must be Catholic, just as only a Catholic could be king of the French.

To understand the diversity of the political uses that have been made of the notion of civil society, it is well to remember that the Catholic

Leaguers seeking to exclude Henri IV were in fact posing the problem in terms similar to those already developed by their opponents, Protestant "monarchomachs," who claimed a right to resist against the political power in place and located political legitimacy not in the people but in the lower-level magistrates (city magistrates, for example) and the Estates General. Defending the right not of mass insurrection—in this they were different from the *fantastiques anabaptistes*[23]—but rather of what they conceived of as legal resistance on the part of instituted elites, resistance to which the political structure of the society gave them the right, the Calvinists found a middle road between submission to royal power and popular uprising, submission to iniquity and fanaticism. The Huguenot theorists thus played a decisive role in the genesis of the modern representative state, characterized as it is by a displacement of sovereignty from the monarch to the people, but on the condition that the people be superintended by its elites.[24]

We have seen that Aristotelian theory has been used to support worship of the power state as well as conceptions of democratic political right, not to mention demogogic populism. But the plurality of readings of Aristotle is not limited to this sphere; it also concerns the very concept of the social tie, as is implied by the different translations of *koinonia politikè*—on the one hand, "political community," on the other, "civil society." The passage from the first of these translations to the second in the various vernacular languages made a useful term available to seventeenth-century theorists of the state of nature. Unlike Aristotle, they did not believe that human beings were naturally political. Even if in their writings "civil society" is not always conceived of as a radical break with the state of nature—Spinoza, for example, called any departure from nature impossible; for him every being, whether its "state" was "natural" or "political," was governed by the fundamental principle of its tendency to continue existing (*conatus*)—"civil society" remained a specified form of organization different from the state of nature. Generally speaking, the translation of *koinonia* as "society" facilitated artificialist conceptions, whereas, as we have said, the communalist and naturalist vocabulary that Aristotle more immediately inspired tended to legitimate an organicist conception of the state.

It was undoubtedly this latter type of conception that led Nietzsche to affirm that the Greeks were fanatical worshipers of the state.[25] His expression may seem deliberately anachronistic, as when he calls Plato "the typical old socialist" for having, in the *Republic*, reduced the individual to an organ that serves the whole.[26] If by "state" we mean not an apparatus specialized in administration or a power machine enjoying a recognized monopoly on violence but rather a political community—that is, a civil society, then Nietzsche's formula fits perfectly into the strong *Machtstaat* tradition (although of course Nietzsche himself was opposed to that position). The question of whether his interpretation of Aristotle was abusive should not obscure the fact that the omnipotence of the state has also been legitimated by Christianity, for if civil society is, like all other things, an effect of God's providence, earthly political order receives thereby a sort of transcendental sanction, and civil society becomes something like the divinely cast shadow of the City of God.

But Christ is not Socrates, although there are similarities. Socrates, the first to desert the polity when he accepted an unjust death—not in the name of the law, but rather of his personal, subjective respect for the laws—transferred the place in which a significant part of life is lived from the boundaries of the public space to the supraspatial dimension of transcendental values. He introduced the Greek world to the principle of consciousness of self over and above the precious order of the polity, universal justice over and above custom, reason over and above tradition. Socrates' "daemon" left behind in Athens a fermenting agent that would degrade and corrupt the real, bringing the ancient world to its ruin by destroying the polis. For if it is true, as Hegel wrote, that Socrates continued up till the end to fulfill his duties as a citizen, when he reached that end his true country was no longer the existing state in which he lived, and his spiritual world was no longer the religion of that state, the Athenian religion. Christ, although he may be said to resemble Socrates in that he too accepted an unjust death, furthermore carried the message that there was an all-powerful Master, the sole Master to be obeyed out of love, and he pointed to a place other than earthly Jerusalem as the locus of good. And Christ established his Church. Situated outside civil society, next to or above the polis, its vocation was to dominate or substitute itself for civil society, rather than to contest or destroy it. The dictum of rendering unto Caesar the things which are Caesar's constituted a recognition of Caesar's legitimacy, which could be accepted as either a sort of regional legitimacy coming directly from God (even if Caesar was animated by the devil) or an instrumental legitimacy according to which Caesar must serve the Church. On this basis, Aristotle and Saint Augustine are by no means incompatible and can readily be brought into a certain alignment: the latter saw the Earthly City, civil society, as fitting into a hierarchy dominated by the City of God, and while this domination devalued civil society, it did not fundamentally call it into question.

City of God, Earthly City

Two of the most important questions that sociology may pose about Western religions, namely, the role Christianity played in the decline of the Roman Empire and the role Protestantism played in the development of capitalism, can be referred back, although of course anachronistically in the second case, to the theopolitical vision of Saint Augustine (354-430). In both these developments the notion of the Earthly City, civil society, and its difference from the kingdom of God are crucial.

Augustine wrote *The City of God* to exonerate the Church from all temporal responsibility in the trouncing that Rome, the *Urbs*, the Earthly City par excellence – Augustine called it a second Babylon – was undergoing at the hands of the barbarians in A.D. 410. Attributing the responsibility for this temporal tragedy to the Earthly City itself, which originated in original sin, Saint Augustine, by affirming the autonomy of evil, also affirmed that of civil society. By underlining its radical separation from the City of God, he opened the way to positing civil society as its own sphere, inferior but irreducible, within which one might act.

Whereas the Stoic emperor Marcus Aurelius (A.D. 121-80), living in a time just as tragic as Augustine's, spending his last days on the frontiers of Europe watching for the arrival of the barbarians, conceived of the individual's reason as part of a single universal reason and called himself a citizen of the world, the cosmos, the sight of Rome being vanquished by looting bands could hardly move the Christian theologian to an integrating, universalizing vision. Nothing is less "cosmopolitan" than Christianity: an irreparable fault precludes thinking that a person inhabits the cosmos as a natural dwelling or city, especially given that the universe is subject not to reason but to God. It was equally impossible for Augustine to follow Aristotle and imagine the human polity as a possible locus of the supreme good. Whereas Aristotelianism and Stoicism are profoundly unitary philosophies, in Saint Augustine's system, closer to Platonic and above all Neoplatonic traditions, a fundamental duality triumphs.

While the Aristotelian conception of civil society evokes the segmentary model, tending toward an apprehension of the polity as a system in which distinctions rather than sharp oppositions come into play, the strong dualism between the City of God and the Earthly City that marks Augustine's political thought was the womb, as it were, from which would be born, sometimes like monstrous offspring, the different political conceptions that establish a strict cleavage between church and state, earthly and religious societies, or even civil society and the state. The separation becomes even more dramatic when we consider how it mobilized and structured political, diplomatic, and military practice during the long medieval struggle between the papacy and the Holy Roman Empire for supremacy and the monopoly on legitimate use of the temporal sword. Lutheranism, as we shall see, formulated this separation between spiritual and temporal reigns in a way that was essential to the genesis of the modern state. As for Marx, who marked the distance beween civil society and its enemy the state by affirming that the supreme value that had been attributed to heaven should in fact go to civil society, while the state, pitched so high, was an illusion, and by demanding that civil society be given the same prerogatives that had abusively been accorded the state, how can we not hear in this analytic separation an ironic echo of the mystic opposition Augustine traced? (And may we not see in Marx's denunciation of the political state an expression of his own fanatical atheism?)

Could the Christian religion be made responsible for Rome's troubles—the most recent being full-scale pillage by Alaric the Visigoth—for having forbidden all sacrifices to the city's gods? Although Saint Augustine responds with both historical arguments, underlining that Rome had already undergone numerous disasters before the Christian prohibition of sacrifices, and a theology of divine providence according to which the glory of the Roman Empire was merely the effect of God's will,[27] the real substance of his interpretation is the distinction he makes between the two Cities. This was not developed into a philosophy of history; his purpose was not of course to make sense out of the positive, concrete world, but rather to construct an eschatological vi-

sion of human temporality as inextricably bound up in God. Augustine
had already presented a first version of this construction when *The City
of God* was nothing more than a project. In the detailed, dramatic
contrast he establishes in the *Literal Commentary on Genesis* between
two kinds of love, "perverse self-love" and charity, we may discern the
explanation for the conflict between the two Cities (predictably, Augustine does not call upon the legend of Romulus and Remus to explain the foundation of the earthly one):

> These are the two loves: the first is holy, the second foul; the first is social,
> the second selfish; the first consults the common welfare for the sake of a
> celestial society, the second grasps at a selfish control of social affairs for
> the sake of arrogant domination; the first is submissive to God, the second
> tries to rival God . . . the first love belongs to the good angels, the second to
> the bad angels; and they also separate the two cities founded among the
> race of men, under the wonderful and ineffable Providence of God, admin-
> istering and ordering all things that have been created: the first city is that
> of the just, the second that of the wicked. Although they are now, during
> the course of time, intermingled, they shall be divided at the last judgment;
> the first, being joined by the good angels under its King, shall attain eternal
> life; the second, in union with the bad angels, shall be sent into eternal
> fire.[28]

The distinction between the two Cities is a mystic one, like that
between grace and nature, for while humanity may be separated into a
great variety of nations (*gentes*), humankind or the human species for
Saint Augustine was divided into two cities, the first peopled by those
who seek to live the peace of the spirit, the second by those who desire
to live the peace of the flesh[29] – Jesus' city versus Adam's, heavenly
Jerusalem versus earthly Babylon. The citizens of the Heavenly City
were born of grace, the same grace that frees nature from sin, whereas
Nature, perverted by sin, gave birth to the citizens of the Earthly City.
The first he called "vessels of mercy," the second "vessels of wrath."[30]
These two cities, heavenly and earthly, would not actually be separated
until the Last Judgment, at the end of human time, this in keeping with
what originally cleaved them apart, the revolt of the evil angels. In
Augustine's vision, the Earthly City was founded by Cain, murderer of
his brother and representative citizen of civil society, whereas Abel, a
stranger to this world, is seen as a pilgrim who, continually advancing
toward heaven, builds nothing on earth.[31] The City of saints was above,

even if it gave birth to its citizens down below; these citizens were only temporary exiles, and on the day of their reunion, rising out of the dust that was once their bodies, they would enter into possession of the promised kingdom, there to reign at the side of their lord, the king of ages. In Augustine's scheme, the inaugural fratricide that was the archetype of the Earthly City was reenacted in the birth of Rome, with the crucial difference of course that both Romulus and Remus were citizens of the Earthly City.[32]

What and where was humanity's good, given that all earthly power, even Rome's, was ultimately brought to ruin? Clearly we are far from Aristotle's belief that humanity's good resided in the polity: for Augustine it was to live united with God. For all citizens partaking of this good, he explained to his Roman reader, and between such citizens and the God they loved, there existed a saintly "society," the unique City of God, which was both that society's sacrifice and its living temple. However, the ontotheological distance between the two cities in no way meant that people should desert the earthly one. First of all, no one could affirm on his own that he partook of God's grace: Who could claim to know himself to be a member of the City of God? Moreover, the human city, humankind—earthly, not divine—possessed its own good, which could procure joy even if it failed to calm that human greed so active among the Romans, the *libido dominandi* or drive for power, that insatiable desire which divided the Earthly City against itself in bloody, perpetual struggle. The good specific to earthly society was peace.[33]

The human city as a possible place of peace against the background of permanent war which was its determining principle and its horizon—such was for Augustine the highest of all possible earthly goods. By no means the highest good of all, he is quick to remind us, for that is the City of God. Peace becomes the criterion for judging political regimes and ranking them according to their merits. The true republic presupposes a foundation of true justice, he affirms, following Cicero, but immediately adds that because true justice exists only in the republic of Jesus Christ, only that republic is worthy of the name. He calls Christ the "ruler" (*rector* in Latin) and "founder" (*conditor*, the title used for Romulus) of the City of God.

But the supremacy of God's kingdom did not, for Augustine, contradict the fact that the Earthly City was the highest good available to

humankind on earth, and since, furthermore, the separation of the two
cities could only be understood as reflecting the will of God, political
authority was doubly legitimate. Just as those who made war at God's
command in no way violated the precept "Thou shalt not kill," so those
who put criminals to death according to the law of a given land, Roman
magistrates for example, had not committed homicide but were as
much instruments of God as the swords they used. It was hardly necessary to demonstrate the functionality of temporal power case by case;
that functionality was founded on the essential affirmation of the omnipotence of the God of love, and it had a correlative that will also be
found in Luther's analysis: Christians had no business rebelling against
the political power in place, even if that power was unjust. Was this the
price to be paid to the Roman Empire for its having allowed the Church
to develop within it? Was it an expression of the masochism inherent in
a religion that finds its love-object in a tortured man? Whatever the
reasons and motives behind this practical equivalent of the "Credo
quia absurdum" [I believe it because it is absurd], Christians were not
to rebel, but to suffer—under Nero, for example, whose extreme vices
made him cruel.[34]

The power to distribute kingdoms and empires was God's alone; he
gave the kingdom of heaven to the good and the kingdom of earth to
both the good and the evil. "It is clear that God, the one true God, rules
and guides these events, according to his pleasure. If God's reasons are
inscrutable, does that mean they are unjust?"[35] Supreme creator and
organizer of the universe, God administered its peace with his laws.
But that peace—"the tranquility of order," which order is "the arrangement of things equal and unequal in a pattern which assigns to each its
proper position"—existed at different levels: it might be the peace of
the body, defined as "a tempering of the component parts in duly
ordered proportion"; the peace of the irrational soul, which was "a
duly ordered repose of the appetites"; or the peace of the rational soul,
which was "the duly ordered agreement of cognition and action."[36]
This vision of distinct orders or levels of peace determined by God's
laws shows that Augustine had a traditional—why not call it Aristotelian?—conception of the Earthly City as naturally composed of various
inferior groupings, the equivalent of the household or the family, each
having its own specific good. For both Aristotle and Augustine the City

as a whole had its own good, as different from it and superior to it as the perfect is to the imperfect; but while for the first this was its potential to be politically organized, for Augustine it was the perfect "sovereign" good to which certain citizens of earth would accede after their resurrection.[37] After the Judgment Day, those who partook of God's grace would be fellow citizens of the heavenly angels and live in eternal bliss: in God's City, mysteriously, "We shall be still and see; we shall see and we shall love; we shall love and we shall praise."[38]

Although Augustine's two cities are radically heterogeneous, they were not, as we have said, absolutely separate from each other; while distinct, they were mixed together on earth, and this contact between two human masses that were radically different in terms of their destinations and destinies, this relation between God's citizens, who were to live in his love as given by his grace, and the earthly, natural city, is expressed in the metaphor of the blessed's stay on earth as a pilgrimage toward heaven. However–and this is crucial–the citizens of God's City, pilgrims only passing through a world that was not theirs, obeying sovereigns who were not their true kings, did not bear any distinguishing marks: during their time on earth they might belong to any nation, profess any religion, be subject to tyrants, or even be tyrants themselves. Rather than describing the Church as the City of God on earth, it is perhaps closer to Saint Augustine's thought to say that the community composed of the citizens of the City of God made its way on earth in the form of the Church–invisibly, mystically. "In truth, those two cities are interwoven and intermixed in this era, and await separation at the last judgment."[39]

The immaterial character of the distinction between the two Cities is underlined by the fact that for Augustine, as we have seen, the cleavage concerned not just humankind but also the angels. The rebellious angels went plummeting out of the City of God in a fall that anticipated humanity's, whereas the City of God, certain of whose inhabitants were exempt from the earthly pilgrimage, was simply there, immortal, in the sky. It was the City of those angels who burn with the holy love of God, who had never betrayed and would never betray his divine friendship, those whom, from the first beginning, God had separated out from the ever already fallen, deserters of the eternal light, which would become darkness for them as they fell into the lowest regions of the air. The two Cities had their origin in these two opposed angelic societies, as well as in the separation between the human lineages of Cain and Abel.

Given the complexity of Augustine's vision, many of the political interpretations, to say nothing of the political uses, that have been made of it may seem reductive; what we can affirm without hesitation is that *The City of God* has been and may understandably be used to nourish dualist visions of society. Although it is generally perilous to try to demonstrate that a certain ideology structures the imagination of a given society or culture, we may without too much risk affirm that the topology of the Christian world is organized by a duality, a bipolarity that opposes Heaven and Earth, high and low, light and darkness, God and the devil. And this structure or arrangement appears to be—that is, circularly, in the sphere of appearance itself, representation, in the sphere of images both sacred and profane—more productive than the trifunctional ideology whose force in the Middle Ages has nonetheless been demonstrated by Georges Duby, working from the analyses of Georges Dumezil.[40]

Although the opposition between heaven and earth can be played out in diverse ways, any notion of an absolute split seems to repress Augustine's central idea of a mystic separation and give preeminence to a division of the two Cities into two separate zones: positing the existence of a City of God seems necessarily to imply tracing its negative and hostile double and establishing a spatial separation between the two. Numerous iconographic examples of this bipolar topology exist, but we should be careful about attributing the physical separation between the two Cities to anything other than representation itself. Indeed, how to paint such an intermingling of the City of God in the Earthly City? The brutality of geometry, always too terrestrial, threatens to overpower any subtle use of color and motif, the dressing of a heavenly and an earthly citizen in the same fabrics, for example. Given that an icon requires its elements to be exposed *partes extra partes* (part next to part), it would seem that mystic separation cannot be represented—unless of course a way could be found to represent clearly such spatial interpenetration. It was Albrecht Dürer, as we shall see in Chapter 4, who first managed to paint the unity of the City of God and the Earthly City without masking the distinction between them.

In general, however, graphic representation of the two Cities gave a dichotomous, Manichaean quality to their separation. An illumination in a medieval manuscript of *The City of God* (Johann Amerbach, Basel, 1490) shows two fortified cities separated by a river. In front of the city on our left, Zion, we see the shepherd Abel, his lambs at his feet, while inside the walls winged angels, one of whom holds his hand up in a gesture of blessing, confront diabolical creatures who threaten them with stones and weapons from the ramparts of Cain's Babylon, Cain depicted as a farmer leaning on his hoe. The relation between the two Cities is slightly more complex in an Adoration of the Holy Trinity that figures in Nicolas Pigouchet's *Heures à l'usaige de Romme* (1498; see Figure 2). The scene is sharply split by a horizontal band of clouds; above we see an assembly of saints and prophets who, together with clergymen and laymen, adore Father, Son, and Holy Ghost, while below, on earth (an effect of perspective shows us the grassy surface of the ground) another group–pope, king, laymen–pray on their knees around a gothic chapel, a church symbolizing the Church, whose spire pierces the clouds separating earth and sky. A similar dualism, likewise marked by a horizontal bar, is to be found in many other compositions, with a more or less perceptible softening of the separation: in *The Fountain of Grace and the Church's Triumph over the Synagogue* by van Eyck (ca. 1420), for example, communication between low–the Church guided by the pope, the emperor, and various princes; the Synagogue led by blindfolded high priests–and high–God the Father, the Lamb, Saint John the Baptist, the Virgin, winged musicians–is ensured by the spire of a sculpted tower decorating a fountain from which springs the water of grace, with its source in the Father's throne.

Such figuration remains far from Augustine's original idea; as we have said, the mystic separation he proposed may well seem impossible to represent, because any such representation would require the combining in one image of things radically different, or, conversely, a cleaving apart of things fundamentally mixed. Another means Augustine used to convey the intermingling of the two Cities on earth was the Old Testament story of Sarah and Hagar. Sarah, Abraham's lawful wife but repudiated by him, gives birth to Isaac, who represents in Augustine's scheme the children of the City of God, while Hagar, Abraham's servant, bears Ishmael, a citizen of the Earthly City. But the opposition between the two women was not Manichaean, for as Au-

2. NICOLAS PIGOUCHET. *The Adoration of the Holy Trinity*, from *Heures à l'usaige de Romme*, Paris, 1498 (photo: Bibliothèque Nationale, Paris).

gustine explains, Hagar is an image of Sarah, herself an image of the City of God. So it was that the Heavenly City could exist symbolically in certain forms of the Earthly City, and the mystic separation between the two could be understood as an intertwining.[41] It was also an anticipation: the split between saved and damned, though radical, nonetheless did not permit identifying the Earthly City with absolute Evil. The Roman Empire may have had to suffer the reign of Nero, but it had also known other perspectives and methods—those of Augustus, for example. By revealing in the prosperity and glory of the Roman Empire all that civic virtues could produce even in the absence of the true religion, God had given men to understand that, by coming to that religion, they would become citizens of another City, governed only and entirely by truth and charity, and lasting not a shorter or longer span of years but for eternity. In a City where God had not yet revealed himself, civic virtues constituted an anticipation of the Heavenly City that attested to its reality.[42]

More complex than any figuration of it, Augustine's mystic theory of the two Cities has allowed for so many different interpretations that reconstituting them would involve an extremely long detour. The influence of Augustinism on Luther, himself an Augustinian monk, will be clarified further on. Whatever form Augustine's theology may have taken among the members of that order in the fifteenth century, it is certain that Luther had read Augustine—specifically *The City of God*[43]—and like him, Luther imagined the Earthly City as bound up in a hierarchical dualism. But when he underlined the cleavage between the two Cities, it was to confer a particular legitimacy on the earthly one. In this respect, Lutheranism turned its back on certain forms of "political Augustinism" that had tended to affirm the complete subordination of the temporal sword to the spiritual one; that is, the submission of states to the papacy and its political strategy.[44]

Spiritual Sword, Temporal Sword

The dualism between state and church allowed for a multitude of doctrinal variations, as complex and subtle as those elaborated about the Eucharist, and the issues at stake were more immediate and visible.

How are we to understand, for example, Charlemagne's coronation in Rome in 800 by Pope Leo III, celebrated in the basilica erected on

Saint Peter's tomb? Was this ceremony consistent with the point of view expressed much later, around 1135, by Hugh of St. Victor, one of the most important theologians of the time, who, following the principle that gave predominance to the life of the spirit over that of the body, asserted that "the spiritual power must establish the earthly power in order that it may exist and must judge it if it has not been good"?[45] Does the fact that the pope crowned the emperor necessarily mean that the temporal power was nothing but an instrument to be used by the spiritual one? Or was that coronation instead an act that made sacred the political power, thereby stripping the Church of its preeminence? Is it not possible to believe that Charlemagne, who is said to have had Augustine's *City of God* read aloud to him during meals, considered himself and was considered to be an agent in the service of the advent of that City of God, having received God's blessing to unify Christendom? This hypothesis is hardly belied by a letter addressed to Charlemagne by his counselor Alcuin in 799, a letter which was most probably instrumental in determining him to go to Rome and be crowned. In it Alcuin spoke of the three qualities of world rulers known up until then: the apostolic sublimity of the pope, Saint Peter's vicar; the imperial dignity of the emperor of Byzantium, who for centuries exercised power over Rome; and finally, in a clear allusion to Charlemagne himself, the royal dignity under which "our Lord Jesus Christ has placed the government of the Christian people."[46] It seems that for Alcuin Charlemagne was greater than the pope or the Byzantine emperor, in that the purpose and end of his political power was to ensure the material survival of all Christendom. Charlemagne's coronation ratified this affirmation because it made real a unique kind of sovereignty, both sacred and temporal.

We should beware of hasty interpretations, however, because the Church cannot be said to have sacrificed its own structures to the Carolingian Caesaro-papist arrangement; it remained fully in charge of the sacraments and all ways to salvation, and with them the professionals and specific organization involved in such administration. Above all, even though it was Charlemagne who, before his coronation, had reinstated Leo III as pope (the man was in prison for several crimes at the time), this did not mean that the political sovereign had become the source of the pontiff's legitimacy any more than that the right to be king originated with the pope—although it did, in its essence, come from God. Nothing prevents us from believing that when he took his crown from the pope, Charlemagne was not absorbing the spiritual power but actually recognizing its autonomy and preeminence. As with the period immediately preceding him, during which the sovereign pontiffs had acquired a temporal right to the Italian territories (accorded them by Pepin le Bref, king of the Franks and father of Charlemagne) and the donation of Constantine (a forgery written in 750), according to which the emperor transferred his powers over the western part of the empire to Pope Sylvester I, it is difficult to see in the coronation of Charlemagne and in the doctrine expressed by Alcuin the triumph of a unitary vision of Christianity, that is, as having only one power, or an attempt to actualize a wayward interpretation of Saint Augustine according to which the Earthly City should try to realize the City of God in the here and now. Alcuin was perhaps describing a real power situation, at a moment when the papacy was relatively weak, rather than propounding a theory of royalty's superior power. It is necessary to remember the complexity of these ideologies and of the actual power relations between the political and sacred orders. Charlemagne, guarantor of the organization and survival of Christendom because the most powerful Western Christian political sovereign, might be seen as realizing in his actions (in a kind of competition with the Byzantine emperor and in a way that seems to go against Augustine's mystical separation) the kingdom of God on earth. It seems more accurate to say, however, that he was the political power accomplishing the spiritual power's mission. In this view he was not claiming to substitute himself for that power but rather continued to recognize its supremacy and the supremacy of the spiritual.[47]

The debate about the interrelations and the respective fields of action of the two kinds of power was often developed in terms of the allegory of the two swords, which as we have said enjoyed immense prosperity and longevity. It was used with particular intensity during the last quarter of the eleventh century in the dramatic conflict between Pope Gregory VII and the German king and later Holy Roman Emperor Henry IV; then again, starting at the end of the thirteenth century during the no less acute confrontation between Pope Boniface VIII and the French king Philip IV. These were two theatrical episodes in which tension peaked. The German king was made to wait three days barefoot, stripped of all royal emblems and in the garb of a penitent,

pleading for papal mercy outside the door of the pope's castle at Canossa before Gregory VII would let him make honorable amends for
having challenged his authority (January 25-28, 1077), and Boniface
VIII was slapped on the face in his palace at Anagni by Guillaume de
Nogaret, a "jurist" sent by the king of France to arrest him with the
help of the noble Roman family and sworn papal enemy, the Colonnas
(September 3, 1303). These two major crises of medieval Christianity
may be understood as resulting from inherent ambiguities in the
Caesaro-papist model born of the fusion of the Holy Roman Empire
with the Church. We have seen with the example of Charlemagne's
coronation that the practical meaning of that fusion remained uncertain, even paradoxical: if, by demanding recognition from the Church–
in the form of a coronation, for example–the political power reinforced the Church, it was conversely true that by claiming for itself a
monopoly on the sacred and insisting on an instrumentalist conception of the temporal sword in the service of the spiritual one, the
Church contributed to the progressive functional secularization of the
state and thereby to its growing autonomy. The state began to be able
to exist on its own and for itself, giving itself some supplementary
legitimacy in the people's eyes by means of a few magic tricks and a
proclamation of its own particular sacredness.

But these two episodes also have the status of founding moments in
the history of Christianity, and they were examined and reinterpreted
each time the temporal status of the Church became a source of acute
tension and conflict. The respective struggles of the French king Philip
IV and the Holy Roman Emperor Henry IV of Germany were regularly
invoked during the sixteenth-century wars of religion in France: the
papacy's pretension to intervene in France's political-religious problems, namely the Protestant Henri of Navarre's accession to the throne
as (the Catholic) Henri IV, was presented with explicit reference to
these medieval episodes. As has been mentioned, the Protestant jurist
François Hotman retrospectively qualified Boniface VIII as a fanatic,
which in his eyes made him the worthy predecessor of Hotman's own
contemporary, Pope Sixtus V, who had excommunicated Henri de
Navarre in 1585.[48]

The conflict between pope and emperor repeatedly touched on a
fundamental problem for Christianity: how much legitimacy and what
breadth of sovereignty for the political power? In the Middle Ages the

question regularly came down to the issue of controlling nominations to religious positions, that is, the problem of the investiture of Church authorities. The problem was an acute one, given the major temporal, civil role of the Church at the time, to say nothing of its immense wealth, especially in the form of land and land revenues. Against the control that had come to be exercised by nonecclesiastics in the matter of investitures–bishops were often named by kings–the papacy first tried to counterattack in the eleventh century through the actions of Gregory VII, attempting to (re)impose its spiritual and temporal hegemony by combating simony, or the selling of episcopal offices, a practice particularly common in Germany at the time.

The conflict between Gregory and Henry, smoldering even before the latter became emperor, exploded when the diocese of Milan found itself with two bishops, one named by the pope, the other by the king, who divided between them the allegiance of the local population (the city and its cathedral were set on fire in 1075 by partisans of the pope's bishop). This was crude evidence that the struggle for control over posts and prebendaries had resulted in two competing *nomenklatura*, two rival bureaucracies. Thus began the period of great agitation and conflict known as the Investiture Contest, which involved repeated excommunications by pope and king, the naming by Pope Gregory of a German anti-king, the calling of a council by King Henry IV to name an antipope; the king's invasion of Rome, where he had himself crowned emperor by his antipope while the original pope took refuge in the Castello Sant'Angelo, to which must be added the intervention by a Norman warlord, Robert Guiscard, who supported Gregory but whose troops put Rome to sack. Gregory VII was to die in 1085 in a kind of exile in the south of Italy.

While the events connected with the conflict were numerous and chaotic–Henry's wait outside Gregory's door at Canossa was the most intense and spectacular of them–the arguments exchanged in defense of the respective parties to it, though complex, followed a clear and strong logic. Indeed, the battle was not just one of clanging weapons; it was juridical, and it produced multiple justificatory briefs, arguments in canon law, in which each camp, anxious to rally its partisans, made ample use of a rhetoric of conviction. Partisans were indispensable because in order to assemble a council to elect a pope, for example (an antipope to those who contested his legitimacy), one had to convince the necessary religious authorities. Money did not always suffice for this purpose, the ecclesiastics in question requiring for their dignity that the arrangement have at least an aureola of theological or canonical phrases, so everyone involved worked painstakingly on their arguments, intellectuals in the service of the German emperor buttressing theirs with Roman law.

In this twelfth-century context it was not of course the purely legal arguments that had the greatest legitimating power; more compelling by far were theological arguments making use of Holy Scripture. In his *Dictatus papae* (1075), a sort of summary of his theocratic ideas, Gregory VII affirmed that the pope, "the only man whose feet all princes kiss" (a clear allusion to his intimate tie to Christ), had the power to depose emperors and release their subjects from their oaths of loyalty when the rulers in question were deemed unjust (this was of course one of the points that sixteenth-century French theorists of the divine right of kings would vigorously contest). When, after an arrogant proclamation in which he immunized himself against any and all criticism by declaring the infallibility of the Catholic Church, "which has never erred and never will," Gregory VII called a synod to excommunicate Henry IV and release his subjects from their oath of loyalty, the Holy Roman Emperor responded (April 1076) with an encyclical letter in which he called the pope by his common name, Hildebrand, because in his eyes Gregory VII was a mere impostor:

> We shall restrict ourselves to saying that [Hildebrand] has laid hold of both the priesthood and royalty against the will of God. By acting thus he has shown his contempt for the order that God has established, for it was God's wish that the priesthood and royalty should not be united in the same hands but on the contrary that they remain distinct and be confided into different hands. This is what our Lord and Saviour in his Passion gave us clearly to understand when he spoke of the two swords. He was told "Lord, here are two swords," and he replied "It is enough" [Luke, 22:38], by which he meant that in the Church there must be a double sword, a spiritual sword and a material sword, by means of which all that is harmful to it should be exterminated: a sacerdotal sword so that, after God, men shall obey the king; a royal sword to fight the enemies of Christ without and oblige all men within to obey the sacerdotal power. In this way there would be ties of charity between the two, the priesthood honoring royalty and royalty in turn honoring the priesthood. This is the economy God established, and it has been destroyed by Hildebrand's madness.[49]

We see that Henry IV used Scripture to affirm a real duality between the two swords and contest the papal pretension to wield them
both. Significantly, he did not position himself outside the Church but
within it—"In the Church there must be a double Sword"—where the
spiritual sword's role was to compel obedience to God and king (but
not to this particular pope, apparently) and where the royal sword
carried with it the obligation to combat external enemies and compel
obedience to the priesthood. In his scheme, royal power was based on
the absoluteness of the divine right of kings:

> He ["Hildebrand"] has tried to deprive me of my kingdom, I, whom God
> has called to the realm, whereas He did not call him to the priesthood, and
> it was because he [the pope] saw that I wanted to reign in His name and not
> in his [the pope's], because he [the pope] did not create me king.[50]

With the exception of a secondary player whose contribution remains obscure,[51] the most important personage to use the analogy of
the two swords in a way favorable to the spiritual power was Saint
Bernard, founder of the Cistercian order. In a letter to Pope Eugenius
III in 1120 he offers the following practical interpretation of the meaning of the two swords:

> Both swords are Peter's: one is unsheathed at his sign [command], the other
> by his own hand, as often as is necessary. Peter was told concerning the
> sword which seemed less his [the temporal sword], "Put up thy sword into
> the scabbard." Thus that sword was undoubtedly his, but it was not to be
> drawn by him.[52]

Saint Bernard was not founding theocratic thought in this passage; his
purpose was not essentially theopolitical. But the distinction that he
made between having a sword in hand (*manu*) and having one at command (*usu*), a distinction that enabled him to argue that the Church
controlled both swords according to two different and precise modalities, was very much appreciated, notably almost two centuries later by
Pope Boniface VIII, who used it in the crucial bull entitled *Unam
sanctam* (November 1302). More precisely, it was used by Giles of
Rome, one of the most important intellectuals among the pope's doctrinal counselors, in arguments against the French king Philip IV
(known as "the Fair"). Giles was a central figure of medieval scholastic
philosophy and, as we have said, the first to translate Aristotle's *koinonia politikè* as *societas civilis*.

Chosen by Philip III as tutor to his son the future king Philip the Fair, Giles of Rome followed a rather unusual path in becoming counselor to Boniface VIII and thereby his former student's adversary. Although his allegiances seem to have followed one another chronologically, we may, for reasons we shall see, understand him to be the symbol of a double allegiance: to king and pope, to civil society and the Church.

Born in Rome in 1243, Giles became a member of the order of the Hermits of Saint Augustine at the age of fourteen; he was sent to study in Paris a short time afterward. There he is known to have followed the lectures of Thomas Aquinas at the University. His intellectual powers came to the notice of Philip III, who, when he chose him as tutor for his son, also commissioned him to write a treatise on the education of princes.[53] Giles responded with *De regimine principum*, which will be discussed in some detail further on. He continued his career in the Augustine order while enjoying the favor of the king, who, among other privileges, allocated to him a large parcel of land on the left bank in Paris on which to build a monastery (destroyed in the nineteenth century) that would house the order of the Grands Augustins after Giles had united several minor orders of Augustinian inspiration. In spite of some difficulties with the bishop of Paris Etienne Tempier in connection with the condemned theological theses of 1277,[54] and by virtue of his abundant and diverse writings, Giles was named Master of Theology at the University of Paris. Proclaimed regent master and then, in 1292 at Rome, elected general of his order, he was made bishop in 1295, at a time when the great majority of France's bishops were born subjects of the king. (Philip IV, who generally complained that the pope attributed the benefices of his realm to foreigners, could hardly protest the appointment of a bishop who had in a way been "naturalized" French.) He was given the important diocese of Bourges, which remained in his name until his death.[55] His was thus a brilliant career, explicable in terms of the support he was given by his royal former student and by Boniface VIII, whose election he defended after Celestine V's resignation.[56]

The dispute between the pope and the French king broke out in 1296 as a result of the papal bull *Clericis laicos*, which forbade the French and English clergy to subsidize their kings. Hostilities deepened with the arrest of the bishop of Pamiers, Bernard Saisset, a partisan of the pope against the king, and his condemnation in 1301. Resolutely and from the outset, Giles of Rome took the side of the pope. In 1302, despite an order from the king of France forbidding all religious dignitaries to leave the realm, Giles participated in the Council of Rome called to prepare the bull titled *Unam sanctam* ("One, holy": the opening words, which may be taken as a definition of the Church), contributing actively to its elaboration. The bull itself seems a theorization of the Jubilee ceremonies of 1300, where Boniface VIII had appeared wearing attributes of both the priesthood and political sovereignty, the pontifical crown and the sword, and was said to have declared, "I am pontiff and emperor, I have earthly and temporal power."[57] It was probably revised by the pope, but even if he did not write all of it, Giles of Rome was at the very least the direct inspiration for it; the few dozen lines read like a condensed and nuance-free version of the treatise he devoted to the power of the Church, *De ecclesiastica potestate*, a polemic which in its argumentation and ideology may be seen as representative of political Augustinism with its refusal to accept the idea that the political order was legitimated by nature and that temporal powers could be autonomous from the sovereign pontiff. Faced with Giles's refusal to adhere to his cause and the blatant support offered to his declared adversary, Philip IV expressed regrets that the pope had ever raised his former tutor to the status of general.[58] A member of the clergy, loyal above all to the pope, Giles of Rome was the living antithesis of Guillaume de Nogaret, jurist in the king's secret council, who, sent to Anagni in 1303 to capture the pope in person, is reputed to have slapped Boniface. In spite of the insubordination to the king committed when he left for Rome to participate in the Council of 1302, Giles of Rome was allowed to return to France, and before dying in 1316 at the court of Pope John XXII in Avignon, he willed his library to the Parisian monastery he had founded. There too, at his request, his body was taken to be buried.[59]

The duality of Giles's allegiance—to king, to pope—can be seen as a kind of practical translation of the double inspiration, Aristotelian and Augustinian, that shaped his political and theopolitical writings. (These constitute only a part of his ample production: his works number in the dozens and were widely circulated, as the existence today of thousands of manuscripts attests.) "Civil society," analyzed in Aristotelian terms, is at the heart of the treatise he wrote for the use of the future king, while his argumentation in favor of the supremacy of the spiritual sword, written for the pope and omnipresent in the *Unam sanctam*, is an Augustinian defense of the subordination of temporal power to spiritual power.

The essay Giles wrote between 1277 and 1279 was one of the most famous "mirrors for princes": numerous Latin manuscripts of it exist, for it was abundantly copied and circulated, but it was also translated – into French, Italian, Spanish, Castilian, Hebrew, German, and English – although as we have noted these translations did not result in vernacular versions of *societas civilis*. One good indication of the essay's repute is the fact that Philip III, who had attentively followed its Latin composition, almost immediately ordered a French translation (1282). As for the Latin original, it was, as we have said, widely copied, then revised – no fewer than eleven times between the first printed edition of 1473 and the last at the relatively late date of 1616. *Li livres du gouvernement des rois*, to give the title of the earliest French translation, may therefore be considered one of the founding texts of political science as a discipline defined by a specific object, method, and purpose.[60]

The text's success, and the fact that Charles V and Philip the Good, duke of Burgundy, ordered new translations of it (in 1372 and 1450) – proving that temporal monarchs found it appropriate and useful – may be explained by the almost technical perspective it adopts; we are far from Augustinian preoccupations here. Addressing himself to the "glorious generosity" of King Philip III, Giles of Rome begins with the affirmation that no political regime can be maintained by violent means. "If a regime is to be transmitted from father to son, it must be founded naturally," and "as the philosopher [Aristotle] tells us, he who has bodily strength but whose mind lacks subtlety and intelligence is a slave by nature, while the man who has an active mind and uses prudence in commanding naturally dominates."[61] The treatise goes on to explain the rules a prince must follow in order to govern first himself, then his household, and finally "civil society." Included are such precepts as that princes should be well dressed so as to impress the people and that princesses should not get married or become pregnant at too young an age because this is bad for their health. The text also explains how to make war. In sum, it enumerates everything that must be done to establish healthy political order, an order the author believed to originate in the fact that human beings are social animals, moved by a "natural tendency" to live in society with others. Isn't this a sort of naive naturalism? One can understand how doubts were raised–misplaced doubts–as to the single authorship of this text and Giles's other major work, the *De ecclesiastica potestate*, in which he affirms, following Augustine to the letter, that the City of God is the only republic in which justice reigns and that where Christ is not ruler and founder, *rector* and *conditor*, there is no justice.[62] Significantly, between the writing of the treatise on education and the theopolitical text of 1301 composed just before he left for Rome in disregard of the king's prohibition, the term "civil society" disappears; it is not to be found in the second work. This absence may be read as confirmation of the belief that temporal power has no purpose or end of its own, that it must be "ordered" by–subjected to and organized by–the imperative of constructing the City of God.

Giles's almost confidential text, written specifically for the pope–it was not translated and was copied only rarely–affirms the supremacy of spiritual power over temporal through a variety of arguments, certain of which were borrowed from the thinking of Denis the Pseudo-Areopagite and Hugh of St. Victor (especially on the concept of hierarchy), others from Saint Augustine. The central theme is that of the two swords, and Giles seeks to legitimate the pontifical power's interventions in the temporal sphere by means of theological doctrine and interpretation. He considers the issue of temporal goods as well as of the Church's relation to civil power, all in the majestic context of a theopolitical conception that elevates papal theocracy into a realization of the City of God. The tone expresses such conviction and determination that Giles's point of view, radically reductive of the autonomy of civil society, was qualified as "fanaticism" by both the first and only German editor of the text in 1929 and *The New Catholic Encyclopedia* in 1967.

The supremacy of the pope for Giles of Rome was founded on his "eminently spiritual" status, which meant that he might judge without being judged in turn and established him as the master of all, subject to none. Spiritual powers, he explained, must not be served in the same way as secular ones: the first made use of the spirit and the will, whereas secular powers might also have recourse to violence–they could make blood flow, administer death. This violence, perfectly legitimate for secular powers, was not fitting for the Church, which, according to Giles, must not have any stain or blemish or "indecency" whatsoever: it would be indecent for the "spiritual sword" to pronounce any judgment that would imply corporal punishment (*judicius sanguinis*). That was why such punishment was to be exercised only by the "material sword."[63] In order to preserve the perfection of spiritual things, a power had been instituted concerned with bodily things; this was the earthly power, particular and material, subordinate to the universal and spiritual power that characterized the spiritual sword.[64] Spiritual authority was the theocratic power's sphere of action, and because violence would soil it, it must use only the spiritual sword (concretely, this meant that it could excommunicate). Following this logic, Giles explained that the sovereign pontiff had the same relation to the temporal power as the soul to the body[65] and that the existence of the two swords was based on a similarly absolute hierarchy between the two kingdoms. It was the spiritual power's superior sacredness that made the sovereign pontiff ruler of rulers and the spiritual sword the most universal weapon.

Giles of Rome therefore categorically rejected the argument that because all power came from God (Romans 3:2), the temporal sword also came from God and thereby enjoyed its own legitimacy, an argument that was to be at the center of the Martin Luther's political doctrine and, of course, that of theorists of the divine right of kings. He insisted that the priority of the spiritual sword was immediately responsible for its primacy: it had come first. The temporal sword in his understanding had been born of a differentiation from the spiritual one; the priesthood historically preceded the political power; the second depended on and was subject to the first because it derived from it.[66] Giles also contested one of the key arguments presented by defenders of royal power when he took on the notion of domination (*dominium*). In the patrimonial model, the king was considered to be master of a domain, with the rights of absolute ownership,[67] whereas Giles maintained that the goods of this world were first and foremost the property of God; they had been put into the hands of the Church and the temporal powers in order that they might accomplish the divine plan, that is, the quest for salvation. The master's right over earthly goods was therefore not absolute and could be taken from him if he was incompetent or unworthy. It followed from this that the pope, in accordance with his function and status, exercised domination over

earthly things and that the Church's power was not limited or circumscribed but rather, once again, universal.[68] And because justice was
intimately concerned with the allocation of earthly goods, there could
be no true justice in a city where Christ—which here comes close to
meaning the Christian Church—was not founder and ruler.

This affirmation was not to be taken abstractly: dominating mother,
the Church's jurisdiction over temporal things was not merely a point
of principle; in certain matters, the denunciation of crimes, for instance, that jurisdiction was "immediate and executive." The positive
nature that Giles attributed to the spiritual power is even more evident
in the Church's recognized right to own earthly goods; it was this right
that was at the center of its conflict with the French royal power. How
could the spiritual power's "domination" not include the right to own
temporal goods?[69] Given that they were "instruments" meant to help
and serve spiritual good, the supreme pontiff, "master of the spiritual
in the mystic universal body," was necessarily also master of all temporal goods.[70] Concretely, this meant that the Church had the divine
right, the divine mandate even, to receive annual dues and collect
tithes.

The doctrine according to which temporal goods had value and
meaning only in relation to spiritual ones necessarily leads, however,
to excluding sinners from any right to own property; it leads to the
legitimation of social death for sinners. This was perfectly consistent
with the assertion that the only political government worthy of exercising power was that of a prince entirely subject to God.[71] The ultimate
consequence of the spiritual sword's supremacy was thus the exclusion
from the political and social order of all those who did not belong to the
City of God. How far we are from the mystic Augustinian conception of
the relation between the two cities: "Infidels cannot justly or truly
possess anything, nor can they justly or truly, but only through usur-
pation and injustice, exercise any domination or power."[72] In other
words, only *Christian* humanity existed, in the same way that in certain
Muslim traditions, only the community of Islam exists. All the rights a
person could have were founded on his membership in the Church and
his obedience to its (earthly) ruler. In a word, fanaticism.

Still, this form of theocracy, by the very sharpness and rigor of the
distinction it drew between the two swords, forbade the papacy to act in
certain ways within the temporal sphere. The very exaltation of the

spiritual power, the requirement that it remain pure, implies the admission of a distinction, within the fixed, sacred hierarchy, between the kingdom of God and civil society. Earthly power in Giles's understanding must indeed be subject to ecclesiastical power and function in its service according to its will.[73] On the other hand, we may insist on how the mere fact of separation and instrumentalization made the Church dependent on the temporal power, which thereby, paradoxically, attained a kind of autonomy.

Let us return for a moment to the beginning of Giles's treatise on the education of princes. He announces from the start that he who reigns and dominates is lord only by "the bounty and acceptance of God": kings and princes serve God and must, like all servants, take their sovereign good to be in this master and find their happiness in him. This is of course a completely different perspective from Aristotle's, for whom civil society itself constituted the supreme good, and Giles's use of the same term cannot disguise his profound reorientation of the concept: civil society's value is in his scheme merely relative. However, as we have said, a certain harmony between Augustine and Aristotle is maintained by the hierarchical integration of civil society into the divine order, and with this in mind the *De ecclesiastica potestate* no longer seems in contradiction with the earlier work. Caesar's power—political power—was legitimate in the author's view only if it was worthy and just; the material sword was under the jurisdiction of the spiritual one. Nonetheless, in temporal matters, those of "cities," "castles," "fields," Caesar imposed a useful "domination" through the practices of collecting taxes and exercising punitive justice. The temporal sword or power was indeed beneath the spiritual sword or power, but because they were distinct, Caesar had real judicial and executive power; we may therefore say that the Earthly City did have its own substance, which was no mere appearance even though it depended on a superior, supreme instance to regulate it. The domination of the temporal sovereign, who enjoyed immediate ownership and exercised immediate control over temporal goods, is not denied, but limited, seen as inferior and secondary—a domination itself dominated. Once again, it was a matter of rendering unto Caesar what was Caesar's, while affirming the subordination of the temporal power to the ecclesiastical one, the only one to have "plenitude of power" (*plenitudo potestatis*).[74] As for the pope, the author appeals to him to allow the earthly powers to exercise their attributes. Let us reiterate that this distinction, although it limits temporal power, does give it complete control in the areas where it may legitimately be exercised. Clearly the spiritual power, whose most immediately usable instrument is the spiritual sword, was concerned with human beings because they had souls, while the temporal power affected them because they had bodies. However, "the temporal authorities have power over man as a whole, which means that he must serve them not only with his body, but also willingly."[75] This is as much as to say that the Christian must consider the temporal order of the world as something of which he is a participating member.

Giles's arguments thus express a sort of compatibility between Aristotle and Augustine, achieved by the insistence on distinctions and relations of dependence within a fixed hierarchy. While the Augustinian conception and the inferior ethical and ontological place it attributes to "earthly society" seem radically opposed to the Aristotelian vision of the political, Giles of Rome managed to put Aristotle in the service of Augustine, a move all the more remarkable in that, oriented toward an affirmation of the absolute supremacy of the spiritual power over the temporal power, it was advanced at the very moment when the position of Philip the Fair and his legists, their proofs against the pope that a king was emperor within his kingdom, were triumphing. Nothing authorizes us, then, to see contradiction or duplicity in the writings of the French king's former tutor; we cannot divide him into, on the one hand, an Aristotelian theorist of civil society and, on the other, an Augustinian monk, fanatical propagandist for the subordination of the Earthly City to the City of God. His Aristotelianism existed only in the framework of a hierarchical vision: the first point of his political science was that a prince must know, above all, how to govern himself. For Giles of Rome, politics was certainly a science, but not, as it was for the Greek philosopher, the science of the highest good.

As for the Boniface VIII, the man in spiritual power at the time, his chances of winning the battle were significantly narrowed by the fact that Philip the Fair enjoyed the support of both political and religious elites: in the assemblies called by the French king, all three estates, including the clergy, endorsed his policy of resisting the papacy. They too wanted established once and for all the king's monopoly over taxation, his control over appointments to positions of responsibility—what we may call in general the bureaucratic and political independence of the state in relation to the imperial, border-crossing papal administration whose interventions had come to be thought of as deleterious to the prerogatives of the monarchy and national sovereignty.

But we are still far from anything resembling a secular state. Philip IV, the miracle-working king who "touched" the scrofulous, was preoccupied with the canonization of his grandfather, Saint Louis, obtained in 1297; and in his dedication of *De regimine principum*, Giles of Rome himself recognized the sacredness of the future king, addressing the book to "Lord Philip, issue of a royal and holy lineage" and inviting him to follow the example of his father and ancestors "in whom holy Christianity and the faith of holy Church have ever been resplendent."[76] In the opposite camp, even though Boniface VIII's successor backed down and reached a compromise with the French king, leaving the celebrated *Unam sanctam* to stand as the last and most extreme manifestation of the papacy's theocratic aspirations, its swan song, it must not be forgotten that the unitarian ideology that subordinates civil society to the Church was to persist in Catholicism and animates it even to this day, not like a kind of peculiar or anachronistic residue, but as a central and dynamic feature (as we can see in the ideology of John Paul II).[77]

The hegemony of the One in the writings of Giles of Rome is manifest in both his conception of the Church as encompassing all and his manipulation of the Aristotelian political conception. His civil society, as we have said, is no longer the most elevated form of community; it includes, of course, segments smaller than itself—the family, the village—but it is itself included in a greater ensemble comprised of several cities: the kingdom.[78] Affirming the primacy of the One, Giles of Rome attributes a key position to the Church, which is to ensure the unity of all kingdoms and thereby to fulfill a similar function in relation to them as a kingdom does for its cities. And there is only one Church: unificatory because itself one and unique, it is declared the highest instance by the very logic of the one and the many. Giles of Rome goes on to proclaim the statutory superiority of the pope, at the head of the Church: his "status is eminently holy and eminently spiritual,"[79] and this places him above any and all earthly and secular powers.

It was of course the same superiority of the spiritual over the temporal power that was so often asserted by Boniface VIII himself. In a letter addressed to the German princes on the subject of one of their dynastic quarrels, he affirmed that all the preeminence and dignity that belonged to the various realms derive from "the grace and the concession of the Holy See, from which kings and Holy Roman Emperors receive the power of the sword."[80] And the *Unam sanctam* is unequivocal: the pope is the head of the Church, and all should submit to him in order to belong to the Church, this being the condition of salvation, for the Church alone had received the mission to guide souls toward God. The unity of the Church and its necessary, inevitable role in salvation are proclaimed and proved with the help of several passages from the Bible, namely references to Noah's Ark and the seamless tunic worn by Christ. This unity is also compared with that of the body, its head being Peter and his successors. It follows that all who desire to be in God must be in the Church, which has only one head, Christ, whose vicar is the pope. That is why the Church controls the two swords, the spiritual one wielded by the Church in the hands of the clergy, and the temporal one, wielded by the hand of the civil authority directed by the spiritual power. Its authority, even if exercised by a man, was not human but divine, given to Peter by God. Therefore, anyone who opposed the power ordained by God was opposing God's law and seemed to be accepting two founding principles, like the Manichaeans. Nothing in this papal bull is particularly original, because the pope only reiterated old and familiar conceptions of the Church, but it mobilized them at a moment of acute crisis. The *Unam sanctam*, whose title went straight to the heart of the problem in proclaiming that papal authority was one and indivisible, presented itself as a universal text with constraining power, affirming in its conclusion once again that, in order to be saved, all creatures must submit to the pontiff at Rome.[81] It is easy to understand how the bull has remained the very symbol of the papacy's theocratic ambitions and why Gallicans in the seventeenth and eighteenth centuries held it in horror.

The Catholic Church and Its Will to Control Civil Society

As we noted in Chapter 1, the archbishop of Paris, Monseigneur Lustiger, used the term "civil society" in 1988 with the intention of reminding his readers that it was utterly impregnated with Christian values. He was not aiming to embrace a wider audience by using a popular expression of the moment: as we have said, the idea is part of the centuries-old tradition of the Catholic Church. We know that Pope John Paul II used the expression in *Centesimus annus*, his encyclical of May 1, 1991, and it had already been used by John XXIII in *Pacem in terris*, and even earlier, in 1891, by Leo XIII in *Rerum novarum*.[82] The fanatic thirteenth-century pope Boniface VIII may seem far away, but the issue raised by the two swords remains entirely relevant today, the terms of the present debate having been set in the nineteenth century, when a new affirmation of papal infallibility combined with the legal separation of the state from the Church made possible a compromise between the two, of which France is a paradigmatic case.[83]

Before discussing the issue as it was defined in the nineteenth century we should underline the general complexity of the debate, in which theological and political stances were not always combined as might have been expected. Denouncing the dangers for France of the doctrine of papal infallibility and the damage already caused at the political level by the papal bull *Unigenitus* (1713), which had limited the freedoms of the Church of France and opened wide the way for Ultramontane pretensions, two of the most important Jansenist writers of the eighteenth century underlined the "ruinous effects that this fatal decree has on civil society." Partisans of the bull, according to these authors, wanted to destroy the calm and tranquility of the state by attacking "our holy freedoms," those of the Gallican Church. To claim, as such partisans did, that a papal bull from Rome had as much value as a position held by the "universal Church," that is, the instituted totality of believers, was equivalent to giving popes the prerogative of deposing kings.[84] Clearly the Jansenists were greatly influenced by the theses of such authors as William Barclay (see Chapter 1, note 28) and Edmond Richer, who in their arguments defending the legitimacy of Henri IV's ascension to the throne had developed a strong Gallican perspective.

Against such radical Ultramontanists as Bellarmin, who explicitly associated his thinking with that of Giles of Rome, Richer affirmed that because the Church was landless—obviously the Church could not be said to be identical with the papacy—and without political structure, it had no power over the temporal sword. The Church's lord, he argued, was Christ and not the pope, who was merely Christ's minister. In diametrical opposition to Boniface VIII's *Unam sanctam*, Richer denied that the pope alone governed the Church, arguing that while the Church was a monarchy with one sole ruler, Jesus Christ, it was governed by two distinct persons, the pope and the king. The pope was merely the Lord's steward and as such had no right to use either the legal or coercive means of the temporal power. The mission entrusted to the Church by Christ concerned a supernatural and spiritual end, and it was up to the political prince alone to act in the defense and for the protection of divine law, this by means of human law and the sword. Papal prerogatives were doubly contested: the Church could wield only the spiritual sword, which meant the pope could not intervene in temporal affairs, and furthermore, within the Church itself, power–more specifically, the power of St. Peter's keys to the City of God–belonged not to the pope but to the universal Church.[85] The defense of civil society in France–let us remember that what was meant by the term then corresponds to what we mean by "state" today–was based on a rejection of two indissociable ideas: that Rome was superior to the national Church, and that the spiritual sword was superior to the temporal one.

The point here is not to signal the importance of the role played by Gallicanism and Jansenism together in the development of a concept of the state as politically autonomous, but rather to underline the continuity and recurrence of the debates. To find a nineteenth-century opponent of this orientation, we need only think of the theopolitical thinker and writer Félicité de Lamennais, who accentuated the opposition between civil society and the Church and wanted to maintain the first in a relation of subordination to the second, as is shown by his fight against the secularization of the school system. To his mind, without a strong influence on the part of the Church, civil society was morally threatened, and the decisive area in which this influence should be exerted was education.[86]

In this sense, the question of the type of political regime in France– monarchy or republic–was secondary to the problem of the hierarchical relation between church and state, which involved the conflict between the localized political power and the transnational Church. Even if by projecting its own structures upon monarchy, the Church had attributed the highest value to that form of government, the crucial point as far as it was concerned was not the nature of political systems, but rather how to control civil society. Pope Leo XIII's 1885 encyclical

Immortale Dei may be seen as breaking with certain doctrinal currents that rejected republican regimes and preached either political abstinence for the Church or else a resolute combat against all secular states. This papal text recommended that Catholics participate in municipal administration, that they work above all to ensure that "as becomes a Christian people, public provisions may be made for the instruction of youth in religion and true morality," and finally that they should "extend their efforts beyond this restricted sphere and give their attentions to national politics." In this way they would "infuse, as it were, into all the veins of the state the healthy sap and blood of Christian wisdom and virtue."[87] The project is clear: to fight against those who, like the Freemasons, worked to make "the teaching office and authority of the Church . . . of no account in the civil state."[88] And the pope did not refrain from asserting, in rhetoric that might have been perfectly at home in the thirteenth century, that the will to "destroy all connection between civil society and the duties of religion" originated in those who, in accordance with the division of humankind into the realm of God and the realm of Satan, belonged to the latter.

What is known as the French Catholic hierarchy's "rallying" to the *fait accompli* that was the French Republic[89] was in no way a recognition of the autonomy of "civil society"; rather we might say that, in order not to alienate all republicans by supporting the royalist faction among the episcopate and the French faithful, the papacy chose to abandon the debate about the nature of political institutions. After all, monarchies had not always shown such goodwill to the papacy that they should be systematically preferred over republics: it was *royal* troops that had invaded the Eternal City in the 1860's with the intention of incorporating it into the new Italian state. The decisive battleground would no longer be that of political structures, but education. Rather than risk having to return to the catacombs for supporting the restoration of the monarchy, the Church decided it would do better to defend territory already won within civil society, meanwhile claiming control over that society.

The encyclicals written by Leo XIII during the last quarter of the nineteenth century–but also John Paul II's, composed a hundred years later–take up the polemics of *The Syllabus of the principle errors of our time* (1864), a gathering of quotations from the writings of his immediate predecessor Pius IX against the autonomy of civil society and all doctrines of free social contract. In them the Church expressed equal approbation of government by one person or several, providing that it were just and applied itself to establishing the common good, and condemned the principle of the people's sovereignty as failing to acknowledge the sovereignty of God.[90] It was from this perspective that they denounced the Protestant Reformation for the effects it had on political doctrine and political reality: its leaders were men who had utterly reversed the respective positions of the temporal and spiritual powers, bringing on civil war and wreaking other damage:

> That harmful and deplorable passion for innovation which was aroused in the sixteenth century threw first of all into confusion the Christian religion, and next, by natural sequence, invaded the precincts of philosophy, whence it spread among all the classes of society.[91]

The sinful fault of the Reformation had been responsible for the development of a new kind of law, one affirming the equality of men, the sovereignty of the people, and freedom of conscience, thought, and published expression—all of which was itself good only if applied to truth and goodness. So much for *liberté* and *égalité*; as for *fraternité*, the pope's affirmation that "it is impossible to reduce civil society to one dead level"[92] gives an idea of how *it* was valued. The theme of civil society's intrinsic debility and its need to be animated and made moral by a spiritual principle is constantly present in this text. And in 1900 Leo XIII pointed out that the religious orders were useful not only to the Church but also to civil society because they taught virtue through word and example.[93]

In general these encyclicals express clear regret that the Christian civilization of the Middle Ages has disappeared: the Church would certainly have preferred God's division of human government between two powers, one ecclesiastical, the other political, to have been harmoniously continued up through the centuries, in a certain agreement about principles, with its own point of view being more docilely followed. Rationalism, naturalism, liberalism, socialism, and communism were all equally to blame for diminishing the Church's influence.

The sixth point of Pius IX's *Syllabus* is a list titled "Errors about Civil Society considered both in itself and in its relation to the Church," among which figure the mistakes of believing that "the best theory of civil society" demands that establishments of learning be "freed from all ecclesiastical authority,"[94] or that church and state must be separate. The pope took up the medieval metaphor of the two swords to affirm that patriarchs, primates, archbishops, and bishops everywhere must fight, armed with the "sword of the Spirit which is the Word of God,"[95] to keep religion from being "banished from civil society." The combat was to be conducted in the field of "freedom of education," that is, against secular schooling, for there must be a school where the truth was told, that is, where the true teacher was God.[96]

It is of course on these grounds that the conflict between church and state continues today, for the "school without God" both makes manifest how civil society has become autonomous from the Church and provides the former with means of further emancipating itself. While the debate in France may take on almost picturesque or even ridiculous aspects (the debate about a weekday where children would not go to school but rather to catechism), the Church nonetheless accords it primary importance. We should not permit ourselves to be misled by the fact that the battle to defend private schooling–in France, this means religious, and therefore essentially Catholic education–cleverly rebaptized "combat for the freedom of education," came to look like a confrontation between the right and the left (this was in part due to the tactlessness with which the issue was handled in 1984 by the socialist government of Prime Minister Pierre Mauroy): the fight for *l'école libre* cannot be considered a merely circumstantial episode in which the right saw how to make the most of an issue that was mobilizing the public. As far as the Catholic Church was concerned it was once again the continuation of a centuries-old conflict. Put another way, though the question of who should control education did not become a crucially important issue in France until the development of mass education that accompanied the rise of industrial society–as if education had replaced the medieval disputes about taxation and investitures as they affected political sovereignty–it may also be seen as the contemporary form of the Church's fight to affirm the priority of the spiritual sword.

In the Church's logic, this is not a rearguard combat, but an absolute priority. Schooling in modern societies has become a fundamental element and condition of social organization. In an industrial society based on universal literacy, this made necessary by the condition of mobility in the division of labor, a society about which we can say, following Ernest Gellner, that the state has the monopoly on legitimate culture, the dispute over education cannot be taken for a marginal or residual phenomenon. As Gellner shows, a modern society cannot function without a mass education system whose purpose is to disseminate a shared culture, the state's function being to assure the existence of that system, which in turn provides the nation with its foundation:[97] there is a manifest tendency in such an arrangement for the political and cultural spaces to overlap. A homogeneous culture whose dissemination is ensured by the school is the basis for the modern nation-state. Meanwhile, from its point of view, the Catholic Church cannot do otherwise than fight for the preeminence of the spiritual sword. So we see that the dispute about education can only be perpetuated, even intensified, even if in countries where a compromise has been reached, necessarily unstable like all compromises, this confrontation can be played out in the form of reconciliations and accommodations.

Pope John Paul II has predictably invoked the students' right to learn "the truths and certitudes of the religion of their choice"; this in turn leads directly to a demand for the teaching of religion in the public schools. He is of course not talking about the transmission of knowledge *about* religion, but rather "confessional" teaching.[98] We begin to see why the Catholic Church now generally accepts the distinction between civil society and the state, between social organization and political authority. Whereas this distinction is absent from the majority of the nineteenth-century papal texts, which, it seems, automatically adopt the Augustinian opposition between civil society and the City of God and take "civil society" and "state" for synonyms, it is present in Leo XIII's *Rerum novarum* (1891) and in John XXIII's *Pacem in terris* (1963), accompanied by a strict hierarchization that makes the state into an instrument of civil society or the political community. And this holds even for the law-governed state discussed by John Paul II in his 1991 encyclical, *Centesimus annus*. The principle of "subsidiarity" according to which a "higher order," in this case the state, must not seek to do what a more basic, fundamental body can do—according to the Church, civil society is such a body—should, in the Church's point of view, be applied in full in order that intermediate structures and bodies can multiply and responsibilities be widely distributed. John Paul II even adopts as his own Leszek Kolakowski's analysis according to which it is the state's absorption of civil society that defines totalitarianism (see Chapter 1, pp. 33-34).

But such praise of civil society and the affirmation of its necessary autonomy, its primacy over the state, is profoundly ambiguous coming from a pope, for it seems to suggest that all states are in danger of becoming totalitarian. This is of course what the present pope believes about all "atheist" states. He even goes so far as to imply that totalitarianism's roots might be found in democracy if that democracy is not in some fundamental way Christian—an affirmation that enables us to measure the depth of the Church's suspicion toward political modernity and of its rejection of Enlightenment philosophy: "A democracy without values easily turns into open or thinly disguised totalitarianism."[99] This thesis of *Centesimus annus* (repeated in 1995 in the encyclical *Evangelum vitae* or *The Gospel of Life*)—wrong at least in so far as no democracy has ever "easily" become totalitarian—clearly shows that democracy is not in itself a value for the Catholic Church. How then are we to interpret the pope's condemnation in this text of the "fanaticism or fundamentalism" of those who, "in the name of an ideology which purports to be scientific or religious," seek to impose upon other men their conception of truth and good? "Christian truth is not of this kind," the pope assures us, for Catholicism is not an ideology that would "presume to imprison changing sociopolitical realities in a rigid schema." No, the Church makes a rule of respecting freedom. The pope is, however, careful to affirm from the outset that "freedom attains its full development only by accepting the truth."[100] There is nothing here of a brutal declaration of the polity's subordination to the Church, and yet we can only take the earlier condemnation of fundamentalism and fanaticism as denial, in the Freudian sense of the term, as soon we realize that the Church considers civil society infirm and suffering from a lack of what the Church, as the vehicle of values and transcendence, can give it. The sincerity of the Catholic Church's acceptance of democracy and human rights is above suspicion, but the value of democracy does remain in its vision—and it would be as absurd to reproach the Church for this as to reproach a circle for being round—secondary, derivative, uncertain. To write in a papal encyclical in 1991, at the moment of the communist empire's fall, that democracy, civil society, needs to be impregnated with Christian values in order to avoid drifting or swerving into totalitarianism is to affirm once again the primacy of the spiritual sword—with all the force left to a Church that no longer has a secular arm, or if so only accidentally, indirectly. "The Kingdom of God, being *in* the world without being *of* the world, throws light on the order of human society, while the power of grace penetrates that order and gives it life."[101] These words, which describe perfectly the role that John Paul II attributes to the Church in routing out European communism and which are the foundation of the messages he delivered during his trip to Poland in 1991, clearly express that subordination in terms of values and an "ultimate purpose" for civil society.

The reason behind the Church's current anti-state position becomes clear: it is the state in its secularity that is being prosecuted and the Church desires to circumvent that state by establishing a direct connection between itself and civil society. Both the Polish and Italian churches have in their ways tried to realize this project recently. Using the dynamic of the social and national combat against communism, a large part of the Polish Church has been tempted to try to take over the role of hegemonic controller of civil society that the old Communist Party tried of late to fulfill. (This of course provoked a backlash in favor of the communists in the 1994 and 1995 elections.) In Italy the anti-statist strategy was clearly laid out by one of the theorists of the Catholic association "Communion and Liberation," who affirmed that "the secular state must not intervene in those sectors of civil society where social forces are already at work." We may see in this a version of Gramscism in which not the Party but the Church is called upon to (re)conquer civil society.[102]

The fact that the Catholic Church has lost a great deal of its capacity to intervene in public policy has not affected the logic that pushes it toward supporting fanaticism. Though it may employ the vocabulary of personalism or some other humanist philosophy, what the Church has to say remains the same: namely, that man without God, atheist man, and society without God, secular democracy, are mutilated, infirm, impoverished. Of course the Church now recognizes that the polity has it own laws, legitimacy, and field of action, and it does not claim to have a program for transforming the world that would make it commensurate with the ultimate good; in this sense it is different from millenarian ideologies such as Leninism. Still, is there not cause to believe that the only reason the Church does not impose its choices, particularly in the matter of moral custom, on all persons, Catholic or not, living in the same political community is that it does not have the political means to do so? The right it claims to being a universal source of illumination; the belief it asserts that one is only fully human when Christian; the affirmation that atheism, tied to Enlightenment philosophy, is a void; the thesis according to which a society cannot even aim to be just if it is not impregnated with Christianity–imperialism in the name of goodness and denigration of civic life–these are still present at the core of Catholic doctrine, even though they are to some degree repressed, thwarted, or combated by the emergence of other ideals, ideals that recognize the universality of human rights regardless of religion or absence thereof, and other institutions, institutions that seek to free the public space from a relation of dependency on the City of God and that affirm the dignity of the profane.

Mahomet the Prophet, or Fanaticism

The word *séide*, a Gallicizing of the Arab word *zayd* defined as a "fanatically devoted henchman capable of committing criminal acts out of religious zeal,"[103] came into French as the name of a character in the play *Mahomet the Prophet, or Fanaticism*, written by Voltaire in 1742.

As we know, Islam was first identified with fanaticism long before the advent in 1979 of the Iranian revolution, the coming to power of the Ayatollah Khomeini, and the rise of Muslim fundamentalism. The linking of Islam with fanaticism was at first meant to signify less an excess or deviation than what was considered the normal quality of Islam, in which no sphere of life, public or private, might be autonomous from the content of revealed faith.[104] But may we say that fanaticism is a part of the nature of Islam, more so than of other religions, because it is in essence theocratic?[105] This was clearly not Voltaire's opinion; suffice it to remember that for him Mohammed and Oliver Cromwell were equally fanatical.[106] His denunciation of Muslim fanaticism applied as well to all fanaticisms, including those of his own century and country, which he could not discuss openly.

Voltaire's play opens with Zophire, sheik of Mecca, refusing to recognize and submit to Mahomet, here portrayed as a brutish camel driver, traitor, and cruel tyrant:

ZOPHIRE: Quoi, moi, baisser les yeux devant ces faux prodiges!
            Moi, de ce fanatique encenser les prestiges!

ZOPIR: What did you say! I should bow humbly before his false miracles! I should pay homage to the miracles of that fanatic! [107]

To be rid of the recalcitrant dignitary who refuses to adopt the Koran, Mahomet orders Séide, a member of his immediate entourage, to assassinate him, at first stirring up his hatred of idolatry, then promising him the lovely Palmire for his bride. This is enough to convince Séide, who sets out to "sacrifice" an old man in a world that generally accords respect to old men.

Reacting to Mahomet's command, he exclaims:

> Je crois entendre Dieu; tu parles, j'obéis.

MAHOMET: Obéissez, frappez: teint du sang d'un impie
Meritez par sa mort une eternelle vie.

SÉIDE: Ange de Mahomet, ange exterminateur,
Mets ta férocité dans mon coeur.

SEID: I seem to hear the voice of God. You speak and I obey.

MAHOMET: Obey, strike him! Stained with his impious blood you will merit eternal life if he dies.

SEID: Angel of Mahomet, angel of death, place your fierceness in the depths of my heart.[108]

And Séide plunges "his consecrated sword" into the old man's breast. But he hesitates before striking, declaring to the woman he has received as payment for the crime he is to commit that he wasn't cut out to be a murderer. Séide nonetheless does the deed, and it turns out to be particularly dreadful, for he and Palmire are in fact brother and sister, and Zophire was their father. Mahomet of course knew all this: the Prophet is a profaner, and not a blind one, as Oedipus is blind to his destiny, but a deliberate one, who knowingly pushes a man to commit parricide, while the only thing that prevents that man from committing incest is Mahomet's intention to keep Palmire for himself by poisoning her brother/husband-to-be. Before the poison has done its work, Séide learns everything and makes a pathetic attempt to rebel, but Mahomet, invulnerable, silences the revolt of the crowd with a few well-chosen words. Meanwhile, to escape the Prophet's bed, Palmire kills herself with the very sword her brother used to kill their father.

If at a literary level, the play demonstrates Voltaire's inability to imagine tragedy as anything other than deliberate manipulation, his message is only the clearer for that: fanaticism violates the most sacred ties, extinguishing the voice of kinship, and its partisans will not shrink from committing the most abominable acts if such is the will of a man who claims to be sent from God. Strangely, then, *Mahomet* prefigures the issue at the heart of the Calas Affair,[109] and, its literary weakness notwithstanding, offers a demonstration of how profanation, here in the form of incest and parricide, is an essential component of fanaticism.

In his hesitation before killing the man he does not yet know to be his father, Séide says, "I don't feel I was made to be an assassin." The word is well chosen, because "assassin" originated, like *séide*, as a proper noun: it designated an Ismaili sect, affiliated therefore with Shiite Islam, active in the eleventh and twelfth centuries, whose leader operated out of the fortress of Alamut, in Persia, communicating instructions to his followers far away in the Lebanese mountains. The sect, known for its meticulously organized and spectacular religiously and politically motivated assassinations, was evoked by Voltaire himself in his "fanaticism" article for the *Dictionnaire philosophique*; he describes them as "weak persons" led by a "knave" called the Old Man of the Mountain.[110] The first text in modern French about the Assassins, *Traicté de l'origine des anciens Assasins-porte-couteaux, avec quelques exemples de leurs attentats et homicides ès personnes d'aucuns roys, princes et seigneurs de la chrestienté* (Treatise on the origin of the ancient knife-wielding Assassins, with some examples of their attacks and homicides against the persons of kings, princes, and lords of Christendom), written by Denis Lebey de Batilly in 1603, proposed to explain the origin of the term a few years after the assassination of the French king Henri III by a monk named Jacques Clément. The word was neither Italian or Spanish, but Arabic, affirmed the author, whose sources were above all eyewitness accounts written in Latin or Old French and dating back to the Crusades.[111] According to these texts, the Assassins were Saracens and Mohammedans subject to the will of their chief, the Old Man of the Mountain:

> A prince feared and dreaded by other princes near and far, whether Christian or Saracen, whom the Old Man often had indifferently killed by messengers whom he had prepared, nourishing them in their youth in his palace, to do his bidding; he had persuaded them that by this means [the assassinations he instructed them to carry out] they would accede to the joys of Paradise.[112]

The sect's first murder victim, affirms the author, was one Raymond, Christian count of Tripoli, killed by an Assassin at the order of his

chief. The Holy Roman Emperor Frederick II is said to have allied himself for a time with the Old Man of the Mountain, with the intention of
dispatching certain Bavarian and Hungarian princes,[113] and Saint
Louis, king of France, to have come close to being one of his victims.
Lebey de Batilly was concerned to underline the contrast between the
conduct of these Saracens and the thinking of certain Christian theologians who condemned summary execution, and thereby indirectly to
censure the French Catholic Leaguers, who in their ferocious readiness to kill resembled in his view the Ismaili sect. The Assassins thus
constituted a vehicle permitting the author to advocate and extol submission to the law by denouncing the mysterious barbarity of the Mohammedans: he gives us to understand that the terrible vices of the
Assassins were in fact to be found at home, as made manifest by a
fanatic monk's killing of a king—for this was the event that had occa-
sioned the book.

A desire to probe the mysterious East stimulated by a dramatic event
originating in and having meaning for the West impelled just about
everything written about the Assassins; from the Crusades on, the
myth was developed, enriched, and complicated by the projection of
theories seeking to account for this particular incarnation of the un-
canny. Marked by a fascination for the "inexpressible dread" inspired
by the "horrible heroism of the Assassins," to use Michelet's words,[114]
the texts that relate the story of the Ismailis, loyal followers of the Old
Man of the Mountain (the first to receive the honor of the title was a
certain Hasan ibn al-Sabbah), in fact reveal more about their authors
than they tell us about their subject. Interpretation was predictably
influenced by the advent of the French Revolution, for example, and
more recently, totalitarian party-sects have been assimilated to the
Assassins and the name of Lenin cited with the idea that just as the
Assassins posited the concrete reality of the kingdom of God, so Lenin
posited that of the revolution.[115]

The first Western accounts underline the Assassins' total devotion
to their chief. In a chronicle of the Crusades written at the end of the
twelfth century, William Archbishop of Tyre describes them thus:

> There is in the province of Tyre . . . a people who possess ten strong castles,
> with their dependent villages; their number, according to what we have
> often heard, is about 60,000 or more. It is their custom to . . . choose their
> chief, not by hereditary right, but solely by virtue of merit. Disdaining any

other title of dignity, they called him the Elder. The bond of submission and obedience that binds this people to their Chief is so strong, that there is no task so arduous, difficult or dangerous that any of them would not undertake to perform with the greatest zeal, as soon as the Chief has commanded it. If for example there be a prince who is hated or mistrusted by this people, the Chief gives a dagger to one or more of his followers. At once whoever receives the command sets out on his mission, without considering the consequences of the deed nor the possibility of escape. Zealous to complete his task, he toils and labours as long as may be needful, until chance gives him the opportunity to carry out his chief's orders. Both our people and the Saracens call them Assissini; we do not know the origin of this name.[116]

In 1809, a French Orientalist named Silvestre de Sacy offered a solution to the etymological enigma posed by the name "Assassins"; his *Mémoire sur la dynastie des Assassins et sur l'origine de leur nom* was read at a public gathering of the *Academie des inscriptions et belles-lettres*. He postulated that "assassin" derived from "hashishins," "hashish" being an Arabic word that designated all types of grasses but more particularly Indian hemp, from which the Ismaili sect was known to have distilled a certain intoxicating liquor. This etymology was adopted by the Viennese Orientalist Joseph von Hammer, who published a history of the Assassins in 1818, then by Moreau de Tours, mentioned in Chapter 1 as a key participant in a highly colorful bit of French romantic activity, in his *Du haschich*, the first fully developed account of the physiological and psychological effects of the drug.[117] We owe one of the more picturesque versions of the myth to Théophile Gautier, who, with some illustrious friends, was a regular member of the aforementioned Club des Haschichins, which met in the Hôtel de Lauzun on the Ile Saint-Louis in Paris, residence of Doctor Moreau de Tours and Charles Baudelaire. There they consumed the hallucinatory substance in the form of a paste, the *dawamesk*, a mixture of the oily hemp extract and ground pistachio nuts; this was prepared and distributed by the good doctor himself to nourish the fantastical visions of the romantic revelers. In his account of the club's doings, Gautier devotes a long parentheses to the Assassins, which is worth reproducing in full:

> In the Orient long ago there existed a formidable order of sectarians commanded by a sheik bearing the title Old Man of the Mountain, Prince of the Assassins.

This Old Man of the Mountain was obeyed without question; his subjects the Assassins set forth to do his bidding, whatever it might be, with absolute devotion, flinching before no danger, even certain death. Upon a sign from their chief they would throw themselves off the tops of towers or stab a king to death in the midst of his guards.

By what artifice did the Old Man of the Mountain obtain from them such utter abnegation?

He knew how to prepare a marvelous drug that had the property of producing dazzling hallucinations. When those who had taken it came out of their exhilarated state, they found real life so drab and faded that they were ready to sacrifice it joyfully to return to the paradise of their dreams, for any man killed carrying out the sheik's orders went straight to heaven by right, while those who escaped death might once again enjoy the felicities of the mysterious concoction.

Now the green mixture that the doctor [Moreau de Tours] had just handed out to us was exactly the same as what the Old Man of the Mountain had his fanatics ingest without their knowing it, giving them to believe that he had at his disposal Mohammed's heaven and the houris [*houris de trois nuances*]–hashish, from which comes the word "hashishin" or hashish-eater, is the root of the word "assassin," whose terrible meaning is perfectly explained by the sanguinary habits of the Old Man's faithful.

Assuredly the people who saw me leave my house at an hour when simple mortals take nourishment had no idea that I was headed for the Ile Saint-Louis, a virtuous and patriarchal spot if ever there was one, there to consume a strange preparation that was used centuries ago by an imposter sheik as a means of exciting his visionaries to commit assassinations. Nothing in my perfectly bourgeois attire could possibly have led anyone to suspect me of this particular Orientalist excess. I looked more like a nephew going to dine with his aged aunt than a believer on the verge of tasting the joys of Mohammed's heaven in the company of twelve Arabs who couldn't have been more French.

If, before the present revelation, you had been told that there existed in Paris in 1845, in an age of unbridled financial speculation and railroads, an order of *Hachichins* whose history has not been written by M. de Hammer, you would surely not have believed it. And yet nothing could be more true, as is so often the case with improbable things.[118]

In contrast to Silvestre de Sacy, the "M. de Hammer" that Gautier mentions had set out to draw a parallel between the Assassins and the modern world, not hesitating to call the Ismaili sect a sort of Freemasonry comparable to the Jacobins (also mountain assassins, he pointed out),[119] and he so clearly drew the analogy between the fanaticism of the Hashishins and that of the revolutionaries of 1789 that in the French translation of his text, published, it is true, just a short time after the July Revolution of 1830, his lines on the Revolution and Robespierre were quite simply struck out. The term "fanatic" is indeed the one that has stuck for describing the medieval sect: it is to be found in the American Orientalist Bernard Lewis's book on the subject, published in 1967, and it received new connotations in a book published in 1923 by the French rightist and xenophobe Maurice Barrès, *Une enquête aux pays du Levant*.

Barrès's trip to Syria and the Lebanese mountains in 1914, his visit to the fortress of the "Hashâshins," were for the native of Lorraine the fulfillment of a childhood dream, a dream in which the charm of alien-sounding words, the mystery of an unknown and distant place, the enchanting cruelty of a barbarian world push the accomplished writer to find, as if it were a duty, the concrete supports behind all those strange names. While his own fascination was to be used to captivate the reader, he also meant to show the profundity of his thoughts, and that he had both preserved the virtues of youth and acquired wisdom. He presented a mixture of selected passages from European and Arab texts on the Ismailis and accounts of his travels, which included encounters with a few of the Assassins' modern-day descendants, now quite pacific, whom this bard of racial roots had pose with him for photographs. But Barrès also wanted if not to explain at least to advance our understanding of the mysterious sect in order to be able to make certain remarks about the modern world and its soul. Though he qualified them as "fanatics," Barrès was far from holding the Assassins in abomination; rather he worked to integrate them positively into his racist vision and into what is—despite the fact that his book is dedicated to the Abbé Bremond[120]—a fundamentally anti-Catholic conception. Barrès was on the lookout for "the subterranean energies of the race," the "ancient layers of Aryan sensibility." For him, the "Persian race," which, like the Indians, the Greeks, the Latins, and "ourselves," was part of the great Aryan family, had been forced with the arrival of Islam to accommodate itself to "Semitic thought, thought that went against its nature."[121] And in the "laboratory of superhumanity" that constituted, according to him, the Ismaili fortress at Alamut, Barrès believed he could hear, in a sort of return-of-the-repressed of the Aryan race, the revenge of Zarathustra: Hasan ibn al-Sabbah, the founder of the sect, that "fanatic devoted to the ideal end, in the service of which he multiplied his crimes,"[122] makes him think of Nietzsche, a Nietzsche with his arm raised not against Christ, but Mohammed. Fortunately, Catholic France was present in this place, so that Barrès could hear a mass for Jeanne d'Arc; this soothed him after an excursion up to Masyaf, in the Syrian mountains, and what was said to be one of the Old Man of the Mountain's castles. At the end of his quest for traces of the ancient fanatics, when some Ismailis show him a photo in a rosewood frame of their venerated Aga Khan, whom the writer had run into at the Ritz and knew to be a regular at Deauville race courses, he ironizes a bit about this adoration, which he finds silly, but he does not let himself go too far, for in his judgment "these peasants, once the assassins of long ago, today decent people who collect donations and adore the portrait of a worldly socialite, possess above all that little flame of religion thanks to which humanity lives and is able to resist the void."[123]

Radically different from such woolly-headed Nietzscheism is the mysticism of Baudelaire. In the passages of his *Paradis artificiels* devoted to hashish, the words "fanaticism" and "enthusiasm" are used interchangeably, with the second occurring more frequently because of its traditional connotation of poetic delirium, a delirium created or reinforced by the virtues of hashish, whose principle, happy, and utterly sophistic quality is to "transform desire into reality."[124]

In "Moral," Baudelaire exposes the terrible morning-after in which one is forced to see "hideous nature" stripped of yesterday's illumination and resembling "cheerless trash left over from a party."[125] Hashish, he explains, is immoral suicide, a magic that dupes the poet, who should instead regenerate his soul through work and contemplation, and Baudelaire evokes Balzac, who, attending one of the club's sessions, reputedly refused to partake of the *dawamesk* because for him the loftiest substance was the human will. But before coming back to earth, the hashishin's "spiritual debauch" seemed to him like a transcendent experience in which one felt a "striving of one's spiritual forces towards heaven," a voyage whose seriousness and intensity makes Gautier's version seem merely picturesque. It culminates in an outrageous thought, unavoidable for the dreaming enthusiast: "I have become God!" In its hallucinatory progression toward the ideal that hashish procures, the user's imagination glows and becomes enflamed "before the beguiling spectacle of his own nature," and he decrees his own apotheosis, affirming himself to be the most virtuous of men. This narcissistic peak of enthusiasm transforms Baudelaire's hashishin into Rousseau, as the poet explains: "The zeal with which he admired virtue, the keen compassion that filled his eyes with tears at the very sight of any noble action, or even the thought of some noble action [that he would have liked to perform], were quite enough to give him a very superlative idea of his moral worth. Jean-Jacques had become intoxicated *without* hashish."[126] It seems as if in what he writes about Jean-Jacques's enthusiasm, Baudelaire had been inspired by the passage in *Emile* lauding fanaticism for its capacity to pull the self up out of its selfish abjection. We shall take up that passage later.

The enthusiastic poet, like the fanatic, is illuminated, inspired; he has fallen prey to an excess of soul that abolishes the distance between humanity and God. "The Man-God": the hyphen in the title of chapter 4 of Baudelaire's *Paradis artificiels* marks the transcendence–false, illusory, gone the morning after–of the orgy, the *fantasia*. It is of course not worth the transcendence a poet may reach through pain.

But the metaphysical, hallucinatory leap here described is the same as the fanatic's compulsion, except that the fanatic is impelled not only to revery but to fury. Revery and fury, the metaphysics of fanaticism with its two poles: self-annihilating fusion of the subject with God; annihilation of the world in the name of God's omnipotence.

*

The impregnable fortress where the Old Man of the Mountain with his magic hallucinatory brew plunged his Assassins into a sleep that made Paradise present to them and from which they left to do his grim bidding, to make truth triumph with a dagger–can it serve as a model of Islam as a whole? Might it not be affirmed that Islam is in its essence a fanatical religion in that it rejects any separation between civil society and the City of God and thereby prohibits the construction of a secular society? If this were true, fanaticism would become not an accident of Muslim history but its very essence.[127] If we chose to follow Bernard Lewis, we would say that Islam, contrary to Christianity, rejects the very idea of civil society.[128] Not that it is "military" or "Pretorian," for the existence today of numerous Arab military regimes must not obscure the fact that there was no professional army in the first centuries of the Islamic era, that caliphs were civilians and the emblem of their

vizirs, in charge of both military and civil government, was an ink pot.
Given then that Islamic society was not originally military, we may say
that civil society may indeed be found in Islam, if what we mean by the
term is a social space in which initiatives whose effect is not strictly
limited to the private realm but which are nonetheless independent of
a central command may be developed. The *waqfs*, charitable associations characteristic of Islamic society that work to organize mutual-aid
systems in the areas of education and health, are manifestations of this
kind of social, even socialistic, vitality. But if we mean by civil society
a society in which there exists a disjunction between social and political rights, then we may say that civil society is unknown to Islam—
except under the influence of the West, as in Atatürk's Turkey; that on
the contrary religion plays the role of "the organizing principle of
society."[129] Where may we locate the origin of this absence of differentiation? Is it to be found in the very content of Mohammed's message, which would imply somehow that a Muslim society cannot be
democratic?

It can be objected that the case of the Assassins alone gives the lie to
any idea that there is *one* Islam, because for its believers that particular
variety of Shiism, heavily implanted in Persia, made them sufficiently
different from and hostile to other Muslims to want to eliminate their
princes. The proliferation of schisms in the Muslim world, the large
variety of ideologies claiming to follow directly from the words of the
Prophet prove that Islam is not so different from other religions. Following the upset in regional power relations represented by the defeat
of Saddam Hussein, did we not see, for example, Persian and Shiite
Iran, citadel of fanaticism à la Khomeini an instant before, applauded
as the land of humanitarian welcome for all those who had been persecuted and oppressed in secular Iraq?

It is therefore not in the dogmatic content of Islam but rather in the
history of its propagation that we should look for an explanation of its
hegemonic role in Muslim societies. Whereas Christianity developed
on the periphery of the Roman Empire and little by little conquered
the center—this initial exteriority followed by a fusion with Caesar was
continually repeated in the Christian West, where the distance between church and state came first, and the state would take its revenge
on the Caesaro-papist arrangement by enabling the secular autonomy
of civil society—the political construction of the state in the Middle

East and North Africa followed a model of conquest involving the importation of a faith, a language–Arabic–and organization into caliphates. "This state," affirms Bernard Lewis, "was defined by Islam, and full membership belonged, alone, to those who professed the dominant faith."[130] It is not then Islam itself but the conditions of its expansion that explain the absence of differentiation between civil society and the state.

Conversely, we must remember that the Christianity of Pope Boniface VIII as well as of Pius IX, Leo XIII, and even John Paul II, though it is fiercely opposed to totalitarianism, is in its essence hostile to any distance between civil society and the Church. An ideology can of course lend itself more or less easily to revision; this is indeed a defining characteristic of ideology–a certain flexibility. The example of Christianity shows the extraordinary plasticity of the dogmatic content of religions, even ones based on a book deemed sacrosanct. Interpretation has its appropriate zone, outside of which it becomes absurd, but like the field of a given metaphor that zone is wide enough to admit a variety of meanings. The best illustration of this point is the innovative political conception proposed by Luther, which made necessary a redefinition of the relations between civil society and the kingdom of God, church and state, as if Christianity had found within itself a principle antagonistic to the fanatical desire of the Church to crush civil society beneath the City of God. This principle, however, would contribute in its turn to the birth of fanatical state worship.

3 Sword Against Flail

The iconoclasts attacking paintings and sculptures in the churches of Wittenberg, the insurgent peasants, the Anabaptists seizing power in the city of Münster to make it over into the kingdom of God—all sought to destroy the established order so as to realize in the here and now the biblical message in all its political, social, and religious aspects. Although they had distinct styles and different declared purposes, they may nevertheless be grouped together: a certain number of these anti-Babylon militants moved from one group to another, and more important, they all called into question, with their words, but also by their violent deeds, the distinction between the Earthly City and the City of God. They desired civil society's death and meant to apply the Bible to the letter toward that end, without delay and without compromise.

In this weren't the *Schwärmer* following Luther's teachings? Hadn't he called for the destruction of Rome, Rome the whore, the pope's city and so the city of the Antichrist, Rome the equivalent of Babylon? Were not those who attacked churches to shatter the "idols" they found there fulfilling Luther's vow to destroy the Roman Church? The sack of Rome in 1527 by troops of the Holy Roman Emperor Charles V has been interpreted as part of the movement to destroy the earthly emblems of the devil and bring on the advent of the City of God, a "fanatic movement," in Michelet's phrase, that was "sweeping everything else up in its path."[1]

Up against the radical "extreme left" wing of the Reformation, however, Luther oriented his doctrine toward a social and political conservatism that some have considered a betrayal of his original project. Such conservatism was, however, an essential part of his thinking; it amounted to theorizing, as Melanchthon and Calvin did, the legitimacy of civil society and political authority. The thousands who, demanding greater justice, fell at the hands of the German princes in the battle of Frankenhausen (1525), Thomas Müntzer decapitated at the end of the Peasants' War, John of Leyde burnt alive for trying to turn the city of Münster into the New Jerusalem–all were swept up in the eschatological dream that Luther combated, at times in tones of burning hatred, as when he denounced the looting hordes of peasants and the false prophets, condemning them to death at the princes' sword.

Thus the first wave of political troubles linked to the Reformation, spanning the years 1521–35, proved a fertile moment for the doctrinal construction of the modern state. The series of strongly similar conflicts that motivated that construction may be summarized in a formula: the fanatics were the iconoclasts of civil society. It involves the following four-part analogy:

$$\frac{\text{City of God}}{\text{Civil Society}} = \frac{\text{God}}{\text{Images of God}} = \frac{\text{Heavenly Jerusalem}}{\text{Babylon}} = \frac{\text{Soul}}{\text{Body}}$$

That is, civil society is to the City of God as images of God are to God, as Babylon is to Heavenly Jerusalem, and finally as the body is to the soul. Iconoclasts and fanatics wanted to eliminate the "interval," represented here by a horizontal bar, that marked the separation between the two Cities, the distance between the two orders. In fact, their project was to abolish the lower terms and leave only the upper ones, following a logic that rejected all institutions and mediations and, more particularly, challenged the theory of divine incarnation and the status of the Eucharist, for it was around the relation between Christ's flesh and bread, Christ's blood and wine, as it pertained to Holy Communion, that the tensions and conflicts of all the other relations crystallized. As we shall see, the metamorphosis of bread and wine was intimately connected to the status of those functions so detested by the fanatics, representation and mediation.

The unbearable wait, the impossible difference, their impatient hopes. The fanatics wanted to be done with all political authorities right away, smash all idols, and institute communal ownership of worldly goods immediately—in short, to turn the world upside down. For them the hour of the Apocalypse had come: Babylon was collapsing and Jerusalem would now descend from heaven to earth.

Luther, Iconoclast

On December 10, 1520, three years after nailing his indictment of papal indulgences on the doors of the local church, the legendary act said to have launched the Protestant Reformation, and standing before a large crowd in that same city of Wittenberg, where he had been established for ten years, Luther threw the papal bull *Exsurge Domine* into the fire. In it Pope Leo X, while not actually excommunicating the Reformer, had given him forty days to toe the line and demanded that his books be burnt. The pope's emissaries meanwhile were circulating the bull, and one of them went to Antwerp to meet Charles V, who agreed to preside over an auto-da-fé of Luther's writings. Other fires would soon be started.

For Luther the pope's decree was blasphemy straight from the Antichrist, and as he threw it into the fire he is said to have declared, "Because you have saddened the Lord's saint, may eternal fire consume you."[2] Just two years later the public disorders had grown from a few protestatory flashes into war, and Luther found himself preaching against the "fanatics," "enthusiasts," "false prophets," and "prophets of death" who had impelled it, seeking thereby to curb the devastating force he had set in motion and which was taking hold throughout Germany, prey at that moment to every sort of convulsion. The move to violent action by those who wanted not only religious but also immediate and wide-reaching political and social transformation threatened to frighten or alienate those who had hesitantly and only recently joined the Reformation into returning to the bosom of the Babylonian whore. But in Luther's case it was not merely a matter of devising a tactic that would ensure the expansion of the Reformation after its brutal and spectacular take-off by diminishing that intensity. The warning he addressed to the iconoclasts and those engaged in related struggles was not simply an opportunistic maneuver designed to rally lukewarm supporters: rather it was perfectly consistent with his theory of faith and the value of the polity. These he reaffirmed spectacularly during the Peasants' War (1525), but the crucial feature of his thought that inspired them, namely the absolute opposition between the king-dom of God and that of the devil, was explicitly present in his doctrine as early as 1520.

From May 1521 to March 1522 Luther lived in imposed seclusion at the Wartburg Castle in the Palatinate; it was probably hoped that this would thwart any further inflaming of the anti-Catholic disorders after his refusal to submit to the newly crowned emperor at the Diet of Worms. Still uncertain about how to impose his power, Charles V had organized the Diet to settle the empire's affairs and more particularly to find solutions to the serious religious and social problems that were tearing up Germany. Even though he had had the Reformer's works burned, the emperor was hesitant about what policy to adopt with regard to the pope and had ended up granting Luther a promise of safe conduct to Worms, thereby enabling him to make a triumphant jour-ney from Wittenberg at the very moment the Sorbonne was expressing its utter condemnation of him by comparing him to Mohammed.

On the second day of his audience before the emperor, Luther proudly claimed paternity for the condemned works and declared that he did not believe either in the pope or the ecclesiastical councils, because, as he put it, it was as clear as day that they had repeatedly erred and contradicted themselves: "I am bound by the Scriptures I have quoted, and my conscience is captive to the Word of God. I cannot and I will not retract anything, since it is neither safe nor right to go against conscience. I cannot do otherwise, here I stand, may God help me, Amen."[3] Furious, the emperor called an end to the tumultuous session, and after some final negotiations–Charles V was too skillful a politician to have the Reformer killed–Luther disappeared under cover of a false kidnapping staged by the Elector Frederick the Wise of Saxony and carried out by his soldiers, to begin a period of captivity that was only half presented as such. If this was done to prevent a possible amplification of the disorders upon Luther's return to Witten-berg, which supported the Reformation, the maneuver failed because the agitation there got worse and only subsided, locally, when Luther was set free and could once again assert his authority.

At the Wartburg Luther first experienced one of his habitual epi-sodes of "melancholy"; then, when the bile had receded, he went to work, writing in both Latin and German and studying Greek and He-brew. In all the correspondence of this period his body is fully, insistently present, a body in pain and prey to desire, for he was "in this leisurely solitude . . . exposed to a thousand devils,"[4] what he called an impure celibacy that condemned men to either a perpetual itching or ignoble pollutions, to say nothing of the persistent, acute constipation from which he suffered.[5] His battle, in which even the guts had their part, was for him a struggle against the devil, a devil that existed physically in the form of temptation. Affirming the existence and presence of the devil had a symmetrical consequence, namely, that Luther identified himself with Christ carrying the cross, his cross being Germany, which he dreamed might one day constitute itself as a nation. He wanted a fight—and criticized Erasmus for being preoccupied not with grace but peace—and at that time he was counting on the common peasant, *Karsthans*, with his wheat flail, to carry the day.[6]

Even without its leader, the anti-Catholic revolt was too well on its way and had struck a chord too deep to lose any of its virulence, much less evaporate. There were other leaders to take up the battle, and their tone and tactics were even more energetic than Luther's. Far from having a calming effect, his absence thus helped spread the fire; propagated as it was now by more radical elements of the movement, the turbulent incidents multiplied. At Wittenberg the former Catholic priest Andreas Karlstadt took the head of the iconoclast movement that had sprung up, while the "prophets," young workers employed in the weaving industry who had come to Wittenberg from Zwickau, in Bohemia, where since 1520 Thomas Müntzer had been preaching radical religious and social reform, played a crucial role in the unrest shaking Luther's city. Its inhabitants began attacking the civic and religious rituals and usages of the time and completely subverted the liturgy, imposing a sort of generalized reversal of the order instituted by the Catholic Church. No more monks: they were to be forced to leave cloistered life. And no more chastity for priests: they must marry. Lent was abandoned, the holy oils burnt to nothing; as convents and monasteries were thrown open and forcibly emptied, Holy Communion began to be celebrated without the clergy. In the churches statues were smashed and paintings destroyed in a wave of iconoclasm that was also crashing through such places as Basel, Ulm, and Strasbourg. These actions may well be noted in the passive voice, because, in Luther's judgment, *Karsthans* had suddenly given way to *Herr Omnes*—the multitude triumphantly imposing its unmediated will on all that it hated.

In his semi-forced seclusion, Luther had undertaken to translate the New Testament into German. His *Septembertestament*, first published in that month in 1522, together with his later translation of the Old Testament, were to play the crucial role of linguistic and cultural unifier–people came to be connected to each other less as members of the same religious institution than as readers of the same book–and thereby further to upset the principle of the Catholic Church's authority.[7] From that moment onward, the traditions and structures of the Church ceased to have priority; each person would direct his personal conscience in accordance with the Bible.

Luther and the iconoclasts seemed to be in a relation of perfect harmony and symmetry: at Wittenberg intransigent disciples battled idolatry through iconoclastic acts, while in Wartburg Castle the master teacher was working to give individual believers access to the Word of God in their own everyday language. Such complementarity existed only in appearance, however, for although Luther accorded an indisputable privilege to the Word and to scripturalism and hardly lauded images, he condemned the iconoclasts, and he retained Latin as the liturgical language for several years. (Thomas Müntzer, for example, had abandoned it immediately.)

The initial ambiguity nonetheless remains patent. Luther's translation of the New Testament would be printed, *after* his preaching against the iconoclasts, with engravings by his friend Lucas Cranach, paradoxical images that canceled themselves out by inviting the viewer to iconoclastic action: the illustrations of the Apocalypse to be found in the *Septemberbibel* were instruments of anti-Catholic propaganda that, directed against the Roman Church and its temporal seat, could only be seen as calling for the destruction of Rome–"Babylon" in the titles (see Figure 3)–as did the images of a slightly later edition of the Bible published at Basel, this one with engravings by Hans Holbein the Younger depicting among other things the collapse of the Castello Sant'Angelo, symbol of papal power, and Rome destroyed by the grinding mill of the Last Judgment (see Figure 4).[8]

Cranach's engravings are in fact reworkings of certain plates done by Albrecht Dürer as illustrations of the Apocalypse; here they have been turned against the Catholic Church, which has become the whore of Babylon (compare Figures 5 and 6): on the head of Revelation's prostitute Cranach has set the papal tiara, in her hand a censer. In

3.   LUCAS CRANACH. *The Destruction of Babylon*, from Luther's *Septemberbibel*, Wittenberg, 1522 (photo: Bibliothèque Nationale, Paris).

4.   HANS HOLBEIN. *The Indictment of Babylon*, from the Thomas Wolff Bible, Basel,
1523 (photo: Bibliothèque Nationale, Paris).

Figure 3 we see Rome falling to pieces, stripped of all pretensions to being an Eternal City: *the* Urbs, *the* "Civitas," comes tumbling down, for this is the grim destiny of the too-earthly City, which cries out to be regenerated. Taken literally, Luther's anti-Babylon discourse, like the other means used in the battle against the pope–Cranach's and Holbein's engravings, not to mention the abundant antipapal iconography, sometimes violent, even scatological, from other sources–could only contradict the Reformer's expressed rejection of iconoclastic action and facilitate the fanatic explosion against which he would also have to fight.

Desiring the destruction of papal Rome, for him the Antichrist, and yet rejecting generalized subversion of the social order, Luther was in an ambiguous position, as is often the case with reformers and revolutionaries when they begin to seek wider support: by mobilizing hatred and resentment, by exciting the desire to destroy, they set in motion a dynamic that is difficult to stop. Luther, who started out as the instigator of protest, was first followed then overtaken by radicals whom he first sought to control and finally turned vehemently, violently against. But by proclaiming the priority of each person's relation to God's word as mediated only by his own conscience, not by any external human player, he had deprived any bureaucratic Church of its foundation. By reducing the number of sacraments he undermined the sacred character of the liturgy. By rejecting transubstantiation he cut the ontological roots of priestly power. By seeking to restrict ecclesiastical rituals and performances he opened the way for a liberated faith, purged of institutional constraints and opposed to mediations, images, and clerics. By preaching the Gospel, he had raised the hope that it be applied here and now. In short, by profaning Rome, he had propelled fanaticism.

Luther left the Wartburg in December 1521 disguised as a Knight of Saint George and paid a brief visit to Wittenberg, where he kept his identity concealed. Deeply worried by what he saw, he returned to his prison and wrote the *Sincere Admonition to All Christians to Guard Against Insurrection and Rebellion*, from which we quoted a passage at the opening of this book in our discussion of Figure 1 representing the Last Judgment. He returned to Wittenberg for good in 1522, "for the sake," as he explained it, not without a certain ambiguity, "of that untoward movement introduced by our friends in Wittenberg to the great detriment of the gospel"[9] and with the aim of reestablishing

5.   ALBRECHT DÜRER. *The Whore of Babylon*, from *Apocalypse cum figuris*, 1498 (photo: Giraudon, Paris).

6.   LUCAS CRANACH. *The Whore of Babylon with Papal Tiara*, from Luther's *Septemberbibel*, Wittenberg, 1522 (photo: Bibliothèque Nationale, Paris).

order, an order that could take hold only locally, because the forces that were leading to the Peasants' War could no longer be stopped.[10]

In the first week of Lent, which began on March 9 that year, Luther gave the eight sermons known as the Invocavit Sermons, in which he reproached both the "prophets" from Zwickau and Andreas Karlstadt, who up until then had fought at his side but who had, as we have said, become the local leader of the iconoclasts, with wanting to impose God's Word through violence. He was able to reestablish order and reinstate the Church in his city, but the iconoclasts would make themselves felt elsewhere for a long time to come. In 1525, while Karlstadt was active in Strasbourg, Luther wrote an open letter to the Christians of that city against false prophets who destroy idols.[11] In February 1529 Holbein reported seeing massive destruction of paintings in Basel, as if the anti-Babylon propaganda to which the painter had contributed was taking its natural, irrepressible course, while Erasmus, who had been teaching at the university there, quit the city. Through the teachings and activities of other Reformers, particularly Calvin, the threats of the image smashers and the general climate of violence they created came to affect all of Europe, with incidents of iconoclasm breaking out in Antwerp in 1562 and Flanders in 1566. With the outbreak of iconoclasm in Bourges in 1562, the French Wars of Religion were fully under way.[12]

Luther Against the Iconoclasts

In everything he said and wrote during his stay at the Wartburg about how sacred matters should be managed, Luther placed preaching at the center of the institution of religion: a preacher–and this profoundly modified his relation to his fellow members of civil society– was not someone who had been ordained, but rather someone who taught the Word. For Luther charisma was not to be exercised by way of any institutional transfer, but only through the preacher's special relation to God's Word. So it was that he asked his friend Melanchthon, a layman in the eyes of the Church of Rome, a married man who had received no special sacrament, to preach in public; this was envisioned as a return to the customs of the early Church.[13] Had Christ needed institutional legitimation to be a preacher? The only authentic sacrament was the Word, and the only power that of Christ: "He is himself (as they say) my immediate bishop, abbot, prior, father, and teacher; I know no other."[14]

But was this not an invitation to destroy all authorities claiming to regulate the sacred, and did it not constitute encouragement to abolish all mediations, henceforth to be considered Babylonian and idolatrous, that might come between the believer and the Word? Contrary to what might have been expected as a natural extension of such radical logic, Luther condemned the violence inflicted against priests' collective houses and the violent reception given a representative of a religious congregation come to collect alms at Wittenberg, declaring publicly that he would prefer monks to leave their monasteries discreetly, not in scandal, and deploring the regrettable events brought on by the "mad visionaries." Did these attitudes result from tactical considerations? To some extent they did, for as we have suggested, Luther had to worry that such excesses might alienate the bourgeois inhabitants of small German cities. But his condemnation of false prophets, iconoclasts, and all the disorders of the moment was above all consistent with the new distribution of power he advocated. The loosening of the Church's temporal hold was to be compensated for by a transfer of power toward the civil authorities. Luther was not announcing the millennium. The fact that he wished to bring about no other destruction than that of modern Babylon—the Catholic Church and its idols in the form of papal indulgences—meant that society was not to be entirely subverted. Thus he could condemn idolatry at the same time as he formally rejected iconoclasm, and although he expressed a preference for churches without statues or images, the preaching of God's Word was the only weapon he approved for abolishing them.[15]

Obviously Andreas Karlstadt had quite a different attitude. Was he trying to take over Luther's place in 1521, or did he believe he was applying the absent Reformer's policies? In any event, when he took over the leadership of the iconoclastic movement in Wittenberg, it was not just to make waves; he founded his action on certain theoretical considerations, assembled in a work published in 1522, in which he justified iconoclastic action with a series of arguments that were not particularly original but were effective in the context of generalized rejection of the institutional framework and liturgical practices of the Roman Catholic Church. Nor should the iconoclast crisis at Wittenberg be seen as a mere accident: in addition to the later incidents already mentioned, there was intense iconoclastic activity in Zwingli's Zurich, where the Great Council decided in 1523 to abolish all images along with mass. Karlstadt himself was taking positions ever closer to those of Zwingli, who went on to develop the thesis that the only two sacraments he recognized, baptism and the Eucharist, were purely symbolic–"sacrae rei signa nuda signa" [sign of sacred things, naked sign]. This rapprochement between the two, which begins to give an idea of the conceptual connection between images and sacraments, led Luther to accuse all those who subscribed to it–the "sacramentarians"–of being fanatics. The three spiritual leaders–Luther, Karlstadt, and Zwingli–had begun with similar practical and theological positions: all of them were hostile to the obligations of eating lean on fast days and of celibacy for priests (they would all three marry), all of them favored reducing the number of the sacraments. But Luther could not follow Karlstadt when the latter incited his supporters to iconoclastic action, and while rejecting the Catholic doctrine of transubstantiation–according to which the wafer and the wine literally become the body of Christ, he nonetheless, as we shall see, believed in and defended Christ's real presence in the Eucharist.

What were Karlstadt's arguments in his tract against images? He demanded that churches be devoted not to the saints but to God, and he disapproved of people going to request good health, advice, and other types of assistance from what he called painted idols. Catholics, according to Karlstadt, throw themselves upon these effigies like "crows and blackbirds on a brigand's cadaver,"[16] flouting Scripture's command to love no foreign God. Karlstadt did not believe in the didactic virtue of images, vehemently disagreeing with Pope Gregory I's argument, most frequently invoked by image defenders, that they fulfilled a pedagogic function as "the layman's prayerbook." Because Jesus, whose authority was obviously superior to any pope's, had said, "Listen to my voice," was not claiming that images should be used to teach the equivalent of saying that the faithful should not be disciples of Christ? More important, images referred only to the flesh, which was useless, indeed harmful, whereas the Word of God was spiritual and therefore truly useful to believers. Word against picture, *Geist* against *Fleisch*, the spirit against the flesh–Karlstadt went as far as accusing "image-lovers" of fornicating with images like truants with whores. What else could be done with idols other than to smash them?

To refute such arguments, and to condemn the iconoclasts' move to violent action, Luther began in the Invocavit Sermons by reaffirming a key point on which all the Reformers agreed: the supremacy of the Word over works. Contrary to Karlstadt, Luther concluded from the hegemony of the Word not that images were base but that the activity of image smashers was spiritually dangerous in that it privileged works over the Word. It was love that must guide our actions against the Catholics; love, according to Luther, was a superior principle that required us to take an attitude of compassion toward the weak–papists were weak–and prohibited coercion. Private masses, for example, should not be abolished by force. A private mass, that is, one said in response to a personal request and celebrated outside the community, was a bad thing because it was mistakenly conceived of as a sacrifice and a good work. One should preach that such masses were sinful, but no physical violence should be used to eradicate them:

> Since I cannot pour faith into their hearts, I cannot, nor should I, force anyone to have faith. That is God's work alone, who causes faith to live in the heart. Therefore we should give free course to the Word and not add our works to it. We have the *jus verbi* [right to speak] but not the *executio* [power to accomplish]. We should preach the Word, but the results must be left solely to God's good pleasure.[17]

Luther proposed as a model attitude, in addition to his own, that of Saint Paul (if he identified himself with anyone other than Christ, it was surely Paul). During his stay in Athens, Paul had entered the temple without smashing images; instead he went up on the Areopagus and preached to the people against idolatry; when his words had penetrated their hearts, the idols fell without being pushed (Acts 17:22-34). As for Luther himself, he opposed the pope of course, but "never with force. I simply taught, preached, and wrote God's word; otherwise I did nothing": it was the Word that had weakened the papacy.[18]

But the supremacy of the Word did not mean it should in all cases be obeyed as an order, that it was comparable to an imperative imposed by earthly authorities. The Word partook of at least two levels of spiritual concern: commandments and remarks on indifferent matters.[19] Necessary things–for example, that we must believe in our Savior Jesus Christ–were commanded or forbidden by the high authority of God, but there were also things that God had left up to human beings, about which a person might choose freely: to become a monk or a nun, to leave the monastery or convent, to eat meat on Fridays–or to make images of God (for profane images, the question was not even raised).

In such areas where there was no command one way or another, one must not behave inconsiderately but rather "subsist," while taking guidance and strength from "God's ordinance," which fortified the heart and the reason: "See to it that you can stand before God and the world when you are assailed, especially when the devil attacks you in the hour of death."[20] Priests could not be forbidden to marry as the pope had decreed; neither should they be required to marry, even though celibacy was impure according to Luther for the reasons he had given in the Wartburg. If the vow of chastity was contrary to God's commandment in that God "has made it a matter of liberty to marry or not to marry,"[21] conversely nothing obliged a priest to marry. In this way Luther demonstrated that the iconoclasts, false prophets, and fanatics confused "must [be]" with "free [to be]": on the one hand, unshakable faith, on the other, what I have freely at my disposition and can use or not as I like. By making "free" into "must," they beguiled or yanked along their weaker brothers, who should instead be treated as a mother treats the child she must wean: first she gives him milk, then porridge and light foods; only later does she begin feeding him bread and cheese. What would happen if she began at once with roast meat and wine? Those who were already weaned would do well to remember that such had not always been the case and to accept even when spreading the Word of God that before it operated on people they might continue to hear mass, fast on Fridays, live in their monasteries and convents–and keep images in their churches: "Thus faith must always remain pure and immovable in our hearts, never wavering; but love bends and turns so that our neighbor may grasp and follow."[22]

Luther called upon those who listened to his sermons that March to defy the one who wanted to strip them of the liberty God had given them–the pope, who had the presumption to erect as a commandment that which God had neither forbidden nor prescribed. But Luther opposed the same argument, the argument according to which "outward things could do no harm to faith if only the heart does not cleave to them or put its trust in them," against all image and altar smashers.[23] Invoking the famous iconoclast dispute that had rent Byzantine Christianity in the eighth century, he explained:

> But now we must come to the images, and concerning them also it is true that they are unnecessary, and we are free to have them or not, although it would be much better if we did not have them at all. I am not partial to

them. A great controversy arose on the subject of images between the [Byzantine] Roman emperor [Leo III] and the pope [Gregory II]; the emperor held that he had the authority to banish the images, but the pope insisted that they should remain, and both were wrong. Much blood was shed, but the pope emerged as victor and the emperor lost. What was it all about? They wished to make a "must" out of that which is free. This God cannot tolerate. Do you presume to do things differently from the way the supreme Majesty has decreed? Surely not; let it alone.[24]

Later in the sermon Luther warns: "You rush, create an uproar, break down altars, and overthrow images! Do you really believe you can abolish the altars in this way? No, you will only set them up more firmly."[25] Once again, what mattered most was to found one's thought and action on strong and clear words from the Gospel, words that one could use against the devil until one's dying day. Whatever one did, without those words a believer was without a weapon, without reason, with an inconstant conscience, in constant danger of being "plucked" by the devil, "like a parched leaf."[26]

Further developing his argument on the issue of images, Luther contended that the iconoclasts could not find endorsement for their actions in the commandment "Thou shalt not make unto thee any graven image, or any likeness of any thing that is in heaven above or that is in the earth beneath, or that is in the water under the earth" (Exod. 20:4): the true meaning of this was that human beings might adore only one God. What was forbidden was not the making or possessing of images, which as we know were not necessarily "Babylonian" or idolatrous in Luther's view, but rather adoring them. This was clarified by the verse that followed, which indeed presumes the existence of such images: "Thou shalt not bow down thyself to them, nor serve them." According to Luther the passage was ambiguous enough not to permit the interpretation that one had the right to smash images in God's name. It is important for our purposes to note that in developing this point Luther accorded a certain competence to legislate in sacred matters to the political powers, to the extent that those matters involved society as a whole. Even if images that had become the object of adoration might well be destroyed, he explained, this must not be done in a reckless way, but rather on the order of the civil authority, as in the Bible, when it is King Hezekiah who destroys the bronze serpent Moses has set high (2 Kings 18:4). Because images could easily be abused—it was abusive for example to place an image in a church with the belief that doing so was itself a good work from which men might hope to receive some kind of divine recompense–it was to be hoped that they would be abolished, and princes, bishops, and important personages would do better to give concrete assistance to the poor than to have statues and paintings rich in silver and gold put up in every nook and cranny of the church: God demanded no such things. But to topple and smash them as the fanatics did was not the right method of getting rid of them. Rather one must preach that they did not serve God: this alone would cause them to fall–into disuse.

The idea that images were in themselves neither bad nor good and that the only thing to be condemned was the false belief that they pleased God was part of a larger framework of thought that constituted an almost naive way of defending the Earthly City:

> God has commanded us in Deuteronomy 4[:19] not to lift up our eyes to the sun and stars, that we may not worship them, for they are created to serve all nations. But there are many people who worship the sun and the stars. Therefore we propose to rush in and pull the sun and stars from the skies. No, we had better let it be. Again, wine and women bring many a man to misery and make a fool of him; so we kill the women and pour out all the wine. Again, gold and silver cause much evil, so we condemn them.[27]

In other words, for Luther–whose liking for good food and consequent stoutness were often ridiculed, while considered by Weber to be among the salient traits of German Protestantism–the world could not be disinvested, even if his critique of the Roman Catholic Church seemed to suggest the contrary.

Luther's argumentation moreover established a distinction between what was represented and representation itself. To destroy an image under the pretext that those who looked at it were identifying it with what it represented, in this case God, would be useless, absurd: surely none of the faithful assembled there was obtuse enough to confuse a crucifix with Christ. Everyone knew that "yonder crucifix is not my God, for my God is in heaven, but this is simply a sign."[28] It was possible to look at images and adore not the images themselves, but that of which they were a sign. And Luther insisted that there were some people, albeit few in number, who knew how to make "good use" of images, although he did not elaborate here; such people could not be accused of idolatry.

Throughout these sermons, Luther's attack was directed not against those who ate fish on Fridays or prayed in front of statues, but rather against the iconoclasts for their lack of love for the weak: they scandalized their neighbor, and in their impatient aggressiveness, had become victims of the devil, who "is after us with all his craft and cunning."[29]

Luther expounded these arguments rapidly, in the first four of the eight Invocavit Sermons. Clearly he was troubled by the depth of the unrest and attached great importance to reestablishing order. He accomplished this: the Church was reinstituted at Wittenberg, as we have said, and the prophets were expelled. Karlstadt continued to develop his propaganda along the lines already mentioned, now preaching in favor of polygamy, which he believed was legitimated by the Old Testament, and above all attacking the doctrine vigorously and relentlessly defended by Luther of Christ's real presence in the Eucharist. After leaving Wittenberg, he settled in Orlamünde and took up his interrupted correspondence with the rebel Thomas Müntzer. He persisted, after a public debate with Luther at Jena (August 21, 1524), in proclaiming that Lutheranism was heresy. He was not alone in this, finding strong support for his ideas in Strasbourg and Basel, as we have mentioned.

Worried to see the deep inroads being made by a doctrine that proclaimed there was nothing but bread in the communion wafer– "What humiliation! But Christ reigns!"–Luther wrote *Against the Heavenly Prophets in the Matter of Images and Sacraments* (1524-25), the title of which clearly underlines the relation between iconoclasm and rejection of the real presence, pointing out that if, in the iconoclasts' view, icons were the cause of idolatry, if loving an earthly representation had the effect of barring access to God, was the doctrine of Christ's real presence in the bread of Holy Communion not analogous? For Karlstadt and Zwingli, accepting the doctrine of the real presence was the same thing as adoring images. The iconoclasts and those who tended to reduce communion to a purely symbolic operation and deny Christ's presence in earthly mediation were the same people. For Karlstadt it was idolatrous to look at paintings and the Eucharist was only a sign; God could not be licitly figured and bread and wine could not be transformed. Luther, on the contrary, did not call for the abolition of the sacrament of mass any more than he wholly rejected images, believing instead that even though the bread did not substantially become Christ, it was as if Christ and the bread had been united in the

Eucharist. He had replaced the Catholics' doctrine of transubstantiation with his own doctrine of consubstantiation.

The arguments that Luther advanced in the Invocavit Sermons were undeniably limited by circumstances: he needed to convince, and quickly, the residents of a highly agitated city. But they nonetheless have a profound and complex theological foundation, the key to which is to be found perhaps in Luther's interpretation of the words spoken by Christ in response to his disciple Philip's request to be shown the Father: "He that hath seen me hath seen the Father" (John 14:9). In Luther's understanding, Scripture forbade us to separate the Father from the Son. Even if, as substances, divinity and humanity are different, when posited as the object of religious acts, as being that which the believer must enter into relation with, Christ is given to the believer in his entirety. The fanatics' mistake was believing that physically seeing Christ meant seeing–and worshiping–only his humanity, whereas "that humanity . . . offered up to the eyes of all . . . was humanity united with divinity." To see Christ for what he is was indeed to focus on what is higher than the visible, and yet the body of Christ, being as it was "the flesh of God," was truly a food for us: "The natures are distinct, but the person is one."[30] The opposition between body and spirit, which Karlstadt was unable to get beyond and which he used to found his hatred of painting, was thus a kind of philosophical error, an intellectualist deviation. By denying the real presence of the invisible in the visible, the fanatics were unable to take seriously the visible humanity of Christ as united with his divinity; they had become blind to the Son of God as the total person he is. In Luther's conception, from the moment the believer's vision of Christ involved apprehending his divine humanity, his human divinity, then Christ's image, and with it every image, stood rehabilitated.

The Peasants' War: Death to the Fanatics!

Peasant revolts like the *Bundschuh* or "clog" rebellion (1503) had been multiplying since the end of the fifteenth century in Europe. These protests repeatedly turned into violent attacks against princes and lords in which the rebels were able to seize several cities, particularly in Central Europe; they were driven by strong forces and often brought down cruel repression. During the same period, the number of "heavenly prophets" or "visionaries" also greatly increased, epitomized in the figure of Thomas Müntzer. Rebellions broke out throughout the area north of the Danube and east of the Rhine, and the movement spread east and also westward into Alsace and France.

In early March 1522, at the very moment of the iconoclast crisis in Wittenberg, Swabian peasants who had gathered at Memmingen formed themselves into a "Christian Union" and wrote out a twelve-article charter of grievances pertaining to both temporal and spiritual matters. To it they attached a list of personalities whom they called upon to judge whether their demands were in conformity with Scripture; Melanchthon and Luther were on the list. The latter responded with a text that was both a *pro domo* plea, reiterating once again his reasons for denouncing the "prophets of death," and an appeal to the Swabian lords to make concessions and so prevent the spark of the peasants' rage from setting fire to the whole of Germany. It was an appeal founded on the Reformer's conception of a prince's duties: "Rulers are not appointed to exploit their subjects for their own profit and advantage, but to be concerned about the welfare of their subjects,"[31] he wrote, and he likewise condemned luxury and waste. Turning to the peasants, he admonished them to beware of the prophets of riot and death, "murder-prophets," who dared invoke God in defense of their rebellion when injustice on the part of an authority could *never* justify such revolt: temporal authority alone might wield the sword; it alone had the right to punish evildoing. The divine law of the Old Testament and the Christian law of the New, together with natural law, forbade acknowledging any kind of legitimacy for the brewing revolt. If everyone made himself judge, there could be no more order or justice, only uninterrupted murder and carnage.[32] By what means could the peasants put a stop to the process, once begun? And what would happen if their troops began to turn on one another?

The false prophets, the propagandists of political subversion, the iconoclasts, were thus envoys from the devil, for the Christian's economy of suffering was completely different from what they suggested and a Christian's path could never be that of rebellion: "We have all we need in our Lord, who will not leave us, as he has promised. Suffering! suffering! Cross! cross! This and nothing else is the Christian law!"[33]

While presenting Christ's endurance of unjust violence as the example to follow, Luther pointed out once again that he himself, despite how he had been persecuted by pope and emperor, had never drawn a sword, no more than he had smashed images; he had rather trusted to God, who had protected him and even favored the spread of his gospel teachings. Luther's message comes through loud and clear: "Suffer wrong and endure evil." Those who rose up in revolt were heathens, because "Christians do not fight for themselves with sword and musket, but with the cross and with suffering, just as Christ, our leader, does not bear a sword, but hangs on the cross."[34] It is true that Luther had biting words for the lords and political authorities in place: they were no different from the peasants, both preoccupied only with the pagan, worldly, earthly meaning of law and justice and caring only for earthly goods. The masters, who squeezed and pressured the poor, were reminded that all earthly empires–Assyrian, Persian, Greek, Roman–had perished by the sword, for "God hates both tyrants and rebels."[35] This equal condemnation seems unjustified to us because the peasants were at the bidding of masters whose unjustness Luther acknowledged, and it would seem all the more difficult to defend given the harsh suppression of the revolt.

Nothing, however, was to change in Luther's analysis of the problem.

Although he estimated that at least one hundred thousand perished in the battle of Frankenhausen,[36] this did not shake his fundamental stance. Indeed, his attitude toward the insurgent peasants was so vehement, his tone ultimately so bellicose, that it has been possible to consider his position as a sort of prototype of totalitarian ideologies. What are we to make, for example, of the well-known passage with which he concluded a text written in May 1525, *Against the Robbing and Murdering Hordes of Peasants*? Addressing himself to the sword-wielding princes, he declares that if they die while exercising the "duties of the sword" against peasants who by rebelling against political authority have taken up the sword against God's Word, they shall be true martyrs and win the realm of heaven:

> Therefore, dear lords, here is a place where you can release, rescue, help. Have mercy on these poor people [threatened by the peasants]! Let whoever can stab, smite, slay. If you die in doing it, good for you! A more blessed death can never be yours, for you die while obeying the divine word and commandment in Romans 13 [:1, 2], and in loving service of your neighbor, whom you are rescuing from the bonds of hell and of the devil. And so I beg everyone who can to flee from the peasants as from the devil

himself. . . . If anyone thinks this is too harsh, let him remember that rebellion is intolerable and that the destruction of the world is to be expected every hour.[37]

That Luther was not incapable of private charity, as shown for example by his taking Karlstadt in for a time to protect him from persecution, or deploring the ghastly death that Müntzer met, or even expressing in a private letter a degree of pity for the stunned and wretched peasants who had survived the carnage,[38] cannot attenuate the virulence of his condemnation. The text he wrote in July 1525 in response to criticism of his "harsh book," far from softening the judgment there expressed, piles on further support for it. Luther quotes Saint Paul—"If you do wrong, be afraid, for he does not bear the sword in vain; he is the servant of God to execute his wrath on the wrongdoer"[39]—and wonders why those who were now demanding mercy for the peasants had not lauded that virtue when those same peasants were setting fires, looting, and trying to exterminate the princes. To all these well-meaning fools, whom he calls in another place "un-Christian and merciless bloodhounds," Luther brutally retorts that what they really want to see is the abolition of prisons and executioners, punishment and authority, that "wickedness go free and unpunished, and the temporal sword [be] made ineffective."[40]

Luther's justifying the bloody repression of a popular movement and reducing the human other to the status of an animal—he called for the slaughter of the rebels as if they were mad dogs (*tollen Hunden*)[41]— have been evidence enough to enable some to conclude that Luther was a precursor to Hitler, all the more so because of his flagrant German nationalism,[42] to say nothing of his anti-Semitism.[43] This conclusion, however, comes up against at least one extremely important obstacle: although Luther did indeed effect what may be called a "zoological" cancellation of the peasants—as Lenin's discourse was to do, destroying the humanity of the bourgeois and the supposed wealthy peasants or *kulaks* by assimilating them to insects, and as the Nazis did when they denied Jews the status of human beings—the logic he was following was not that of totalitarian terror: he did not, at least in this context, identify certain groups as "objective enemies" to be destroyed for what they *were* rather than for what they *did* (see Chapter 9, pp. 327-28). The distance between totalitarian logic and Luther's logic is clearly marked by his injunction to spare the lives of prisoners taken in battle. In other words, he reasoned according to the categories of war and peace and not in terms of mass extermination: to kill an enemy who is fighting against you is not the same sort of action as to undertake the methodical destruction of a stigmatized group.

Luther's conception of political authority, upon which his attitude toward the rebellious peasants was based, can be disengaged from its theological frame of reference and the imprecatory rhetoric he couched it in—although the legitimacy of such a procedure is open to discussion—whereupon it appears as a rational theorization of such authority, a prototype of Weber's famous characterization of the state as the human community that holds the monopoly on legitimate physical violence within a given territory.[44] From this perspective, Luther may take his place in the long line of theoreticians of the power state, and Weber, who took as inspiration for his definition the remark made by Trotsky in 1918 at the moment of the Brest-Litovsk peace agreement that in the end violence determines everything, might just as coherently have placed himself under Luther's patronage, for on this point the Reformer's ideas clearly seem to anticipate what we may call Weber's cynical conception of the political.[45] The crux of Luther's demonstration that the violence being inflicted by the princes on the peasants was legitimate is in fact the disjunction he established between a criminal and a rebel: the first violated the law, but without calling into question the principle of the authority he had not obeyed, whereas the *Schwärmer* rebel, by combating authority and seeking to abolish any and all power of command and sanction, damaged and threatened the very foundations of organized political existence.[46] The rebel was thus more dangerous than the brigand, and crushing the fanatics was vital for the very existence of civil society.

The principle of a monopoly on legitimate physical violence was indispensable, because without force, authority was stripped of everything it had. This principle admitted no exceptions, and as it was a law both natural and divine, it must be respected even by Turks and Jews— that is, universally, by the whole of humankind—in order for there to be peace and order on earth. Someone who violated the law, which was organized social life's condition of possibility, was not even worthy to be called a "heathen."[47] Luther did indeed exclude the rebel from the rest of humanity, but he did not naturalize that difference: as soon as the madman who violated the law either voluntarily submitted to it as before or was made to submit by force, he became part of humanity again. The power of the sword, *Macht des Schwerds*, was a monopoly so strict, however, that the prohibition imposed on those who had not been institutionally permitted to take it up applied as well to the victims of a bad king, and even to those who suffered religious persecution.[48] This was one of the radical consequences of the affirmation that political authority emanated from God.[49]

The Two Kingdoms

Luther applied this logic in his point-by-point commentary on the *Twelve Articles*, the list of grievances drawn up by the future insurgents that had been submitted to him for a judgment on its conformity with Scriptures. In response to the article objecting to the principle of the *corvée* on the grounds that "no one is to be the serf of anyone else, because Christ has made us all free," Luther affirmed that it went directly against the Gospel, which in no way called for overturning the order of the Earthly City. No, the master could not be deprived of the body that had become his property; however, a serf could be a Christian and thereby enjoy a Christian's freedom, in the same way that a prisoner or sick person could.[50]

Luther's demonstration hangs on a distinction between the two kingdoms, a distinction he had already discussed in a variety of texts and to which he returned time and again as the central point of his theory of the nature of political authority. It overlaps, though not completely, another distinction, that between the two governments or regimes, each characterized by a particular type of laws and rights, which organized the two kingdoms. These two distinctions are tied to a third, with which once again they do not coincide, namely the more clearly Augustinian one between the kingdom of God or Christ, on the one hand, and the kingdom of the devil or this world on the other. Like Saint Augustine, Luther separated humanity into those who belonged to the kingdom of God or Christ and constituted the community of saints, the Church, and those who were under the devil's command. The two types could not be distinguished by their appearance or by their works, and all external criteria such as being a man or a woman, circumcised or not, prince or peasant, monk or layman, were irrelevant because perfection resided within, in the heart, in faith and love. Nonetheless, all humanity belonged eternally to one or the other kingdom. But considering the issue from a different angle, it must also be understood that because human beings were both soul and body, each person partook of the double status of the two kingdoms, each part being regulated by specific principles. The governments or regimes of the two kingdoms should therefore each be regulated by principles specific to these two parts, the spiritual and the corporal, of which human beings were made. The spiritual and the temporal should thus be managed differently, in accordance with their different natures. This distinction was of course first used not against the fanatical insurgent peasants but against the papacy, the Catholic Church, which, perversely in Luther's eyes, was organized like an earthly kingdom.

In *The Freedom of a Christian*, a theological treatise written in 1520 and addressed to Pope Leo X, Luther began by positing two indissociable definitions:

> The Christian is a perfectly free man, lord of all things, subject to no one.
> The Christian is a serf, servant in all things, subject to everyone.[51]

This opposition between freedom and servitude is to be understood in reference to a person's double nature, spiritual and corporal. The spiritual, inner person may be united with Christ; the soul needs only God's Word to become a lord. Indeed, Christ came among us with no other function than to preach that Word. Thus it was that faith alone, of its own strength, unaided by works, together with the Word acting inside the believer and uniting his soul to Christ as to a spouse–for Christ agreed to take that sickly harlot for his wife–brought justice, freedom, and felicity. Through this union with Christ we possessed an immense good, for Christ enjoyed in his relation with God the Father all the prerogatives of a firstborn son.[52] Because Christ shared his dignity with all Christians, they became, in the spiritual domain, lord of all things, reigning over all things, and nothing could harm them: the freedom and power of a Christian were thus unlimited. But the Christian was also, like Christ and thanks to Christ, a priest, and it was this that made Christians worthy to "appear before God to pray for others and to teach one another divine things."[53] The separation between preachers and laymen could therefore no longer have institutional content: the Church did not make priests; rather the priests made the Church. The "ecclesiastical state" was thus not founded on a distinction between priests and the laity but instead resulted from the fact that, even though all Christians were priests, not all of them could practice the divine service of publicly preaching the Word of Christ. Those who did so devote themselves were called by Scripture "servants," "serfs," "stewards" (*ministri, servi, oeconomi; Diener, Knecht, Schaffner*),[54] although up to now they had called themselves popes, bishops, and priests: according to Luther the divine office had abusively given birth to a temporal domination and force more tyrannical than any earthly empire, namely the papacy, and Christians had become serfs of the vilest of men.

But human beings lived in the external world, on earth, where each had to govern his body and have dealings with the people he lived among. For this reason a person could not give himself over to idleness but had also to do good works—to fast, to labor—in order to control his concupiscent body, serve his neighbor, and thereby please God.[55] Luther insisted, however, that works and their goodness could not have any kind of retroactive effect on the person who accomplished them; they could bring no recompense. Once again, a person was either good or bad before he had done any works, be they good or bad. Works, legitimated by faith, could thus only be done freely, without hope of spiritual reward. They had no weight in the economy of salvation, which was ensured only by faith and grace, thanks to Christ and his Word. Christians must devote themselves to their neighbors by performing useful services, and they must accept the temporal authorities, not because doing so procured them any spiritual benefit, but because they existed for the good of all. They did not participate in the life of civil society hoping for benefit but because they believed in the validity of the two kingdoms and of each one of them separately.

To clarify the status of works in his system, Luther draws an analogy that seems pedagogically designed to convince pope and papists. They would undoubtedly agree that the acts accomplished by a bishop—blessing a church, for example, or baptizing a child—were not what consecrated him; rather it was because he had been consecrated, had been made bishop, that these acts had value. If we borrow notions used by the philosopher of language John Austin to distinguish between affirmative and performative utterances, we might say that a performance—in this case, baptizing someone, blessing a church—can only be accomplished by someone whose status confers on him a specific competence. If someone other than the president of an assembly declares the session open, his utterance cannot be performative because he does not have the recognized competence required to make it so. If saying is to be the equivalent of doing, the utterer must have the corresponding competence, certified by the necessary status. Following out Luther's demonstration in these terms, if the performance equals a person's works and the competence at issue is salvation, clearly works do not create salvation, neither do they bestow grace upon the performer; performing good works does not make one saved. Of course, for Luther—in contrast to how the Catholic Church would generally interpret it—the competence that enabled one to accomplish certain performances was not tied to any *institutionally legitimated* status: no other authority but God could attribute or delegate the competence that validated performances or deduce from accomplished acts that they *were* valid performances; that is, that they either corresponded to a real competence or created one. In this sense, performances could only be freely done, without hope of spiritual recompense: they did not increase competence, much less produce it. But this gratuitousness did not mean they were useless: a performance, a work, was either a service done for others or a good from which the outer part of ourselves, the body, could benefit. We performed good works to please God.

Christians were thus raised above themselves in Christ and lowered beneath themselves by charity to their neighbors, and Christian freedom, like heaven, hovered above the earth.

In 1525, in *De servo arbitrio* (The Bondage of the Will), written in Latin and conceived as an answer to Erasmus,[56] Luther reaffirmed that salvation was a gift of God that came from Christ—"sola gratia, sola fide" [only by grace, only by faith]—and compared man to a horse that two men fight to possess: there can be only one rider, God or the devil. Those who belonged to the kingdom of Christ followed him and were united with him, whereas the members of this world's kingdom followed and were united with the devil; the devil was the head of the kingdom of this world just as Christ was the leader of the Church, his spiritual body composed of the faithful. Obviously for Luther it was no more possible than for Augustine to identify the two governments with, on the one hand, the visible, instituted Church and, on the other, the political state; each was composed of both sinners and true Christians chosen by grace, mixed up together. Kingdom of this world and Earthly City were not identical. The temporal regime involved humanity in a different way than did the kingdom of the devil, because the true Christian, who in eschatological terms belonged to the kingdom of God, was nonetheless a member of the Earthly City.

There was of course a crucial link between the devil's kingdom and the Earthly City: the existence of the first explained that of the second. Given that humanity was massively sinful, only force could govern it, and this was the principle role of the temporal kingdom (*Reich*) and the temporal government or regime (*Regiment*). This is the first point of Luther's *Temporal Authority: To What Extent it Should Be Obeyed* (1523) in which he affirms, with the support of numerous biblical texts, that "it is God's will that the sword and secular law be used for the punishment of the wicked and the protection of the upright."[57] The fact that the existence of earthly government based on the use of force was founded in the existence of evil hardly meant that such government should, like the devil's kingdom, be considered evil in itself. On the contrary, that government was willed by God as a means of battling Satan, for the temporal sword, which would be useless if there were only "true Christians" in this world, was absolutely necessary to sinful, sinning humanity. It was of course not the only instrument for fighting evil, nor the main one: as he had explained in the treatise on Christian freedom, only the Word of God, the Word of Christ, who had come on earth with the sole purpose of preaching it–and not to brandish a physical sword or fight against the temporal one–could propel humanity first toward a deep acknowledgment of its sinful nature and then to the determination to have faith. The Word of God was divided, in accordance with the shift from the Old Testament to the New, into commandment and promise. Commandment led humanity to a consciousness of its own impotence by causing the believer to wonder with anxiety (*anxius*; *Angst*) how one could possibly follow the commandment and satisfy the commander. This in turn had the effect of reducing the believer to "nothing" in his own eyes, because "he finds in himself nothing whereby he may be justified and saved."[58] It was then that the second Word of God came to bear, for it told the believer that he must believe in Christ, who accords all grace, and that faith, the promise, is all. It was of persons who had undergone this type of spiritual trial that the true Church–invisible, spiritual–was made. Furthermore, only the Word of Christ could be used to fight heresy, whereas force, incapable of expelling the devil from sinners' hearts, could only fortify it.

It was this same argument, at first used against the papacy, that is to be found at the core of his critique of iconoclasm and the *Schwärmer*—namely, that violence was impotent in spiritual matters. This is equivalent to saying that a militant Church wielding the temporal sword was inconceivable, impossible. That sword belonged to the sovereigns of the earthly kingdom.[59]

The role of temporal government legitimately armed with the sword, government whose existence was an effect of God's goodness, was completely different from that of the Church: such government, of this world, ensured not this world's salvation but its very survival. Because "scarcely one human being in a thousand is a true Christian," without a temporal government human beings would tear each other to pieces and "the world would become a desert."[60] The two regimes were however constantly threatened on earth by the devil, who transformed princes into tyrants and subjects into rebels, and was responsible for a confusion between the temporal regime and the spiritual one, such as when princes sought to intervene in spiritual matters—as, for example, when they tried—unsuccessfully—in certain regions of Germany to ban Luther's German translation of the New Testament. This perversion was found first and foremost in the Catholic Church, which borrowed the methods of the temporal regime and had the arrogance to claim that temporal authority belonged above all to pope and bishops.

Luther was particularly vehement in his denunciation of the emperor Charles V and those princes who, at the urging of pope and bishops, sought to prescribe to their subjects in the matter of religious belief when the laws and rights that were the specific substance of the government (*Regiment*) of the temporal kingdom (*weltliche Reich*) forbade it to express judgment on anything that did not have to do with the body, property, the outer man. They could not be concerned with the soul, over which God "cannot and will not permit anyone but himself to rule."[61] Nonetheless, it was God's will that there be bad princes, tyrants, and executioners, who, serving his divine wrath, had the effect of chastising the wicked, even hurting the innocent, and in all cases maintaining a sort of external peace in the city (princely cruelty appears in this text above all as punishment and as a necessity for countering the potentially devastating effects of existence in the earthly kingdom).

The true Christian, who was a member of the kingdom of God,

understood these dangers and that it was for this reason that God willed the temporal authority. It was in this spirit that true Christians obeyed temporal laws, not out of respect for them, or fear of them, not for their personal gain, either spiritual or material, and certainly not with the intent of deifying kings, but according to the same principle that made them carry out charitable works; that is, through a higher obligation, the knowledge that this was what God willed. Thus, even supposing they belonged to the kingdom of God (which of course no one on earth could know), they obeyed the rule of the temporal sword, paid their taxes, served the political authority and, when they had a vocation to do so, played a role in the government of the polity, for although they themselves had no need to do these things, the services they performed—their vocation—were of vital use to others. Christians thus could and should accept the role of hangman, judge, or prince; in this way they helped to ensure that the civil power and with it civil society did not perish, all the while fully aware that this type of good works did not ensure salvation any more than any other.

Political obligation was thus more a matter of commandment than promise. Addressing now rather his left than his right, the *Schwärmer* or those tempted to join them rather than the pope, Luther reminded them that Christians too were by nature sinners:[62] they also must bow before the temporal sword, this being of course exactly what the fanatics refused to do. The figure of Christ could not serve as an example in the matter of what *civic* attitude a Christian should adopt, because, as we have said, Christ was sent to fulfill one single "function" or "state": to spread the Word of God, in other words to wield the *spiritual* sword, as he is represented doing in Figure 1. Once again, he had not been sent to abolish the temporal one. And since it could not be the function of all Christians to spread the Word, they had to fulfill other functions—carpenter, farmer, hangman, prince.

If a Christian could be a prince, it followed that a prince could be a Christian: it could happen that the Earthly City was governed by a member of the City of God. This did not mean that it would thereby be transformed into the City of God, but simply that a Christian's regime would be different from an earthly city governed by a non-Christian prince. How does Luther portray this Christian prince? What defined his particular art of governing? It carried the imprint of his being a Christian: he would give priority to the Word of God, meaning that he could not be guided by the words of jurists or law books. Just as Plato's statesman based his legitimacy on having direct access to what was true, the *logos*, this leading to a distinction between political regimes based on the written word and mere legality and political regimes based on the spoken word and true legitimacy,[63] so the Christian prince according to Luther in this relatively early text would reject "dead books," turning instead only to God, praying for wisdom.[64] And rather than placing his trust in the "living heads" who were his counselors, he would ensure that his conduct and decisions were determined by the quest for what was useful to his subjects; he would take charge of their needs as if they were his own. His decisions would aim to minimize the quantity of pain and discord, of evil: for example, he would never seek revenge or even punish an injustice if the punishment would create a greater wrong: widows and orphans of enemies, for instance, would be left alone. In other words, he would be commanded entirely by the principle of service, itself founded on his relation to Christ's Word.

And what constituted just government of the spiritual kingdom, the Church? For Christians in the fullness of that identity–as souls, inner consciences–there could be no superior authority to whom they need bend, because only Christ was superior to other Christians. The government practiced by priests and bishops would consist only in spreading the Word, for only the Word, and not recourse to any exterior means, could govern Christians as such: priests had neither authority or power, but rather fulfilled a function, performed a service. As for non-Christians, they existed in the temporal kingdom and were subject to the temporal sword, forced by it to do what true Christians did of their own will. To refute the Anabaptists, according to whom the Christian lived only in the Word of God and thus could be neither prince nor subject, and to reinforce the legitimacy of the temporal authority without at the same time rehabilitating the Roman Catholic Church, which imposed a temporal administration on its followers, Luther insisted that during one's time on earth a human being was a double person: a person in relation with Christ (*Christ-person*) and an earthly person (*Welt-person*). As a *Christ-person*, the Christian must obey perfectly what Christ said in the Sermon on the Mount. However, because they lived in human time, Christians had obligations that, regardless of their potential incompatibility with the prescriptions of the Sermon or other Christian texts, had to be fulfilled. In this fallen world, God had determined that the Christian should have a function, a vocation, which could well be that of a political or military leader; this in turn authorized him to put a criminal to death, for example. The imperative to fulfill one's earthly role, one's vocation or calling (*Beruf*) assigned by God,[65] applied to all, but once again Christians obeyed it because they respected the law of charity: the performance of one's earthly role was a service useful to one's neighbor.

We see that the two regimes do not correspond to the two kingdoms. Because they too were first creatures of nature and therefore sinners, Christians were to be subjected to the temporal regime; conversely, the spiritual kingdom did not exist solely for those who were already Christians. The Word of God, his promise, concerned and was addressed to all humanity. Each was therefore a "citizen of both kingdoms," *Bürger beider reiche*: Christ's Word was addressed to all; likewise, no one could escape the temporal sword. Some had to seize and brandish it; others had to fear it and suffer from it. Christians obeyed it.

In this sense Luther's political message may be interpreted as proposing an exchange in which the Christian's internal freedom would be acknowledged and the political authorities cease intervening in that sphere, while the Christian would abdicate even the will to contest the political authority in place, instead abiding by, supporting, even exercising the power of the sword. Are we to understand this theological doctrine as corresponding first and foremost to the political interests of the Reformation in that it guaranteed to princes the loyalty of their subjects (from the moment they refrained from dictating in spiritual matters), whereas Catholics necessarily found themselves in a system of split loyalties, loyalty to a given sovereign but also to the pope? With his violent rejection of the *Schwärmer* in 1525, Luther has been said to have exchanged revolution for reform; it was from this moment, according to Marx and Engels, that the interrupted (true) course of German history would have to be rewritten. If we are more concerned with the internal logic of Lutheranism than with its effects, Marx's imputation is debatable, at the very least because Luther had already developed the conceptual framework for his political positions in *The Freedom of a Christian*—before, that is, the peasant unrest, before the rise of fanaticism and Anabaptist anarchism. What we can say with certainty is that Luther's project was intended to upset, and thereby set right, what he believed to be the perversely inverted order of things in which princes sought to reign over the spiritual and spiritual lords over the temporal.

The Fanatics Against Civil Society

The vehemence with which Luther expressed his disapproval of the fanatics was perfectly in keeping with the mood of the particular moment, in which a multitude of discontents rumbled and exploded: iconoclast violence, social strife, even private wars, like that conducted by Michael Kohlhaas, later made famous by Kleist's short story in which the author has Luther address a letter to the protagonist explaining that a rebel may not claim the right to brandish the sword of justice.[66]

It was against this convulsive background that the Anabaptist movement developed, more structured than the others at least in terms of its doctrinal content. It had its immediate origins in the activities of 1520-21 at Zwickau (though, as is the case for all these movements, its roots went much deeper in German spiritual and social history), whence it was brought to Wittenberg by a number of self-appointed prophets, who as we have said, played a crucial role in the iconoclast crisis there. Müntzer's questioning of the validity of infant baptism, along with his call for violent action, makes it possible to consider him a precursor of the Anabaptist movement, which culminated in the 1534 attempt led by John of Leyde to establish the kingdom of God in the Westphalian city of Münster. The project was carried out with the intention of applying certain principles taken from the Old Testament, such as community ownership of property and polygamy, for these millenarians, who contested the validity of infant baptism and the sacraments in general, also rejected all social institutions in place in their desire to make immediate, brutal, total use of the evangelical message. The movement was crushed in 1535. Meanwhile, another group had formed around certain schismatic disciples of the Swiss Reformer Huldrych Zwingli (Luther was no more inclined to approve of them than of their inspirer), this time characterized, contrary to its bloody origins, by an ethic of nonviolence.

The political elements of the dispute that opposed Lutherans and Anabaptists cannot be dissociated from the religious ones. And the Anabaptist movement, like the peasant movement preceding it, compelled the Reformers to develop a more systematic doctrine on the subject of civil society, which Philipp Melanchthon soon defined very precisely. Whereas Luther's positions were of central importance in the four-year period between 1521 and 1525 marked by the iconoclast trouble and the Peasants' War, in the period that followed, dominated by the Anabaptist issue, Melanchthon was the main theorist; it was he more than Luther who emphasized and defended the legitimacy of civil society. This was perhaps because by the mere force of reiteration the threat to such society seemed more menacing at this later time, but it had also become more radical. The fact is that Luther, who, as we have seen, strongly disapproved of the feudal lords' selfishness, did not entirely reject the demands made by the peasants in 1525. While condemning unconditionally any contestation of the political authorities' monopoly on legitimate political violence, he nonetheless acknowledged, at least before the beginning of massive violent action, the soundness of certain of the peasants' demands. But while Müntzer's involvement and the prophets' activity provide indisputable evidence that the Peasants' War was a millenarian project, it was the Anabaptists who made fully apparent just how radical a transformation was being sought: as Michelet noted, they wanted to change the very nature of the social tie. By calling into question the political powers in place and the very notion of political dominance, by calling for communal–communistic–ownership of goods in a demand that went beyond mere economic or fiscal reform, Anabaptism in its first, violent form was less a contestation of the earthly sphere in the name of the City of God than the expression of a will to substitute the City of God for civil society. It was, in short, total subversion.

Melanchthon could be all the more direct in his critique of Anabaptism and its goal of destroying the Earthly City because unlike Luther, who denied that human beings could play any role in their own salvation, Melanchthon accorded a certain efficacy to human works. Civil society was for him, as for Aristotle, the place where humanity might seek its own good–not the ultimate good, to be sure, but one eminently worthy of respect. Melanchthon's attachment to and broad knowledge of the writings of antiquity, his commentaries on Aristotle's *Politics* and preface to Cicero's *De officiis*, his writing of the *Augsburg Confession*, the Lutheran religious credo signed by a Diet assembled by the Holy Roman Emperor Charles V in 1530, to say nothing of his school manuals for the study of Latin, textbooks that would be used for centuries, won for Melanchthon the title of *praeceptor Germaniae* (Germany's teacher)—a title brilliantly illustrated by the younger Cranach's portrait showing him with a book in his hands printed in Latin and Greek, not reading it but rather holding it open, as if he were a living lectern, to the viewer, who thereby becomes himself a reader. In this way the artist effected a passage from the image in the painting to the letter of the book, creating an image which may be said to symbolize his subject's intellectualized iconoclasm: Reformed humanism anchored in scriptural culture. Melanchthon may well be thought of as a sort of synthesis of Erasmus and Luther: though he sought to purify Christianity, he was also a humanist whose regard for the Greek and Latin heritage was inseparable from his defense of the polity and made all fanaticism hateful to him. We can understand how Freud was moved to hang Dürer's engraving of him on the wall of his consulting room alongside portraits of Charcot and Helmholtz, and how, on the other side, Engels lambasted him in *The Peasant War in Germany* for manifesting what he considered the lukewarm attitude of an inconsequential revolutionary and the blatant opportunism of a petit-bourgeois.

In his battle against the fanatics Melanchthon forged a sort of alliance between Aristotle and Jesus.

We know that our key terms are to be found together in his commentary of Aristotle's *Politics*, which he quoted in Greek but discussed in Latin following Leonardo Bruni's translation; under the auspices of the Greek philosopher and with his Ciceronian Latin, Melanchthon may thus be said to have furnished a connection between the German Reformation and the first moment of Florentine humanism.[67] In his commentary he denounces the Anabaptists for their will to obliterate the "interval" between the City of God and "civil society." Precisely the same idea is to be found in *Loci communes theologici* (which as we know was translated into French in 1546 and prefaced by Calvin in 1551)—a fact that enables us to propose that it was with Lutheranism, not Calvinism, that the spirit of capitalism was born, for without taking up this question in detail, we may underline the continuity from Luther to Calvin of the defense of civil society. In this respect, the initial particularity of the Reformation is its opposition not to Catholicism but rather to the fanaticism of the *Schwärmer*. By affirming against the millenarians the relevance of the split between the two Cities and by positing the legitimate autonomy of civil society, Luther and Melanchthon, and only after them Calvin, founded the validity of centuries-old political and civic practices that did not pertain exclusively to economic activities but most certainly included them.

According to Melanchthon, the political sphere was no more a matter for the Gospel than medical science was: the political sphere involved a particular domain (just as the medical art concerned the body) and aimed at a particular good (analogous to health). The fanatics were guilty of sedition because in the name of the Gospel they were intruding into areas that they had no business concerning themselves with: the Gospel's subject was the heart's justice, not the polity. Melanchthon's rejection of a theocratic state of course concerned not only the mad visionaries who had sprung up in the wake of the Reformation, but also the Roman Catholic Church. There had been, he asserted, too few voices in the Catholic Church affirming the heterogeneity of politics and religion as practical spheres—not enough, in any case, to have stopped the popes from invading the state and claiming the right to behave like kings. "This is why we have underlined the fact that there is a maximal interval between the Gospel and the political, and that all political things are in accordance with the Gospel as long as they are in accordance with reason."[63] It was not Melanchthon's intention to have theologians thrown out of the polity (the fate that Socrates advocated for poets), but he did wish at the very least to keep them at a distance from the activities of governing the republic, and he reminded his readers that neither Christ nor the Apostles had sought to abolish Roman law.

To counter the Anabaptists it was necessary to explain that no civil society could exist without power (*imperium*). More important, he argued, natural right was divine right: everything that was natural in civil society should be considered the equal of divine law. No, civil society was not artificial; to affirm that it was was to undermine the very bases of such society and open the way for contestation of it on the grounds of principle. To refute any such contestation Melanchthon overlegitimated civil society by basing it on a natural right whose origin and foundation were to be found in God. He thus combated Anabaptist subversion with a double defense of civil society, both Aristotelian and Christian: by affirming the natural but also divinely ordained character of civil society, it was possible to argue against the fanatics while at the same time steering clear of idolizing society, political authority, the state. When Aristotle made the polity–civil society–the place of humanity's supreme good, had he not made the mistake of elevating the state into a sort of absolute value? By affirming both the natural inherent value of civil society and the divine foundation of natural law, Melanchthon rescued civil society from the Anabaptists while at the same time relativizing it.[69]

Let us follow out the practical consequences of his doctrine in a particular area: the issue of property ownership. Social life, the *vita civilis*, implied work, the family, magistrates; the exercise of a craft, the ability to establish contracts, and property–all to be accompanied by fear of God and faith.[70] Charity did not consist in upsetting the social order in which goods were divided up, for Christian perfection was in no way a matter of externals, wealth or marriage, for example, but consisted rather in faith–and charity correctly understood. At the same time this meant that though keeping one's virginity all one's life or handing out one's goods were indeed perfections, they could only be a matter of personal maxim; that is, they could not be erected into universal laws. Indeed, all "sedition" that might disrupt "the social organization" by redistributing property was vigorously to be rejected: it was out of the question for human beings to follow Socrates' model of a communal republic. In fact, Scripture itself legitimated the right to "economy": had not Solomon said "I bless your garden," and didn't this mean that there existed a divine blessing for the "faculties" of those who "managed" their property?[71]

But while civil society possessed in and of itself a legitimacy based on universal natural law, it also had a function to fulfill in relation to religious faith. For Luther–and as we shall see at the end of Chapter 4 the same thing may be said of another important figure of the period, Albrecht Dürer–it was the state's duty to organize and put in place the general conditions that would permit the existence of a Church in harmony with the Word of God. The state was therefore universally necessary to humankind as the condition of possibility for the exercise of the true faith; this was its highest value. Although Melanchthon argued more pointedly than Luther that the nonreligious ends of civil society were sufficient to legitimate it, he did insist that the essential purpose of civil society was to maintain the preeminence of God within society and to enable humanity to seek the *ultimate* good. It was not fitting that people should devote themselves essentially to pursuing and enjoying "the belly's benefits"; they should rather be seeking "eternal goods."

There is then nothing in Melanchthon's thinking that could be understood as an assertion that owning property was an essential condition for belonging to civil society and nothing resembling encouragement of the capitalist ethic, if by that we mean an ethic of accumulation or commodities exchange, though we do encounter here a form of secularized asceticism such as Weber claimed characterized the Protestant ethic.[72] Clearly for Melanchthon the world should not be deserted, and while it was not meant to be a place of pleasure and even less of salvation, one was allowed to be rich; the important thing was to remember that wealth had no value in itself. Melanchthon thus defended private property against the Anabaptists' communism in a mode similar to Luther's when, seeking to protect painting against iconoclast attacks, he compared images to wine and women (see p. 116): they could not be violently, summarily done away with. The kinds of reasoning and argumentation used by the two central figures of the Reformation in their theories of political power are also quite similar.

Ten years after the Anabaptist crisis, Melanchthon undertook to examine the validity of Pope Boniface VIII's doctrine as formulated in *Unam sanctam* (1302), a theocratic and hierarchical vision according to which the pope held both swords, that of the Church as well as that of earthly empire. For Melanchthon, Boniface was wrong on at least two points: first, both church and state—and this included the political powers in place among Jews and pagans—had their origin in God; second, there was only one sword. It was the work of the political power to use coercion—the sword—to maintain civil peace, preserve good moral conduct, and protect the true religion. The magistrate's power, that is, the maintenance of "external discipline," was limited once again by natural, positive, divine laws: it could not aim to change impious minds. But it *was* incumbent upon it to punish blasphemers. This was also the duty of priests and laymen—in short, it was everyone's duty to fight against false prophets. Furthermore, it was incumbent on princes in their domain—external discipline—to execute those decisions of the Church reached by synods (of course Melanchthon's scheme included no pope). The magistrates' role could not be restricted to protecting the bodies of their subjects from the likes of robbers and murderers; as defenders of the law, it was also their duty to sanction impious persons:

"The magistrates, therefore, who hold the sword, must forbid heresies, that is, impious dogmas, and punish heretics, the authors of such dogmas."[73] And the political power, which had the function and duty of taking action against those who publicly attacked the true religion, must of course itself submit to the true religion.

As for ministers of the gospel, their particular functions were to administer the sacraments, proclaim the remission of sins, and "excommunicate, with words, not by physical force, those who fall into manifest disobedience." Against what he understood to be Boniface's vision, Melanchthon affirmed that "the Apostles and their successors do not have a sword by divine right; that is, they do not have the right to coerce through physical force"[74]—there could be no Inquisition. The two functions, that of the Church and that of the state, were thus absolutely distinct, even though the civil power was to serve the Church by taking disciplinary action "in the same way that the father must be the minister and agent of the Church within his family."[75] Whereas in Boniface VIII's conception, political power was a subordinate part of a totality dominated by the Church and the temporal sword was meant to serve the spiritual and was legitimated by divine right only through the Church's mediation, Melanchthon followed a logic of division of labor according to which there existed but one sword, that of the state, in a relation with the Church that was less one of dependence than complementarity. Melanchthon's thinking thus opened the way for the close association between the respective bureaucracies of the state and a popeless local church which is characteristic of Northern Europe.[76] It was of course out of the question in his scheme that any sword be used to institute the City of God here below.

Calvin Against the *Phantastiques*

There is a striking similarity between these lines by Melanchthon, which we have reason to believe Calvin read, and what the French Reformer wrote in "On Civil Government," chapter 20 of the *Institutes of the Christian Religion*. The first edition of Calvin's major work appeared in the general context of what is known as *l'Affaire des placards*: on the night of October 17, 1534, anti-papists posted bills against the saying of mass, going so far as to tack one on the gate of François I's chateau at Amboise, bringing down royal fury, repression, and the burning of heretics.

The German Lutheran princes with whom François I was allied at the time protested against such violent retaliation, and the king justified his actions in a *Manifeste*, about which Calvin would later say, recalling the dramatic atmosphere of the moment, that it assimilated – wrongly, of course – the victims of the repression to the "Anabaptists and seditious persons who, with their reveries and false opinions, upset not only religion but also the entire political order."[77] The *Institutes*, which was first published in Latin in 1536, then rapidly translated into French by the author before appearing in various greatly amplified versions, was first and foremost a response to the king's defamation of the French Protestants, whom Calvin sought to exonerate in the epistolary dedication to François I and at several points in the work itself.

A significant difference between Luther and Calvin was that, while believing unshakably with the German Reformer in the legitimacy of political authority, Calvin unconditionally condemned religious images. His arguments against them, delivered in a classic Protestant style that probably owed much to Zwingli, are based on an affirmation of the primacy of the Word, but are also marked by a desire for moral purity and asceticism. Anyone who dressed or behaved the way religious images depict the saints as dressing or behaving would be fit for whipping: "Surely the brothel houses can show harlots more chastely and soberly attired than their temples show images of these whom they would have called virgins."[78] And there was more than one such creature to be found in the house of prayer, particularly in Germany, whose churches were encumbered with altarpieces, frescoes, statues, paintings, gilt, carillons and organs, chasubles and surplices – in Strasbourg Cathedral alone one might count fifty different altars. Even before Luther, critics had raised their voices against practices in that city which they considered extravagant, wasteful idolatry, preparing the ground for Karlstadt, who as we know would hold religious sway there in 1525.

But the wellspring of Calvin's attack against images went deeper than a will to take on Catholicism, which he accused of transforming virgins into whores. That attack was based on an elaborate theology of representation. If it was indeed attested that God had shown himself to be present by means of certain "signs," these were fleeting, transitory: no "visible figure" was fitting to represent the "invisible,"[79] and there was nothing less fitting than to "bring to the measure of five foot" our

God who was "above all measure and incomprehensible."[80] The wings
of the cherubim that concealed God when he came to the mercy seat on
the Ark of the Covenant to give Moses the orders to be followed by the
people of Israel (Num. 7:89) served to "foreclose" (*foreclore*) human
sight and all other human senses.[81] We may well speak of foreclosing
the image of the Father, for anything that claimed to be his image was a
corruption of his Name, his Word; it was an indecency that the temples
must be purified of. Could one agree with Saint Gregory (Pope Gregory I) that images were the prayer books of the ignorant? If people had
to be taught in this way it was because the *Word* of God had not been
adequately "imprinted" (*imprimée*) upon them.[82]

To prevent "corrupting" God's grandeur and majesty by "phantoms" utterly improper to him, it was necessary to limit painting and
sculpture to things seen by the eye.[83] These arts could illustrate "sto-
ries" or even make for "delectation," but they could not teach anything; only the Word of God could teach. If people were to be protected
from idolatry, images would have to be banned from the temple, for
given humanity's propensity for superstition—a theme to be encountered later in the thinking of Spinoza, for whom the *Institutes* was a
crucially important text—such simulacra simply could not be put to
good use. The only "images" that could be present in a temple were
those of baptism and Holy Communion, which "God has consecrated
by his Word; such images are imprinted with his true mark."[84] The
coincidence of the Reformation with the increased availability of books
has often been pointed out: Protestant scripturalism was made possible
when culture became portable thanks to the reduced size and price of
books and the use of vernacular languages. This development certainly
has a role in explaining how for Calvin the field of legitimate images
was determined by the Word: the only licit images were those that
"imprint" or "impress" *its* "mark." On this issue, Luther's conception
of a religion founded on the Word of God—the printed Word—was less
radical than Calvin's, for as we have seen, and unlike Zwingli, whose
influence is also present in Calvin's writings, Luther did not believe
that as soon as one prostrated oneself before an image one was invited
to commit idolatry, and certainly not that images *were* idolatry.

Calvin seems hardly to have distinguished between images and religious relics, to which he devoted a frankly comic work in the manner
of his contemporary, Rabelais.[85] It includes a catalog of the effects of

superstition, nourished by stupidity and swollen by avarice, superstition he saw as inevitable as soon as the Word was abandoned, for this was the grim consequence of the Fall, which had radically changed human nature: no one could venerate God through images without sinking into idolatry. He ridiculed the notion that paintings might come to exist through miracles, such as those at Lucca, which were said to have been done by angels: Was painting any activity for angels? And did Christ really wish to be known and kept in "our memory" by means of "carnal images"? Relics were always too fleshly: if one were to assemble all the limbs and body parts of the saints, the sum of their bones dispersed among a multitude of churches and places of pilgrimage, one could easily construct all sorts of outrageous beings—creatures with five heads and ten arms. There were indeed saints that had several bodies scattered among different cities, each more than ready to prove that the body it possessed was the real one for the simple reason that exploiting the credulity of the faithful was so lucrative.

While composing the text on relics, Calvin learned that Christ's prepuce had just been discovered—the third on record. And that elsewhere it had been shown that those who thought they were adoring a martyr's bone had been thrown a dog's. And that he who believed he was kissing Our Lady's ring had put his lips to one worn by a whore. Calvin himself, when a child, had kissed a part of one of the multiple bodies of Mary's mother, Saint Anne, in the Abbé d'Orcamps near his native city of Noyon. And yet common sense, the most basic knowledge of physiology and history should have enabled people to reject such absurd pretensions, for even a simpleminded man or woman was capable of understanding that the "dagger [*braquemart*] which looks very much like one boys play with" that was reputed in Carcassone to have belonged to Saint Michael, was nothing but a farce[86] (which the reader would be careful not to confuse with *bracquemars* in Rabelais).[87] The conclusion to be drawn from this sarcastically enumerated list of deceptions was clear: the canonization of relics was "a pollution and defilement" that "ought not on any account to be tolerated in the Church."[88] How could the fable have been invented that Saint Luke was a painter when "it was certainly not the practice at that period for Christians to have idols, nor was it introduced till long after, when the Church had been corrupted with superstition."[89]

In his thinking about Christian freedom, Calvin agreed with Luther that it was not necessary to follow either Old Testament law or what was then the law of the Catholic Church, but he differed from the German Reformer in that the use of images did not figure along with eating meat and possessing wealth on his list of indifferent matters, matters of choice. While condemning those who ate meat on Friday just to make a show of their freedom, he said little against the iconoclasts. If we take the status of images as an index of the interval between the two juris-dictions, the spiritual and civil kingdoms, we conclude that Calvin's affirmation of the separation between the two was more radical than Luther's. Although with his position on the Eucharist he may have deepened that gap, he nonetheless firmly rejected all conceptions that announced that the hour of Judgment was nigh: Calvin rejected the millenarian perspective.

While Melanchthon insisted on the interval between the two king-doms and rejected the belief that it could be overcome, Calvin as we know reproached the fanatics or *phantastiques* for daring to consider everything touching the "business of this world" as foul and profane. For him, fanaticism was just this hatred of the profane world, hatred that made all involvement in transitory life seem superfluous and which seemed underwritten by the idea that human beings were per-fect. Those who rejected the "utility of the polis" would lead humanity into "inhuman barbarity," whereas those who filled the "office" of magistrate were obediently practicing a "legitimate vocation approved by God." The utility of political organization, what he called the *police* and which could just as well be called "civil society," was that much easier to insist upon in that it was for Calvin, as for Luther and Me-lanchthon, the condition of possibility for the true religion. Indeed, it was the existence of such a *police* that made it possible for us to "fash-ion our manners to civil righteousness" and that enabled the develop-ment of a "public form of religion amongst Christians."[90] The polis then was what held barbarity at bay; thanks to it, "humanity consisted amongst humans." To give substance to people's humanity by enabling human beings to live in concord with one another to the furthest extent possible, including, of course, in their religious beliefs—this was the function of the polis, a function so lofty that it forbade our considering it soiled or worthless.

Moreover, while, like Luther, Calvin distinguished two regimes or governments affecting humanity, one concerning eternal life and the inner person, who was free, the other whose work was to organize civic justice and reform morals; while he distinguished the spiritual reign of Christ from that of the polis, he did not believe–and here he differed with Luther–that the two regimes or reigns were in contradiction with each other: the "company of men" was in no way the devil's City. Taking up Saint Augustine's comparison that on earth human beings were like pilgrims yearning for their true "country," Calvin deemed that they needed help on this voyage and that to deny them that help was to deprive them of their "human nature."[91] The temporal regime was in no way "distasteful" to the spiritual reign of Christ: "For the civil government doth now begin in us upon earth certain beginnings of the heavenly kingdom, and in this mortal and vanishing life doth as it were enter upon an immortal and incorruptible blessedness."[92] We have here a rejection of any attempt to flee the world, affirmed in the following terms: the polis would only be useless if God's reign, within us, had "extinguished" our present life.

It was, of course, in their conceptions of the Eucharist that Luther and Calvin most differed, a disagreement similar to the one that divided them on the issue of images. Luther as we have said rejected the Catholic theory of transubstantiation. The term, inherited from Aristotle, designates in Catholic doctrine the change in substance effected in the Last Supper and believed to be repeated each time Holy Communion is celebrated; the concept may likewise be understood as the very source of the value Catholicism accords to images. For Luther there was no such transformation of substance: the bread and wine remained bread and wine, and to adore them in the mass was to commit idolatry. Rather what took place was what has been called consubstantiation (though Luther himself never used this term): the bread and wine remained unchanged in substance while the body and blood of Christ was added to them; it was in them and with them, sustaining them. Consubstantiation was similar to what happened when metal was heated: the hot iron has all the properties of iron, plus the heat. Clearly Luther and the Catholics agreed that Christ was really present. For Calvin, on the other hand, the words spoken by Christ during the Last Supper were not meant to change the nature, matter, or substance of the bread and wine; if this were the case, then Christ was a magician, and priests were sorcerers, using words to act upon inanimate objects–an unworthy conception of Jesus, reduced thereby to a kind of fairground quack.

When Christ spoke the words, "This is my blood, this is my body," he was hardly addressing the wine and bread–it would be mad to talk to things as if they were animate creatures. No, he was speaking to his disciples. The Word of Christ acted on their hearts: the bread and wine became his body and blood for *them*:

> But Christ speaketh not to the bread that it may be made his body, but [rather] commandeth his disciples to eat and promiseth to them the communicating of body and blood. . . . We ought not here to imagine any magical enchantment, that it be sufficient to have mumbled up the words, as though the elements did hear them: but let us understand that those words are a lively preaching, which may edify the hearers, which may inwardly pierce into their minds, which may be imprinted and settled in their hearts, which may [bring] them forth effectualness in the fulfilling of that which it promiseth.[93]

The "substance" of the mass was therefore not in any substantial transformation of bread into the body of Christ, but instead in the explanation of the mystery to the people and the recitation of the promise.[94]

As a virulent critic of magic, Calvin contributed to what Weber called the dis-enchantment of the world: his rejection of fanaticism, as elaborated in his fight against the *phantastiques*, expressed his will for an acknowledged split between the order of the world and that of grace and explains his abomination of all magicians, sorcerers, diviners.[95] It likewise led him to devalue priests: the administration of the sacraments might no longer be, as was affirmed under the "tyranny of the pope," a matter merely of their intention–as if consecration were in no way dependent on "the people" but only on religious professionals. This transfer of authority from priest to people represented a return to the living God: it was necessary to put an end to idolatry, which made people adore what was given instead of the giver. The "adoration" of the sacraments was contrary to God's Word: kneeling before the wafer of Holy Communion instead of taking it and eating it–that was idolatry and "superstitious worship."[96] Jesus Christ was indeed the matter and substance of the Holy Eucharist, whose effect was to absolve believers of their sins; they consumed his body and blood under the "signs of bread and wine" without having to *fantastiquer* that his body was contained therein.

The passage from a substantialist to a symbolic conception of the Eucharist is clearly marked by the vocabulary Calvin used in attempting to explain the mystery: the fact that the word "body" was attributed to the "symbol" of the bread was to be explained by a similarity between them; this was a "metonymy," like that which led us to say that circumcision *was* the covenant with God. Undoubtedly the sign, corporal, visible, earthly, differed in "substance" from the spiritual, invisible truth that it figured; this did not, however, make it a "vain and useless memorial" but rather a "true and real exhibition" of the signified thing. And if signs invented by human beings sometimes took the "name" of the things they signified, how much more applicable was this principle to signs instituted by God, which might "borrow the names of that to which they attest without any fallacy and by the truth of which they are always accompanied."[97]

There was "metonymy" in the mysteries.[98]

The mystery of the Eucharist then must be understood in terms of symbolic efficacy, where words genuinely act on people, and not magical effect, where words give the illusion of acting on things. In this denaturalization—to chew and swallow the Eucharist was not to chew and swallow Christ's flesh—the status of images was determined by the preeminence of the Word: the only relevant images were tropes, the only valid figuration, the rhetorical figure. Religious beliefs and rituals are structured like a language. God is literary style. And once symbols had received the name "image," painted images would fall to so low a station that their destruction would be inevitable. Signs, Calvin had said in discussing the Eucharist, were "images of things absent" that took their "names" from the things they signified. One could therefore say of Holy Communion that it was a "mirror" or a "picture," but that image which was the sacrament bore no relation of resemblance or imitation to that to which it referred. Holy Communion was an image that *represented* nothing, for it mirrored the invisible. And if the sacrament was a painting that figured the invisible, painting itself, when it sought to show the invisible, was "foreclosing" the Word of God. Painting was therefore, like the adoration of relics, an execrable sacrilege in which "we have adored dead and insensible creatures instead of the unique, living God." Because the sacraments acquired their value only from the uttered Word, the papists' mass was "pure aping and quackery":[99] by celebrating the mass through "mimes," its mystery was veiled over rather than explained; the people were mystified rather than edified.

It was for the same reason that Christians had to break with the logic of Old Testament Jewish ceremonies. Because we had Christ's body, we had to abandon the shadows.[100] Christ's incarnation and his death had radically changed the status of sacrifice: the animal sacrifice of the Old Testament figuratively anticipated the Son's "perfect" sacrifice, but after him there was no reason to continue figuring it with images. Christ's humanity must not lead to a kind of anthropomorphic naturalizing of the sacrament where one would be chewing on God's Son as on a piece of meat while contemplating his face in a picture. Instead, that humanity had put an end to "the time of figures." The incarnation was not some sort of mixture: Christ had assumed our humanity on earth and uplifted it to heaven by freeing it from the condition of mortality, "not by changing its nature."[101] Human nature and the glory of the ascension–Christ was double, as were the kingdoms. He could not really be present in a multitude of bits of bread, nor could he exist locally in any one of them. Fragmenting Christ's body, making it ubiquitous, would mean stripping him of that body and transforming him into a "phantom."[102] One must not then prostrate oneself before the sacrament as before an idol, for Christ was not there; he was in the truth of the sign born of his commandment, "Take and eat." For this reason religious ceremonies should be reduced to a minimal function, the same one that Spinoza would accord them, as we shall see in Chapter 5. As long as they were sober and fitting, they had the effect of deepening reverence for the sacrament–not the same thing as adoration–and served "decency and the public order."

The status of painting was thus directly correlated with the doctrine of the Eucharist: the more Holy Communion partook of carnal substance, the greater the legitimacy of images. At one pole was Catholicism, with its substantialist conception of the Eucharist and full legitimacy for pictorial representation; at the other Protestantism, with its symbolist conception of the Eucharist and corresponding rejection of images. From the Roman Catholic Church to Calvin and Zwingli, with Luther in between, we have a sort of desubstantializing of the Eucharist, which in turn deprived images of their ontological value. For Zwingli the sacrament was merely a "commemoration" of the sacrifice on the Cross, whereas for Calvin, as we have seen, the Eucharist remained a sacrament, but without any transformation of the substance.[103] In the middle position, Luther deemed that some degree of anthropomorphism was inevitable when the Christian thought of

Christ, a position that led him to accept images while condemning idolatry. This complex attitude is reflected in the strategy that Cranach followed in composing his post-Reformation altarpieces: they no longer show a central figure, be it that of Christ or the Holy Trinity, which the faithful might adore, but rather represent a personage in an attitude of adoration: the painting thus invites the viewer to adore not by presenting him with an image of the thing to be adored but by following the example given.

Although Luther and Zwingli were engaged in raging theological battle against each other, the latter did accord a certain spiritual reality to the presence of Christ in the wine and wafer given to the believer, whereas the radical iconoclast Karlstadt, with whom Zwingli too fell out in 1525 (though Luther deliberately continued to confound the two) went so far as to interpret "this" in "This is my body" as referring not to the bread but rather to Christ's own body. This conception, which eliminated all sacrificial content from the mass as well as the faintest suggestion of Christ's presence, is consistent with his hatred of images, expressed as we know not only in theory but in action. In contrast, both Zwingli and Calvin, the latter in the context of his vehement condemnation of the Anabaptists, had some, if not many, disapproving words for iconoclast practices.

Clearly Luther's critique of the iconoclasts in 1521 and his combat against Karlstadt were not anecdotal or marginal battles against excesses threatening the social order; they went straight to the heart of his theology. It is not then surprising to find together in a text praising civic life, which we shall now consider in some detail, both an attack against the Swiss Reformer and a defense of painting: Luther's doctrine of the Eucharist conferred validity on images and a legitimacy—conditional but incontestable—on civil society.

Luther's Cemetery

In 1525 the plague was raging at Breslau.

How should Christians respond to the danger and, more particularly, should they leave their city? This was the question asked of Luther by its pastors; the Reformer published his answer, *Whether One May Flee from a Deadly Plague*, two years later, when Wittenberg itself was touched by the disease and he could witness the devastating effects of people's fear.

Because death was a God-sent punishment for our sins, some advised facing it wherever one happened to be. Luther, however, consistent with the argument he had used against the iconoclasts, declared this attitude appropriate only for the strong; not everyone could be expected to stay in place and fight what might come. Members of the spiritual ministry, of course, had no choice: "[They] must remain steadfast before the peril of death";[104] they must stay at their posts. The same was true for those exercising a civic function: "To abandon an entire community which one has been called to govern and to leave it without official or government, exposed to all kinds of danger such as fires, murder, riots, and every imaginable disaster is a great sin. It is the kind of disaster the devil would like to instigate wherever there is no law and order."[105] This proclamation is of course consistent with his sense of political legitimacy as including the right to put down peasant rebellion in the name of public order. It was forbidden to desert those "offices" in which one performed a "service" or "duty" that followed a master-servant, parent-child model of relations, characterized, it must not be forgotten, by *mutual* obligation, in that the master might not abandon his servant and children's duty was to help their parents if the need arose. Municipal employees, including doctors paid by the city, mercenaries, mayors, judges, and the like had to fulfill their roles by staying put, unless there were already enough of them in a given community. Everyone else might leave if they wanted to, for "to flee from death and to save one's life is a natural tendency, implanted by God."[106]

There could hardly be a better illustration than this of the principle of civil society's autonomy: civil society must not seek to bring on the kingdom of God by indulging in abusive sacrifice; it must function according to profane principles. Even in cases other than epidemics or, similarly, famine and fire, and more specifically, even in the case of religious persecution, fleeing to save one's life was not unworthy behavior for a Christian: should the Turks come, no Christian was obliged to sit in his village waiting to receive divine punishment from the heathen's sword.

We may say that Luther refuted the Christian version of the "laziness" argument, a refutation first formulated in reaction against the Stoics and their doctrine of necessity. If the order of the world was an ineluctable chain of causes, then if I fell ill, sending for a doctor would in no way change my destiny—it was in these terms that the Stoics' opponents sought to expose their thesis as untenable: it was obvious that seeing a doctor could change my condition. Transposed into the terms of the Christian problem of evil, the laziness argument would have it that, because God wished to punish humanity, it must accept that punishment, leaving God's will to express itself through the actions of Turk or plague. Completely opposed to this view, Luther exhorted people to act, to make politically and socially useful decisions: he underlined their obligation to help each other—though not to sacrifice themselves uselessly—and called on them to fight together against their fear. Although it was true that everyone had the right to try to ensure his own survival, it was also his duty to help those who were in danger—and this applied to all, not just to civil servants. If my neighbor's house was on fire, I must help him put it out, even if that meant risking my life. But Luther did not believe that solidarity should depend solely on the individual good will. He did not believe, for instance, that the responsibility for the care of deprived or elderly people should fall to private individuals alone but that the public authorities should contribute, and he called for the establishment in all large cities of hospitals where the sick would be cared for by professionals. This was not merely a matter of managing charity and solidarity more rationally, but of a more general will to be socially and practically effective. One can and should intervene in the events Providence imposed.

This attitude is perfectly illustrated by the ways Luther proposed for combating the plague. Keeping the disease from spreading necessarily meant acting in the common interest. Helping the sick was a duty to be performed in the name of charity, but it was also a service that protected the community by preventing the spread of the plague. It was thus entirely out of the question to limit the fight against physical affliction to mere prayer. On the contrary, it was necessary to make full use of professionals and experts—to let the city's doctors decide, for example, whether by burying the dead in cemeteries situated at the center of town there was not a real danger of bad air circulating and contaminating others. "God has commanded us to care for the body, to protect and nurse it so that we are not exposed needlessly."[107]

Does this call for the institution of public services in matters of hygiene and aid to the sick and elderly—what we would call today the establishment of public policies—contradict the Lutheran theory of salvation as completely independent of works? Not if we remember

Luther's insistence on the necessity for a Christian to act and behave in accordance with the demands inherent in the reality of this world's kingdom, his belief in the existence of a community of believers. Natural law, impulses due to nature, could not be overlooked or ignored; rather Luther integrated them into an ethics whose first purpose was to affirm the substance of this world. That substance could not be confused with the kingdom of Christ; it would be absurd to decree rules and regulations for civil society drawn from a false analogy between it and the City of God. The fact that works were not instrumental in salvation ensured their autonomy in relation to the kingdom of grace and gave them a specific consistency endowed with its own rationality and validity. It was up to human beings to make the Earthly City as good a place as possible.

There was to be no denying of the interval between the kingdom of the here-and-now and the kingdom of God; no parodying the Last Judgment here on earth by uselessly risking one's life–Luther's reflections on what attitude Christians should adopt when confronted with plague was an occasion for him to reaffirm what may be called his concern for this world, its ontological reality, which was not mere appearance. Death was a serious thing and one must not risk it for nothing. To understand the desire to flee death as reasonable was to recognize the value of life. If indeed it may be said that, like Socrates, Luther privileged individual personal conscience, this was only in the matter of the individual's relation to God's Word; it was in no way meant to open up a philosophical way for flight from this world or to dissolve community and its tasks in the acid of the subjective consciousness.

Far from exhorting people to practice vain heroism, Luther valued the care and concrete measures they took to survive. The feeling they might have of a threat weighing on all and each must not give way to desertion or panic; fear and trembling made sense only as a reaction to God's power and his judgment, whereas fear of earthly things, anxiety about the things of this world, had no spiritual value. On the contrary, the fright that caused us to turn away from the battle against suffering, the horror that made us tremble at the sight of sickness–these were provoked by the devil. Luther utterly avoided terror-charged rhetoric that would remind people of their wretchedness, because he saw in the fear that paralyzed people and kept them from fighting for survival a ruse of Satan.

This acceptance of the world in all its weight, the world in which we must live, is consistent with his vehement rejection of the conception of the Eucharist as developed by the visionaries, enthusiasts, fanatics. Despite a few attempts at reconciliation, Luther's break in 1525 with Karlstadt, Zwingli, and all those who denied the real presence of Christ in the sacrament of the Eucharist, who denied that mass was a sacrifice, proved absolute. Luther wanted to maintain the fullest meaning for Christ's declaration, "This is my body," and as we have seen, this put him into irresolvable conflict with Karlstadt and Zwingli. For Karlstadt the first "this" referred not to the bread and wine but to Christ's own body, the Savior's meaning therefore being to announce his Passion: "I am the body that shall be sacrificed for you." For the Reformer from Zurich, the verb "is" in Christ's statement meant "signifies" and the Savior was saying "This bread signifies my body," so that in the Last Supper Christ's flesh was eaten not "naturally and literally, but only spiritually."[108] Luther, as we know, underlined the words "my body": the incarnation was real and God had become flesh. Holy Communion could therefore not be reduced to commemoration or a symbolic ceremony in which Christ was "purely spirit." Holy Communion meant that Christ-made-man was really present, and he denounced the "sacramentarian fanatics," thereby establishing a tie between the insurrectionary peasants, the Anabaptists, and Zwingli's followers, all *Schwärmer*–"They are like a bedbug which itself has a foul smell, but the harder you rub to crush it, the more it stinks"[109]–whose spiritual error was perfectly symmetrical to the pope's. He called upon his followers to combat them, just as he had called for the peasants' rebellion to be squelched, because for him the dead Müntzer's spirit lived on. It is with this exhortation that he concludes the text explaining Christian duty in a time of plague:

> In closing we admonish and plead with you in Christ's name to help us with your prayers to God so that we may do battle with word and precept against the real and spiritual pestilence of Satan in his wickedness with which he now poisons and defiles the world. That is, particularly against those who blaspheme the sacrament, though there are other sectarians also. Satan is infuriated and perhaps he feels that the day of Christ is at hand. That is why he raves so fiercely and tries through the enthusiasts [*Schwärmer*] to rob us of the Savior, Jesus Christ. Under the papacy Christ was simply "flesh" so that even a monk's cap had to be regarded as sacred. Now he is nothing more than sheer "spirit" and Christ's flesh and word are no longer supposed to mean anything.[110]

In fact, Luther so deeply detested those who believed that reenactments of the Savior's meal were nothing but commemorations that "sooner than have mere wine with the fanatics, I would agree with the pope that there is only blood."[111] For him the wine of Holy Communion was as different from wine made from grapes as such wine is from wine mixed with water: just as in the mixture the water disappears and the wine is changed, so the wine of Holy Communion underwent a change. And while for Zwingli during the ritual of Communion Christ's body was present only for the believer (because it was to the believer that the bread and wine "signified" Christ), for Luther the Savior's body was present even for the unbelieving, who, though it had no meaning for them, did not merely drink wine and eat bread, but ate Christ's flesh and drank his blood—for their eternal damnation. Luther, then, contrary to Zwingli, saw in the Eucharist not an issue of signification but one of substance (he might have accepted discussion of it not as a metaphor but a synecdoche: "My body is *in* the bread").

Luther's condemnation of the sacramentarians for their denial of the Incarnation should not lead one to believe that their leader Zwingli was not preoccupied by life in the polity; his moves to intervene in public life in Zurich, culminating in his death in 1531 as a "soldier for Christ" in the second battle of Kappel against the Catholic cantons, prove the contrary. While Luther fairly quickly came to enjoy a strong local position, enabling him to leave the matter of managing the affairs of the city and protecting the "true religion" in the hands of the rich and powerful elector of Saxony, Zwingli's mission of reinforcing the Christian Civic Union (*das Christliche Bürgerrecht*) and ultimately creating a wholly Protestant Switzerland required his involvement in all political struggles there. He did not, however, seek to take over the role of the legitimate political authorities, as Müntzer had, and on this point he was in agreement with Luther. The primary difference between the two persuasions—which explains the failure of attempts, in Marburg in 1529 under the aegis of the Protestant Prince Philip of Hesse to bring together Lutherans and Zwinglians—was that for the Zwinglians and all those whom Luther called fanatics, the Word of God might or should be the only guide to social and civic life, whereas for Luther that Word could not stand as a program in such matters but rather reinforced humanity in its fight against the devil.

The preceding quotation makes it very clear: to Luther's way of thinking, reducing Holy Communion to a symbolic practice was the equivalent of increasing evil's power. Luther did not believe in the possibility of reorganizing civil society in supposed accordance with commandments to be found in the Word of God. In his view, saying that the wine of Holy Communion was merely wine did indeed mean radically rejecting idolatry, but at the same time it deprived civil society of all sense of the sacred. If what the others said was to be believed, that there was no physical, fleshly substance in the Incarnation, this meant that anything which perpetuated that illusion–real presence in the Eucharist, images–would have to be reduced (Zwingli) or destroyed (Karlstadt)–at the risk, to Luther's mind, of throwing all social order into a kind of chaos in which neither the real presence of Christ or any political authority would exist. In the face of this grim prospect, Luther conferred substantial reality on the Eucharist, attributed to images the value of signs, maintained the full relevance of civil society in Christian life, and committed himself to social and political conservatism. It is as though, by insisting on fleshly presence in the Eucharist, he were maintaining the last barrier preventing human beings, doomed to evil, from plunging headlong into it. Indeed the troubles caused by the fanatics, the social disorder provoked by the followers of Karlstadt, Zwingli, and Müntzer–whom Luther, with his tendency to label "fanatic" anyone who was not Catholic but not with *him*, put in the same pot despite their differences–might well seem to prove him right. Martin Luther rejected the rationalist and political radicalism of his rivals and did not follow out to its logical conclusion his belief in the preeminence of the Word, continuing to have what may be called an accommodating attitude toward the flesh.

*

Luther's defense of the fleshly nature of Christ's Incarnation, upon which he founded his argument for the legitimacy of civil society, was also, and more particularly, an argument for the necessity of taking care of one's body at that crucial moment when not doing so, not fighting contagion, made one in his eyes a murderer. His concern for earthly well-being was further expressed in the ideas on cemeteries he developed in the same text.

Although he would not make it an obligation, Luther would prefer that the dead be buried outside the city, in a tranquil place conducive to meditation. He complained that the Wittenberg cemetery was noisy and dirty and that all sorts of unspeakable things went on there day and night, declaring that even the Turks had more respect for the dead than did his fellow citizens. Given the present conditions, he himself would prefer being thrown into the Elbe to burial in such a place.

The cemetery he wished to see built would be a revered, sacred place where the visitor might devote himself to religious contemplation, pray, and reflect on the Last Judgment and the Resurrection. On its walls he imagined frescoes representing religious subjects, images that would move their viewers to meditate on death.[112]

So it was that, thinking on his own death in a moment of universal anguish and anxiety, Luther concretely affirmed the importance and validity of painting in the economy of the sacred, rescuing images from the iconoclasts' fury as he had rescued civil society from the fanatics' violence.

4 The Painter of the Two Cities

An engraving done at the beginning of the Reformation depicts the practitioners put out of work by the movement, among them a churchbell maker, a fishmonger, and a painter. We have seen, however, that Luther, who along with other Reformers had no difficulty accepting painting in profane contexts and for profane uses, also accorded it a role in religious edification; this defense of the relative legitimacy of images was consistent with the autonomy he recognized for civil society. Might he have agreed that painting could be so effective a vehicle for theological content that it deserved a status similar to that of Scripture?

An analysis of the crisis for German art that ensued from the Reformation movement, a crisis involving the decline of the plastic arts in favor of music—and this in not only Protestant but also Catholic Germany—would necessarily involve a discussion of the very different cases of Matthais Grünewald, Hans Holbein the Younger, and Lucas Cranach. Albrecht Dürer alone, however, evoked the deep complexities of the problem in several of his works, and more particularly in an engraving he did in 1525 representing a project for a monument to victory over the insurgent peasants (see Figure 7). The engraving stands as an enigma, but may be interpreted with the help of certain other works by the painter, works which themselves require interpretation.

Dürer was a Lutheran of firm convictions, and like Lucas Cranach

7.   ALBRECHT DÜRER. "Project for a Monument to the Peasants' Defeat," in *Unterweisung der Messung*, 1525.

he was an admirer of the Reformer, to whom he sent various engravings. But he did not become a propagandist for him as other artists did, though he did read Luther's texts early on and discuss them with those he was close to in Nuremberg and during his stay in Antwerp in 1520, which coincided with that of Erasmus.[1] It was in this city that he learned of Luther's confinement in the Wartburg and heard the rumor that he had been assassinated and his body found at the bottom of a mine pit, covered with stab wounds. The artist's reaction may be guessed from the flow of eloquence that suddenly interrupts his otherwise dry journal and its string of bookkeeping details. Dürer compares Luther to Christ:

> And whether he yet lives I know not, or whether they have put him to death; if so, he has suffered for the truth of Christ and because he rebuked the unchristian Papacy, which strives with its heavy load of human laws against the redemption of Christ.–But 'ere thou judgest, oh Lord, Thou willest that, as Thy Son, Jesus Christ, was fain to die by the hands of priests, and to rise from the dead and after to ascend up to heaven, so too in like manner it should be with Thy follower Martin Luther. . . . Him wilt thou quicken again. And as thou, oh my Lord, ordainest thereafter that Jerusalem should for that sin be destroyed, so wilt thou also destroy this self-assumed authority of the Roman Chair. Oh Lord, give us then the new beautified Jerusalem, which descendeth out of heaven, whereof the Apocalypse writes, the holy, pure Gospel, which is not obscured by human doctrine. Every man who reads Martin Luther's books may see how clear and transparent is his doctrine, because he sets forth the holy Gospel.[2]

Desiring the destruction of papal Rome, assimilable for him to the earthly, theocidal Jerusalem, and longing to receive the Holy Gospel without mediation, Dürer was of course in perfect harmony with the Reformer, who at the Wartburg was working on translating the New Testament into German, a project that clearly unified the Reformist elites. But by supporting the destruction of Catholicism's seat and affirming the primacy of God's word, was not Dürer taking the side of the iconoclasts? Certain painters of the period did in fact renounce their art, while others applauded the image destroyers, who seemed to be obeying the paradoxical injunction of the iconoclastic images that served as antipapal propaganda and had been created by still other artists. Though he knew he had to take the iconoclast threat seriously, Dürer in no way abandoned his art; quite the contrary, he explicitly criticized the iconoclasts. Are his attacks against those who sought to annihilate painting and sculpture – "gifts of God" as he called them – to be interpreted as a corporatist defense of his craft? Didn't painters, together with bell makers and fishmongers, have to watch out for their livelihoods now? Dürer's praise for the arts is rather to be understood in terms of his vision of the spiritual tie between civil society and the City of God, a tie his own creations make visible.

One of the artist's major works, an altarpiece designed and executed between 1507 and 1511, before the Reformation was in full swing, is a complex, subtle, and innovative interpretation of the very theme we have been discussing here, the Earthly and Heavenly Cities, as inherited from Saint Augustine and repeatedly rethought and manipulated throughout the Middle Ages. Dürer's *Adoration of the Holy Trinity*, commissioned by a rich merchant named Matthäus Landauer and destined for the chapel of a home for old and indigent citizens that Landauer had founded in Nuremberg – the painting, now at the Kunsthistorische Museum in Vienna, exemplifies the sumptuousness of German religious art in that period – illustrates the fecundity of this dualist system for the Western visual imagination (see Figure 8). The dualism may well become complicated, be refined in a great variety of ways, but once again it is always stronger than any trifunctional vision: the relevant distinction, that which is productive of schemes of representation and interpretation, involves the ways in which the two Cities might articulate with each other rather than the three functions of priest, warrior, and peasant (see Chapter 2, note 40). Such trifunctional distributions may be present, sometimes powerfully so, but binary tension, which has taken the various forms of conflict between pope and emperor, between church and state, between the French monarchy and the Roman Church, civil society and religious societies, and civil society and the state, is perennial, and it may be affirmed that what that binary tension is fundamentally about is the specific nature and breadth of the distance between the two Cities. In other words, dualism in its different metamorphoses compels us to interpret the history of humanity, both spiritual and temporal, as that of the ontological and theological differences between the two kingdoms and how those differences have made themselves felt. The particular scheme of the interrelations between the two Cities that Albrecht Dürer produced was highly innovative and quite remarkable.

8.　ALBRECHT DÜRER. *Adoration of the Holy Trinity*, 1511. Kunsthistorisches Museum, Vienna (photo: Roger-Viollet, Paris).

Dürer, Painter of the City of God

In the *Adoration of the Holy Trinity*, Dürer combined a model for understanding the tie between civil society and the City of God, which is the eschatological vision at the heart of the work, with a theory of painting whose key is to be found in a small portrait of himself as painter included in it. In the lower-right-hand corner, we see the artist standing alone and holding up a cartouche by means of which he signs the painting (Figure 8). His place is tiny, but crucial, in a whole powerfully structured around a traditional representation of the Trinity, the throne of Grace.[3]

Sitting on a celestial rainbow that does not touch the ground is God the Father; above his head we see the dove that represents the Holy Ghost encircled by cherubim. God holds Christ on the cross he was sacrificed on; he holds him between his knees and in front of another rainbow, offering his son for adoration as his own mantle of mercy is held wide open by two angels, whose companions, symmetrically grouped, hold up the instruments of the Passion: the column to which Jesus was tied to be flogged, the lance that pierced his side, the vinegar-soaked sponge.

On God's right (the viewer's left) stands a group of female saints, all carrying palm leaves, some identifiable by their attributes or the objects associated with their martyrdom: Agnes with a lamb, Dorothy holding a basket, Catherine and the wheel upon which she was tortured, Barbara holding a chalice with the Eucharist wafer. In front and set off against them but linked to them in that she also carries a palm leaf, is the Virgin Mary, robed in blue, crowned, kneeling.

On God's left and arranged similarly to the women stands a group of men. John the Baptist, barefoot and wearing a green mantle over a brown tunic, kneels on the clouds, hands clasped in prayer, while behind him press figures from the Old Testament: Moses holding the tablets of the law, David playing the harp, prophets and sibyls.

Below the Holy Trinity and the saints and prophets, Dürer has painted the community of the faithful, among which two groups can be clearly distinguished: on the one hand, members of the clergy–priests, monks, nuns, ecclesiastical dignitaries–in whose midst may be seen, kneeling between a purple-robed cardinal and a hooded monk in what looks like Franciscan garb and holding his fur hat in hand, the rich bourgeois Matthäus Landauer, who commissioned the painting, and on the other, laymen of all types and ranks, some of whom are turned toward the object of adoration. Positioned opposite the merchant of Nuremberg is a knight in gilded armor, believed to be a member of the powerful Haller family; he is praying, his sword is sheathed.

Among the faithful assembled together in the love of God and the mediation of Christ we may identify a king wearing a crown and an ermine mantle, two popes, German prince electors, a Venetian doge, and three emperors, one of whom is wearing the chain of the prestigious order of the Golden Fleece, which may be seen around the necks of the Holy Roman Emperor Charles V or other princes in numerous other paintings.

The presence of so many emperors and popes may be explained by the fact that what is given form here is not the contemporary world in its political and social reality but rather an eschatological vision of the City of God. The rainbows—less visible here than in the engraving at the front of this book or those by Dürer treating the same subject—clearly show that the adoration scene takes place after the Last Judgment. Moreover, the Last Judgment is the theme depicted in the work's painted and sculpted frame.[4]

Of vast dimensions (as is generally the case for an altarpiece), the frame shows Christ in his majesty separating the saved from the damned: in a preparatory drawing we may see an image of Christ with, on one side of his mouth, a sword, on the other, an olive branch, just like the one in Figure 1. The frame then serves not primarily as ornament, but rather to deepen the meaning of the painting at its center. The painting is bounded not spatially but spiritually: it offers a vision of what will be after the Last Judgment.

There are numerous points of comparison between the anonymous *Last Judgment* of Figure 1 and Dürer's *Adoration of the Holy Trinity* (Figure 8): the rainbow Jesus is sitting on, the angels carrying the instruments of the Passion, John the Baptist in prayer. But the meaning of the two works is completely different. By placing the Last Judgment in the surrounding frame and the assembly of the City of God at the center, Dürer points out the shared destiny of all the City's members, saints and prophets, priests and laymen, the latter not naked as they would be if they were on their way to Hell or Heaven, but dressed once again in the clothes, jewelry, arms, spurs that are the attire of members of civil society. From a point situated beyond the end of human history, Dürer has constructed one of the forms that the relation between the Earthly and Heavenly Cities might take: the harmonious final reuniting of the various members of the City of God. This anticipation of a substantially different future does not fail to say something about the present; it shows, for example, the spiritual destination of the merchant donor of the work and the richly armored warrior, and reminds us, by showing us individuals of widely varying rank and social status, that making their way on earth among the damned are pilgrims of the City of God, who may be drawn from among both the powerful and the humble.

The inhabitants of civil society that Dürer has painted have completed their earthly pilgrimage and been raised above the earth by the love of God, whose sacred power, which is also the power to make sacred, is clearly indicated by his robe and face. In God the Father the two sovereignties, political and religious, are united, just as he unites the Old and New Testaments: his crown is nearly identical to that of the emperors, who themselves resemble conventionalized portraits of Charlemagne; the face of one of the emperors is identical to God's; the external surface of God's golden mantle resembles that of the popes' while its lining is blue like the Virgin's cape and green like John the Baptist's. In the image given of him here, God the Father gathers all sacred and profane history in a sort of microcosm that reminds the viewer that all is in him.

The members of the community of the once earthly faithful are disposed in such a way to show that they are not cut off from more highly placed members of the divine City: they stand or kneel on the upward-curving band at whose summit Dürer has placed the Holy Trinity. All are thus equidistant from God, and those positioned lower down meet up with the inhabitants of the Heavenly City pictured above–the saints and prophets, Mary and Saint John–neither mixing with them or remaining separate from them, as is illustrated by the superimposition of the women's heads and the Virgin's robe on the left.

The new geometry–etymologically the term means "measurement of the earth"–that Dürer proposes of the Earthly City thus resolves by means of a single form–a circle, a single ribbon of laymen and clergy where all citizens of the community of the faithful are distributed equidistant from God–the contradiction between the separation of the two cities and their proximity: they are distinct but not cleaved from one another. Moreover, the continuity of laymen and clerics, who do not form two isolated groups but rather succeed one another on the ring of adoration, is in harmony with the connection established between the two reigns. There is no confusion possible between the two Cities, but rather a proximity between the saintly citizens of the City of God and those erstwhile of civil society; they are all gathered together after the Last Judgment in the eternal sovereignty of God.

The iconographic and theological specificity of this altarpiece becomes clear when we compare it to other works in the adoration genre (though the artists of these works were not necessarily imagining the scene as taking place after the Last Judgment); examples abound. In the Gothic tapestry of the Apocalypse at Angers, created at least a century before Dürer's time, Christ is adored by three horizontally separated groups: the highest band is composed of angels, below whom are the nobles, sharply distinguished from the clerics, with the common people making up the lowermost band. More complex are *The Fountain of Grace* by van Eyck, described earlier, and especially the *Adoration of the Holy Trinity* that illustrates Pigouchet's Book of Hours, also discussed earlier, in which communication between heaven and earth is established by a Gothic church steeple, which, because it passes through the earthly sky and enters that of heaven, can symbolize the godly institution of *the* Church (Figure 2). Comparison with earlier or contemporary German compositions enables us once again to observe the originality of Dürer's vision: in the *Holy Trinity Above a Landscape Surrounded by Angels* by Lucas Cranach (among many other examples), the utter separation between the Holy Trinity and the world is underlined by the ring of angels that isolates the Holy Trinity from the earth and the city we see below.[5] The same distance may be remarked between Dürer's work and Italian paintings of the period, such as Perugino's *Gonfalone della Giustizia*, where citizens of the Earthly City may adore the Virgin only from below and across a wide space, metaphysical, insuperable. In Titian's *Assumption*[6] the holy vision is reserved for saints and apostles only (whereas Perugino allowed it to ordinary citizens). And Dürer's painting retains its specificity when compared to later works, for example *The Trinity in Glory* by Rubens.[7] Here the duke of Mantua, wearing the chain of the Golden Fleece, and his family contemplate the Trinity from a plane that is not only lower than but also cut off from that holiness; the interval may be crossed only by love and the adorer's gaze.

The contrast between Dürer's work and *The Coronation of the Virgin* by Raphael (Figure 9) is particularly striking: the latter, completed before Dürer's second trip to Venice (1505-7), is marked by a horizontal band that divides two spaces that only the gaze can join—no physical contact is possible. While all these other representations imagine a radical discontinuity between the two domains, heavenly and earthly, in Dürer's *Adoration* there is no river between the two Cities, no horizontal bar separating the two reigns, no angelic band isolating the Holy Trinity or cloud bank breaking up the sky, no empty space that distances the suprasensory world from the human one.

The visual break that introduces a clear duality here is not between the two types of City but rather between those two Cities, closely linked in peace and spiritual communion, and what is below them—the ground on which the solitary painter stands. Civil society's promotion to the realm of God has raised it above the ground; its separation from God has been transcended in a move to which it was ultimately destined. Only the painter remains in the landscape, looking straight ahead with an expression resembling that of Melancholy (see Figure 13). Might not the Trinity catch his eye and pull it upward? Instead it is as if Dürer did not see what he painted, for, as a member of the Earthly City painting the City of God, it is possible for him to imagine and represent it, but not to contemplate it or participate in it. Though he may paint the man who commissioned the painting into it, the artist with his name has no place there. Earthly, the painter makes the invisible accessible to our sense while at the same time indicating that the real presence is neither here, on earth, or now: the hour of Judgment has not yet sounded. But in painting the Earthly City not as it is but in accordance with its destiny, its eschatology, its ontological eminence, to come yet already here by an anticipation accessible to our sense, he makes us mindful of its future and eternal dignity, and he demonstrates, by depicting it, that it is even from this moment representable and worthy of adoration. In this sense, the painting transcends the painter: Dürer cannot situate himself among the chosen, but he can paint them. The paradox by which the painter can make visible what cannot be seen—and here that impossibility is deepened in that the painting shows what is the most ontologically and chronologically

9.   RAPHAEL. *The Coronation of the Virgin*, 1502–3. Pinacoteca Vaticana, Rome (photo: Roger-Viollet, Paris).

distant, what is beyond the world and time, transcendence in its essence—underlines the dignity of painting as a means of acceding to a
superior order, while the sad blindness of the painter demonstrates
how that order remains beyond the grasp of this world.[8]

But if painting can also fulfill the role of intercession and figure
what is highest, making visible what the painter's eye cannot look at,
does not this very power justify it against the iconoclasts' attacks?
Without being themselves what they represent, icons still receive value
from that of which they are the image: to smash them would be to
destroy the image of God inscribed in the order and end of his creation.
Such work thus legitimates itself by legitimating the spiritual relevance of human image-making. It is painting that indirectly, above and
beyond its own mere existence, can refute the iconoclasts' arguments
by means of a metaphysics of the image: Dürer, unlike certain painters
of his time,[9] was no iconoclast. In the dedication of his *Unterweisung
der Messung* (*Painter's Manual, A Manual of Measurement of Lines,
Areas, and Solids by Means of Compass and Ruler*),[10] Dürer explicitly
condemned Karlstadt's iconoclasts in what may be taken as a response
to the treatise that leader had written in favor of iconoclastic action.
Dürer wrote this text in German, like Luther, thereby secularizing
knowledge. He began it by underlining the necessity for the painter of
anchoring his art in the art of measurement:

> It is this skill [measurement] which is the foundation of all painting. For
> this reason, I have decided to provide to all those who are eager to become
> artists a starting point and a source for learning about measurement with
> ruler and compass. From this they will recognize truth as it meets their
> eyes, not only in the realm of art but also in their proper and general
> understanding, not withstanding the fact that at the present time the art of
> painting is viewed with disdain in certain quarters, and is said to serve
> idolatry. A Christian will no more be led to superstition by a painting or a
> portrait than a devout man to commit murder because he carries a weapon
> by his side. It must be an ignorant man who would worship a painting, a
> piece of wood, or a block of stone. Therefore, a well-made, artistic, and
> straightforward painting gives pleasure rather than vexation.[11]

To the extent that there is a risk of idolatry or crime, it comes not
from the existence of images or swords, but from the way they may be
misused. This affirmation is all the more remarkable in that, at the
moment the *Manual of Measurement* was published, in 1525 just after

the battle of Frankenhausen, thousands of insurgent peasants had already died by the sword. Soon after demanding that the looting bands of peasants be crushed, Luther wrote in a letter:

> We pity these poor people who have been so cruelly treated. But what could be done? It is necessary–and God wants it so–that they be filled with fear and awe. Otherwise Satan would do much worse things. For such is the judgment of God: "Qui accipit gladium, gladio peribit."[12]

In another letter, written late in the summer of 1525, he observed:

> The affair of the peasants has quieted down everywhere after almost a hundred thousand have been killed, so many orphans made, and the rest, so robbed of their livelihood that the appearance of Germany was never more miserable than now. The victors rage in such a way they complete the wickedness [of the peasants].[13]

In the same letter he announced his marriage to the former nun Katharina von Bora, a marriage that would be, he said, a testimony to the Gospel–not in words, but in deed.

The Monument to the Peasants' Defeat

In the third book of the *Painter's Manual, A Manual of Measurement*, Dürer explains that it is his intention to satisfy the wish of those seeking to erect a column in the place where they have vanquished enemies, a column that shows who those enemies were by being constructed out of weapons taken from them. We then are shown three engravings, accompanied by a descriptive text, which represent respectively a monument to military victory, a monument to victory over rebel peasants, and a funerary monument dedicated to an anonymous drunkard. The text includes a series of instructions on the art of erecting monuments, explaining precisely what their proportions must be (these measurements are given in the engravings themselves) and what objects they should be built of, these too identified with great precision. The second monument has proved particularly mysterious.

"The person who wishes to erect a victory monument [*victoria* in the German original] because he has vanquished rebel peasants might take inspiration from the following monument,"[14] Dürer writes, and at the bottom of the page we find an engraving of the base of the monument, while the model for the column itself takes up the whole of the following page. (Figure 7 is a montage reuniting column and base.)

On the stone pedestal surrounded with sculpted domestic farm animals – cows, sheep, pigs – shown tied up, we see woven baskets full of cheese, butter, eggs, onions, and herbs. The column itself is a stack of agrarian objects: from the bottom up we may discern a rough-hewn grain chest, a large overturned cooking vessel with its handle hanging downward, a cheese bowl covered with a plate, upon which rests a wooden butter churn, and on top of this a milk jug resembling an amphora. Resting on the milk jug is what looks like a sheaf of wheat concealing a tall earthenware pot from which emerge the teeth of several rakes for collecting cow dung, while a variety of other farm implements have been bound to the outside of the sheaf: a hoe, a pick, a pitchfork for moving manure and a flail for threshing grain. Set on top of the rake teeth is a cage containing a rooster and a hen; the birds might have been taken in such a cage, along with other animals and things to eat, to a market such as Dürer had drawn elsewhere: scenes in which a peasant man and woman sell the two or three products of their labor.

At the summit of the monument we see, sitting on a lard tub, back hunched over and head down, an "afflicted peasant" (*trauretten Bauren*), with an immense sword (*Schwerd*) plunged into his back, a sword disproportionate to his body, as long as a butterchurn is tall.

Are we meant to understand this precarious, brutal edifice as a declaration of Dürer's satisfaction at the announcement that the yokels' movement has been crushed,[15] his joy at the sword's violent supremacy over the wheat flail as it has just been confirmed? An illustration of the unappealing wretchedness of shit-shovelers living in such close contact with animality that they can't pull themselves out of it, even once dead? Must we, as Stephen Greenblatt has argued, beware of any retrospective illusion and avoid seeing in this bloody georgic any sign of sympathy on Dürer's part for the oppressed, acknowledging that we are only projecting our own sympathy onto the artist? The monument could even be interpreted as "a wish-fullfilment fantasy": in a period of generalized and personal anxiety – at Whitsuntide 1525, Dürer had a nightmare in which he saw columns of water falling from the sky and flooding everything; deeply shaken, he later made an image of it in a watercolor depicting a landscape and town under black clouds – he might have found some satisfaction in representing peasants defeated by the sword.[16]

But numerous objections can be made to the affirmation that what we have here is the image of a wish or a satire on the peasants.[17] We might first consider the effects of placing the monument project between another project in honor of victory over the strong and powerful (Figure 10)–a solid column of bronze made of mortars and a cannon barrel, decorated with breastplates and crowned with helmet plumes– and a third project for a monument to a dead drunkard (Figure 11). The three monuments, explicitly linked in that all of them are in the shape of a standing column and bear the same date, 1525, are also indirectly linked by similarities observable between them: in the military monument, to the right of the column, we see the same keg as in the one for the drunkard's tomb (we of course presume that the first is used for powder and the second for wine, but is the first assumption necessarily true?), while the cheese bowl in the peasant monument is also to be found in the drunkard's. Thus both the monument to more conventional military victory and the monument to military victory over peasants have an object in common with the obviously grotesque monument to a drunkard. We might then venture to affirm that Dürer is saying that there is something grotesque about building a monument to a military victory over peasants, and that what is mocked is not the vanquished but rather the victors who would build such a thing. Considering the problem from a slightly different angle, we could say that given the date they all bear, 1525, the first and third could only be meant to clarify the second: only the second represents the full, precise meaning of that date, referring as it does to a concrete, unusual, painful event of the immediate past: the Peasants' War. If the first is what seems like a straightforward monument to military victory while the third is clearly grotesque, we could say that what we see in the second is a particular combination of these, that is, a grotesque victory. This is all the more plausible in that, as Dürer has drawn and described it, the monument to victory over peasants could only come tumbling down: how could a stack of uneasily balanced objects–a load-bearing chicken coop on top of the splayed teeth of farm implements, for example– support the ultimate weight of death?

It seems to me that we are justified then in rejecting any reading of the engraving as illustrating Dürer's approval of Luther's violently hostile attitude toward the peasants. Let us rather try to understand it with the help of other works by the painter, works that preceded it and which seem to clarify its meaning.

In fact, Dürer had already painted the peasant we see at the summit

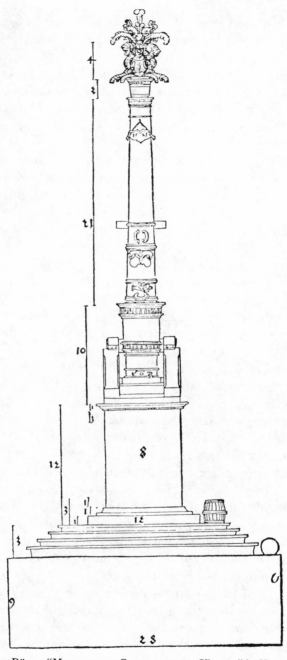

10.   ALBRECHT DÜRER. "Monument to Commemorate a Victory," in *Unterweisung der Messung*, 1525.

11.   ALBRECHT DÜRER. "Monument to a Drunkard," in *Unterweisung der Messung*, 1525.

of his project for a monument. Downcast in death at the top of that imagined column, in the altarpiece of the *Adoration of the Holy Trinity* he is shown enjoying the eternal life of the inhabitants of the City of God after their pilgrimage on earth. Placed next to the richly and powerfully armored knight, he carries his wheat flail as an insignia and has respectfully removed his cap in the same love of the three-person God that has moved the important man, spurred and armed with a sword, to kneel. Rustic and soldier are placed at the same height among the citizens of the old earthly kingdom who have attained the Heavenly City (see Figure 12).

Ironically enthroned on his overturned lard pot at the top of the monument of 1525, the bearded peasant is bent over in the death inflicted on him by the warrior's terrible sword. But what glory could the knight in his gilded armor expect to receive from such a victory? The arms of the vanquished are merely implements for working the earth—hoe, wheat flail, manure forks—made useless now by the peasant's death. Humble takings, which can only be seen as ironically offered to the military hero; laughable takings that degrade the victor.

On the cartouche of the monument project we read "Anno Domini 1525"–a way of placing it under the Lord's aegis and a reminder that time is to be computed in God's terms, for he is the only true sovereign of this world. The engraving shows a vanity, not a triumph, not the glory of the soldier but the spiritual and temporal disaster into which civil society is plunged once the sword has been unsheathed. Dürer does not show us a man who, having lived by the sword, has now perished by it but rather the desolation of a man who met that death while brandishing only a flail.

Perhaps more significant, the posture that Dürer has given the victim—head supported by the right hand, arm bent, and elbow pressed against the thigh—reproduces that of Melancholy, in an engraving done in 1514 (Figure 13). The man who worked the earth is shown with his nose pointing down toward his torn pants and worn-out shoe, while Melancholy, a crown of watercress and renunculas around her head to fight off the aridity that threatens saturnine natures, looks straight ahead; her gaze both intense and empty. She has a compass in her hand, for she measures the earth the peasant works. Clearly Dürer, following an old tradition both popular and learned that distinguished four temperaments–sanguine, irascible, phlegmatic, and melancholic–

12. ALBRECHT DÜRER. *The Adoration of the Holy Trinity*, 1511, detail (photo: Roger-Viollet, Paris).

13.　ALBRECHT DÜRER. *Melencolia I*, 1514, detail. Musée du Petit Palais, Paris (photo: Giraudon, Paris).

each associated with an element—air, fire, water, earth—placed both Melancholy and the peasant under the somber influence of the planet Saturn. Saturn, the earth god who devoured his children and brings on black and bilious moods, dooming those born under his sign to morosity and labor. Melancholy has wings in her back, not a sword, but it seems unlikely that she will ever fly, remaining instead eternally gloomy, like all children of Saturn, despite the fact that she has knowledge and knows how to use instruments of measurement, the very ones for which Dürer would give the rules in the *Painter's Manual*. If *Melencolia I* can be seen as an intellectual and spiritual self-portrait of the artist,[18] who, in the *Adoration of the Holy Trinity* is abandoned on the deserted ground of this world—as we may conclude from his horizontal and empty gaze—then the engraving of a vanquished peasant chosen to illustrate a treatise on how to use geometry to represent the world could hardly signify disgust at or rejection of the one who has been cast down. Dürer may not have supported the peasant's cause, but his work expresses a compassionate identification with his fate.[19]

No interpretation of Melancholy makes of her a laughable creature in a contemptible position, and we have no indication in Dürer's work in general, even though he did fantastical work, that he ever ironized or satirized figures in his own work. If we take Melancholy as a self-portrait of the artist plunged not into depressive inactivity, but rather a kind of visionary trance,[20] is it not an honor for a humble wheat thresher to be shown in an analogous attitude? And this remains so even though the figure in *Melencolia I* can only represent an inferior moment of meditation, the first level, as it were, whereas in *Saint Jerome in His Study* Dürer gave an image of a superior level of thought, in which man is shown seeing divine truth.

Another of Dürer's works, the frontispiece of *The Little Passion* (see Figure 14),[21] should persuade us that the artist was moved by something other than hatred and contempt or fear when he designed the monument to victory over the peasants. Here Christ is shown in the same attitude as Melancholy, wearing the crown of thorns at a moment of his martyrdom, which, though it does not correspond precisely to any of the gospel accounts, may nonetheless stand as a general emblem of the Passion.[22] The very analogy between Christ about to die and the slaughtered peasant, both victims of the strong, forbids us to see in the 1525 monument project a mockery of the meek.

14.   ALBRECHT DÜRER. "The Man of Sorrows Seated," woodcut; frontispiece to *The Little Passion*, 1511 (photo: Giraudon, Paris).

A painter of earthly society as oriented by its divine end, Dürer did not inscribe the victory over the peasants into the same configuration as Luther did. After 1521 he no longer referred directly to the Reformer who with violent imprecations would call for the defeat of the peasants. Following that defeat, Luther proclaimed that the kingdom of this world was merely the minister of God's wrath against sinners, and that, as a preliminary sign of hell and eternal death, its tool was "not a wreath of roses or a flower of love, but a naked sword."[23] Whereas the fanaticism of the peasants and Anabaptists desirous of instituting the City of God on earth led Luther to support as legitimate, by force of theopolitical conviction and defensive reaction, the established order of civil society regardless of the cost in blood and to demand that the temporal authority fulfill its function without mercy, it is hard to believe that Dürer could applaud the repression of one of the elements of the Earthly City, whose eschatological dignity and ultimate elevation to the City of God in which men with swords and men with flails would live side by side, founded the right of pictorial representation.

The very reasons for which he condemned the iconoclasts would, it seems, forbid him to hate the "fanatics" and even more strongly forbid him to cheer on those who had vanquished them. The Earthly City was where saved pilgrims made their way toward the City of God, and it was possible that some of the impoverished rebels massacred by the lords of this world figured among those pilgrims.

The Four Apostles

In 1526, a year after the *Manual of Measurement* was published, Dürer made a gift to his native city, Nuremberg, of two painted panels, on one of which he had represented Saint John and Saint Peter, on the other Saint Paul and Saint Mark. The work is known as *The Four Apostles* (Figure 15) and though its subject is religious, Dürer gave it not to a church but to the city council.

Saint John, on the far left, holds open a book in which we may distinguish, though they are partly covered by his fingers, the first words of Luther's German translation of the Scriptures, words that are the clarion call of Lutheranism: "Im Anfang war das Wort . . . "(In the beginning was the Word . . .). Though largely hidden by the saint's hand, the verses that follow in the biblical text are clearly identifiable.

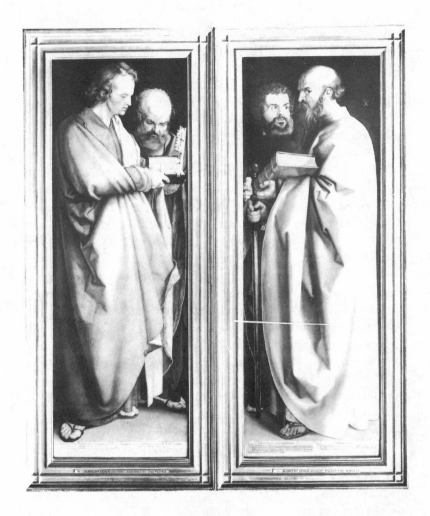

15.   ALBRECHT DÜRER. *The Four Apostles*, 1526 (Alte Pinakothek, Munich).

Standing behind John, carrying a golden key, is Saint Peter, whose head is bent to read in the Holy Book that John is holding: the attitude of the Church's founder clearly indicates that the Church is founded upon the Word of God.

On the right-hand panel Saint Paul is shown holding a sword and a Bible, while behind him Saint Mark has a scroll on which is written MARCI CAP I ("Mark, Chapter 1").

The four saints either read or carry the Gospel; they either point to or carry the Holy Book. Clearly the organizing principle of this painting is the word of God, and the painting receives its religious legitimacy from the fact that it uses figuration in the service of that word. We might speak of a paradox that functions in the opposite way from that of Cranach's or Holbein's engravings of the hoped-for destruction of Rome: those works were an invitation to apocalyptic destruction and a sort of incitation to iconoclastic action; Dürer's shows the value of painting as handmaiden to and vehicle of God's Word.

Each of the four saints assembled here in their shared love of the Word has a face evoking one of the four temperaments—Saint Peter is phlegmatic, Saint John sanguine, Saint Mark irascible, and Saint Paul melancholic. The four taken together thus come to represent all humanity. The left panel is painted in warm tones, red and gold, while the one on the right displays colder colors, blues, and the sword's steel gray. Below the painted saints we find texts, calligraphed by one of Dürer's apprentices, Johannes Neudörffer, but chosen and edited by the painter himself, a montage of quotations from Luther's *September-bibel*, which Dürer read in the edition that Cranach had illustrated with radicalized adaptations of Dürer's own engravings of the Apocalypse.

The four saints themselves are thus supported, as it were, by the word of God that is inscribed at the base of the painting like a predella composed of letters instead of images. The left panel figures an exhortation based on Revelation 22:18-19: "All worldly rulers [*weltliche Regentem*] in these dangerous times should give good heed that they receive not human misguidance for the Word of God, for God will have nothing added to His Word, nor taken away from it. Hear therefore, these four excellent men, Peter, John, Paul, and Mark, their warning."[24] This text takes up and is a reworking of the following passage in 2 Peter 2:1-3: "There were false prophets also among the people, even as there shall be false teachers among you, who privily shall bring in damnable heresies, even denying the Lord that bought them, and bring upon themselves swift destruction. And many shall follow their pernicious ways: by reason of whom the way of truth shall be evil spoken of."

The inscription placed under the Apostle Peter, who may be seen in one of Dürer's engravings readying his sword to cut off Malchus's ear, also denounces the "false prophets," following this time 1 John 4:1-3, while the other texts declare that men who are enemies of good have appeared in recent days (2 Tm 3:1-7) and lash out against the Pharisees: "Beware of the scribes which love to go in long clothing, and love salutations in the marketplaces, and the chief seats in the synagogues, and the uppermost rooms at feasts; Which devour widows' houses, and for a pretence make long prayers: these shall receive greater damnation" (Mark 12:38-40).

The collage of biblical texts assembled by Dürer thus warns both against false prophets, visionaries, and fanatics and against professional priests, prebendary bureaucrats of the sacred–the Catholic Church. While some of those who had encouraged Nuremberg to "give the pope notice" had returned to Catholicism,[25] Dürer's text appears as both a reminder of the spiritual dangers constitutive of the Roman Church with its priests cut off from God's Word and a warning against the radical extremists who sought to abolish all institutions.

But how to be free of the institutional framework of the Catholic Church without losing the guarantee of order that the Church provided and thereby allowing false prophets to flourish? By presenting his painting to the magistrates of the city, the political authority, Dürer seems to have indicated the solution. Placed in the Nuremberg city hall, the painting and its words come to identify and symbolize the role of the civic authorities, the "worldly rulers." Liberated from the Catholic Church, cities and principalities must ensure not only political but religious order. It was thus the business and duty of the political powers to combat the false prophets, as they had done since 1525, the year that Nuremberg rallied to the Reformation and all social agitators–"false prophets," insurgent peasants, and iconoclasts–were put down.

Hung in a public building, *The Four Apostles* could convey a warning to and against those who would disturb order in the name of their religious vision, and it expressed the new distribution of religious and political power that the Reformation had achieved. While political authority was to be supported by religion, the two were now separate, and the political authority must from now on provide certain guarantees to believers. The state was no longer to be contested in the name of God, and no church might claim to have or be an authority superior to the state. (The Roman Catholic Church for its part would continue to affirm that the state was only an instrument for its own spiritual mission and end, while presenting itself as the earthly image of the City of God.) But the effect of this change was almost to sanctify the magistrates: secular power, civil society, was dramatically reinforced by the Reformed Church's retraction into its own specific sphere. There being no other earthly authority to compete with or contest it, much less to dominate it, political power emerged as a kind of absolute power, believed to emanate from the will of God, who desired that there be political authorities and that they have a specific mission, to be accomplished according to a logic specific to themselves while they would at the same time guarantee a kind of monopoly for the true religion.

But the meaning of the painting is deeper than its strong and visible political implications and has to do with the place given in it to letters and books. It is as though it were itself an illustration of the text Peter reads in the book John holds: "In the beginning was the Word."[26] By representing love of the Word, Dürer in *The Four Apostles* shows that which is superior to representation; by making the intellectual and visual principle of his painting the Word gathered into a book, and by bending all his human characters to the inaugural word of God, the artist transcends—not in spite of representing it but indeed because he represents it—the opposition between image and God's Word, between pictorial representation and language. Just as he had overcome—in painting and by painting—the separation between the Earthly City and the City of God in the altarpiece of the *Adoration*.

5   The Mouth of God

In April 1640 Uriel da Costa took his life shortly after submitting to the sentence passed on him by the Jewish community of Amsterdam: 39 lashes. Born into a Marrano family and raised a Christian, da Costa had reconverted to Judaism, then returned for a time to Christianity: the flagellation was the price of readmission to the Jewish community.[1] It is probable that Baruch Spinoza, then 14 years old, was present at the ritual whipping.

In 1656 Spinoza himself became a victim of religious fanaticism. Under suspicion by the Synagogue because he was known to follow the lectures of a certain Van Den Enden, a former Jesuit and freethinker, the philosopher came close to being killed when a zealous Jew attacked him with a knife, ripping it through his coat. Accused of "abominable heresies" and "enormities," Spinoza was expelled from the Synagogue with these terrible words:

> With the judgment of the angels and of the saints we excommunicate, cut off, curse, and anathematize Baruch de Espinoza, with the consent of the elders and of all this holy congregation, in the presence of the holy books, by the 613 precepts which are written therein, with the anathema wherewith Joshua cursed Jericho, with the curse which Elisha laid upon the children, and with all the curses which are written in the law. Cursed be he by day and cursed be he by night, cursed be he in sleeping and cursed be he in waking, cursed in going out and cursed in coming in. The Lord shall not

pardon him. The wrath and fury of the Lord shall henceforth be kindled against this man, and shall lay upon him all the curses which are written in the book of the law. The Lord shall destroy his name under the sun and cut him off for his undoing from all the tribes of Israel, with all the curses of the firmament which are written in the book of the law. . . . And we warn you that none may speak with him by word of mouth nor by writing, nor show any favor to him, nor be under one roof with him, nor come within four cubits of him, nor read any paper composed or written by him.[2]

The violence of these words reminds us that the religious plurality, the multiplicity of churches and sects that characterized the Netherlands in the seventeenth century, was not a sign that tolerance had become a fundamental value, but rather corresponded most immediately to a multiplication of intolerances and fanaticisms within the different religious groups. Spinoza sought to determine what kind of political arrangement might protect people against the type of attack he had undergone.

In a letter to the philosopher, who was constantly being denounced and threatened, Albert Burgh, one of his former disciples and a convert to Catholicism, accused him of being deceived by the Evil One. Burgh strung together a series of arguments meant to show the wretchedness and anxiety of atheists and invited the philosopher to repent.[3] In his response to the freshly zealous Catholic militant, Spinoza allowed him one point: the advantage of the political order instituted by the Roman Church, adding "I should think there was none [no Church] more suited [than the Catholic Church] to deceive the people and to constrain the minds of men, were there not the order of the Mohammedan Church, which far surpasses it. For from the time that this superstition began there have arisen no schisms in their Church."[4] We are not concerned here with the obvious inaccuracy of Spinoza's assertion about Islam (we mentioned the schisms within Islam in our discussion of the sect of the Assassins). More significant for our purposes is the fact that Spinoza's "hierarchy" of churches—the uppermost being the least desirable—is determined by their relative capacities of integration, of resistance against internal division: obviously the homogeneity of the mass of the faithful that resulted from "deceiving the people and constraining the minds of men" did not represent any absolute value for Spinoza; in his understanding, the phenomenon of sects at least reflected the nature of human passions. The grave problem with sectarians, however, was that they refused others freedom and, judging their followers to be God's chosen people, considered "enemies" of God anyone whose opinions differed from their own.[5] Himself a victim of excommunication and in all probability witness to Uriel da Costa's grim punishment, Spinoza tried to find a solution that would affirm the superiority of "true knowledge" without condemning what he took as inferior forms of thinking, including the passions, which were grounded in human nature itself. It was necessary to deduce from human nature the doctrine most likely to conform to human practice. This global approach is perhaps most clearly expressed at the beginning of the *Political Treatise*, published posthumously in 1677, where he explains: "On applying my mind to politics that I might investigate the subject matter of this science with the same freedom of spirit [impartiality] as we generally use in mathematics, I have labored carefully not to mock, lament or execrate but to understand human actions."[6] We might say that in his analysis of social phenomena we encounter Spinoza as reader of both Machiavelli and Descartes.

It was possible, he asserted, to identify the universal content of faith; it consisted of seven dogmas themselves ensuing from a single fundamental affirmation: "There is a Supreme Being who loves justice and charity, whom all must obey in order to be saved, and must worship by practicing justice and charity to their neighbor."[7] But given that attempts at authoritarian control of the passions, attempts which would necessarily seek to homogenize systems of belief and forbid the existence of groups of believers particularized by their own dogmas and ceremonies, were just as irrational as that which they meant to control or combat, it was necessary to imagine a regime in which the existence of sects would not preclude a communal life regulated by reason in which wisdom has an acknowledged place. By underlining that the Roman Catholic Church did not have a monopoly on the holy life any more than did any other church, but rather that such a life was available to all, Spinoza refused to denounce either sects in general or the sects of his time, some of which he enumerated in his response to Burgh: "the Lutherans, the Reformers, the Mennonites, and the Enthusiasts." We might greatly lengthen the list of religious groups visible in the Netherlands at the time, composing a picturesque tableau of Quakers, Borrelists, Muscovites, Orthodox, Anabaptists, and other varieties of Lutheran, by following an inventory given by a former Calvinist named Jean-Baptiste Stouppe, a soldier in the French army who served under Condé in the Siege of Utrecht in 1670.[8] Spinoza would not, of course, have accepted Stouppe's including *him* in the category of sectarian, for his theological-political project was to find in the political order, and based on a universal credo, a means of giving an institutional, hence stabilizing, status to the diversity of beliefs and believers. The Spinozan solution may well appear a paradigm for modern practices of instituting tolerance (though the author of the *Ethics* did not himself use the word), based as it was on a will to treat rationally even that which is irrational. In a free commonwealth, "freedom of judgment" must be guaranteed: individuals could not be deprived of the freedom to express their thinking, and such freedom of thought, far from being a threat to the political power, was in fact necessary to "public peace, to piety, and to the right of the sovereign."[9] However, though the political authority in place did not have the right to legislate in the domain of speculative thought, that authority must not be physically contested, lest civil society be destroyed.[10]

The problem was to define a type of social functioning that would take into account the existence of superstition while preventing it from escalating into fanaticism.[11] Though neither the Latin word *fanaticus* nor its derivatives are to be found in Spinoza's text, "fanaticism" renders fairly exactly what in the Latin text would be translated word for word as "superstitious fervor," or "the anger of the Pharisees."[12] Fanaticism is burning, active superstition, superstition coupled with anger, "a desire by which we are spurred, from Hate, to do evil to him we hate."[13] In his *Political Treatise*, Spinoza pointed to that person who, "because he is attached to this or that religion judges the laws of a dominion [*imperium*] worse than any possible evil."[14] How could we not think of the Anabaptists, and the danger represented by the sects that, more or less covertly, desired that there be one and only one law in the City—the one dictated by their beliefs? The Mennonites of Spinoza's time, descendants of the Anabaptists, were undoubtedly quite peaceable; the "Enthusiasts" he spoke of in his letter to Burgh provoked no social unrest, but they were still the descendants of the fanatics denounced by Luther, Melanchthon, and Calvin, and sectarian logic—as the dramatic events connected with the Synagogue made only too clear—always posed a threat. Holland in the second half of the seventeenth century was certainly not Germany in 1525—one was more likely to meet "Christians without a Church" than "fanatics of the Apocalypse."[15] But the first of these could become the second. From a perspective similar to that of Lucretius and not unrelated to Calvin's, Spinoza underlined the pathological dimension of superstition and the mixture of anxiety and avidity that gave it its strength: superstition was a feeling (*affectus*), a phantasm (*phantasmata*), based on fear and anger: "Superstition, like all other instances of hallucination and frenzy, is bound to assume very varied and unstable forms, and . . . finally it is sustained only by hope, hatred, anger, and deceit."[16] Volatile in nature, superstition provoked troubles of all sorts and ghastly wars, faith often manifesting itself in fury instead of the practice of virtue.

All religious prejudices sprang, according to Spinoza, from a single one: the anthropomorphizing belief that nature was governed by final causes. Because human actions were shaped in accordance with goals that human beings set themselves, they believed that this logic was equally applicable to God—no one doubted that if triangles could think they would imagine God as triangular. This illusion became superstition when human beings not only took it into their heads that there were several masters (*rectores*) of nature but that these masters, the gods, had disposed the world in such a way as to force their creatures to worship them. Superstition was an illusion about final ends, the illusion that God tended toward a goal, that he therefore was lacking something and wanted people to love him in order to make up for his deficiency—all of this being of course a contradiction of the idea of a perfect being. The illusion of a God at once jealous, cruel, and weak was accompanied by rituals through which humanity sought to make itself loved. Superstition was in its very principle quarrelsome, every sectarian being in competition with others—a competition that had its source in "blind desire" and "insatiable avidity"—to win the good graces of a God who, for his part, was not paying attention. In this sense, superstition was pathological, a kind of madness springing from the illusion, constitutive of human beings, that the images they have of the world correspond to the way the world actually is.

This "construction" could be dismantled by means of the new rule of truth that had come to light with mathematics. Mathematics did not concern itself with ends, but with essences and the properties of figures. It was absurd and vain to wonder, for example, *why* someone had been knocked down and killed by a shingle torn off the roof by the wind. Absurd to suggest that it was to punish him for not having observed some ritual, or so that others might take warning that life was a fragile thing and repent of their sins. All such questions, through which people tried to sound out the will of God—that "asylum for ignorance"—were in their essence illusory and wrongheaded. What we *could* know was that the wind was blowing the day of the accident, and the direction it was blowing from—that is, the series of antecedent causes; the rest was not mysterious or hidden from the eyes of men, but rather had no reality: as Wittgenstein would warn, it could not be uttered, so it should be kept silent. Of God who was infinite we could not know all, but we *could* know that he could not be irrational and capricious. Superstitious madness, on the other hand, was a destructive passion.

A passion. Unlike the shingle falling off the roof, like human error, the illusion about final ends was neither an accident nor a contingent phenomenon (error being precisely the fact of believing in God's contingency) but rather necessary; it followed from human nature: even though I know that the sun is at an enormous distance from the earth, I cannot help seeing it as if it were only two hundred paces away. Human beings went on to make the gods rave just like them, giving them the faces of kings. In truth, God was neither a master nor a prince, because his will was not distinct from his understanding.[17] If God's decrees were perceived adequately, as they were meant to be perceived, that is, not as laws but as eternal truths, they would be understood to concern *jus* (right), and not *lex* (law), for God was *potentia*, potential, capacity, and not *potestas*, power. God did not command, ordain, or require. He was not a "power," external to his creature and commanding him; rather all things that were, were in God (who might also be called Nature). They were in him through a free necessity of his nature; and their "conatus," their being, and their perfection were in him. God was free necessity, for he was subject to no external constraint: what he was, and all the things that were in him, followed from his essence.

Spinoza's rejection of superstition is accompanied by a theory on reading Scripture whose main idea is that, to avoid raving dangerously, human beings should not look for "profound mysteries" in Scripture, wearing themselves out in sounding them only to attribute their inventions to the Holy Spirit:

I hold that the method of interpreting Scripture is no different from the method of interpreting Nature, and is in fact in complete accord with it. For the method of interpreting Nature consists essentially of composing a detailed study of Nature from which, as being the source of our assured data, we can deduce the definitions of the things of Nature. Now in exactly the same way the task of Scriptural interpretation requires us to make a straightforward study of Scripture, and from this, as the source of our fixed data and principles, to deduce by logical inference the meaning of the authors of Scripture.[18]

Three rules governed the "historical" reading of Scripture. It was necessary to analyze the nature and properties of the language in which the books of Scripture had been written; this meant knowing Hebrew (Spinoza himself wrote a Hebrew grammar), which was needed for reading the texts not only of the Old Testament but also the New, full of Hebrew expressions: in his philologic procedure, Spinoza was looking for the text's meaning first and foremost *in* the text. Second rule: assemble from each book all statements about a given object and note the contradictions or ambiguities that emerged in relation to the different contexts; this would enable the reader to determine, for example, if a term was being used metaphorically or not. From this procedure one would conclude, for instance, that when Moses said that God was a fire or that God was "jealous," he believed or wanted to teach that God had human passions–an idea that was of course contrary to the teachings of reason and was to be understood in terms of the fact that he was speaking as a political leader of a people with a specific culture. It was necessary, therefore, to discover and take into account the conditions in which these statements had been written–who were the authors of the texts? for what purpose had they been written?–and their history: How had they been transmitted? Had they been altered? In this way we could understand why Christ's teaching of nonresistance to injustice and impiety so differed from Moses', who called for taking an eye for an eye. Christ was speaking at a time when the City, ruled by a corrupt state, was threatened with ruin, and the oppressed could have no thought for improving their lives on earth but could only be preoccupied with attaining the kingdom of God, whereas Moses was concerned to organize a healthy and stable political society on earth, namely the Israelite state.

These three rules may be telescoped into one general rule, which the philosopher expressed thus: "All knowledge of Scripture must be sought from Scripture alone."[19] An anti-paranoid method, we might say. To the paranoid everything is a sign, in a world that is perfectly transparent and where everything talks to him, imperiously commanding him, even calling him to a mission. Those who were superstitious read into nature instead of reading nature, and subjected themselves to the power of a transcendent master-signifier, an anthropomorphic projection, with the difference that in it their own finitude had become God's infinitude. Spinoza's method of history-based interpretation, where deductions would be based on the observation of data and definitions constructed from "facts," rejected any break between Nature and Scripture, and this continuity was analogous to that which existed between the state of nature and the social state. Spinoza explained what differentiated his thinking from Hobbes's in the following words: "With regard to Politics, the difference between Hobbes and me . . . consists in this that I ever preserve the natural right intact so that the Supreme Power [Magistrate] in a State [*Urbs*] has no more right over a subject than is proportionate to the power by which it is superior to the subject. This is what always takes place in the state of Nature."[20]

For Spinoza there was no gap between the state of nature and civil society or break between the natural order and Scripture, either in terms of their content or how to interpret them: one always came back to the eternal substance.

Inspiration, Prosopopoeia, Critique

We are not directly concerned here with the place of Spinoza's recommendations for how to read Scripture in the history of biblical exegesis, but shall try instead to grasp its impact by establishing a partial typology of contemporary treatments of scriptural quotation. More particularly, our point is to demonstrate the specificity of Spinoza's method by considering two of his French contemporaries, one renowned, the other obscure; one showered with honor, the other with opprobrium: Jacques Bénigne Bossuet, archbishop of Meaux and sermonist at the court of Louis XIV, and Isabeau Vincent, a fifteen-year-old Calvinist shepherdess living in the Cévennes.

The young peasant woman could not have been more different from the prelate. She is known to few beyond those interested in the history of Protestantism in southern France and in the prophecy movement that manifested itself there at the end of the seventeenth century, then was transplanted to England in the eighteenth by the exiled Camisards. In fact, Isabeau Vincent may be considered the first case in an epidemic of prophesying by which the Camisards incurred the accusation of fanaticism. She exemplifies, if mildly, the entire movement.

On February 3, 1688—that is, less than three years after the Revocation of the Edict of Nantes by which Louis XIV annulled the right of Protestants to the religious freedom accorded them by Henri IV in 1598—at Crest in the Dauphiné, the fifteen-year-old shepherdess, Calvinist but illiterate, was heard "speaking in her bed the magnificent things of God." She continued to prophesy for several months, and people pressed around her. Witnesses transcribed her words, which were speedily disseminated throughout Protestant Europe, namely by a certain Pastor Jurieu, who had calculated with the aid of Revelation that the Beast, the Roman Church, would be vanquished in 1689. From his exile in the United Provinces Jurieu sent out his tract, in which Louis XIV figured as Nebuchadnezzar. Isabeau was quickly arrested—taken while watching her sheep—and imprisoned at Crest, where, continuing to prophesy, she was declared insane and finally taken to a convent in Grenoble. But the movement had been launched, and new prophets were already making themselves heard on the other side of the Rhône, in the Vivarais region. Here the phenomenon prospered, propelled by its own increasing momentum, and culminated, in June 1689, in the massacre of a group of Protestants gathered in the mountainous country near Serre-de-la-Salle by soldiers of the "Most Christian King." Despite this repression, the "prophets" continued to multiply.

In all her exhortations, Isabeau Vincent was said to express herself in excellent French, except on the frequent occasions when she "lashed out against the abuses of the Roman Church," in which case she used her "natural language." When she came to, she never remembered having spoken and was unable to express herself in French. The following are excerpts from her prophesies:

> It is not I that speak, but the Spirit that is within me. In the latter days your sons and your daughters shall prophesy, and your old men shall dream dreams.[21]
>
> Heaven and earth shall pass away, but the Word of God shall not pass away; the evildoer shall be cut down like the grass is cut down; this is why, Christians, let us remain firm, and may your faith be ever founded in Jesus Christ who shed his blood for our sins; for he that shall endure unto the end

shall receive eternal life. It is necessary to suffer for the Word, for he said: he who loves me shall take up my Cross. It is to Jesus Christ that we must give all our love; it is he who said: he that loveth someone other than me is not worthy of me.[22]

All words spoken by Isabeau that are not direct quotations from Christ come either from the Old Testament or elsewhere in the New;[23] her virtuoso display of memorization testifies, as it were, to the success of Protestant evangelism in Southern France: it had managed to eradicate the local culture and substitute its own–a bible culture expressed in the French language–even among illiterates. But more significant than this sociological feature is the fact that Isabeau the prophetess cancels herself out both as uttering subject and as subject of the utterance. It is not she who speaks, and she does not speak directly about herself. The foreignness of her speech attests to the alienation of all those of her faith; her possession by the Word of God testifies to their dispossession. Her words are empty, in the sense that they are pure repetition, but this monotony gave them their value and the meaning with which they would mobilize crowds of people who had been dispossessed of their legitimate faith–Protestantism–the faith for which they would soon risk their lives.

Let us listen now to Bossuet, prince of the Catholic Church, shepherd of a noble flock, who also cited the Bible with great frequency, but from a cultivated memory that mastered the sacred texts, deliberately set them in relation to one another, edited them, used them as instruments of conviction in a strategy of edifying persuasion rather than a morbidly disputatious harangue. The opening of the prelate's *Oraison funèbre* for Henriette de France, widow of Charles I of England (which, in passing, attacks the Quakers as "fanatical people"), delivered in 1669 in the church of the Sisters of Saint Marie of Chaillot, where the heart of the former queen lay, reads as follows:

> He who reigns in Heaven and has jurisdiction over all empires, to whom alone belong glory, majesty, and independence, is also the only one whose glory it is to lay down the law to kings and to teach them, when it pleases him, great and terrible lessons. He erects thrones or brings them low; he communicates his power to princes or takes it back from them, leaving them only their own weakness; he teaches them their duties in a sovereign manner that is worthy of him. For in according them his power he commands them to use it as he does himself, for the good of the world, and he

gives them to know, by taking it away, that all their majesty is borrowed, and that though they may be seated on the throne, they are nonetheless under his hand and his supreme authority. Thus it is that he instructs princes not only by means of speeches and words, but also by effects and examples. *Et nunc, reges, intelligite; erudimini, qui judicatis terram.*

The Latin injunction, of which Bossuet only later gives a French version, recurs like an incantation:

The heart of a great queen, once raised high by such a long series of prosperities, then plunged suddenly into an abyss of bitterness, shall speak loudly enough; and since a common person is not permitted to give lessons to princes about such strange events, a king shall lend me his words so that I might say to such princes: *Et nunc, reges, intelligite; erudimini, qui judicatis terram*: Understand this, O great men of the earth; instruct yourselves in this, arbiters of this world.[24]

While quotation, translation, and prosopopoeia do not constitute an exhaustive catalog of Bossuet's rhetorical methods, they do form the core of them: reiterated quotations are used to support a point or advance an argument or demonstration, and may be taken, as here, from the Vulgate text of the Old Testament or from the New, but also from the church fathers (Augustine, Tertullian, Gregory of Nazianzus). Quoting the Word in Latin, a language intelligible to his particular listeners, nonetheless enabled Bossuet to accentuate the distance between himself and the speaker, who thereby became a kind of disembodied voice from elsewhere, captivating the ear with its psalmody. Prosopopoeia enabled him to transmit the Word of God as if it were being spoken here and now, to make persons heard who could no longer speak, to attribute the power of the Word to things that might only have it metaphorically, such as the "heart" of Henriette de France. Bossuet could further complicate this game, as for instance when he has her "cry out with the prophet," putting a series of quotations from Jeremiah in her mouth. And in the 1683 oration for Maria Theresa of Austria, he announces that he has become the dead queen's vehicle of expression, openly pretending to be the victim of a sublime possession:

Hear the pious Queen who speaks louder than all preachers. . . . She is telling you through my mouth, and in a voice you know, that greatness is a dream, joy an error, youth a flower that fades, and health a deceptive word.[25]

Words and names have even greater powers than to make kings tremble and convert; for they can stir in people "that je-ne-sais-quoi for which no language has a word" when, during the funeral ceremonies devoted to the heart now dust of the deceased queen, Bossuet speaks to her of her husband Charles Stuart, decapitated on the English fanatics' scaffold–Charles, who "showed great heart during his final ordeal":

> Great queen, I satisfy your most tender desires when I celebrate this monarch. Your heart, which lived for nothing else but him, awakes, dust though it is, and becomes capable of sense even beneath this shroud, at the name of the spouse so beloved of it, to whom even his enemies must accord the title of wise and just, and whom posterity will rank with the great princes when his story finds readers whose judgment will not let itself be mastered by events or fortune.[26]

How can such theatrical staging of the word–a word that claims the power to make dead hearts speak, a voice that lends itself to the dead and resuscitates them, a word that animates as much as it edifies–not be seen as the epitome of what Calvin would have called magic, and recall Spinoza's assessment at the beginning of the *Tractatus Theologico-Politicus*, published a year after the funeral oration for Henriette de France, that "the very temple became a theatre where, instead of Church teachers, orators held forth, none of them actuated by a desire to instruct the people"?[27] It is not surprising that on his side, Bossuet had the first edition of a rationalist exegetical work by the Catholic scholar Richard Simon seized and burnt (1678),[28] afterward having him expelled from his order and forcing him to pursue his work in hiding.

Both the Protestant shepherdess from Crest and the Catholic "eagle" of Meaux, each in their particular tone and style, used the Word of God as that of a transcendent Master commanding them to mobilize or edify. Spinoza on the other hand worked to persuade others to abandon the tone and register of "sacred cause" and take up that of causality: he naturalized the Word of God.

Spinoza's Antifanatical Political Order

According to Spinoza, nothing in Scripture justified an individual or group's claim to a privileged relation with God that conferred some kind of special legitimacy: such legitimacy could be founded only on ethical perfection and the virtue of the message—these were what made Christ an exception. Spinoza denounced belief in miracles as dangerous, for nothing might occur that went against the ways of nature; believing in miracles was just another way of transforming God into a capricious prince—and would ultimately lead to atheism.[29] He also rejected the idea that prophecies had any truth value: natural, ordinary knowledge was not inferior to prophetic knowledge, whose proper field was that of practical morality, the sociopolitical sphere. The prophets, more often ignorant and uncultured than wise, had only grasped what they claimed to be divine truths with the help of their imaginations, a faculty that varied from person to person. Their imaginations were excited either by visions or by words. The meaning of these types of signs, contrary to that of mathematical signs, which followed from the things perceived or seen, changed with the prophet's temperament and opinions: sensitive natures' imaginings of God were refined in style, while military men made him into the leader of an army; courtiers took him for a king, and those who believed in the absurdities of astrology imagined Christ's birth to have been revealed by a star. Some prophets had more vivid imaginations than others, and they could be further distinguished from each other on the basis of other psychological and sociological criteria. Was this brutal reductionism on Spinoza's part? The alternative to his materialist analysis was to admit that God was insane and that reason did not exist—and also to recognize the legitimacy of the sects in the sects' own terms. For Spinoza, the only prophet who had heard the voice of God was Moses, and Christ alone had received a revelation from God without the help of imagination, without images and without words, in a communion of "mind to mind."[30] But while all prophets should be understood in the framework of this critique of prophesying, conversely one could not accuse prophets of being false out of loyalties to one religion or sect. It was reason that showed us who was a real prophet, who had a real message—Moses, Christ, and Mohammed, for example.

The radical nature of Spinoza's position emerges clearly in a letter written after the publication of the *Tractatus Theologico-Politicus*, in which he challenged a Christian interlocutor's affirmation that the philosopher's theories would not enable him to demonstrate that Mohammed was a false prophet. The philosopher's response was complex, both strategic and ironic. He explains that Mohammed was clearly an

"impostor" because "he entirely took away the freedom which the
Catholic Religion, as revealed by natural and by prophetic light, allows
and which I have shown ought to be allowed."[31] Mohammed is excluded from the ranks of the prophets for precisely what seems to be
the distinguishing feature of all prophets, that they limit or deny the
freedom to think, and Spinoza ironically explains to his intolerant
Christian correspondent that it is Mohammed's lack of tolerance—
there is no freedom of thought in Islam—that makes him a false
prophet. However, he continues—after adding that it is not *his* responsibility to demonstrate that Mohammed was not a true prophet—if one
objected that Mohammed had taught "a divine law" and that he had
given "sure signs" of his mission, then we would have no reason to
deny that he was a "true prophet." It is undoubtedly because he was
writing a private letter that Spinoza allowed himself to draw out clearly
all the lessons of his doctrine and to affirm the universality of "the
spirit of Christ," not the fleshly Christ, but Christ conceived of independently of ethnic or religious borders, a Christ present also in Islam:
"As regards the Turks and other Gentiles, if they worship God by the
exercise of justice and charity toward their neighbor, I believe that they
have the spirit of Christ and are saved, whatever convictions they may
in their ignorance hold about Mahomet and the oracles."[32]

If there was no cursed people, no nation of infidels, neither could
there exist a chosen people: the Israelites' alliance with God was, in
Spinoza's eyes, more political than religious, and the "election" of the
Jews involved only matters of society and state; it conferred no spiritual superiority on them. Israel was distinctive as a temporal society,
not as the mooring point of transcendence: "The Law revealed by God
to Moses was simply the laws of the Hebrew state alone, and was therefore binding on none but the Hebrews, and not even on them except
while their state still stood."[33] If then even the Israelites were not a
chosen people, no one and no group—neither person, sect, or nation—
could claim for his relation with God a privileged status. By denying to
the Jews any particular excellence in science or piety, Spinoza dismissed *a fortiori* any claim to any superior inspiration that did not
derive from the light of reason. But it did not suffice to invalidate
fanatical pretensions to a monopoly on truth. Against the sectarian's
fury, his fevered zeal, against exacerbated superstition, it was necessary to develop means for protecting civil society.

Regulating social life required technologies that took into account the fact that, in the searing pronouncement of the *Ethics*, "The mob is terrifying, if unafraid" [terret vulgus, nisi metuat],[34] while ensuring that men were not treated as slaves.

Such was the function of religious ceremonies, for example, which, from the perspective of reason, fell into the category of superstition, but were nonetheless effective as a means of procuring obedience, as was the poetic style: religious ceremony and the figurative rhetoric of the prophets, which inspired devotion, were both useful conventions that functioned by stimulating people's imagination and awe. With this in mind, what should religion be and how should it be organized from the perspective of the political order? To all of the existent religions Spinoza accorded only private status, affirming that their houses of worship might be numerous but could be neither too big nor too physically close to one another at the risk of bringing on the "mob" effect. Above all he imagined and affirmed the necessity of what he termed the "homeland religion" (*religio patriae*), a public religion to be celebrated in the public space. In contrast to private churches, those dedicated to the homeland religion were to be large and ornate. In an aristocratic regime only "patricians or senators" might preside over worship and ritual ceremonies such as baptism, marriage, and the laying on of hands.[35] It was necessary for all patricians to share this unique religion, once again in order to avoid any escalation of sectarianism. Civil society in general could not function without the obedience of its subjects: this meant not the ruin of the various existing religions but rather that the only worship that was compulsory in the framework of the polis was to assist one's neighbor as much as possible; no one had a public mandate to practice any other public form of worship than "loving one's neighbor." This meant in turn that no one had the right to proselytize or disseminate propaganda in favor of a given religion: propagating a given faith could only have grievous results, as past centuries had demonstrated (the expulsion of the Jews from Spain and Portugal, the Wars of Religion). What was conventionally meant by worship and religion was thus an activity of the private sphere: "Everyone, therefore, wherever he may be, can worship God with true religion, and mind his own business, which is the duty of a private man."[36]

The only licit religious propaganda in Spinoza's scheme was propaganda in favor of the minimalist credo of the public religion. And while no church could claim a monopoly on truth in sacred matters or legitimacy as a political apparatus, the democratic state that Spinoza imagined above and beyond the aristocratic one would institute a "political order" that would guarantee freedom to the sects; as we have said, sectarianism was for Spinoza part of the very nature of human passions and it would be vain to try to prohibit it. Civil society could not effectively protect itself from fanaticism by instituting a hard and fast separation between the two Cities, because this would result in unconditional, unchallenged acceptance of the state. Spinoza's vision involved less a secularizing of the political, where it would be reduced to a profane if imperative order, than the instituting of a political order that allowed freedom of thought, religious and otherwise, and gave certain individuals access to reason.

Nothing could be further from the Spinozan solution to the problem of sects than that proposed at almost the same time by Bossuet, once again in his funeral oration for Henriette de France. He deemed the fragmentation of the people into sects to be the essential cause of the English Revolution and concluded: "It is clear that since separation and revolt against the authority of the [Catholic] Church have been the source of all evils, the remedy can only consist in returning to the former unity and submission."[37] Bossuet expressed an even more fervent desire for unity, the One, and in terms that almost justify citing him among the precursors of totalitarianism—which would be a mistake of course, for a good Catholic believes he is moved only by love of his neighbor, which Bossuet pushed even to the point of proposing a kind of cannibalistic model of the Catholic Church (there is nothing shocking in this if we keep in mind that consuming the flesh of its God is Catholicism's essential ceremony). In the funeral oration for Père Bourgoing (1662), Bossuet writes:

> All the grace of the Church, all the efficacy of the Holy Ghost, resides in unity: the treasure is in unity, in unity is life; outside unity lies certain death. The Church is . . . the mother, ever giving birth to all the persons of whom she is made. So it is that she unites everything she engenders most intimately with herself, in this being unlike other mothers, who put outside themselves the children they produce. On the contrary, the Church can only engender her own by receiving them into her bosom, incorporating them into her unity. She imagines that she hears unceasingly from Saint Peter's mouth the same commandment that he receives from on high: "kill

and eat," unite, incorporate: *occide et manduca*. . . . And when she sees heretics tearing themselves from her very entrails . . . she redoubles her maternal love for the children who have remained, binding them and attaching them ever more closely in her spirit of unity.[38]

This cannibal mother, this incestuous ogress that was the Catholic Church, this sadistic orality, this model of community that operated through fusion and incorporation, is precisely what Spinoza rejected in the interest of a secularized, intellectualized, symbolicized conception of the social tie.

The "preservation of the organized human community" was the supreme good because without it the passions of fury and impiety would run rampant. "Piety for the homeland" was a superior affect. Because "the preservation and well-being of the homeland is the supreme law" [salus patriae suprema lex est], the sovereign powers, that is the magistrates or the individual who ruled this homeland, the polity, had a crucial function: he or they were the legitimate "interpreters" of religion. This was why, as Spinoza affirmed, "none can truly practice sincere piety or obey God if they do not abide by the decrees of the sovereign powers." This conception remains, however, a source of tension within Spinozan doctrine, because the philosopher also affirmed that there belonged "to every man the sovereign right and supreme authority to judge freely with regard to religion, and consequently to explain it and interpret it for himself."[39] The right to think freely belonged to all, including in the matter of religion: the eternal word of God was written in the human heart—a tablet of flesh. How might the imperative of social regulation and protection against sectarianism and fanaticism that was satisfied by the political authority's control of the public religion be reconciled with freedom of conscience?

To overcome this difficulty Spinoza distinguished between "public" and "private law," *jus publicum* and *jus privatum*. In order to avoid the decomposition of the body politic, magistrates must have the exclusive right to interpret the laws, even those concerning public religion, whereas authority in the matter of private religion was part of private law. Moses had a right to command because the laws he imposed constituted the public law of the Israelite homeland. The popes, then, who claimed to interpret what for Spinoza was a matter of private religion, could not impose their political authority by claiming Moses as a precedent. "There is no light superior to nature, and no authority external

to men"[40] either in the institutional order of religion–there could be
no sovereign pontiff–or in the spiritual domain: each person was himself the highest authority in the matter of interpreting Scripture. Political power could not be founded on the sacredness of those who held it,
and conversely, sacredness could not found a given power. With Spinoza we are following a different logic than that of Luther's project for
destroying Babylon and founding a ministry of the Word, for Spinoza,
with his *Natura sive Deus* (Nature = God) abolished all transcendence
and all sacredness, and with them all sacrilege. Scripture was to be
observed and understood in the same way one observed and understood nature; there was no higher authority than human society. This
radical affirmation of the "sovereign right to judge freely"[41] was the
logical consequence of the fact that all was in God, which itself followed from the fact that God, cause of himself, and nature, including
humanity, were one and the same, that nothing cleaved the Creator
from the creature. There was not, on the one hand, a creating God, all-
powerful agent, and on the other an ontologically lesser creation.

But against this rationalist interpretation of Spinoza's thought, can
one not object that he was first and foremost a kind of mystic metaphysician? Doesn't the primacy accorded the Word of God, and even communication without words–that between God and Christ–mean that
his position was similar to that of the "Enthusiasts"? By opposing
divine law as pronounced by "the mouth of God," *os dei*,[42] to idolatry
of the fixed letter, and by lauding Christ for having liberated humanity
from servitude to the law as commandment (*lex*) by writing it in their
hearts, Spinoza gave supreme value to the immediacy of God, who was,
by definition, present in humanity as a part of nature. Once again,
though humanity was indeed a finite mode of nature, this did not mean
that people were cut off from the infinite and eternal substance by
some kind of irremediable difference, because man was of that substance and, more important, could raise himself to a kind of knowledge of all things from "a species of eternity" (*sub quaedam specie
aeternitatis*).[43]

Isn't this the equivalent of giving everyone the right to be a visionary, and couldn't the beatitude that Spinoza in part 5 of the *Ethics*
defined as the supreme form of loving and knowing God also be the
equivalent of false illumination? This is what Kant would claim, as we
shall see in Chapter 8. For Spinoza, however, the Word of God was not

received from without; its source was not external to and above humanity, but within each, immanent, given that each was in God: "Whatever is, is in God, and nothing can be or be conceived without God."[44] Spinoza's God could not be used to found fanaticism because he was not an authority: neither prince or master, he was rather a fixed order, the concatenation of natural things. Let it be mentioned in passing that while Spinoza considered God, cause of himself, to be the only substance, he nonetheless defined distinct attributes of God (thought, extension), affirming that he had both infinite and finite modes. This precludes understanding his system as a sort of pantheism where all is God, and thus from using the philosopher's thought to open the way for a kind of fanaticism where everyone could claim to be God. Spinoza's idea was quite different, and was formulated by turning Hobbes around: "Man is a God for man." Given Spinoza's definitions of human beings as natural and of God as identical with nature, this conclusion follows from Aristotle's affirmation, which Spinoza took as his own: "Man is a social animal."[45]

It might be argued that the initial assessment from which Spinoza worked was close to Hobbes's: human beings are agitated by passions such as anger, envy, covetousness, that put them into conflict with one another. Being more powerful, skillful, and clever than the other animals, their nature makes them one another's enemies.[46] But every person "is striving to persevere in his being to the extent that that being is in him" [unaquaeque res quantum est in se perseverare conatur]. This effort, what Spinoza called the conatus, led humanity to adopt, involuntarily, a strategy of rescue: isolated, an individual had zero chance of surviving the danger that others presented and little capacity for meeting vital needs and even less for leading any kind of life of the mind. In order to maintain and develop their potential strength, individuals came around to helping one another, collaborating, accepting common legislation; rights, that is the supplementary power they acquired in effecting this passage from the state of nature to the social state, "civil society," were great in proportion as the number of people so associated was great.[47] Above all, individuals were strengthened to the extent that they came to agreement with beings identical to themselves, because the effectiveness of any aggregate was great, its conatus strong, in proportion to the number and similarity of its composite parts: those who were dominated by passions fell into discord, whereas those who were led by reason came naturally into agreement. Nothing was more useful to a person than another who was likewise seeking that which was useful to him, a person, that is, who lived by reason. Even if all people could not live by reason, even if some of them–certainly the greater number–lived guided by their passions, the impossibility of solitary life could not but confer superiority on life in society, legitimating Aristotle's definition of the human being as a social animal and making individuals wish for a life with other individuals in which, necessarily, the passions, which could not be eradicated, would be rationally organized. Passion, the fear felt by the weak and isolated person in the state of nature for whom all other human beings seem, at first, like enemies, or reason, which moved that person to cooperate with another–in either case, social life imposed itself on individuals as a necessity of their nature, a necessity internal to their conatus, for it permitted them to persevere in their being and increase its strength, to raise themselves to perfection.

Empire of the One: The Secret of Tyranny

Not all political regimes, not all types of political authority, result in an equal increase in potential strength. We shall pass over the positive examples Spinoza gave–for him democracy was the best of all regimes– and consider instead the worst, which was tyranny, the worst of bad systems. A free multitude must guard extremely carefully against entrusting its preservation and well-being to a single person (*Unus*). The Turks offered a perfect illustration of this danger: Mohammed was perhaps an authentic prophet, but the Ottoman emperor was unquestionably a tyrant. While it was true that the purpose of society was peace and a safe life, such life could not be reduced to silent immobility, nor was peace equal to the absence of all conflict. To be sure, no state (*imperium*) had known greater stability than the Ottoman state, especially in comparison to the sedition and uprisings that took place in democratic states. But was this a convincing argument for conferring political power on a single individual? "Is it then to servitude and barbarity, to the desert, that we must reserve the name of peace? If one were to concur with this opinion, that would make peace the most wretched of all human conditions."[48] There would be fewer clashes in family life if paternal authority consisted in complete domination (*dominium*) and children were treated as slaves, but in fact "slavery, . . .

not peace, is furthered by handing over to one man [*unus*] the whole authority."⁴⁹ Given the volatility of human passions, superstition was the surest means of governing the masses, making them love kings as if they were Gods or detest them as plagues of humankind. The Turks knew this so well that they had sought to embellish religion with a ceremonial that ensured constant respect on the part of the faithful– the Turks, for whom a simple discussion about religion was sacrilegious profanation, in whom prejudices crushed all power of judgment, and whose reason was reduced to the silence of the desert, for it had not even the right to utter doubt.

The Ottoman Empire was thus the paradigm of regimes in which an absolute monarch manipulated religion in order to ensure his power:

> Granted, then, that the supreme mystery [*arcanus*] of despotism, its prop and stay, is to keep men in a state of deception, and with the specious title of religion to cloak the fear by which they must be held in check, so that they will fight for their servitude as if for salvation and count it no shame, but the highest honor, to spend their blood and their lives for the glorification of one man [*unus homo*].⁵⁰

Human beings fighting for their servitude as if it were their salvation–this was the perversion in which despotism resulted; perversion in that it could be said to go against nature, for in such a situation the conatus malfunctioned, plunging people into dependence, weakness, impotence, where all their strength seemed enslaved to the desire of a Master who would have himself taken for a God and whose first act of mystification was to have persuaded them that God *was* a Master.

People subservient to a single person and sacrificing themselves for him. Triumph of the One over Union, the *Unus* over the *Unio*, over the concord of people together. Fanaticism.

6 The Voice of the Prophets

The epidemic of convulsive prophesying of which Isabeau Vincent was the first case crossed the Rhône, as we have said, and spread from the Vivarais south toward the Languedoc.

Wonders were to be seen: the visionaries were guided by gleams of celestial light, walked on burning embers without suffering pain or injury, cut themselves with knives and did not bleed. Contempt of death and a capacity for self-sacrifice manifested themselves in spectacular fashion–in heroic and bloody contradiction to the recantations made directly after the Revocation of the Edict of Nantes by great numbers of Protestants in the south of France.[1] The Protestant prophets left three hundred of their number dead near Serre-de-la-Salle in 1689, having held their chests out to the bullets of the king's soldiers while crying "Back Satan." For the Camisards, the world had become an enchanted place. And by 1702 convulsive prophesying had become a guerrilla movement. Throughout the Guerre des Camisards, attacks by resolute little bands fighting in the Cévennes were punctuated by convulsive fits in which the Word of God made itself heard in the voices of hundreds of visionaries.

Immediately after the dramatic events at Serre-de-la-Salle, the bishop of Nîmes, Esprit Fléchier, wrote his "Faithful account of what happened in the assemblies of the Vivarais fanatics."[2] The term he used to designate the prophets was, as we know, a great success; moreover, it enabled him to denigrate the Protestant prophesying by reducing it to a matter of earthly passions–the author did not hesitate to speak of sexual promiscuity among the young "prophets." Using all the means of ideological warfare open to him, Fléchier fueled his arguments against the "rebels" with open allusions to the disapproval expressed by Protestants in Geneva, who saw the French prophets as impostors: Hadn't a most celebrated Swiss professor sought to demonstrate that these children could not be inspired by God, only by the devil, and that their illness, if it was not a "possession," was at the very least an "obsession"? The Genevan Protestants' technique for exposing the imposture of the "little prophets" seems to have been inherited from the witch hunts practiced there. The so-called prophet would be pricked in the arm with a needle during one of his or her transports, upon which he or she would be heard to cry out loudly. The conclusion was that the transport had been faked. After being exposed, the prophets were thrown out of the city with the threat of being hanged if they kept up their activity.

Fléchier's information and analyses were taken up by David de Brueys in *Histoire du fanatisme de notre temps* (1692).[3] The author was a Huguenot from the south of France who, after first polemicizing against Bossuet, then met several times with the prelate and ended up converting to Catholicism, taking orders in the year of the Revocation (and just after his wife's death) from the bishop of Meaux's own hands. While pursuing a successful career as a playwright (among other works, he adapted *La Farce de maître Patelin* into modern French), he also wrote numerous anti-Protestant tracts meant among other things to justify his own spiritual journey. The term "fanaticism" is at the core of his attack, developed well before the Camisard war, against the Calvinists of southern France and their convulsive prophesying. In it he used both etymology[4] and a great deal of jargon to advance a complicated medical explanation of the phenomenon: he "diagnosed" fanaticism as a kind of "melancholia or mania" that persuaded those afflicted with it that they had the power to prophesy and perform miracles. He proposed a model that borrowed from mechanistic biology and Cartesian vocabulary: the body was a machine, and in the case of overly strong thoughts or overly prolonged thinking about miracles during a long period of tired wakefulness and fasting, the blood became overheated and dried out, with the result that animal spirits "fall upon the fibers of the brain, already weakened by energetic application to the subject of miracles and prophesies, and force these mad beings to dream constantly about them until they become persuaded that they can themselves accomplish miracles and prophesies." It was clearly a matter of "alienation and insanity," and even if the demon would sometimes mix his "seductions" with the fanatics' madness, the illness in itself remained banal; its symptoms, though they might seem surprising, had causes thoroughly familiar to the medical profession and might be treated with fitting remedies like any other disorder. All this scientistic rationalization did not change the fact that the only medicine actually applied to the "fanatics" was repression.[5] This type of explanation moreover allowed the prophecy movement to be presented as the result of a deliberate enterprise; the reader was led to imagine the existence of a "manufactory" of little prophets who, fasting and closed off from the world, would be led to the brink of delirium and hallucination–a drug-free version of the Old Man of the Mountain's Assassins.

Doctors arrived on the scene to diagnose the visionaries. In 1701, a group of them from Montpellier went to Uzès near Nîmes to examine the "little prophets" at the earnest request of the authorities, in this case the governor of Languedoc Nicolas de Lamoignon de Bâville, who was to become known to the Protestants as the "tyrant of Languedoc." The doctors observed the young visionaries with astonishment, arguing with each other in Latin and even coming to blows; their opinions about the phenomenon differed widely. Surprised to hear adolescents speak so well and quote Scripture with such method and relevance, they themselves could do no better than to pronounce highly ambiguous oracles about what they had seen, applying to the prophets "the vague name of fanatic."[6] Later the term "hysteric" would take its place. The morbid element in their behavior was thus patent, and seemed to invite the examiners to develop explanatory systems for what appeared to be psychopathological manifestations.

De Brueys, the first to apply the term "fanatic" to the Camisards, also contributed to the doctrine of civil society. By the end of the War of the Camisards, besides having published a second edition of his book to which he had added a volume on the "troubles in the Cévennes," he had also written the *Traité de l'obéissance des Chrétiens aux puissances politiques et spirituelles*, explicitly linked to the Camisard war and prefaced by Fléchier.[7] In this book the earlier medical conception of fanaticism is nowhere to be found; here its theopolitical meaning is uppermost. According to de Brueys, all Christians–Catholics, Lutherans, Calvinists, and all sects existing in Europe–must admit that they had to obey the temporal powers in charge of civil government, even if those powers were associated with a religion opposed to their own. The Fanatic sect, however, as distinct from the *Religionnaires* (all other Protestants)[8] refused to do in France what all Christians agreed to do in Rome and Geneva. Fanaticism was thus characteristically a *political* attitude, and the definition that de Brueys gave of the *Fanatiques* harks back to Luther's: they were people who refused, in the name of their faith, to recognize the legitimacy of the political authorities, according primacy to religious membership over political loyalty. De Brueys accused them of wanting to subject political life to the exigencies of the City of God; in other words, while the Christian belonged to two societies, "spiritual society" and "civil society"–the author used the term–his membership in the first gave him no right to contest or disturb, as the fanatics were doing, the political government that was in charge of the second. De Brueys's analysis of the Camisard war is thus made to serve as a certain type of apology for the political power in place. The argument is simple: a Christian must obey God; Holy Scripture affirms that we must render unto Caesar what is Caesar's; therefore, it was part of "divine law" to render unto the temporal powers what belonged to them and to obey them. The syllogism was irrefutable.

In fact, the use of "fanatic" as synonymous with "hostile to civil society" should be inscribed in a much larger lexical and conceptual field, which takes us some distance from the Cévennes.

Fanaticism: Fury and Mysticism

In 1661, well before Fléchier, the word *fanatique* had been used as we know in Renaudot's *Gazette*, in the translation of an English account of the violent unrest stirred up by visionaries and zealots in London in 1660. A few years later, as we have mentioned, Bossuet applied the word to the Quakers in his list of sects born of "a secret adversion to all that possesses authority, and an itching for endless innovation,"[9] whose proliferation had enabled Cromwell to come to power. Bossuet also made use of the word in his *Histoire des variations du protestant-*

isme, and in 1680 Père Louis Maimbourg used it in his history of Lutheranism to designate Karlstadt and the Anabaptists.[10]

"Extravagant madman, person of alienated mind, who believes he has visions, inspirations. The word is hardly used outside the context of religion"–thus read the entry "fanatic" in the *Dictionnaire de l'Académie* of 1694, which went on to cite *illuminés* and *trembleurs* as examples. The definition clearly shows how pejorative the term was; it had been made to bear both the weight of insanity and the destruction wrought by the English Revolution. *Fanatique* was being used intensively in France once again after its earlier importation from Germany and German via Latin, this time arriving from England, where it was often spelled the same as in French.

At the very moment that Fléchier and his followers applied it to Protestants in the south of France, the word was being used in quite a different context, to refer to private mystic ecstasies among certain aristocrats and their circle, rather than to public convulsive prophesying and semirural rebellion, and far from the harsh landscape of the Vivarais or the Cévennes, at the court of Louis XIV in Versailles. The issue was that of "pure love," and the term "fanaticism" was used, by Bossuet and numerous others, to discredit Madame Guyon and her confessor and defender, François Fénelon, archbishop of Cambrai.

In his *Maxims of the Saints Explained*, Fénelon defined five types of love for God, beginning with the "servile love" of the "carnal Jews" for "the gifts of God distinguished from him, and not for himself" and ending with the following definition of the fifth, highest form: "love to God alone, considered in itself, and without any the least mixture of an interested motive, or of hope . . . is pure love or perfect charity."[11] It was just this absence of mediation and motive that made such love theologically problematic. Considered from the angle of semantics, the dispute about "pure love" might be summed up as follows: Bossuet assimilated "pure love" to "fanaticism" whereas Fénelon qualified its tenets as "mystical." The "fanatic" label was also applied to the new spiritualists and their defender by the Abbé de Rancé, who alluded to the erotically charged nature of such worship, and by Jansenists such as Antoine Arnauld even before Bossuet used it,[12] as well as by Leibniz (see Chapter 7), who was deeply interested in the dispute, which he could have read about in detail in the pages of the periodical review *Histoire des ouvrages des savans*.[13] The controversy echoed throughout Europe.

The general outlines of the story, whose French elements include court intrigues, personal dramas, and theological disputes, are well known. In 1675, the Spanish theologian Miguel de Molinos published at Rome his *Guia espiritual* (Spiritual guide), which was rapidly translated into Italian, French, and Latin; its success cannot be isolated from that being enjoyed by other spiritual innovators.[14] Rome conducted an offensive against such "contemplatives," the name given to followers of Molinos's teachings, and in 1686 the author himself was arrested. In August the papal authorities issued a decree against him, and his works were put on the Index. Quietism, from the Latin *quies*, repose, which affirmed the possibility and validity of praying, worshiping God through a kind of quietude in which the passive soul would be immersed in him, corresponded to an ancient tradition that already had practitioners in France and which became matter for a confrontation whose principal actors were, on one side, Madame Guyon, author of the controversial *Moyen court et très facile de faire oraison* (Quick and very simple method of prayer), and Fénelon; on the other, Bossuet, who enlisted the aid of the king and was not adverse, despite his Gallicanism, to setting Rome against his colleague. It has even been suggested that his objections to the doctrines of the French Quietists were just a pretext and that his primary aim was to crush Fénelon and his supporters.

At first, Bossuet was little concerned about or informed on the matter, despite the fact that his library was well stocked with books discussing it. He hardly went further than to advise the Charitable Daughters of La Ferté-sous-Jouarre, who came under his spiritual tutelage as bishop of Meaux and whose list of allowed reading material he had been asked to look over, to be wary of a few rather strong expressions in the writings of certain "mystics" that seemed to affirm that in the contemplative life the soul was utterly passive.[15] A short time later he was accusing the Quietists of considering active love for Christ to be mere self-love and reaffirming in no uncertain terms–against Fénelon's idea of a love for God unmotivated by a desire for happiness on the part of the lover[16]–humanity's global vocation for happiness.

The archbishop of Cambrai began to come to his attention. Tutor to the royal sons and implicated on account of this high position in a multitude of court intrigues, Fénelon had met Madame Guyon in 1689 just after she was released from the convent of Sainte-Marie, rue Saint

Antoine in Paris, to which she had been confined for her writings. Solicited and influenced by some of Madame Guyon's lady friends, Madame de Maintenon, who had secretly become Louis XIV's wife, had interceded with her husband for her release. When Madame Guyon came to thank her protectress, with whom Fénelon was intimate, we may say that she charmed the prelate.

"He saw her: their spirits pleased one another, the sublime in each of them fused"–it was thus that in his *Mémoires* the duc de Saint-Simon described their meeting,[17] which had all the appearance of a lovers' encounter–but need we insist on that point? In the shared logic of the persons involved their relation was indeed one of love, love of the highest kind: "pure." In fact, Fénelon was not the only one to succumb to the "prophetess"–the term is Saint-Simon's[18]–for she was later received at the school for young impoverished noblewomen that Madame de Maintenon had founded at Saint-Cyr, where she provoked general enthusiasm. This was only to continue for a limited time, however: when the bishop of Chartres warned Madame de Maintenon to be wary, she went to consult (among others) the bishop of Meaux.

Bossuet read Madame Guyon's writings and talked with her, then with Fénelon, who gave him his own notes and writings on certain mystics, materials he had assembled to demonstrate that there had been a gnostic, mystic tradition in the Catholic Church since very early on.[19] The effect of all this was, however, to strengthen Bossuet's feeling that "pure love" was a deviation similar to Quietism–he was soon calling it fanaticism. And to his mind it was Fénelon who was responsible for the ideas behind it: passive souls, whose passivity resembled too much that of Quietism, believed themselves to be directed by "inspiration, and that by it they would know what God wanted from them at every moment." Didn't this reduce to nothing all active hope and desire for salvation?[20] But in addition to the theological reasons for opposing it, Bossuet did not at all appreciate Madame Guyon's relating how God had given her "such abundance of grace that she burst out with it in a literal sense, so that they were fain to unlace her."[21] The bishop of Meaux was hardly at ease with the "hysterical pious-woman," ecstatically overflowing with God.[22]

An attempt at a compromise between the two camps failed.[23] Madame Guyon was inundating Paris with her ideas and had to be stopped; she was arrested again, this time on Bossuet's orders, and confined to the Château de Vincennes outside Paris for six months. Fénelon, for his part, refused to pronounce what was supposed to be an absolute condemnation of the woman he had "revered as a saint," and the dispute began to take on more vehement tones: Bossuet went to Louis XIV to ask pardon for not having exposed his colleague's fanaticism earlier; meanwhile Fénelon asked permission to submit to the authorities at Rome the work in which he defended himself against the accusation of fanaticism; he hoped he would be allowed to go to Rome to make his case. After forbidding this, the king sent a letter to Pope Innocent XII denouncing the archbishop of Cambrai's work as dangerous; the letter had been written by Bossuet. Outraged, Fénelon continued to defend himself in a multitude of new books and pamphlets in which he asked why Bossuet had deemed it necessary to "denounce him to the Church as a fanatic, like a second Molinos."[24] For his part Bossuet explained that while he could perhaps accept the existence of a "pure love" for God, he could not agree that this might be one's "habitual state."[25] At Rome, where the respective allies of the two prelates were confronting each other, Bossuet had the stronger position; Fénelon was unable to clear himself and Madame Guyon of the accusations of fanaticism,[26] and he and his family were banished from Court. The author of *Télémaque* submitted to Rome's verdict and made the required public amends.

We see that in the last decade of the seventeenth century "fanatic" had two meanings, different but susceptible to being combined into one. If a "fanatic" could just as well wear the face of a Madame Guyon—whom, as we have said, Fénelon characterized not as a Quietist but a mystic—as that of an insurgent peasant from the Cévennes, the face of "pure love" as well as one distorted by violent convulsions, what the two cases have in common is an abandoning of oneself to God in a movement where the subject strips him or herself of will, alienating him or herself in God, as it were, in order to receive from him the communication of his being.[27] Moreover, the two cases shared a rejection of images, of figuration—of representation. Fénelon affirmed the possibility of contemplation without representation, as if God's Being, by its very excess, could only appear as nothingness.[28] As for the Camisards, the fact that they only marginally engaged in iconoclast activity is surely to be explained by how efficiently French Calvinists had practiced it the century before:[29] the Camisards' religious universe had already been purged of images, and steeped as they were in a French-language biblicalism that had eradicated their local culture, God was for them the Word, a voice that penetrated them and spoke through them—God as cause of desire.

Hysteria

On the stage of the "sacred theater" of the Cévennes, the Word of God took hold of an entire community and threw them into convulsions and prophesying, then into a bloody guerrilla war for "God's cause." The excessive quality of these events evokes the extremes of the Old Testament, not the mildness of the Gospel, the God of armies not of love. The various testimonies assembled in *Le Théâtre sacré des Cévennes* are bathed in an atmosphere of unreality, as alluring as a dream but as strange and frightening as a nightmare. The war, in fact, had its beginning in a dream—one that came to Abraham Mazel, who would become a leader of the movement, and which was interpreted for him by the divine spirit as an order to take up arms. He obeyed and with a group of friends in the night of July 24, 1702, launched an attack against a church that was being used by its abbot as a prison for a handful of Protestants. The "visionaries" killed the priest after forcing him to free the prisoners, castrated him, and destroyed whatever pious images they found. Some time later, Jean Cavalier, at the head of sixty Camisards, put seven hundred royal troops to rout near Alès, and it proved necessary to mobilize a real army and devastate the upper Cévennes in order at last to put down the insurrection in 1704.

Soon after that first night, the entire Protestant community of the mountains was fighting—in what Emmanuel Le Roy Ladurie has called a "rebellion sauvage"[30]—against the soldiers the king had sent to crush them. Shepherds, masons, wool carders, cobblers, plowmen, hog gelders; men, women, children; masters and servants gathered together, and in between battles where, believing themselves invulnerable and singing psalms all the while, they hurled themselves against the dragoons of the Most Christian King, they would praise the Lord and be seized with convulsions that threw them to the ground, where they began to speak. Or rather, they were spoken through by a Spirit that took hold of their organs of speech and used them to reveal the future and the ultimate meaning of things.

So it was that God had "made his marvels shine forth" on the stage of the "sacred theater of the Cévennes." In the book bearing that title we have the testimony of the visionaries themselves, assembled by them with the intention of defending themselves against the accusation of fanaticism. (That term so stuck that Voltaire, for example, who later changed his opinion on Protestantism, at first looked disapprovingly on the Camisards and, sixty years after Fléchier, used the same epithet for them.)[31] The accusation of being fanatics, and not the true prophets they believed themselves to be, followed those Camisards who had made it to relative safety in London, where they continued openly to convulse. Though they were not free from attack in England – verbal for the most part – the response of the earl of Shaftesbury, one of the first representatives of philosophical, enlightened thinking and a friend of Locke, was instead one of mild and generalized ridicule and a certain analytic interest in the phenomenon of convulsion. "They have set afoot the spirit of martyrdom to a wonder in their own country, and they long to be trying it here," he writes in "A Letter Concerning Enthusiasm,"[32] and remarks that "they are at this very time the subject of a choice droll or puppet show at Bart'lemy Fair":

> There, doubtless, their strange voices and involuntary agitations are admirably well acted, by the motions of wires and inspiration of pipes. For the bodies of the prophets, in their state of prophecy, being not in their own power, but (as they say themselves) mere passive organs, actuated by an exterior force, have nothing natural or resembling real life in way of their sounds or motions; so that how awkwardly soever a puppet-show may imitate other actions, it must needs represent this passion to the life.[33]

Meanwhile, the Camisards who had taken refuge in London wanted the authenticity of their prophesying recognized, and it was in the interest of winning a certain legitimacy that they published, among other texts, *Le Théâtre sacré des Cévennes*.[34] Interestingly, they sought to prove the veracity of their inspiration simply by relating their experiences. The access they themselves offered to the existential dimension of their story was what permitted and continues to permit clinical hypotheses to be advanced about them.

Fléchier had underlined the erotic element of the Camisards' prophesying, obviously in order to denigrate it; only later would the physician Philippe Hecquet speak in the Camisards' case of hysteria. For him the hysterical character of their prophesying episodes was so apparent and the cause, "hysterical vapors," so clear, that he used the

Camisards as a precedent on which to found his diagnosis of the Saint-Médard convulsives.[35] And despite his having read the *Théâtre sacré*, which includes several accounts of men in convulsions, he spoke only of "vaporous girls."[36] "Hysteria" is also mentioned in the writings of John Wesley, the founder of Methodism, who in January 1739, as he explained in his diary, paid a visit to "one of those persons commonly called French prophets," whom he found afflicted with "strong workings in her breast" and whom he heard pronounce sentences broken up by "convulsive motion" about which he hypothesized that it was "either hysterical or artificial."[37]

There is nothing surprising in his application of the term, for the phenomenology of Camisard prophesying corresponds well to that of hysteria: the subject falls to the ground, then utters prophetic words in a kind of glossolalia. The Camisards' seizures were generally public and often contagious within the group; they were patently theatrical, and the subject's acceptance of, even complicity with, the experience was visible. Interestingly, he or she was never injured in the fall to the ground. The frontispiece of de Brueys's *Histoire du fanatisme de notre temps* shows a man and a woman on the ground in the midst of a rocky desert landscape; in the throes of an epileptic-like seizure, they are watched by a large crowd, which includes an executioner–a brutal and naive version of the spectacle that would later be on view at Charcot's ward in the Salpêtrière.

It is worth recounting in full one of the descriptions given in the *Théâtre sacré*. It was written by a woman who had observed the fit of a fifteen-year-old servant girl at Anduze. The young girl, explains the author, is suddenly seized with convulsive movements, becomes pale; her eyes close, head and chest heave, her breathing becomes spasmodic. After several moments she begins to speak in a distinct but jerky voice–in French, a detail that astounds the witness given that in those parts people of her rank and age know only the local patois. "Without affectation" the young prophetess calls on sinners to repent. And she has a revelation the truth of which will immediately be confirmed: the Spirit says, "My child, my child, I say unto you that your brothers are at present grappling with the enemy. But it is I who fight for them, have no fear; I promise you they will be the victors." Shortly thereafter, reports the witness, a Camisard victory was announced.[38]

The fit is always presented by those who have witnessed one as following a similar pattern. Its visible climax is designated by a multitude of similar terms: "agitation," "twitchings," "tremblings," "transports," "quiverings," "shudderings," "shiverings," "jerks," "convulsions" throw the subject on the ground and bring him or her to "ecstasy." The clearly hysteric appearance of such fits seems to allows for an explanation in Freudian terms in which sexual repression plays a determining role.[39]

However, a major aspect of the phenomenon cannot be accounted for by such an explanation. The hysterics, their bodies convulsed, never stopped talking. It is true that some of them spoke in an apocalyptic tone resembling that of Jurieu when he denounced Louis XIV and papism and predicted the fall of Babylon and the death of the Beast: the exile's imprecations, largely disseminated in written form throughout Languedoc, were taken up and embroidered on by itinerant, self-appointed preachers journeying through a region the Revocation had emptied of established pastors. Still, the imprecatory, millenarian, let us say fanatical, talk is not the essential element reported in the *Théâtre sacré*. What emerges from the Camisards' own testimony is that the Spirit was generally quite prosaic; he had immediately useful and everyday things to say. Talkative, he was not above discussing the most minor items and inscribed the entire life of the visionaries and their companions into a network of advice and instructions. Their God was an organizer, a schemer, a calculator and computer of the things of this world. He prescribed that meals be prepared for the brothers in arms, warned of the enemy's arrival, and told how to avoid ambushes, indicated where battles would take place and how to escape arrest. He commanded Elie Marion to take up arms and pointed out to Jean Couderc which soldiers had to be expelled if the Camisard ranks were to be kept pure. He let Jean Cavalier know that he would speak to Louis XIV. And all this was realized, done. He was a God who sympathized with those who loved him and were penetrated by him, who watched over the troops so that sentinels became unnecessary, and who protected them from the bullets' lead. Such an attentive Spirit proved his "paternal bounty" by answering all the questions he was asked:

> Should we attack the enemy? Were we being pursued? Would the night take us by surprise? Should we fear ambushes? Would there be an accident? Should a given place be marked by our holding an assembly there? First we set ourselves to pray: "Lord, give us to know what pleases you that we may

do it for your glory and our good!" Straight away he would answer us, and his inspiration guided us in everything.[40]

The two sons, the two daughters, a grandson, a brother, and a sister of a certain Marliaut were massacred by the Catholics during a Camisard meeting. "The most remarkable thing," writes Isabeau Charras, "is that all the martyrs had been warned by the Spirit what was going to happen to them. They had told their father about it before they left that night, and asked his blessing, before going to a meeting that should have taken place the following night."[41] Standing over the dead bodies of his family, the father "showed a pious resignation."[42] The Word of God thus had a more important function than the practical one of warning and prevention; its power of anticipation served less to allow for an appropriate adjustment of actions and behavior than to make bearable the unbearable, to make possible the real, by veiling it over with the divine Word. The real was thus buried away under a kind of speech that organized it and smoothed it over with euphemism. Delirium and hallucination, far from cutting those who experienced them off from the real, enabled them to assimilate the horror of their particular everyday life. The Word of God domesticated that horror.

Paranoia

But a world in which everything is a sign, where everything *says* something, is the world of paranoia, and its two interlinked constituents, "communication" and "persecution," both of which abound in the Camisards' accounts. The four main autobiographical testimonies contained in the *Théâtre sacré des Cévennes* all have one episode in common: the discovery of a traitor, whose presence is revealed by divine inspiration, by the Holy Spirit.

Elie Marion receives a warning from the Spirit accompanied by a vision of the traitor in conversation with an agent of the forces of repression. The next day the Spirit seizes him again during a meeting and makes him expose the traitor, a "false brother." Abraham Mazel also receives information from the Spirit denouncing a conspirator. After the battle of Gaverne, Jean Cavalier, the military commander of the moment, hears his cousin of the same name declare that he has been kissed by a Judas. Later, when the little group is at table in what might so readily have seemed to the participants a repetition of the

Holy Supper, he himself is seized by the Spirit and in great agitation pronounces words accusing one of the diners of treachery. Then another one of his relatives falls in "ecstasy" and through his mouth the Spirit announces the presence of a traitor, whereupon Ravenel, a future martyr, is invested by the Spirit, who reveals that there is a Judas among them who seeks to poison them. The task of revealing the traitor's identity will fall to another of the Camisards, who then turns to address the man in question: "Know you not, miserable creature, that I see all things?" The traitor is, however, not immediately punished, and he goes on to denounce sixty persons to the Catholic authorities, including Jean Cavalier, who meets up again with him in prison at Perpignan and watches him sink into a deep melancholy, then die as befits his abject state, vomiting a flow of filth. Durand Fage, who had born arms against the Camisards against his will before joining up with them, recounts another case: the discovery of two traitors by Jean Clary, who, in order to prove that he had had a revelation, chose for himself the ordeal of standing in a fire–he came out without a burn.[43] Fage next gets involved in the search for another traitor whom numerous revelations had accused. Hunting down traitors was a collective activity, constant, obsessive, involving the entire community. This time the traitor in question was put to death, but only after an intense moment of hesitation on the part of Cavalier, a "terrible ecstasy" in which the Spirit threatens to abandon him if he does not obey by executing the traitor.

Why this obsession with betrayal? Why this repeated undermining from the inside by "false brothers"? There might conceivably have been traitors among the Camisards, but what made them so numerous and so easy to unmask? Might we not justifiably suspect that such permanent betrayal itself belied an unconscious desire, that it was a kind of exorcising projection?

Being a victim of actual persecution is not enough to immunize one against delusions of persecution. The accounts assembled in the *Théâtre sacré* are organized, as we have suggested, by a belief in the perfect transparence of the world. In the throes of his or her inspiration, the prophet apprehends phenomena as if they were a group of divine signs, the Word of God made concrete. Whereas the hysteric disturbs the world with his protestation, his unsatisfied desire, the paranoid is part of an order of which he wants to be the agent, the hero, or the victim.

To use Lacan's formula, the hysteric protests against a world in which there are no sexual relations (by which we mean more particularly that there is neither harmony between the sexes nor harmonious sexuality for the *parlêtre*, the speaking human being), whereas the paranoid believes that sexual relations *do* exist (he believes, then, in the world's ultimate and absolute intelligibility). The prophet is directly plugged into the source of Truth, directly plugged into the Other, God, the Absolute, the *sujet du savoir* or knowing subject, who reveals its secrets to him, lets him in on the plan. Separation and exile are over, and the creature is reintegrated into the Word of the great knower, who makes truth flow from the prophet's mouth. Ecstasy. Not the ecstasy of the mystic, white, imageless, and stupefying, but a terrifying, brutal intrusion. Thrown to the floor in convulsions, the prophet is dispossessed through a total alienation: his "organs are agitated by the Heavenly Angel"; a "superior power" that he does not know takes control of his mouth.[44] He has become God's ectoplasm. The Holy Spirit is not a parasite, unwelcome guest living at the expense of the person who shelters it, nor is it a noise that brings on confusion. It is a nourishing, creative word.

And it has the same power as hallucination: it is real. For the real is certainly not what common sense might think: the landscape of the Cévennes, the plain of the Languedoc, the scrubland, the chestnut trees—all this has become unreal. The administrator Lamoignon de Bâville's soldiers, twenty thousand men mobilized to fight a few thousand poorly armed visionaries, lose their consistency, weakened in the light of a new comprehension, a sort of eternal light that will not leave the rebels in peace and that authorizes all sorts of audacities in the fight against their enemies. The military exploits of the Camisards were founded in their certitude of being soldiers for God:

> We had neither strength or counsel; our only recourse, the only thing we depended on, was our inspirations. They alone elected our leaders and guided them. They were our military discipline. They taught us to take our enemies' first fire on our knees and to attack them while singing psalms to put terror in their souls. They changed our lambs into lions and made them perform glorious deeds.[45]

Paranoia works. It works where common sense would fail and hysteria wouldn't even try. The Camisards' madness should thus be taken not as the limit of their story but as its very center.

There was democracy in Camisard prophesying–all might know inspiration–but this democracy was only the reverse side of divine despotism: God spoke to whomever he wanted and when it pleased him; no virtuoso could make him appear at will and no one might elude his injunctions. God was both utterly distant and utterly present, which ensured that a double circuit of communication was kept open: the libidinal tie–desire for God–was maintained and his words kept coming; communication was open between each member and God and between each member and every other member of the group. God the utter stranger was also the closest of the close. And from this it followed that the closest of the close could also be an utter stranger. A false brother. Being stuck in the mirror image of the other.[46]

A traitor.

A traitor is not an ordinary enemy: he is here, belonging to the same world, and yet he is hidden; next to you, similar to all the rest of you, and yet radically different, a difference that is invisible except to the One who sees all, Himself the same and yet utterly different. Treachery is the passage from a same to an other effected in the shadows; it silently, insidiously breaks up the harmony of the group, shakes the naive confidence upon which their spontaneous social contract rests. Each had confided his trust in his supposed likeness; the "false brother" perverts the public space. The traitor exposed, on the other hand, gives new authority to the group by permitting it to reaffirm its unity through the exclusion of what is now waste material. A temporary end to the group's anxious fear of being undermined by someone identical to its members, an obscene same-but-not-the-same element. The chasm of specular representation may close up again.

Above all, the traitor enables each one to deny reality in a delusionary mode, or to ward off the threat of discovering himself that he has failed. According to Freud this was what explained the betrayal myth forged by the French after their defeat at Sedan in 1870: "The *grande nation* cannot face the idea that it can be defeated in war. *Ergo* it was not defeated; the victory does not count." How could this be explained? After 1870, in Freud's understanding, France invented a "delusion of betrayal," offering the world an example of "mass paranoia." Freud made these remarks in 1895 as an illustration of his theory of paranoia,[47] which he would fully develop in the celebrated case study of Doctor Schreber (1911). Uncovering a new sexual etiology of paranoia,

Freud presented its different clinical forms as four modalities of negating the formula "I (a man) love him (a man)." The negation can be applied to either term of the proposition and is accompanied by a projection. This gives

erotomania:	*I* don't love him, it is I who am loved, by *her*;
delusions of jealousy:	*I* don't love him, *she* loves him;
megalomania:	I don't love anyone, I only love *myself*;
delusions of persecution:	I don't *love* him, I *hate* him, because he persecutes me.[48]

By analogy, the Camisards' variety of persecution delusion might read: "I, a Protestant, don't love him, a Catholic, because he persecutes me." Or more exactly, "I, a Protestant, don't love him, a Catholic, my father."

This was in fact the proposition that had to be denied, because it was the truth. The Protestants active from 1690 to 1704 belonged to a community marked by betrayal. There is no doubt that that community was being persecuted, martyred, but could the reality of its suffering, of the repression it brought down upon itself, really make up for the exile of the Protestant elites, the acceptance by many of forced conversion, their recanting of Protestant truth? It is as if the whole story of the Cévennes Protestants was structured around the negation of an original betrayal. In fact, the young Camisard leaders did not hesitate to speak of the "cowardice" of their fathers. They suffered from what might be called a failure of the *Non-du-Père*, the Father's "No": their fathers had not been capable of saying no to the official rejection of their faith. This unbearable knowledge necessitated a rectification of the real that involved instituting harmonious communication with the *Nom-du-Père*, the Father's Name. The young visionaries often felt guilt, suffered depression. The first "inspiration" was often accompanied with a keen feeling of having somehow committed an offense, a feeling that remained with them for a time. But this sense of culpability did not have the effect of weakening the subject; it did not lead to the impotence that may afflict someone invaded by remorse. Their sadness and depression were quickly overtaken by hallucination—in the midst of which they acted, and acted out. Guilt feeling gave way to the certitude of being persecuted: in paranoia, melancholy receded.

The fathers were not only traitors; they, too, were persecutors, and persecutors of their own children, according to those children. There was the peasant who allied himself with the parish priest against the "inspirations" of his son, the father who had his prophesying daughter put in prison, the "cruel parents" who would not let their children be, but beat them and persecuted them in the interests of their own worldly reputation.[49] There were, of course, parents who supported their children's resistance or who accompanied them in their prophesying, but in general the situation resembled that described by Elie Marion: "I had been raised, as one might think, in keeping with the wretched usage of the time: forced by some, from the beginning of my childhood, to go regularly to mass, and educated otherwise by my father and mother, but ineffectually, given the necessity in which they found themselves, because of the persecutions, to be for me themselves the example of what they disapproved of."[50] The impossibility of identifying with parents who were traitors to themselves. How could a parental imago that rubbed itself out fulfill the function of "ideal self"? In the victims of the Revocation of the Edict of Nantes we discover subjects who canceled themselves out as carriers of a true Word, who forbid themselves to be the means by which another subject might accede to that Word.

Jean Cavalier was the incarnation of this crippling configuration. In 1686 his father had signed papers drawn up for the inhabitants of his village declaring that they regarded "all those who failed in their duty to go to mass, hear sermons, and follow catechism as sworn enemies of religion and the state."[51] The son rebelled against the state and the imposed religion and escaped to Geneva; in retribution, his parents were imprisoned, his father at Carcassonne, his mother in the terrible Tower of Constance at Aigues-Mortes. When he hears the news, and fully conscious that he risks the noose, he returns to Languedoc. In the meantime his parents have been freed, and upon arriving of a Sunday at the paternal home, he finds his parents getting ready to go to mass:

> My father told me that they had been freed on condition that they fulfill their duty to the Roman Church. I pointed out that they were buying their freedom dear, for they were losing their souls, and that I would rather rot in prison than so damn myself. He retorted that my opinion was beside the point because he had promised to go to mass, that it was because I had fled that he had been persecuted, that he would be tortured if they found out I

had come back, and that if I didn't want to go to mass, he didn't want me to set foot in his house ever again.[52]

The father who throws his son out of the house with the reproach that he, the father, is in danger of being persecuted because of his son, whereas the son thought to rescue his father from persecution. An inextricable situation to which madness seems an appropriate response. The son must pay a debt, that of the father's betrayal, the reality of which the father denies at the same time as he affirms that he, the father, is paying for the son's fidelity to *his* faith. The father, a traitor to his own cause, accuses the son of supporting it.

We have here the elements of a model enabling us to understand the "fanatic" crisis: it is the pathology of a generation whose fathers have not sacrificed themselves. Fanaticism, an extreme form of loyalty to an idea or a person—let us call it the ideal self—may be seen as an attempt to compensate for paternal failure, a failure not on the order of weakness or deficiency, but rather of a betrayal by the father of his own ideal self, which in turn leads him to persecute his son, to seek to kill in his children any possible transmission of that ideal. In this sense, fanaticism may be seen as the children's response to being persecuted by their own persecuted parents.

Are other examples to be found that confirm this hypothesis? The classic mechanisms of "return," where new converts or individuals who have seized on the faith they were born into distinguish themselves by their radicalism—certain American Jews, for example, remarkable in Israel for their virulence, one of the most extreme cases being Meir Kahane—might stand as further illustrations. The appearance of religious fundamentalism in certain Muslim countries after a phase of modernization and Westernization might also be understood in this sense. One generation's abandonment of traditional ideals (or at least ideals assumed *a posteriori* to be traditional), an abandonment that took the form of its adherence to a modernist ideology during the crucial period of decolonization, is somehow being compensated for, redeemed, by the next generation's return to those ideals, for it is restoring to its proper place what has been betrayed, making restitution of what had been, it seemed, forgotten. Fanaticism is to be understood in this sense not as an immediate effect of repression but a restoring of what has been "foreclosed."

This line of reasoning makes it impossible to explain fanaticism by referring to the specifics of a given religion or doctrine, showing it rather to be a generational phenomenon, more exactly, an effect of the interaction between generations. Fanatics can be seen as reconstituting a continuity (imaginary, imagined, to be sure, as is the case in all processes of identification) with the generations preceding that of their fathers. Their violence against what their fathers loved or adopted (Catholicism for the fathers of the Camisards; Marxism or Westernism for the fathers of some of today's young Muslim fundamentalists), a love or adoption that constituted murder of *their* fathers, manifests itself all the more easily when the paternal betrayal has yielded little. The failure of "socialism" and the triumph of the bureaucracy in certain Arab countries fuels the return to ideals supposed authentic; indeed, the fathers' abandonment of these ideals is understood by the sons as the cause of the fathers' failure. This feeling can easily be galvanized into a mass movement if "modernization" has not only produced aspirations and frustrations but also defined social groups who, expecting and counting on benefits, instead find themselves stripped of both resources and cultural touchstones. Great expectations, terrible disappointments. The student who believed in the well-foundedness of his father's Westernization, who followed him on that path and even tried to go further, and who ends up suffering personal defeat because he cannot attain the social status he seeks, who is not recognized either by those who trained him or the public he was trained to serve; the frustrated apprentice bureaucrat, especially if he has spent some time in a European country and suffered humiliation there, will be ready to change paths. He will forget the language of the colonizer and return to that of his "people" and his ancestors, reject the intellectual's ideals for those of the cleric, hang up any plans to buy a new three-piece suit and slip on a jellaba instead, and even declare himself ready to make the supreme sacrifice for the faith (a faith he did not have before his terrible disappointment). Fanaticism thus appears as a deferred reaction to persecution, an effect of relations between generations. At the same time, it might be said that the history of the Camisards' war—its significance—is that of the partial and progressive acknowledgment, in the course of the eighteenth century, that Protestants had been persecuted under Louis XIV. Thus Voltaire could observe in *Le Siècle de Louis XIV* that "persecution never fails to make proselytes, especially when it is exerted against a spirit of enthusiasm."[53]

The shift in interpretation perceptible in this remark was not unanimously adopted in France, and even in the second half of the eighteenth century we may find pamphlets stigmatizing the Camisards for their fanaticism. But by then there were also French authors who portrayed the Protestants as *victims* of fanaticism.[54] If, however, fanaticism may be thought of as an effect of fanaticism, then fanatics cannot be called rebels. In fact, the principle of tolerance reached a radically new stage of development when it was constructed as a doctrine meaning precisely *tolerance of fanaticism*. This idea had been postulated as early as the end of the seventeenth century in the context of the multiplication of fanatical sects during the English Revolution. At the very moment that Bossuet was attacking such sects, John Locke, as we shall see in the following chapter, was formulating the idea that they should not be persecuted, and when the bishop of Meaux set out for Rome to mobilize support for a condemnation of Fénelon, the Toleration Act had already been passed in England (1689).

Let us return a moment to Shaftesbury and his letter on enthusiasm. Shaftesbury's purpose was not to preach tolerance *to* the fanatics, to convince them of its necessity—that would have been a waste of time:

> To prescribe bounds to fancy and speculation, to regulate men's apprehensions and religious beliefs or fears, to suppress by violence the natural passion of enthusiasm, or to endeavor to ascertain it, or reduce it to one species, or bring it under any one modification, is in truth no better sense, nor deserves a better character, than what the comedian declares of the like project in the affair of love: "You will manage it no better than if you undertook to be rationally insane."[55]

Rather he counseled tolerance *of* them, tolerance that made sense only if fanaticism found a worthy competitor in reason: "Not only the visionaries and enthusiasts of all kinds were tolerated by the ancients; but, on the other side, philosophy had as free a course, and was permitted as a balance against superstition."[56] Against those who would have the sacrilegious fanatic burned at the stake must be opposed the spirit of charity and tolerance, the spirit of philosophy, whose weapons were those of reason.

Such an optimistic view of reason reflected a belief in the progress of civilization and nourished the hope that civil society, through its own evolution, would purge itself of intolerance.

7 The Absolute Bourgeois

In November 1712, Peter I, Czar and Autocrat of all the Russias, named as his close personal adviser in matters of justice the German philosopher Gottfried Leibniz (1646-1716), who was already performing the same function for the prince elector of Brunswick-Lüneburg. Peter the Great wanted to use the philosopher, who he knew was responsible for great advances in mathematics, in his project of "making the arts and sciences flourish ever further in this empire."[1] Leibniz, who wished to help the czar "de-barbarize" his nation, submitted a variety of projects to him, at the core of which was a plan for the creation of an academy (similar to the one he designed for Berlin in 1700) with a library; collections of paintings, engravings, and medals and of mineralogical, botanical, and zoological specimens; and instruments for mechanical engineers and architects.[2] This institution was to serve as a basis for the development of schools that would teach "languages, arts, and sciences."[3] In the matter of higher education–religious, civil, military, and technical–Leibniz drew up precise curricula. His purpose in attempting to organize knowledge thus into encyclopedic, systematic, communicable form went beyond that of stimulating students' curiosity or satisfying a desire to be educated: it was necessary to "provide new discoveries in the fields of administration, the polity, commerce, the navy, crafts and manufacturing, and health," and, as he put it, "no one is participating more gloriously at present [in this cause] than His Czarian Majesty, who has a natural inclination for the sciences, has acquired great knowledge about them, and has set himself the project of making them flower in a great empire, for which he may avail himself of the advantages of Europe and China combined."[4]

For Leibniz it was a matter of practicing an "advantageous application of the sciences,"[5] which would perfect the arts and improve the lot of the empire's inhabitants, while at the same time diffusing God's infinite glory so that order and morality would be propagated among pagans, barbarians, and even savages. From this Leibnizian perspective, which we may call typical of modernity, "civil society" was an effect of scientific-technological progress, which, through the flourishing of good policies, brought about the advancement of the City of God on earth.[6] The barbarians were not to be evangelized or converted but rather introduced into the universal process of civilization.

Leibniz was sufficiently concerned that his projects succeed to have devised means of financing them. In a project for a Society of Sciences similar to the one he envisioned for the czar, this time to be established in Prussia, he imagined a financing solution in perfect harmony with the plan in that it required technical progress to fuel itself. Recently, he pointed out, water pumps for putting out fires had been invented that allowed an operator to shoot a continuous stream of water in any direction through a leather hose: "In this way, with the divine blessing, we now have a remedy for the trouble."[7] The Prussian Society of Sciences was to provide such pumps to different cities in the empire and collect a tax in exchange; every *Bürger*, every bourgeois, would be invited to contribute a sum proportionate to the value of his house—a tax that people would pay with pleasure because it was "advantageous and economical," like an insurance premium. Leibniz—who moreover proposed to extend this type of taxation, pleasant and harmonious in his estimation, to pay mathematicians to calculate the optimal paths of rivers and streams, which would then be modified or carved out accordingly to avoid future flooding[8]—was following a logic according to which progress was cumulative and civilization, founded on science, became the defining characteristic of the Earthly City. There is no trace in his scheme of a division or split between the two kingdoms, because science was rational knowledge of the world as God, through a rational choice, wished and meant it to be; from among all possible worlds, it was the one in which the quantity of evil was at its lowest possible level. Science was civilizing; it was bourgeois–if we take the bourgeois to be not only someone who possessed political rights in the city but also a rational entrepreneur, an owner who knew how to calculate.

The *Bürger als Bourgeois*, or "citizen as bourgeois," is the equation that Hegel would propose later, but there is no foreshadowing of the Hegelian revolution itself, the nonconflictive distinction between civil society and the state, to be found in Leibniz's thought. Though he may be considered the founder of modern rationality, Leibniz's political ideas seem in some respects more like a continuation of medieval thought, because, as we shall see, for him the political sphere was in no way autonomous. His vision remained hierarchical, with the City of God as its summit, even though he was active at the beginning of that century when political economy based on technology and science came to seem to many thinkers the primary or sole locus of civilization. In fact, if for Luther or Spinoza the issue of civil society was a theological and political one, in Leibniz's time a new idiom was emerging, that of political economy.

Whereas for Aristotle economy was a private matter (as the term itself, *oikos*, "household," makes clear), the passage from an agrarian society, in which writing-based culture was the monopoly of a few, to an industrial society based on universal literacy and the rationalizing of technologies that become more and more independent of any natural context and thus create their own ecology, tends to bring about the overlapping of the economy and the public space. Political economy may be taken to mean the politicization of the economy: as the domestic economy ceases to be the principal locus of production and consumption, the economic sphere and the political community, the market and civil society, begin to intersect. Through a shift, undoubtedly slow but with spectacular results, the citizen, one of whose defining characteristics in the ancient world was to be a soldier, became a bourgeois–a merchant, an industrialist operating in the public sphere, a member of civil society and an agent of the market–and the quality of being a bourgeois came to find its guarantee in that of being a citizen. The process was extremely complex, because, while citizenship continued to imply participation in civil society, that civil society itself had come to be defined as the sphere in which each one of its members sought what was useful to him, and it was this pursuit which was now guaranteed by civil and political rights. So what began as a politicization of the economic sphere resulted in the distinguishing of civil society, the economic sphere, from government, the political one.

The separation or distinction between the political sphere and civil society, which led to the latter's being defined in economic terms, reminds us that the split between the economic and the political cannot be thought of as a primordial separation, but rather as the result of a disentangling of the two through the course of history: this is demonstrated by Locke's conception of property, a conception that is consistent with his rejection of fanaticism, as we shall see.

Civil Society: Mirror of the City of God

Leibniz's belief in the effectiveness of technical progress was not unrelated to preoccupations that were, in the commonest sense of the term, political. His encouragement of the czar and various German princes reflected his concern to reinforce other European powers in the face of French domination, for in Louis XIV he saw a determined imperialist. In an effort to divert the French monarch from his grim designs, Leibniz even tried to incite him to invade Egypt–and thereby leave the Netherlands alone. The philosopher's efforts to unite all Christians, which resulted in his making a wide variety of contacts, notably Bossuet, and maneuvers, were all ultimately doomed to failure; his attempt to find some common ground between Protestants and Roman Catholics that would enable an institutional rapprochement between them– all seem designed to contain the French monarchy by finally obliging it to submit to a pontiff of all Christendom. Leibniz would have preferred Christendom united under a pope who, in contrast to the situation in the Middle Ages, would not claim infallibility to a Europe under French domination, which would cripple Germany. In a pamphlet that parodied Bossuet's style, he accused Louis XIV of having affirmed the priority of sovereignty founded on the sword. And the letters he wrote to the Palatine princess after the French monarch's death clearly expressed his judgment that the reign of the great king–the "Most Christian Mars"–had been disastrous for France and Europe.

A keen nationalism bursts through his writings from time to time, as for example when he expresses the wish that a society of German sciences would fix its sights on "the glory of God and the general prosperity of our beloved homeland, the German nation." He deplored the fact that, as the "force" of its neighbors was growing, Germany was becoming weak and that "while God has endowed the Germans with a variety of reason which, more than that of other peoples, tends toward realities"—as was shown by their language—instead of deploying this practical intelligence, they gave themselves over to drink and gambling.[9]

But Leibniz's political project cannot be analyzed primarily as a mobilization of science and technology for the sake of increasing German political force. It is less the vocabulary of mechanics or force than that of optics—light—that shaped his model of power. This paradigm allows for conceiving differences without contradiction—light being itself comparable to sound or music, we may speak, for instance of harmonic intervals—and it is this design that is to be found in his particular theory of society, which, while affirming unity, is conceived in terms of hierarchy. Leibniz could not have approved of the iconoclasts because the image, vision, and light have a highly positive value in his system. His panoptimism is a panopticon of the divine light; human subjects, to his mind, were differentiated less by their respective amounts of force than by their varying aptitudes for reflecting that divine light; that is, their power of reflection: their capacity to be as mirrors of God. We knew God's nature thanks to the same principle that enabled us to demonstrate his existence: without God there would be no causation, and without causation, nothing could be explained. It was through God that we might explain why the things that were were, and why they were not confused and mixed up every which way but rather existed together in an ineffable harmony.

The nature of God was such that he was the ultimate cause of a harmonious world: the supreme power and supreme harmony of all things. Thus it was that love for God was above all other things love of universal harmony, and therefore of the public good (*bonus publicus*), an expression of that harmony. Between universal harmony and the glory of God there existed a relation identical to that between the body and its shadow, the person (*Person*) and the image (*Bild*), between a direct ray of light and a reflected one: for universal harmony was in the facts of the world, and the glory of God was in the soul of those who knew him. But God had not endowed his creatures with reason only so that they might be a mirror in which were reflected and infinitely multiplied the rays of his infinite harmony.[10] Full knowledge and love

of God consisted in a blissful vision or celestial joy that had the effect of
concentrating that infinite beauty into a tiny point in the soul—like a
concave mirror in which the converging rays of the sun's light ignite a
fire. We are far from Calvin, for whom the Eucharist, while a mirror of
God, could yet give back no image of the invisible: here what is at issue
is not the possibility of seeing God but of seeing as God sees, by the
same light. With Leibniz, it is no longer a matter of a figurative conception of God; rather he developed the idea of an illuminative perspective, actually rewriting the laws of optics Descartes had established, changing them from geometrical formulas to trigonometrical
ones—a break with figuration in favor of reason as symbolic computa-
tion and creation.

Love of God and eternal bliss consisted in each person's grasping
God's beauty according to the particular capacity of his or her reason
and reflecting that beauty onto others. Each person might illuminate
other people and creatures in proportion to his aptitude: as we have
said, people were distinguished from one another not by their respective amounts of energy but by their capacity to catch and reflect the
divine light. They contributed to the glory of God and the public good—
contributing to the second necessarily meant contributing to the first—
according to a hierarchy of luminous intensities that represented their
different aptitudes; these constituted specific contributions to the
progress of civil society, which society in turn was born of the integration of people of differing capacities. Even those people in whom
"shadow" dominated in that their reason and potential were inferior,
who could only serve other people as mechanical instruments, were
valuable because according to the principle of universal harmony,
shadows, folds in the light, represented not a defect or lack but rather a
good and a necessity—in paintings, for instance, where they set off
areas of light.

Some were counselors. Others, who possessed both reason and
power, were orators and priests. With their grand and sublime work
they honored God by making him accessible to the senses of ordinary
people—through their sermons, music, hymns, cathedrals, but also
through their church ornaments, which brought glory to the Church as
an institution. Ornaments for Leibniz were not vain additions but aspects of God's glory, and he repeatedly attributed positive value to
images, which were also part of how the philosopher honored God.

Like priests, philosophers spoke of the power and wisdom of God in a manner that made them available to the senses, for none of God's marvels, "images" of his majesty, must be left "without reflection." But the word "philosopher" in the seventeenth century, and as Leibniz used it, also referred to theorists in science and technology, and he regarded making progress in these domains as the most valuable of human activities. Its value for him was not, as in classical political economy, connected with work crystallized into commodities nor, as for misers, with the value of money, but rather was to be calculated as light, its principle being more "luciferian" (*luciferum*: "made by light") than "lucratiferian" (*lucriferum*: "made by lucre"): "If we were to discover a new mirror of God's beauty, it would be more priceless than the most brilliant diamond."[11] Nonetheless, as we have seen with the example of the fire pumps, the luciferian quest for perfection was in no way incompatible with improving the lot of human beings, as if light were in fact being transformed into diamonds, reason into a practical instrument.

The third and highest way of expressing God's glory and honoring him was that of moral philosophers and political actors who were governors of the *res publica*, civil society–people who added good deeds to thoughts and words and who contributed concretely to the general welfare. What we have in the following passage is a paean to technology, be it the technology that perfects nature or that which perfects the life of the polity:

> Yes, it is those people who have discovered the marvels of nature and art, invented medecines, machines, and the commodities of life, discovered materials with which to help and feed the poor, to turn men away from idleness and crime and incite them to justice, to winning rewards and avoiding punishment, to preserving their repose, in general bringing about the good of the homeland, ending times when goods were dear, times of plague and war to the extent that it is in our power and to the extent that it is our duty; it is they who have diffused true religion and awe before God throughout the world, and who above all have sought only humanity's happiness and to imitate what God has made in the world.[12]

The enchantment of the world was in no way dispelled by rationality because it was rationality that enabled humanity to imitate God; concurrently, the world became a place in which the profane was made sacred–if we consider that fire wagons conventionally belong to the profane world. A certain felicity was thus possible for the human species, not that of Thomas More's *Utopia*, but one brought about through everyone's putting to use in his or her given sphere means that were small and not costly but which would nonetheless contribute to the general good. In fact, imitating God did not mean copying what he had made, but rather imitating his rational way of thinking and acting by calculating what would be the best of all possible worlds. With his concern for the improvement of general well-being or welfare (*Wohlfahrt*), which stood as the expression of divine providence in the world, Leibniz may be considered a precursor of developers of modern techniques of government meant to rationalize the welfare state through an optimal management of public policy. Conceiving a wholly calculable world and believing that these calculations might be usefully applied, Leibniz put reason and its systematic use into the service of a better "polis," one that would aim at maximizing well-being.

But at the same time as he founded a rationalist vision of society, a kind of social engineering, Leibniz also ordered the different "associations" making up that human society in a hierarchy that seems closer to Giles of Rome than to Hegel or Weber. If his vision of progress in the arts and sciences makes him the theorist of a certain continuity between civil society and the City of God, facilitating an analogy between theodicy and sociodicy, it also explicitly established the different associations that compose society along a continuum. In the political order, any kind of dichotomy "civil society/the state" would go against Leibniz's very definition of universal harmony: harmony was unity in multiplicity, and it was maximized when the greatest number of elements, seemingly disordered, were brought through an admirable configuration into the greatest agreement.[13]

In many of Leibniz's French and German texts we find no term corresponding to our notion of "the state": he distinguished territorial political units according to their size and the degree of sovereignty they might claim. In his system the city (*cité, Stadt*) was situated above the clan but below the province or kingdom. As for associations, they were not contrasted according to an Aristotelian political/nonpolitical criterion; rather in his conception of different types of association or society, civil society existed as one of the six forms of natural society that began with the family and continued up to the Church, each constituting something like a level and including all the lower levels. What

differentiated associations from one another was the particular function of each and the type of relations that obtained between those who
were part of a given association: the family, for instance, united man
and woman for the perpetuation of the species, whereas the Church
united all people for their eternal happiness. Leibniz's hierarchy took
the form of an inverted pyramid, where what was most worthy was also
most universal. Moving upward along the pyramid we find associations
whose components are more and more numerous while the functions
that they fulfill are less and less tied to the vital exigencies of the
species: reproduction in the individual couple is at the bottom of the
pyramid; followed by education of the children within the family; then
satisfaction of needs within the household (this involved the work of
servants controlled by masters); welfare in civil society, and finally,
perfect happiness at the top in the City of God. Each association conditioned the one above it while orienting the preceding one, so that
the whole system was in fact circular: the reproduction of humankind
within the couple had meaning only in relation to humankind's destiny, which was to be part of heavenly society.

Whereas Augustine opposed the two Cities and Aristotle distinguished the city, or civil society, by the type of power it implied (different from that of the master over his household or of husband over
wife), for Leibniz the path from marriage to the City of God was
straight and unbroken. His belief in structural homogeneity is marked
by the general principle upon which he based all associations—justice—
and by the fact that all six types of association were natural. Nothing
could be more alien to his conception than the idea that political association was an artifice. While he believed in technological progress
resulting from the application of science to practical problems and
in the possibility of improving life thanks to the full development of
knowledge and a more rational management of public policies, he did
not think of society as founded on an artifice such as the contract. No
association—and this was just as true of civil society as of any other
form of human aggregation—broke with nature.[14]

Leibniz worked out another way of classifying societies, this one
according to a method of conceptual differentiation; as is generally the
case, we find Leibniz more interested in the relations that obtain between things than in the things themselves. First, societies could be
either egalitarian or inegalitarian, depending on whether or not each

person in them possessed as much power as all the others. Second, they could be unlimited or limited, depending on whether or not they were concerned with the whole of life and the common good (*gemeine Beste*) or had a particular purpose (for example commerce or warfare). These distinctions enabled him to conceive different possible modalities of association. In one and the same human aggregation, different types of social ties might be found: thus it was that the family as a group could be interpreted in different ways, on the one hand, as "egalitarian-unlimited"–a group of individuals, both children and parents, endowed with reason; on the other hand, as unlimited but inegalitarian in that children must obey parents.[15] To these two distinctions, which could produce four types of social ties, he added another, that between simple and composite societies, which took into consideration, although not exclusively, the number of members in a given association. Because an unlimited society's means of reaching the common good could be very specific (education, for example, aimed at the common good but through the very specific association of teachers and students), in order to attain universal welfare different simple and composite associations had to combine with one another to form a single society, which ultimately became "a community [*Gemeinde*] under the rule of God."[16]

Because of the existing multiplicity of types of society, "society" served as a paradigm for Leibniz of false unity, that is, unity which existed only in appearance, which, instead of emanating from the nature of what was being looked at, was created by an undiscerning eye. Phenomenological unity was not real unity: the rainbow was not a substance. We have here the main postulate of Leibniz's theory of monads: "What is not truly *a* being is not truly a *being*."[17] A monad was a simple substance, without parts, whereas a thing composed of parts could not be a member of the category "substance"; to use Leibniz's metaphor, such things were foreigners in the world of monads and he was against according them "the bourgeois' right" or "citizenship rights" (*droit de bourgeoisie*) in the nation of substances.[18] While a "regulated society" was more united than a "confused mob" it was nevertheless not a substance, which differed as much from an entity formed through aggregation as a individual differed from a community such as "a people, an army, an association, or a political assembly, which are mental entities that have something imaginary about them, something that depends on a fiction created by our minds."[19] Societies, society, must be put in the category of the nonsubstantial, the phenomenal.

Among what Leibniz called substances, that is, beings that were truly one, he distinguished between corporal substances, which expressed the world rather than God, and thinking minds (*esprits*), which expressed God rather than the world. The republic of minds was under God's government; this republic was the City of God and there perfect justice and order reigned: no bad action went unpunished, nor good action unrewarded, in due proportion. Leibniz's City of God, the sum of all substances "expressing" each other under the guidance of a just God, may well seem an anticipation of the Hegelian state, which as we shall see in the following chapter is defined as morality-made-substance.[20] At other moments in his thinking, far from developing his vision of a necessarily composite larger society, the philosopher picturesquely appropriates Plato's organicizing vision of a trifunctional division of the "City": attributing the meaning "government" to "the political," he writes, "I am in the habit of comparing the political to the head, the military to the heart, and the financial to the stomach; if [the stomach] has a poor constitution, it soon spoils all the body's food and impedes the functioning of the nobler parts."[21]

As we have seen, Leibniz did not consider civil society the most elevated form of association: all the different societies, including civil society, found their end in the City of God.[22] Every soul was a living mirror of the universe, but minds, that is reasoning souls, were images of the author of nature himself. They could therefore enter into a "sort of social relationship with God,"[23] who stood in relation to them not only as an inventor in relation to his machine but also as a prince in relation to his subjects and a father for his children. The gathering in of all minds formed the City of God. Though he used the vocabulary of Saint Augustine, Leibniz was nonetheless far from sharing his eschatological vision: the point at which human history began was not for him the Creation and the Fall, but rather God's choice of the best of all possible worlds, the best, that is, from among all those that he had the capacity to conceive thanks to his infinite intelligence. At the core of this natural world created by a calculator God, an engineer God, and in which the creator's wisdom and strength were everywhere manifest, there existed a moral world: it was in this world that God's glory truly consisted, because there his grandeur and bounty were known and admired by minds; in this most elevated part of his creation God manifested his goodness. And there was harmony between the Reign of Nature and the Reign of Grace, between God, architect of the universe, and God, monarch of the divine city of minds. While observing an "economy" with regard to material substances–the economy of the architect for his construction, a relation of exteriority to what he built– God was with regard to the republic of human minds the sovereign monarch, and that republic was composed of "so many little gods under this one great God."[24]

We see that there can be no opposition between the City of God and the natural world, and obviously none between the City of God and the Earthly City. Nothing is more repugnant to Leibniz's system than discontinuity and dualism: far from presenting the City of God as in opposition or contradiction to the Earthly City, Leibniz made "humankind" into a part of the City of God, a whole too vast for us to know. And by affirming the Earthly City's inclusion in the City of God, he gave the former full value and dignity. The City of God did not stand above the Earthly City; on the contrary, it was born of the Earthly City's fulfillment.

At the same time that Leibniz's thinking greatly helped tighten the knot binding together the ideas of civil society and civilization, his contribution to the genesis of modernity–to the extent that economy would be at the core of that modernity–is also due to the fact that in his conception of the world, his "Theodicy," he used modes of reasoning that would be at the heart of the discipline of political economy–if we agree that the essence of this discipline is expressed by three purposes: maximizing the mean, maximizing the minimum (producing the least amount of evil), and maximizing equality.[25] But Leibniz's world was not one that God had in any way abandoned; the icy waters of selfish calculation did not there drown the soul. On the contrary, it was in that world that God's warmth was concentrated.

The Sovereign Is Not a God:
Leibniz as the Anti-Hobbes

An ensemble of segmented, hierarchically structured associations oriented toward the common welfare and destined to become the City of God–this theory of difference and continuity has its parallel in Leibniz's conception of sovereignty, which was to be measured by degrees.

His idea runs explicitly counter to that of Hobbes and stands as a critique of the absolutist pretensions of monarchs, essentially Louis XIV, and as an expression of the political heterogeneity that characterized seventeenth-century Germany, divided as it was into principalities, cities, and kingdoms, a mosaic of different political entities with overlapping competences and powers. We can also understand it as anticipating the modern idea of the law-governed state, if by this term we mean a state in which the sovereign's sovereignty is subject to the law.

Leibniz himself asserted that his conception of sovereignty was irreconcilable with Hobbes's. Before presenting his argument, it should be remembered that for Hobbes civil society–a generic term denoting all types of "political society" such as city, kingdom, state, and every type of political association–was the result of an "accident" rather than a "necessary disposition." Hobbes did not anchor political sociability in human nature as Aristotle had; for him human beings were not political animals but, according to the celebrated formula *homo homini lupus*, wolves to one another. "We do not by nature seek society for its own sake," but rather for the "honor and profit" that having it brings.[26] In group life we found what was needed to satisfy our self-love, our desire for glory. One need only remark the meanness of social life as manifested by mutual spite: scandalmongering and perfidious actions proved that as soon as human beings came together each sought to come out on top. This was much more than a superficial defect, even though it was best illustrated by social life in the trivial sense of the term; it was rather an anthropological structure: "in the state of nature," the will to do harm existed among all human beings. By "nature" here we should understand "essence," that which defines and characterizes and which is therefore neither temporary or accidental. It was not benevolence, good will toward the other, but fear that functioned as the cement of social life: discipline, not nature, made humanity sociable. And it was through fear of one another that individual human beings were pushed, by rational calculation, to "contract" a civil society that would bring them security. What made such civil society necessary was its capacity to procure peace–peace, which the laws of nature could not guarantee. But human beings agreeing among themselves was not enough to found a society contractually, because they were, by nature, hostile to one another. In a society that had been contracted, there had to be "some common power whereby particular men may be ruled through fear of punishment" so that peace might reign, "one will of all men" that would organize the maintenance of peace. In order for that single will to exist, individuals had to subject their individual wills to that of another individual or to that of a council, "that whatsoever his will is in those things which are necessary to the common peace, it be received for the wills of all men in general, and of every one in particular."[27] By this "submission of the wills," each person made the commitment not to oppose the will of the leader or council; the sum of all such individual commitments formed a "union." If everyone subjected his will to that of another, delivered to him "the right of his strength and faculties," and if all made the same transaction—we might say accepted the same alienation—"he to whom they have submitted hath so much power as by the terror of it he can conform the wills of particular men into unity and concord."[28] It was upon this economy of fear, this balancing of the costs (the individual's abandoning his will) and benefits (security), that civil society rested, and it represented a radical break from the state of nature.

Civil society, a *union* of wills that formed the body of the state, the Society, was also definable as "a civil person . . . *one person*": "A *city* therefore . . . is one person, whose will, by the compact of many men, is to be received for the will of them all; so as he may use all the power and faculties of each particular person to the maintenance of peace, and for the common defense."[29]

*

In a move consistent with the rest of his thinking, Leibniz rejected both this radical opposition between the state of nature and civil society (a rejection that put him more or less on the side of Aristotle) and, even more significant, the theory of political sovereignty as absolute and unitary. He proposed a vision of sovereignty as shared or limited, in the same way as he posited degrees of territorial domination—a gradualist conception diametrically opposed to that of the state as enjoying absolute, indivisible sovereignty. What he called globally "lords" (*seigneurs*) did not have identical powers, and in this diversity of degrees of sovereignty there existed no absolute sovereign power—either political or religious. There could be neither political infallibility or political absolutism.[30]

In Leibniz's opinion the concept of sovereignty had remained unclear and above all bogged down in the "deplorable mania" of jurists to concern themselves only with what was "ancient," with scholarly Roman law rather than with modern empirical knowledge and logical demonstration. He developed his definition of sovereignty or "supremacy" using territorial criteria and taking into account the type of domination exercised. This led him to distinguish three degrees of "lordship" (*seigneurie*; we might say today "domination"): the lord of jurisdiction, the territorial lord, and the potentate or sovereign. A lord of jurisdiction was competent in all matters and instances of justice but did not have the right to keep an army. What defined a territorial lord was his ability to have armed forces capable of protecting him against internal disorder or foreign attack. Finally, sovereigns or potentates are defined as "those larger powers which can wage war, sustain it, survive somehow by their own power, make treaties, take part with authority in the affairs of other peoples: powers which are somehow exempt from the commerce of private persons and which, as human affairs now stand, cannot easily fall to lower persons, or persons of lesser standing."[31] Such a sovereign benefited from the prerogatives conferred by international public right, such as embassies and ceremonies. A political territory, which could be a republic, city, dominion, region, province, was thus a space in which one type of sovereignty–even if limited and partial–was exercised.

The distinction between a lord of justice and a territorial lord is clear. The first had a jurisdictional capacity, which gave him the right to sit in judgment or apply decisions of justice, including "mild coercion against stubborn private persons." This capacity, which the jurists of antiquity had called *imperium*, gave the right to use force to the degree, here strictly limited, required to enforce legal judgments. The right to military domination belonged to an entirely different order, much higher: it was not merely a capacity to exercise coercion, even violent coercion–for example, a prince's right to have executed a person who has been condemned to death–but rather the right to mobilize a military force in order to maintain one's domination of a given territory. Finally, only the person who could assemble an armed force within his larger political territory to fight against another large political territory was a sovereign. This did not mean that domination could be exercised only through the use of armed force; the opinions of a lord's subjects also constituted a foundation for domination: reverence, worship of the lord, and recognition of his legitimacy might also found his right to rule and ensure his authority, without the use of force, for as long as his subjects were of the opinion that they must obey. There was therefore no need for a sovereign to have numerous standing forces; rather he must have the ability to mobilize great force if necessary. On the basis of this definition, territorial hegemony was identical to what the French called "sovereignty": a prince did not have to possess the right of coinage or taxation, because what mattered was "that he have in readiness the power to obtain from his subjects, either by his dignity or, when necessary, by *force majeure*, whatever rights do remain his."[32]

This conception allowed for recognizing as politically sovereign what in Germany were called prince-electors (local sovereigns who participated in the election of the emperor), whose territories other political authorities could partially control without the princes' monopoly of the use of legitimate force being infringed upon. This in turn allowed for supporting political entities whose sovereignty was not complete (because, for example, though they could mobilize troops in the interest of their own internal security or to protect themselves from foreign attack, they could not coin money) in their demand for recognition and their aspiration to play a role on the international scene, if only through the exchange of ambassadors. This is precisely what Leibniz arranged for the prince-elector of Brunswick-Lüneburg, whose sovereignty was of course limited but for whom Leibniz sought recognition at an international level.

The contrast is radical between Hobbes's conception of the "sovereign power" as one and without degree and Leibniz's conception of sovereignty, which admits the existence of corporations, royal courts, assemblies, orders. As shown by his analysis of the multiplicity of association types, Leibniz not only accepted but accorded positive value to diversity among social groups. It would be absurd to try to rule a society, necessarily diversified, as if it were an undivided substance. And his gradualist vision made him reject Hobbes's way of thinking as logically impossible: "Hobbes' fallacy lies in this, that he thinks things which can entail inconvenience should not be borne at all—[a judgment] which is foreign to the nature of human affairs."[33] The "division of supreme powers" or plurality of authorities within one political entity could indeed bring about dissension and even war. But through experience people learned to keep to a middle way, to act with prudence and moderation and avoid the extremes to which their obstinacy might push them. We might, Leibniz pointed out, observe the absence in civilized Europe of any republic (*res publica*) obeying the principles set forth by the English philosopher, as well as the absence of that anarchy which Hobbes's doctrine of the necessity of individuals' totally alienating their rights in favor of an absolute sovereign predicted for states otherwise constituted. Leibniz cited in support of his argument the various examples of Poland, Holland, and the German Empire. In contrast to Samuel Pufendorf, he did not consider this last a monster, even though the making and applying of decisions in Germany did not always require unanimity (whereas in Holland the dissent of a single city was enough to block a decision when the problem under discussion was a major one, such as peace, war, and treaty-making or signing). Even in France, "which some people put forward as an example of an absolute kingdom," the order of the *noblesse* and *les notables* were called upon to give their opinion in the context of a public assembly about the fundamental laws of the kingdom and the limits that should be imposed upon royal power, while another order of the realm, the clergy, might also intervene through "demands, negotiations, and discussions." Moreover, half the territory of France was made up of *les pays d'états*, regions with parliaments or assemblies, in which the sovereign did not have the right to levy special taxes without first consulting the opinion of the different orders. The same was true in England. In these kingdoms "anything further, exceeding custom or law, can have force only if it succeeds in the king's councils."[34]

Leibniz went further: even the emperor of the Turks was not, in the minds of his subjects, above the law. Indeed, Ibrahim, father of Mohammed IV (the Ottoman Sultan in Leibniz's time), had been condemned in accordance with a judicial procedure that involved deliberation by the highest military and civic authorities. It was the Chief Priest, the Mufti, who, following the emperor's condemnation, had ordered him to appear before God's Court, the *Shar-Allah*. His refusal would have freed his subjects from their oath of allegiance to him. In short, a power such as Hobbes had described was not any more to be found among barbarian nations than among civilized ones, and this state of affairs had nothing to do with contingency: Hobbes's sovereign was neither possible or desirable. In order for such a situation to exist, it would be necessary for those possessing supreme power to be likewise endowed with angelic virtues: if not, it was inconceivable that anyone would agree to abdicate his will to them. Who would agree to put himself utterly into the hands of any power other than God?

> For men will choose to follow their own will and will consult their own welfare as seems best to them, as long as they are not persuaded of the supreme wisdom and capability of their rulers, which things are necessary for perfect resignation of the will. So that Hobbes' demonstrations have a place only in that State whose king is God, whom alone one can trust in all things.[35]

And for Leibniz, no human being could be God, nor claim the status of divinely appointed delegate.[36] The philosopher mocked Louis XIV and his swollen pretension to being the agent of the City of God on earth in a text that he ironically attributed to an imaginary German defender of the king of France, *Mars Christianissimus* (*Most Christian War-God*). This artifice enabled him to expose the monarch's diverse turpitudes–treaty violations, disregard for promises, diverse villainies, of which his attacks on possessions of the Hapsburg monarchy at a time when it was nearly overcome by the Ottoman power were the most heinous–then use arguments to refute such accusations that made the king appear that much more monstrous. The putative author, to whom Leibniz lends his pen and wit, intends to show why the king should be excused from obeying the law, and he claims by means of his theoretical construction to be preserving Louis XIV from any criticism about his "beautiful invention":

> But, since the vulgar know nothing of this beautiful invention, one should not be surprised if those who have been freshly despoiled are tormented and move heaven and earth with tragic words, if they show us fields inundated with Christian blood to satisfy the ambition of a nation [which is the] sole disturber of the public peace, if they make us see the thousands immolated by iron, hunger, and miseries, only so that they have some cause to write on the gates of Paris the name of Louis the Great in letters of gold.[37]

The "beautiful invention" said to justify Louis XIV is the "absolute right" of which he disposed as God's "true and sole vicar of the world with respect to all temporal matters."[38] Had he not received the gift of performing miracles thanks to a holy phial of Christ's blood, and of healing the sick, which was the mark that heaven set on those who had been put on earth to extend the two kingdoms? Parodying Bossuet and his taste for demonstrations based on Holy Scripture and quotations from the Vulgate, the German apologist for Louis XIV claims to find in Christ's words a prophecy that the kings of France were destined one day to liberate the Church. Thus when Christ, in Matthew 6:28, said, "Lilia agri non nent" [The lilies of the field do not spin], his words announced that "the Kingdom of France [whose symbol was of course the fleur de lis] must not fall to the distaff side ['be ruled by a woman' but also 'fall apart'], so that the scepter not be taken away from this warlike nation and that she never submit either to foreigners or to women."[39] Let all then throw themselves into the French king's arms — the Austrians and the Germans, threatened from within by rebellion and from without by the Turks; the Dutch, who had been punished with floods for their resistance; and the Italians, who suffered from the ardors of the sun. To protect themselves against such chastisements and perform prompt repentance, each of these countries should hurry to take its place in the bosom of the anointed Lord, Louis Quatorze, whose mission was "the general restoration of the affairs of a corrupted Christendom." Appearances must not deceive: everything the king did was a miracle performed by the hand of the Omnipotent, and it was clear therefore that "French arms are destined to [support the] expansion of *religion*," not that of the *region* occupied by the French king. As for the Commonwealth of Germany, it was patently so monstrous that it must have an "absolute master" without delay to re-establish a "good government," for the term fatherland was pleasing only to idiots and the German nation should give way to "the general good of Christendom and to the orders of heaven."[40] In fact, since enlarging the kingdom of France was the same thing as enlarging that of Christ, the person who lost his freedom by becoming a subject of the French king could only rejoice.

It was by looking into the soul of the great king that one might grasp his designs, not by looking to "common right" for arguments to defend France's enterprises. And when we looked, we found a magnificent spectacle:

> This great prince has foreseen everything: he knows the evils which he does or which he permits, [and] he himself groans when he envisages the loss of so many thousands of souls. But what do you want? How can he resist the vocation from on high which obligates him? He sees that all other ways of curing the ills of Christendom, except those that he undertakes by iron and fire, would be only a palliative: gangrene cannot be cured except by means

which involve cruelty. . . . Jesus Christ himself said that he had come to bring the sword, and not peace, in order thereby to establish a true peace.[41]

We must then, together with the king's confessor, absolve the king, even pitying him (almost) for the obligation he had to fulfill of being the pitiless sword of the kingdom of God.

In this satirical pamphlet written in 1683 against Louis XIV's expansionism we are presented, in a quite different tone, with the same issues as were treated in the critique addressed to Hobbes. Indeed, Louis XIV seems the incarnation of Hobbes's sovereign, an absolute monarch resolved to "acknowledge as his judge only God, that is, the sword," a sort of monstrosity in which the pagan god of war acted as if he were the earthly vicar of Christ and consequently devastated Europe and Christendom. For the philosopher, sovereignty could be founded only on respect of natural law and, as we have said, must be limited by being divided among several loci of power: no sovereign was a God, at least not a Christian God, and the way God became effective, present, in the City was not through war and oppression, but progress and the exercise of reason.

The Fanatic Rejects the Universality of Reason

If working to perfect the Earthly City through its different forms of association was how people realized the City of God, any kind of fanaticism, the will to substitute the City of God for civil society, was absurd—as absurd as believing that a sovereign could be God. Leibniz accordingly attacked fanatics for rejecting the principle that reason is universal; their mistake was to believe that certain articles of faith might be exempt from the principle of contradiction and the principle of mathematical reasoning according to which the opposite of a true proposition was a contradictory proposition. While a given truth, such as the Holy Trinity or God's choice of the best of all possible worlds, could be above reason, it could not go against reason.[42] A fanatic was someone who misused reason by seeking to subtract the domain of faith from its legislation.

Leibniz thus gave a definition of fanaticism that would lead to the Kantian conception, a definition that we may call secular and rationalist in that it conceives of fanaticism as characterized by a logical (rather than theological) error. Unlike Bossuet or the anti-Camisard polemicists, Leibniz did not see fanaticism as involving deviance in the content of belief; it was not the raving of a false prophet. Just where he differed with the bishop of Meaux became clear at the time of the dispute about "pure love": though Leibniz did not agree with Molinos, whose *Guia espiritual* hardly satisfied him,[43] in his judgment what was needed to resolve the dispute and any "theological war between the pietists and the anti-pietists" was an adequate definition of love, and he warned against being "sectarian and schismatic"[44] in spirit when fighting against "abuses"–a "fierce and tumultuous style" may have worked well for Luther but it was not an example to be followed.[45] Unlike Bossuet, Leibniz did not appeal to the authority of the church fathers or tradition; his response was predictably more philosophical than theological. Though he found the German mystic Jakob Böhme, who had "quite surprising things to say for a cobbler,"[46] Saint Teresa of Avila, and other mystics muddled or extravagantly visionary at points, and though he even satirized William Penn, the ardent English Quaker who had founded the colony of Pennsylvania in 1681, he did not entirely reject their writings or projects. "If quietude does not go beyond contemplation of eternal truths as understood in divine perfections and a fixed gaze upon the infinitely perfect Being in his perfection, without any regard for our particular interest and for earthly things," there was nothing to be said against it.[47] In this sense, Quietism was a "spiritual artifice" that allowed "the act of divine love" to last longer than usual. But if Quietism consisted of "abandoning one's body to doing evil actions" it would be a ridiculous abuse.[48]

This danger was one of the reasons Molinos had been condemned: in "pure love" the soul, at least its superior part, was imagined to escape sin through its mystic union with God; it no longer made an effort to be virtuous, to mortify the body, and was in danger of believing that it had reached a state where it was exempt from all sin. This was the argument that the French moralist La Bruyère put in the mouth of his Quietist director of conscience–rejecting it of course:

> Our school is a school of im-pecc-ability. . . . Mystics are impeccable on earth because, being united to God by a pure faith and an essential mission, they can enjoy the pleasures of the Creature without cutting themselves off from the Creator.[49]

The satirist poet Nicolas Boileau was equally ironic in "Sur l'amour de Dieu":

C'est ainsi quelquefois qu'un indolent mystique,
Au milieu des péchés, tranquille fanatique,
Du plus parfait amour pense avoir l'heureux don,
Et croit posséder Dieu dans les bras du démon.

Thus it is from time to time an indolent mystic,
In the midst of his sins, tranquil fanatic,
Thinking to have the happy gift of most perfect love
Believes, while in the devil's arms, that he possesses God.[50]

Leibniz rejected this soul-body split, which might be used to autho-
rize licentiousness, just as he rejected a love of God that would somehow disdain Christ as incarnated mediator. Contemplation of the blessings God had given us in Jesus Christ was the best possible way of
preparing ourselves for the grace of divine love. The Incarnation–and
this was as we know one of Luther's affirmations against the fanatics–
was not a degradation, no more than was a love that brought pleasure
to the one who loved. As long as what Molinos was counseling was a
pure and disinterested love that fixed its gaze only on all that was to be
loved in God without the lover reflecting on himself or herself and the
blessings they might obtain from such love, Leibniz, contrary to Bossuet, accepted it. But he disapproved of it if "pure love" meant rejecting the obligation to think on Jesus Christ, his sacred humanity, if it
meant failing to worship the Virgin–and if it meant rejecting images.

Put another way, Leibniz rejected "pure love" to the extent that it
was iconoclastic. And it is precisely through an analogy with the love of
art that he illustrated his idea of love. The philosopher gave several
versions of his definition, but without ever changing it essentially: to
love was not in contradiction with the lover's taking pleasure on condition that the lover's pleasure was not in contradiction with what was
good for the beloved. In a letter to Bossuet he explained his thinking
thus: "To love is nothing other than to find one's pleasure (I say pleasure, and not utility or interest) in the good, the perfection, the happiness of others, and thus, though love may be disinterested, it cannot be
detached from our own good, for happiness enters into it in an essential way."[51] With this conception, Leibniz deemed it possible to resolve
the significant theological difficulty underlined by Fénelon, among
others, of achieving "non-mercenary" love. It was necessary to distinguish between utilitarian good, which was desired through self-interest, and that which was good in and of itself and was desired for itself:

"So it is that the contemplation of beautiful things is pleasant in and of itself, and that a painting by Raphael touches the person who looks at it with enlightened eyes, even though he gets no profit from it."[52] The word "profit" must here be understood to have its most commonplace monetary meaning: "If I bought a painting by Raphael in order to sell it at a profit, I would not be disinterested, but if it was for the pleasure I would have in looking at it, that would correspond to pure love."[53] Pure love, as Leibniz used the term, was disinterested love that found its pleasure in the beloved object itself without wanting to change it, obviously, and without wanting to love it for anything other than what it essentially was. Love of beauty and love of God's glory were both loves of this kind—a purified love that was not part of a strategy in which the beloved object would be reduced to a mediation enabling the lover to obtain a worldly or pecuniary benefit, but rather a love in which the beloved object enabled the lover to benefit from its (the object's) essence—in the case of the Raphael painting, its beauty; in the case of God, the universal harmony he has created.

> A person who takes pleasure in contemplating a beautiful painting and who would be grieved to see it damaged, even though it belonged to someone else, loves it, we may say, with disinterested love; this would not be the case for someone who only had his sights on profiting by selling it or being applauded by showing it off, without worrying, furthermore, about whether it will be damaged when it is no longer his.[54]

There were thus two ways of loving painting, that of the speculator who bought a painting to lock it away in a safe, hoping that it would increase in value, and the lover of painting who enjoyed it just as much in a museum as he would if he were the owner. To say that the person who does not speculate on the art market gets no pleasure from painting when in fact it is *his* love that is pure was to utter an absurdity. Pure love could be detached from our "mercenary interest," not from our "good";[55] because it was a kind of love, pure love implied pleasure and happiness.

When Leibniz read the account by William Penn (whom he designated "chef des Couakers d'Angleterre") of the trip he took to Holland and Germany after returning from America, where according to Leibniz he had been playing the "little tyrant of Pennsylvania,"[56] he did not entirely dismiss the text. Even though Penn's "magnificent" words explained almost nothing, passion and imagination could, in Leibniz's view, compensate somewhat for a lack of true light. Without true light one could not of course have true love for God, which necessarily involved knowing "his beauties," that is, the "great order and wonderful universal harmony that stands in relation to the divinity as the ray to the sun."[57] And though he liked Saint Teresa of Avila's mystic affirmation that "the Soul must conceive things as if there were but God and the soul in the world,"[58] it must be understood in terms of the definition of the reasoning soul as the mirror of God, for this was how we came to have "reason in common with God, reason which establishes not only the ties of the whole society and of friendship between men, but also [the ties] between God and man."[59] It was to be understood in accordance with the definition of God as the creator of the best of all possible worlds, a world whose beauty, visible to our eyes, was continually and ever more fully expressed thanks to progress in the arts and sciences, through a historical effect of providence:

> Now that providence has enriched our age with so many new lights resulting from the wonderful discoveries that have been made about nature and revealing to us more and more of its beauty, we should benefit from them by applying them to the ideas that Jesus Christ gives us of God. For nothing could better mark out divine perfections for us than the admirable beauties that are to be found in his works.[60]

The danger inherent in the ways of Quakers and mystics was that of turning us away from the search for "natural truths," when in fact "the more we know nature and the solid truths of the real sciences, which are so many rays of divine perfection, the more we are capable of truly loving God."[61] In the dispute about the value of pursuing intellectual work in monasteries that developed between the Benedictine monk and scholar Jean Mabillon and the reformer of the Trappist monks, Rancé, it was clear whose side Leibniz took; he found it strange that one could prefer ignorant monks to learned ones.[62]

Nothing could be more repellent to Leibniz than obscurity; there was nothing he loved more than light. He could conceive of shadow only as part of an aesthetic of chiaroscuro: it was chiaroscuro that made the art of painting special and that corresponded best to the principle of universal harmony.[63] Imagining a world without shadow would be as absurd as imagining a painting void of all form. Still, our gaze upon the world must not be merely that of an art lover, originating from one fixed point: we might better see the world if our way of looking was improved: "Since we cannot notice the beauty of a given perspective when the eye is not placed in a fitting position for looking at it, we should hardly find it strange that the same thing happens to us in this life."[64] But this correct way of looking at the world, which would enable us to discover its harmony, must not plunge us into passive contemplation, for "true morality or piety, far from supporting the idleness of certain lazy Quietists, ought to incite us to cultivate the [practical] arts."[65] In short, the true struggle against fanaticism consisted in contributing to the progress of civilization.

Locke and the Birth of Tolerance

Around 1690, Leibniz struck up an imaginary dialogue with Locke, part of which concerned fanaticism. Locke is important for our genealogical study not only because he was a major contributor to the development of the notion of toleration but also because he played an important role in the history of the notion of civil society.

Indeed, in the 1667 *Essay Concerning Toleration* we find a reflection on both the "fanatiques" and "civil society," in which Locke sought to show the "danger of establishing uniformity" and considered "how it comes to pass that Christian religion hath made more factions, wars, and disturbances in civil societies then any other, and whether toleration and latitudinism would prevent those evils."[66] In the course of the English Revolution, as we have noted, the term "fanatic" was used to attack Cromwell and designate extremist political-religious groups.[67]

The issue of tolerance was, in this context, a political one, and took the following form: What opinions did the political power have the right to prohibit? It was not a matter of political powers questioning religious authorities about what *they* might accept as variations in interpretation of dogma (their exclusionary response was entirely predictable), but of discovering the principle that would allow for the determination of which opinions might have *legal* status and legitimacy. By posing the problem of tolerance not as a religious, theological one but as a political, civic one, Locke was positing the principle of "freedom of conscience" from the point of view of "civil society." The purpose of the political power was to ensure the general well-being of individuals in society; a monarchy, even one claiming "divine right," was not absolute and it could have no other end than the preservation and "welfare" of its subjects during their lifetime. The magistrate's

power and authority derived from the "grant and consent" of its subjects (Locke was writing ten years after the publication of Hobbes's
Leviathan), and its sole purpose was their preservation. With this in
mind, it became appropriate to distinguish between different types of
opinion. "Purely speculative opinions," which could not disturb the
commonwealth (state) and did not wrong my neighbor, had a "just
claim to an unlimited toleration";[68] likewise, the political power had
no business interfering in the way I worshiped "my God" or in anything concerning "my private interest in another world," for if that
power had nothing to say about the house I bought or my choice of a
wife, choosing my religion was even less a matter for its concern: if God
had wanted to force his creatures into heaven, he would hardly have
made use of the magistrate's "outward violence on men's bodies, but
the inward constraints of his spirit on men's minds."[69] Everyone, then,
had the right to determine his religion according to his own criteria;
this was a matter for the private sphere: if someone chose to be rebaptized, that would not provoke a tempest in either the river or the state.
Whether I observed Friday as my day of rest, with the Mohammedans,
Saturday with the Jews, or Sunday with the Christians; whether I followed the "pompous" religious ceremonies of the papists or the more
sober ones of the Calvinists—none of these choices could make me a
bad subject for my prince or a bad neighbor to my fellow citizens. What
was needed therefore was "perfect uncontrollable liberty":[70] as soon as
a religion was permitted at all, Judaism in a Christian realm, for example, the magistrate might no longer interfere in its forms of worship.
This was the opposite of what would happen if ambition or factiousness
ran free. To put it briefly, what threatened toleration was uncivil, un-
civic passions.

It was not conviction, faith, that was at issue in toleration: no matter
how strong one's beliefs might be about what sin was, what duty was,
this level of belief was not relevant to the political point of view. The
only rule that the sovereign must follow in his choices was to consider
"the civil good and welfare of the people."[71] The welfare state's first
responsibility of taking into account the people's well-being provided a
principle for guiding political choice; at the same time it set a limit on
the prince's powers: he could not privilege his own convictions to the
point of seeking to impose them on all his subjects. From the point of
view of the King of kings, the difference between the temporal sov-

ereign and his subjects was not so great that the former might establish himself as an absolute master in this matter. This meant that while the "lawmaker" did have the right to limit the *expression* of opinions that could disturb the public order, he could not force anyone to renounce his opinion.

Acknowledging its strangeness, Locke then made the following affirmation: "The lawmaker hath nothing to do with moral virtues and vices": "God hath appointed the magistrate his viceregent in this world, with power to command; but 'tis but, like other deputies, to command only in the affairs of that place where he is viceregent." Locke was referring of course to the political sphere, whereas the relation between the soul and God was "private" and belonged to a "superpolitical" order: the state of the public weal was to concern itself only with peace and respect for property, with the "quiet and comfortable living of men in society one with another," not with the welfare of the human soul.[72] The magistrate therefore was not to oblige anyone to practice virtue for itself, but rather because it was "advantageous" for communal life. Religious membership was even less of a threat than membership in a guild: "Men united in religion have as little and perhaps less interest against the government than those united in the privileges of a corporation."[73] On the other hand, the freedom of believers who recognized a political authority other than the magistrate–namely, the Roman Catholics–must be strictly limited.

Locke was specifically interested in the English case, which involved both "papists" and "fanatiques," and his conclusions were intimately tied to the immediate English historical context. "Papists are not to enjoy the benefit of toleration because, where they have power, they think themselves bound to deny it to others."[74] They were bound by "a blind obedience to an infallible pope," that is, to a "foreign enemy prince." Moreover, the exclusion of the papists would make the king of England chief of all Protestants and would win him international support. In regard to those designated by the "opprobrious name" of fanatics, that is, members of extremist religious sects, Locke, still reasoning in political terms, predictably proposed a completely different attitude: while papists must be rejected, fanatics must be made into supports for the government, because, contrary to the Catholics, they were not caught up in a mechanism of mixed loyalties. Above all, they must not be persecuted.[75]

Locke's defense of tolerance would be less convincing were it not accompanied by a critique of persecution, here conducted in terms of feasibility and profitability: persecution could only fail, because having an opinion constituted "the dignity of a man." This might be empirically verified by considering the persistence with which Christians captured by the Turks and made into galley slaves clung to their faith. Persecution would reduce England to one vast galley where none would be protected. More important, while persecution was powerless to change the beliefs of the person who suffered it, it had the effect of aggravating the danger by transforming a visible, honest adversary into a secret, treacherous enemy. Persecution gave energy to its victim and ended up uniting all dissidents into one camp—with the shared status of state enemy. In other words, in the fight against the fanatics, the Puritans, it was imperative not to adopt the logic of war: to reduce England to "uniformity" would involve a degree of violence incompatible with Christianity—only "total destruction" could accomplish it.

While fundamentally political in nature, the problem of fanaticism for Locke was also philosophical and demanded conceptual elaboration. This was the object of book 4, chapter 19 ("Of Enthusiasm"), of *An Essay Concerning Human Understanding*, published nearly thirty years later, in 1690. The word "fanatic" is not to be found in it, undoubtedly because of the highly polemical charge it had acquired during the English Revolution. An enthusiast, according to Locke, was someone who, seeking to establish revelation without reason, destroyed both at the same time and "substitute[d] in the room of them the ungrounded fancies of a man's own brain, and assume[d] them for a foundation both of opinion and conduct."[76] The enthusiast took "the conceits of a warmed or overweening brain" as an illumination from God, that is, a divinely authorized illumination, and let himself be guided by the firmness of his persuasion as by an "*ignis fatuus*, that leads [him] continually round in this circle: it is a revelation because [he] firmly believes it, and [he] believes it because it is a revelation."[77] Reason, the natural power of revelation that God had planted in humanity, was the ultimate means of evaluating the supernatural: "God when he makes the prophet does not unmake the man. He leaves all his faculties in their natural state, to enable him to judge of his inspirations, whether they be of divine origin or no. When he illuminates the mind with supernatural light he does not extinguish that which is natural."[78] Locke was not denying the existence of divine revelation, but rather demonstrating that a revelation could not be considered divine without its first being submitted to reason's examination; only this procedure enabled us to determine that our illumination was not false.

In the imaginary dialogue Leibniz pursued with Locke as a response to this text, under the title *New Essays on Human Understanding*,[79] the German philosopher was understandably in complete agreement with him about enthusiasm. Unlike Locke, he did use the term "fanatic" and even listed certain precise examples, including the Quakers, Jakob Böhme, and Antoinette Bourignon.[80] Fanatics and enthusiasts could also be mystics, and fanaticism could be defined as the mystic's claim to having an immediate relationship with God. In his preface to the *New Essays*, in which he denounced the Quietists for imagining that "the soul is absorbed into and reunited with the sea of the divinity,"[81] Leibniz criticized the "fanatical philosophy" that "saves all phenomena by ascribing them immediately and miraculously to God." Immediate, unmediated God–this was the motor of fanaticism.[82] Leibniz could therefore only adhere to Locke's formulation, "Reason must be our last judge and guide in everything," even though the metaphysical foundation that he proposed for such a conclusion was quite different. Both philosophers' diagnoses of the problem of enthusiasm or fanaticism underlined the influence of a disproportionately large degree of figurative power–fancy, imagination–in relation to reason.

Taking reason as a guarantee rather than one's own fancy as a guide meant acknowledging that "the firmness of our persuasions is in no way proof of their being right"–the very acknowledgment that zealots of all camps refused to make. If reason was not considered the only means of judging what was true, each would be persuaded that his light came to him from God and it would be impossible to maintain a peaceful public space.

Government and Civil Society:
The People Are Endowed with Reason

Locke appears in the genealogy of the concept "civil society" primarily because of the place he accorded to property in social organization: it was in order to preserve their property that people formed communities and placed themselves under governments, for this could not be accomplished in the state of nature. Property, which should here be understood broadly, as an anthropological rather than economic reality–for Locke freedom and life itself were as much property as personal possessions–could only be guaranteed in civil or political society, the two terms being synonymous. The relevant distinction to be established was between civil society and the family: the master of a family had only certain distinct, circumscribed powers over the other members, whereas in civil society the power to punish occupied a crucial place. The state of nature gave birth to free individuals possessing equal rights: everyone had received the power not only to preserve his property–"life, liberty, and estate"–from depredation at the hands of others, but also to judge and punish infractions of this law, even by death. The right to property was reciprocal; I recognized it as a right of others, and also as giving me the right to protect myself from attacks others might make on my property. Civil society existed only where private property was guaranteed by the possibility of punishing "the offenses of all those of that society": it was therefore necessary for each of civil society's members to have "resigned" his natural power to punish "into the hands of the community in all cases that exclude him not from appealing for protection to the law established by it." The right to judge and punish was the monopoly of the political community, which had the status of "umpire." The essence of civil society resided not, then, in the actual possession of property but in the *right* to own property: in the state of nature everyone was judge and executioner, whereas "those who are united into one body, and have a common established law and judicature to appeal to, with authority to decide controversies between them and punish offenders, are in a civil society with one another."[83]

Political society's monopoly of force was thus a consequence of its juridical and judicial monopoly, and Locke defined civil society in terms of the legal limitation of power. Let us remark first of all that this places it in quite a different perspective from that of the power state: domination by an absolute prince was incompatible with the existence of civil society, which supposed an authority that everyone might refer his case to if he believed himself injured and that everyone must obey, so that none might be both judge and party to the case. The transition from the state of nature to civil society was also the transition to a mode of collective organization that included law, a judge to apply it, and force to ensure that it was respected. What was beyond the state of nature, then, was not the erecting of an absolute power capable of putting an end to the war of all against all, but the emergence of law and the institutions bound up with it.

What founded civil society was the "agreement which every one has with the rest to incorporate and act as one body, and so to be one distinct commonwealth."[84] This is why only conquest by a foreign power could dissolve a political society: in such a case, each person would return to his prior state and seek his security by associating with other persons in a new society. In the case of such dissolution and recomposition, it was justified to affirm that the conqueror's sword "cut up government by the roots and mangle[d] societies to pieces."[85] However, though the government (the equivalent of a political regime) found in civil society the ultimate condition for its existence, the converse was not true.[86] Disintegration of governments from within–not at all the same sort of upheaval as conquest from without–might be caused by several types of social dysfunction.[87] The consequence of this is crucial: if as Locke affirmed civil society had primacy over government, the "community" over the "state," individuals associated into a body over the political authorities, and if the end of civil society was to ensure the security of its members, then the people had the right to judge whether or not the legislative power or the prince was acting in a way that went counter to that mission. From this followed the people's right to active resistance and to "resume their liberty."[88]

Just as reason was the supreme legislator and should have the last word over and against enthusiasm, so civil society rejected all absolute power, which flouted its very raison d'être–the security of its members –and claimed against the absolute prince its ability to know what was best for it and the right of the people, endowed with reason, to have the final say. There was no need to fear that the right to resist governments would open the way for demagogues and troublemakers. As long as the "ill designs" of their leaders did not move the "masses," the "people, who are more disposed to suffer than right themselves by resistance, are not apt to stir."[89] But if the people

> universally have a persuasion grounded upon manifest evidence that designs are carrying on against their liberties, and the general course and tendency of things cannot but give them strong suspicions of the evil inten-

tion of their governors, who is to be blamed for it? . . . Are the people to be blamed if they have the sense of rational creatures, and can think of things no otherwise than as they find and feel them?[90]

It was because the people, that collective singular noun, that singular collective, was capable of reasoning that its right to resistance was well founded. We could say that the people's situation in an absolute monarchy, where they would be utterly deprived of the right to use their reason to criticize the political power, is analogous to that of enthusiasts, who for Locke have renounced their reason (the difference being that the first are dominated by a power external to them, the second by a power they have in a way internalized):

> Reason is lost upon them . . . they see the light infused into their understandings, and cannot be mistaken; it is clear and visible there, like the light of bright sunshine; shows itself and needs no other proof but its evidence; they feel the hand of God moving them within, and the impulses of the Spirit, and cannot be mistaken in what they feel.[91]

For both the people under absolute monarchy and the enthusiast under the absolute spell of inspiration it is absolutely impossible to use reason as a critical faculty.

We may thus discover a similarity between Leibniz and Locke in their common rejection of the Hobbesian solution to the problem of the transition from the state of nature to the social state: the sovereign could not be considered absolute; civil society had preeminence over the king. Reason claimed for itself the authority to judge in all things, and if Locke could allow Revelation, it was because he judged it to be in accord with reason. This meant that whatever the institutional relations between church and state, the religious power and the civil one, the City of God and the Earthly City, the Church could no longer be erected above the earthly realm, and if there was an entity that could play, in relation to the government, the role claimed by the medieval Church, it was the people. The transfer of sovereignty from which civil society benefited by its identity as the locus of civilization–it was the effective and progressive realization of the City of God–composed of citizens endowed with reason guaranteed its autonomy in a system where the Church, its status profoundly affected, had lost the monopoly on truth and goodness. Reason, the individual's faculty for conceiving the universal, founded the people's political claim to be the foundation of civil society.

Civilization and Its Discontents

Having placed Leibniz and Locke at the center of the development of toleration, we could show how the concept's value was progressively affirmed throughout the eighteenth century, namely by Voltaire – but it is perhaps more interesting to consider a counterexample, that of Jean-Jacques Rousseau, apologist for fanaticism.

Rousseau deals directly with fanaticism as a political problem: "fanaticism" is what would result from the "science of salvation" embracing that of "government."[92] To his mind, true Christian religion did not involve an institutional system (this affirmation obviously places him within the Protestant tradition, in opposition to the Catholic Church), and it did not have to do with the state or civil society, the two terms being for him synonyms.[93] Whereas philosophers had denounced fanaticism, Rousseau criticized "proud philosophy," whose dogmatism itself was to him a source of fanaticism. And pitting himself against "the philosophical turn" of the likes of Pierre Bayle, whose *Dictionary* included a series of attacks against intolerance, he set out to defend fanaticism. Though "delighting in cruelty and blood," fanaticism was "a magnanimous passion" that "animates the human breast, inspires it with a contempt of death, and gives it an extraordinary spring," whereas the reasoning mind of the philosophers abased and demeaned the soul and sapped society's strength, "concenter[ing] all the passions in the mean principle of self-interest and that abject thing called self." Rousseau thus sought to rehabilitate fanaticism for the ethical and political effects it had of extracting the subject from his particularity and creating "the sublimest virtues."[94] "Sublime" – the same word that Kant, a great reader of Rousseau, would associate with enthusiasm in his favorable assessment of the French Revolution. Was that not a moment in history when the subject, torn from his clammy and gastric ad nauseam little self, committed himself to realizing humanity's moral destiny? For the author of *Emile*, as for the author of the *Critique of Judgement*, the sublime was an actualizing of the ethic sense, which acted by exacerbating the emotions. (It becomes clear why Baudelaire evoked Jean-Jacques in *Les Paradis artificiels* apropos of enthusiasm.)

It wouldn't be exact to affirm that fanaticism for Rousseau restored something that had been lost with the state of nature; it was rather a sort of compensation for the brutal shift to civil society, for this disaster was irreversible and any attempt to go back to what had been, absurd. Among the "depravations" that characterized civil society for Rousseau–language, reflection, rational calculation, luxury, and the list continues–the most remarkable was the swelling of *amour-propre* (egotistical self-love), which Rousseau was careful to distinguish from the right kind of self-love, the duty of self-preservation, which, together with piety, was the source of all natural law. Civil society, which was based on property, developed *amour-propre*, whereas fanaticism pulled one up out of such narcissism. Fanaticism was thus a way of surpassing the distinction "be/appear," which had permitted the development of luxurious display, cunning, and all the vices that went with them;[95] it represented a break with narcissism and the specular antagonism that characterized social relations. The constant, appalling paradox was that once the march toward civil society had begun, life in society always led to its opposite. It was precisely because social life developed ties of solidarity among individuals that it accentuated their withdrawal into self, selfishness, and rivalry:

> The isolated individual is so weak a being–at the very least we can say that his strength is just barely sufficient for his natural needs and his primitive state–that should that state change in the least or his needs increase, he could no longer do without his fellows. And when, as a result of progress, his desires embrace all of nature, the whole of humankind working together hardly suffices to satisfy them. Thus it is that just as the same causes that make us mean also make us slaves, and just as our weakness is born of our cupidity, so our needs bring us together in the same measure as our passions drive us apart, and the more we become enemies the less we can do without one another.[96]

Presented thus *within* the framework of civil society, wasn't fanaticism a way of setting one's sights on the universal? An aim that, let it be said in passing, would have to be qualified as "savage" if considered from the perspective of that regulated, policed universal that is the Hegelian state. The fanatic, according to Rousseau, was a virtuous being who went beyond a life reduced to a mediocre routine, who sought to transcend that limit. It is understandable that he particularized it by the word "sublime"; his excessiveness is both a demand and a sign–the demand for a civil society where the ethical content inscribed by nature in humanity would not be denatured or eclipsed, and a sign–the very fact that fanatics existed–that to hope for such a society was not absurd. Rousseau's iconoclasm is accountable to his seeing in the arts and sciences not an abusive mediation between humanity and God that would lead to idolatry but rather a corruption that weakened peoples and polities: had not the Romans lost their military virtues in the course of becoming lovers of engravings and paintings? The fanatic and the iconoclast thus manifested, through their civic virtues, the persistence within civil society of the state of nature, even though that state had been perverted by civil society itself. But while Rousseau was clearly nostalgic for Roman-style citizenship based on virtue as inculcated by fathers whose "government" was more severe than that of any magistrate's, he knew that the "continual miracle" that had been Rome would never take place again; that type of citizenship was thus more useful in bolstering his critique than in shaping a model for the modern political state based on alienation of the individual will and the sovereignty of the people. In fact Rousseau agreed that within the state as he knew it, religious fanaticism was a threat that had to be put down.

How? Rousseau's solution, similar to Spinoza's, was the establishment of a state religion: "External worship should be organized with the purpose of maintaining peace in the state," he wrote in the final chapter of *Du Contrat social*, "On Civil Religion." The "true citizen" is presented as a "fanatic," transformed by civic religion and hoping to receive "the life to come" as his reward for "virtue." The apology of "fanaticism" was accompanied by a paean to tolerance as a social principle: Rousseau defended the *ethical* relevance of fanaticism, but in no way conceived of it as a *social* value. The fanaticism we find in *Emile* is, moreover, that which might arise from taking individual virtues to an extreme – Roman-style fanaticism – rather than the fanaticism of the believer for whom "outside the Church there is no salvation." *That* formula Rousseau clearly condemned as founding an equation between state and church and instituting theocracy.[97] The social pact accorded rights to the sovereign, whose sole aim was public utility: the sovereign could have nothing to say about people's opinions except as they might affect the community as a whole. It was important for the state that the citizens had a religion, but religious dogma pertained to civil society only to the degree that it touched on moral principles and constituted a profession of faith involving sociability, for religion was in a way sociability's condition of possibility. It followed from this that all those who rejected religion and fought against it must be banished from the state. The religion in question, however, could not be Christianity, "a wholly spiritual religion, taken up only with things of heaven" and incapable of providing a foundation for citizenship, because, quite the opposite of Roman citizens, "true Christians are made to be slaves."[98] The religion the state was to take charge of as its own foundation was reduced to a few essential dogmas, fixed by the sovereign; everyone could add their own dogmas, provided these did not contradict the sovereign's. The positive dogmas included existence of the divinity, life after death, the sanctity of the social contract and the laws. As for the dogmas expressed in negative terms, they came down to one: the absolute rejection of intolerance. There was no need to distinguish between civic and ecclesiastical intolerance: since one could not live in peace with people one believed to be damned, religious intolerance necessarily became political intolerance. And intolerance could only provoke the war of all against all, because the intolerant person and the person conceived by Hobbes as bringing on a generalized state of war were one and the same. Since in Rousseau's estimation an exclusive national religion had become impossible, all religions that tolerated other religions must themselves be tolerated: toleration alone was what allowed civil society to subsist.

Rousseau's particular rejection of fanaticism is consistent with his apology for it: both are based on his condemnation of the inflated self. While Roman-style civic fanaticism provided a way of freeing oneself from egocentrism, being tolerant was the equivalent of admitting that the other was not "obligated to think as I do to be saved." Being Christian, a citizen, a person implied that "I do not believe anyone to be guilty before God for not having the same ideas about worshiping him as I do."[99]

As was demonstrated by the appalling persecution of the Protestants—the mildest and most sociable of sects, in Rousseau's judgment—intolerance not only deprived those who were persecuted of their rights as citizens, but it reduced them to less than human.[100] Once the process of denaturalization had been set in motion—for the human being could be considered a depraved animal[101]—a person's humanity seemed no longer guaranteed by the possession of a kind of essence, but had to be actively defended and promoted: the purpose of civil society and citizenship was to ensure the conditions of humanity, and this in turn meant that in the absence of *natural* sociability, human beings could only remain human because they were citizens. It was not that civil society emanated from human nature, but rather that civil society guaranteed "de-natured" persons access to their humanity:

> Though there is no natural general society between men, though they become bad and unhappy in becoming sociable, though the laws of justice and equality mean nothing to those who live both independent of the state of nature and subject to the needs of the social state, rather than believing that there can be no more virtue or happiness for us and that heaven has abandoned us without resources to the depravity of our species, let us strive to find in the evil itself the remedy that may cure that evil: let us repair the internal vice of the general association by forming new associations.[102]

*

Rousseau's vision of civil society provoked a multitude of dissenting responses, among them that of Adam Ferguson, the Scottish political economist and author of *An Essay on the History of Civil Society* (1767).[103] For Ferguson civil society did not constitute a break with nature. He established a parallel between the development of the individual and that of the species: just as a person advanced from infancy to maturity, so humanity progressed toward civilization, the state of nature and civil society being situated on a continuum—a palace was not natural, of course, but neither was a thatched cottage. Against Rousseau, Ferguson affirmed that the attributes of human nature, among them articulated sounds—language—were social in character and that the human species must be considered in terms of groups, for this was how it had always existed. But though he believed humanity to be naturally sociable, Ferguson did not consider human beings animals, because what characterized them was the artificiality of their existence. There was then no "analogy" to be made between human beings and animals; "art itself is natural to men," who, contrary to animals, did not have instincts but were moved instead by interest.[104] As for knowledge, it was the result of sensation and practice. One could not speak of any state of nature, for if one accepted that human beings were *by nature* able to perfect themselves, one could not turn around and say that their first steps toward that perfection were steps *away* from nature. In the vocabulary of modern anthropology, we would say that for Ferguson, culture was humanity's distinguishing characteristic, and that even as savages, human beings had never lived in natural surroundings. In this artificial world, the human species did not develop linearly, because history was characterized instead by perpetual tension, namely between contradictory tendencies within individuals, who were "to one another mutual objects both of fear and love."[105] History had successively produced the savage, the barbarian, and civilized man. But though there was evidence of humanity in the savage's condition, full freedom had only come to be within governed and civilized nations. The savage had personal freedom and lived in a state of equality with the other members of his tribe, and the barbarian had a kind of independence because he had "courage and a sword,"[106] but only a good government could provide for the regular administration of justice or form a force within the state for defending the rights of its members. Furthermore, following through on the model of individual development, every society might after "childhood" and "adulthood" fall into decline and decay—in fact, Rousseau and Ferguson have in common a pessimistic vision of civilization:

> To the ancient Greek, or the Roman, the individual was nothing, and the public every thing. To the modern, in too many nations of Europe, the individual is every thing, and the public nothing. The state is merely a combination of departments, in which consideration, wealth, eminence, or power, are offered as the reward of service. It was the nature of modern government, even in its first institution, to bestow on every individual a fixed station and dignity, which he was to maintain for himself. Our ancestors, in rude ages, during the recess of wars from abroad, fought for their personal claims at home, and by their competitions, and the balance of their powers, maintained a kind of political freedom in the state, while private parties were subject to continual wrongs and oppressions. Their posterity, in times more polished, have repressed the civil disorders in which the activity of earlier ages chiefly consisted; but they employ the calm they have gained not in fostering a zeal for those laws and that constitution of government to which they owe their protection, but in practising apart, and each for himself, the several arts of personal advancement, or profit, which their political establishments may enable them to pursue with success. Commerce, which may be supposed to comprehend every lucrative art, is accordingly considered as the great object of nations, and the principal study of mankind.[107]

Ferguson nonetheless insisted that society was based not only on individual interest but also on affection and friendship, as might be seen in the Greeks' love for their country or the patriotism of the Romans—in fact he exalted civic virtues not unlike those associated with the fanaticism touted by Rousseau.[108] And he underlined the value of war:

> Without the rivalship of nations, and the practice of war, civil society itself could scarcely have found an object, or a form. Mankind might have traded without any formal convention, but they cannot be safe without a national concert. The necessity of a public defense has given rise to many departments of state, and the intellectual talents of men have found their busiest scene in wielding their national forces.[109]

War was not evidence of the cruelty or barbarity of human nature, but rather of the human capacity for feeling disinterested love; their patriotism attested that they were endowed with sensibility and compassion. In Ferguson's estimation, giving primacy to commerce in civil society degraded it,[110] and he contrasted this state of affairs with that of the Native American tribes: "The principal point of honour among the rude nations of America, as indeed in every instance where mankind are not greatly corrupted, is fortitude."[111] Going against doctrines that founded civil society not on ethics and civic conscience but on the blind play of individual self-interests, the economy, Ferguson acknowledged that if it were true, as was said of all commerce-practicing nations, that people in them were dominated by self-interest,[112] it did not follow that this natural penchant of theirs turned them away from society or from mutual affection. There was, he asserted, evidence to the contrary, even in places where self-interest held the strongest sway. Ferguson pointed out the necessity for something other than interest to regulate civil society, and he situated this means for humanity to perfect itself in a society's government and the virtue of its citizens.[113]

Kant and Hegel would theorize this anchoring of morality in public law, taking into account the social and political transformations brought about by the French Revolution, a moment when political fanaticism and the ideal of legal regulation both combined with and confronted each other.

8 The Citizen as Bourgeois

Polite, civilized, urbane–adjectives that trace the figure that Hegel called the *Bürger als bourgeois*, "the citizen as bourgeois." This was the equation he posited a little more than a hundred years after Leibniz had made reason-in-practice the active principle of civilization and progress. The triumph of the *Bürger-bourgeois*, practical in the case of the French Revolution, theoretical with Hegel, would be vigorously invalidated by Marx, who condemned citizenship for being necessarily bourgeois and who sought to return to Luther's original inspiration: according to Marx and Engels, as we shall see in Chapter 9, Luther had betrayed himself by abandoning his project for the revolutionary unification of Germany. Hegel, on the other hand, took Luther to be the spiritual founder of Germany.

Leaving Marx's reading of Hegel for a moment in order to grasp the latter's idea, we may say first of all that the Hegelian bourgeois was not a citizen *because* a bourgeois; rather he could only be a bourgeois because he was a citizen. To put it another way, it was less actually owning property that defined the bourgeoisie than the *right* to own property. Civil society, the bourgeois's civil society, only existed thanks to the law-governed state. Hegelian civil society was neither the origin or the whole of society: the philosopher carefully theorized the distinction between civil society and the state, placing the state in the dominant position, attributing to it the key role. For his part Marx claimed to be expressing civil society's protest against being put in a subordinate position, a protest that in his opinion both Luther and Hegel had repressed. Marx wished to return civil society to what he considered its primary place in social structure and the dynamic of history.

What we have called the Hegelian revolution, namely the nonconflictual distinction between civil society and the state, is all the more remarkable in that it is hard to find any anticipation of it. On the other hand, we have no difficulty perceiving a continuity between Kant and Hegel (even though the latter did not distinguish civil society from the state), in the sense that both may be taken as theorists of the law-governed state. In this perspective, what defined the bourgeois was less his wealth than the legal status of property as tied to civic and political rights. For Hegel, citizenship meant participation in civil society, which he defined as the sphere in which each member sought what was useful to him, but a member's very status as a self-interested individual was guaranteed by his political and civic rights. The legal guarantees emanating from the state made economic life and the bourgeoisie's existence possible. Rather than seeing in Hegel an interpreter of Ricardo's political economy, it is well to rediscover, to recover, the weight of the political and juridical in his definition of civil society. Still, it would be at the very least a methodological error to reduce Hegel to the status of Kant's successor, for despite the crucial role given by both philosophers to right and law, they differed radically in their ways of theorizing fanaticism.

Upon learning of the outbreak of the French Revolution, Kant, according to the celebrated anecdote, departed from the immutable routine of his life, modified his schedule. His was an enthusiastic reaction: the epithet could not be more exact.

Kant's Revolutionary Enthusiasm

Almost ten years after the wave of affect that crashed over Europe with the events of 1789 had reached Königsberg, Kant wrote the following assessment in *The Contest of Faculties*, "An Occurrence in Our Own Times Which Proves This Moral Tendency of the Human Race":

> The revolution which we have seen taking place in our own times in a nation of gifted people may succeed, or it may fail. It may be so filled with misery and atrocities that no right-thinking man would ever decide to make the same experiment again at such a price, even if he could hope to carry it

out successfully at the second attempt. But I maintain that this revolution has aroused in the hearts and desires of all spectators who are not themselves caught up in it a *sympathy* which borders almost on enthusiasm, although the very utterance of this sympathy was fraught with danger. It cannot therefore have been caused by anything other than a moral disposition within the human race.[1]

Enthusiasm such as that excited by the spectacle of the French Revolution was the "idea of the good to which *affection* [affect] is superadded,"[2] "a tension of forces produced by ideas." Aesthetically, enthusiasm was "sublime"; it arose from a moral cause—there was for Kant no necessary contradiction between the aesthetic and the moral—and even though it was an emotion and therefore not to be entirely approved of, it had to do with "the ideal"—in the case of the French Revolution, a people's right to endow itself with a republican political constitution. Kantian enthusiasm was not so much a mobilizing emotion commanding an active type of energy as it was a feeling that revealed with certainty that humanity was progressing and would continue to progress toward what was better, the sign of a faculty for self-improvement in the human species. Enthusiasm brought about a certain exaltation, including in those who contemplated the Revolutionary armies' victory from the outside, a victory itself made possible by the enthusiasm of the players, whose aim was to win certain rights for their people. As an ethical emotion, enthusiasm could not be excited by self-interest; the mediocrity of written-for-hire attacks against the French Revolution amply testified to this. The sublime in history was analogous to the sublime in nature, where the triumph of one force over another—rocks against a stormy sky, erupting volcanoes, raging oceans—filled us with fear. In such spectacles nature outdid itself, making us apprehend what was superior to it. The sublime, which pleased us immediately precisely because of what Kant described as the resistance it opposed to the interest of our senses—an Alpine chasm cannot easily be overcome or appropriated for human use, it is somehow incommensurable with our capacities for mastery—thus went against a certain mediocrity and selfishness, against the mercantile spirit. The peaceable bourgeois was a person without enthusiasm: How could he accept the fact that aesthetic judgment favored the warrior-leader over the statesman? Or that war itself, provided that it was conducted with respect for civil rights, had something sublime in it and made the attitude and ideas of those who were waging it sublime? For Kant, the wars of the French Revolution only reinforced the sublimity of the revolutionaries' project to found a republican government. In short, enthusiasm, even bellicose, revolutionary enthusiasm, was worthier than flaccidity–"a mere commercial spirit, and with it a debasing self-interest, cowardice, and effeminacy."[3]

As we have said, Kant was careful to distinguish enthusiasm from fanaticism, *Schwärmerei*.[4] Whereas enthusiasm was a passing state characterized by use of the imagination, *Schwärmerei* was raving insanity, a sickness, a madness that consisted in trying to see beyond the limits of what the senses could apprehend, a "delusion that would will some VISION beyond all the bounds of sensibility; i.e. would dream according to principles (rational raving)."[5] The relevant term today is psychosis. While in enthusiasm the imagination was *used*, in *Schwärmerei* it was *unleashed* and took over like a disease, "a deep-seated, brooding passion." Far from signaling the presence of an ultimate tendency toward good in nature or history, *Schwärmerei* illustrated the fundamental danger involved in human thinking, the problem that legitimated Kant's critical project–namely humanity's propensity to misuse its reason by exceeding the limits of that reason.

A Citizen Is a Bourgeois

While exciting Kant's enthusiasm, the French Revolution also played a crucial role in the elaboration of his political theory, leading him to found "civil society" on "civil status," political institutions: he saw the good political regime–a republic–as characterized less by its degree of civilization than by its mode of political organization.[6]

As we have said, Kant did not distinguish between civil society and the state any more than the authors that preceded him did. What sets him apart from them, however, is the fact that his theory encountered and took into account the transformations brought about by the French Revolution:[7] for him "civil society" was a "political society" in which citizens benefited from political rights, whereas the state of nature was one in which there were neither civil rights nor distributive justice. What was to be opposed to the natural state was not a social or "artificial" one,[8] because in the state of nature it was possible to regulate legally the relations between members of different societies or associations (within the family, for instance), but rather "civil status," the civil state, the state of public right and law. The birth of civil society might well change nothing in the way that different particular societies functioned, but it did make apparent a "public right" that concerned the "cohabitation" of its members and gave that cohabitation a legal form. In other words, a civil society was a society in which there existed a constitution (already for Aristotle the polis was characterized by the *politeia*):

> The members of such a society who are united for giving law (*societas civilis*), that is, the members of a state, are called *citizens of a state* (*cives*). In terms of rights, the attributes of a citizen, inseparable from his essence (as a citizen), are: lawful *freedom*, the attribute of obeying no other law than that to which he has given his consent; civil *equality*, that of not recognizing among the *people* any superior with the moral capacity to bind him as a matter of Right in a way that he could not in turn bind the other; and third, the attribute of civil *independence*, of owing his existence and preservation to his own rights and powers as a member of the people. From his independence follows his civil personality, his attribute of not needing to be represented by another where rights are concerned.[9]

The contract by means of which a "civil constitution" was established and a "civil state" formed was not different in type from other contracts. But while every contract focused on a common chosen end, only the social pact was at the same time a duty, and even the condition *sine qua non* of all other external duties: it was the right of those living under coercive public laws by which each could be given what was due to him (distributive justice), and it guaranteed justice for the individual against any encroachment upon it by others. Public right was "the distinctive quality of external laws that made it possible to bring the freedom of each into agreement with the freedom of all"; the "civil constitution" or *pactum unionis civilis* was a relation between individuals who were free at the same time as they were subject to these coercive laws. The civil condition was based on the freedom of each of its beneficiaries, on their equality, and on their independence in relation to any community.

Mensch. Subjekt. Bürger. Human being. Subject. Citizen.

Freedom. Equality. Independence.

Freedom. Each individual human being had the right to pursue his own happiness. A paternalistic government under which the people were treated like a group of minors was despotic; what was necessary was not a paternal but a patriotic government where all might see the political body as the "maternal womb" or the "paternal ground."[10]

Equality. Every subject had rights of coercion over all others, with the exception of the head of state, who could coerce without being coerced. But such universal freedom was perfectly compatible with the most striking inequalities: physical or intellectual superiority, for example, and superiority in terms of fortune and "external property." Nonetheless, everyone must be able to attain to all the "degrees of rank" that his particular talents, industry, and luck allowed him: his fellow subjects could enjoy no prerogatives based on birth, for birth was a fact of nature and not an act of the subject (this argument served to prohibit slavery). One had the right to inherit property but not privileges.

Independence. Every member of the Republic was "co-legislator," citizen, *Bürger*. The source of legislation could never be a single will, but only the united will of the people–this was the sense of the original contract. "Anyone who has the right to vote on this legislation is a *citizen* (*citoyen*, i.e., citizen of a state [*Staatsbürger*], not *bourgeois* or citizen of a town [*Stadtbürger*])."[11] Kant specified the "natural" condition of a citizen–neither woman nor child–and the fact, already suggested by this, that he had to be his own master. In order to possess this status he had to possess property. This did not mean that only men who possessed real estate or other material goods could be citizens: as with Locke, Kant's definition of property included everything that enabled one to earn a living–skill, talent, competence, knowledge–providing that the owner of such property might sell it without alienating himself from himself, that is, without allowing someone else to make use of him. This condition excluded barbers, for example, who like all other servants labored but created no commodity, but not wigmakers, whose labor resulted in a salable product: "In this respect, artisans and large or small landowners are all equal, and each is entitled to one vote only."[12] Property, then, while it could not be considered the source of citizenship, was its condition, because citizenship presumed the citizen's independence: his status must in no way be that of a dependent.

Considering the distinction between *Staatsbürger* and *Stadtbürger* from Marx's point of view in "On the Jewish Question," we may equate it with that between formal freedoms and real inequalities, whereas Kantian civil society is based on the affirmation of the equal rights of all citizens as guaranteed by the *real* freedom conferred on them by their economic and statutory independence–an independence whose conditions were not easy to delimit, as Kant himself pointed out. Were the philosopher who sold his services as a private tutor and the philosopher paid by the state both citizens? Whatever the answer, the Republic, founded on an original contract in which individuals had "completely abandoned their wild and lawless freedom in order to find again their entire and undiminished freedom in a state of lawful dependence (i.e. in a state of right), for this dependence is created by their own legislative will,"[13] did not accord the right to rebel or make revolution, for rebellion would thrust them back into the state of nature: "At this point, the state of anarchy supervenes, with all the terrors it may bring with it. And the wrong which is thereby done is done by each faction of the people to the others."[14]

Considering the historical order of things, we may say that from Kant's viewpoint the Revolution of 1789 was legitimate in that it led to a people's constituting itself as a state whose functioning was to be regulated by the original civil pact and in which the Idea of that original contract stood as the unique and infallible standard. However, the revolt that toppled the monarchy, more particularly the execution of a king after what his accusers considered a valid legal procedure, constituted one of the gravest crimes possible because it destroyed the very "foundations" of civil society.[15] While a revolution whose end was to establish a constitution excited the laudable emotion of enthusiasm, no constitution could include a law allowing for and organizing its own overthrow: that would be the equivalent of instituting a sovereign other than the sovereign. However, the people did possess certain inalienable rights whenever they found themselves in conflict with the chief of state, rights not of exercising coercion against a monarch or of rebellion, but operative rather in the sphere of opinion and reason. The people had no right to criticize the king with arms; what they did have was a right to the arm of criticism. Kant then was not in agreement with Hobbes; in fact his argument on this point is hardly different from Leibniz's. For Hobbes, those who governed the republic were not bound by any "compact to any man,"[16] and the chief of state could therefore never be considered unjust in his treatment of the people–a terrifying affirmation, in Kant's view. One of the citizen's inalienable rights was that of deeming that he had been the victim of an injustice, and the sovereign had to concede to the citizen the right to "make public his opinion about whatever of the ruler's measure's seem to him to constitute an injustice" understood not merely as an injustice against himself but against the commonwealth as a whole.[17] Not acknowledging this right meant assuming that the sovereign was omniscient and infallible, implying that "he receives divine inspiration and is more than a human being."[18] Like Leibniz, Kant considered fallacious Hobbes's attributing the *soul* of a God to the *body* politic, civil society. On the contrary the sovereign must be posited as fallible: he should conceive of himself as such and, like Frederick II, give the citizens, among their other freedoms, "freedom of the pen," that is, freedom to think and to communicate one's thought:

> In every commonwealth, there must be *obedience* to generally valid coercive laws within the mechanism of the political constitution. There must also be a *spirit of freedom*, for in all matters concerning universal human duties, each individual requires to be convinced by reason that the coercion which prevails is lawful, otherwise he would be in contradiction with himself. . . . For it is a natural vocation of man to communicate with his fellows, especially in matters affecting mankind as a whole.[19]

The important place attributed to reason in civil society leads one to conceive of it from a wider perspective: civil society was only fully intelligible in terms of that final end which was human culture. Nature—this was its ultimate purpose—could give humanity the means to culture. The diversity of human abilities meant that the mechanical skills of certain individuals—plowmen, blacksmiths, weavers—enabled others to work in areas of culture less directly necessary to survival, namely, the sciences and the arts. Those who devoted themselves to knowledge and the beautiful "oppressed" the first type by keeping them in a state of "hard work and little enjoyment" and yet "in the course of time much of the culture of the higher classes spreads to them also."[20] Culture continued to progress despite the contradictions it engendered, the perverse effect in which the superfluous began to threaten the necessary. But in order for that progress to continue there must be an organizing structure:

> The formal condition under which nature can alone attain this its real end [culture] is the existence of a constitution so regulating the mutual relations of men that the abuse of freedom by individuals striving one against another is opposed by a lawful authority centered in a whole called *civil*

society [*bürgerliche Gesellschaft*]. For it is only in such a civil society that the greatest development of natural tendencies can take place.[21]

A cosmopolitan whole, the creation on a worldwide scale of what civil society was for each nation, would enable humankind to avoid war, such "cosmopolitical society" being in a way the universalization of civil society. But universal peace established on such a basis demanded an intelligence and wisdom that human beings did not have, or at least not yet. War itself, meanwhile, forced them to develop their talents. Imagining that the advance of culture would "prepare man for a sovereignty in which reason alone would hold sway"[22] was not idle dreaming but rather the discovery of a regulating Idea. We can understand why a great world-historical event such as the French Revolution served to bolster the optimism of the onlooker, excited a feeling of "enthusiasm" in the same way as a "sublime" natural spectacle. Indeed, nothing was "more metaphysically sublime" than the Idea of a constitution in which power rested not with persons but in the laws: Wouldn't such an idea enable humanity, through a process of successive approximations, to reach perpetual peace, the sovereign political Good?[23] This on condition that such peace was instituted not by the revolutionary overthrow of a defective constitution, Kant explained, but by imperceptible reform. This restriction, however, did not apply to the French Revolution because, through the revolutionary abolition of a constitution, which was to be condemned for (temporarily) creating a juridical void, what the French Revolution accomplished was precisely the worthiest of all transformations: that of a "great people into a State," a "body politic" with political institutions that, like a body, was organized by a living force into a whole.[24]

The Meaning and Value of Freedom of Thought

Civil society was a public space regulated by laws in which individuals benefited from certain guarantees and rights. In order to ensure equality before the law—the term used by Socrates in the *Gorgias* was *isonomy*—there had to be a guarantee of *isology*, equality in the use of words: the primacy of rational discussion. The condition of possibility of the republican political regime was to be found at the discursive level (the practice of human communication known as discourse); this was what ensured the prevalence of reason. And the "*transcendental formula* of public right" was as follows: "All actions affecting the rights of other human beings are wrong if their maxim is not compatible with their being made public."[25] A maxim is a Kantian term corresponding to a formula for a universal (or universalizable) rule of behavior. Fanatics had nonuniversal, nonuniversalizable maxims that were incompatible with their being made public– "All books that criticize religion should be destroyed" for example–and this was why, unlike enthusiasm, *Schwärmerei* was to be condemned: it had a destructive effect on society.

Kant clearly outlined the political dangers involved in *Schwärmerei* in *What is Orientation in Thinking?*, a book written for a large readership and published in 1786, a few months after the death of Frederick II. At a time when intellectual exchanges within Germany were characterized by tension, the king's death deepened the threat to freedom of thought and expression. Spinoza and Spinozism, were at the center of a debate known as the "pantheism dispute" that bitterly divided German intellectuals. The details of the dispute are complex.[26] We may say that it began with Friedrich Jacobi affirming that the great thinker of the *Aufklärung*, Gotthold Lessing, had privately confessed to him his Spinozist convictions, Spinozism in this context referring to the negation of God's transcendence, of God as creator, and of free will. For Jacobi, the principle element of all knowledge and human activity was faith; reason, faith's opposite, could only lead to atheism with a Spinozan-pantheist face.[27] Concerned to defend Lessing, who had died in 1781, Moses Mendelssohn in turn accused Jacobi of *Schwärmerei*, to which Jacobi retorted that if he was a *Schwärmer*, so was Kant, because Kant called for setting limits on the power of reason. Caught in the fray of accusation and counter-accusation, Kant responded with his pedagogic *What Is Orientation in Thinking?* in which he sought to clarify and defend his position against what he understood as a charge of Spinozism. "Spinozism" and "*Schwärmerei*" may seem like radically opposed accusations: the first implies a condemnation of Spinoza's absolute rationalism; the second condemns a perspective in which reason is subordinate to inspiration. But they were not so for Kant, as we shall see, and they may be reasonably linked together in that Spinoza made man an element of the divinity.

The idea of associating Kant's thinking with *Schwärmerei* may seem strange; it can nonetheless be defended convincingly, for could it not be said that Kant had founded a negative theosophy? By limiting reason, excluding the possibility of knowing God, was he not opening the way for fanaticism? For Kant only intuition or faith, not reason, could posit existence because, according to the formula he gave in the *Critique of Pure Reason*, reason was the power of reaching conclusions, that is, of "judging mediately."[28] This was why he was so concerned to show the impossibility of a positive proof of the existence of God. But didn't the affirmation that reason was silent on God amount to turning over the right to speak to the heart, the emotions, unbridled subjectivity–in short, to fanaticism? On the subject of "my rational concept of God," Kant affirms:

> Even if nothing is found to contradict that concept in the whole manner in which the phenomenon in question made itself immediately apparent to me, this phenomenon, intuition, or immediate revelation–or whatever else one wishes to call a representation of this kind–would never prove the existence of a being whose concept (unless it is imprecisely defined and hence liable to be associated with every possible illusion) requires that it be of *infinite* magnitude to distinguish it from all created things; but no experience or intuition whatsoever can be adequate to this concept, or ever prove the existence of such a being in an unambiguous manner.[29]

Does this leave any other alternative to atheism–God does not exist because his existence cannot be demonstrated–than fanaticism: God cannot be known by reason, only by illumination?

Kant believed it possible to escape this vicious circle by means of critical philosophy. *Schwärmer* must be attacked for rejecting the principle of "reason as the sovereign legislator," and the limits of freedom of thought must be set by reason itself. What Kant was insisting upon was the "civil right" of communication: in order to be thought, an idea must be capable of being thought with others, in common. Freedom of thought was not a sort of extra or fringe benefit, the right to communicate one's thought; it was rooted in nothing other than itself; it was not part of a more general demand, a demand for universal freedom, for example. Freedom of thought was the very condition that made thought possible, because without intercommunication, thought could not be thought: "How much and how accurately would we think if we did not think, so to speak, in *commun*ity with others to whom we *commun*icate our thoughts and who *commun*icate their thoughts to us!"[30] Against the claims of capricious and fanatical "genius," against the pretensions of inspiration, the arrogant pride of illumination, all of which invalidated the supreme legislation of reason and fell under the category of *priv*ate thought–which therefore de*priv*ed itself of thinking and thought nothing–Kant made the following affirmation: "The inevitable result of *self-confessed* lawlessness in thinking (i.e. of emancipation from the restrictions of reason) is this: freedom of thought is thereby ultimately forfeited and, since the fault lies not with misfortune, for example, but with genuine presumption, this freedom is in the true sense of the word *thrown away*."[31] Freedom of thought, if it tried to act "independently even of the laws of reason, eventually destroys itself."[32] In order to be protected from this loss of orientation, it was necessary to determine the limits-of-power of pure reason and give "reason its due right to make the initial pronouncement in matters relating to supra-sensory objects such as the existence of God."[33]

Kant included Spinozism in his condemnation of fanaticism, declaring it to be one of the paths to *Schwärmerei*.[34] Spinoza's *Deus sive natura* ("God or nature"), his affirmation of the immanence of both creator and creature, his rejection of a sovereign God external to the order it created implied the possibility of a kind of knowledge in which humanity, which was in God, could know all things from the point of view of eternity, from the point of view of God himself: my consciousness and God's consciousness are identical in that I know nature, which is God, just as God knows it/himself. Absence of mediation: "I" is in God; "I" is God: fanaticism.

For Spinoza, superstition was born of imperfect knowledge; when it took phenomena that should be understood as obeying the eternal laws of nature for signs emanating from God, it raved. But it was precisely Spinoza's affirmation of the power of reason–human reason being, in Spinoza's view, a mode of God's reason–that Kant criticized as being a possible root of fanaticism. Logically, Spinoza had to assert that all thought is in God, of God, and to constitute the "intellectual love with which God loves himself" as the supreme value.[35] It is true that this could lead to a kind of illuminism: What was stopping anyone and everyone from giving himself permission to present himself as a kind of God? Spinoza's supposed atheism paradoxically resulted in the deification of every person, who, to the extent that he thought *in* God, attained to God's perfection. When reason, while not in the least repudiating itself, passed from what Spinoza called the second kind of knowledge, that is, knowledge attained through reason and in keeping with common notions, to the third—the intuition of every thing as it is in God—it overtook itself in a "beatitude" in which God was himself in humanity, whose potential was thereby increased to a kind of infinity. When humanity knew the world under the "species of eternity," then God loved himself with an infinite love.

In appearance, nothing could be further from Kant's limiting of knowledge, which in principle precluded human beings from having a relation with God, let alone *in* God, by way of reason. Still, the enthusiastic exaltation excited by the French Revolution was not a mere quivering on the surface of the Kantian subject, and we should not be surprised to find a certain proximity between Spinoza and Kant, as suggested by the particular status Kant reserved for images.

The Imageless Sublime

As we indicated in Chapter 5, prophesying for Spinoza involved having a particularly powerful imagination; the prophet was a visionary who illustrated, figured, expressed. His capacity as prophet did not derive from the value of his message, which was in no way superior to what natural reason might elaborate, but rather from his ability to give perceptible form to religious and ethical messages, forms, that is, perceptible to the people and which were necessarily projections of his own sensibility and condition. Spinoza's break with anthropomorphism was a break with figuration: Spinoza's God did not have a human face; he was not like a king. Both the false idea of God as a *rector* and all figurative representation of him were anthropomorphic. The Spinozan conception of God—*more geometrico*, "in the manner of mathematicians"—was in its essence iconoclast.

Kant did not believe any more than Spinoza that images were ethically necessary, and he too founded an iconoclast metaphysics—not in arguing against the right to figure what was invisible but in affirming that human beings had the ability to grasp what was beyond the perceptible and that images could only hamper that ability. If the Kantian sublime was indeed to be found in landscapes, and also in *spectacles* (he used the French word) such as the French Revolution, this was to be explained by the fact that his sublime caused the subject to experience a sense of infinitude—we have only to think of his celebrated comparison of the moral law within us to the celestial vault above. Taken to its logical conclusion, this conception would permit him to qualify the destruction of images approvingly as "sublime": perhaps, he opined, there was no more sublime passage in the Old Testament than the commandment forbidding the creation of images: "Thou shalt not make unto thee any graven image, or any likeness of any thing that is in heaven above, or that is in the earth beneath, or that is in the water underneath the earth" (Exodus 20:4). The verse brings us back once again to the connection between iconoclastic feeling and enthusiasm, for Kant affirmed that religions which prohibited images—the sublime commandment—were also those touched with enthusiasm: "This commandment can alone explain the enthusiasm which the Jewish people, in their moral period, felt for their religion when comparing themselves with others, or the pride inspired by Mohammedanism."[36] And what was true about humanity's relation to God, namely, that it was in the absence of images of God that religious feeling was not only activated but reinforced, exalted to the point of excess, was also true of the representation of moral law in relation to the moral tendency we have within us. In other words, the absence of images, far from causing a lack of fervor, actually warmed religious and moral feeling, to the point that we had cause to worry about excessive feeling:

> The fear that if we divest this representation [of moral law] of everything that can command it to the senses it will thereupon be attended only with a cold and lifeless approbation and not with any moving force or emotion is wholly unwarranted. The very reverse is the truth. For when nothing any longer meets the eye of sense, and the unmistakable and ineffaceable idea of morality is left in possession of the field, there would be need rather of tempering the ardour of the unbounded imagination to prevent it rising to enthusiasm than of seeking to lend these ideas the aid of images and childish devices for fear of their being wanting in potency.[37]

Imageless sublimity in morality and religion was thus not without risk, but it was risk worth taking. Renouncing images meant trusting that human beings would make good use of their inclination toward enthusiasm. It was in this iconoclast sublimity that human activity, and thereby human freedom, could enjoy their fullest development. This Kant affirmed negatively, among other ways, in the following condemnation of images:

> Governments have gladly let religion be fully equipped with these accessories, seeking in this way to relieve their subjects of the exertion, but to deprive them, at the same time, of the ability required for expanding their

spiritual powers beyond the limits arbitrarily laid down for them and which facilitate their being treated as though they were merely passive.[38]

Far from finding support in images, enthusiasm was reinforced by their absence, because true enthusiasm was a response only to what was ideal, purely moral–to the "concept of right" in the case of the French Revolution.[39] This was why, even though the theory of the sublime involved aesthetics, the sublime had nothing to do with an analysis of taste. Beauty was the essence of taste, whereas it was merely the condition that allowed human beings to have access to sublimity: the sublime did indeed have to be beautiful in order not to be savage, rough, repellent, barbarous, for in such a case it would excite not admiration but horror and would fail to awaken in the subject a feeling of his own grandeur and strength.[40] But beauty was not the essence of the sublime. And obviously Kant did not put his hopes in any kind of aestheticizing of the political or the moral. Law must be loved for itself in all its rigor, and without its being ornamented by grace: the majesty of the law, similar to that of the commandments given on Mount Sinai, must inspire veneration, respect for a master we carried within us; the feeling of the sublime in our personal destiny was awakened, and it delighted us more than any other beauty. What was at work in the sublime was humanity's immediate grasp of its purpose and end, and of the freedom that guaranteed the humanity of the subject in its destined progress toward good under the guidance of reason. Kant's optimism was founded on a belief in the power of reason. With this in mind, rather than scrutinizing the differences between critical philosophy and Spinozism, we may insist on their shared rejection of figurative thought, of the imagination as a substitute for reason–of the figurative representation of the Holy Trinity as an old man, a young man, and a bird, for the painting by Dürer that we examined in Chapter 4 would have seemed puerile to Kant.[41] There was no risk that pure morality might lead to fanaticism, extravagance, raving madness. Indeed, fanaticism and terror went against enthusiasm and the sublime: on the one hand the French Revolution, on the other the terroristic conception of humanity's history that was to follow it: "It seems that the day of judgment is at hand, and the pious zealot [*Schwärmer*] already dreams of the rebirth of everything and of a world created anew after the present world has been destroyed by fire."[42] The fanatic stigmatized by Kant and the one Luther denounced appear to be one and the same, both illuminated prophets of an apocalypse they ardently desire. Their sameness is only seeming, though, for while those who Luther called fanatics sought to abolish the interval between the Earthly City and the City of God, the other type refused to believe in reason's being realized through history. The first did not believe in the virtues of civil society, while the second had no confidence in the virtues of civilization.

The Tip of the Fakir's Nose and the
Cabbage Head

Kant had seen a sign of progress in the enthusiasm excited by the French Revolution; Hegel put the later Jacobin Terror—which had also been condemned by Kant—at the very center of his analysis of fanaticism.

A lexical change, a different assessment. For Kant the positive word associated with the French Revolution was *Enthusiasmus* (as opposed to *Schwärmerei*), whereas for Hegel the French Revolution was a compelling illustration of *Fanatismus*. It is possible to see in the adoption of the word *Fanatismus* (also to be found in his contemporary Hammer's work on the Assassins) an effect of the French Revolution itself. As we have indicated, fanatic, fanaticism, and the verb *fanatiser*, meaning "make fanatic; make into a fanatic," were used frequently by those who participated in the Revolution, and they stigmatized anyone they were applied to—refractory priests, Jacobins, Terrorists. As these examples suggest, the word tended to overflow the field of religion, coming to serve in attacks on ideological and political enemies. In a speech of November 21, 1793, for example, Robespierre denounced the "fanaticism" of those who wanted to pursue an earlier policy of forced de-Christianization against the "fanatics."[43] The link between the problem of fanaticism and the concept of civil society is as crucial in Hegel's thinking as it is in Kant's,[44] and like Kant, Hegel theorized them both: in fanaticism as in political organization what was expressed was how individuals use their will. Hegel's originality is patent in his discussion of this question as in all others. He distinguished civil society and the state without opposing them and thus proposed a new conception of civil society; like those defined by earlier authors, Hegel's civil society regards fanaticism as a threat, but the Hegelian state, linked as it is to civil society is, as we shall see, strong enough to accept the existence of religious sects.

Fanaticism according to Hegel was to be understood as a pathology of the will, with the will defined as the unity of two moments—pure indeterminacy, or the " 'I' 's pure reflection into itself"—and the transition to being determined in one way or another. The will could not remain a "pure thinking of oneself," undetermined, but rather had to be realized in some content, an object, found either in nature or the mind, by means of which the "I" entered into finitude, became particularized. The self necessarily wants something. In the case where the self is incapable of wanting anything delimited, precise, it remains indefinitely in this false infinitude that is indetermination, absence of content, unlimited shapelessness: "This is the freedom of the void, which is raised to the status of an actual shape and passion."[45] This free will, which wants nothing more than to will, may result in two forms of fanaticism: the fanaticism of religious contemplation and the "active fanaticism of both religious and political life."[46]

According to Hegel, Hindus engaged in the first form of fanaticism. The aim of Hindu systems of philosophy was to "teach the means whereby eternal happiness can be attained before, as well as after death." For those who were not born Brahmins, this might be accomplished through "excessive acts of penance . . . to which a retreat within themselves is added";[47] further efforts to achieve happiness and special powers—"the power to expand into a gigantic body; the power to become light enough to be able to mount to the sun on a sunbeam," and other such—might involve "a profound meditation, accompanied by holding back the breath and inactivity of the senses, while a fixed position is constantly preserved."[48] Or as Hegel put it in another version of these lectures, Hindus might remain seated immobile for years in the same place considering nothing but "the tip of their nose."[49] The Hindu sought thereby to smother all desires, all needs, all passions with his absolute indifference, his emptied mind: he retreated into himself in order to find "Brahma" in his unconscious and, attaining thus to felicity before death, to escape metempsychosis after it.[50]

But Hegel lived at a time when philosophical thought was less concerned with the bleak daydreaming of fakirs staring at the tips of their noses or sleeping standing up in the bliss of the void or the belief that they had or might become one with the absolutely universal One than with heads rolling off the guillotines of the French Revolution. Accordingly, next to the contemplative fanaticism of the Brahmin, who sought only to persevere in his empty interiority, where his "I" attained the inanity of a forgotten trinket, there was a fanaticism born of the void but turned toward action. In this second type, freedom, having no other content than the void it projected, sank into willing the elimination of all social order. Political fanaticism, in this conception, sought to eliminate anyone who willed a certain order; it engendered fury and a crazed desire for "annihilating any organization which attempts to rise up anew."[51] The French Terror sought to cancel out all distinction between talents, opposed any and all authority, and deployed a hatred of differences, "intolerance toward everything particular."[52] It was Will devoid of all content but itself, abstract and undifferentiated; such fanaticism would allow no substituting of a new order for the old, of an untried hierarchy for a past one. Active fanaticism was the will to destroy all particularities, all singularities—a desire for nothingness:

> The sole and only work and deed accomplished by universal freedom is therefore *death*—a death that achieves nothing, embraces nothing within its grasp; for what is negated is the unachieved, unfulfilled punctual entity of the absolutely free self. It is thus the most cold-blooded, mean and meaningless death of all, with no more significance than cleaving a head of cabbage or swallowing a draught of water.[53]

It may be said that active fanaticism as Hegel defined it makes civil society impossible, given that such society can only exist as a regulated system of differences. The religious fanatic denounced by Luther and Melanchthon, who in his own understanding was seeking to abolish civil society in the interests of the City of God, could be stigmatized from a Hegelian perspective as desiring to institute the dictatorship of the universal void; to put it anachronistically, he—like the French Terrorist—was a nihilist. When the Anabaptists in the sixteenth century denounced all political organization and all legal order, seeking to banish private property, marriage, the situations and activities characteristic of civil society, from a Hegelian perspective this was because they deemed them "unworthy of love and the freedom of feeling."[54] But because real action and existence required making decisions, it was necessarily up to subjectivity in the case where all political order had been abolished to make those decisions, and they thus became arbitrary, based on nothing but the subject's volition. The religion of active religious-political fanatics was not genuine religion; on the contrary, a genuine religion, that is, one that went well beyond arbitrary subjectiveness in that "the business of its worship consists in *actions* and in *doctrine*," would hardly reject the state–quite the reverse, it needed the state, finding in it a regulating structure that would guarantee protection for the religious community. But the need was mutual. Because the state found in religion that which could anchor *it* in subjectivity, because religion guaranteed the state the stability of private spiritual belief, the state might require all of its subjects to be affiliated with a religious community–this without concerning itself with the content of any given faith. A state whose organization was fully developed, perfected, might because of its strength be liberal and tolerate religious communities that did not recognize themselves as having duties toward it (the duty of fighting to defend it, for example). It could be satisfied with a passive respect for the duties owed it and leave the followers of such religions to civil society, of which they were, Hegel pointed out, active members. They might fulfill their obligations to the state in different, specified ways: by paying a special tax in place of serving in the military, for example, even though defending the nation against its enemies was a citizen's highest duty.[55]

Here we may best measure the gap separating Luther's doctrine from Hegel's. Whereas Luther's fanatics were a threat to civil society, that is, to the state, and this fact legitimated using force against them, the liberal Hegelian state could tolerate subjects within civil society who claimed their specialness. We can begin to appreciate the originality of Hegelian civil society: a sphere or moment of the state in which individuals could find a guarantee for their singularity as individuals. What was universal in the state did not crush the particularities of civil society, even when they were those of an entire community–the Jews, for example. Hegel approved of Jews' being granted the status of legal persons in civil society, explaining moreover that it was from their "self-awareness" of this status, "infinite and free from all other influences, that the desired assimilation in terms of attitude and disposition arises."[56]

Hegelian Civil Society and State

Hostile to any and all order, active fanaticism engendered more than disorder: as nihilistic capriciousness, it made any and all organization impossible. In this sense the state, which can be defined as the organizer of organization, was an anti-fanatic device. But while it was the *organization* that ensured the functioning of the social whole, the

Hegelian state was not an englobing, absorbing *organism*; it was instead a differentiated, constituted totality.[57] Rather than absorbing the individual, it ensured his existence and fulfillment *as* an individual.

Civil society was where the tension between the individual and the whole that characterized the Hegelian state was resolved. It was the sphere in which the individual's selfish interest could assert itself, but that civil society itself could only be maintained through the individual's integration into institutions—classes or estates (*Stände*) regulated by "corporations" (professional associations) in the framework of what he called a *Polizei*, "police" or "public authority."[58]

The first point to be underlined is that civil society was the moment—organizational rather than chronological—which Hegel situated between those of the family and the state. The state preceded civil society both logically and chronologically, coming into existence before civil society (ancient Rome had a state but no civil society) as civil society's condition of possibility: without the state, civil society would not subsist.[59] The state brought necessity to civil society, otherwise a terrain of multiple and spreading contingencies. The state instilled the universal in civil society, a place in which singularities might otherwise run rampant. Civil society seen from the point of view of the patriarchal family was the space of freedom, and as such a threat of anarchy emanated from it. In fact, civil society broke family ties and alienated family members from one another: it substituted itself for "the external inorganic nature and paternal soil from which the individual gained his livelihood," with the result that the family had come to depend for its subsistence on the economic contingency that characterized civil society. In this transition from the soil to the social, from the geopolitical to political economy, "the individual becomes a son of civil society."[60] Civil society made humanity enter a system regulated by needs and work. And through this emancipation, which we may say corresponds to the passage from feudalism to capitalism, civil society became a type of family in which the children, minors, might, by acceding to their legal "majority," rise to the status of "free personalities." The creation of this new family meant that the family into which an individual had been born receded to become a mere origin. In the modern state, the individual could not be owned by his family nor could he own it, as had been the case in ancient Rome; rather each and every son could become an heir, an owner, a citizen.

This "dissolution" of the family—in the sense that the children went on to produce other families—brought about the emergence of "legal persons,"[61] who, to satisfy their selfish purposes, had to enter into a system of mutual dependence in which culture was liberation and work the ultimate liberation. Hegel called this world in which work brought the individual a satisfaction dependent on his ties to other individuals and in which individuals were tied to each other for that satisfaction the "system of needs." Private persons, preoccupied with their personal interests, were obliged to appeal to other private persons in order to satisfy those interests: in this way the individual with his particularities was bound to the universal. And the function of the state was to ensure that this bond was made solid and lasting. In doing this, the state realized morality: it made social relations and social life moral by subsuming them in reason.

Hegel found in political economy as described and conceptualized by Adam Smith, Jean-Baptiste Say, and David Ricardo an account of civil society's concrete content, characterized by a diversity that, thanks to progress in the arts and sciences, had become deeply sophisticated. Their work enabled him to expound on such important aspects of civil society as the division of labor and the nature of the different classes—principles of political economy.[62] But this modern-times science could not exhaust what there was to know about civil society. At one end of it people worked, acquiring and accumulating wealth, while at the other the poor increased in number to the point of becoming a surplus "rabble."[63] Furthermore, in civil society immediate natural needs were modified by what might be called the spiritual need of representation. Clearly, civil society could not be reduced to a complex machinery of needs. It was not merely economic.

Second, then, civil society, existing in and by means of the state, could not be reduced to matters of economy: it was also juridical, or legal, and political.

Hegelian civil society includes "rights" in the form of law and a "police" not as accidents or parasites but as vital, substantial elements. This is made perfectly clear by the outline of the section in *Elements of the Philosophy of Right* devoted to civil society: after "The System of Needs," we find "The Administration of Justice," followed by "The Police and the Corporation." The expositional order is not rhetorical; rather it reflects the logic of Hegelian civil society itself. In civil society individuals sought to satisfy their selfish needs–this was individualistic atomism. If it were not for the regulatory devices found within it, civil society would give way to the war of all against all, a return to the state of nature. The administration of justice gave property its legal status and guaranteed it protection: regulating civil society with good laws was crucial if the state was to flourish. But justice was too abstract, in that it gave only the framework in which my particularity became manifest; it did not directly concern my welfare (*Wohlfahrt*):

> Through the administration of justice, *infringements* of property or personality are annulled. But the right *which is actually present in particularity* means not only that *contingencies* which interfere with this or that end should be *canceled* and that the *undisturbed security* of *persons* and *property* should be guaranteed, but also that the livelihood and welfare of individuals should be *secured*–i.e. that *particular welfare* should be *treated as a right* and duly *actualized*.[64]

Actualizing particular welfare conceived as a right was the work of the "police," whose global function was to maintain the universal. In order to fight against particularist fragmentation, it was necessary to have recourse to corporatist organizations. This would not be useful to the peasant class, whose ties to the soil and familial mode of living guaranteed it concrete stability. Nor did the "universal estate" of civil servants have need of the corporations, because it was destined by its very nature to be entirely taken up with the universal. For the industrial class, however, the corporation provided a counterweight to particularities, and in this it was the second ethical anchoring of the state, together with the family.[65] The corporation was not a cast, turned inward on itself, ossified; rather it raised individual particularities toward the universal.

The tasks to be performed in modern society by civil society were to guarantee permanent security and to ensure the protection of private property and personal freedom.[66] But it could not accomplish these tasks if it did not go beyond itself: the bourgeois in his corporation was already no longer an isolated individual. The trace of universality that could be discerned in the corporation became fully realized in the state, whose interest, we may say, was universal; its purpose was to maintain the universal: right (*Recht*) and legality. The corporatist spirit born of the legitimacy of different groups' particular interests was transformed into the spirit of the state, for it was in the state that individuals found, thanks to the mediation of the corporations with which they were affiliated, that which made it possible for them to satisfy their particular interests. The state was not a kind of dollop of soul decorating civil society; we can say rather that it had its roots in civil society's contingency. But we should add that the state in turn rooted the particular in the universal: without the legislative framework, without civil servants to manage the general interest of the state, the corporations would be ruined by conflicts about hierarchy and more generally by the petty passions, desires, and fantasies of their particular members. This was the secret of the patriotism felt by the *Bürger als Bourgeois*: he recognized his substance as being in the state, for without it, particular interests would no longer be protected–they would lose their legitimacy. If he did not partake of the general organization of the state and its universalist focus, if he were not a citizen, the bourgeois or corporation member would disappear as such, for, abstractly posited, in and of itself, "civil society is the field of conflict in which the private interest of each individual comes up against that of everyone else."[67] Thanks to the state, civil society meant instead civil, bourgeois peace. The state, Hegelian civil society, knew no class struggle, let alone the "more or less veiled civil war" that according to Marx characterized bourgeois society.[68]

Internally regulated, primarily by the family and the "estates" under the control of the civil servants, the state was a system under central control, but its functioning could only be fully understood by considering it in relation to its exterior: it existed in relation to other states. While war against a foreign enemy was not the unique destiny of the state–it must also, as we know, ensure the individual welfare that civil society made possible–it *was* the state's supreme destiny. Contrary to the ancient City, then, the Hegelian state was not entirely destined for and devoted to war: if it was true that it could require the individual to sacrifice himself, it was equally true that it guaranteed him the satisfaction of his needs and the possibility of attaining well-being. Like the Greek polis, the state was based on the distinction between *stasis* and *polemos*, internecine war, which destroyed the City, and war against an external enemy, which founded the City's legitimacy. However, it did not subordinate the individual to the whole: as we have said, the bourgeois citizen was not essentially a soldier, as was the Greek or Roman citizen. It was as if the state had taken the possibility of war against an external enemy in exchange for the internal peace that reigned in civil society: it located the state of nature, the war of all against all, outside of itself, in its relations with different states, all the while ensuring the well-being of the individual within.

Hegelian civil society is thus radically different from that formulated by Aristotle in that it makes autonomous the political sphere and affirms the individual's right to seek what is useful to him. Hegel's vision of the state also places him at a great distance from Augustinian preoccupations: he did not conceive of the state as inferior to the Church. An arrangement in which spiritual life had its seat in the Church and in which the state was the regime of the arbitrary, of passions and violence, was indeed to be found in barbarian historical epochs, not necessarily in the modern civilized world, where the state actualized effective morality or ethics. The unity of church and state was therefore in no way imperative. Incontestably, the content of both was truth, but their differences could not be annulled, because in order for the state to attain the universality of thought, it was necessary that it be independent of all other authorities, that it exist in and of itself: fusional unity of church and state, of their respective contents and organizations, was the equivalent of "oriental despotism."[69] There was probably no contradiction in principle between religion and the state, but clearly there could be one at the level of factual reality should the Church ever seek to usurp the state's mission: "Everything in religion invariably has reference to the totality. And if this totality sought to take over all the relations of the state, it would become fanaticism."[70] The Church's sphere was that of spiritual truth, but it had no business trying to actualize such truth in a concrete institution: "If, then, religion constitutes . . . the nature of the state as the divine will, it is at the same time only a *foundation*; and this is where the two [i.e. the state and religion] diverge. The state is the divine will as present spirit, *unfolding* as the actual shape and *organization of a world*."[71] It was not in the Church that the divine will was actualized; reason and the spirit were incarnated in the state.[72]

So it is that the Hegelian state could accept within it the likes of Anabaptists and Quakers. These two groups, typical fanatics for Lutherans but also of course for all Catholics (Bossuet for example), had rights, legal status in the Hegelian City—we see how radically different Hegel's position was from Luther's. Once the relevant distinction was no longer between civil society and the kingdom of God, but rather between civil society and the state, the problem was no longer to protect civil society against those who sought to impose the kingdom of God. Instead, the state organized civil society so that everyone might seek what he believed to be his own good. The liberal Hegelian state—and in this it is of course utterly distinct from the totalitarian state—guaranteed personal freedom, including that of "fanatics." By advancing a judgment that may be summarized in the phrase "no fanaticism against the fanatics," Hegel went against Luther.

And yet what proximity to Luther! The Hegelian state pursued the movement of secularization Luther had launched. His Reformation had already begun to replace sanctity with ethical life: the vow of chastity with the family and the vow of obedience with obedience to the laws of the state. Yet for Hegel, as we have said, the state could only have a veritable foundation if its principles did not remain abstract and artificial; that is, if they were anchored in the general religious consciousness. In order for those who governed and administered to respect the spirit of the laws, it was necessary that this spirit coincide with their religious spirit. This was why Revolution without Reform(ation) could only fail.[73]

But because the state had to have a foundation in subjectivity, the individual consciousness, it had to recognize the right to subjectivity, even if that subjectivity involved what it might consider error or deviation. To say that the moral truth of the state had to be recognized as an ethical-religious principle was to say that those who did not recognize it as such also had to be accepted—the Quakers and Anabaptists, for example, who were only passive members of the state because they refused to defend it against its enemies, but who were nonetheless active members of civil society. And the state's tolerance was to go well beyond accepting sects. To the proposition of giving Jews full civil rights it might be objected that, unlike other sects, they considered themselves not only a religious community but a people. Still, it must be remembered that they were "primarily *human beings*" and that this was "not just a neutral and abstract quality": "*A human being counts as such because he is a human being*, not because he is a Jew, Catholic, Protestant, German, Italian, etc."[74] Because a Jew was recognized as a person, he must be recognized as a "legal person in civil society." Furthermore, excluding the Jews from that status precluded reproaching them for not assimilating.[75]

Civil society in Hegel's terms was an entity that allowed for the flexible management of multiplicity, heterogeneity. The unified state was in a position to approve a diversity that was not accidental, but essential. Civil society authorized the existence not only of the individual as a person seeking to satisfy his subjective interests, but of groups that stood in a relation of dissidence to the state—that dissidence was legally founded. At the opposite pole from any and all theories anchoring citizenship in ethnicity, Hegel's theory founded citizenship on civil society, and civil society on right.

9 Civil Society and Civil War

Gorbachev's perestroika had numerous semantic effects on official discourse as well as on that of the intelligentsia, one of the most remarkable of which was the reappearance of the terms "civil society" and "law-governed state," or, more exactly, the appearance of two perhaps self-contradictory formulas: "socialist civil society" and the "socialist law-governed state."[1] The nineteenth conference of the Communist Party of the Soviet Union (CPSU), held from June 28 to July 19, 1988, declared the "formation of a socialist law-governed state" to be a "question of principle" at a moment when calls for the bringing into existence of a civil society were multiplying. Though not made explicit by the new Soviet ideologues, the relation between these two objectives—creating a civil society and creating a law-governed state—was obvious. Indeed, Soviet history has frequently been characterized as lacking just these two elements: the absence of civil society, absence visible in the USSR, has often been given as the defining trait of totalitarianism, while the absence of a state founded on the rule of rights-based law has been designated as what distinguishes a despotic state from a democratic one.[2] According to this argument, the Russian and Soviet past underline, negatively of course, how civil society and the law-governed state are related: the existence of a society of citizens supposes that the state subjects itself to the law and recognizes those citizens as having certain inalienable rights. This was precisely what both the czarist autocracy and the Communist regime, using of course quite different modalities, had refused to do.

The construction of a state governed by rights-based law was and, during the first presidency of Boris Yeltsin, continued to be that much more crucial for former Soviet society in that it conditions not only all political transformations but also to a large extent the transition to a decentralized and competition-based economy. The chaos that threatens the former USSR and its inhabitants is exacerbated by the absence of economic rules. We know that the problems posed by the legal regulation of this particular society are enormous. Socialism destroyed the already weak juridical and civic culture that existed in Russia before the Communist Revolution; under communism Russia knew law only as an instrument in the service of apparatuses of violence. The Soviet-Russian judicial and penal system has been marked by a will to brutal repression, barbarous punitive measures, and the total absence of protection for the accused—witness the penitentiary system, still in operation in the 1990's. Given such realities, it is extraordinarily difficult to find answers for the innumerable practical questions that must be asked: Where are lawyers to come from? and judges? and legal codes enabling the defense of civil rights and the regulation of social relations? How may efficient and dependable contractual relations be established, for example in the practical fields of private and commercial law? On what bases and by what means might a civic culture be established that would make it possible to eradicate corruption? And the innumerable concrete difficulties involved in constructing a civil society and law-governed state are deeply complicated by the issue of determining the status of national minorities—we have already seen how readily this problem can escalate into war and bloodshed. What is to become of minority groups in the former federated republics, now on the path to independence? What political rights will the Ossetians have in Georgia (supposing that the Caucasus region does not become a kind of Lebanon)? Or Russian-speakers in Moldavia and the Baltic nations? A good test of whether a society is indeed a civil society is how well it is able to avoid ethnicization of conflicts. It would appear that the embryonic civil society of the former Soviet Union, liberated from the brutal, mind-destroying weight of the party-state, is now in danger of being crushed by the religious and nationalist fanaticism being fomented in the CIS. The war in Chechnya is grim evidence of how difficult it is to build a federal state based on civic culture.

As we know, Gorbachev's project of instituting a "*socialist* law-governed state" failed; it represented a sort of contradiction. Communism was ideologically founded on the rejection of the concept of personal and civil rights; the political mode it assumed was dictatorship; it consolidated itself through a rejection of citizenship with the ambition of attaining civilization by destroying the City. In Lenin's phrase, communism was characterized by its will to use barbarity to fight barbarity. As long as the Communist Party was presented as the only remedy for the evil of which it was the cause, the situation in the Soviet Union could not change; it remained a prisoner to its totalitarian past. This explains why, after March 1990, when Gorbachev finally made up his mind to surrender the Party's monopoly on power and the Party lost its official status as the core of Soviet society, there were only two possible outcomes: definitive decline or restoration. The unsuccessful attempt in August 1991 to reinstate the old order by force accelerated the Party's fall. The maneuver designed to reverse the course of reforms whose progress at the time can only be characterized as slow, timid, and vague brought about the opposite result from what its instigators were hoping for, and with it the disintegration of the old federal structure. By obliging Gorbachev to choose between his political survival or that of the CPSU—as we know, he chose the former option—the leaders of the putsch helped liberate the embryonic civil society from the parasitic Communist Party and thereby advanced the laborious process of constituting a civil society and law-governed state. But this also brought to the fore the major problem, by no means exclusive to the former USSR, of the compatibility of a law-governed state with nationalism. We will return to this problem.

"Civil society" thus played the role of a concrete political end to be achieved, together with the construction of a law-governed state, but it has also functioned, as we have said, as an explanatory concept, both in the post-totalitarian Soviet Union and in a majority of the other formerly communist countries, particularly Poland, where, as we have suggested, the social, antitotalitarian meaning and usage of the term were in a way invented. But the term is also relevant for all systems of the same type, regardless of cultural distance—namely China. As we said in Chapter 1, "civil society" is at the heart of all analysis of development for those who understand modernization not primarily in terms of economic growth but rather as the appearance of a civic space: political modernization presupposes the instituting of contrac-

tual relations in both private and public life and the politicizing of social life. The student struggles in China have shown the universal relevance of the battle to institute civil society, and that no culture is in its
essence (if cultures have essences) incompatible with the emergence of
democratic ideals. After the events in Tienanmen Square (spring 1989)
and with the collapse of the Soviet empire, an explanatory paradigm
can be proposed according to which communism, appearing in societies where civil society was in the process of constituting itself, then
brought that process of differentiation to a halt by means of the single
party.[3] Through an irony based on the real movement of history, the
expression "civil society," which flourished in part due to Marx's use of
it, is being turned against those regimes which claimed it as their
inspiration. It is used to propose social relations regulated by law, and
it privileges civil rights. It is thereby serving completely to reverse the
project cherished by the founders of the communist regimes.

If we want to measure the enormity of the reversal that has taken
place in the Soviet Union (and has thus far failed to take place in
China), we have only to read Lenin's *Declaration of Rights of the Working and Exploited People*,[4] written at the end of 1917 and placed in
preamble to the first Soviet constitution. The Bolshevik leader there
contradicts in deliberate and systematic fashion the French *Declaration of the Rights of Man and Citizen* of 1789, making it excruciatingly
clear that the Soviet regime was not founded on any temporary suspension or overlooking of *les droits de l'homme et du citoyen* but on their
deliberate negation. We cannot insist too strongly on this: the negation
of civil rights does not tell a story of measures hastily adopted as necessary in the heat of the Revolution, then abusively rigidified, institutionalized, and codified later on. From the moment the Communist
regime began, the Party confiscated all legitimate power and with it
the right to speak, instituting mass terror as the normal tone and
substance of social and political life. As early as December 1917 Lenin
pronounced his watchword and battle cry, emblematic of the Revolution's destiny, that it was necessary to "cleanse the Russian soil of
harmful insects."[5] The vision of Lenin as dedicated to the ideals of
emancipation but forced to take exceptional measures to ensure the
revolution's survival, in contrast to the coarse peasant Stalin, who prolonged the useless terror, is an apologetic construction: from the beginning Lenin had decided, taking as his models the French Revolu-

tion, the Revolution of 1848, and the Paris Commune, that civil war was an inevitable phase in the revolutionary process. He meant to preclude all counterrevolution by taking forceful, terroristic initial measures, then found in the counterrevolution he had thereby helped to engender the confirmation that his political logic was right. This explains why, without any hesitation, Lenin instituted the extermination of objective "enemies" as a fruitful moment of communist revolution.

The Communist regime in the Soviet Union, constituted by its founder as the dictatorship of the party-state, was a regime without law whose initial legitimacy resided in the force it deployed against the former exploiters. The Party, or more exactly its leaders, sought to gather all power into their hands. According to Russian legend, Prince Potemkin, a favorite of the empress Catherine the Great, constructed fake villages for the sovereign's pleasure during a trip through the Crimea; the state in the USSR was as fake as one of those villages: the soviets, mere shadows; elections, mere mystification; the unions, Party transmission belts. Though certain supporters of Gorbachev claimed the contrary, there could be no law-governed state in the Soviet Union as long as the Party dominated society while asserting a principle giving it the right to do so, like a demiurge claiming the right to control its creature. Article 6 of the Soviet constitution of 1977 posited that the Party, armed with "Marxist-Leninist doctrine," was the "core" of all institutions and the "force" that "orients and leads" society; it recognized the Party as the only legitimating institution, the only effective locus of power in the system of which it was the womb. The Gorbachevian experiment involved searching for the means of calling the Party's monopoly into question by transferring sovereignty to the state—that is, to the Supreme Soviet, the parliament—but at the same time preserving the Party, hoping thereby to recover the propulsive force it could no longer find in an exhausted ideology, or in a Soviet nationalism that was dissolving into a multitude of distinct nationalist, separatist demands. But the operation that aimed to revitalize the Party by means of the state failed, and the Party was forced to give up its power, not to a full-fledged state but to an ill-formed, weak political apparatus. The 1990 revision of the Constitution of 1977, particularly the modification of Article 6 which made political party pluralism legal (in the absence of real parties), was necessarily fatal to the Party: How could the former central agent of totalitarianism with all its heavy machinery possibly be integrated into a pluralist system? Either it had to be reinstituted in its full force or it had to disappear. As we know, Gorbachev was forced after the putsch to make choices that entailed its disappearance.[6]

But the Party did not vanish in September 1991 like a junta or a group of oligarchs retreating after a failed power play. The Party was not something at the summit of a society that it merely surveyed from on high; rather it penetrated the whole of that society. The communist system had not been added on to a confirmed and relatively autonomous civil society; rather it had sought since its birth to destroy–without perfect success–whatever seeds of such society might exist. It is infinitely easier to pull out Matisse, Chagall, and Malevich paintings hidden away in the basements of Russian museums and reopen a few churches for the faithful than to bring into existence the bases of a modern democratic society. The problem has nothing to do with some supposed deeply rooted or essential Russian barbarism, but rather with the effects of an enterprise pursued for dozens of years designed to prevent, by barbarous means, the advent of "civil society," whatever meaning is assigned to the term.

Marx Overturns Hegel's Civil Society

It would be a mistake to impute to Russia the role of source for the political model that Bolshevism brought to triumph. Indeed, the dictatorship of the single Party had its essential source not in the Russian past, but in Lenin's terroristic radicalization of Marx's analysis of the Bonapartist state as the parasite of "civil society." It is true that for Marx the secret of modern "civil society" was civil war; but Lenin took up Marx's notions and watchwords while leaving aside the elements that founded them, for he did not take into account what Marx had said about how the state and civil society fit together.

The Leninist and Stalinist party-state reversed completely Aristotle's definition of the human being as a political animal: it reduced the human being to a *mere* animal. Marx may be said to have begun that reversal *theoretically* with, on the one hand, remarks of the type that the art of heraldry proved that the secret truth of nobility was zoology and, on the other, his claim that through the process of production that split the worker into both an instrument of forced labor and an organism with needs to satisfy, modern civil society turned that worker into a beast. The Leninist Party, however, put that reductive view into *practice* when it put in place a politics of civil war and social hygiene. Lenin could not have ousted civil society from his system, however, had it not been for Marx's critique of Hegelian political philosophy.

In 1859 Marx gave a certain number of indications about the "course" of his analyses. He explained how in 1843 he had undertaken to revise Hegel's *Philosophy of Right*, with the following result:

> Legal relations as well as forms of state are to be grasped neither from themselves nor from the so-called general development of the human mind, but rather have their roots in the material conditions of life, the sum total of which Hegel, following the example of the Englishmen and Frenchmen of the eighteenth century, combines under the name of "civil society" [*bürgerliche Gesellschaft*]; that, however, the anatomy of civil society is to be sought in political economy.[7]

There follows the celebrated passage in which, after affirming that the real foundation of society is its economic structure and that it is only on top of this that the legal and political edifice rises, Marx puts forward the canonical formulas of "historical materialism."

In the commentary he wrote between 1842 and 1843 of Hegel's *Philosophy of Right*, Marx retained for his own concept of civil society only a part of what made up Hegelian civil society. Thirty years later, he underlined that his dialectic method was "exactly opposite" to Hegel's and that what he had criticized before was above all the mystical element of Hegelian dialectic.[8] In fact, if we go back to the unfinished commentary of 1843, it is clear that Marx's deposing of Hegelian idealism was first and foremost a rejection of Hegel's subsuming civil society in the state, the individual in the universal, the particular in the "general"; a rejection of what Marx considered the fading away of the real in favor of "consciousness." For this reason Marx retained only those elements of Hegelian civil society that had to do, in his opinion, with "life," while excluding all that was a matter of consciousness. He criticized the "logical, pantheistic mysticism"[9] of the philosopher, in whose thought "the family and civil society appear as the dark natural ground from which the light of the state arises."[10] Speculative philosophy mystified by presenting as mere "appearance, as phenomenon" what was in fact the "real relation": the family and civil society were for Marx "active elements," "the premises of the state," "the driving force,"[11] whereas for Hegel the opposite held. Marx explained that what he was doing was standing Hegel's "very method . . . on its head."[12] Politically, Marx's rejection of Hegelianism for, among other things, its putting a hereditary monarch at the summit of the state, was based on his valuing direct democracy as the union of universal and particular.[13] This is consistent with his general denunciation of all mediation, be it monetary, religious, or political, as alienation: "In democracy, no moment acquires a meaning other than what is proper to it. . . . Democracy is the generic constitution. Monarchy is only a variety [of constitution] and a bad variant at that."[14] The coinciding of the subject with himself was for Marx the very principle of humane social life.

So it is that Marx radically rejected the Hegelian legitimation of the state and the bureaucracy (this last being for Hegel "state consciousness" or "state will")[15] in terms of "general interest" (*allgemeine Angelegenheit*)[16] or "matters of general concern," because this legitimation was based on the false opposition between the "in itself" and the "for itself," where "the people does not know it wants"[17] and the estates (*Stände*) were "mere form." Moreover, the Hegelian solution to conflicts between individuals within civil society, conflicts which threatened to turn it into the war of all against all, was inoperative: How could it be imagined that conflicts evacuated at the level of individuals would not reappear at the level of the corporations?[18] Corporation battles, both internal and against the state bureaucracy, would take the place of struggles between individuals, and this made Hegelian society, modern liberal society, nonviable.[19] The Hegelian state was the speculative sanction of the "abstraction" of private life, its loss of substance, its impoverishment, which the modern world was leading up to. Whereas in the Middle Ages everything–property, trade, society, human beings themselves–was political and the life of the people and the life of the state were identical,[20] the modern world, which Hegel claimed to theorize, though according to Marx he was only dissimulating its truth, instituted the dualism of civil society and the political state.

In his commentary on *The Philosophy of Right,* Marx sought to expose the aporia in Hegel's reasoning. Hegel had presupposed the separation of civil society and the political state, then tried to posit that bourgeois life and political life were identical because mediated by the estates or corporations. But when he made the bureaucracy the basis of objective freedom, Hegel in fact gave it an illusory foundation and therefore could provide nothing better than an empty, formal solution to the problem of subjective freedom, namely the distinction between the estates and the political state: "The separation of the *in itself* and the *for itself*, of substance and subject, is abstract mysticism."[21] For Marx, every solution to the separation of civil society and the state was illusory, as was any attempt to find a mediated solution to the separation of the *in itself* from the *for itself*, objectivity from subjectivity: it was vain to try to find a good working relation of civil society with the state, because no functional coordination or complementary relation could exist between these two spheres. Marx was not looking, as Hegel had been, for a better means of organizing modern society; rather the lesson he took away from the aporia of Hegelian political analysis was that Hegel's whole way of conceiving the problem must be rejected. He did, however, retain a part of the other's vocabulary.

Marx transformed the structure of the relation "civil society-the state" as posited by Hegel by making that which conditioned, namely the state, into that which was conditioned. But he also attacked the Hegelian content of the two terms, excluding from *his* definition of civil society all that could be classified as juridical-political. The effect of evicting right, law, and the political from civil society, the only effective locus of real history as he saw it, was radically to devalue them, reducing them to temporary obstacles that humanity would have to clear out of its path. Marx's overturning of Hegel consists essentially in an interpretation that went willfully counter to the meaning Hegel attributed to civil society. Reducing it to the sphere of needs, only one of its elements in Hegel's conception, and granting it the one crucial role in history and the role of foundation for the political and the state, Marx developed a logic that could not free itself of its initial anti-Hegelian perspective.

Civil Society or Bourgeois Society?

Though Marx eradicated from civil society the juridical and political connotations so prominent in Hegel's notion, this hardly means that *his* concept of it is simple. Indeed, Marx's "civil society" is marked by an ambiguity, what could even be called an internal contradiction–the fact that *Bürger* can mean citizen and/or bourgeois–which has produced absurdities in translation and interpretation (facilitated, it is true, by the difficulty of the concept). For his part, Marx does not seem to have wanted to clear up the equivocation: far from obscuring his own logic, it functioned positively in his system as a conceptual resource.

Marx himself may have derived benefits from the ambiguity; for his translators and interpreters, as we have said, it has caused numerous problems. In 1888, when Engels published the *Theses on Feuerbach*, which Marx had written more than forty years earlier during the same period as his critical rereading of Hegel's *Philosophy of Right*, he added quotation marks to his friend's manuscript and underlined certain words; this explains why in the ninth thesis the text reads *die bürgerliche Gesellschaft*, whereas in the tenth we find *die "bürgerliche" Gesellschaft*. Following the text as Engels thus modified it long after Marx wrote it, the tenth thesis may indeed be translated as follows: "The standpoint of the old materialism is bourgeois society."[22] But the other possible translation–"The standpoint of the old materialism is civil society"–is closer both to Marx's manuscript, and, as we hope to show, to the logic of his theory; truer as it were to Marx's signifiers and signifieds.[23] And clearly the meaning of the sentence that follows– "The standpoint of the new [materialism] is human society or socialized humanity"–and of the eleventh thesis–"The philosophers have only interpreted the world in various ways; the point, however, is to change it"–is radically different depending on what meaning of *Bürger* has been retained. Indeed, the declaration that philosophers must "change" the world means one thing if what is to be transformed is "bourgeois" society, quite another if it is "civil" society. Was not the great originality of the "new materialism" Marx inaugurated precisely to attack, above and beyond bourgeois society, the very foundation of all alienation–namely, in his view, civil society? It was not a matter of changing the type of power in place but of profoundly reorganizing society, making it globally, radically different from anything humanity had ever known: the end of the opposition town/country, of the distinction between intellectual and physical labor; indeed, the end of the division of labor; and the disappearance of social classes and the political superstructure–all of this relevant for the slave-holding and feudal periods of "civil society" as well as the bourgeois capitalist one.[24]

The term Marx generally used to designate "bourgeois society" is "*modern* civil society." If the difference between civil society as a

whole and bourgeois or modern civil society is not understood, then
the critique Marx constructed against mere "political emancipation,"
which, by erecting human beings into "citizens" (*Staatsbürger*) did not
truly enable them to find their generic essence but rather reduced
them to, on the one hand, selfish individual members of "civil society"
and on the other to abstract "moral persons," remains unintelligible.
Political revolution for Marx–and his model of it was the French Revolution–was merely a revolution of "modern civil society," and the
"rights of man" that it promoted were merely those of the "bourgeois."
If the Marxist critique were aimed only at bourgeois society, it would
remain prisoner to civil society's point of view, partaking of its alienation. In short, we may say that it is because Marx agrees with Hegel
that in "civil society" the object is the *Bürger als Bourgeois* that he
protests against it; in other words, he protests against civil society to
the extent that it is, in its very principle–that is even before the existence of the bourgeois class–bourgeois. The person for Marx cannot
be split into "citizen" and "bourgeois," an abstract being and a selfish
individual. That scission, which the French Revolution with its *Declaration of the Rights of Man and Citizen* had stabilized, magnified,
glorified, had to be overcome, together with the one between the political state and civil society.

When his interpreters confuse civil society and bourgeois society,
not only do they fail to understand what was for Marx philosophically
and anthropologically true, they miss the specificity of the "standpoint
of the new materialism" and cast his enterprise into a kind of shadow
where all distinctions become blurred. Let us consider, for example,
the celebrated passages in *The German Ideology* defining civil society:

> Already here we see how this civil society is the true source and theater of
> all history, and how absurd is the conception of history held hitherto, which
> neglects the real relationships and confines itself to high-sounding dramas
> of princes and States. Civil society [*die bürgerliche Gesellschaft*] embraces
> the whole material intercourse of individuals within a definite stage of the
> development [*Entwicklung*] of productive forces. It embraces the whole
> commercial and industrial life of a given stage, and insofar, transcends the
> State and the nation, though, on the other hand again, it must assert itself
> in its foreign relations as nationality, and inwardly must organize itself as
> State. The term "civil society" [*bürgerliche Gesellschaft*] emerged in the
> eighteenth century, when property relationships had already extricated
> themselves from the ancient and medieval communal society [*Gemein-*

wesen]. Civil society as such only develops with the bourgeoisie [*Bourgeoisie*]; the social organization evolving directly out of production and commerce, which in all ages forms the basis of the State and of the rest of the idealistic superstructure [*Superstruktur*], has, however, *always been designated by the same name*.[25]

This text becomes absurd if, instead of being translated "civil society," *bürgerliche Gesellschaft* is rendered as "bourgeois society" (though this has been done).[26] It obviously makes no sense to claim that "bourgeois" society is the scene of all history, or that history came into being only with the development of the bourgeoisie.[27] Nonetheless, at the heart of this absurdity lies a truth: civil society has indeed existed throughout history, according to Marx, but it only came to exist *fully* with the triumph of the bourgeoisie.

Above and beyond the ambiguity inherent in the signifier *Bürger*, Marx's texts may well seem self-contradictory. In one place he affirms that civil society was born only recently; in another that it has always existed.[28] It can even seem like the two affirmations are being made simultaneously. The confusion is, however, only an illusion, and translating *bürgerliche* according to context as either "civil" or "bourgeois," a false solution.[29] The difficulty of interpretation–is it "bourgeois" or "civil" society?–and of the conceptual status of civil society is eliminated when we consider the status of categories in Marx's thinking. Civil society falls into the category of an abstraction: though it was historically produced, it is nonetheless universalizable. How in fact does Marx conceive of the categories of political economy? They arise from determined historical conditions; it is in these conditions that they have their full and entire validity, because it is there that they correspond to reality. The category of "abstract human labor," for example, came into being at the same time as the modern world–was born of and with it–for in the modern world, where commodities reign, labor produces wealth-in-general. In other words, labor is no longer particularized or linked to the capacities of a given individual, who would thereby create a specific use-value. This was not so in ancient Greece, where heterogeneous activities existed for which there was no applicable generalization, since they were neither socially and economically unified or subsumable under a single concept. Still, the economy of ancient Greece could not be understood without recourse to this concept of abstract labor, or to that of commodities, even though the market only existed then in a very limited form. Knowledge always came after the fact, for knowledge itself could only be born in specific historical circumstances that enabled what was obscure to come to light. Nonetheless, its value was not merely local. Like Hegel's philosophical bird, political economy appeared only at the end of the day, when modern society would divulge the secrets of all past history; it appeared at the moment of past history's death. The truth of history for Marx was retrospective and recapitulative–as Hegel's owl of Minerva would see it. But this ultimate knowledge was not nostalgic wisdom come too late. It was infused with the green sap of life.

Civil society, then, had existed through all time, even in ages when it was not and could not be known. In Marx's words, the "real" was only "adequate to its concept" in the modern world. Civil society only existed as such, fully deployed, revealed, manifest, in social formations where the capitalist mode of production dominated: it was there that civil society was itself–modern, that is, bourgeois. Two of Marx's formulas may be used to illuminate each other: one we have already quoted–"the anatomy of civil society is to be sought in political economy" (see p. 295)–and the following, which must be understood *cum grano salis*: "Human anatomy is the key to ape anatomy."[30] Though categories do have retroactive relevance for Marx, the differences between historic forms could not be denied: that which comes at the end was always already there, but only from the analytic point of view. The notion of class was thus indispensable for understanding history, but for understanding it as the history of class struggle, that is, as the history of different historical modes of formation of social groups and confrontation between them (casts, orders, and also classes), a history that was only intelligible in terms of the struggle between classes. But this did not mean that all forms of aggregation into social groups might be reduced to classes. Before modern civil society, for example, the bourgeoisie did not exist as a "class" but rather as an "estate" or "order" (*Stand*). Marx underlined that the passage from one to the other type of aggregation, which came about with the French Revolution, represented a break, a discontinuity.[31]

Misinterpretations of Marx's theory of the abstract category as always-already-there may provoke a desire to poke fun at the eternal Marxist "bourgeois." Before the "bourgeois-bourgeois," the real, full bourgeois of modern civil society, wasn't there a *bourgeois-gentil-*

homme? And before that, a bourgeois-slaveholder? And isn't the bourgeois-early communist, prototype of the dis-alienated bourgeois of fully developed communist society, waiting for us in the depths of history, already ready to reappear, renewed, on his particular scene, and so to bring history full circle?[32]

Such irony must be resisted, however. For Marx, the human being was not an ape, and the feudal lord was not a bourgeois, even if humanity, the final stage of ape development, was the only way to understand apes, and the feudal lord could only be understood with reference to the bourgeois. While the process by which each of the categories of political economy (class, labor, commodities, money) was constituted was a process of abstraction made possible by the universalizability of certain forms, civil society involved a very specific process: civil society emerged through a progressive "split" (*Spaltung*) from the state in which the two entities, conceptually distinct, gradually became separate in the real. In at least one concrete case, that of France, the two had become so completely differentiated from each other that their relation had become one of mortal antagonism, engendering civil war, real modern civil-bourgeois war (*Bürgerkrieg*)–the Paris Commune of 1871. The history of the relation between the state and civil society was, for Marx, the history of a contradiction, in fact the history of several contradictions, whose modalities varied; but his providing the key that makes them intelligible–namely, the permanent epistemological validity, from an analytic and decontextualized point of view, of a category nonetheless historically produced–precludes our finding a contradictory duality in his political theory.[33] Instead we can assume that Marx deliberately conceived of a contradictory reality, which he subsumed under a single concept, "civil society," a reality whose unity was that of a contradiction, that between civil society and the state.

The History of Civil Society Is the
History of the State

Though when Marx applied his political theory to different existing states the resulting analysis was often quite complex, that political theory itself is in large part based on a relatively simple explanatory factor: the status of property. A detailed analysis of political development would of course involve, among other variables, the development of the division of labor, but, following Marx, we may consider that the history of civil society and the state, on the one hand, and the history of property, on the other, are the same story. Put in the space of a formula, political development led from community (*Gemeinwesen*) to modern civil society (*die bürgerliche Gesellschaft*), that is, from the owner-state to the owners' state.

The first historical form that property took was that of tribal ownership of land, based on cattle raising in the case of the Germanic tribes and on war for the Romans. When several tribes came to coexist in one town, landed property became state property; individuals did not have property rights but rather a right of *possessio*, the right to use, not to own. Under these conditions, civil society was the state, and vice versa. Real private property first appeared as movable property, then progressed through a number of developmental stages—portable personal property, immovable personal property, capital invested in manufacture—which culminated in the appearance of modern capital, which was "determined by big industry and universal competition, i.e. pure private property, which has cast off all semblance of community (*Gemeinwesen*) and has shut out the state from any influence on the development of property."[34] Thus the movement that leads from community to civil society is that of a differentiation between civil society and the state, the latter being, in the initial stage of its history, not a mere reflection or superstructure but, on the contrary, an active player in real history. Marx insisted repeatedly on the decisive function of the state as the creator of conditions allowing for the existence of capital, notably in England under the rule of Henry VII and Henry VIII. In this context he underlined the role of force in history, particularly during the stage of primitive accumulation of capital, explaining thus:

> All [methods used during this period] employ the power of the State, the concentrated and organized force of society, to hasten, as in a hothouse, the process of transformation of the feudal mode of production into the capitalist mode, and to shorten the transition. Force is the midwife of every old society which is pregnant with a new one. It is itself an economic power.[35]

To put it briefly, in the stages preceding the advent of modern civil society, that is, before the triumph of private property and the bourgeoisie, the state played an economic role. But all this changed with the formation of modern civil society, characterized by the decline of the state, whose role became strictly political. Indeed, with capitalism and the hegemony of the bourgeoisie, the state had become the owners' property: they bought it on the stock market (in the form of state treasury bonds).[36] The state in capitalist society was therefore no longer an agent of real, that is, economic, history, but rather the instrument of a given social class.

At the very moment that the developmental process of property and the division of labor resulted in the victory of the bourgeois as a class, the state became bourgeois. This was its destiny: existing now distinct from civil society, it was reduced to the role of an instrument useful to the dominant class of that society. In the modern world the state's independence was no more, except where hybrid situations were in effect, in which no segment of the population could manage to dominate another. When the "splitting" process was accomplished, when the state had acquired a particular identity next to, outside of, civil society, it had lost its autonomy to the bourgeois class. It had become "the form in which the individuals of a ruling class assert their common interests, and in which the whole civil society of an epoch is epitomized."[37] But this definition was only fitting to the situation found in modern times. It was only in bourgeois society that civil society lost all elements of community and the atomized individual appeared, separate from other individuals; such a being had not existed in precapitalist societies.[38] In the state, the individual members of modern civil society, the "bourgeois," constituted themselves into "we," a moral person, which then presented itself as the manager of "the general interest." The state gave the bourgeoisie the means of management, together with armed force to protect it from the ascendant proletariat. The state, then, did play a role in the economy, but no longer the active role it had, for example, in the ancient Germanic tribes or sixteenth-century England, but rather a superstructural one, merely legal and political. It might, for example, institute legal procedures of expropriation in order to facilitate the private construction of railroads. Even though this would adversely affect certain individual bourgeois owners, it was hardly the same thing as intervening in the economy or using force to redistribute property; rather it was politically managing the general interest of the bourgeoisie. And of course it was the opposite extreme from a state that accumulated capital and used it to build railroads, as was the case in czarist Russia. The modern, political state was a harmonizer, regulator, organizer of the "general common interest," that is, the interest of the bourgeoisie as a whole, but this in no way made the state an owner, and to believe in its omnipotence was to fall victim to an illusion.[39] In the same way, Marx distinguished the state as an apparatus of violence fulfilling an economic function by means of force (the accumulation of capital in England) from the state as an apparatus of violence in the political service of a social class (the military dictatorship of General Cavaignac during the 1848 Revolution in France). One could not consider a state that directly structured the relations of production by forcibly distributing property to be the same as one that could be bought by individual private owner-citizens at auction on the stock market thanks to the mechanism of public debt and which served their common interests as an instrument of regulation and repression when confronted with the rise of the proletariat. Nor was a state that used its force to maintain people in slavery or serfdom the same as one that used violence against workers struggling to improve their salaries or working conditions. The first was an economic state; the second a merely political state. The modern worker was kept enslaved not by the state's direct violence but by the free market.

However, these two different types of state must be analyzed with the same explanatory tool: *The state was born out of civil society's differentiation from itself.* An entity primitively both political and economic, civil society evolved through definable stages to become adequate to its concept, that is, purely economic, thereby bringing into being, outside of itself, an autonomous, purely political sphere, instrumentalized by the bourgeoisie. Civil society only became truly itself—autonomous in nature, identical with itself and its concept—when it became bourgeois and when the state, which had been *of it* at the beginning of history, became detached from it. In the capitalist mode of production the economic sphere was no longer politically controlled—no political law could change the law of value or the market. Rather the state, through the use of law, harmonized divergent interests within the bourgeois class and provided it with administrative means and apparatuses of violence whose functions were purely political in the sense that they could not change the factors which structured the mode of production.

This general theory gave Marx a principle with which to analyze all existing states: each social formation would be characterized by the degree of separation between civil society and the state that had been achieved through historical development and the nature of the ties existing between the two.

Typology of States

Determining the degree to which the split between state and civil society has been accomplished, the weight of the past in the present enables us to distinguish different forms of the state according to an archaeological method whereby the past is conceived as having determined the present, giving it its particular configuration, just as the ruins of an old and buried city still have an effect on the new one that has been built on top of them.

Marx analyzed two societies representing opposite extremes of political development: North America in the 1850's and the Russia in the 1880's.

In America, more exactly in the northern industrial states of the United States, civil society had not developed on a foundation of feudalism; rather, the state had been from the beginning subordinate to civil society, which here—and the case was unique—existed as pure, adequate to its concept.[40] The North American state had no end of its own, in contrast to France where the state was as strong as civil society was weak, the latter being a mere "caricature" of itself, or to the English situation, although there the differentiation between the state and civil society was further along than in France. On the contrary in America, civil society was "emancipated" from the state.[41] At least this was Marx's assessment midway through the century; he of course modified it accordingly as economic development in the targeted countries progressed. Thus it was that in 1871 he came to insist on the extreme separation between the state and civil society in France, at the same time vigorously attacking Mikhail Bakunin as a "coffee-house politician" for not having taken into account his (Marx's) analysis of England as the "true apex of civil society in Europe."[42]

At the opposite extreme, Russia had no civil society, properly speaking; the term is nowhere to be found in Marx's 1881 analysis (in French) of the Russian case, which he had been studying for a long time.[43] In answer to questions asked by the celebrated Russian revolutionary Vera Zasulich about the destiny of the agricultural commune (*mir* or *obshchina*), more specifically whether or not it was necessary for Russia to pass through all the stages of capitalism before it could reach com-

munism, Marx refused to say whether capitalism might be skipped
over, especially the process of primitive capital accumulation, which in
England was synonymous with expropriation of peasant land, but he
did say that the "historical inevitability" he had studied at work in
Western Europe was not relevant to Russia.[44] Elsewhere, he put limits
on how far English history could stand as a model and formulated the
hypothesis that the order of the stages of primitive accumulation of
capital could vary.[45] Marx saw the state in Russia during the 1870's as
playing a decisive economic role: "At the expense of the peasants, the
state has cultivated, in a hothouse, branches of the Western capitalist
system";[46] it was helping a new "capitalist vermin" to grow rich, suck-
ing the already meager blood of the people of the "rural commune,"
sterilizing the land and torturing the peasants—all to the capitalists'
great advantage. Engels would later take up this analysis and underline
the directly political origin of the czarist state's erecting itself as an
active agent of economic development. Like Colbert in seventeenth-
century France or Bismarck in Germany's then very recent past, the
Russian autocracy was using "artificial means" to facilitate the growth
of capital. Indeed, its defeat in the Crimean War had made it clear to
the Russian autocracy that in order to play a central political role it
needed to have a modern army; that is, an army based on industry,
particularly the railroad. It had learned that it had to transform its
economy by facilitating the development of capitalism, and having no
civil society, no bourgeoisie, the Russian state itself was fulfilling the
role of active economic agent, in the interest of attaining political-
military power.[47] In doing so it was operating in quite the opposite way
from the American state, which was strictly closed off in its own sphere
simply because it had not been necessary to the appearance and development of a capitalist economy and civil society there.

In comparison to the clearly contrasted cases of North America and
Russia, Prussia's situation after 1870 was, in a muddled way, somewhere in between. Neither a purely political or a purely economic
agent, the Prussian state was a combination of different outdated political forms with certain energetic new features; Marx described it as
"a police-guarded military despotism, embellished with parliamentary
forms, alloyed with a feudal admixture, already influenced by the bourgeoisie and bureaucratically carpentered."[48] In fact, the states of "civilized countries" (including Prussia) all had a common basis, which was

"modern civil society," though capitalism was unequally developed in them and capitalist society "more or less free from medieval admixture."[49] For Marx and also for Engels, Germany–a constant theme for both of them–was characterized by its backwardness in relation to other European countries: political backwardness in comparison to France; economic backwardness in comparison to England. Capitalism, wrote Marx in 1873, had developed only very recently in Germany, and it might be observed that "modern civil society" was late in developing there: German capitalism was just coming to "maturity," whereas in England and France class struggle had already become intensely antagonistic.[50]

Without insisting on the weight of the French revolutions in Marx's thought, or, for example, on the particularly French origin of the concept of "dictatorship of the proletariat," we may nonetheless underline the fact that Marx's most detailed analyses of a particular state concern France. But wasn't it Bonapartist imperialism's originality to have "brought out in all its purity the antagonism that exists between the state and the society" and to have in a way divulged to us the secret of that antagonism and made us understand the "anatomy of all apes" that had preceded this ultimate state? Marx's study of the history of the state in France begins with the appearance of absolute monarchy, in which the state played a necessary and positive role, and ends with the civil war that was pitting the state against civil society at the time he wrote it. At the end of the feudal period, the state in France took over, progressively but massively, the common interests of society and created global institutions that, in place of the "motley pattern of conflicting medieval powers," established the "regulated plan of a State."[51] The French Revolution had accentuated and increased the state's functions: it "swept away all these relics of bygone times" and thereby made possible the construction of a modern state whose "political character changed simultaneously with the economic changes of society."[52] Based as it was on the division of labor and centralization, the state no doubt continued to play an essential role in the organization of all social life, itself structured along the lines of modern industry, but as class antagonism between the bourgeoisie and the proletariat deepened, the state came to look more and more like a repressive apparatus of domination, an "engine of class despotism."[53]

Beginning in February 1848, the state had became an instrument of open civil war; then, during the phase of the Second Republic when Louis Napoleon Bonaparte was in power, this became "avowed class terrorism."[54] Civil war could not, however, be society's normal form, and so it gave way to the Bonapartist empire with the coup d'etat of December 2, 1851, which created a "reinforced" state, over and above both dominant and dominated classes, a state above civil society. Bonapartism represented the most "prostitute" and at the same time the final form of the state: the parasite state.[55] Above and beyond the support of the "small holding peasants" (*Parzellen*), for whom Bonapartism was a "religion,"[56] Louis Napoleon was careful to secure another type of political support, that of the bureaucracy, whose development he facilitated. Bonaparte's bureaucracy, supernumerary petty officers and functionaries, was a "caste" rather than a class in that it was defined not in terms of a place in the relations of production—it had none—but by a political function.[57] Up through the reign of Louis Philippe the bureaucracy had been a useful instrument of the dominant class; with Louis Napoleon it became autonomous, existing by the state and for the state, at the same time approved by the small peasantry, which, like itself, was characterized by the homogeneity of its members in terms of status and living standards.

It was in the Empire, on the backs of the bureaucracy, that the "orgies" of the imperial elites, an obscene display of money mixed with pleasures, flourished in a *jouissance* that fed itself on the society below.

This was the state that the Paris Commune had destroyed. Marx called it a "monster," a term Nietzsche would use a short time later when he qualified the state in its essence as the "the coldest of all cold monsters."[58] This "parasitic excrescence," where "state vermin" in the form of standing armies swarmed and "leeches" and judiciary "vampires" prospered, was like a "boa constrictor" squeezing and suffocating civil society. When the Paris Commune was brutally crushed in May 1871, class antagonism was brought to paroxysm: the Versaillais preparing to restore the Empire or an equivalent political form, as their predecessors had in 1848 and 1849, were "ghouls," "cannibals."[59] And Marx predicted that Bismarck, applauding and fraternizing with Thiers, thinking he was witnessing the "definitive squelching of a new, rising society," would in fact see the "complete disintegration of the old bourgeois society," because even if a military dictatorship managed to keep the bourgeoisie and the proletariat under its oppression, their struggle would break out anew and unceasingly: the class struggle could not be suppressed. The civil war of 1871 was therefore a war both of the bourgeoisie against the proletariat (as in 1848–49) and of the parasite state against civil society. With the Commune, the iron grip of centralized power, which under Bonaparte had been used to control society instead of serving it, had been broken, and the working class had accomplished its "emancipation," and with it the young Marx's dearest wish. For even though the Commune was only the "organic means" of an action that would regenerate humanity and not the larger "social movement" that would accomplish that action on a global scale, it was nonetheless a kind of first attempt at forming such a social movement: it stood as a kind of beginning-of-the-end of the political. The Commune had put into practice the democratic society of which Marx had written, where each person was really only a moment of the people as a whole.

At the opposite pole from this regime where individuals' political relations with one another would be ones of immediacy, the secret truth of modern civil society was civil war. Even if not all states were parasite states, the splitting movement by which civil society produced something other than itself could only result in the emergence of an antagonistic double, a monstrous ogre that the proletariat–the class that in fighting for itself, fought for all humanity–must confront. The proletariat would have to institute its own dictatorship; it would have to transfer all administrative functions over to the people and destroy all specialized apparatuses of violence, to be replaced by universal armed masses. The dictatorship of the proletariat would thus bring about the withering away of the state, which meant the end of all coercion, but also the abolition of all law–in short, the abolition of the political sphere.

Denunciation of the prostitute–we may call it Babylonian–state, vampire of civil society, is a remarkably constant feature of Marx's anti-statist, anti-juridical stance. That stance proceeds out of the same logic as his critique of religion or money: all mediation must be condemned as essentially alienating. As we have said, he denounced what he called delusions of "consciousness" in the name of "life"; work was the main-spring of life, and he called upon humanity to reappropriate its essence, its generic being.

Marx took the relation "state-civil society" to be analogous to the relation "heaven-earth," and accepting this opposition, a distant heritage from Saint Augustine, between the kingdom of God and the kingdom of this world, used it to make his point: in the opposition "earth" (civil society)/heaven (the state) he reversed the Augustinian values, making the valued term, of course, "earth" and denouncing the political "heaven." But his affirmation of the primacy of civil society (and corresponding denunciation of the political "heaven") could only lead to a rehabilitation of fanaticism, a fanaticism whose project was not to substitute the City of God for the Earthly City, but rather to destroy–in the name of the true City, civil society–the city of illusion, the political state.[60]

The Peasant War: Long Live the Fanatics!

Given that the French Revolution, because merely political, was only an illusory, mystical, and mystifying solution to human alienation, where might a way out toward real revolution be found for those who, like the Germans, had not even had their 1789? The answer for Germany was to take up again the solution Luther had been moving toward:

> Even from the historical standpoint theoretical emancipation has a specific practical importance for Germany. In fact, Germany's *revolutionary* past is theoretical–it is the *Reformation*. In that period the revolution originated in the brain of a monk, today in the brain of the philosopher.[61]

The philosopher as Marx conceived of him was not an interpreter but rather a transformer of the world, as he put it in the celebrated eleventh thesis on Feuerbach. The radical advances of the Reformation, as expressed by the Peasants' War, had been brought to a halt by theology, but today radical revolution was possible: thanks to the Reformation, religion was no longer an obstacle.

The possibility of revolution in Germany involved two contradictions: that between civil society and the state, and the contradiction within civil society itself. The solution that would allow these two contradictions to be overcome was itself made possible by the existence of a class of civil society itself paradoxical: though it was indeed a class, produced by and thus a part of civil society, it existed at the same time outside civil society, excluded from civil society, the negation of such society. This class was "a *total loss* of humanity . . . which can only redeem itself by a *total redemption of humanity*. This dissolution of society, as a particular class [*Stand*], is the *proletariat*."⁶² It was through the proletariat that humanity would emancipate itself.

What might appear as Germany's backwardness—it had not known, as France had, the end of the Old Regime and the advent of the political state, but rather the religious Protestant Reformation—became in fact a forward developmental position. Germany, which had lived through all the suffering involved in the history of modern peoples without experiencing their evolution, could only accomplish an even more radical revolution than they. This idea enables us to understand clearly the particular interpretation of the German Peasants' War that Engels presented in a work devoted to that historical event.

In the summer of 1850, after the Revolution of 1848 had failed and he had gone into exile in England, Engels undertook a rereading of German history that brought him back to the year 1525. He sought to bolster the hope and energy of the communists and the German radicals by demonstrating that Germany too, like the other major European countries, had a revolutionary tradition. Though it is true that this text, more a narrative than a conceptual construction and manifesting Engels's particular taste for military history, was written in response to what the author judged were the needs of the revolution at the moment, he also thought it relevant enough to have it republished nearly 25 years later, this time with a critical preface.

Engels began by putting the 1848 revolution into both genealogical and analogical relation with the Peasants' War: the past could serve as a foundation for hopes for the future and had lessons to teach us. This explains why the author is constantly drawing parallels, either explicit or implicit, between nineteenth-century and sixteenth-century Germany, parallels that go beyond mere pedagogic artifice, for Engels sought to reveal what he saw as genuine structural similarities. The class struggle that had been activated in the Peasants' War, at a time when Germany was fragmented into a multitude of little states, was, according to Engels, a historical anticipation of the revolutionary movement that had also not succeeded, at the moment of writing, to give birth to a unified republic.

In his preface to the 1874 edition, Engels would explain that in writing *The Peasant War in Germany* he had sought to show, following the same principle that had guided Marx in the *Eighteenth Brumaire*, that the specificity of Germany's political constitution, the contradictions between political unification and the political and religious theories of the 1520's, were not the causes but the "results" of the degree of development of such concrete fields of activity as agriculture, industry, communications, the commodities market, and finance. His materialist conception is entirely structured around the notion of civil society: political and religious controversies are shown to be a "reflection" of the class struggle, and the notion of civil society is what founds his explanation of both historical phenomena and the insurgents' aspirations in 1525. At that moment in time, he explained, the "bourgeois heresy" was accompanied by a "peasant and plebeian" heresy that demanded that the conditions of equality characterizing early Christianity be reestablished between the members of the "community" and that they become the norm of civil society.[63] This heresy sought to institute equality in civil society for all God's children: civic equality, but also the equalizing of fortunes, or at least the diminishing of great differences. To Engels's mind this other heresy was just as easily observed during this period as the bourgeois heresy was (although this was not so in the much earlier case of the Albigensians): it was to be found among the extremist Hussites of Bohemia at the beginning of the fifteenth century. Beneath the theocratic embellishments of the peasant-plebeian heresy—and this was the postulate behind Engels's entire interpretation, the whole of his religious sociology—one could discern the communist and nationalist tendencies that were developing in Germany at the end of the fifteenth and the beginning of the sixteenth centuries.[64] In short, Engels interpreted the heresies that emerged at the end of the Middle Ages and the beginning of the Renaissance as anticipations of modernity that had to be freed of their theological or mystical shell, a shell that had meaning only because of its function, which was to enable men of the time to say something above and beyond what the realities of the time allowed. Although inadequate to the reality of class relations, the language of heresy was not false like an error; rather it contained the truth of an illusion to be understood by considering the conditions in which the plebeians of the time found themselves. Because their stage of economic, political, and social development forbade them to make their own revolution in their time, the plebeian "class" could only manifest its aspirations in terms of prophesying. This was, in Engels's words, a "violent and fantastic" historical anticipation.[65] The result of the disparity between the visionaries' aspirations and the historical capacities that would be necessary to realize them—capacities unattainable at that moment—was fanaticism.

The situation of the modern proletariat was analogous to that of the plebeian at the time of the Reformation: a class negated by the whole of society and which would negate its negation with the revolution. Though civil society was indeed the anatomy of all social formations, modern civil society, based on division into classes, must be gotten beyond. Still, it was necessary for a given civil society to be developed enough to be qualified as "modern," a stage that Germany, as we have said, only reached relatively late, in the last third of the nineteenth century, after England, France, and North America.

But what was the situation of the plebeians in Germany at the beginning of the sixteenth century?

They constituted during that period the only class entirely outside official society. Plebeians had no privileges, and, unlike the peasants and the petty bourgeois, not a single possession, not even one for which they would have to pay heavy and regular charges. Under such conditions, the plebeians had no contact with any existent institutions, and conversely, such institutions did not take their existence into account. They were the living symptom of the decomposition of feudal society and of a world structured around guilds, and at the same time, the precursors of modern civil society. It was this situation that explained why, even this early in time, the plebeian faction could not limit itself to the struggle against feudalism and the privileged bourgeoisie but had to, at least in imagination, go beyond the modern civil society that was just beginning to come into existence. It explained why this segment of the population, excluded from all ownership of property, had to call into question *already* the institutions, conceptions, and ideas common to all forms of society based on class antagonism. "In this respect, the chiliastic fanaticism [*Schwärmerei*] of early Christianity offered a very convenient starting point,"[66] Engels wrote. This way of conceiving the plebeians at the time of the Reformation is of course exactly the same as the way in which Marx presented the status of the proletariat in modern society.

What was a revolutionary class? When part of the class that was in the process of emancipating itself attained general supremacy and was thereby recognized as the "general representative" of society, it excited "enthusiasm," both within that class, among its other elements, and outside it, in the whole of society.[67] This upsurge of enthusiasm had already been observed in the case of the French bourgeoisie (we have seen how it touched Immanuel Kant). But in Germany, according to Marx in 1843, no similar process could be expected to take place because no class felt the need for it; no class possessed the ability to bring about general emancipation simultaneously with its own emancipation; there was no class whose own fight for freedom could coincide with the revolution of an entire people. This move from the particularity of a group to the universality of the revolution could only take place if a class of civil society came into existence which would be universal in that its sufferings were universal. The revolution depended on the emergence of a social class so completely dehumanized that its emancipation would bring about the full restoration of humanity for all. This class was the proletariat. And it was of course with features similar to those of Marx's description that Engels, a few years later, painted the rebellious plebeians of the beginning of the sixteenth century. Thomas Müntzer, the prophetic leader of the peasants, in whose thinking and writings might be discerned communist resonances that expressed the aspirations of a real social group and "anticipated modern civil society,"[68] could justly appear the ancestor of the proletarian revolutionaries. In his analogy Engels even described the German nation during the period of the Peasants' War as divided into three camps: Catholic conservatives, Lutheran moderates, and the revolutionary party. He portrayed Luther as being at the center of "sordid trafficking" that resulted in the Augsburg Confession of 1530 and the constitution of the bourgeois Protestant Church, and as manifesting the petty bourgeois spirit to be found later, in 1850, in the Erfurt Parliament, which, assembled at the initiative of the king of Prussia with the aim of proclaiming German unity, had not dared to confront Czar Nicholas I. Whereas Luther showed "cowardly servility to the princes,"[69] Müntzer was the leader of the popular, revolutionary party, which identified the kingdom of God as a society without class differences, without a state power foreign to the members of society. For Müntzer not the princes but "the entire community has the power of the sword."[70]

In his analysis of the Anabaptist phenomenon, Engels explained the fact that this "fanatical" (*fanatische*) sect[71] had rallied round Müntzer for reasons both social—their hostility to the dominant classes—and

religious–their call for a second baptism. It was the combination of
these attitudes and beliefs that gave the group its internal cohesion.
Luther and Müntzer were emblematic of two classes: Luther's hesi-
tations, and to an even greater degree Melanchthon's, were those of
the bourgeoisie, whereas Müntzer possessed revolutionary energy and
steadfastness, and he saw beyond the insurgents' immediate demands.
The "wild fanatic form"[72] of asceticism that characterized this sect,
then, was of a nature completely different from that preached by Lutheran morality or the English Puritans, the secret of which resided in
saving money: it enabled the lower strata of the population to "develop" its "revolutionary energy"[73] and to become clearly conscious of
its hostility to all other elements of society. In fact, we can say that its
function was the same as the "unity of will" that, in Lenin's expression,
had to organize the Bolshevik Party.

As we know, Müntzer's fate was rather different from Lenin's. What
happened to him, explained Engels, was the worst thing that could
happen to a revolutionary leader: he had been obliged to take power at
a moment in history when the movement was not yet ready to be dominated by the class it represented or to apply the measures implied by
the domination of that class. A leader in this situation was doomed to
suffer a terrible fate, because what little he had it in his power to do
could not accord with all his past, more radical actions and the principles and immediate interests of his party. Given that what he should do
could not be done, he found himself compelled not to represent his
party, his class, but rather the party and the class–not his own–for
whose domination the movement was in fact ready: "In the interests of
the movement he is compelled to advance the interest of an alien class
and to feed his own class with talk and promises, and with the assevera-
tion that the interests of that alien class are their own interests."[74]
What had happened to Müntzer was that the transformation that
haunted his imagination could not be anchored in the material conditions of the period he lived in; in fact these conditions were propitious
for the development of a social order that was the opposite of the one
he dreamed of instituting.

His defeat could thus be understood as a revenge of the laws of
historical materialism on fanaticism. Tragically, against the visions,
the phantasms of those who dreamed of building the kingdom of God,
civil society had imposed its law: in the end it was always civil society

that won. The only way Müntzer had at his disposal for trying to overcome the "chasm" between his theories and reality was to become, unreservedly, the fanatical, exalted prophet of the revolution – the premature prophet of a revolution that could only take place a long time after him – and to inflame and nourish the people's hatred for the dominant class – princes and landowners – a hatred that filled his mouth with the religious and nationalistic ravings of the Old Testament prophets.

The failure of the 1848 revolutions to bring new nations into existence, more particularly a unified Germany, and Engels's ensuing choice at this moment of disappointment to narrate an edifying story, that of a hero – Germany – who must overcome ordeals, had the effect of accentuating the nationalistic tenor of his retrospective analysis: the insufficiency of Germany's economic development, both weak and irregular, and the fragmentation of German society into different "estates" themselves internally divided "ruled out any centralization of Germans into a nation,"[75] Engels wrote with regret of 1525, and the situation in Germany after the revolutions of 1848 was analogous to this earlier one. Worse yet, the Peasants' War had reinforced the princes' domination and thus stabilized a Germany broken up into numerous units. In fact, Engels made two affirmations that could be seen as contradictory: one, that the German "nation" did not exist because there was not and there had never been any centralization; two, that Germany existed nonetheless, despite its divisions. According to the second of these visions, the German nation was emerging as the progressive realization, carried out under the determining influence of economic conditions, of an entity preexisting the political form known as the nation-state, preexisting industrial capitalism, preexisting "modern civil society." Engels thus seems to have hesitated between two conceptions of "nation," the idea that a nation is an effect of the prevalence of the capitalist mode of production, and the idea that a nation somehow exists prior to capitalism, that it is the development of capitalism that in some way awakens it or brings it to realization. The affirmation that founds *The Peasant War in Germany* is, in any case, sharply marked by a substantialist conception of "nation": "The German people, too, has its revolutionary tradition."[76] What immediately follows is a clear expression of romantic nationalism:

> There was a time when Germany produced characters that could match the best men in the revolution of other countries, when the German people

displayed an endurance and vigour which would in a more centralised nation have yielded the most magnificent results, and when the German peasants and plebeians were full of ideas and plans that often made their descendants shudder.

The text is clearly a contribution to the myth of the eternal Germany,
which though it may be characterized by its revolutionary spirit, is
nonetheless understood from the perspective of an ethnic conception
of "nation." There are however other passages that could be used as
arguments to support the hypothesis that a given nation-state results
from random processes.

Much of the debate within Marxism about the status of nations
oscillates between these two visions, the one emphasizing that they are
sociopolitical constructions, the other that they are the actualization
of a quasi-eternal reality. It is true that in conceiving of social laws as
laws of nature, having the same kind of necessity and truth, Marxism
may tend toward an ontological and substantialist vision of nations,
though this is sometimes contradicted by a more artificialist vision.
Marx's retrospective epistemology–according to which, as we have
seen, "work" as a category, though emerging only with the modern
world, was what made the economy of ancient Greece intelligible to
us–if applied to societies, tends to produce a conception of "the nation" as a sort of invariant or essence whose conditions of realization
or actualization alone are historically determined. It becomes understandable why Müntzer, or the Marxist interpretation of him, was used
in attempts by the communist German Democratic Republic to legitimate itself: it was the heir to Germany's heroic revolutionary past. The
last manifestation in Communist Germany of this will to find chronologically distant and thereby supposedly profound roots for oneself in
accordance with the commonest of nationalist prejudices was the organization of ceremonies for the five-hundredth anniversary of the birth
of Thomas Müntzer–the totalitarian bureaucracy would celebrate the
fanatic hero. While the exact year of his birth is not known (it was
either 1488, 1489, or 1490), the ceremonies were held in 1989 to coun-
terbalance those in commemoration of the French Revolution of 1789.
There were exhibitions, books, artists' commissions–the Communist
bureaucrats meant to deploy all devices necessary to a full theatricalization of the national memory: the state's construction of the national
past. The irony of history was of course that with the fall of the Berlin

Wall in December 1989 the GDR would disappear, at the very moment it sought to celebrate its five-hundred-year-long revolutionary past. Leading the fight against communism in the country were the Lutherans: Luther against Müntzer, defenders of civil society against admirers of the fanatic, with Erich Honecker, general secretary of the Party and president of the committee charged with organizing the anniversary ceremonies, at their head.

But interpreting the Peasants' War and the activity of Thomas Müntzer could result in quite a different figure from that of the heavy Stalinoid millenarianism of East Germany.

Using largely the same material as Engels, Ernst Bloch in *Thomas Müntzer, Theologe der Revolution* (1921) gave quite a different vision of the revolutionary prophet. Unlike Engels, Bloch was writing not after a counterrevolutionary victory but rather just after the Russian October of 1917. For him, despite the "positivist spirit" that had enabled Marx to save communism from being theology, one could not forget that "dreams," "oriented enthusiasms," in short millenarianism, were not "hollow ideology" but rather "spring up from a primordial point in the soul, creating and determining values."[77] He saw in Müntzer a brother of Karl Liebknecht, the great social-democrat leader of the Spartacus movement together with Rosa Luxemburg, but also of Lenin: "capable of illuminating the revolution not solely with the idea of earthly happiness but with the strongest of finalities." "At present," wrote Bloch, "the time of the Kingdom cannot fail to come; toward this time radiates a spirit within us that rejects all renunciation and will not know disappointment."[78] And he chose to see in Müntzer an anticipation of "that most inward of men, the Russian man":

> He who carries within himself a Russian man will hear within himself the *homo archifanaticus* [Müntzer] . . . : and the true spirit of the Reformation will awaken, close to the humblest, the flame growing into the magic of love, into the spirit of Russian fanaticism, to the point where, through force and reason, apocalyptic Catholicism will open the way out of the old world toward the ultimate myth, the absolute transformation.[79]

But the millenarian hope that Bloch saw rising up with the Russian Revolution would quickly be crushed, in the very place it had been born. Civil society would be cast into oblivion–an oblivion at the very heart of Bolshevism.

Barbarity and Civil Society

Civil society was not one of Lenin's concepts. Or rather, just as the
bourgeois class had been missing from Russian political and economic
development, we may say that in Lenin's thinking "civil society" is a
missing concept.

The fact that the expression so frequently found in Marx's writings
does not once appear in Lenin's analysis is due not to a problem of
terminology or translation but to a conceptual gap between the two
thinkers, though it is true that both of them rejected the idea of right
and law and denounced political representation.[80] Situating himself
elsewhere than in the constellation of issues structured around the
notional pair "civil society/the state," Lenin instituted his own program, then installed at the core of Soviet institutions the monopoly of
the monolithic party-state. To legitimate his revolutionary strategy for
Russia, Lenin leaned heavily on texts in which Marx made intensive
use of the concept of civil society, particularly on his analyses of the
state in France, but he retained only one lesson from what Marx said in
them: the state was the apparatus of violence; violence was its very
essence. At least it is in this brutal nakedness that his doctrine appeared in the critical summer of 1917, just before the Bolshevik coup
d'etat that, in the void created by the implosion of the old society,
would lead to the emergence of the first single-party dictatorship.

It is no doubt true that before he wrote *The State and Revolution*
that summer, Lenin's assessment of the czarist state was more complex
than what we may read in that text. In 1913, the Bolshevik leader had
begun to theorize the stages of development that constituted the history of the Russian state: he characterized the period that began with
the 1905 revolution as that of a transformation from autocracy to a
constitutional monarchy modeled along the lines of both the Prussian
and French states, both Bismarckian and Bonapartist. But it is clearly
impossible to present the czarist state as "independent" of civil society. It is, moreover, possible to hypothesize that it was the interpenetration or interweaving of state and civil society in Russia, in
other words the absence of a modern civil society there, that prevented
Lenin from positing them as separate entities. In this case, the extremely high value attributed to the political as expressed by his demi-
urgic theory of the Party could be explained in terms of the absolute

dominance exercised by the state in Russian society. The transformative crisis inaugurated by Gorbachev–and its prolongation in Yeltsin's Russia–together with the intensive use that has been made in the former Soviet Union of the formula "civil society" since the middle of the 1980's have shown that the present political entity is confronted with a similar problem, a kind of constant, radical difficulty: Can a civil society be built from above?

At the end of the nineteenth century Lenin affirmed, against the populists, that capitalist development was indeed under way in Russia: the country could not possibly follow a noncapitalist path, namely because agriculture was penetrated with market relations. But contrary to "economist" Marxists, who wanted to concentrate the activity of the Party on defending the economic interests of the proletariat and whom Lenin accused of leaving the monopoly over political struggle (essentially the combat for civil rights) to the liberals, Lenin sought to show that capitalism in Russia was severely impaired by the autocracy, by what he called Asianism.[81] Despotism was not only a way of organizing political power; it suffused all social relations–Russia was not civilized, or at least not sufficiently so. The process by which class consciousness was spontaneously created through the class struggle of the workers against an educated bourgeoisie, the process Marx had described as taking place in Western Europe, was impossible in Russia. The autocracy had the effect of curbing the spontaneity of economic transformation in Russia, and what was worse, there could be no political element in that transformation because there was no coherent bourgeoisie making decisions that were logically consistent with its interests. As if it were anticipating in a way a later stage of the class struggle in which it would be directly threatened by the proletariat, the Russian bourgeoisie had failed to throw itself resolutely into combat against the despotic system to promote its own political interests, namely the instituting of civil rights. In fact it was using the present despotic regime to protect itself from the future threat. Because of this failure on the part of bourgeoisie, because of the absence of a civilized bourgeoisie due to that class's social and political weakness, the revolutionary Party would have to have a program both socialist and democratic: socialist in order to attain its social objectives, democratic in order to obtain the political freedoms for which the Russian bourgeoisie was fighting only half-heartedly. It was therefore the Party's task to inject the workers with social-democratic class consciousness and to organize them in order to multiply their force. In short, Lenin attributed to the Party the function of agent of historical transformation: the Party had to compensate somehow for the absence of a civilized bourgeoisie–a modern civil society, we may say–in Russia.

In the name of its civilizing mission, the Party had both the right and the duty to be barbarous. It would roundly fulfill this duty once in power by organizing, as one of its first tasks, the combat against "parasites": "He who doesn't work doesn't eat." The harmful elements in Russian society left over from the old system had to be destroyed to permit the advent of the new society. But what Lenin called a parasite was not the same as a Bonapartist parasite, either bureaucrat or reveler, as designated in Marx's anti-statist zoology. The insects the dictatorship of the proletariat, a regime of civil war, had to destroy in Soviet Russia did not form a "caste" as had the supernumerary personnel of Bonapartism; they were not the artificial products of a political system erected above society, but rather members of classes or segments of classes condemned by history. People with wealth, hysterical intellectuals, elements of the working aristocracy, *kulaks*–the types of people Lenin called parasites had more to do with an analysis of the modes of production than a study of the character of the state at a given moment.

For Marx, the Paris Commune was civil war waged by civil and civilized society against the parasite state; for Lenin, dictatorship was the civil and civilizing war of the party-state against the parasites existing in barbarian society. The Soviet power continually gave itself "tasks," to use one of Lenin's favorite words, which required total mobilization, even during periods of peace such as the spring 1918 truce. The models for such mobilization were the modern army and big business; its apogee was to be seen in the closely planned warfare of World War I, with general staffs commanding the movements of what seemed then vast and technically mighty armies. In this warfare the Bolshevik leader read the triumph of his organizational ideals.[82]

Because it was organized in accordance with the principle Lenin called "unity of will," the Party produced an exponential increase in the force of its members. As was the case in all modern, efficient organizations, each Party member had to alienate his individual will completely in the interest of the whole. There was a hierarchy, division of labor, and a central management imposing absolute discipline. Just as in the modern army and the capitalist factory, individuals were the gears and cogs of a machine that, like a lever, produced a miraculous effect: the force of each element—soldier, worker, or professional revolutionary—was not simply added to that of the next; rather their respective forces, because organized, multiplied each other. But what kind of energy fueled them?.

Hatred.

Hatred as a desire to kill, destroy, purify.

As a will for nothingness, a desire for death.

Hatred seeking not to vanquish the enemy but to annihilate evil, in a movement where the organized proletariat's energy must attain such force that it topples and razes the old to create the new.

Mass terror: terror on a mass scale: terroristic and terrorized masses.

Massive, regenerative terror against the enemies, terror to be deployed by purifying revolutionary masses who must rise up, in a gesture of absolute self-sacrifice, as high as death if need be. A call to heroism: during the civil war, at the Ninth Congress of the Communist Party in March 1920, Lenin affirmed that the workers' battle-cry—"Rather perish than surrender"—was the determining factor for attaining victory. The love of death as the decisive element of victory: fanaticism erected as a positive historical factor. We may consider for example the advice Lenin gave to Mussolini's Italian socialists in 1921: "In order for communism to triumph in Italy your Party must be incapable of hesitation, a true avant-garde, uniting within itself the greatest fanaticism and devotion without limits, resolute, firm, inflexible."[83] In order to be so, the Party had to both reinforce its own cohesion by purging itself—in this way it multiplied the efficiency of its hatred—and instill contempt for death in the masses. Its ultra-centralized organization and the fanaticism of the masses would reach their maximal power in civil war, which was the apogee of the political.

Leninism's Enemies

The Soviet regime as Lenin instituted it was a regime of "civil" war, ineluctable according to his doctrine, which functioned like a self-fulfilling prophecy made that much more effective because the enemies of Bolshevism symmetrically proclaimed an identical assessment of the situation. As the example of the French Revolution had demonstrated to Lenin, a given social class would always fight to the end to defend its interests and resist, actively or passively, the new power. Political power could only be conquered and preserved by force. To make it absolutely clear that the rifle was in charge and despite the reluctance of several Bolshevik leaders, Lenin signed the proclamation announcing his coup d'etat on October 25, 1917, in the name of the Military Revolutionary Committee of the Soviet of Petrograd, not in the name of the Party. He preferred to take power by armed force than to receive it from the Congress of Soviets, which was to be held a few weeks later and in which the Bolsheviks had the majority. The terror that held sway, terror whose duration, extension, and methods largely exceeded the few duly voted legal texts that were its framework, was not, as we have said, Leninism gone haywire but rather, from the outset, one of the regular modes of communist functioning. We have a clear indication of this in the fact that at the Party's Tenth Congress (March 1921), after open hostilities had ceased, after the end of war communism, at the beginning of the famous New Economic Policy or NEP, the Bolshevik leader brandished mass terror as a threat against the "bad" communists he knew had infiltrated the Party. At the same moment, he was proclaiming that the only choice left to the entire world was white, fascist terror or red, revolutionary terror, demanding not only that class struggle be continued under socialism but even that it be exacerbated. By rejecting, in favor of the absolute preeminence of the class struggle, any distinction between internecine warfare and war against an external enemy, *stasis* and *polemos*; by denying all sovereignty or legitimacy to the state in the interests of the Party; by erecting civil war as the regulating Idea of political life to the absolute detriment of representation, Lenin can only be said to share the conception of the political affirmed later by the rightist German political philosopher Carl Schmitt—at what we may call the midnight hour of Europe's brown and red century—that "the era of the state is in decline" and that "the specific political distinction to which political actions and motives can be reduced is that between friend and enemy."[84]

But enemy and friend were not simple categories for the Bolshevik leader. Leninist policy may be called an intellectual and practical, moral and material technology of otherness that organized systematic classification and treatment of all types and species. Under cover of the single term "enemy," fatal for all to whom it was applied, it refined the taxonomy of hostility, inventing new varieties, bringing to light entities before unknown or ill-known. Marx had said in discussing the art of heraldry that the science of nobility was zoology; for Lenin the "living soul" of Marxism, "the concrete analysis of a concrete situation," was a kind of purifying, purging zoology.

For Lenin the Party's maximal centralization was to be combined with an ideology of civil war and social hygiene–all in the interests of promoting mass terrorism. Once we know this, do we really need, for example, Raymond Aron's analysis of the three historical stages of the Soviet regime to understand the nature of totalitarianism? Might it not be preferable to underline that as early as October 1917 the organizational and conceptual matrix of totalitarian terror was already in place? Aron analyzed the history of the Communist Terror in concrete terms. The first form, identical to that of the French Revolution, was civil war, in which the Party in power was not mistaken when it saw enemies everywhere: they were there. Thus, between 1917 and 1921 Lenin followed the same procedures as Cromwell and Robespierre. In the second period, 1929-30, what took place was the elimination of "class enemies," this being in Aron's view explicable in rational terms, if not excusable, as the adequate means of reaching the fixed end: collectivization. But the third and most astonishing aspect of terror according to Aron was that the Party should have turned against itself: the Great Terror, though interpretable in terms of Party structure and the existence of an orthodoxy, was nonetheless irrational and unreasonable. For Aron it was to be understood mainly with reference to the role of the personality cult (an explanation not very different from the one given by Khrushchev in his 1956 "secret" report).[85]

Before Aron, Hannah Arendt had in fact proposed a similar periodization of Soviet history. For her totalitarianism only really triumphed in the 1930's, whereas she saw in Lenin an authentic statesman who, when he died, left a completely unresolved situation, notably because he had made possible an alliance between the peasantry and the proletariat and permitted the development of the middle-level peasantry. Totalitarian regimes reached their maximal intensity with the notions of "objective enemies" and "undesirables."[86] We cannot take up here all the elements of the debate on Soviet totalitarianism, the relevance, for example, of an equation between Nazism and Leninism. But we can underline the fact that totalitarianism does not, and cannot, exist, any more than any other political and social system, in some kind of pure form, and this is even truer given that it defines a program whose application collides with social reality not by accident but precisely because its intention is to remodel that reality entirely, all the way down to its biological foundations. In any case, it is impossible to understand the historical significance of the Leninist period of the Russian Revolution, the logic that animated it, the intention that oriented the decisions made by its promoters, without taking into account the crucial phase of spring and summer 1918: a tragic episode of "the class struggle" that ended up in the "anti-*kulak* crusade"–the kulaks are an example of an "objective enemy"–conducted under the slogan "Death to the vampire kulaks." This campaign, together with the brutal intensification of the fight against the Whites, resulted in the official opening, on Lenin's explicit order, of the first Soviet concentration camp, the first element in the system whose operation would soon be handed over to the newly formed General Camp Administration, or Gulag. A fecund moment for totalitarianism.

Let us put parentheses around the Russian civil war proper, which, after the supposed class struggle, developed into the deployment of pure violence by an apparatus of repression whose only purpose was to provoke even greater terror, and consider for a moment the NEP. It is often presented as a period both of economic truce and of greater political freedom and less police repression, perhaps because of the freedom enjoyed during this moment by the segment of the intelligentsia that had rallied to the regime. There is, however, no evidence to prove that the repression was discontinued; it may have changed techniques and targets, but there was no change in its scale or intensity: the dictatorship of the single Party remained just as strong and the police organs did not stop their work for an instant. If we lose sight of this, perhaps because the economy was no longer that of war communism and the market had been granted a minor role, we are in danger of creating the illusion of a break between Leninism and Stalinism; of masking over the fact that the inaugural moment of the Bolsheviks' coming to power also gave birth to the totalitarian system. Periodizing totalitarian terror, as Raymond Aron does, means considering only a single, visible aspect of it, while the other aspects, mighty but in shadow, continue to act and structure the system; it means seeing only one of the targets and one of the methods, whichever ones happen to be on center stage at a given moment.

It is necessary instead to bring to light what was at the core of the system, namely, the Leninist classification of "enemies." Who must be fought? Following the model of the French Revolution, the Bolsheviks had to fight against the "enemies of the people"–an explicit use of Jacobin signifiers. Just after the Party came to power, for example, the Constitutional Democrats (Kadets), a typically bourgeois party according to Lenin, were declared "enemies of the people." This formula, like "class enemy," seems to have designated enemies that were both "subjective" and "objective"; that is, elements hostile to communism as much by what they thought and wanted as by what they did, both hostile to the Bolsheviks and willing to combat them actively. But it was fitting, in Lenin's view, to distinguish two varieties, for "enemies of the people," objective-subjective enemies, could either appear in full daylight or in disguise; they might try to "mask" their faces–the word coming this time not from Lenin but from Joseph Stalin, who in 1937 opened the hunt for residues of Trotskyism hidden within the Party and the fight against activities of sabotage, espionage, and terrorism by "Trotskyite-Zinovievist fascist agents." Open enemies were enemy soldiers (White Army soldiers and the English expeditionary corps that supported them) or members of parties openly hostile to the Bolsheviks. As for "masked" enemies, they were "saboteurs" or "spies" who might be encountered anywhere, even inside the Party. At the beginning of the NEP, at the very moment of the Kronstadt insurrection, Lenin affirmed in a speech to the Tenth Party Congress that the Party could well be infiltrated with White guards in the guise of "communists of the extreme left," and he attributed part of the responsibility for the failure a year earlier of the Hungarian revolution to reformist communists who had sabotaged the Party and the Hungarian soviets from within. From the very first years of the Revolution, the framework for bloody repression against the Party itself had been put in place by the denouncing of enemy presences within it. There was then no safe place for anybody, because even the Party was not a shelter and its members enjoyed no immunity. Once again, this logic did not result from the specific conditions of the Revolution. As early as 1908-10, Lenin had denounced "bad" revolutionaries inside the Party, accusing them of wanting to "liquidate" it. The pre-1917 history of Bolshevism was already one of denunciation and purges.

In addition to "objective-subjective" enemies, there were what Lenin called simply "objective" enemies, for whom the term "enemy" doesn't quite fit in that they were not animated by anti-Bolshevik sentiment. These groups quite simply were not conscious of the evil they constituted. Rich citydwellers and *kulaks* constituted such innocent threats, to which corresponded a particular type of qualifier: they were "parasites," "vampires," "harmful nuisances," and what condemned them was the "necessities of history." Vast groups left over from outdated modes of production, they encumbered the Russian soil, which had to be "cleansed" of them much like the soil of England had been by "estate-clearing" (purging the English countryside of excess peasants was, of course, the operation Marx had cited as giving birth to the early accumulation of capital). What Lenin had in mind was a class-cleansing operation: the *kulaks*, for example, had to be eliminated "as a class," and it was the Bolsheviks' task to see that this was done. Designating enemies of this type, ignorant of their malfeasance, depended on a rationalizing kind of knowledge in which hatred was legitimated by means of a kind of objectivizing neutrality.

But White soldiers and "saboteurs," on the one hand, the "parasites," on the other, were not to be confused with a third type of "objective" enemy who was at the same time a "subjective" friend, that is—this time—declared allies or partisans who, because of what they did or said, were in truth against the Bolsheviks and therefore against the Revolution. In fact, they were enemies more by what they said than by what they did, and sometimes by the mere fact that they dared to speak at all. While the bureaucratized communists, mainly from the former Menshevik ranks, who had rallied to the communist revolution but who remained mute while parading their haughty demeanor had to be expelled from the Party, as Lenin explained in 1922, those "objective enemies–subjective friends" who were noisy and agitated, some of them going so far as to be openly rebellious, were "hysterics": the Menshevik Julius Martov, who supported the revolution and had been in friendly contact with Lenin during their shared Siberian exile at the end of the 1890's but who had opposed him at the Second Congress of the Russian Social Democratic Party in 1903; Bukharin and his leftist revolutionary romanticism of the winter of 1917-18; the leader of the Left Socialist Revolutionaries, Maria Spiridonova, and her comrades at the Sixth Congress of the Soviets in July 1918. Hysterics disturbed the Party's functioning and frustrated the "unity of will." Political judgment, which was also judicial judgment that could condemn without appeal, must never consider what supposed friends thought were their motives or intentions. Lenin always knew better than those friends what their desires, thoughts, and political intentions were. By declaring that those who did not speak as he spoke should not speak at all, he claimed for himself the role of absolute master of the signifier.

Each one of these classified groups of enemies was to be treated in a specific way. For "hysterics" there was the psychiatric hospital. For the objective enemies—parasites and harmful nuisances—concentration camps. Against open objective-subjective enemies, war. For "the enemy's infiltrated agents" and all "saboteurs," death was the appropriate punishment: execution was the only acceptable way to deal with the hundreds of traitors among the Kadets, those without a party, the socialist-revolutionaries, all of whom "acted," either with weapons or through disorganizing maneuvers, against the power of the Soviets—like the Moscow typographers and railway workers, all supporters of the Mensheviks, who had gone on strike in November 1917 to protest against the Bolsheviks' forming a single-party government that excluded other socialists. The most fitting form of repression for spies, however, was the trial. By avowing his guilt, the traitor, an enemy both objective and subjective, objectively recognized his subjective hostility. By confessing, he honored the absolute power of the one who had known how to penetrate his disguise of good communist or old Bolshevik and uncover the soul of an enemy of the Soviet power. By his own words, the accused annihilated himself in a perfectly transparent world where his life was offered as a sacrifice to the omniscience and omnipotence of the chief. He canceled himself out in the paranoid other.

These three species of the genus "enemy" did not leave much room for the genus "friend." Indeed, Leninist logic exonerated from the crimes of hostility, otherness, or deviance only one element of the system: the one who pronounced sentence on the adequacy of the real to its concept, who decided what had to be so that those parts which science had designated as negative and politics as dangerous could be removed from the world. Only the chief corresponded to the true, and this in turn ensured his power, while around him absolutely nothing was secure, for an enemy could be hidden in the very features of a friend. After Lenin, Stalin complained—as one who had become a victim of the paranoid-making machine—that it was possible for an enemy disguised as a good communist to accuse a good communist of being a disguised enemy and that, thinking to get rid of a traitor, one had in fact fallen victim to a saboteur and had thus disorganized the Party at the same time as one had ensured the triumph of its enemies whereas what one had really wanted to do was to punish them![87] "An ignoble two-faced man, the camouflaged enemy of this type does his best to create a climate of excessive distrust in the Party organizations, a climate in which all members who take up the defense of a calumnied communist are immediately accused of lacking vigilance and having relations with the enemy."[88] The principle of Leninist objectivism, that people must be judged without taking into account what they themselves as subjects think but only on the basis of what they do, and that words must be confirmed by actions, becomes pure subjectivism and madness as soon as the action that verifies the words can only be an act of accusation made either against another or oneself.

The sense of objectivism, the primacy of actions over words, is perfectly condensed in Lenin's stigmatization of hysteria. "We do not need hysterical outbursts," he proclaimed at the beginning of the Revolution, "what we need is the cadenced march of the iron battalions of the proletariat." For Lenin, hysteria, connoting as it does emotion, tears, cries, and denoting the behavior of petty-bourgeois revolutionaries, was dangerous in that it accorded a privilege to theatrics, *mise-en-scène*–representation. If indeed Lenin's fanaticism was not iconoclast, it was made of an absolute hatred of all images that correspond to the conditions of modern political life: an absolute hatred of representation, political democracy, which for him could be nothing other than vaudeville, foolish and dishonorable theatricalization. We may understand his dissolution of the Constituent Assembly in January 1918 as a consequence of this hatred; in his eyes, he was putting a halt to a farce. The same hatred of words, discussion, protestation, are evident in his stigmatization of the delegate Maria Spiridonova as a hysteric–for which crime she would soon be incarcerated in a psychiatric institution–for having denounced Bolshevik peasant policy on the stage of the Bolshoi Theater at the Sixth Congress of Soviets. Words were always dangerous and fallacious, delegation was always deceptive and mystifying, representation was always dispossession and illusion. In representation, delegation through words, culminated the deception of bourgeois politics, the effect of which was to disarm the proletariat.

In politics, to speak was always to lie, because speaking in politics meant denying primacy to force in action. By placing insurrection at the summit of revolutionary action, Lenin not only indicated that violent coup d'etat was the privileged technical means for taking power, he also underlined that the essence of the political, the truth from which everything else followed, was war. That war was to be conducted, in the case of civil war proper, with soldiers marching in time against enemies who had declared themselves, but it was also to be waged, in the form of a program of social hygiene, against designated individuals and groups in society and the Party, who were to be treated as psychiatrically deranged human beings or as destructive animals, harmful insects—to be either locked away or exterminated.

*

Lenin and Stalin might not have engaged so readily in constructing their political taxonomy had they gone more often to the zoo. There they might have found matter for meditation, in the same way Friedrich Engels once did. One day in 1843 Marx's friend found himself at the Manchester zoo admiring a platypus egg. The platypus is a philosophical animal if ever there was one, Darwinian and anti-Hegelian, for, both mammalian and oviparous, it belies the idea that the world is rational, demonstrating that the world is not always adequate to its concept, and that without the inadequation of the living being to itself—the platypus is living proof of this—there would be no evolution. Hegel, Marx once said critically, had proposed not a logic of the Thing, but rather the Thing of logic. With Lenin and Stalin what we have is the logic of Thingifying, and it created a terrible new zoology, where platypuses were monsters.

10 Civil Society and the Law-Governed State

The state is the opium of civil society. That formula may serve to condense Marx's political theory: the state offered people imaginary compensation for their alienation in civil society. By proposing illusory liberty and equality, illusory in that they did not correspond to the earthly condition of real people, the *Declaration of the Rights of Man and Citizen* played the same role as religious "phantasmagoria" that promised eternal happiness in the hereafter.

Both religion and politics were "opiates of the people," who lived on the "real *ground*" of civil society, and we can condense Marx's theory into the following three-part analogy:

$$\frac{\text{Heaven}}{\text{Earth}} = \frac{\text{the Political}}{\text{the Economic}} = \frac{\text{the State}}{\text{Civil Society}}$$

An atheist, Marx radically condemned the domination exercised by the superior term "Heaven," which he assimilated to fantastic illusions emanating from a world that had to be not merely interpreted but transformed. He maintained the dualism theorized by Augustine, but with the express purpose of criticizing it, and therefore inverted the hierarchy of values, just as he reversed the logic of fanaticism as Luther and other Reformers had characterized and stigmatized it. That logic, let it be recalled, rested on the following series of analogies:

$$\frac{\text{City of God}}{\text{Civil Society}} = \frac{\text{God}}{\text{Images of God}} = \frac{\text{Heavenly Jerusalem}}{\text{Babylon}} = \frac{\text{Body}}{\text{Soul}}$$

Whereas Luther had defended, against the fanatic iconoclasts, the legitimacy of the interval between the upper and lower terms, Marx contested the very notion of that interval. He did not of course, in the manner of the sixteenth-century *Schwärmer*, call for eliminating the distance between civil society and the City of God through a zealous, instantaneous instatement of God's kingdom, but rather for the Earth to rebel against Heaven, the economic against the political, civil society against the blood-sucking state. In this sense the Paris Commune of 1871 was for Marx the resumption of an interrupted moment of history: it realized the hopes that had mobilized the German peasants in 1525. The Parisian proletariat had for a brief moment succeeded where the iconoclasts had failed, namely in the practical destruction of illusion, the abolition of the "split" between civil society and the state.

Marx's denunciation of the political state as a false solution to the problem of real human wretchedness was radical and entire; it was not especially aimed at oppressive regimes, but as we know targeted the democracy that had resulted from the French Revolution. Even though Marx preferred a certain degree of political freedom to dictatorship (he hated the Russian autocracy), he abhorred so completely what he saw as the fundamental lie of the political state that he preferred dictatorship of the proletariat exercised in the name of civil society. The political state's attitude toward civil society was to him just as spiritualist as Heaven's toward Earth, and combating it required the same atheism.[1] In the political sphere, the profane individual of civil society was as lost as he was in religious "fantasy."[2] And "political democracy is Christian," because, while man was indeed a sovereign, supreme being in such a system, the sovereign man of the political state was "corrupted, lost to himself, alienated" and "subjected to the rule of inhuman elements and conditions by the whole organization of our society."[3] Citizens as such were religious in their worship of the State and of law, in that modern man found his truth not in the material conditions of his life but rather somewhere else, in the life of the state, situated above and beyond the real individuality of each particular person. Human beings were politically religious to the extent that in a world dominated by the capitalist mode of production, politics, like religion, was the expression of what separated one person from another.[4] The so-called sphere of "general interest," where the ideal of the rights of the individual reigned, was really just the spiritualist aroma, the incense, of the private sphere in which individuals in fact treated one another as means to ends.[5]

The state, then, and more especially the democratic state, fulfilled the spirit of Christianity. The state was Christ. Just as Christ was the mediator to whom humanity attributed its own divine nature even as it was dehumanized, so the state was the mediator, artificial and unnecessary as were all mediators, between the individual and his own human freedom.[6] Yes, the state ensured the triumph of "man," because he held the supreme power in it–except that "man," this citizen who was a political sovereign, was in fact a false sovereign because a false man, cut off from his own humanity and from the rest of humanity by the conditions of modern society. What was political freedom other than the right to be limited to oneself, to be reduced to a selfish individual? Modern civil society's individual was an atom. A person dehumanized in that he was deprived of relations with other people. An individual without community, turned in on his private interest and pleasure. Thus it was that the French Revolution had simultaneously constituted the political state and, through the dissolution of feudal civil society, created a bourgeois civil society of selfish individuals–equal, free, and human in the political and legal abstract, quite the opposite in the concrete, material particularity of their lives.

To give people back their humanity, to ensure that it would not be stolen from them by any mediator, be it Christ or the state, it was necessary to get beyond bourgeois civil society, composed as it was of selfish monads above which loomed religion and the state. It was necessary to rise up to community, to communism.

Critique of the Political Illusion

The relation between the real world and the world offered by religion, between the economic and the political, civil society and the state, was for Marx less a relation between two distinct terms than a mechanism of illusion modeled on the *camera obscura*: what we see projected on the far surface of the box is an image of the real object, but inverted, upside down.[7] The relevant opposition, then, the one that summed up all the others, was that between the real and what Marx qualified as the fantastical, or what we may call phantasmal. The phantasmal world produced by false consciousness (*Nebelbildung*)[8] was a false world, one where, for example, money made the stupid and ugly who had it handsome and smart in direct proportion to how much they had. Religion, a flower in a flowerless world, was a consoling deception that depicted humanity as having a grandeur that was the opposite of the wretchedness of real life. As for the state, it was the form of "illusory general interest" that permitted the conflicts between particular interests and collective interest to be "resolved" through mystification: "It follows from this that all struggles within the State, the struggle between democracy, aristocracy, and monarchy, for example, the struggle for the franchise, etc., etc., are merely the illusory forms in which the real struggles of the different classes are fought out against one another."[9] Therefore—and this was true regardless of the type of state and for the whole matter of right—freedom and equality as the French Revolution had promoted them engendered a citizen whose solemnly declared abstract universality constituted a denial of the fundamental inequality existing within modern civil society, that between the bourgeois and the proletarian.

In order to thwart this phantasmal vision, it was necessary to place civil society at the base of history, as its foundation, for it was civil society that explained all theoretical productions and forms of consciousness, and revealed the state to be "divorced from the real interests of individual and community."[10] With its "*earthly* basis for history,"[11] the Marxist conception of historical development could account for all the "idealist twaddle"—religion, philosophy, moral philosophy—and all the superstructures—law, state, ideology—in terms of the material production of existence. To be a victim of political illusion, as the English had been since 1688 and the French since 1789, or of religious illusion, which was typical of the Germans since Luther, was to be a victim of "representation"; representation was responsible for handing the driving role of history over to supraterrestrial forces.

Marx presents two examples of the mechanism of illusion at work: Kant's philosophy and the French Constituent Assembly of 1789.

German history after Luther was the history of the *bourgeoisie*'s incapacity to constitute itself into an active, dynamic class.[12] It was technologically behind, cut off from the international market; its interests, economic, political, ideological, were heterogeneous, fragmented. It had neither estates (they had disappeared) nor classes (they had not yet come into being). Because the conditions for economic centralization were lacking, political centralization could only come to exist outside civil society, in the sphere specialized in administration, which therefore played the role of a Will imposed on the weakness and atomization of a yet retarded civil society. The modern state in Germany was thus not the political effect of an economy unified by the market, but, quite the contrary, the deliberate agent of social unity: since the period of the absolute monarchy it had possessed an apparent autonomy that had engendered all sorts of illusions about the supposed independence of the political in relation to the economic. And the philosophy of Kant, spokesman for the German bourgeoisie, was the illusory ideological reflection of this real process: his theory of the categorical imperative had prettied up the bourgeois ideas of the bourgeoisie, isolating the "autonomous will," the "free will," while neglecting to consider that that will was determined by the material conditions in which people found themselves. Kant's theory, which founded morality on the self-determination of the will, omitted or rather dissimulated the fact that each will was particularized by specific interests. The omission was analogous to that at the very core of the modern state, which claimed to represent the general interest, whereas what it really did was veil the conflictual divergence of particular interests. Kant was thus the philosopher of that illusion of freedom which allowed for the perpetuation of material conditions engendering real slavery.[13]

The second example of illusion, which had of course also been promoted by Kant, was the historic document of 1789 establishing the *citoyen* as the truth of the *bourgeois*, whereas in reality the *bourgeois* was the truth of the *citoyen*. In the French Revolution the French bourgeois, that is, the owner, had thrown off his prior status of monarch's subject and conquered that of citizen. So it was that the transformation of the Estates General in June 1789 into a National Assembly and then, in July, a Constituent Assembly marked the passage from representation in terms of estates to representation in terms of classes, in other words, from feudal society to modern civil society: bourgeois society. From that moment on, the regulation of social conflicts between individuals was no longer founded on privileges but rather on the rights and laws imposed by the democratic, representation-based state. Marx's analysis of the metamorphosis of owners into citizens, of privileged persons into individuals equal before the law, led him to the following conclusion, decisive for the concrete political fate of Marxism: "The representative system is a product specific to modern civil society; it is as inseparable from modern civil society as the isolated individual of that society is."[14]

Political representation in modern civil society was the correlative of social atomization, of the conflict of particular interests that characterized such society; political representation enabled the bourgeoisie to represent its own interests as being universal interests. One might even say that it was analogous, in the institutional order of things, to Kant's philosophy in the theoretical order: in Kantism, as in the French Revolution, the mystification that consisted in affirming the sovereignty of the will triumphed. We know the watchwords and battle cries that resulted from this condemnation by Marx and his successors of representation in general and political representation in particular: hatred of what was considered parliamentarian cretinism and the whiners and bawlers of bourgeois democracy, and the absolute primacy of power relations and force, whose absence or omission from the analysis—or action—could only be understood as deceit or treason.

In illusion, a form—the state or right—detached itself from the concrete lives of persons and turned against them. Marx reproached those who merely criticized illusions for not really attacking the root of the problem: it was not enough to denounce illusions; the conditions that engendered them had to be changed. Given that the illusion had its source in material life, the arm of criticism would have to give way to criticism by arms: it was not enough "not to believe what one is told"; one had to seek out in the real (in the concrete matter of civil society) the reasons for the lie, the interests it spoke for, and then engage the battle to transform the world that had engendered such phantoms. To criticize religion as if it were an autonomous sphere was merely to denounce the "spiritual aroma" of material conditions—religion was merely the "enthusiasm" of civil society[15]—instead of fighting those conditions in their profane form; and in order to attack effectively the "rights-of-man" mystification, which disguised the bourgeois as citizen, it would be necessary to fight against the system of social relations based on private property. This was what "communists" would do—for such was the name that Marx and Engels took for themselves in the middle of the 1840's. For communists, only the profane was real: it was on this assumption that they founded their atheist fanaticism.

We can say that critiques of Marx miss their target when they seek to rehabilitate the sacred against the profane, Heaven against Earth. Let us consider the example of right and law. Communism's absolute refusal to recognize the value of civil and human rights and of law, be it private or public, that originated in Marx's thinking and was reinforced and systematized for practical use by Lenin, led to reducing law in the USSR to a mere instrument in the hands of the single Party, a fact grimly illustrated by the Moscow show trials under Stalin and the repeated recourse made to Article 58 of the Soviet penal code, written by Lenin himself, in order to fill up the concentration camps. But how to go about reversing Marx? By returning to Kant? By rehabilitating the state? By reinstituting the law?

Inverting Marx's thesis on inversion can result in theories and practices that, because they employ a symmetric, inverted logic, are in fact a continuation of Marxism. We may observe some of the coarsest effects of this mechanical inversion in the former communist countries of Eastern and Central Europe, where the supposed setting back on its feet of a world turned upside down by Marxism has resulted in bizarre post-totalitarian combinations—religion and money, God and the market, nationalism and profit, for example, where religious and political fanaticism and money-worship mutually exalt one another. This restoration of Heaven, the term denounced by Marx as illusory, as part of a logic of human emancipation does not get beyond Marx but rather remains locked up in his presuppositions, a naive revival of his logic. Reversing Marx cannot consist in rehabilitating the forms that he condemned as mystification—money, religion, law—but rather in affirming the *value* of illusion, reestablishing the value of mediation and representation, refusing to devalue them as mere phenomena in the name of some reality that somehow *is*, and is all there is. By denouncing the law as illusion, on the one hand, or singing its praises as real, on the other, we remain prisoner of the ontological, realist illusion. The only way out is to affirm that if law is indeed a reality this is because it *is* an illusion, that representation is not ontologically degraded, infirm, or sickly. It must be recognized that representation, what we may call with Levi-Strauss and Lacan the symbolic sphere, is itself effective. Its effectiveness is not an expression of material effectiveness; the symbolic sphere itself acts.

We can illustrate this point by rapidly considering how violence may be regulated within a society, making use of a simple sociological observation: the more armed policemen on duty there are, the more crimes are committed. Not that policemen are criminals–this is only exceptionally the case. Rather, if the state's only reaction to the violence of those it should be able to make respect and obey it is to deploy more violence, it can only increase general recourse to violence. How can ordinary individuals not involved in writing laws or putting them into effect be expected to be more virtuous than the state and not resort to violence when the authority that claims to allocate value doesn't abide by what it teaches and, through its policing example, makes violence the normal means of social regulation? The state that uses violence is less effective against violence than the state whose law, necessarily mediation and representation, forbids the use of violence. It is not the *presence* of state violence that can limit violence; what can limit violence is rather the state's *representation* of violence as forbidden. If the state believes in using force, why shouldn't everyone believe that the use of force is legitimate? And how could the example of immorality given by the state not be the most pernicious of all? This is what Freud's critical reflection on the state at the time of the First World War led him to conclude, as we shall see.

Condemned by Marx as illusion in his critique, both nominalist and empiricist, of ideology, vilified by Lenin with the accusation of hysteria, representation–both figuration and mediation–does not accord priority to religion, politics, or money, but rather institutes the non-coincidence of the subject with himself or herself, the non-coincidence of need with its object, of the signified with its signifier. Positing as real what Marx posited as illusion does not enable us to break with the iconoclast indignation with which he denounced representation as masking and denaturing the real. By erecting the state, law, the political, or money as the only reality, we close ourselves up in a logic that is just as monistic as Marx's was when he posited as possible and true the reduction of all history to the history of civil society. We may observe, moreover, that the substance of Marx's critique has been so little engaged by many of those who claim to refute it that they end up proposing a kind of neo-Marxism, unconscious and ultrasimplified, in its place: the idea that all social life has its origin in the economy, its principle in the business corporation, its truth in production. Many of the champions of anti-Marxism remain in an attitude of denial, still warming themselves at the hearth of that old liberal thought from the tradition of which Marx's own thought was born.

Marx used to compare ideologues, navigators of the speculative ocean, to Cervantes' hero. While denouncing their confinement in the world of phantoms that made them read Hegel like the ingenuous Hidalgo de la Mancha had read *Amadis of Gaul*, he took their idealist illusions seriously: he did not confuse them with error, and he knew very well that they would not be dispelled by the mere knowledge of truth, but that illusion was constitutive of a situation that prevents the truth from appearing. To fight against illusion was thus to fight its conditions of production and reproduction. Marx, moreover, did not hesitate to propose a materialist explanation for Don Quixote according to which the knight of La Mancha was locked up in an outdated ideology, chivalry: the economic conditions of his time had changed.

In fact, the logic of illusion in Cervantes rests on principles quite different from Marx's. In Don Quixote the subject who has illusions himself appears as a phantom to the other: Don Quixote, who attacks those he thinks are phantoms, is himself taken for a phantom (*fantasma* in Castilian) by those he charges with his lance.[16] His phantasm then is imposed on other subjects: if a barber on a donkey sees himself charged not by a poor fool with a sad face but a frightening phantom, this means that Don Quixote, the fantasizing subject of the other's phantasm, is *real*. A common barber of la Mancha, who has not read chivalric romances, like a materialist and communist economist who criticizes speculative philosophy, cannot escape phantasm any more than any human subject can: phantasm is not an imaginative, imaginary addition to the world, but its very warp and woof. There is no need to set up once again an elaborate opposition between Marx and Freud (who as an adolescent learned Castilian to be able to read *Don Quixote* in the original). Suffice it to say that Marx believed it was possible to reduce the world and the subject to their profane forms, that is, to strip them of all phantasm, whereas Freud granted a fundamental place to phantasm as the mark made on the subject by the object of desire.[17] We may nonetheless underline the fact that for Marx, as opposed to Freud, phantasm was in no way linked to the structure of a person's desire but to his history, his transitory contingency. Illusion had no future, to the extent that the end of capitalism, the final class society, necessarily implied the decline of the very conditions that engendered illusions. Thus with the advent of the dictatorship of the proletariat, all illusions would slowly perish, at the same pace as the state withered, and persons would find themselves, and "find themselves," on the real ground of civil society.

In *Capital* (1867), Marx took up once again the religious question to which he had devoted so much space in his work of the 1840's. This time he dealt with it not from an anthropological perspective but in terms of an analysis of "the fetishism of commodities" characteristic of the capitalist mode of production. It might be said that the "mystical character of commodities" derived from the fact that the relation between the use value and the exchange value was the same as that between the real and the phantasmal: people believed that commodities were exchanged in accordance with qualities they inherently possessed, whereas in fact merchandise was exchanged in accordance with the quantity of work that went into it (it takes so many hours to make a table, a dress). In the capitalist market economy, a determined social relation between persons took the "fantastical form" of a relation between things, in the same way as in religion products of the human brain appeared as autonomous beings. The mystification of capitalism transformed the real inequality of different products of human labor—the "sensuously varied objectivity" of tables and clothing, for example, as "articles of utility"[18]—into an equality: a table can be exchanged for a certain quantity of clothing. The mechanism of abstraction that Marx describes in this text closely resembles his critique of political abstraction as making unequals (a worker and a bourgeois) seem equal. But the illusion that made people fetishize commodities was not any more inevitable than the political illusion in Marx's view. In a society regulated by the time spent working, such as communist society would be, people's social relations with each other and with useful objects would be "transparent in their simplicity": when working conditions and practical life were rational, when social life was based on the work of freely associated persons, the religious and political reflection of the world would fade away.[19] With this we touch on a key point of Marxism: civil society was both the first and the last reality of history. After history, a new kind of humanity would appear.

Marx refuted the hypothesis that civil society was necessarily, in its essence and principle, composed of separate individuals–this was merely the form it took in bourgeois society. Indeed, the atom, self-contained and isolated, was sufficient unto itself, and for it the external world was empty and silent, whereas the individuals of civil society needed one another: their stomachs reminded them that needs created interactions between people in which they acted as *material* mediators for one another. They needed one another to be able to satisfy their needs. Even linked by false, alienating mediations–notably money–people were by "natural necessity" bound together in civil society by interest. They were only atoms in and for the sake of the political illusion, in the sky of their imagination, the universal azure of the "rights of man" that canceled out the differences of earth. In fact, the idea that social life had to be maintained by the state could only have been forged by political superstition, Hegelian superstition. The reality was the opposite: the state was maintained by civil society.[20]

The Power State

The refusal to consider the clash of individual interests as an essential feature of civil society is to be found, though with different consequences, in the thought of Emile Durkheim (1858-1917), for whom belief in the atomistic nature of civil society was not the principle of political illusion, but rather the source of the power state. It was in the name of such a state that Germany stood "over all": *Deutschland über alles.*

In an anti-German propaganda tract published in 1915 that stands as French sociology's contribution to the war effort, Durkheim explained German cruelty as a "social pathology" connected to a Nietzschean will to power; one form in which this will expressed itself was the doctrine of the power state.[21] In this theory the state was defined by power; this in turn explained and legitimated its acting in order to increase that power, mainly through war, in which it realized itself. At the core of Durkheim's analysis of the German doctrine of the power state is a critique of the opposition that doctrine had formulated between civil society and the state, an opposition which established the superiority of the state and placed it above morality. The German theorists had mistaken the nature of the state and committed a radical error concerning the nature of civil society: they deemed civil society to be the theater of a "confused medley of all imaginable interests in conflict one with another,"[22] interests that if left to themselves, would bring on the famous war of all against all. In order to keep civil society under control, for its very principle was the *bellum omnium contra omnes* of Hobbes's "state of nature," the state, according to this theory, had to be strong and use that strength. And the state that behaved like a conqueror in order to dominate its civil society could, by logical extension, only be military and warlike in its relations with the outside. *Der Staat ist Macht.*

Durkheim contested the idea that the state, which in his scheme was not might but rather organization and order, the response to a "need," could have a kind of unshakable stability in contrast to the kaleidoscope of civil society. Individuals were moved by more than their own interest: "By uniting, by linking themselves with one another, they become conscious of the groups they form . . . and thus those social sentiments which the State expresses, defines, and regulates, but which it assumes to exist, come spontaneously into being."[23] In short, collective consciousness, whose place was in civil society, played the role of a community tie founded on what Durkheim considered the "real factors of historic development," namely ideas, beliefs, economic life, technology, and art, whereas the sphere in which the state intervened–diplomatic negotiations and war–was more superficial. There was, then, no need for a state that would impose its law on the supposed atomistic anarchy of civil society by demanding a kind of formal obedience to which citizens might superficially assent without their intimate personal acquiescence being required.

The arrogant, brutal consequence of the affirmation that "the State is above civil society" was "Germany is above all." The country that so proclaimed itself was a "monster" whose monstrosity resulted from the fact that its only ideal was the exaltation of its power: "not a word of humanity, of the duties the State has toward it" from the theorists of the power state. This led Durkheim to contrast Germany with Christian peoples, whose morality had for its object "the realization of humanity, its liberation from the servitudes that belittle it, its growth in loving-kindness and fraternity."[24] If we disengage the Durkheimian program from its chauvinist underpinnings and patriotic pathos, we can see that it was designed to limit the state by imposing on it an ethical purpose, with Kantian resonances, whose roots, which others situated in the state of nature, were here placed in civil society. To the (German and pagan) conceptual couple "atomistic civil society/the power state" might therefore be opposed the (French and Christian) couple, "organized society/the ethical state." We can understand how Durkheim could impute primary responsibility for the war of 1914 to an ideological factor, namely the "Nietzschean" overvaluing of the state's will. His belief that war was caused by bad ideas is consistent with the place he attributed to representation, collective conscious- ness, in the functioning of society, and which he reproached the Ger- mans for underestimating when they reduced civil society to the sphere of selfish competition. On this point he was of course at opposite poles from Marx (even though, like Marx, he posited the primacy of civil society and contested the ideal that such society was necessarily atom- istic), for he imputed to moral representations, social ideologies, the role of essential historical causes.

While the First World War led Durkheim to denounce the theory of the power state, it also facilitated the rise of what we have called cyn- ical sociological theories, according to which the very heart of the state consisted in its holding and wielding of force: the state as apparatus of violence for Lenin; politics as the discrimination of enemy from friend for Carl Schmitt; and the most famous of these theories because, un- like the first two, it is not often suspected of having affinities with either communist or Nazi totalitarianism, namely Max Weber's defini- tion, in which, after explaining that the state fulfills all possible func- tions, he identifies the *means* of fulfilling them specific to it and it alone in the celebrated phrase "the monopoly of legitimate physical violence within a certain territory." As we noted earlier, the genealogy of this idea goes back at least to Luther, for whom the existence of a political authority that in turn prohibits the deployment of private violence appeared as a natural human right. As we know, Weber cited as an authoritative source Trotsky–"Every state is founded on vio- lence"[25]–hardly surprising words coming from the founder of the Red Army at the very moment that Lenin was defining the dictatorship of the single Party as a regime based on violence and following no other laws than those it gave itself. In the Marxist-Leninist vulgate's defini- tion of the state, the Weberian conception, and that of Treitschke and Schmitt we find the same cynicism, producing what it claims to de- scribe and legitimating tyrants, boiling social life down to power relations and fully excusing states for their use of power, power being their essence and the use of it their only means of fulfilling their historical destiny.

Against them, Durkheim's vision is to be inscribed in the tradition of the law-governed state, not in the juridical sense of a theory of the hierarchy of norms, but rather in the ethical and political sense of limiting the law's sovereignty by a particular type of higher law. Although the law by which the state limits itself may vary in content and in the source of legitimacy accorded it, a law-governed state is nonetheless subject to a law it recognizes as governing its decisions and actions. The substance of this law is civil rights, the rights of the individual. A state that presents itself as law-governed because the legality of the law is therein verified by a constitutional or supreme court is not necessarily limited thereby in its sovereignty, and it is for this reason that a law-governed state must be characterized not only in juridical terms but also in ethical and political ones: that which is antagonistic to the sovereignty of the state is the sovereignty of the individual human being and the citizen. A state that recognizes this other sovereignty yields its own to the rights of the individual and the citizen. Though he does not structure his argument in precisely these terms, the state valued by Durkheim is based on the same type of principle, because it is, as he put it, the "subject" of the "great human community" and "cannot subsist when all humanity is arrayed against it."[26]

Freud formulated his indictment of the power state at the same moment as Durkheim, but using quite different arguments and reaching quite different conclusions from those of the French sociologist. Using the magnifying glass of the war, during which *la raison d'Etat* abolished all morality in the state, Freud underlined the danger to civilization constituted by such a state. The state's immorality, patent during the war, was not accidental. It was not merely to be accounted for by the exigencies of the hostilities between it and other states, where it came through so garishly—in the inversion of the commandment "Thou shalt not kill" into the obligation to kill, for instance. What became evident was that the "state has forbidden to the individual the practice of wrong-doing, not because it wants to abolish it, but because it desires to monopolize it, like salt and tobacco."[27] Indeed, by requiring obedience and sacrifice from its citizens, the state transformed adult individuals into minors, and it made use of patriotism (what we may call nationalist fanaticism) to legitimate its thirst for power. But because moral consciousness was nothing other than the superego, whose origin was to be found in social anxiety, when that anxiety could no longer fulfill its role as a moralizing factor on account of the blood-stained immorality of the state, brutality was born among the citizens of the civilized world, who were thereby divided and abased. Civilization's discontents were both expressed and promoted by the power state, which ate like an acid into the already thin veneer of civilization that was all there was to make the subject moral.

The Law-Governed State *Is* Civil Society

No need to insist on the distance between Durkheim's optimistic idea of the possible morality of social life and Freud's pessimistic vision of the fragility of civilization, a pessimism whose appropriateness was to be so grimly confirmed by the rise of Bolshevism, then Nazism. What is most striking is that in his text of patriotic mobilization, Durkheim seemed to believe that the state and civil society, in France and elsewhere, could somehow not end up corroded in their ethical foundation and collective morality by war. Obviously the climate of nationalism present both generally and within professional circles had a kind of anesthetizing effect on French sociologists, among others.[28] Though war might well have constant and universal roots in a timeless drive, its most immediate cause in the modern world was, as Freud repeatedly indicated, a kind of nationalism based on religious or ethnic affiliation that the individual found difficult to steer clear of. Far from those fanatics who, in Luther's time, sought to pull down political authorities and abolish the state, the fanatics who assimilated "foreigner" with "hostile"–a type Freud watched rise triumphantly during the war–were state worshipers, who organized themselves into states in order that their cause might triumph and sought to purify civil society of any deviant or simply different elements. So it was that Freud asked what the Bolsheviks would be able to do after killing all their bourgeois in order to ensure an internal cohesion based on hatred. Stalin's answer, as we know, was to undertake a generalized, large-scale massacre of Bolsheviks, among others. While blatant and terrifying in the context of totalitarianism, the logic of hatred as a means of social organization is also a threat within democratic regimes.

If we may say that totalitarianism is characterized by the state's imposing a kind of general mobilization against its own citizens, it is also true that democracies can be perverted by a state's turning its means and powers against civil society. The possibility of war, impossible to exclude, is constantly present even for a pacific state, necessarily pulling it toward the blood-shedding aspect of sovereignty—from civilization toward barbarity, Freud might have said. The horizon of war acts like a constant potential corrupting agent of human rights: the frontiers between peace and war, between the interior and the exterior of a given political territory, become blurred, and we may observe that the methods of war, involving the suspension of the individual's rights in the so-called interest of the state, are made to serve the passion for excluding others that runs through modern societies: groups arbitrarily constructed by the assimilation of social traits to objective or natural characteristics are stigmatized, threatened, oppressed, in certain cases annihilated. It is in this way that the threats of *polemos*, war against an external enemy, and *stasis*, internecine division, are activated and intensified, and a general mobilization is instituted, which results in the state battling those it was meant to shelter and protect. The fact that a given regime is based on the principle of the people's sovereignty is not sufficient to thwart that corruption of which the nationalist power state, not to mention the totalitarian state, is the most visible instance. Even those democracies which respect most attentively the formal procedures by which a government is chosen are capable of stripping certain of their citizens of their rights or of treating noncitizens like enemies. In France, for example, the principle of the state's secularity is sometimes understood not as prohibiting the state from privileging any particular religion or giving any particular religion a specific place in the institutions of the Republic, but as obliging certain religious groups to show indifference to their own beliefs.

Against what we have called the nationalist power state, whose image haunts the whole of post-totalitarian Europe, there is only one institutional answer, whose effectiveness is based on the political mobilization of citizens—in some cases violent mobilization—to affirm their political rights. That answer is of course the law-governed state, in which democracy takes its most concrete form.

The extension of the notion of the law-governed state, both the widening of its meaning and the multiplication of its uses, its transition from the status of scholarly category to that of mobilizing theme, is contemporaneous in France and other countries with that of the expression "civil society." Neither one of them, however, should be considered a mere matter of fashion; they both require the same type of genealogical study. Neither the concept nor the reality of the law-governed state is new, even though the term came into existence much later than "civil society" (*Rechtstaat* appeared at the beginning of the nineteenth century). But the genealogy of civil society as we have expounded it here shows that the notion has at certain key moments in its history been meshed with that of law-governed state; one would indeed not be mistaken in affirming that the demand for a "law-governed state" on the one hand and a "civil society" on the other are one and the same demand. In its very essence civil society is a society composed of individuals endowed with civil rights (this is, as we have seen with Aristotle, what distinguishes it from the family or the *ethnos*); that is, civil society is a society founded on the civil and political rights of citizens. At the risk of distorting it, let us quote once again the definition Aristotle gives in the *Politics*: "Justice is political; for justice, which is the determination of what is just, is the ordering of civil society."[29] This is not the technical definition of the law-governed state – according to which such a state is based on a hierarchy of norms that requires legislation to conform to the criteria of a supra-constitutional legality usually determined by a court with precisely this expertise – but rather its ethical and political meaning. The citizenship that exists in a law-governed state stands as the absolute limit of the political power. This power cannot violate the rights of citizens without legitimating their desertion or insurrection, for if citizens had no right to combat violation of their rights, including by violent means, the law-governed state would be an empty signifier. We may therefore say that state sovereignty in a law-governed state is radically weakened, the state becoming the mediator between "supra-state" political imperatives and its citizens (or, put another way, between human rights based on natural right and civil society). In this state of affairs the process of limiting power begun by the mechanisms of representation (the vote, representative government) finds its complement. Analyzed in these terms, however, the law-governed state comes to appear as the concrete mode of organizing civil society. As the authority that defends the rights of individuals, in their name and subject to their verification and approval, the law-governed state is not the instrument of what Hegel –

and Marx by way of criticism–called "the general affair," but rather of concrete individuals, to whom it ensures the framework within which they can effect their undertakings and receive protection for their liberty. We may indeed underline the facts that political right, that is, justice and the procedures and institutions by which it is realized and enforced, is the infrastructure of civil society, and that the law-governed state is a state made up of individuals who are citizens, by positing the following equation: law-governed state = civil society.

Not only is the equation conceptually sound, it also corresponds to concrete political realities, to the anti-authoritarian, antitotalitarian political mobilization in Eastern Europe, for example, in which the fight for civil rights and the autonomy of civil society against the dictatorship of the single Party has brought about a practical surpassing of the opposition between civil society and the state in the recognition of the common enemy, the Leninist party-state. The attempt to find institutional guarantees against all ways of crushing citizenship–for it is this that engenders all forms of oppression, the insidious as well the massive, which communism multiplied from the moment it took power–is in turn rehabilitating the representative state and juridical systems as institutions that effectively protect individuals and promote human emancipation. The abrogation in 1990 of Article 6 of the 1977 Soviet constitution–Sakharov's last battle–a pure product of Leninist logic which attributed to the Party the role of society's ruling center, and of similar measures in the satellite countries, was the symbol of the destruction of the Party's monopoly and of the acceptance, neither easy to elicit or put into practice, of the logic of democracy and the law-governed state. And the anti-Party movement could only lead–the only alternative would have been to turn backward and restore Party dictatorship–to the official self-liquidation of the Soviet Communist Party, which as we know Gorbachev was forced to recognize after the failed coup d'etat of August 1991. The Leninist or Weberian idea of the state as defined first and foremost as an apparatus of violence was replaced in the Soviet Union by a program for constructing mediated political relations. In short, a new content and tone were adopted that–instead of cynically accepting the existence of inegalitarian power relations that reduced the individual to a set of needs, society to a system of interests, and the political to a force field, the whole dominated by the Party, organizer of all organization–manifested the will to inscribe the political in a kind of *mise-en-scène* or staging. In August 1991 what we witnessed was the abandonment of paranoia in favor of hysteria, symbolized by the failure of the tanks to take over the Russian parliament, itself defended by the *words* of Boris Yeltsin: a sort of reversal of the dissolution of the Constituent Assembly of January 1918, when, after the sailor on watch had announced that the military men were tired and wanted go to bed, the deputies had dispersed, never to reassemble, replaced by the absolute dictatorship of the party-state. In 1991 the Red Army, on the contrary, seemed so weary that it didn't even have the strength to disperse the feeble parliament. In that moment, the history of the USSR refuted any antagonism–dogmatically promoted in the West but already belied in Poland, Czechoslovakia, and Hungary– between state and civil society, offering instead images of an embryonic civil society fighting for the survival of an embryonic representative state based on the rule of law.

Against Lenin and Marxism as enemies of right, figuration, and mediation, what we are witnessing after the collapse of European communism is a rehabilitation of the juridical illusion and, more broadly, political representation. In Bolshevism's rejection of all procedures of delegation and negotiation, considered as mere deception in the context of a logic of interests, mere noise in comparison to the march of the iron battalions of the proletariat, we may find a desire for objective truth that accords well with the ambition of making politics a science like the natural sciences: Leninist and Stalinist politics, as we have seen, oscillate between the most radical naturalism (groups classed according to their social status or profession, this being the only criterion taken in consideration in determining their fate, which could well be, as it was for the kulaks, to disappear from the face of the earth) and completely uncontrolled subjectivism (the Party as multiplier of force attributes to itself the ability to provide socialism with a material basis that corresponds to the "unity of will"). Social science of this type is always rooted in paranoia, because it conceives of behaviors and actions that can only be rooted in concrete subjectivities as if they were objects, while at the same time according itself a specific status, that of being a science, which immunizes *it* against the reproach of subjectivism. In a word, Bolshevism was founded on the fantasy of a world without phantasm. The very principle of democratic society, which seeks to found the political tie not on some absolute truth, but rather on what is equitable and just, with all the conflicts and approximations that this involves, is thus in formal contradiction with the Leninist desire for a kind of perfect social unity where the deployment of mute, naked force is the only real constituent of the political. So it is that at the core of civil society we find the street demonstration, the political march, with all its banners, slogans, and sloppiness. It is there in all its noisy theatricality like an essential "demonstration" of the belief in the effectiveness of representation, showing with gestures and words a way of struggle for civil society within the law-governed state.

But bringing a law-governed state into existence presupposes a series of complex conditions and institutions, diversified technologies, and also a certain civic culture, a constant investment on the part of the citizens, a constant battle to conserve the primacy of the word in politics; otherwise it is in danger of remaining purely formal. I do not speak ill of formalism here as residing in the nonmaterial character of political rights (universal suffrage is not always accompanied by real political participation, and obviously the act of voting has never filled a voter's stomach, even one of meager appetite). The formalism of political rights resides in putting limitations on citizenship—in terms of both what it means to be a citizen and who may accede to citizenship. A state that excludes certain groups from the possibility of becoming citizens—as was the case in the West for women, who until recently enjoyed only a kind of partial citizenship, not to mention the present situation of women in the majority of patriarchal Islamic societies—or that does not offer certain guarantees and protections to noncitizens—minors, prisoners, the mentally ill, immigrants—is not a law-governed state. We have a clear contradiction of the principles of the law-governed state in the idea that the practice of "policing" foreigners should be an administrative matter rather than a legal one. This results in foreigners present in the territory of a given state being for the most part deprived of recourse to judicial procedures for defending their human rights. It is a different experience to have the opportunity to present one's case before a judge than to be "handled" exclusively by the police. The status of foreigners in France, where the ideology of the Vichy government still presses with all the weight of its negation of the universality of human rights, is a good indicator of this discrepancy between the formal proclamation of a law-governed state and its effective reality.

Considering the category of the nationalist state, which attributes political rights and legal guarantees in accordance with ethnic membership, we may say that it is as remote from the law-governed state as is the power state, the two types tending moreover to become indistinguishable. When, in the matter of citizenship, which is in essence political, civic, civil, primacy is accorded to criteria of nationality, ethnic membership, religious affiliation, native language, roots, ancestors' blood–the particular salient trait (arbitrarily) privileged is of little importance–that primacy contradicts the principle of the law-governed state and goes against democracy, which on the contrary abstracts individuals from their concrete particularities. And that contradiction is all the more dangerous in that, as has often been pointed out, loss of citizenship and the rights that constitute it so often entails loss of human rights–witness the generally grim situation of refugees and displaced persons throughout the world.

A law-governed state cannot be based on a naturalist or biological determination of nationality; it is necessarily founded on a legal and political definition of citizenship. The primacy of citizenship over nationality, the political over the biological, collides with the most virulent of modern fanaticisms, that based on a certain fantasy of community, be it a community of blood or religion, in which individuals exist not as possessors of political rights but as bearers of glory-charged emblems or shameful stigmata: in such a system individuals are confined within an identity that absorbs their personal rights and, with a stone-like rigidity, inscribes them into a group from which they cannot dissociate themselves, even after death.

To the extent that what may be called communitary fanaticism, under the auspices of either religion or nationality, is the most powerful fomenter of war in the modern world and the most virulent agent of exclusion within states, it seems logical and right to believe that the strengthening of civil society as the society of political rights is the best way of protecting the state from the exigencies of war and individuals from exclusionary measures. In short it may be said that the law-governed state, unlike the nationalist power state and the totalitarian state, subjects itself to the demands of civil society, composed of individuals who enjoy political rights. The political in civil society thus subverts naturality, which means that in the matter of citizenship it posits the primacy of culture over blood ties, language over biological ties–with the idea that a language is something that is learned and can be translated–and gives priority within language to what Saussure called *langue* rather than *parole*, that is, language as an impersonal institution of which no one is the exclusive master or possessor, rather than a subjective practice or the emanation of a given community.

In the aftermath of the collapse of the Soviet communist system, we see that civil society, and with it the law-governed state, is affirming itself throughout Europe. It is newly urgent and relevant–witness "ethnic cleansing" in the former Yugoslavia–given the rise of nationalisms, long repressed, exacerbated, reborn from the ashes of communism. The present mobilization for democracy, supported by long and mixed traditions, particularly the defense of civil society that developed out of Luther's battle against the iconoclasts, is in fact affirmed as the conflict of two antagonistic notional pairs: nation–police state and civil society–law-governed state.

Translation, Mediation, Representation

In civil society, representation weaves a fundamental social tie, whereas for the fanatic, representation is always a parasitic excrescence, target of his hatred. For the fanatic, mediation is a loss of strength or meaning that necessarily entails a degradation: he seeks to abolish figuration and translation, profanations to his mind, so as to impose, violently, his fantasy of the unique language of truth.

In Hegel's opposition to political romanticism we may discover the principle argument against the organicist conception of the state, which privileges the biological over the political, the life of "the people" over the constitution of the state. Hegel pulled the nation and the state up out of the dark ground of naturality, at least in part. We may of course find in Hegel's writings the themes of nationalistic thought: he believed that it was only in the state that a nation might fulfill its destiny, and he praised war as the culminating moment of history. But we may also discern a rejection of all naturalistic objectivations of nations, peoples, the state, and all doctrines that assimilate them to living beings. The Hegelian state is indeed organized, but this does not make it an organism: it does not annihilate the individual by reducing him to the role of an organ in the service of the whole, and this led Hegel, as we have seen, to accept the existence within civil society– where everyone pursued his own interests–of heterodox religious groups, including fanatical sects.

It is worth returning to the origin of this conception by way of the definition Hegel gave of Germany. He characterized it by its language, to which he attributed eminent value. But what founded, in his view, the superiority of the German language? It was not that it emanated from a people with ancestral virtues flowing through its veins. Rather it was born from Luther's work, and more particularly his translations of the Bible, a project undertaken at the same time as the iconoclasts were smashing images similar to that shown in Figure 1. Following out the implications of this affirmation, we may say that it was the combining, through Luther's mediation, of Germanic and Judaic heritages that endowed the German language and post-Reformation Germany with their eminent spiritual relevance. Hegel denaturalized notions of people and language and refuted theories of national identity by founding German supremacy on the self's difference from itself. Germany was not Germany, in the sense that it could not be reduced to its Germanic element, but was exalted by its relation to the Other as a treasure of signifiers. Luther's German Bible held the same Word as the founding Hebrew and Greek Books. Luther, wrote Hegel, *gave* Germany its "People's Book."[30] It was not that Luther had received something–the German spirit–in deposit from the Germans, but that by translating and disseminating the Bible he procured for them a language. A people's truth or reality was not then to be found in the land or the blood, or even in the word as form, expression, or reflection of the life and soul of a people, but rather in language as the means of instituting the spirit of a people. The German people's true identity resided in difference, a particular type of difference: a translation whose source was, among others, the Hebrew Bible, the language of the Other. The Germans thought in foreign languages that had become their language through Luther's mediation. Without a doubt this is alienation, but an alienation that founds identity. The relevance Hegel accorded to translation is consistent with the affirmation that a person's humanity is inscribed in civil society. When he translated the Bible, when he fought against fanatic iconoclasts, Luther was expressing the same acceptance of discrepancy, non-coincidence, inadequation–a translation is not the same as the source text, a painting is not the same as what it figures–not as humanity's failure, or as a failure of the subject, but as their positive essence.

We have here an affirmation of the irreducibility of the "interval" between the City of God and the Earthly City, affirmation upon which both the conviction of civil society's relevance and the rejection of fanaticism are based: earth separated from heaven is not radically infirm, it can live according in its own code and ways. Was not God, through Christ's mediation, made flesh? The non-coincidence of social life with the kingdom of God was not a distance to be reduced at any cost, and even if God's substance reached us only metaphorically, this did not prevent it from being nourishing through his Word. The sign was worth the substance.

A representative presents an absence. He may be a delegate who usurps a role, but he can also replace, entirely and without degradation, that or those to whose place he has come. The absence of what is represented is not a deficit, simply a distance. *Mise en scène* is as valuable, and as strong, as force, but without its terrible effects. It is thus representation, in all its diverse forms, that is legitimated: representation translates force into signs and founds the possibility of constructing a specifically human world. Mediation is not imposture, absence of force is not a lack, distance from the first language is not a loss. Rather they open up a space in which the human subject may constitute itself, a discrepancy, an absence, a distance that liberate.

Reference Matter

Appendix A

*Significant Occurrences of "Civil Society"
and/or "Fanaticism"*

	"Civil Society"	"Fanaticism"
Cicero (106-43 B.C.)	*De republica*	*De divinatione*
Giles of Rome (1243-1316)	*De regimine principum*	
Luther (1483-1546)		*Ein Brief an die Christen zu Strassburg wider den Schwärmergeist* (*Letter to the Christians at Strassburg in Opposition to the Fanatic Spirit*)
		Das diese Worte Christi "das ist mein Leib" noch feststehen wider die Schwärmgeister (*That these words of Christ, "This is my Body," etc., still stand firm against the Fanatics*), and other texts
Melanchthon (1497-1560)	*Commentarii in aliquot Politicos libros Aristotelis* *Loci communes theologici*	*Commentarii in aliquot Politicos libros Aristotelis* *Loci communes theologici*

	"Civil Society"	"Fanaticism"
Rabelais (1494-1553)		Le Tiers livre des faicts et dits héroïques du bon Pantagruel Le Cinquiesme et dernier livre
Calvin (1509-1564)		Institutio Religionis Christianae Institution de la religion chrétienne Contre la secte phantastique
Montaigne (1533-1592)	Essais	Essais
Barclay (1546-1608)	De potestate papae (Of the Authority of the Pope)	
Richer (1559-1631)	De ecclesiastica et politica potestate libellus (A Treatise of Ecclesiastical and Politike power)	
Codurc (1580-1660)	Traicté de l'obéissance des chrestiens	Traicté de l'obéissance des chrestiens
Hobbes (1588-1679)	Leviathan De cive The Citizen Elémens philosophiques du citoyen, traicté politique où les fondemens de la société civile sont descouverts	Elémens philosophiques du citoyen, traicté politique où les fondemens de la société civile sont descouverts
Bossuet (1627-1704)	Politique tirée des propres paroles de l'Ecriture sainte (Politics Drawn from the Very Words of Holy Scripture)	Avertissement sur les écrit suivants et sur un nouveau livre . . . Oraison funébre de Henriette de France, and other texts
Spinoza (1632-1677)	Tractatus politicus	
Vauban (1633-1707)	Projet d'une Dixme royale	
Pufendorf (1632-1694)	De officio homines et civilis juxta legem naturalem (The Whole Duty of Man according to the Law of Nature)	

	"Civil Society"	"Fanaticism"
Locke (1632-1704)	*Two Treatises on Government*	*An Essay Concerning Human Understanding*
	An Essay Concerning Toleration	*An Essay Concerning Toleration*
De Brueys (1640-1723)	*Histoire du fanatisme de notre temps*	*Traité de l'obéissance des Chrétiens aux puissances temporelles*
Penn (1644-1718)	*The Christian Quaker and his divine testimony vindicated by Scripture, reason, and authorities, against the injurious attempts lately made to render him odiously inconsistent with Christianity and Civil Society*	
Leibniz (1646-1716)	*Divisio societatum* "*Sur Isaac Papin*"	*Essai de Théodicée* *Nouveaux essais sur l'entendement humain*
Fénelon (1651-1715)		*Explication des maximes des saints sur la vie intérieure*
Mandeville (1670-1733)	*The Fable of the Bees, or Private Vices, Public Benefits, Containing several discourses that demonstrate that human frailties may be turned to the advantage of the Civil Society*	
Burlamaqui (1694-1748)	*Principes de droit naturel*	
Hume (1711-1776)	"Of the origin of government," in *Essays, Moral and Political*	"Of superstition and enthusiasm," in *Essays, Moral and Political*
Voltaire (1694-1778)		*Dictionnaire philosophique* *Le siécle de Louis XIV* *Traité sur la tolérance* *Mahomet ou le fanatisme*

	"Civil Society"	"Fanaticism"
Rousseau (1712-1778)	*Discours sur l'origine et les fondements de l'inégalité entre les hommes* *Emile, ou de l'education* *Du contrat social* (Geneva manuscript)	*Lettres écrites de la montagne* *Emile* *Du contrat social, ou des principes du droit politique*
Ferguson (1723-1816)	*An Essay on the History of Civil Society*	
Diderot and D'Alembert, *Encyclopédie* (1751-1772)	s.v. "Société"	s.v. "Fanatisme"
Kant (1724-1804)	*Kritik der Urteilskraft* (*Critique of Judgement*) *Die Metaphysik der Sitten* (*Metaphysics of Morals*) *Über Theorie und Praxis* (*Theory and Practice*) *Anthropologie in pragmatischer Hinsicht* (*Anthropology from a Pragmatic Point of View*)	*Kritik der Urteilskraft* (*Critique of Judgement*) *Der Streit der Facultäten* (*The Contest of Faculties*) *Was heisst: Sich im Denken orientieren?* (*What Is Orientation in Thinking?*) *Anthropologie in pragmatischer Hinsicht* (*Anthropology from a Pragmatic Point of View*)
Burke (1729-1797)	*Reflections on the Revolution in France*	
Bonald (1754-1840)	*Théorie du pouvoir politique et religieux dans la société civile*	
Fichte (1762-1814)	*Beitrag zur Berichtigung der Urteile der Publikums über die französische Revolution* (Considerations destined to rectify public judgment on the French Revolution)	
Haller (1768-1854)	*Restauration der Staatswissenschaft* (Restoration of political science)	

	"Civil Society"	"Fanaticism"
Hegel (1770–1831)	*Rechtsphilosophie (Elements of the Philosophy of Right)*	*Phänomenologie des Geistes (Phenomenology of Mind)* *Rechtsphilosophie (Elements of the Philosophy of Right)*
Lamennais (1782–1854)	*De la religion considérée dans ses rapport avec l'ordre politique et civil*	
Pius IX (1792–1878)	*Syllabus*	
Michelet (1798–1874)	*Histoire de France*	*Histoire de France*
Leo XIII (1810–1903)	*Rerum novarum*	
Marx (1818–1883)	*Aus der Kritik der Hegelschen Rechtsphilosophie (Contribution to the Critique of Hegel's "Philosophy of Law")* *Misère de la philosophie* *Die deutsche Ideologie (The German Ideology)* *Manifest der Kommunistischen Partei (The Communist Manifesto)* *Der Bürgerkrieg in Frankreich (The Civil War in France)* *Kritik des Gothaer Programmentwurfs (Critique of the Gotha Programme)*, and other texts	
Engels (1820–1895)	*Die deutsche Ideologie (The German Ideology)* *Manifest der Kommunistischen Partei (The Communist Manifesto)* *Der deutsche Bauernkrieg (The Peasant War in Germany)*	*Der deutsche Bauernkrieg (The Peasant War in Germany)*

	"Civil Society"	"Fanaticism"
Baudelaire (1821-1867)		*Les Paradis artificiels*
Durkheim (1858-1917)	*"L'Allemagne au-dessus de tout." La mentalité germanique et la guerre*	
Bloch (1885-1977)	*Thomas Münzer, Theologe der Revolution*	*Thomas Münzer, Theologe der Revolution*
Gramsci (1891-1937)	"Appunti et note sparse per un gruppo di saggi sulla storia degli intellettuali e della cultura in Italia" (Notebook 12 of *Quaderni del carcere*)	
John Paul II (1920-)	*Centesimus annus*	*Centesimus annus*
Lyotard (1924-)	*La Condition postmoderne*	
Gellner (1925-95)	*Conditions of Liberty: Civil Society and Its Rivals*	
Foucault (1926-84)	*Surveiller et punir* (*Discipline and Punish*)	"Médecins, juges et sorciers au XVIIe siècle"
Derrida (1930-)	*Glas* *Politiques de l'amitié*	

Appendix B

Translations of koinonia politikè *and* polis *in*
Translations (t) of and Commentaries (c) on
Aristotle's Politics *and* Nicomachean Ethics

	koinonia politikè	*polis*
Hermann the German		
Ethics, ca. 1240 (t)	communicacio politica	
Robert Grosseteste		
Ethics, ca. 1246-47 (t)	politica communicacio	police
William of Moerbeke		
Politics, the "imperfecta," ca. 1260-64 (t)	communitas politica	civitas
Politics, the "perfecta," ca. 1265 (t)	communicatio politica, civilis communitas	civitas
Albertus Magnus		
Politics, ca. 1265 (c)	communitas politica	
Thomas Aquinas		
Politics, books 1-3, 1269-72 (c)	communicatio politica, civilis communitas	civitas
Peter of Auvergne		
Politics, books 4-8, 1274-90 (c)	communicatio politica	civitas

	koinonia politikè	*polis*
Giles of Rome		
Politics, 1277–79 (c)	societas civilis, civitas	civitas
Walter Burley		
Ethics, 1333–45 (c)	communicatio politica	
Politics, 1338–39 (c)		
Jean Buridan		
Politics, ca. 1350 (c)	communicatio politica	
Nicole Oresme		
Ethics, ca. 1350 (t)	communication politique	cité
Politics, ca. 1370 (t)		
Leonardo Bruni		
Ethics, 1416 (t)	societas civilis	civitas
Politics, ca. 1438 (t)		
Don Carlos de Viana de Navarra		
Ethics, 1509 (t)	societat de cuidadanos, policia	ciudad
Politics, 1509 (t)		
Philipp Melanchthon		
Politics, 1529 (t & c)	societas civilis	civitas
Simon Abril		
Politics, 1534 (t)	compaña civil	ciudad
Antonio Brucioli		
Politics, 1547 (t)	civile società	città
Bernardo Segni		
Politics, 1549 (t)	civile compagnia, republica	Stato
Ethics, 1550 (t)		
Pietro Vettori		
Politics, 1552 (t & c)	communio civilis	civitas
Louis Le Roy		
Politics, 1568 (t & c)	compagnie civile (t) société civile (c)	cité

	koinonia politikè	*polis*
anonymous English trans. of Le Roy's French trans. of and comm. on the *Politics*, 1598	civill societie	cittie
William Ellis *Politics*, 1778 (t)	political society	
Champagne *Politics*, 1797 (t)	commune république	cité
J. G. Schlosser *Politics*, 1798 (t)	bürgerliche Gesellschaft	Staat
Charles Millon *Politics*, 1803 (t)	société civile	Etat
M. Thurot *Politics*, 1824 (t)	association politique	cité
Jules Barthélemy Saint-Hilaire *Politics*, 1837 (t)	association politique	Etat
Jacob Bernays *Politics*, 1872 (t)	staatliche Gemeinschaft	Staat
V. Costanzi *Politics*, 1918 (t)	associazione politica	città
Jean Voilquin *Ethics,* 1940 (t)	société civile	
Ernest Barker *Politics*, 1946 (t)	political association	state
Jean Tricot *Politics,* 1962 (t)	communauté politique	cité
Carnes Lord *Politics,* 1984 (t)	political partnership	city
Terence Irwin *Ethics,* 1985 (t)	political community	
Pierre Pellegrin *Politics,* 1990 (t)	communauté politique	cité

Notes

Preface

1. An example of such, to my mind, ill-founded interpretation is Ralph Miliband's *Marxism and Politics*.

2. It follows from this that Louis Althusser's idea in *For Marx* of a break between the young Marx, still primarily a philosopher and proposing a humanist philosophy of alienation, and a truly Marxist Marx constructing a science of the modes of production is not relevant for the political domain of his thinking, in particular his theory of the state.

3. My "Civil Society: From Utopia to Management, from Marxism to Anti-Marxism" gives a highly condensed version of the history of the term.

4. See the works by Baron, Garin, and Pocock listed in the bibliography.

5. On this point see Aby Warburg's "Dürer und die italienische Antike," in *Gesammelte Schriften*, 2: 443–49.

6. *Of the Jews and Their Lies*, in *Luther's Works*, ed. Pelikan and Lehmann, 47: 268, 269 (hereafter abbreviated *LW*). This grim text, a kind of compendium of anti-Semitic stigmatizations and projects, includes an appeal to expel Jews from Germany. In chapter 10 of *Luther: Man Between God and the Devil*, in the section "Darkness at Noon: Luther and the Jews," Heiko Oberman attempts to situate Luther's anti-Semitism theologically: though the Reformation was rooted in part in a valorizing of the Old Testament, for Luther the Word of God given in the New was unconditionally superior, and it condemned those who refused to recognize the divinity of Christ. A Jew who did not convert was therefore an enemy of the true religion. Oberman notes that for Luther, popes, Jews, and Turks formed a "coalition" of opponents to the Holy Gospel (p. 294).

7. Aristotle gives a clear definition of the Athenian citizen and the role of compulsory military duty in male citizenship in *The Athenian Constitution*, chap. 42.

8. On women's social and political status in ancient Greece see the works of Nicole Loraux, particularly *The Children of Athena*.

9. Jacques Derrida, *Glas* (in English version see for example pp. 13-14, 16) and his preface to *Politiques de l'amitié*, p. 13.

10. See *Surveiller et punir: Naissance de la prison*, pp. 90 and 170. Jean Cohen and Andrew Arato are thus mistaken in affirming (*Civil Society and Political Theory*, p. 257) that Foucault did not use "civil society." There are several occurrences of the term in *Dits et écrits*: "Naissance de la biopolitique" (1979), 3: 820; "Entretien avec Michel Foucault" (1980), 4: 89; "Un système fini face à une demande infinie" (1983), 4: 374. The term is also to be found in notes from a lecture he gave on January 31, 1979, as part of a series on "la biopolitique," published under the title "La Phobie d'Etat" in the French daily *Libération* at the time of his death (issue of June 30–July 1, 1984, p. 21). This text is not included in *Dits et écrits*.

11. Jean-François Lyotard, *Instructions païennes* (published in English as "Lessons in Paganism," in *The Lyotard Reader*, pp. 122-54; see for example pp. 132, 135, 140) and *L'Enthousiasme*.

12. Among the many books on the concept published after this one, we should mention *Civil Society: Theory, History, Comparison*, ed. John Hall, which includes articles on Poland, China, Islam, and Latin America and closes with an incisive essay by Salvador Giner, "Civil Society and Its Future."

13. For a brief discussion of civil society with special reference to Ferguson see also Robert F. Miller, *The Developments of Civil Society in Communist Systems*.

14. See Michel Foucault, "Medecins, juges et sorciers," in *Dits et écrits*, 1: 753-66.

15. The notion of implosion is key in the thinking of Martin Malia, who frequently uses the concept of civil society in his analysis of Soviet history; see *The Soviet Tragedy*.

16. See, among others, Z. A. Pelczynski, "Solidarity and the 'Rebirth of Civil Society' in Poland, 1976-81," and Andrew Arato, "Civil Society Against the State: Poland, 1980-1981," and "Empire vs. Civil Society: Poland, 1981-1982." For a different assessment, see Miklos Molnar, *La démocratie se lève à l'Est*.

17. See Steven Fish, *Democracy from Scratch*.

18. On the definition of ethnic group and for a critique of supposed ethnic "purity," see Jean-Loup Amselle, *Mestizo Logics*, forthcoming from Stanford University Press (1998).

19. *Les Temps modernes* 29, no. 318 (January 1973).

20. The English version was published in *Sartre in the Seventies. Interviews and Essays*, pp. 198-210.

21. The text Bourdieu published in *Les Temps modernes* was that of a talk he gave in 1972; it was republished in 1984 in *Questions de sociologie* (English translation, *Sociology in Question*, 1993) with some significant modifications. In 1972 he had hypothesized that elections tend to "attenuate conflicts and cleavages" and *"naturellement à servir la conservation"* ("serve naturally to conserve"). The second hypothesis was omitted from the 1984 version.

22. See Claude Lévi-Strauss, *Introduction to the Work of Marcel Mauss.*

23. On the need to break with "mimetic" politics, see F. R. Ankersmit, *Aesthetic Politics: The Political Beyond Fact and Value*, forthcoming from Stanford University Press (1997).

Introduction

1. Martin Luther, *A Sincere Admonition to All Christians to Guard Against Insurrection or Rebellion*, 1522, in *LW*, 45: 59-60.

Chapter 1

1. Melanchthon, *Commentarii in aliquot Politicos libros Aristotelis*, in *Corpus reformatorum*, vol. 16. Melanchthon's commentary covers books 1 through 3 of the *Politics*. At points he quotes the Greek (bk. 1, chap. 1, §16) on justice, where, following Leonardo Bruni, he translates *koinonia politikè* as *societas civilis* (col. 423). The term occurs repeatedly in this text (see cols. 422, 424).

2. The English terms used here are translations from the Latin version of Melanchthon's *Loci communes* (Basel, 1545). Melanchthon wrote numerous versions of the text in both Latin and German, developing and changing it significantly over time. The first Latin version is dated 1518 and the last 1559; we are interested primarily in the 1545 version. The work was translated only much later into English: there exists a nineteenth-century translation of the 1518 Latin version and a twentieth-century translation from the German version of 1555 (Manschreck, *Melanchthon on Christian Doctrine*). Given that the English terms in this latter translation often do not correspond exactly to the Latin terms, we have translated directly from Latin, also consulting the 1551 French version prefaced by Calvin. The relevant passage from the commentary on the seventh commandment reads as follows: "Indeed, by this commandment God forbids stealing; he wishes each to own what belongs to him. And this affirmation confutes the raving of the fanatics, who commit a great and pernicious error when they affirm that property is forbidden in the Gospel" (*Loci communes theologici*, Basel, 1545, p. 159). "Political order" appears more frequently in this text (at least thirteen times) than "civil society" (four times). *Societas politica, politica vita*, and *politia*, as well as *gubernatio politica*, also occur. A typical passage reads: "Political order, as I have said, is good, beautiful, pleasant to humankind, a singular work of God, who wishes men to live under common laws in civil societies" (p. 623). In the second French

edition, published in 1551 with a preface by Calvin, both *société civile* and *compagnie de citoyens* are to be found as translations of *societas civilis*; "fanatics" has been translated *insensés* or "insane people." We also find the terms *esprits fantastiques* and *enthousiaste*. The Anabaptists are qualified as *furieux*, a translation in adjectival form of *furor*, meaning extreme madness. In the Latin original *fanaticus* is used repeatedly.

3. On the first French translations of Luther's texts in France, see Moore, *La Réforme allemande et la littérature française*.

4. In bk. 4, chap. 15, of the first edition of the Latin text (1536) of Calvin's *Institutes*, as well as in the later editions (chap. 20, §2), the term used is *fanatici*. In Norton's 1560 translation we find "fanaticall men" (20v) and also "phrentike man" (491v). In 1547 Calvin wrote a virulent pamphlet, *Contre la secte phantastique et furieuse des Libertins*, in which he accuses this group from the north of France of seeking to mix up "heaven and earth and annihilate all religion."

5. For Tocqueville's conception of civil society, see Keane, "Despotism and Democracy."

6. Cicero used *fanaticus/-a/-um* as a synonym for "superstitious" or "raving" (see *De divinatione* 2.118), as did Juvenal (see *Satire* 2, line 112).

7. In his pamphlet attacking the Anabaptists (1545), *Brève Instruction pour armer tous bons fidèles contre les erreurs de la secte commune des Anabaptistes*, Calvin used the *ph-* spelling (*phantastiques*) more frequently than the *f-*; we also find *phantaisie* (p. 88) and *phantosme*. A significant passage reads: "The Manichaeans have fantasticated [*phantastiqué*] that Jesus Christ brought a celestial body into the belly of his Virgin mother. The Marcionites had a slightly different reverie, that he did not have a truly substantial body but only the appearance or semblance of a body—as if Christ were a phantom [*phantosme*]" (p. 103). Calvin's political reasons for condemning the Anabaptists are made clear in the following passage: "We see then . . . how false and perverse are the Anabaptists' allegations when they condemn the vocation of the Magistrates, whom God has so well approved. . . . As for the end they call for, I will say only this: that they reveal themselves by it. For to vituperate against what God has honored is to make war on God, to seek to trample underfoot what he has exalted, and we could hardly machinate the world's ruin better, and introduce brigandry everywhere, than by trying to abolish the civil government or the power of the sword, which is indeed cast low if it be not licit for a Christian man to exercise it" (p. 92). As for the "libertines," those "miserable *phantastiques* who boast so loud that they have the word of God for them" (p. 53), Calvin deemed their doctrine an "incomparable labyrinth of reveries so absurd that it is a marvel how creatures who bear a human face can be so lacking in sense and reason as to so deceive themselves that they sink into worse than brutish fantasies [*phantaisies*]" (p. 52). Among Calvin's uses of the Latin *fanaticus* there is one referring explicitly to Karlstadt (see *Pro Farello adversus Petri Caroli Calumnias*, 1545, p. 306).

8. Melanchthon, "On the Number of the Sacraments," in *Loci communes theologici* (Basel, 1545), p. 296. The word "enthusiasts" is in Greek in the original. The French translation of 1551 adds a number of picturesque details: the "enthusiasts" take "everything they dream while snoring away to be divine inspiration"; their "rabid reveries" are "forged in the hollow brains of baboon monks and furious Anabaptists" (p. 224).

9. In Rabelais, *Le Cinquiesme et dernier livre des faicts et dicts heroïques du bon Pantagruel*, chap. 46, "Comment Panurge et les autres riment par fureur poétique," we find the expression *cerveau phanatique* ("fanatic brain"; in *Œuvres complètes*, ed. Marty-Lavaux, 3: 175). Rabelais also used *fanaticque* twice to describe convulsively nodding prophets (*Le Tiers livre*, chap. 45; in *Œuvres complètes*, ed. Boulenger, pp. 510 and 511).

10. See J. Bellenden, *Livy's History of Rome* (1533). We do however find "fanatike" as early as 1534. Other English examples: "the Anabaptists and other phanatical spirits" (Th. Cooper, *An Admonition to the People of England*, 1580); "Enthusiasts, Anabaptists, fanaticks and Familists" (J. Gaule, *Sapientia justificata*, 1657).

11. The proximity between "fanatic" and "fantastic" is also attested in English: in a text from 1644 we read "Saving grace, as some fanatickes and fantastickes fondly imagine" (Maxwell, *Sacro-sancta regnum, or the Sacred and Royal Prerogative of Christian Kings*). It is interesting to note that even after the *f-* spelling came to dominate, the word retained the meaning accruing to it from the etymological error: Shaftesbury in his *Letter Concerning Enthusiasm* (1708) clearly associates fanaticism with "apparitions" (pp. 34–35).

12. Calvin, *Institution of Christian Religion*, bk. 4, chap. 20 (Norton, 491v).

13. Ibid.

14. "Les particularités du soulèvement des Fanatiques en la ville de Londres, contenues en la lettre d'un Anglais à un de ses amis," in *La Gazette de France*, no. 15, 1661, p. 109.

15. From Bossuet, *Oraisons funèbres*, p. 126. On the Puritan sects of the "left" see Christopher Hill, *The World Turned Upside Down*. It would appear that the term "fanatic," present in English since the sixteenth century, did not come to be used in the context of the English Civil War until 1660, and more particularly in 1666 with the wave of apocalyptic prophesying. In the Bodleian Library's copy of *Mirabilis Annus* (1661), we may read the following handwritten commentary, presumably added later: "produced by fanatics to rouse the vulgar" (Hill, *The World Turned Upside Down*, p. 286).

16. See Maimbourg, *Histoire du luthéranisme* and *Histoire du calvinisme* (both published in 1686).

17. The Camisard revolt at the very beginning of the eighteenth century brought on the bloody War of the Cévennes (1702–5) in the south of France. The name is in reference to the white shirts (*camiso: chemise*) they were said to wear over their other clothing in order to recognize one another.

18. *Robin Hood and the Stranger*, in *Robin Hood; a Collection of all Ancient Poems, Songs, and Ballads now Existent Relative to that Celebrated Outlaw*, ed. Ritson (1795).

19. In Melanchthon's German *Schwärmer* is the equivalent of *fanaticus*, which is also to be found in Latin translations of Luther. The caption for a portrait of Thomas Müntzer, considered by Luther the very type of the *Schwärmer*, reads "Arch-fanatic leader and captain of the seditious peasants" (archifanaticus patronus et capitaneus seditorsiorum rusticorum).

20. Locke, *Essay Concerning Toleration* (1667), p. 97.

21. *Mechanical Operation*, in Swift, *Writings*, pp. 411 and 413.

22. *Gulliver's Travels*, pt. 1, chap. 4, in Swift, *Writings*, p. 31. *Brundrecal*, the title Swift gives to the (Protestant) Little-Endians' prophet's holy book, comes to mean "call back to the Bible" (see *A Voyage to Lilliput*, p. 113).

23. Leibniz, *Opera omnia*, 5: 55. See also Shaftesbury (to whom Leibniz explicitly refers): "For as some have well remarked, there have been enthusiastical atheists" (*Letter Concerning Enthusiasm*, p. 37).

24. Kant, *Critique of Judgement*, pt. 1 (Meredith, p. 128).

25. *Les Politiques d'Aristote* (Le Roy, p. 35); translated anonymously into English from Le Roy's French under the title *Aristoteles, Politiques, or discourses of Governement*, p. 21. The text is a gloss of the key passage on justice in the polity (*Politics*, bk. 1, chap. 1, §16). In addition to Aristotle, Loys Le Roy (Regius in Latin) translated several works of Plato, including *Timaeus* and the *Symposium*. His own texts include *De l'Origine, antiquité, progrès, excellence et utilité de l'art politique*, *Considérations sur l'histoire françoise et universelle de ce temps*, and *Des Troubles et différents advenans entre les hommes par la diversité des religions*. As far as we know he did not use the term "civil society" in his own political writings, employing instead *police* (polis) or *estat publique*. He deplored the wars of religion and dreamed of a peaceful solution along Platonic lines where a divine king would gather all religions into one. He remarked on and likewise deplored the persecution of the Jewish people. He died in 1577.

26. Montaigne, *Essais*, bk. 2, chaps. 10 and 12, pp. 454, 600. The second example reads: "ce sont tous songes et fanatiques folies" (Screech translates "frantic folly"; *Complete Essays*, p. 602).

27. Bodin, *De republica* (Frankfurt edition, 1586), bk. 3, chap. 6, p. 77.

28. In 1600 the English jurist and professor of law William Barclay published *De regno et regali potestate*; Bellarmin responded with his *Tractatus de potestate summi pontificis in rebus temporalibus, adversus Gulimun Barclay* (Power of the pope in temporal affairs, against William Barclay, 1610), to which Barclay in turn retorted with *De Potestate papae* (*Of the Authority of the Pope, whether and how far forth he has power and authority over Temporal Kings and Princes*, 1611; translated into French the same year). In this last text we find the following affir-

mation: "Therefore in those matters which belong to the safety of the commonwealth, and to the civil society, and are not against the divine ordinance, the Clergy
is no less bound to obey the sovereign Prince temporal than other citizens are"
(chap. 14, p. 76). Among other works in which the term "civil society" is used we
may cite François Hotman, *P. Sixti V Fulmen Brutum in Henricum serenis* (1603).
On the Catholic Leaguers' side, texts by partisans of popular sovereignty who used
societas civilis include *De justa reipublicae christianae* (1590), attributed (probably
erroneously) to Guillaume Rose, bishop of Caen (p. 3), and Mariana's celebrated
1599 *De rege et regis institutione* (p. 22). Both of them affirmed the naturalness of
civil society as an entity whose purpose is the common good.

   29. Philippe Codurc's *Traicté de l'obéissance des chrestiens envers leurs magistrats et princes souverains*, published in 1645, includes a partial translation of
Luther's *Admonition to Peace*, addressed in 1521 to rebelling Swabian peasants
(see Chapter 3 of this work), in which we find the following affirmation: "To
submit to the order of justice and recognize the Magistrate's authority does not
make men Christian. It is necessity that obliges men to do so, for the subsistence of
civil society. You who seek to eradicate the law of nature and the law of nations are
worse than the profane nations." Codurc used Luther's text, among others, to
demonstrate that a Christian did not under any circumstances have the right to
rebel against the temporal prince–not even in the case of persecution. He offers
Luther and Calvin as models: they never behaved like military or political chiefs,
unlike young "harebrained, fanatical orators." A Calvinist pastor who had converted to Catholicism, Codurc, like Luther and Melanchthon before him, defended
the legitimacy of the existing political order against fanatics, and he was a precursor of de Brueys, who wrote against the Camisards at the turn of the seventeenth
century (see Chapter 6).

   30. In the later English version of Hobbes's *De cive*, the term is present in the
title of the first chapter: "Of the State of Men Without Civil Society."

   31. Article 2 of book 1 of Riley's translation of Bossuet's *Politique tirée des
Propres paroles de L'Ecriture sainte* reads: "The society of mankind gives birth to
civil society, that is to say, to states, peoples, and nations" (p. 8). Civil society, a
synonym for state, is linked to Cain: "God was the bond of human society. The first
man having separated himself from God, by a just punishment division was cast in
his family, and Cain killed his brother Abel" (p. 8). Though Bossuet did not relate
the notion of fanaticism to civil society, we can say how they were connected for
him: civil society was born of division; the fanatics were to be blamed for pushing
that division to an extreme. Against them and it, Bossuet holds up "human society," whose unshakable foundations Jesus Christ had shown us by forming his
Church: "one same God, one same object, one same end, one common origin, one
same blood, one same interest, one mutual want, alike for the affairs as for the
enjoyments of life" (p. 8).

32. Vauban used the term (*Projet d'une dixme royale*, p. 50), distinguishing between king and civil society, an anticipation of the distinction between the state and the economic sphere. (My thanks to Emmanuel Le Roy Ladurie for calling the usage to my attention.) Montesquieu used "civil society" only exceptionally (*Esprit des lois*, bk. 26, chap. 25, p. 777).

33. In a comment included in his French translation (1707) of Samuel Pufendorf's *De officio hominis et civis* (The duty of man and citizen), Barbeyrac raised the issue of how best to translate *civitas*: whether by *Cité*, *Etat*, or *société civile*. He chose the last of these.

34. [The term *droit politique* (political right), which figures in the subtitle of Rousseau's *On the Social Contract*, may be loosely defined as the ensemble of principles on which the state, the polity, civil society–all these were synonyms for Rousseau–should be founded (see the conclusion of *On the Social Contract*; Cress, p. 227). Both *droit* and the German *Recht*, which may in many instances be translated "law," also serve to designate the founding principles and juridical norms on which laws are–or should be–based. To mark this distinction, *droit* and *Recht* have been rendered at appropriate points–and following recent translators of political philosophers such as Rousseau, Kant, and Hegel–by "right" rather than "law." In these instances, the word designates abstract or universal principles and norms of superior moral and judicial validity–in the sense of "right" as opposed to "wrong"; it is from these principles that specific laws may be derived. Trans.]

35. The sharing of vocabulary and conceptual definitions is due in great part to the fact that the later authors read and took seriously the earlier ones: Spinoza and Rousseau read Hobbes; Fichte in his work on the French Revolution (*Beitrag zur Berichtigung der Urtheile der Publikums über die französische Revolution*, 1793) used *bürgerliche Gesellschaft* as a translation for *société civile* when directly discussing Rousseau (pp. 61-62).

36. French historians of late antiquity and the Middle Ages have regularly used the term in this way. See, for example, Cavallera, "La doctrine d'Origène sur les rapports du christianisme et de la société civile"; Le Bras, *Institutions ecclésiastiques de la chrétienté médiévale*, bk. 5, chap. 3, §3; and de Lagarde, *La naissance de l'esprit laïque*. For the same usage in a more recent work, see Merle, "Sociologie comparée du pouvoir dans l'Eglise et dans la société civile."

37. Melber von Gerolzhoffen, *Vocabularius predicantium*. Several editions exist; I consulted the Strasbourg edition of 1486.

38. See Huntingdon, *The Soldier and the State* and *Political Order in a Changing Society*. But the civil/military opposition is sometimes obliterated: in Tobon, *Estado, violencia, y democracia*, we read: "Guerrilla warfare is part of civil society."

39. *Politics*, bk. 1, chap. 1, §1 (Barker, p. 1).

40. The text in question is *De regimine principum*; the author is also known as

Aegidius Romae and Egidio Romano or Egidio Colonna. Gauchy's 1282 French translation used the expression *communauté de vile ou de cité*; in Italian we find *communitade civile*; in Spanish, *compaña civil*. (My thanks to Jean-Philippe Genet for calling Giles of Rome to my attention.)

41. Aquinas (here glossing *Politics*, bk. 1, chap. 1), *In octo libros Politicorum Aristotelis expositio*, §37.

42. To my knowledge Cicero used the term *societas civilis* only once, in *De republica* 1.32.

43. Moerbeke's translation of bk. 1, chap. 1, §16, of the *Politics*—"Diki enim civilis communitatis ordo est. Diki autem iusti iudicium"—became in Bruni's translation "Nam jus ordinatio et civilis societatis Iudicatio autem iusti iudicium" ("Justice belongs to the polis, for justice, which is the determination of what is just, is an ordering of the political association"; Barker, p. 7). Moerbeke's contemporary Roger Bacon underlined the difficulties of translating Aristotle into Latin in *Opus majus*, pt. 3, p. 45.

44. Weber, *Economy and Society*, vol. 2, chap. 16.

45. See Bruni's preface to Aristotle's *Economy*, in *Aristotelis Ethica, Politica, Œconomica* (ca. 1438).

46. On Bruni and civic humanism see the works of Hans Baron. We may note that the very term *stato*, used extensively by Machiavelli, derived from the city-states' conception of citizenship: " 'All active citizens,' under the conditions of the Renaissance city-state, of course means those who possess 'lo stato,' i.e., the full-citizen rights–a group which excludes some of the lesser guilds and the laborers in the Florentine industries" (Baron, *The Crisis of the Early Italian Renaissance*, p. 560, n. 41).

47. See Bec et al., *L'Italie de la Renaissance*, and Garin's *Educazione umanistica in Italia* and *L'Umanesimo italiano*, both of which discuss Bruni.

48. Moerbeke's translation nonetheless benefited from the technology of printing; an edition of it (among others) was published in Cologne in 1493. Aquinas's commentary was sometimes published jointly with Bruni's translation, as for example in Leipzig in 1493. (In addition to the usual catalogs I also consulted Miroslav Flodr's *Incunabula classicorum* [Amsterdam, 1973] and F. E. Cranz's *Bibliography of Aristotle Editions* [Baden-Baden 1984].)

49. See Warburg, "Dürer und die Italienische Antike," in *Gesammelte Schriften*, 2: 443-49.

50. Benveniste, *Le vocabulaire des institutions indo-européennes*.

51. Kolakowski, "The Myth of Human Self-Identity: Unity of Civil and Political Society in Socialist Thought."

52. See, for example, Lefort, *L'Invention démocratique*, in which totalitarianism is defined as the absorption of "civil society" by the state.

53. " '*L'Etat, c'est moi*' [I am the state] is almost a liberal formula by com-

parison with the actualities of Stalin's totalitarian regime. Louis XIV identified himself only with the State. The Popes of Rome identified themselves with both the State and the Church–but only during the epoch of temporal power. The totalitarian State goes far beyond Caesaro-Papism, for it has encompassed the entire economy of the country as well. Stalin can justly say, unlike the Sun King, '*La société, c'est moi*' [I am Society]" (Trotsky, *Stalin*, 2: 255).

54. See Rupnik's "Dissent in Poland, 1968-78"; also see Erard and Zygier, eds., *La Pologne, une société en dissidence*, and, for a recapitulation of the history of civil society in Poland, Arato's "Civil Society Against the State: Poland, 1980-1981" and "Empire vs. Civil Society: Poland, 1981-1982."

55. For an analysis in these terms of the situation in Poland, see Fenchel and Weiss, "Staat, Partei, Gewerkschaft." In the course of their discussion the authors suggest replacing *bürgerliche Gesellschaft* with the word *Zivilgesellschaft*.

56. Among other texts, see Miliband, *Marxism and Politics* (at the index entry "civil society" we read "see bourgeoisie"–evidence of a not uncommon misunderstanding of Marx's notion of *bürgerliche Gesellschaft*); Cohen, *Class and Civil Society: The Limits of Marxian Critical Theory*; Pelczynski, ed., *The State and Civil Society: Studies in Hegel's Political Philosophy*; Quelquejeu, "K. Marx a-t-il constitué une théorie du pouvoir d'Etat?"; Riedel, "Hegels 'bürgerliche Gesellschaft' und das Problem ihres geschichtlichen Ursprungs"; and Lefebvre's edition of various texts by either Hegel or his students, *La Société civile bourgeoise*.

57. Speaking of Nicholas II's reformist prime minister Pyotr Stolypin during an interview about his novel *The Red Wheel*, Solzhenitsyn affirmed: "Actually, he was a liberal. He thought that before creating civil society, we had to create the citizen, and therefore before giving the illiterate peasant all sorts of rights, you had to elevate him economically" (interview in *Time*, Jul. 24, 1989, p. 56).

58. The expression is Claudio Ingerflom's in his book of the same title: *Le Citoyen impossible*.

59. Molnar, *La démocratie se lève à l'Est*. In *Cinquante Idées qui ébranlent le monde, Dictionnaire de la glasnost* (Fifty ideas that are shaking the world, a glasnost dictionary), we have an example of how "civil society" was used by some of the first partisans of perestroika; a key expression among radical Gorbachevians was "the development of civil society" (see my entry *société civile* in *Cinquante Idées*; also the article *société civile* in Niqueux, ed., *Vocabulaire de la perestroïka*).

60. Shils, *Political Development in the New States*. Discussing the role of education in the new states, the author affirms that the condition for the emergence of a stable and progressive civil society is the active presence of groups of intellectual-technicians and groups animated by a spirit of public service. He uses the term "political society" to distinguish civil society from a society based primarily on kinship. In "Society and Societies: The Macrosociological View" (in *Center and Periphery*) Shils concludes: "Integrated societies in which the authoritative institutional and

cultural systems are well established can become civil societies with a wide diffusion of the virtues required for the effective practice of citizenship" (p. 46).

61. Earlier, Gurvitch had used the notion in his *Traité de sociologie* (1: 31); it was then taken up by Bottomore in *Sociology*, who affirmed that Adam Ferguson's theory of civil society (as developed in the *Essay*) played a key role in the eighteenth-century development of the discipline of sociology by directing attention for the first time to nonpolitical issues: population, the family, kinship, customs.

62. Among other works, see Bobbio, *Gramsci e le concezione della società civile*.

63. Badie and Birnbaum, *The Sociology of the State*; Barret-Kriegel, *L'Etat et les esclaves*.

64. Karady uses the term in "A l'Est la grande transformation," published in Bourdieu's journal *Actes de la recherche en sciences sociales*. See also Lochak, "La société civile: du concept au gadget." Alain Touraine has of course accorded much place to the notion of civil society in his works. See also Garreton.

65. Rosanvallon, *Le libéralisme économique. Histoire de l'idée de marché*. The passages on Marx rely on translations where *bürgerliche Gesellschaft* has sometimes (absurdly) been translated "bourgeois society."

66. Abensour, "Le procès des Maîtres rêveurs."

67. See Cannac, *Le Juste pouvoir. Essai sur les deux chemins de la démocratie*. According to the author it was "political society" that triumphed in 1981 with Mitterrand's election as president, marking a significant advance in its "centuries-old rivalry against civil society."

68. This is Alain Lancelot's analysis (from an interview in *L'Express*, Oct. 21–27, 1988).

69. "In any case, starting now I shall see to it that the government is more open to civil society, that in the choice of those to be in charge, and at all levels, the impartiality of the state dominates, and that the parliamentary minorities accede to the responsibilities to which they have a right" (declaration by President Mitterrand, June 6, 1988).

70. Rocard's circular to his ministers of May 27, 1988, was a kind of charter for governing differently; it was composed of five points: (1) respect for the law-governed state, (2) respect for the legislative body, (3) respect for civil society, (4) respect for the coherence of governmental action, and (5) respect for administrative functions. The Rocardian vision of civil society can be understood through the six principles included in point (3): (a) the more the state shows itself capable of understanding civil society, the more readily civil society will accept the state's authority; (b) it is necessary to dispel the illusion that state intervention is the solution to all evils; (c) government ministers must make good use of the good will, ideas, and initiatives abundantly present in civil society; (d) negotiation should be preferred to affirmations of superior authority; (e) civil society may be justly irritated by the excessive and complicated rules the state itself imposes on it, as well as

by the difficulty it has getting access to the state; and (f) civil society has a right to demand from the state a better "cost-efficiency" ratio.

71. On the controversy provoked by appointments of this type and for general discussions of the term "civil society" in the French press, see, for example, *Le Nouvel Observateur*, Jul. 8, 1988; *Le Figaro*, Aug. 8, 1988; *Libération*, Aug. 9, 1988; and my article, "Les avatars de la société civile," *Libération*, Jul. 16, 1988.

72. Interview in *Le Monde*, Oct. 5, 1988.

73. Debray elevates civil society to truly mythic dimensions in his book *A demain de Gaulle*: the pair civil society/the state corresponds to and determines a whole series of other oppositions: economic/political, oral/written; democracy/Republic; Mitterrand/de Gaulle. The author, undeceived, prefers the state: "When the *Cité* is confounded with society, law with mores, right with fact—when, in sum, the imported notion of 'civil society' has supplanted the revolutionary one of national sovereignty—then the people becomes the population and the leadership elite is able to convince everyone that in being *people* [sic] it is doing politics" (pp. 55-56). There is nothing in the work about where the notion "civil society" might have been "imported" from (the importation fantasy is itself rather strange), and it should be specified that the opposition civil society/the state is nowhere to be found in de Gaulle's own thought: by interpreting Gaullism with this conceptual grid, Debray imposes quite external concerns on it.

74. According to the journalist Samir al-Khalil, "Saddam's regime has severed the ties of civil society" ("C'est aux Arabes de combattre les Arabes," p. 92), whereas the political scientist Ghassan Salamé affirmed the opposite (in "Raison du régime et raison d'Etat," *Libération*, Jan. 16, 1991). We should also note that the Ibn Khaldun Center in Cairo has been publishing a newsletter titled *Civil Society: Democratic Transformation in the Arab World*, in the tenth issue of which (Oct. 1992) we may read an article called "Civil Society in Egypt" and an editorial in support of "secular forces." The newsletter also features a column called "Civil Society in Brief," with news about political parties, elections, and the progress of democratic institutions and practices in Egypt, Sudan, Tunisia, Jordan, Iraq, and Kuwait, among other countries.

75. Interview with Minc, in *L'Express*, Apr. 14, 1989.

Chapter 2

1. Biblical quotations are from the authorized King James Version unless noted otherwise.

2. Aristotle, *History of Animals* 487b33-488a13.

3. Aristotle, *Politics*, bk. 1, chap. 1, §12 (Barker, p. 6).

4. Ibid., bk. 7, chap. 7, §2-4 (Barker, p. 296).

5. Ibid., bk. 4, chap. 1.

6. Aristotle, *Nicomachean Ethics*, bk. 8, chap. 12 (Irwin, p. 229).

7. Aristotle, *Politics*, bk. 3, whole of chap. 1 defining the citizen; chap. 7, §5, last sentence; and chap. 9, §14 (Barker, pp. 92–96, p. 115, and p. 120). See also Aristotle, *Nicomachean Ethics*, bk. 8, chap. 9.

8. Aristotle, *Politics*, bk. 3, chap. 6, §4 (Barker, p. 111).

9. Aristotle, *Nicomachean Ethics*, bk. 8, chap. 9 (Irwin, p. 225).

10. Ibid. (Irwin's translation of key terms *koinonia* and *koinonia politikè* modified).

11. Aristotle, *Politics*, bk. 1, chap. 7, §1 (Lord, p. 43).

12. Gellner, *Saints of the Atlas*, p. 43.

13. Aristotle, *Nicomachean Ethics*, bk. 8, chap. 9 (Irwin, p. 225).

14. Aristotle, *Politics*, bk. 3, chap. 6, §9 (Barker, p. 112).

15. Ibid., bk. 1, chap. 2, §16 (Barker, p. 7). It should however be pointed out that Aristotle believed justice to be present in all forms of community: "In every community there seems to be some sort of justice, and some type of friendship also" (*Nicomachean Ethics*, bk. 8, chap. 9; Irwin, p. 224).

16. Aristotle, *Politics*, bk. 2, chap. 2, §2 (Barker, pp. 40–41).

17. Ibid., §4 (Lord, p. 56).

18. The word *politeia* has several meanings in Aristotle's writings: it can designate either all the citizens of a given polis; a political regime; the *good* political regime; or a written document defining political institutions (what we most commonly understand by the word "constitution"), as in *The Athenian Constitution*. On the importance of written constitutions for Aristotle and others, see my "Grammaire politique de l'Occident."

19. This is the understanding expressed at the beginning of the *Nicomachean Ethics*.

20. Aristotle, *Nicomachean Ethics*, bk. 1, chap. 2 (Irwin, p. 3).

21. See Colliot-Thélène, "Les Origines de la théorie du *Machtstaat*."

22. *De justa reipublicae christianae in reges impios autoritate* (see Chapter 1, note 28).

23. In general the French Calvinists, desirous of advancing politically through the favor of noblemen and city magistrates, sought to discredit the Anabaptists— and dissociate themselves from them—with the charge of fanaticism. Théodore de Bèze thus protested, in his *Confession de la foi chrétienne* (1560), against any assimilation of Protestants with "the fanatical Anabaptists, who seek to abolish the magistrates' authority" (chap. 45). In the epistle to François I that precedes his *Institutes of the Christian Religion*, Calvin coined the word *catabaptiste*, the Greek prefix *cata* signifying "disastrous change."

24. See Bèze, *Du droit des magistrats*; Hotman, *Franco-Gallia*; and the anonymous *Vindiciae contra tyrannos*.

25. Nietzsche, "The Wanderer and His Shadow," §232, in *Human, All Too Human* (Hollingdale, p. 369). The German term is *Staats-Narren*.

26. Ibid., §473 (Hollingdale, p. 173).

27. Augustine, *City of God* 1.36 (p. 46) and preface to bk. 5 (p. 179). (All page numbers are for the Penguin edition, Bettenson translation, unless otherwise indicated.)

28. Augustine, *De Genesi ad litteram* 11.15, 20, in *Patrologia Latina*, vol. 34, col. 437. The translation quoted here is Bourke, *Literal Commentary on Genesis*, in *The Essential Augustine*, p. 201. On the two cities in Augustine see Gilson, *Les Métamorphoses de la Cité de Dieu*; Brown, *Augustine of Hippo*; and Marrou, *Saint Augustine and His Influence Through the Ages*.

29. Augustine, *City of God* 14.1 (p. 547).

30. Ibid. 15.2 (p. 598).

31. Ibid. 15.1 (p. 596).

32. Ibid. 15.5 (pp. 600-601).

33. "It would be incorrect to say that the goods which this city desires are not goods, since even that city is better, in its own human way, by their possession. For example, that city desires an earthly peace, for the sake of the lowest goods; and it is that peace which it longs to attain by making war. For if it wins the war and no one survives to resist, then there will be peace, which the warring sections did not enjoy when they contended in their unhappy poverty for the things which they could not both possess at the same time. This peace is the aim of wars, with all their hardships; it is this peace that glorious victory (so-called) achieves. Now when the victory goes to those who were fighting for the juster cause, can anyone doubt that the victory is a matter for rejoicing and the resulting peace is something to be desired? These things are goods and undoubtedly they are gifts of God. But if the higher goods are neglected, which belong to the City on high, where victory will be serene in the enjoyment of eternal and perfect peace—if these goods are neglected and those other goods are so desired as to be considered the only goods, or are loved more than the goods which are believed to be higher, the inevitable consequence is fresh misery, and an increase of the wretchedness already there" (ibid. 15.4; pp. 599-600).

34. "The man who despises glory and is eager only for domination is worse than the beasts, in his cruelty or in his self-indulgence. Some of the Romans were men of this kind, who, while caring nothing for the opinion of others, were possessed by the passion for domination. History shows that there were many such; but it was Nero Caesar who first scaled, as it were, the heights of this vice, and gained the summit. So debauched was he that one would have supposed that nothing virile was to be feared from him; such was his cruelty that one would not have suspected anything effeminate in his nature if one had not known about it. Yet even to men like this the power of domination is not given except by the providence of God, when he decides that man's condition deserves such masters" (ibid. 5.19; p. 213).

35. Ibid. 5.21 (p. 216).

36. Ibid. 19.13 (p. 870).

37. "Peace between men is an ordered agreement of mind with mind; the peace of a home is the ordered agreement among those who live together about giving and obeying orders; [the peace of the City is the ordered agreement among fellow citizens about giving and obeying orders;] the peace of the Heavenly City is the perfectly ordered and perfectly harmonious fellowship in the enjoyment of God, and a mutual fellowship in God" (ibid.). We have restored the clause in brackets which, present in the original Latin, has somehow been omitted from the Bettenson translation. For the Latin, see the text of *De Civitate Dei* established by B. Dombart and A. Kalb (edition of the Latin text used here is the bilingual *Bibliothèque augustinienne*, 37: 110).

38. Ibid. 22.30 (p. 1091).

39. Ibid. 1.35 (p. 46).

40. In his comparative analysis of Indo-European religions, pursued in *L'Idéologie des trois fonctions dans les épopées des peuples indo-européens* and *Destiny of the Warrior*, among other texts, Dumezil identified as common to all of them what he called three functions: the sacred, the military, and the productive. These are just as surely to be found in Plato's ideal republic and Roman mythology as in the division of the French ancien régime into three Estates. The French medievalist Georges Duby sought to understand how this schema operated in a particular place at a particular time in his well-known sociohistorical study of the north of France during the eleventh and twelfth centuries (in English *The Three Orders: Feudal Society Imagined*).

41. With Sarah there had appeared on earth a prophetic image of the Heavenly City, an image that was "servant" to this "free City" in that it pointed to or symbolized "something other than itself." In this connection Augustine quotes Paul's Epistle to the Galatians : "We are told in Scripture that Abraham had two sons, one by a slave-woman, one by his free-born wife. The slave-woman's son was born in the course of nature, the free woman's as a result of the promise. These facts are allegorical. For the two women stand for the two covenants. The one bearing children for slavery is the covenant from Mount Sinai; this is Hagar. Now Sinai is a mountain in Arabia and it stands for the present Jerusalem; for she is in slavery with her children. But the Jerusalem above is free; and she is our mother" (Gal. 4: 22–26 as quoted by Augustine). Sarah was of course Abraham's freeborn wife, who, barren when young and having reached an age when she could no longer become pregnant, mysteriously gave birth to Isaac, born thus not of "nature" but as "a result of the promise," while Hagar, the servant Sarah had sent to Abraham's bed, gave birth to Ishmael, born of nature and in servitude. Allegorically, Hagar was the earthly Jerusalem of Paul's time, which from a Christian perspective could only appear enslaved, while Sarah, who gave birth supernaturally as it were and whose descendants were free, symbolized by these attributes the heavenly Jeru-

salem. "Thus we find in the earthly city a double significance: in one respect it displays its own presence, and in the other it serves by its presence to signify the Heavenly City." Because of the conditions of his birth, Isaac symbolized the children of grace, "citizens of the free city . . . who form a community where there is no love of a will that is personal, and, as we may say, private, but a love that rejoices in a good that is at once shared by all and unchanging, . . . a love that is the wholehearted and harmonious obedience of mutual affection" (*City of God* 15.2, 3; pp. 597–99).

42. See Augustine, *Epistolae*, letter 138, addressed to the recently converted Roman official Marcellinus (to whom the *City of God* is also addressed), in *Patrologia Latina*, vol. 33, col. 533.

43. An early occurrence of *phanaticus* is to be found in one of Luther's glosses of the work (see *Weimarerausgabe* [hereafter abbreviated as *WA*], 9: 15).

44. On medieval political theorizing of Augustinian inspiration see Arquillière, *L'Augustinisme politique*.

45. *De sacramentis* 2.418; quoted in Burns, *Medieval Political Thought, c. 350– c. 1450*, p. 300.

46. "In qua vos domini nostri Iesu Christi dispensatio rectorem populi disposuit" (Alcuin, letter 174, in *Monumenta Germaniae Historica. Epistolae Karolini Aevi*, 2: 288).

47. On the meanings of Charlemagne's coronation, see Pacaut, *La Théocratie*, pp. 31–36.

48. Hotman, *P. Sixti V Fulmen Brutum*, p. 168.

49. Henry IV, encyclical letter of April 1076, in *Monumenta Germaniae Historica. Constitutiones et Acta Publica*, 1: 112.

50. Ibid., p. 113.

51. Hildebert du Mans, letter 7 (1110), in *Patrologia Latina*, vol. 171, col. 153.

52. St. Bernard of Clairvaux, letter 256 (1150), in *Patrologia Latina*, vol. 182, col. 464; quoted in English in Burns, *Medieval Political Thought*, pp. 372–73.

53. This version of the facts is also to be found in Neiderman and Forhan, eds., *Medieval Political Theory, A Reader*. Burns, on the other hand, contests the assertion that Giles was tutor to the dauphin, later Philip the Fair, (*Medieval Political Thought*, p. 669).

54. See Hissette, *Enquête sur les 219 articles condamnés à Paris le 7 mars 1277*.

55. For more information on Giles of Rome as bishop of Bourges, see Devailly, *Le Diocèse de Bourges*. Gérard Pigalotti, bishop of Arras from 1296 to 1316 and later bishop of Spoleto, was like Giles of Rome a foreigner. According to a letter by Cardinal Porto, discussed in Dupuy, *Histoire du différend d'entre le pape Boniface VIII et Philippes le Bel, roy de France*, p. 72, Philip the Fair admitted to having named the two foreigners, *nourris sans la France*, to their respective posts.

56. Giles devoted a long treatise, *De renuntiatione papae*, to defending Boniface VIII's right to be pope.

57. "Ego sum pontifex et imperator, terrestreque ac coeleste imperio habeo"– the formula Hotman attributed to him (*P. Sixti V Fulmen Brutum*, p. 74).

58. For details of this conflict, see Dupuy.

59. The library of the monastery of the Grands Augustins, which in the eighteenth century contained some three hundred manuscripts, was confiscated at the time of the French Revolution. Since no catalog exists, we cannot know what manuscripts Giles of Rome owned. There is however a manuscript known to have belonged to him at the Bibliothèque de l'Arsenal in Paris.

60. A manuscript of the first French translation of *De regimine principum*, done by Henri de Gauchy in 1282, was edited and published in the United States in 1899. For a comprehensive catalog of manuscripts by Giles of Rome, see the first three volumes of *Aegidii Romani Opera Omnia*, the last of which is entirely devoted to manuscripts of *De regimine principum* in the Vatican library and other Italian libraries.

61. Unless otherwise noted, this passage and all others from Giles of Rome, *De regimine principum*, were translated for this work from the 1607 Latin edition.

62. Giles of Rome, *De ecclesiastica potestate* 3.10 (p. 198) (all page numbers are for the Scholtz translation), and 3.11 (p. 201). Giles is here quoting *The City of God* 2.22 (p. 75).

63. Ibid. 2.13 (pp. 115–16).

64. "Why then was it necessary to institute another power and another sword? We say that this necessity rose from the too great excellence and the too great perfection of spiritual things. The nobility and excellence of spiritual things is such that, to ensure that no defect might blemish them, it was well to institute a second power to preside especially over corporal matters, so that the spiritual power could more freely take care of spiritual ones. The spiritual power is thus general and widespread, because it extends not only to spiritual matters but also corporal ones, whereas the material and earthly power is particular and limited because it was instituted especially for corporal matters. The second sword was thus instituted not because of any weakness in the spiritual sword but in accordance with the right ordering of things and with decency" (ibid. 2.13; p. 113).

65. "The power of the sovereign pontiff is that sublime power to which every soul must be submitted, . . . which has more excellence and nobility than any earthly and secular power in the same way that the soul is more excellent and more noble than the body and the spiritual more excellent than the earthly" (ibid. 1.3; p. 11).

66. Ibid. 2.5 (p. 56), and 3.1 (p. 148).

67. Pacaut in *La Théocratie* underlines the importance of Giles's critique of the notion of *dominium*. Giles also uses, though less frequently, the term *imperium* (see, for example, *De ecclesiastica potestate* 2.10; p. 92).

68. Giles of Rome, *De ecclesiastica potestate* 2.12 (p. 102); 1.5 (p. 13); 2.6 (p. 66).

69. Ibid. 3.6 (p. 175), and 2.1 (p. 32).

70. Ibid. 1.4 (pp. 51-52).

71. Ibid. 2.8 (pp. 63-64), and 9 (pp. 68-69).

72. "Nullam possessionem, nullum dominium, nullam potestatem possunt infideles habere vere et cum iusticia, sed usurpative et cum iniusticia" (ibid. 2.11; p. 96).

73. "Therefore the art of governing according to the earthly power, and the earthly itself, must be subject to the ecclesiastical power, so that it may itself function, together with all its organs and instruments, with the respect due to the spiritual power and in its service (*ad nutum*). And because the organs and instruments of the earthly power are the public force (*potentia civilis*), the armies, temporal goods, laws and constitutions that it establishes, all this and itself must be established in such a way as to respect the ecclesiastical power and in accordance with its will" (ibid. 2.6; p. 69).

74. Ibid. 3.10 (p. 195).

75. Ibid. 1.4 (p. 11).

76. These two phrases have been translated from Gauchy's translation of 1282.

77. The supremacy of the Church over civil society was most recently underlined in John Paul II's 1995 encyclical *Evangelum vitae* (*The Gospel of Life*). On questions of Church doctrine on political power see Arquillière, *L'Augustinisme politique*; Landry, *L'Idée de chrétienté chez les scolastiques du XIIIè siècle*; and Rivière, *Le Problème de l'Eglise et de l'Etat au temps de Philippe le Bel*.

78. On the primacy of the One in the polity see Giles of Rome, *De regimine principum* 3.2.

79. Giles of Rome, *De ecclesiastica potestate* 1.2 (p. 8). According to Rivière, Giles's thinking "foreshadows the doctrine of infallibility with remarkable precision" (*Le Problème de l'Eglise et de l'Etat*, p. 194).

80. See Boniface VIII, "Letter of the 13th of May 1300 to the German princes after they deposed Adolf of Nassau as King of Germany and designated in his place Albert of Austria," in *Monumenta Germaniae Historica. Constititiones et Acta Publica*, vol. 4, pt. 1, p. 80.

81. Boniface VIII, *Unam sanctam*: "Porro subesse Romani Pontifici omnem humanam creaturam declaramus, dicemus, dissinimus et pronuntiamus omnino esse de necessitate salutis" (We [hereby] declare, say, determine, and affirm that it is necessary for men to submit to the Roman pontiff). In the Lateran Council of 1516 we find a similar formula: "Declaratio quod subesse Romano Pontifici est omni humanae creaturae de necessitate salutis" (It is [hereby] affirmed that it is necessary for every human creature's salvation that he submit to the Roman pontiff).

82. John Paul II's encyclical was published on the centenary anniversary of *Rerum novarum* and cites it explicitly.

83. *Société civile* as a synonym for state as opposed to church is to be found in pontifical texts written in French; see, for example, Leo XIII's *Lettre à M. le président de la Règublique française pour revendiquer les droits des catholiques* (May 12, 1883).

84. See Maultrot and Ney, *Apologie de tous les jugements rendus par les tribunaux séculiers en France contre le schisme* (1752–1753), 1: 417 and 420. "State" and "civil society" were of course interchangeable terms for these authors.

85. In *De ecclesiastica et politica potestate libellus*, Richer made the following affirmations on the relation between spiritual and temporal powers: "The Church taken either for the whole company of the faithful or for the Christian commonwealth is contented with her sole only head and essential foundation, our Lord Jesus Christ. Nevertheless, in the matter of exercise and execution of government in this Christian commonwealth, she is differently ruled by two diverse persons, that is the Pope, and the Civil Prince" (§10); "The Church is within the commonwealth as it were upon another man's ground, territory, and dominion" (§12); it has "neither territory nor use of the material sword" (§18). As for relations within the Church, Richer wrote: "The Church is ruled by Canon, not by an absolute power" (§18); "The power of decreeing and making canons" belonged to "a general counsel." The pope could not have "infallibility of decreeing," for this ran contradictory to the very structure of the Church, "a monarchical polity tempered by an aristocratical government" (§15). Not surprisingly, Richer judged Boniface VIII's *Unam sanctam* "extravagant." His arguments explictly refuted those of the Jesuit Bellarmin, whose *Tractatus* had been published in Rome a little more than a year earlier (1610) and who referred directly to Giles of Rome's *De ecclesiastica potestate* (among a host of other texts) to support his defense of the pope's spiritual and political supremacy (Bellarmin, *Power of the Pope*, p. 4).

86. For Lamennais there existed two societies, one without God, which prevailed in political administration and government, and the society of Christians united under the authority of the Church, who had to struggle unceasingly against political atheism and its consequences in order to maintain faith, worship, and moral order on earth (*De la religion*, p. 58). Because religion in France was situated entirely outside political and civil society and because the state was atheist (p. 30), the fight against public schooling was particularly necessary (p. 58).

87. Leo XIII, *Immortale Dei*, §44, §43, §45, in Carlen, 2: 116–17.

88. *Leo XIII, Humanum genus* (encyclical against the Freemasons, April 20, 1884), §13, in Carlen, 2: 94.

89. The Catholic Church was at first hostile to the Third Republic in France and openly expressed its hope that the monarchy would be reinstated. Around 1890, however, in a move known as the *ralliement*, the Catholic hierarchy reversed its attitude, acknowledging, if not wholeheartedly approving, the legitimacy of the Republic.

90. See, for example, Leo XIII's *Diuturnum* (On the origin of civil power, 1881), in Carlen, vol. 2.

91. Leo XIII, Immortale Dei, §23, in Carlen, 2: 112.

92. Leo XIII, Rerum novarum, §17, in Carlen, 2: 245.

93. Namely in a letter to S. M., cardinal archbishop of Paris, titled *Au milieu des consolations* (Sept. 23, 1900). The following is a characteristic passage from another text of the same period: "We are told that [civil] society is quite able to help itself; that it can flourish without the assistance of Christianity, and attain its end by its own unaided efforts. Public administrators prefer a purely secular system of government. All traces of the religion of our forefathers are daily disappearing from political life and administration. What blindness! Once the idea of the authority of God as the judge of right and wrong is forgotten, law must necessarily lose its primary authority and justice must perish: and these are the two most powerful and most necessary bonds of [civil] society" (Leo XIII, *Tametsi futura prospicientibus*, 1900, in Carlen, 2: 471; *civilis societas* in the Latin original; see *Allocutiones, epistolae, constitutiones*, vol. 7, p. 441).

94. Quoted in Fremantle, *The Papal Encyclicals in Their Historical Context*, p. 148.

95. Pius IX, *Quanta Cura*, quoted in Fremantle, p. 141.

96. Pius IX, *Quanta Cura*. See also Leo XIII, *Libertas praestantissimum* (On the nature of human liberty) 1888: "There can be no doubt that truth alone should imbue the minds of men . . . and therefore nothing but truth should be taught both to the ignorant and to the educated. . . . [I]t is manifest that man's best and surest teacher is God, the Source and Principle of all truth. . . . In faith and in the teaching of morality, God Himself made the Church a partaker of His divine authority and through His heavenly gift she cannot be deceived. She is therefore the greatest and most reliable teacher of mankind, and in her swells an inviolable right to teach them" (Carlen, 2: 176–77).

97. Gellner, *Nations and Nationalism*, pp. 35–38.

98. From a declaration issued by the pope on April 15, 1991, upon the conclusion of a meeting of the Council of the Episcopal Conferences of Europe.

99. John Paul II, *Centesimus annus*, chap. 5, §46, pp. 70–71.

100. Ibid., p. 70.

101. Ibid., chap. 3, §25, p. 39.

102. In an interview given to the French Catholic newspaper *La Croix* in 1991, Salvatore Abbruzzese made the following affirmation: " 'Communion and Liberation' retrieves the concept of civil society's autonomy that was in vogue in the 1960's and thereby calls into question the secular state as conceived of today: we deny the ethical character of that state." Gramsci in fact formulated the revolutionary party's strategy for conquering a hegemonic position within civil society in accordance with the particularities of the Italian situation, taking fully into ac-

count the Church's role in controlling that country's civil society. We might add that the "centrists" of France's Christian Democratic party (Union Démocratique Française or U.D.F.), who are the politicians most audibly in favor of according preeminence to "civil society," are also among the most active partisans of religious schooling.

103. [Translation of definition given by the nineteenth-century French lexicographer Emile Littré. Trans.]

104. Among the numerous signs of this link that the West seems so easily to establish between the Muslim world and fanaticism figures the classic narration of the English traveler Charles Doughty, who from 1876 to 1880, starting in Damascus, traveled with Muslim pilgrims all the way to Mecca without dissimulating the fact that he was a Christian, an infidel. "Fanaticism" plays the role of master signifier in his *Travels in Arabia Deserta*, the story of his peregrinations among the tribes of the Arabian peninsula, of which a 1936 version with a foreword by T. E. Lawrence opens with the following question: "Tell me, . . . how couldst thou take such journeys into the fanatic Arabia?" (vol. 1, p. 39).

105. The French Orientalist Louis Massignon has called Islam a "secular [in the sense that it has no real priesthood] and egalitarian theocracy" (*La Passion d'al-Hallaj*, p. 23).

106. See Voltaire, *Essai sur les mœurs et l'esprit des nations*, vol. 2, chap. 6.

107. Voltaire, *Mahomet the Prophet, or Fanaticism*, p. 3.

108. Ibid., p. 37.

109. Jean Calas, a French Calvinist, was accused of killing his son for wanting to convert to Catholicism (the son had in fact committed suicide) and was condemned to die on the wheel (1762). Voltaire among others denounced the judicial error and stigmatized Catholic intolerance in the matter (see his *Traité sur la tolérance*).

110. See *The Works of Voltaire*, vol. 5, pt. 1, p. 19.

111. Among the texts in Old French cited by Lebey de Batilly figure the chronicler Jean Joinville's memoires and accounts of Marco Polo's voyages.

112. Lebey de Batilly, *Traicté de l'origine des anciens Assasins-porte-couteaux*, p. 6.

113. The historian Ernst Kantorowicz recounts how it was said of Frederick II that he explicitly took the Old Man of the Mountain for a model. On the relations between the German emperor and the Assassins, see *Frederick the Second, 1194–1250*, chap 4.

114. Michelet, *Histoire de France, Le Moyen Age*, bk. 4, chap. 3, p. 259; Michelet speaks of the "fanatic" Ismailis.

115. See the renowed Orientalist Maxime Rodinson's foreword to the French translation of Bernard Lewis's *Assassins*, p. 30. Rodinson uses his expert knowledge of Marxism, more particularly Leninist Marxism, to interpret Ismaili history.

116. Translated from the Latin text, *Historia rerum in partibus transmarinis gestarum*, in *Patrologia Latina*, vol. 201, col. 811; quoted in Lewis, *Assassins*, pp. 3-4.

117. Moreau de Tours, who adopts the drug-related etymology of the word, speaks of the medieval Ismailis's "fanatic devotion" (*Du Hachisch*, p. 12).

118. From *Le Club des Hachichins*; our translation. Reprinted in Baudelaire, *Les Paradis artificiels*, p. 53.

119. [During the French Revolution, *la Montagne* was the name by which the radical revolutionary party was known; its members, the Jacobins, and most notably Robespierre and Saint-Just, decided upon and organized the Terror. Trans.]

120. Between 1916 and 1936 Abbé Bremond published the monumental *Histoire littéraire du sentiment religieux en France*.

121. Barrès, *Une enquête aux pays du Levant*, p. 180.

122. Ibid., p. 205.

123. Ibid., p. 281.

124. Baudelaire, *Les Paradis artificiels*, p. 150. *Fanatique* appears on p. 149; *enthousiaste* or *enthousiasme*, on pp. 139, 149, 152, and 155.

125. Baudelaire, *Artificial Paradise*, p. 77.

126. Ibid., p. 75; translation modified to conform more closely to the original.

127. For an analysis of the political specificity of Islam compared to Christianity, see Badie, *Les deux Etats*.

128. See Lewis, "State and Society under Islam": "The very notion of something that is separate or even separable from religious authority . . . is totally alien to Islamic thought and practice" (p. 41). Further on the author affirms that in the Muslim perception "the primary meaning of civil is non-religious, and the civil society is one in which the organizing principle is something other than religion" (p. 45).

129. Ibid., p. 46.

130. Ibid., p. 42.

Chapter 3

1. Michelet, *Histoire de France. Renaissance et Réforme*, p. 337. In a different context Michelet comments that the Anabaptists wanted to change "civil society, property, even marriage–the whole of the external world" (p. 462).

2. See Lovy, *Luther*, p. 133.

3. *Luther at the Diet of Worms* (1521), in *LW*, 32: 112-13. For this and all other quotations in English we have followed Pelikan and Lehmann's U.S. edition; for any Latin or German references, see *WA* unless otherwise indicated.

4. Luther to N. Gerbel, Nov. 1, 1521, in *LW*, 48: 319.

5. "Today, on the sixth day, I had elimination with such difficulty that I almost passed out. Now I sit aching as if in labor confinement, wounded and sore, and shall have no–or little–rest this night. Thanks be to Christ who has not left me

without any relic of the holy cross. I would have been healed from all soreness if the elimination had moved more easily. But whatever heals in four days is wounded again by elimination. I write this not for sympathy but that you may congratulate me, praying that I may be worthy to become fervent in the Spirit. Now is the time to pray against Satan with all our strength; he is threatening Germany with some fatal tragedy" (letter to G. Spalatin, Sept. 9, 1521, in *LW*, 48: 307).

6. See Luther's letter to Melanchthon from the Wartburg, May 26, 1521: "If the Pope will take steps against all who think as I do, then Germany will not be without uproar. The faster he undertakes this, the faster he and his followers will perish and I shall return. God is arousing the spirits of many, especially the hearts of the common people. It does not seem to me likely that this affair can be checked with force; if [the pope] begins to put it down, it will become ten times bigger. Germany has very many *Karsthansen*" (*LW*, 48: 233). For Luther's critique of Erasmus, see his letter to Spalatin from the Wartburg, Sept. 9, 1521, in *WA*, 2: 287.

7. Throughout his life, Luther gave numerous courses on the Bible (he was professor of Bible studies at the University of Wittenberg from 1512 to 1517). He began translating the New Testament in 1521 and published a first complete edition of the Bible in 1534 (other complete editions were published in his lifetime). The Reformer was greatly assisted in this monumental project, namely by his friend Melanchthon, both Hellenist and Latinist, and by other professors at Wittenberg, among them specialists in Hebrew. The group constituted a veritable translating workshop (see *The Cambridge History of the Bible*, vol. 3, chap. 1, and Bedouelle and Roussel, eds., *Le Temps des Réformes et la Bible*, chap. 6).

8. On the use of iconography during the Reformation, see Scribner, *For the Sake of Simple Folk* and *Popular Culture and Popular Movements in Reformation Germany*.

9. Luther to Elector Frederick, March 5, 1522, in *LW*, 48: 389.

10. The name "Peasants' War" is somewhat misleading given that other social groups, namely certain elements of the urban petty bourgeoisie, took arms against the nobility as well.

11. Luther, *Letter to the Christians at Strassburg in Opposition to the Fanatic Spirit*, in *LW*, vol. 40.

12. On the incident in Bourges in 1562 see Cristin, "Iconographie de l'iconoclasme. A propos de la mutilation du portail de la cathédrale de Bourges."

13. "For if we have broken all laws of men and cast off their yokes, what difference would it make to us that Philip is not annointed or tonsured but married? Nevertheless he is truly a priest and actually does the work of a priest, unless it is not the office of a priest to teach the Word of God. . . . Since, therefore, Philip is called by God and performs the ministry of the Word, as no one can deny, what difference does it make that he is not called by those tyrants—who are bishops not of churches but of horses and courtiers" (*LW*, 48: 308–9).

14. Letter to his father, Hans Luther, Nov. 21, 1521, in *LW*, 48: 336.

15. In a letter to Count Ludwig of Stolberg written at Melanchthon's request and dated April 25, 1522, Luther explains: "Your Grace may rest assured that I do not like what the iconoclasts are doing. Even if images were more worthy of condemnation than they are, such means of being rid of them is in no way proper. There are indeed people who misuse the bread and wine, as Paul says (Romans 16:18): 'quorum Deus venter est' [Their belly is their god]. Should we for that reason attack and cast opprobrium on all bellies, just as for the gold and wine? If so, we should also tear the sun, moon, and stars down from the sky, for the Gospel rigorously forbids us to adore them. What is more, we should let no authority subsist, neither father or mother, for we sometimes honor them by bending the knee, as before God himself. In truth, true serving of God is internal; it resides in trust and love" (*WA*, 2: 513).

16. Karlstadt, *Von abtuhung der Bilder* (Wittenberg, 1522).

17. *LW*, 51: 76.

18. "I did nothing; the Word did everything. Had I desired to foment trouble, I could have brought great bloodshed upon Germany. . . . What do you suppose is Satan's thought when one tries to do the thing by kicking up a row? He sits back in Hell and thinks: Oh, what a fine game the poor fools are up to now!" (ibid., pp. 77-78).

19. Luther here takes up a distinction first theorized by the Stoics.

20. *LW*, 51: 79-80.   21. Ibid., p. 81.

22. Ibid., p. 72.   23. Ibid., p. 83.

24. Ibid., pp. 81-82. On the Byzantine crisis see Grabar, *L'Iconoclasme byzantin*.

25. *LW*, 51: 83.   26. Ibid., p. 80.

27. Ibid., p. 85.   28. Ibid., p. 84.

29. Ibid., p. 85.

30. Luther, *Distinctae sunt naturae sed una persona* (see *Vorlesung über den 1 Brief des Johannes*, in *WA*, 20: 602-4).

31. Luther, *Admonition to Peace, A Reply to the Twelve Articles of the Peasants in Swabia*, in *LW*, 46: 22-23. See Cargill Thompson's stimulating discussion in *The Political Thought of Martin Luther*.

32. In the *Admonition to Peace*, Luther condemns individual recourse to violence by citing several scriptural texts but also with reference to "the natural law of the world, which says that no one may sit as judge in his own case or take his own revenge" (*LW*, 46: 25).

33. Ibid., p. 29.

34. Ibid., pp. 31-32.

35. Ibid., p. 41.

36. Luther to John Briessmann, Aug. 5, 1525, in *LW*, 49: 124-25; see Chapter 4, p. 167.

37. *LW*, 46: 54-55.

38. See Chapter 4, p. 167.

39. Romans 13:4; quoted in Luther, *An Open Letter on the Harsh Book Against the Peasants*, in *LW*, 46: 68.

40. Ibid., p. 69.

41. Such language is typical of *Against the Robbing and Murdering Hordes of Peasants*.

42. "I am born for my Germans, whom I want to serve" (Luther to Nicholas Gerbel, Nov. 1, 1521, in *LW*, 48: 320). The nationalism of the Swiss Reformer Huldrych Zwingli was defined to a degree by the particularities of the Swiss Confederation: he called on his compatriots to renounce the self-interest (*eygennutz*) that made them take high-paying work as mercenaries, most notably in the service of the pope; this is linked with the pacifist element in his thinking. But while affirming that the term "right to make war" could only signify "violence," he nonetheless acknowledged the necessity of war in the defense of one's country and the legitimacy of using violence against those who disobeyed or refused to submit to the law (see *Ein Göttliche Vermahnung an die Eidgenossen zu Schwyz* [Exhortation from God to the confederates of Switzerland, 1522], and *Eine treue und ernstliche Vermahnung an die Eidgenossen* [A loyal and earnest exhortation to the confederates, 1524]).

43. In a deterministic interpretation of German anti-Semitism, the French historian Léon Poliakof affirms that Luther was a precursor of Hitler (*History of Anti-Semitism*). In his *Luther*, Oberman proposes to analyze the meaning of Luther's brutal, hateful anti-Semitism as expressed in one of his last texts, *Of the Jews and Their Lies* (1543), and in his last sermons, such as that of February 14, 1546, four days before his death, and underlines the historical consequences of his attitude (see pp. 292–97). It is fair to say that Luther's aggressive hostility toward Jews was not one of the more salient features of his discourse in the period of his career considered in this book, namely the 1520s.

44. See Weber, *The Profession and Vocation of Politics*, in *Weber: Political Writings*, pp. 310–11.

45. See Chapter 10, p. 344–45.

46. "A murderer or evildoer lets the head of the government alone and attacks only the members or their property; indeed, he fears the ruler. So long as the head remains, no one ought to attack such a murderer, because the head can punish. Everyone ought to await the judgment and command of the head, to whom God has committed the sword and the office of punishment. But a rebel attacks the head himself and interferes with the exercise of his sword and his office, and therefore his crime is not to be compared with that of the murderer" (Luther, *Open Letter*, in *LW*, 46: 80).

47. Ibid., p. 27.

48. Zwingli expressed a similar attitude. In his *Exposition of the Christian*

Faith, addressed to the French king François I (written in Latin in 1531 and translated into French in 1539), the Reformer from Zurich explained that because "rebels and obstinate people" existed who must be reprimanded and corrected, "magistrates and administrators of justice" must likewise exist. Referring then to ancient political systems, he distinguished three forms of government–monarchy, aristocracy, democracy–and their degenerated versions–tyranny, oligarchy, demogogy–and corrected the Greeks: if the prince dominated he must be obeyed; if he degenerated into a tyrant he should be reprimanded, but if he became violent and cruel, his iniquity must be borne until the Lord God deposed him. Zwingli also reiterated the obligation for subjects to pay all taxes required of them.

49. This is an essential point of Article 16 of the *Augsburg Confession*, composed by Melanchthon in 1530: "Of civil affairs, they [Reformed Christians] teach that legitimate civil ordinations are good works of God. . . . And so Christians ought necessarily to obey their magistrates and laws, unless they command them to sin; and then they must obey God more than men. Acts 5[:29]" (*A Melanchthon Reader*, p. 104).

50. *Admonition to Peace*, in *LW*, 46: 39. Luther answers thus: "This article [of the peasants' demands] would make all men equal, and turn the spiritual kingdom of Christ into a worldly external kingdom, and that is impossible. A worldly kingdom cannot exist without an inequality of persons, some being free, some imprisoned, some lords, some subjects, etc." (ibid.).

51. "Christianus homo, omnium dominus est liberrimus, nulli subiectus. / Christianus homo, omnium seruus est officiousissimus omnibus subiectus" (*Martin Luther. Studienausgabe*, 2: 264). [As was often the case, Luther wrote versions of this text in both German and Latin; the version destined for the pope was in Latin. We have modified the English translation given in *LW*, which seems to attribute an inner subjectivity to Luther's Christian not inferable from the Latin formulation of his definition. Trans.]

52. "The first-born brother was priest and lord over all the others and a type of Christ, [who is] the true and only first-born of God the Father and the Virgin Mary and true king and priest, but not after the fashion of the flesh and the world, for his kingdom is not of this world. He reigns in heavenly and spiritual things and consecrates them–things such as righteousness, truth, wisdom, peace, salvation, etc. This does not mean that all things on earth and in hell are not also subject to him . . . but that his kingdom consists neither in them nor of them" (*LW*, 31: 353-54).

53. Ibid., p. 355.

54. *Martin Luther. Studienausgabe*, 2: 283.

55. Luther in no way advocates the accumulation of riches or the maximization of productivity; rather he approves economy and work for their role in making human beings moral. As Marx pointed out, he condemned usury. Calvin's position on usury was quite different.

56. *De servo arbitrio* (*The Bondage of the Will*, in *LW*, vol. 33) was a response to what Luther called Erasmus's diatribe on free will (*De libero arbitrio*) in which the humanist had affirmed that a person might cooperate in his or her salvation.

57. *LW*, 45: 87.

58. Luther, *Freedom of a Christian*, in *LW*, 31: 348.

59. When Paul said that all things work together for good for the elect, Luther explains, "This is not to say that every Christian is placed over all things to have and control them by physical power–a madness with which some churchmen are afflicted–for such power belongs to kings, princes, and other men on earth" (ibid., p. 354).

60. Luther, *On Secular Authority* (Höpfl, pp. 9–10).

61. Luther, *Temporal Authority*, in *LW*, 45: 105.

62. "No man is by nature a Christian or just, but all are sinners and evil" (Luther, *On Secular Authority*; Höpfl, p. 10).

63. Plato, *The Statesman*. I discuss this distinction in "La Grammaire politique de l'Occident."

64. Luther would later insist on the importance of written law, analogous in the political domain to Scripture in the domain of faith (see *A Sermon on Keeping Children in School*, 1530, in *LW*, vol. 46). For an interpretation of this change in attitude, see once again my "Grammaire politique de l'Occident."

65. Luther, *On Secular Authority* (Höpfl, pp. 19–22). In chap. 3 of *The Protestant Ethic and the Spirit of Capitalism*, "Luther's Conception of the Calling, Task of the Investigation," Weber gives only a sketchy idea of Luther's notion of *Beruf*. Calvin used the word *vocatio*, *vocation*.

66. Kohlhaas was a Brandenburg merchant who was insulted and abused by a Saxon nobleman. Unable to obtain reparation, he formally declared war on the prince elector of Saxony and the principality as a whole in 1534. Despite Luther's exhortations, he acted on his word, committing several acts of banditry with the help of troops he had recruited. He was captured and imprisoned, then put to death in 1540.

67. Aristotle's works with a commentary by Melanchthon, including the *Politics* in Bruni's Latin translation, were among the books in the library of the Academy of Geneva founded by Calvin and Théodore de Bèze. It was thus partly through Melanchthon that Florentine humanism reached the French Protestants.

68. Melanchthon, *Commentarii in aliquot Politicos libros Aristotelis*, col. 420.

69. Melanchthon's dualism may be interpreted as a precursor to all doctrines seeking to determine a universal principle superior to civil society that would legitimate it in and of itself while englobing it within a superior sphere. It may thus be understood as a source of Hegel's political thinking (see Chapter 8).

70. Melanchthon, *Commentarii*, col. 419, and *Loci communes theologici* (1545), p. 657, among numerous other places in Melanchthon's work.

71. Melanchthon expounded his theory of property in Latin in *Adversus anabaptistas iudicum*, in *Corpus reformatorum*, vol. 16.

72. See Weber's celebrated analysis of the birth of capitalism in *The Protestant Ethic*; also see Weber, *Economy and Society*, 1: 541.

73. See Melanchthon, *Philosophia moralis epitomes* (1546), in *CR*, 16: 122; this and all quotations to the end of this section were translated from the Latin.

74. Ibid.

75. On the role played by Protestant churches in the building of nation-states in Europe, see Eisenstadt and Rokkan's classic study, *Building States and Nations*, 2 vols., particularly Rokkan, "Cities, States, and Nations: A Dimensional Model for the Study of Contrasts in Development," 1: 73–96.

76. Melanchthon, *Philosophia moralis epitomes* (1546), in *CR*, 16: 124.

77. Calvin, preface to *Livre des Pseaumes. Commentaire sur les Pseaumes* (1558), in *Corpus reformatorum*, 13: 24.

78. Calvin, *Institutes*, bk. 1, chap. 11, §7 (Allen, 1: 103; see also Calvin, *Traité des reliques*).

79. Calvin, *Institutes*, bk. 1, chap. 11, §3 (Allen, 1: 100).

80. Ibid.

81. "Hiding the mercy seat with their wings, they should not only keep back the eyes of man but also his senses from the beholding of God, and to correct his rash hardiness" (ibid.; Norton, 23v).

82. *Institution de la Religion*, bk. 1, chap. 11, §13.

83. "We conclude, therefore, that nothing should be painted and engraved but objects visible to our eyes: the Divine Majesty, which is far above the reach of human sight, ought to be not corrupted by unseemly figures" (*Institutes of the Christian Religion*; Allen, 1: 108).

84. Ibid.

85. The English title of this work is *An Admonition Showing the Advantages Which Christendom Might Derive from an Inventory of Relics* (first translated 1561). Calvin was not above making a sexual joke or two, like his remark in the *Traité d'astrologie judiciaire* (1549, translated into English in 1561 as *Admonicion against Astrology iudiciall*) about preserving the maidenhood of the "Virgin" constellation.

86. Calvin, *Admonition*, p. 321.

87. See, for example, Rabelais, *Pantagruel*, bk. 2, chap. 15, "How Panurge prescribed a Highly Original Way to Build the Walls of Paris." Panurge proposes using women's "pleasure-twats" as stones to build the walls: "These should be made to dovetail and interlace, diamond-shape, like the great tower of Bourges, with as many horny joy-dinguses [*braquemars*], which now reside in claustral codpieces" (*Gargantua and Pantagruel. The Five Books*, trans. Leclercq, p. 61).

88. Calvin, *Admonition*, p. 339.

89. Ibid., p. 320.

90. Calvin, *Institutes*, bk. 4, chap. 20 ("On Civil Government"), §3 (Höpfl, p. 50).

91. Ibid.

92. Ibid., §2 (Norton, 491v).

93. Ibid., chap. 17, §39 (Norton, 409r).

94. Calvin, *Petit Traicté de la saincte Cène*, p. 124.

95. Divination is the subject of Calvin's *Traité d'astrologie judiciaire* (1549), in which he denounces belief in the power of the stars as one characteristic of the *phantastiques* (here used for those given over to superstition) and stigmatizes the "devilish superstition" and "folly" of "charmers and sorcerors," "phantastical fellows," to which he opposes useful and effective science (a fact which suggests that Calvin's famous Protestant "secular asceticism" was of less importance than his apology for practical life): "That learned men do give themselves to good and profitable studies and not to foolish curiosities which serve for none other end than to make fools to muse at them. That little and great, learned and unlearned, may think that we are not born to the end that we should occupy ourselves about unprofitable things: but that the end of our exercises ought to edify both ourselves and others in the fear of God. . . . No good science is contrary to the fear of God. . . . That we have this wisdom that we use these arts to serve us, whether they be liberal or handycraft, while we pass through this world, to haste continually towards the heavenly kingdom" (*Admonicion against Astrology iudiciall*, 1561, unpaginated).

96. Calvin, *Institutes*, bk. 4, chap. 17, §36 (Allen, p. 570).

97. Ibid., p. 546. [We have modified Allen's translation slightly, omitting the words "faithful representation," which are present neither in the Latin or French versions of Calvin's text. Trans.]

98. The Latin text of the *Institutes*, bk. 4, chap. 17, contains many more technical rhetorical terms than the subsequent French version: *metonymia* in Latin becomes *translation de nom* ("transfer of names"), an expression that more directly resembles our definition of metaphor. If the statement that the rock from which water pours forth in the desert *is* Christ is an example of Calvin's "transfer of names," clearly we are dealing with metaphor.

99. The French original is "pure singerie et bastellerie" (*Institutes*, bk. 4, chap. 17, §43). Allen translates "insignificant and theatrical fooleries" (p. 579).

100. Ibid., chap. 14, §25.

101. "But it is clearly ascertained from the Scriptures, that in the one person of Christ the two natures are united in such manner that each retains its peculiar properties undiminished" (ibid., chap. 17, §30; Allen, p. 560).

102. Ibid., §7.

103. According to Zwingli, images were forbidden by God (though we must show patience in the struggle to eradicate them); they led to idolatry. Only the

word of God could teach, and only images that could not be taken for God or the Lord Jesus might be admitted in the church–this is the main idea of his essay, "On Images," in *Short Christian Instruction*.

104. "We have a plain command from Christ, 'A good shepherd lays down his life for the sheep' " (Luther, *Whether One May Flee*, in *LW*, 43: 121).

105. Ibid.

106. Ibid., p. 123.

107. Ibid., p. 136.

108. Zwingli, *Exposition of the Christian Faith*, p. 254. He developed his explanation of the Eucharist as follows: "Thus it seems to me that several of the early Fathers termed the body and blood a sacrifice, not as if it were their sacrifice or offered up by them, but because Christ offered himself. Thus it is nothing other than a memorial of that which once took place, in the same way in which Easter, which likewise took place only once, is called the day of resurrection" (*Writings*, 2: 121). Calvin differentiated his position from Luther's on the one hand, Zwingli's and Œcolampadius's on the other. He reproached Luther for using his "habitual vehemence" in the form of "hyperboles of speech" against the other two (whom Luther had qualified as heretics). Furthermore he deemed Luther's doctrine of consubstantiation inadequate to refute the papal thesis of "local presence" (*Petit Traicté de la saincte Cène*, p. 129).

109. Luther, *Whether One May Flee*, in *LW*, 43: 137.

110. Ibid., pp. 137-38.

111. Luther, *Confession Concerning Christ's Supper*, in *LW*, 37: 317 (see also *WA*, 26: 462: "Und ehe ich den Schwermern wolt entel Wein haben, so wolt ich ehe mit dem Papst entel Blut halten"). See also Luther, *That These Words of Christ, "This is my body," etc. Still Stand Firm Against the Fanatics* (1527), in *LW*, 37: 3ff.

112. Luther, *Whether One May Flee*, vol. 43, pp. 136-37.

Chapter 4

1. See Waetzoldt, *Dürer and His Time*, chap. 10.

2. *Albrecht Dürer, Diary of His Journey to the Netherlands*, pp. 90-92. Somewhat further on in the same entry, dated May 17, 1521, Dürer addresses a plea to Erasmus to take over, if necessary, where Luther left off.

3. The first occurrence of this iconographic type, according to the French historian of Romanesque art Emile Mâle, dates back to 1100 in the *Evangiliare* of Perpignan. The term "throne of Grace" was proposed at the end of the nineteenth century by F. X. Graus for images in which the Father supports the Son nailed to the cross. Approximately 300 such images from the twelfth to the fifteenth centuries have been catalogued (see Boespflug, "Les images de Dieu dans l'art occidental").

4. A preparatory drawing done in 1508 (now at the Musée Condé in Chantilly)

provides a view of the altarpiece's global design; the finished frame is at the Germanisches Nationalmuseum of Nuremberg.

5. In Cranach's work, dating from between 1516 and 1518 and now at the Kunsthalle in Bremen, as in his *Holy Trinity Adored by the Virgin and Saint Sebastian* (1515), there is no place for the former pilgrims of the Earthly City.

6. In Venice at the Chiesa di Santa Maria Gloriosa dei Frari.

7. Mantua, Palazzo Ducale.

8. Titian used a similar approach in the *Ca' Pesaro Altarpiece*. Here the Virgin, Child, and Saint Peter are quite invisible to mortals, and while the donors are shown on their knees unseeingly adoring them in a rigid attitude of prayer, a boy located in the lower-right-hand corner has his head turned instead toward the viewer, while in contrast with them all a Franciscan monk, clearly positioned as intercessor, gazes at the holy grouping. The same principle may be observed in the composition of Caravaggio's *Madonna of the Rosaries* (Vienna, Kunsthistorisches Museum).

9. Georg Breu, for example, who expressed a certain sympathy for the Augsburg iconoclasts in his diary (quoted in Wittkower and Wittkower, *Born Under Saturn*, chap. 2, §3, p. 27).

10. Dürer dedicated the *Unterweisung der Messung* to his close friend and adviser Willibald Pirckheimer.

11. Dürer, *Painter's Manual, A Manual of Measurement*, p. 37.

12. Luther to Johan Rühel, May 23, 1525, in *WA, Briefe*, 3: 507.

13. Luther to John Briessmann, Aug. 15, 1525, in *LW*, 49: 124-25.

14. Dürer, *The Painter's Manual, A Manual of Measurement*, p. 227 (translation slightly modified).

15. This is the thesis of the Wittkowers in *Born Under Saturn*. The authors affirm that Dürer was a conservative and that after the crushing of the peasant movement he gave free rein to his feelings in a "scathing design," namely this project for a monument (chap. 2, §3, p. 27). Arguing from a quite different perspective in "Murdering Peasants," Stephen Greenblatt is in agreement with the Wittkowers concerning Dürer's attitude toward the peasants (pp. 101-12).

16. The dream-inspired watercolor is in the Kunsthistorisches Museum in Vienna. Greenblatt ("Murdering Peasants," p. 107) proposes an interpretation of the monument in terms of wish-fulfillment.

17. Panofsky holds that the three columns are "elucubrations," and that Dürer "went out of his way to ridicule the revolting peasants in his Treatise on Geometry of 1525" (*The Life and Art of Albrecht Dürer*, 1: 233). He describes the second of the three monuments as "a triumphal column satirizing the revolting peasants" (2: 57).

18. This is part of Panofsky's interpretation, which he supports by citing Melanchthon's remark on Dürer's "most excellent melancholy" (*Life and Art of*

Albrecht Dürer, chap. 5). With Raymond Klibanski and Fritz Saxl in *Saturn and Melancholy* he has shown that the painting's composition closely follows a passage from Agrippa's *De occulta philosophia* (pt. 4 on Dürer). Aby Warburg suggested that in *Melencolia I* Dürer shows the demon of Saturn made inoffensive through the exercise of reason and underlined how the Reformation had to combat fear of monsters and projective thinking ("Heidnischantike Weissagung" [1919], in *Gesammelte Schriften*, 2: 534). Gombrich quotes and discusses this article in *Aby Warburg: An Intellectual Biography*, p. 214.

19. In "La *Mélancolie Paysanne* d'Albrecht Dürer" (1956), an article with which my analysis has points in common, Bialostocki suggests reading the two works in relation to each other.

20. See Frances Yates, *Occult Philosophy in the Elizabethan Age*, chap. 6, for this interpretation.

21. The work is a series of woodcuts done in 1511. In *The Limewood Sculptors of Renaissance Germany*, p. 99, Baxandall points out the existence of a statue in wood done by Hans Leiberge that follows the same model.

22. Dürer also did an *Ecce Homo* in the same attitude (1505), now in the Kunsthalle in Karlsruhe.

23. Luther, *Open Letter on the Harsh Book Against the Peasants*, in *LW*, 46: 70.

24. This and the other biblical texts included in the *Four Apostles* are assembled in Conway, *The Literary Remains of Albrecht Dürer*, p. 134. For the original German, see *Altdeutsche Malerei*.

25. This was the case of Dürer's longtime close friend Pirckheimer.

26. In a preparatory drawing for another work, *The Great Crucifixion* (1523), Dürer gave Saint John Luther's features (Vienna, Albertina).

Chapter 5

1. On Uriel da Costa and his writings, see Strauss, *Spinoza's Critique of Religion*, and Meinsma, *Spinoza et son cercle*.

2. Quoted in Pollock, *Spinoza, His Life and Philosophy*, pp. 17-18.

3. *The Correspondence of Spinoza*, letter 75.

4. Ibid., letter 76, p. 354.

5. See Spinoza, *Tractatus Theologico-Politicus*, chap. 14 (Shirley, p. 220) (hereafter abbreviated *TTP*).

6. Spinoza, *Political Treatise* (hereafter abbreviated *PT*), 1, §4, in *Chief Works of Benedict de Spinoza*, 1: 288.

7. *TTP*, chap. 14 (Shirley, p. 224).

8. See Stouppe, *La Religion des Hollandais*, 1673.

9. *TTP*, chap. 20 (Shirley, p. 299).

10. The term most often used by Spinoza is *status civilis* (see *PT*, chap. 1, §7; chap. 2, §21; chap. 3, §§1, 3, 6; chap. 5, §2, chap. 6, §1; chap. 7, §§22, 26), though he also uses *Civitatis* and, more rarely, *Urbs*.

11. Francès and Misrahi use the word *fanatisme* in the 1954 Pléiade translation of Spinoza, the existence of the word in seventeenth-century French being fully attested (see pp. 871, 896, 920, 931, 958, and 960 of *Traité des Autorités théologique et politique*, in *Œuvres complètes de Spinoza*).

12. *TTP*, chap. 18 (Shirley, pp. 274, 276); *ardore superstitionis* and *Pharisaeorum irae* in the original.

13. See Spinoza, *Ethics*, pt. 3, §36 (Curley, p. 539).

14. *PT*, chap. 3, §8, in *Chief Works*, 1: 304.

15. See Kolakowski, *Chrétiens sans Eglise*, and Cohn, *The Pursuit of the Millennium* (published in French under the title *Fanatiques de l'Apocalypse*).

16. *TTP*, preface (Shirley, p. 50).

17. Spinoza, *Ethics*, appendix to pt. 1, and the scholium to prop. 17.

18. *TTP*, chap. 7 (Shirley, p. 141). In the original Latin: "Nam sicuti methodus interpretandi Naturam in hoc potissimum consistit, in concinnanda scilicet historia Naturae, ex qua, utpote ex certis datis, rerum naturalium definitiones concludimus; sic etiam ad Scripturam interpretandam necesse est ejus sinceram historiam adornare, et ex ea tanquam ex certis datis et principiis mentem authorum Scripturae legitimis consequentiis concludere."

19. Ibid., chap. 7 (Shirley, p. 142): "Tota itaque Scripturae cognitio ab ipsa sola peti debet."

20. *Correspondence of Spinoza*, letter 50, p. 173. In the *Political Treatise* Spinoza had written: "Inasmuch as all men, whether barbarous or civilized [*culti*], everywhere frame customs and form some kind of civil state [*status civilis*], we must not, therefore, look to proofs of reason for the causes and natural bases of [*Imperium*], but derive them from the general nature or condition of mankind" (chap. 1, §7, in *Chief Works*, 1: 290). On Spinoza's political vocabulary see Moreau, "La notion d'*Imperium* dans le *Traité politique*." Letter 50 dates from 1674; Spinoza's belief in the continuity between "state of nature" and "state of society" is more firmly expressed here than in the *Tractatus Theologico-Politicus* (1670), a text in which the influence of the Hobbesian thesis of a break between the two states is clearly perceptible.

21. Manen and Joutard, *Une foi enracinée, la Pervenche*, p. 70. See also Schwartz, *The French Prophets*, pp. 17-22.

22. Manen and Joutard, *Une foi enracinée*, p. 72.

23. The exact biblical references are given in ibid., pp. 70, 72.

24. All texts by Bossuet have been translated for this work; for the original see *Oraisons funèbres*, pp. 111-13. The king Bossuet cites in Latin is David, Psalm 2.

25. Bossuet, *Oraisons funèbres*, pp. 238-39.

26. Ibid., p. 123.

27. *TTP*, preface (Shirley, p. 52).

28. Simon's work was the *Histoire critique de l'Ancien Testament*.

29. See *TTP*, chap. 6, "Of Miracles" (Shirley, p. 130). On Spinoza's critique of

procedures used in religion see Barret-Kriegel, "Spinoza et la doctrine de la liberté publique," in her *Chemins de l'Etat.*

30. *TTP*, chap. 1 (Shirley, p. 35).

31. *Correspondence of Spinoza*, letter 43, p. 259 (translation slightly modified).

32. Ibid.

33. *TTP*, preface (Shirley, p. 54).

34. *Ethics*, pt. 4, prop. 54 (Curley, p. 576).

35. *PT*, chap. 8 , "Of Aristocracy," §46, in *Chief Works*, 1: 368.

36. *PT*, chap. 3, §10, in *Chief Works*, 1: 306.

37. Bossuet, *Oraisons funèbres*, p. 128.

38. Ibid., pp. 53–54.

39. *TTP*, chap. 7 (Shirley, p. 159).

40. "Non ullum supra naturam lumen, neque ulla externa authoritas" (*Tractatus Theologico-Politicus*, in *Opera*, 2: 190).

41. This is affirmed more forcefully in the *Tractatus Politicus* and the *Ethics* than in the *Tractatus Theologico-Politicus*, which was published relatively early.

42. Spinoza, *Tractatus Theologico-Politicus* (1670), chap. 4; for the original Latin see Spinoza, *Opera*, 2: 140.

43. Spinoza, *Ethics*, pt. 5, prop. 29 (Curley, p. 609).

44. Ibid., pt. 1, prop. 15 (see Curley, pp. 94–97).

45. Ibid., pt. 4, scholium to prop. 35.

46. See *PT*, chap. 8, §12, in *Chief Works*, 1: 351.

47. Ibid., chap. 2, §15, in *Chief Works*, 1: 296–97.

48. *TTP*, preface (Shirley, p. 51).

49. *PT*, chap. 6, §4, in *Chief Works*, 1: 317.

50. *TTP*, preface (Shirley, p. 51).

Chapter 6

1. Of the estimated one million French Protestants (around five percent of the total population at the time), 300,000 left the country after the Revocation. The remaining 700,000 found ways to live with the Revocation (if not entirely without their religion), including recanting. See Garrisson, *L'Edit de Nantes et sa révocation.*

2. "Récit fidèle de ce qui s'est passé dans les Assemblies des Fanatiques du Vivarais; avec l'histoire de leurs Prophètes et Prophétesses, au commencement de l'année 1689," published in Fléchier's *Lettres choisies* (1715), 1: 350ff. Fléchier also wrote the "Mémoire touchant la bergère de Crest et deux autres filles du diocèse de Castres mises au rang des nouvelles Prophétesses" (in *Lettres choisies*, 1: 399ff).

3. A second edition in four volumes of de Brueys's *Histoire du fanatisme de notre temps* was published between 1709 and 1713. Yet another author to link the Camisards with fanaticism was Louvreleuil in *Le fanatisme renouvelé.*

4. De Brueys refutes the erroneous assertion that "fanaticism" derived from the Greek word *phos*: the fanatics were in no way illuminated.

5. The question of the treatment of the Camisards as fanatics is discussed by Foucault in "Medecins, juges, et sorciers au 17è siècle" (an article that came to my notice after the French publication of this work).

6. See *La Nécessité de donner un prompt et puissant secours aux protestants des Cévennes*, published anonymously in London in 1703.

7. Interestingly, the work was later censored and republished without Fléchier's preface.

8. De Brueys used the capital letter to make the *Fanatiques* an entity apart, distinguishable from the *Religionnaires*, a synonym for the global terms "Reformed" or "Protestant." For Saint-Simon, the term "fanatic" was applicable because "these rebel Protestants . . . have among them alleged prophets or prophetesses who . . . lead them where they will with confidence and inconceivable fury" (*Mémoires*, 11: 80).

9. From Bossuet's funeral oration for Henriette de France, *Oraisons funèbres*, p. 126. The text continues thus: "So it is that the Calvinists, more brazen than the Lutherans, served to establish the Socinians, who went even further than they; the Calvinists now join them in greater numbers each day. The infinite Anabaptist sects come from the same source, and their opinions, mixed together with Calvinism, have given birth to the Independents, among whom we find the Quakers, fanatical people who believe all their reveries inspired in them, and those called the Seekers because seventeen hundred years after Jesus Christ they are still looking for religion, having no clear one of their own."

10. Maimbourg, *Histoire du luthéranisme* (1686), p. 88.

11. Fénelon, *The Maxims of the Saints Explained, concerning the interior life*, pp. 32-33.

12. In 1688 the Abbé de Rancé, founder of the Monastery of the Trappe, wrote: "Nothing is more worthy of compassion than these poor fanatics [*phanatiques*] who fashion their own piety for themselves and who, under the pretext of being entirely spiritual, have discovered the secret of making abstractions and separations that could only be imagined by people who have renounced the life of the spirit and given themselves over to that of the senses. There is no one more qualified to write about this matter than M. X if he wanted to bother [probably Pierre Nicole, Jansenist and moralist, teacher at Port Royal], he being perfectly familiar with all the cunning and subterfuge involved." Antoine Arnauld, Jansenist theologian active at Port Royal, rejected the "false spirituality–demonstrated to be false–of the Quietists," calling the spiritualist writer François Malavalle "fanatic" and dubbing Jean de Bernières, author of *Le chrestien intérieur*, "the great doctor of the Fanatics of Caen" (letter of April 10, 1687, in *Œuvres*, 2: 770-71).

13. *Histoire des ouvrages des savans* was a thrice-yearly publication written in

French and printed in Rotterdam which included debates by intellectuals from throughout Europe and reviews of their writings. The Oct.-Dec. 1698 issue, for example, reviewed a text by Fénelon in which he defended himself against Bossuet's attacks. The reviewer concludes that Fénelon had never "digested" Bossuet's calling him a "Fanatic" (review of *Réponse de Mr l'Archevêque de Cambrai à l'Ecrit de Mr l'Evêque de Meaux, intitulé Relation de Quiétisme*, art. 6, p. 496).

14. The full title of Molinos' work: *Guia espiritual que desembaraza al alma y la conduce por el camino interior para alcanzar la perfecta contemplacion y el rico tesoro de la paz interior.*

15. See Le Brun, *La Spiritualité de Bossuet*, p. 462.

16. Fénelon, *Explication des maximes des saints*, in *Œuvres*, 1: 1011.

17. Saint-Simon, *Mémoires*, 2: 340-41.

18. Ibid., p. 344.

19. Among the writings Fénelon gave to Bossuet was a short work on the gnosticism of Clement of Alexandria. Bossuet proceeded to refute in detail Fénelon's interpretation of gnosticism, rejecting namely the ideas that the Catholic Church included a tradition of secret mystical thinking and that perfection resided in the absence of desire.

20. "The extraordinary and particular instinct by which our 'perfect ones' are guided is found in the [following] false principle taken from [Fénelon's] *Instruction pastorale*: 'The will of God, his good pleasure [*la volonté du bon plaisir*] is made known to us by actual, present grace [*grâce actuelle*].' In order to discover in this principle all the fanaticism of the new mystics the following brief demonstration suffices. God's will includes all the ways that God wants us to act in each particular event. If we say that actual grace makes God's will known to us, that means that actual grace knows the side that God wants us to take in each of these events. But a grace that would make all this known to us in detail is not habitual grace, it is rather an extraordinary and particular instinct: our alleged 'perfect ones' are thus delivered up to that instinct, which governs them on every occasion, as the Monsieur from Cambrai assures us. It is no wonder that its own industry precludes action. . . . Obviously this is how our false mystics are moved and urged– they admit as much themselves. They are therefore pure fanatics and their Quietism is inexcusable" (Bossuet, *Avertissement sur les écrits suivants et sur un nouveau livre de Mgr l'Archevêque de Cambrai*, in *Œuvres complètes*; Bar-le-Duc, 10: 38). See also Bossuet, *Tradition des nouveaux mystiques*, in *Œuvres complètes* (Lechat, vol. 19).

21. English translation of one of Bossuet's letters in *Quakerism A-la-Mode; or a History of Quietism, particularly that of the Lord Archi-bishop of Cambray and Madame Guyone* (1698), p. 10. For the original, see Bossuet, *Correspondance*, 6: 47-51.

22. *Dévote hystérique*–the expression is Kolakowski's in *Chrétiens sans Eglise*, chap. 8, sec. 3, "Madame Guyon, autoportrait," p. 521.

23. A meeting of three high-level ecclesiastics, including Fénelon, was held at Issy on the outskirts of Paris and resulted in a text of compromise composed of 34 articles. The effort proved ineffective, however; the compromise short-lived.

24. Fénelon, *Réponse de Monseigneur l'archevêque de Cambrai à l'écrit de Monseigneur l'évêque de Meaux intitulé "Relation sur le quiétisme"* (text reviewed in the *Histoire des ouvrages des savans*; see note 13).

25. The term is Fénelon's; see *Maxims of the Saints Explained*, p. 12.

26. Fénelon returns again and again to the accusation in his *Réponse de Monseigneur l'archevêque de Cambrai* (see *Œuvres complètes*, 1: 1102, 1105, 1106).

27. The distinction between mystics and fanatics intersects another, that between "enthusiasts" and "fanatics." Whereas Leibniz used the two terms as synonyms, Voltaire would draw a clear separation: enthusiasm, which "agitated" the "bowels," was above all characteristic of false religious devotion, but when accompanied by reason could give rise to great poets. Quite different from the light wine of enthusiasm was fanaticism. The fanaticism that had inspired Jacques Clément, Henry III's assassin, that had led to the Saint Bartholomew's Day massacre and animated the Old Man of the Mountain, was a nearly incurable disease. Whereas the enthusiast was inspired to believe that he had privileged access to truth, the fanatic was an enthusiast who believed himself called to perform a bloody mission, and "the spirit of philosophy" was capable of combating fanaticism only early on, "for when the disorder has made any progress, we should, without loss of time, fly from the seat of it, and wait till the air has become purified from contagion" (*Philosophical Dictionary*, in *Works of Voltaire*, vol. 5, pt. 1, p. 17). This terminological distinction, which is not quite the same as Kant's between *Enthusiasmus* and *Schwärmerei* (see Chapter 8) was of crucial importance for Mme de Staël, who declared the Germans to be the race not of fanaticism but enthusiasm. Hegel rejected the distinction, grouping religious mysticism and political fanaticism together, the first as empty desire, the second as the desire for emptiness (see Chapter 8). The rationalism of the Enlightenment and of an author such as Voltaire led to a global rejection of both enthusiasm and fanaticism in the service of "the spirit of philosophy," of tolerance, whereas the romanticism of Kant and Mme de Staël led them to defend enthusiasm.

28. Even if Bossuet could accept the possibility of "the act of contemplation not being attached to images," he clearly drew the line between himself and Fénelon on the matter of imagination: "As for the exclusion of images, which is called for in many places by Saint Clement [the Gnostic], he usually means corporal images of God, which are indeed so many idols that carnal men forge for themselves in their minds, and in some cases he is referring to all perceptible images that come between us and God. But the new mystics take things even further because among the images they exclude are all distinct ideas, often even that of Jesus Christ: these are things whose exclusion, as we have seen, is completely opposed to God the Father" (*Tradition des nouveaux mystiques*, in *Œuvres complètes*; Lechat, 19: 23).

29. On the iconoclastic activity of the early Calvinists, see de Sainctes, *Discours sur le saccagement des églises catholiques par les hérétiques anciens et nouveax calvinistes* (1562), which denounces the "knights of disorder." Also Cristin, "Iconographie de l'iconoclasme" (see Chapter 3, note 12) and on the violent episode of 1566 in Flanders, Deyon and Lottin, *Les Casseurs de l'été 1566.*

30. Le Roy Ladurie, *Les Paysans du Languedoc.* See pt. 5, chap. 5, "Rebellions sauvages," in which the author discusses the Camisards.

31. See *Le siècle de Louis XIV* (1751), chap. 32 (in the 1752 English translation, *The Age of Lewis XIV*, pp. 219, 222, 226). In the same text Voltaire qualified the convulsives of Saint Médard as "enthusiasts." However, in the addition that he made to the *Essai sur les mœurs* (1763), "Du Protestantisme de la guerre des Cévennes," he affirmed that the war that had been launched in the Cévennes by the "wild mob" was "the fruit of persecution" (2: 933).

32. Shaftesbury, "A Letter Concerning Enthusiasm," in *Characteristics of Men, Manners, Opinions, Times, etc.* (1708), p. 20. Among the English pamphlets written against the Camisards should be noted one called *Enthusiastik Impostors no divinely inspired prophets* (1707).

33. Ibid., p. 21.

34. *Le Théâtre sacré des Cévennes ou Récit des diverses merveilles nouvellement opérées dans cette partie de la province de Languedoc* (1707) is a series of autobiographical testimonies.

35. The convulsives of Saint-Médard were men and women who, starting in 1730, regularly gathered and went into convulsions around the tomb of a Jansenist deacon believed to work miracles. The church cemetery of Saint-Médard where the deacon was buried was closed by royal order in 1732.

36. Hecquet, *Le Naturalisme des convulsions dans les maladies de l'épidémie convulsonnaire* (1733), pt. 1, p. 193. The author links the "Fanatiques des Sévennes" (*sic*) to the "possessed" of Loudun, among others, and refers directly to the Camisards' *Théâtre sacré* (pt. 1, p. 176). He furthermore associates all these groups with the Quietists. For him the Paris convulsives were a matter for medical science, though they were less abominable than the possessed of Loudun with their "stigmata and immodest speech," and he ranks their "artifices and similar pranks" with "the prophesies, convulsions, prayer states, and pathetic speeches of the fanatics of the Cévennes" (pt. 1, pp. 182-83). Further reference is made to the Camisards in pt. 2, p. 181.

37. "Two or three of our company were much affected, and believed she spoke by the Spirit of God. But it was in no wise clear to me. The motion must be either hysterical or artificial. And the same words any person of a good understanding and well versed in the Scriptures might have spoken. But I let the matter alone, knowing this, that 'if it be not of God, it will come to nought' " (Wesley, *Journal*, 2: 137).

38. *Théâtre sacré des Cévennes*, pp. 182-83.

39. The term "hysteria" was used by Charles Bost in 1935, but the most important analysis in these terms is of course Le Roy Ladurie's in *Les Paysans du Languedoc* (1965). Le Roy Ladurie, to whom my own interpretation owes much, applied the Freudian theory of neurosis to the Camisards and convincingly demonstrates the sexual motive in the prophets' convulsive fits.

40. *Théâtre sacré des Cévennes*, p. 175.

41. Ibid., p. 155.

42. Ibid.

43. Ibid., pp. 162-70.

44. Ibid., pp. 65, 84, 162.

45. Ibid., pp. 138-39.

46. *Engluement imaginaire*–the expression is Lacan's (see "R. S. I." [Réel-Symbolique-Imaginaire], seminar of Apr. 8, 1975, text established by J.-A. Miller, in *Ornicar?* no. 5, p. 42).

47. See Freud, "Draft H.–Paranoia" (1895), in the *Standard Edition of the Complete Psychological Works*, 1: 210.

48. [A condensation of pp. 165-68 of Rieff, ed., *Three Case Histories*. Trans.]

49. *Le Théâtre sacré des Cévennes*, p. 179.

50. Ibid., p. 123.

51. Cavalier, *Mémoires sur la guerre des Camisards* (editor's note), p. 47.

52. Ibid.

53. Voltaire, *The Age of Lewis XIV*, p. 218.

54. The entry *fanatiques* in the *Dictionnaire théologique portatif* of 1756 provides an example of the traditional view of the Camisards. Conversely, in *Mémoires pour servir à la vie de Nicolas de Catinat, maréchal de France*, published in 1775, the Court of Louis XIV is said to have manifested "inconceivable fanaticism" in levying ever more onerous taxes on the new Calvinist converts of Dauphiné (p. 133).

55. Shaftesbury, "Letter Concerning Enthusiasm," p. 14. The "comedian" in question is Terence (*Eunuchus* 1.1).

56. Ibid.

Chapter 7

1. Czar's decree appointing Leibniz as his adviser, in *Œuvres*, 7: 553.

2. Leibniz expounded his projects for the czar in a series of drafts and letters, written either in German or in French, the majority of which are to be found in *Œuvres*, vol. 7. The project to *débarbariser* the Russian Empire is mentioned in a letter dated July 13, 1698 (*Œuvres*, 7: 451).

3. Ibid., p. 485.

4. "Projet d'un conseil supérieur des sciences et arts pour le Czar" (Project for a council on technical arts and sciences for the czar, 1712; original in French), in *Œuvres*, 7: 516.

5. The expression is to be found in "Denkschrift über die Errichtung einer Kurfürstlichen Societät der Wissenschaften" (1700), a report addressed to the prince elector of Brandenburg (*Œuvres*, 7: 600).

6. Leibniz used the term "civil society" in several different languages: for examples from *Textes inédits*, see 2: 578 (French), 2: 596, 615 (Latin), 2: 564 (Greek; *koinonia politikè*, used explicitly in reference to Aristotle); and 2: 602 (German; *bürgerliche Gemeinschaft*); see also note 14.

7. "Einige Vorschläge pro Fundo Societatis Scientarum," report to the prince elector of Brandenburg, in *Œuvres*, 7: 621.

8. "Denkschrift über die Errichtung einer Kurfürstlichen Societät der Wissenschaften," in *Œuvres*, 7: 606-7.

9. "Plan zu einer deutschliebenden Genossenschaft" (Plan for a German academy of sciences), in *Œuvres*, 7: 389.

10. Throughout this paragraph we have been closely following Leibniz's ideas as developed in another plan, *Grundriss*, for the creation of a German academy of sciences (1680) (see *Œuvres*, 7: 33-34).

11. Ibid., p. 43.

12. Ibid., p. 45.

13. Leibniz, *Confessio philosophi*, p. 40.

14. The following is a long excerpt from the very brief but important text *Divisio Societatum*, in which Leibniz expounds his hierarchical vision (original in German):

Justice is a social duty, or a duty which preserves society.

A society [*Gemeinschaft*] is a union of different men for a common purpose.

A natural society is one which is demanded by nature.

The signs by which one can conclude that nature demands something, are that nature has given us a desire and the powers or force to fulfill it: for nature does nothing in vain.

Above all, when the matter involves a necessity or a permanent utility: for nature everywhere achieves the best.

The most perfect society is that whose purpose is the general and supreme happiness.

Natural law is that which preserves or promotes natural societies.

The first natural society is between man and wife, for it is necessary to preserve the human race.

The second is between parents and children; it arises at once out of the former; for when children are once created, or freely adopted, they must be reared, that is governed and nourished. In return they owe their parents obedience and help after they are raised. For it is in the hope of such gratitude that such societies are preserved and promoted, though nature demands them primarily for the sake of the children. For they may one day reach perfection. Parents then, exist primarily for the sake of children, and the present, which does not last long, for the future.

The third natural society is between master and servant, which is conformable to nature when a person lacks understanding but does not lack the strength to nourish himself. For such a person is a servant by nature who must work as another directs him. . . .

The fourth natural society is the household, which is composed of all the above-mentioned societies—some or all. Its purpose is the satisfaction of daily needs.

The fifth natural society is the civil society [*bürgerliche Gemeinschaft*]. If it is small, it is called a city; a province is a society of different cities, and a kingdom or a large dominion [*Herrschaft*] is a society of different provinces . . . whose members sometimes live together in a city, sometimes spread out over the land. Its purpose is temporal welfare.

The sixth natural society is the Church of God, which would probably have existed among men even without revelation and been preserved and spread by pious and holy men. Its purpose is eternal happiness. And it is no wonder that I call it a natural society, since there is a natural religion and a desire for immortality planted in us. This society of the saints is catholic or universal, and binds the whole human race together. If revelation is added, this bond is not torn, but strengthened (in *Leibniz: Political Writings*, pp. 77–79).

15. "Every society is either equal or unequal. It is equal when one [person] has as much power in it as another, unequal when one rules another. Every society is either unlimited or limited. An unlimited society concerns the whole life and the common good [*gemeine Beste*]. A limited society concerns certain subjects, for example, trade and commerce, navigation, warfare, and travel. An unlimited society exists between true friends. And such a society exists particularly between man and wife, between parents and grown children, between masters and freedmen, and in general between all intelligent men who are adequately acquainted with each other" (*Divisio Societatum* or *Classification of Societies or Communities*, in *Leibniz: Political Writings*, p.79 [original text in *Leibniz Deutsche Schriften*, 2: 417–19]).

16. *Divisio Societatum*, in *Leibniz: Political Writings*, p. 80 (*Leibniz Deutsche Schriften*, 2: 419).

17. Leibniz to Arnauld, Apr. 30, 1687, in *Discourse on Metaphysics; Correspondence with Arnaud; Monadology*, p. 191 (hereafter cited as *Discourse*).

18. Ibid., p. 199.

19. Ibid.

20. Still, Leibniz is less a direct precursor of Hegel than a successor to the German jurisconsult Johannes Althusius (1556-1637), who on rare occasions in his *Politica* used the term *societas civilis* (see *Politica*, pt. 1, §33) and who characterized political life as a "symbiosis," "consociation," or "mutual communication." Indeed, his analysis of "symbiotic consociations" would seem to announce Leibniz. (Althusius refers to numerous authors, namely Augustine, Calvin, and Gregory of Toulouse.)

21. Leibniz to Landgraf Ernst of Hesse-Rheinfels, Mar. 4, 1685 (in French), in *Sämtliche Schriften und Briefe*, Reihe 1, *Allgemeinen politischer und historischer Briefwechsel*, 4: 351.

22. Both Leibniz's *Monadology* (see §84ff.) and his *Discourse on Metaphysics* (§35ff.) close with an invocation of the City of God.

23. Leibniz, *Monadology*, §83, in *Discourse*, p. 270.

24. Leibniz to Arnauld, Oct. 6, 1687, in *Discourse*, p. 231.

25. If we substitute for the divine Architect of Leibniz's system an immanent causality that includes only individual intentions, either directly realized or altered by the course of events, his theory can be read as a first version of Joseph Schumpeter's theory of capitalism. Schumpeter accepts the Weberian notion of the individual entrepreneur, underlining the irrationality of individual, anarchic decision making, but whereas for Marx and his successors that irrationality is the very mark of capitalism and cannot be overcome within it, Schumpeter emphasizes the long-term rationality and effectiveness of the capitalist system. In this way Schumpeter's optimism is a version of the Leibnizian theodicy, in which the irrationality of capitalist decision making in fact explains its long-term efficiency: in the long run the optimal order becomes apparent. But the analogy is also strong between Leibniz's vision and Mandeville's in the *Fable of the Bees* (see Elster, *Leibniz et la formation de l'esprit capitaliste*). Elster has shown the importance of Leibniz's *Theodicy* in the genealogy of political economy.

26. Hobbes, *The Citizen*, chap. 1, §2 (*Man and Citizen*, p. 111).

27. Ibid., chap. 5, §5 (*Man and Citizen*, p. 169).

28. Ibid., §8 (*Man and Citizen*, p. 170).

29. Ibid. Civil society, the formula Hobbes used most in the 1651 English translation of this text (occasionally he used "commonwealth"), corresponds to *societas civilis* or *civitas* in the original Latin (1642) and *société civile* or *Etat* in Sorbier's 1649 French translation from Latin, which Hobbes reread and corrected. The work (whose full French title is *Elémens philosophiques du citoyen, traicté politique où les fondemens de la société civile sont descouverts*) was instrumental in diffusing the term "civil society." In *Leviathan*, however, written in English in 1651, "civil society" appears only once (bk. 2, chap. 29), the preferred term being "commonwealth."

30. Even though in his wish to facilitate a rapprochement between Lutherans, Calvinists, and Roman Catholics Leibniz envisaged the possibility of a practical compromise on this point, he nonetheless rejected the principle of papal infallibility on the same grounds as he rejected the idea of an infallible absolute prince.

31. See *Caesarinus Fürstenerius* (*De Suprematu Principum Germaniae*), chap. 10, in *Leibniz: Political Writings*, pp. 114-16.

32. Ibid., p. 116.

33. Ibid., p. 119.

34. Ibid.

35. Ibid., p. 120.

36. The German jurist and philosopher Samuel Pufendorf (1632-94), for whom, like Leibniz, the sovereign was no god, attributed an important function in civil society to religion and the fear of death: they "contain unruly men within the bounds of their duty" (*De officio hominis*; translated into English as *The Whole Duty of Man*, bk. 1, chap. 4, p. 53). He did however oppose "civil society" to the state of nature, after defining the latter as "that condition wherein [man] is placed by the Creator pursuant to his Divine Will that he should be the most excellent animal in the whole creation" (bk. 2, chap. 1, p. 187). However, a person abandoned in that state without the help of his fellows would be in a sorry condition: "There [in the state of nature] the passions rule, and there is continual warfare, accompanied with fears, want, sordidness, solitude, barbarity, ignorance and brutishn ss; here [community, civil society] reason governs, and here is tranquillity, security, wealth, neatness, society, elegancy, knowledge and humanity" (bk. 2, chap. 4, p. 192).

37. See *Leibniz: Political Writings*, p. 141 (translation slightly modified).

38. Ibid., p. 126.

39. Ibid., p. 127.

40. Ibid., pp. 134-35.

41. Ibid., pp. 144-45 (translation slightly modified).

42. Leibniz, *Theodicy*, §24 (for the original French, see the Aubier edition, *Essais de Théodicée*, pp. 67-68).

43. See Leibniz, "Au Landgrave" (after 1690), in *Textes inédits*, 1: 80. See also Naert, *Leibniz et la querelle du pur amour*.

44. Leibniz to Morell, Sept. 1, 1699, in *Textes inédits*, 1: 144.

45. Leibniz to Morell, Dec. 17, 1699, ibid, p. 145.

46. Leibniz to Stenon, Mar-Apr 1677, ibid., p. 161.

47. Leibniz, draft of a letter (addressee unknown), probably written the same year that Molinos, arrested in 1685, was condemned by the Inquisition (Sept. 3, 1687), ibid., p. 79.

48. Ibid., p. 80.

49. La Bruyère, *Dialogues poshthumes sur le quiétisme*, p. 704.

50. Boileau, *Epitre XII*, lines 87-90.

51. Leibniz to Bossuet, Oct. 1698, in *Œuvres*, 2: 195.

52. Leibniz, preface to *Codex*, in *Die philosophischen Schriften*, 7: 149.

53. Leibniz to Spanheim, Feb. 20, 1699, in *Textes inédits*, 1: 142.

54. Leibniz to Nicaise, May 4-14, 1698, in *Fragments philosophiques*, 4: 176-77.

55. Leibniz to Mme de Brimon, May 15, 1699, in *Textes inédits*, 1: 208.

56. Leibniz to Morell, Sept. 1, 1699, ibid., p. 143.

57. From Leibniz's commentary on Penn's *An Account of W. Penns Traevels in Holland and Germany Anno MDCLXXVII [1677] for the Service of the Gospel of Christ*, ibid., p. 89.

58. Leibniz to Morell, Sept. 1, 1699, ibid., p. 103.

59. From "Parallèle entre la raison originale ou la loy de la nature, le paganisme ou la corruption de la loi de la nature, la loi de Moyse ou le paganisme réformé et le christianisme ou la loi de la nature rétablie" (1704), ibid., p. 47.

60. Leibniz's commentary on Penn, ibid., p. 91.

61. Ibid.

62. Leibniz's note on Rancé and Mabillon, Apr.-May 1692, in *Textes inédits*, 1: 83.

63. Leibniz, *Confessio philosophi*, p. 28.

64. Leibniz to the Electress Sophie, Aug. 1696, in *Textes inédits*, 1: 380.

65. Leibniz, *New Essays on Human Understanding*, bk. 4, chap. 12, §12 (Remnant and Bennett, pp. 455).

66. Locke, *An Essay Concerning Toleration*, in *Scritti sulla tolleranza*, p. 103 (spelling standardized). Locke conceived the essay as a response to Edward Bagshaw Jr.'s *Great Question Concerning Things Indifferent in Religious Worship* (1660). He probably worked on it during a stay in Shaftesbury's London home; the two may have collaborated on the seven-point summary that appears at the end.

67. See, for example, Samuel Pepys's *Diary*, entry for Feb. 1, 1660.

68. Locke, *Essay Concerning Toleration*, p. 83.

69. Ibid., p. 84.

70. Ibid., p. 85.

71. Ibid., p. 87.

72. Ibid., p. 91.

73. Ibid., p. 92.

74. Ibid., p. 95.

75. Ibid., pp. 97-98.

76. Locke, *Essay Concerning Human Understanding*, bk. 4, chap. 19, p. 429.

77. Ibid., p. 431.

78. Ibid., p. 432.

79. This text, written in French, was not published until 1765, long after Leibniz's death.

80. On the French visionary mystic Antoinette Bourignon, quite well known in her time especially in Scotland, see Knox, *Enthusiasm*, pp. 352-56, and Kolakowski, *Chrétiens sans Eglise*, chap. 10.

81. Leibniz, *New Essays on Human Understanding*, preface (Remnant and Bennett, p. 59).

82. Leibniz is here directly attacking the English "fanatical" theosopher Robert Fludd and his *Philosophia Moysaica* (1638), as well as the "barbarous philosophy" that invented "demons or imps which can without ado perform whatever is wanted" (ibid., p. 58).

83. Locke, *Two Treatises on Government*, bk. 2, chap. 7, §87 (p. 159).

84. Ibid., chap. 19, §211 (p. 224).

85. Ibid.

86. Aristotle already posed the problem of distinguishing society from government or political regime (*politeia*) (see the *Politics*, bk. 3, chap. 3, and Chapter 2, p. 49, herein).

87. Rousseau, who like Locke distinguished the state or civil society from government, imagined the possibility of government destroying civil society. The government (or executive power) acted as an intermediary body between sovereign (or legislative power) and subjects "for their mutual relations," and was "charged to execute the Laws and the maintain both civil and political Freedom." It partook of the general will that constituted it but also had a will of its own, and the fewer its members, the stronger it was. Since sovereignty had a tendency to "slacken," the executive body tended to take over from the legislative power, and "when the Law is finally subject to men, there remain only masters and slaves; the State has been destroyed" (*Lettres écrites sur la montagne*, in *Œuvres complètes*, "La Pléiade" 3: 808). Moreover, how could we imagine that a state could be immortal, given that Sparta and Rome had perished? But unlike the "constitutions" of human beings, there were ways to thwart the aging of the "constitutions" of political bodies (Rousseau, *Du Contrat Social*, bk. 3, chap. 11). The possibility of civil society's disintegrating due to the corruptibility of government follows from Rousseau's strict artificialism: because as he saw it civil society had no roots in nature, it is more vulnerable in his theory than in those that posit a natural origin for civil society.

88. For Locke's line of argument, see *Two Treatises on Government*, bk. 2, chap. 19, §215-22 (pp. 226-30).

89. Ibid., §230 (p. 233).

90. Ibid. (p. 234).

91. Locke, *Essay Concerning Human Understanding*, chap. 19, §8 (p. 430).

92. Rousseau, *Lettres écrites sur la montagne*, in *Œuvres complètes*, "La Pléiade" 3: 706.

93. *Société civile*, *corps politique*, and *Etat* are equivalent terms for Rousseau as for all eighteenth-century authors; they are alternative translations of the Latin *civitas*. *Société civile* is to be found in Rousseau's *Discourse on the Origin of Inequality*, though not in the final version of *Du Contrat social*. We know from the first version or "Geneva Manuscript" of this text that the author was at one point considering calling it *De la société civile* and subtitling it *Essai sur la constitution*

de l'Etat; he frequently used "civil society" in this earlier draft (see Derathé, *Jean-Jacques Rousseau et la science politique de son temps*, pp. 380-86).

94. Rousseau, *Emile ou de l'éducation*, bk. 4, p. 387. The English is from a contemporary translation: *Emilius, or an essay on Education* (1763), trans. Nugent, 2: 96.

95. Rousseau, *Discours sur l'origine de l'inégalité*, in *Œuvres complètes*, "La Pléiade" 3: 174.

96. Rousseau, *Fragments politiques*, in *Œuvres complètes*, "La Pl]éiade" 3: 479.

97. Rousseau, *On the Social Contract*, bk. 4, chap. 8, "On Civil Religion," in *Basic Political Writings*, p. 227.

98. Ibid., bk. 4, chap. 8 (p. 225). (A definition which may, ironically, recall the second part of Luther's definition of a Christian in *The Freedom of a Christian*.)

99. *Du Contrat social* (Geneva Manuscript), *Œuvres complètes* 3: 341.

100. Ibid., pp. 341-42.

101. "If nature has destined us to be healthy, I almost dare to affirm that the state of reflection is a state contrary to nature and that the man who meditates is a depraved animal"(Rousseau, *Discourse on the Origin of Inequality*, pt. 1; *Basic Political Writings*, p. 44).

102. Rousseau, *Fragments politiques*, in *Œuvres complètes*, "La Pléiade" 479.

103. In a foreword to the French version of this text, the contemporary translator attacked Rousseau and his "would-be philosophical" productions, taking him for a pure and simple enemy of civil society, as was often done.

104. Ferguson, *Essay on the History of Civil Society*, pt. 1, sec. 1, p. 10.

105. Ibid., pt. 1, sec. 3, p. 26.

106. Ibid., pt. 6, sec. 5, p. 437.

107. Ibid., pt. 1, sec. 8, pp. 92-93.

108. "Men are so far from valuing society on account of its mere external conveniencies, that they are commonly most attached where those conveniencies are least frequent. . . . Hence the sanguine affection which every Greek bore to his country, and hence the devoted patriotism of an early Roman" (ibid., pt. 1, sec. 3, p. 31).

109. Ibid., pt. 1, sec. 4, p. 39.

110. On this point Ferguson criticizes Mandeville and the *Fable of the Bees*.

111. Ibid., pt. 2, sec. 2, p. 151.

112. "It appears, therefore, that although the mere use of materials which constitute luxury may be distinguished from actual vice, yet nations under a high state of the commercial arts are exposed to corruption by their admitting wealth, unsupported by personal elevation and virtue, as the great foundation of distinction, and by having their attention turned on the side of interest, as the road to consideration and honour" (ibid., pt. 6, sec. 3, p. 425).

113. "Liberty results, we say, from the government of laws" (ibid., pt. 6, sec. 5,

p. 440). The late Ernst Gellner devotes a chapter of his last book, *Conditions of Liberty: Civil Society and Its Rivals* (1994)–a characteristically brilliant and pithy text that came out after this work was first published–to Ferguson's ambivalent perception of the society emerging in the eighteenth century (pp. 61-80).

Chapter 8

1. "An Occurrence in Our Own Times Which Proves This Moral Tendency of the Human Race" (*Contest of Faculties*, sec. 2, §6, in *Kant: Political Writings*, p. 182).

2. Kant, *Critique of Judgement*, pt. 1, bk. 2, §29 (Meredith, p. 124 [N.B. that in Meredith each part of the *Critique of Judgement* is paginated independently]).

3. Ibid., §28 (Meredith, p. 113).

4. Ibid., §29 (Meredith, p. 128). Translating Kant's *Schwärmerei* as "fanaticism" is not without its problems (to the point where the renowned French historian of philosophy Alexei Philonenko chose to leave it in German in his French translation of the *Critique*). What we can say, following Kant's own lexical clarification, is that *Schwärmerei* may be associated with psychosis: "If enthusiasm is comparable to *delirium* [transitory], fanaticism may be compared to *mania*" (*Critique of Judgement*, pt. 1, §29; Meredith, p. 128). The comparison confirms Kant's earlier analysis of *Schwärmerei* in *Dreams of a Spirit-Seer*, where he dismantled the doctrine of the Swedish mystic Emanuel Swedenborg. This text, of seminal value for understanding Kant, asks how we are to distinguish between Swedenborg, clearly in the *Schwärmer* category, and Leibniz, a true metaphysician (see David-Ménard's *La Folie dans la raison pure. Kant lecteur de Swedenborg*).

5. Kant, *Critique of Judgement*, pt. 1, §29 (Meredith, p. 128). "Insanity (*dementia*) is that disturbance of the mind, wherein everything which the insane person relates is in accord with the possibility of an experience, and indeed with the formal laws of thought; but, because of falsely inventive imagination, self-concocted ideas are treated as if they were perceptions" (Kant, *Anthropology from a Pragmatic Point of View*, §52; Dowdell, p. 112). This text was translated into French by Michel Foucault in 1954.

6. In *Conjectures on the Beginning of Human History*, a critical response to Herder, Kant opposes the "civilized state" (*kultivierter Zustand, gesitteter Zustand, zivilisierter Zustand*) to the state of nature but affirms that the solution to contradictions *within* civilization, its discontents as it were, is not to be found in the expansion of economy and technology but rather a "perfect civil constitution" (*Conjectures*, in *Kant: Political Writings*, p. 228).

7. *Société civile* figures prominently in the vocabulary of the revolutionaries of 1789, namely in the drafts of the declarations of the rights of man written in August of that year by Servan, Duran de Maillane, and also Marat, for whom *Etat, peuple, nation*, and *société civile* were synonyms (see Fauré, *Les Declarations des droits de l'homme de 1789*). For the fairly widespread use of *fanatisme* and *fanatique*, namely

to stigmatize the Church and royalists, see Bianchi, *Dictionnaire des usages socio-politiques, 1770-1815*.

8. The terms Kant uses are *status naturalis* and *status artificialis* (*Die Metaphysik der Sitten* [*Metaphysics of Morals*], §41).

9. *Metaphysics of Morals*, §46 (Gregor, p. 125).

10. *Imperium non paternale sed patrioticum* (*Theory and Practice*, pt. 2, §1, in *Kant: Political Writings*, p. 74).

11. Ibid., p. 78. As his use of the terms *citoyen* and *bourgeois* makes clear, Kant's political idiom was that of the French Revolution.

12. Ibid.

13. *Metaphysics of Morals*, pt. 1, §47, in *Kant: Political Writings*, p. 140.

14. *Theory and Practice*, pt. 2, conclusion, in *Kant: Political Writings*, p. 83.

15. Ibid., p. 81.

16. See Hobbes, *The Citizen*, chap. 7, §14, in *Man and Citizen*, pp. 198-99.

17. *Theory and Practice*, pt. 2, conclusion, in *Kant: Political Writings*, p. 84.

18. Ibid.

19. Ibid., pp. 85-86.

20. Kant, *Critique of Judgement*, pt. 2, §83 (Meredith, p. 95).

21. Ibid. (Meredith, p. 96; translation modified).

22. Ibid. (Meredith, p. 97).

23. Kant, *Metaphysics of Morals*, §62, conclusion (Gregor, p. 161).

24. Kant, *Critique of Judgement*, pt. 2, §65, note (Meredith, p. 23). Kant opposes such an "organization" to an inanimate machine, whose different parts are, in his conception, merely juxtaposed.

25. *Perpetual Peace: A Philosophical Sketch*, append. 2, in *Kant: Political Writings*, p. 126. Kant also provides an affirmative version of this principle: "All maxims which *require* publicity if they are not to fail in their purpose can be reconciled both with right and with politics" (ibid., p. 130).

26. For a complete account of the "pantheism dispute" see Zac, *Spinoza en Allemagne*.

27. Jacobi, *Ueber die Lehre des Spinoza*, in *Briefen an den Herrn Moses Mendelssohn*, 1785.

28. Kant, *Critique of Pure Reason*, "Transcendental Dialectic," bk. 1, sec. 2: "Reason, if considered as a faculty of a certain logical form of knowledge, is the faculty of concluding, that is of judging mediately, by bringing the condition of a possible under the condition of a given judgment" (Müller, p. 268).

29. *What is Orientation in Thinking?* in *Kant: Political Writings*, pp. 245-26.

30. Ibid., p. 247; emphasis added.   31. Ibid., p. 248.

32. Ibid., p. 249.   33. Ibid., p. 246.

34. "The highest degree of fanaticism [*Schwarmeren*] is [thinking] that we are ourselves within God, and [when] we intuit and contemplate our being in him. The

second degree is seeing all things according to their true nature, with God alone as their origin and his ideas as archetypes. The third is not looking at things in God but rather deducing them from the very concept of God, that is, deducing his existence from our being and our notions of reason, in the first of which that existence can have only an objective reality. And now, from the lowest degree [back] to the highest: Spinoza." (For the original see *Kants Gesammelte Schriften*, vol. 18, sec. 6050, "Von der philosophischen Schwarmeren," p. 438).

35. "Amor intellectualis quo Deus seipsum amat" (Spinoza, *Ethics*, bk. 5, prop. 35).

36. Kant, *Critique of Judgement*, pt. 1, §29 (Meredith, p. 127).

37. Ibid. (pp. 127-28).

38. Ibid. (p. 128).

39. *Contest of the Faculties*, in *Kant: Political Writings*, p. 183.

40. Kant, *Critique of Judgement*, pt. 1, §29 (Meredith, pp. 118-24).

41. "The picture book, like the pictorial Bible, or indeed one of the illustrated compendiums of law, is a visual treasure chest for the childish teacher, so that he can make his pupils still more childish than they were before" (Kant, *Anthropology from a Pragmatic Point of View*, §34; Dowdell, p. 75). "Therefore, the Trinity, an old man, a young man, and a bird (the dove), must be understood not as actual forms which resemble their objects, but rather as mere symbols. Pictorial expressions of the descent from heaven and the ascension to heaven are just such symbolic expressions. We cannot proceed in any other way; we have to anthropomorphize if we want to provide our notions of rational being with illustrations. It is, however, unfortunate and childish if as a consequence, the symbolic representation becomes the notion for the object as such" (§30; Dowdell, p. 62).

42. *The Contest of the Faculties*, sec. 2, §3a "The Terroristic Conception of Human History," in *Kant: Political Writings*, p. 179.

43. See Bianchi's *Dictionnaire des usages socio-politiques, 1770-1815*.

44. The most developed version of Hegel's interpretation of the 1793 Terror in France is to be found in the *Phänomenologie des Geistes* (1802); eighteen years later, in *Elements of the Philosophy of Right*, the text in which he presents his theory of civil society and the state, he discusses and defines fanaticism.

45. Hegel, *Elements of the Philosophy of Right*, §5 (Nisbet, p. 38).

46. Ibid. (Nisbet, p. 39).

47. Hegel, *Lectures on the History of Philosophy* (Haldane, 2: 129).

48. Ibid. Hegel is quoting Henry T. Colebrook (1765-1837), a scholar of Sanskrit and the Hindu religion.

49. *Vorlesung über die Geschichte der Philosophie*, in *Hegels Sämtliche Werke*, 15a: 288.

50. "The Soul . . . is exempt from metempsychosis and likewise bodily form so that it does not after death make its appearance in another bodily form. This

blessed condition therefore is . . . a perfect and eternal release from every kind of ill. . . . Now when the Indian thus internally collects and retreats within his own thoughts, the moment of such pure concentration is called Brahma" (Hegel, *Lectures on the History of Philosophy*; Haldane, 2: 129). Voltaire had called "Gymnosophists and Brahmins" "the most fanatic of mankind" (*Le Siècle de Louis XIV*, chap. 36; for the English, see "Calvinism" in *Works*, vol. 11, pt. 2, p. 107). He did not consider violence an essential characteristic of fanaticism, believing that religious violence had its origins in the struggle for political power.

51. Hegel, *Elements of the Philosophy of Right*, §5 (Nisbet, p. 38).

52. Ibid., addition (Nisbet, p. 39).

53. Hegel, *Phenomenology of Mind*, pt. 6, sec. B, "Absolute Freedom and Terror" (Baillie, p. 605).

54. Hegel, *Elements of the Philosophy of Right*, §270 (Nisbet, p. 293).

55. Ibid. (Nisbet, pp. 294-95; pp. 302-3).

56. Ibid., Hegel's note (Nisbet, p. 296).

57. We insist on the difference between organization and organism, even though Hegel explicitly affirms that "the State is an organism, i.e. the development of the Idea in its difference" and that "this organism is the political consitution" (*Elements of the Philosophy of Right*, §269; Nisbet, p. 290): the metaphor enables Hegel to insist on the unity of the state despite the multiplicity of its parts. However, it is the syllogism, not the body, that stands as the model of articulation of the different parts—a logical body, as it were. Obviously Hegel rejected all criticism of the state as creating an artificial gap with "nature." He is particularly vehement in the case of his contemporary, the authoritarian romantic reactionary Karl Ludwig von Haller, and his affirmation that domination of the weak by the strong was an eternal ordinance of God, explaining that from there Haller was led to reject law, the role of the state, and all taxes (§258, Hegel's note; Nisbet, pp. 280-81). In his *Restauration der Staatwissenschaft* (Restoration of political science), Haller predictably attributes a sinister role to the expression "civil society": "social relations" ought to have been explained in terms of "natural societies," and not those "so-called civil societies" with all they implied of false theories (the state of nature, the social contract, etc.). The expression *societas civilis* reflected the reality of Rome, where the citizens formed a "corporation," a "bourgeoisie," a "true civil society," but this singular case had been wrongly extrapolated to other political aggregates. At the same time, Roman laws had been adopted, "even though the ancient customs of the Germans, so close to simplicity and nature, were possibly superior to them" (translated from the author's French version, *Restauration de la science politique ou Théorie de l'état social naturel et social*, pp. 97-100). In sum, it was to be wished that "this expression 'civil society,' which has slipped from the language of the Romans into our own, be quickly and entirely banished from science" (p. 542). (The original of this text is in German, but Haller himself translated it into French almost immediately.)

58. Nisbet translates *Stände* as either "Estates" (when it refers to the "supposedly natural divisions" of "feudal and absolutist society") or "estates" (when used in a wider sense to refer to other "distinct social groups"; see translator's preface, p. xliii. The three "estates" are presented in §§202–6 of Hegel's *Elements of the Philosophy of Right* (Nisbet, pp. 234–38): "the substantial estate" (*der ackerbauende Stand*) or cultivators of the soil; "the formal estate" (*der Stand des Gewerbes*) or "estate of trade and industry . . . giving form to natural products"; and "the universal estate" (*der allgemeine Stand*) or civil servants, whose concern is with "the universal interests of society." On Hegel's term *Polizei* see Nisbet's clarification: "It refers to an authority whose responsibility extends beyond the upholding of law and order to such matters as price control, public works, and welfare provisions" (p. xlii). One of Marx's essential criticisms of Hegelian political theory concerns the role of the corporations: Hegel thought to resolve the political problem of intrasocial conflict by the roles given to the different estates, but because of the necessary contradictions that pit corporations against one another, he had in fact only displaced the problem. For Marx of course no ruse of reason could evacuate the problem of the contradictions between classes within civil society (see Chapter 9, p. 299).

59. "Civil society is the [stage] of difference which intervenes between the family and the state, even if its full development occurs later than that of the state; for as difference it presupposes the state, which it must have before it as a self-sufficient entity in order to subsist itself. Besides, the creation of civil society belongs to the modern world, which for the first time allows all determinations of the Idea to attain their rights" (Hegel, *Elements of the Philosophy of Right*, §182, addition; Nisbet, p. 220).

60. Ibid., §238 (Nisbet, p. 263).

61. Ibid, §§177, 178 (Nisbet, p. 214).

62. In 1799 Hegel read and wrote a commentary on the English thinker James Steuart's *Inquiry into the Principle of Political Economy* (see Chamley, *Economy politique et philosophie chez Steuart et Hegel*). He was familiar with Smith's *Wealth of Nations*, already twice translated into German, and refers to it several times in the Jena manuscripts of 1805–6. He had also probably read Ferguson's *Essay on the History of Civil Society*, translated into German in 1768; Schiller's *On the Aesthetic Education of Man* (1795), a work influenced by Ferguson, must have sharpened his interest in the Scottish philosophy professor. (On the importance of the Scottish school for German thought, particularly Hegel's, see Dickey, *Hegel, Religion, Economics, and the Politics of the Spirit*.) Manfred Riedel's article "Hegel, 'bürgerliche Gesellschaft' und das Problem Ihres geschichtlichen Ursprungs" has understandably been of great use to me.

63. Against the spread of poverty Hegel proposed that the "rabble" be sent to the colonies which civil society was "driven" to establish; see *Elements of the Philosophy of Right*, §§243–48 (Nisbet, pp. 266–69).

64. Ibid., §230 (Nisbet, p. 260).

65. Ibid., §255 (Nisbet, p. 272).

66. The law had no abstract existence, however, but was related to the concrete life of civil society, and this affected how the gravity of crimes was measured; penal codes were necessarily tied to a given age and could not remain fixed.

67. Hegel, *Elements of the Philosophy of Right*, §289, addition (Nisbet, p. 329).

68. *Communist Manifesto*, in the *Marx-Engels Reader*, p. 345.

69. Hegel, *Elements of the Philosophy of Right*, §270 (Nisbet, p. 301).

70. Ibid. (Nisbet, p. 304).

71. Ibid. (Nisbet, p. 292).

72. This is why the state—more exactly, the states, because the Hegelian perspective embraced a multiplicity of nation-states—could hardly regret the schism within the Church: such divisions only weakened it and strengthened the state.

73. See *Enzyklopädie der philosophischen Wissenschaften*, §552.

74. Hegel, *Elements of the Philosophy of Right*, §209 (Nisbet, p. 240).

75. Ibid., §270, Hegel's second note (Nisbet, pp. 295-96).

Chapter 9

1. On contemporary Russian political vocabulary, see Niqueux, ed., *Vocabulaire de la perestroïka*.

2. See Barret-Kriegel, *L'Etat et les esclaves*, and Colas, *Textes constitutionnels soviétiques*.

3. On the history of China in terms of civil society and the state, see Bergère, Bianco, and Domes, eds., *La Chine au 20ème siècle*.

4. Lenin, *Collected Works*, vol. 26.

5. See, among other texts, *How to Organize Competition?* in Lenin, *Collected Works*, vol. 26. On enemies assimilated to insects see my *Léninisme*, chap. 8, "Epuration."

6. On the constitutional problems of the Gorbachev period see Sharlet, *Soviet Constitutional Crisis: From De-Stalinization to Disintegration*, and Malia, *The Soviet Tragedy*.

7. *A Contribution to the Critique of Political Economy*, in the *Marx-Engels Reader*, p. 4.

8. Marx, *Capital*, postface to the second ed., 1873 (Fowkes, 1: 102).

9. *Contribution to the Critique of Hegel's "Philosophy of Law,"* in *Collected Works of Marx and Engels*, 3: 7 (hereafter abbreviated as *CW*). This is Marx's commentary—never published by him—on §§261-313 ("The State") of Hegel's *Grundlinien der Philosophie des Rechts*, or *Elements of the Philosophy of Right* (translated in *CW* as *Philosophy of Law*).

10. Ibid.

11. Ibid., pp. 8-9.

12. Ibid., p. 40.

13. Ibid., pp. 38, 40. We may discern in this criticism the influence of the young Marx's reading of Spinoza.

14. From the unpublished critique of Hegel's *Elements of the Philosophy of Right*, published under the title "Critique of Hegel's Doctrine of the State" in *Karl Marx: Early Writings*, p. 87.

15. *Contribution to the Critique of Hegel's "Philosophy of Law,"* in *CW*, 3: 45. These are Marx's versions of Hegel's definitions.

16. Ibid., p. 42. Marx quotes Hegel's *Elements of the Philosophy of Right*, §301.

17. Ibid., p. 43. Once again, this is Marx's version of Hegel's *Elements of the Philosophy of Right*, §301.

18. Ibid., p. 42 (see Chapter 8, note 58).

19. "The identity which he [Hegel] has constructed between civil society and State is the identity of two hostile armies, where every soldier has the 'opportunity' to become by 'desertion' a member of the 'hostile army'; and indeed Hegel herewith correctly describes the present empirical position" (ibid., pp. 50–51).

20. Ibid., p. 32. Further on Marx explains: "One can express the spirit of the Middle Ages in this way: The estates of civil society and the estates in the political sense were identical, because civil society was political society–because the organic principle of civil society was the principle of the state" (p. 72).

21. Ibid., p. 63.

22. The text as Marx originally wrote it (in 1845) together with Engel's version (1888) are in *Marx Engels Werke*, vol. 3, pp. 5–7 (Marx), pp. 533–35 (Engels). Editions where *bürgerliche Gesellschaft* was translated as "bourgeois society" include *Marx, Early Political Writings*, trans. O'Malley, pp. 134–35, and, in French, *L'Idéologie allemande*, trans. Cartelle and Badia.

23. The version of the tenth thesis on Feuerbach cited here is in the *Marx-Engels Reader*, p. 109.

24. Marx clearly underlines the radical newness that is to characterize society after the proletarian revolution in a text written in French in 1847, in which he uses the words *société civile*: "The condition for the emancipation of the laboring class is the abolition of all classes, just as the condition for the emancipation of the Third Estate, the bourgeois order, was the abolition of all estates and all orders. In the course of its development, the laboring class will substitute for the old civil society an association that will exclude classes and their antagonism, and there will be no more political power properly speaking, for the political power is precisely the official summing up of antagonism in civil society" (*Misère de la philosophie*, in Marx, *Œuvres*, 1: 135–36).

25. *German Ideology*, pt. 1, in the *Marx-Engels Reader*, p. 127; emphasis added. The translator here, S. Ryazanskaya, regularly and, to my mind, correctly uses "civil society."

26. We find *bürgerliche Gesellschaft* translated *société bourgeoise* throughout this passage in Cartelle's 1953 version of *The German Ideology*, p. 28.

27. The editors of the English translation of Marx and Engels's *Collected Works* maintain that *bürgerliche Gesellschaft* has two different meanings in Marx's theory: (1) "to denote the economic system of society irrespective of the historical stage of development" and (2) "to denote the material relations of bourgeois society, of capitalism" (5: 593 n. 25). They translate the term as either "civil society" or "bourgeois society" according to context. In spite of the terminological clarification, however, we observe that in the index of this volume, at "bourgeois society" the reader is repeatedly referred to pages where the only term to be found is "civil society." The translators for Rubel's three-volume French edition of Marx's works also chose which term to use on the basis of the immediate context. A rare example where the German term has been systematically translated "civil society" is the 1968 annotated French edition of the complete text of *The German Ideology* (published under the title *L'Idéologie allemande*); it is the work of several translators, among them Jean Baudrillard.

28. Compare Marx's *General Introduction to the Critique of Political Economy* (1857) and his *Critique of Political Economy* (1859).

29. We would propose the following, albeit not exactly elegant, solution: *bürgerliche Gesellschaft* to be translated systematically as "civil society"; *moderne bürgerliche Gesellschaft* as "modern civil-bourgeois society."

30. Marx, *General Introduction to the Critique of Political Economy*, §3, "The Method of Political Economy" (1857).

31. See Marx, *On the Jewish Question*.

32. For one such ironic perspective on Marx, see Descombes, "Pour elle un Français doit mourir."

33. Badie and Birnbaum see a clear dualism in Marx's political theory (see *The Sociology of the State*).

34. Marx, *German Ideology*, pt. 1, "The Relation of State and Law to Property," in the *Marx-Engels Reader*, p. 150.

35. Marx, *Capital*, pt. 8, chap. 31: "The Genesis of the Industrial Capitalist" (Fowkes, 1: 915–16).

36. *German Ideology*, in the *Marx-Engels Reader*, p. 151.

37. Ibid.

38. This is the general theme of *On the Jewish Question*.

39. As the philosopher Max Stirner, among others, had (Marx, *Die Deutsche Ideologie*, pt. 3, Sankt Max; in *MEGA*, 5: 334).

40. Marx, "Bastiat und Carey," in *Ökonomische Manuskripte, 1857/58*. Marx specifies:"Die bürgerliche Gesellschaft existirt nicht rein, nicht ihrem Begriff entsprechend, nicht sich selbst adaequat in England" (In England civil society does not exist in a pure state; it is not adequate to its concept or its nature) (p. 4).

41. Ibid., p. 5.

42. See Marx's notes on Bakunin's book, *Statehood and Anarchy*, in *CW*, 24: 498. The English translation of *bürgerliche Gesellschaft* as "bourgeois society" has been modified.

43. See Marx, *Drafts of the Letter to Vera Zasulich* (Feb.-Mar. 1881), in *CW*, 24: 336-72, and the text Zasulich actually received, Mar. 8, 1881, in *CW*, 46: 70.

44. Ibid., 24: 346, 370.

45. Marx, *Capital*, bk. 1, pt. 8, chap. 26: "The Secret of Primitive Accumulation" (Fowkes, 1: 876). Marx added a sentence to the French translation of his book that restricts the validity of the English model: he affirms that in Western Europe the process of capital accumulation could follow "different orders of succession" (ibid.). In his letter to Zasulich Marx refers to the French translation of *Capital* (1872-75), quoting to her an addition he had made to this French edition: "At the core of the capitalist system, therefore, lies the complete separation of the producer from the means of production. . . . [T]he basis of this whole development is the expropriation of the agricultural producer. To date this has not been accomplished in a radical fashion anywhere except England. . . . But all the other countries of Western Europe are undergoing the same process." Marx concluded thus: "Hence the analysis provided in *Capital* does not adduce reasons either for or against the viability of the rural commune, but the special study I have made of it, the material for which I drew from original sources, has convinced me that this commune is the fulcrum of social regeneration in Russia, but in order that it function as such, it would be necessary to eliminate the deleterious influences which are assailing it from all sides, and then ensure for it the normal conditions of spontaneous development" (*Letter to Vera Zasulich*, in *CW*, 46: 72). The original French texts of Zasulich's letter to Marx and Marx's answer and the drafts of his answer can be found in Marx, *Ouevres*, 2: 1556-73.

46. *CW*, 24: 355

47. Engels, *Afterword to "On Social Relations in Russia"* (1894), in *CW*, 27: 432.

48. *Critique of the Gotha Program*, in *The Marx-Engels Reader*, p. 395.

49. Ibid., p. 394. We have modified the translation of *bürgerliche Gesellschaft* as "bourgeois society."

50. *Capital*, postface to the second German edition (Fowkes, 1: 98). For Marx's use of *moderne bürgerlich Gesellschaft* see *Marx Engels Werke*, 23: 18.

51. *Eighteenth Brumaire of Louis Bonaparte*, sec. 7, in the *Marx-Engels Reader*, p. 514. This text was written between late 1851 and early 1852 but important passages of sec. 7 were added in 1869.

52. *Civil War in France*, pt. 3, in the *Marx-Engels Reader*, p. 552.

53. Ibid.

54. Ibid., p. 553.

55. "The Communal Constitution would have restored to the social body all the forces hitherto absorbed by the State parasite feeding upon and clogging the free movement of society" (ibid., p. 556).

56. *Eighteenth Brumaire of Louis Bonaparte*, in the *Marx-Engels Reader*, p. 517. In the version of this text printed in the *Marx-Engels Reader*, *bürgerliche Gesellschaft* is systematically translated "bourgeois society." (We find the same misinterpretation in an anonymous French version published by the Editions sociales in 1963.)

57. Ibid., in the *Marx-Engels Reader*, p. 520.

58. Nietzsche, *Thus Spoke Zarathustra*, pt. 1, "On the New Idols" (Hollingdale, p. 75).

59. *Civil War in France*, sec. 3, in the *Marx-Engels Reader*, p. 563. Throughout this passage we have also referred to Marx's first draft of this text, which can be found in vol. 17 of *Marx Engels Werke*.

60. In his 1891 introduction to the *Civil War in France*, Engels suggests that in attacking the state, the Paris Commune had attacked the "superstitious belief in the State" held by philosophers, among others, for whom—here he is explicitly quoting Hegel—the state had been " 'the realization of the idea,' or the Kingdom of God on earth" (*Marx-Engels Reader*, p. 536).

61. Marx, *Contribution to the Critique of Hegel's "Philosophy of Right,"* intro. (1843), in the *Marx-Engels Reader*, p. 18.

62. Ibid., in the *Marx-Engels Reader*, p. 22.

63. Engels, *The Peasant War in Germany*, in *CW*, 10: 414.

64. Ibid., p. 432.

65. Ibid., p. 415.

66. Ibid. In what seems to be the authoritative English version of this text, this occurrence of Engels's word *Schwärmerei* is translated "dream-visions." We have restored the translation "fanaticism."

67. Marx, *Contribution to the Critique of Hegel's "Philosophy of Right": Introduction*, in the *Marx-Engels Reader*, p. 20.

68. Engels, *The Peasant War in Germany*, in *CW*, 10: 461. Translation slightly modified (once again the English version rendered *bürgerliche Gesellschaft* by "bourgeois society"; see also p. 408 and p. 471).

69. Ibid., p. 427.

70. Ibid., p. 423.

71. Ibid., p. 425.

72. Ibid., p. 429

73. Ibid.

74. Ibid., p, 471.

75. Ibid., p. 480.

76. Ibid., p. 399.

77. Bloch, *Thomas Münzer, Theologe der Revolution*, p. 75.

78. Ibid., p. 297.

79. Ibid., p. 151. In calling Müntzer *homo archifanaticus*, Bloch is quoting the caption of a contemporary portrait of him (see Chapter 1, p. 374, note 19).

80. The formula *bürgerliche Gesellschaft* is found only in certain passages that Lenin copied in German directly from Marx's *Holy Family* as part of a summary of that work made for personal use rather than publication (see Lenin, *Polnoe sobranie sochinenii*, vol. 29). Lenin translates Marx's *bürgerliche Gesellschaft* as *burzhuaznoe obshestvo*, the Russian equivalent of "bourgeois society," namely in *The State and Revolution.*

81. See Ingerflom, *Le Citoyen impossible.*

82. On Lenin in general and more particularly on his theory of organization see my *Léninisme* and *Lénine et le léninisme.*

83. Lenin, *Polnoe sobranie sochinenii*, 41: 418.

84. Schmitt, *The Concept of the Political*, p. 26. See also Derrida, *Politiques de l'amitié*, pp. 93ff.

85. Aron, *Democratie et totalitarisme.*

86. See Arendt, *The Origins of Totalitarianism.*

87. This difficulty was the theme of a short text by Stalin written in 1930, in the period of forced collectivization, in which he warns against the danger of attacking good communists; see "Dizzy with Success."

88. Extract from a decree of the Communist Party Central Committee Plenary Session (of which Stalin was the General Secretary), Jan. 1933; quoted in Rittersporn, "L'Etat en lutte contre lui-même."

Chapter 10

1. Marx, *On the Jewish Question*, in *CW*, 3: 154. (We have slightly modified this English translation from time to time and have occasionally used instead the translation published in the *Marx-Engels Reader*, pp. 24–51.)

2. Ibid., p. 159.

3. Ibid.

4. "The members of the political state are religious owing to the dualism between individual life and species-life, between the life of civil society and political life. They are religious because men treat the political life of the State, an area beyond their real individuality, as if it were their true life. They are religious insofar as religion is the spirit of civil society, expressing the separation and remoteness of man from man" (ibid.).

5. Ibid., p. 154.

6. Ibid., p. 152.

7. Marx, *German Ideology*, vol. 1, pt. 1, "Feuerbach," in *CW*, 5: 36. Marx adds: "In direct contrast to German philosophy which descends from heaven to earth, here it is a matter of ascending from earth to heaven."

8. *Deutsche Ideologie*, in *Marx Engels Werke*, 1: 212.

9. *German Ideology*, vol. 1, pt. 1, in *CW*, 5: 46.

10. Ibid.

11. Ibid., p. 42.

12. Marx regularly used the French word in the *German Ideology*, and he distinguished explicitly at one point between the two meanings of *Bürger*, indicating that the word could refer either to *bourgeois* or *citoyen* (see *German Ideology*, in *CW*, 5: 201).

13. For Marx on Kant, see *German Ideology*, in *CW*, 5: 193-96.

14. Ibid., p. 200 (we have modified the translation in a way certainly familiar to the reader by now).

15. Marx used the word *Enthusiasmus* (see *Zur Kritik der Hegelschen Rechtsphilosophie. Einleitung*, in *Marx Engels Werke*, 1: 378).

16. Cervantes, *Don Quixote*, bk. 1, chaps. 19 and 21. Marx refers explicitly to these two chapters in *Die Deutsche Ideologie*, pt. 3: Sankt Max, sec. 6C: Der humane Liberalismus, in *MEGA*, 5: 214-19.

17. What Lacan formalized as $\mathcal{S} \lozenge a$ (see *Télévision*, p. 64).

18. Marx, *Capital*, bk. 1, chap. 1 "The Commodity," §4 "The fetishism of the commodity and its secret" (Fowkes, 1: 164-66).

19. Ibid. (Fowkes, 1: 172-73).

20. Marx, *The Holy Family: A Critique of Critical Criticism*, chap. 6.

21. Durkheim is here explicitly attacking Heinrich von Treitschke's *Politik*. The work in question is *"L'Allemagne au-dessus de tout." La mentalité germanique et la guerre*, written in 1915 and translated into English and Italian that same year. On Durkheim's activities during World War I, see Lukes, *Emile Durkheim*.

22. Ibid., sec. 3, "The State Above Civil Society," p. 29 (Durkheim is quoting Treitschke's *Politik* directly).

23. Ibid., p. 30.

24. Ibid., pp. 23-24.

25. See Weber, *Politik als Beruf*, p. 8.

26. Durkheim, *Germany Above All*, p. 45.

27. Freud, *Reflections upon War and Death*, pt. 1 (Rieff, p. 112).

28. Such nationalism is patent, for example, in Marcel Mauss's conception of the nation as the endpoint of historical development (see *La Nation et l'internationalisme*, in *Œuvres*, 3: 573-639).

29. Aristotle, *Politics*, bk. 1, chap. 1, §16 (Barker, p. 7; translation modified).

30. Hegel, *Philosophy of History*, pt. 4 "The German World," sec. 3, chap. 1 "The Reformation" (Sibree, p. 418).

Bibliography

This bibliography includes all texts cited in the chapter notes as well as a number of works that make an important contribution to my subject in one way or another. Often, and especially in the case of older texts, when an individual text is not quoted directly it has been identified simply by author, title, and date of publication.

Research for the French original of this work was principally done at the Bibliothèques Nationale, de l'Arsenal, and Mazarine in Paris, as well as at the British Library. In the preparation of the English edition, the libraries of Stanford University and the University of California at Berkeley were of inestimable assistance.

Abbruzzese, Salvatore. Interview in *La Croix*, May 12 and 13, 1991, p. 7.

Abensour, Miguel. "Le procès des Maîtres rêveurs." *Libre* 4 (1978): 207-30.

Albertus Magnus. *Commentarii in octo libri politicorum Aristotelis*. Ca. 1265. Commentary on the *Politics*.

——. *Super Ethica Nicomachus*. Ca. 1248. Commentary on *Nicomachean Ethics*.

Alcuin. Letter to Carolus Magnus, June 799. Letter 174, in *Monumenta Germaniae Historica. Epistolae Karolini Aevi*, vol. 2. Ed. E. Duemmler. Berlin: Weidmann. 1895.

al-Khalil, Samir. "C'est aux Arabes de combattre les Arabes." *L'Autre Journal* 9 (Feb. 1991): 92-101.

Allen, J. W. *A History of Political Thought in the Sixteenth Century*. London: Methuen, 1964.

Altdeutsche Malerei (Catalog 2 of the Alte Pinakothek, Munich). Ed. Christian A. zu Salm and Gisela Goldberg. Munich: F. Bruckman, 1963.

Althusius, Johannes. *Politica Methodice digesta, atque exemplis sacris et profanis illustrata.* 1603.

Althusser, Louis. *For Marx.* Trans. Ben Brewster. London: Penguin Books; New York: Pantheon, 1969. Originally published as *Pour Marx* (Paris: François Maspero, 1965).

Amselle, Jean-Loup. *Mestizo Logics.* Stanford: Stanford University Press, 1998. Originally published as *Logiques métisses: Anthropologie de l'identité en Afrique et ailleurs* (Paris: Payot, 1990).

Anderson, Perry. *Lineages of the Absolutist State.* London: Verso, 1979.

Ankersmit, F. R. *Aesthetic Politics: The Political Beyond, Fact and Value.* Stanford: Stanford University Press, 1997.

Arato, Andrew. "Civil Society Against the State: Poland 1980-1981." *Telos* 47 (1981).

——. "Empire vs. Civil Society: Poland, 1981-1982." *Telos* 50 (1982).

Arendt, Hannah. *The Origins of Totalitarianism.* New York: Harcourt, Brace & World, 1951.

Aristotle. *Aristoteles latinus.* Ed. L. Minio-Paluello, then G. Verveke. Bruges and Paris: Desclée de Brouwer; Leiden: E. J. Brill, 1957- .

——. *The Athenian Constitution.* Trans. P. J. Rhodes. London: Penguin Books, 1984.

——. *History of Animals.* 3 vols. Vols. 1 and 2, trans. Arthur Leslie Peck. Vol. 3, trans. D. M. Balme. Cambridge: Harvard University Press, 1965-91. Bilingual edition.

——. *Nicomachean Ethics* (translations in chronological order).

Ethica Nicomachae (Ethica vetus, Ethica Nova, Hoferiana, Borghesiana). Trans. Hermann the German, ca. 1240. Text ed. R. A. Gauthier. Leiden: E. J. Brill; Paris: Desclée de Brouwer, 1972.

Ethica Nicomachae. Trans. Robert Grosseteste, ca. 1246-47. Text ed. R. A. Gauthier. Leiden: E. J. Brill; Paris: Desclée de Brouwer, 1972.

Les Ethiques d'Aristote. Trans. Nicole Oresme, ca. 1350. Paris, 1488.

Ethica ad Nicomachum. Trans. Leonardo Bruni, ca. 1416. Rome, 1473.

L'Ethica d'Aristotile tradotta in lingua vulgare fiorentina et commentata da Bernardo Segni. Trans. Bernardo Segni. Florence, 1550.

Les Ethiques d'Aristote stagyrite à son fils Nicomache: nouvelement tradittes de Grec en Français par le P. L. Gentilhomme de la Maison de Monsieur le Conte d'Aran. Paris, 1553.

L'Ethique à Nicomaque. Trans. Jean Voilquin. Paris: Garnier, 1940.

Nicomachean Ethics. Trans. Terence Irwin. Indianapolis: Hackett, 1985.

——. *Politics* (translations in chronological order).

Translatio prior imperfecta. Interpreta Guillelmo de Moerbeka edidit Petrus Michaud Quantin Aristotelis latinus. Trans. William of Moerbeke, 1260-64. Paris: Desclée de Brouwer, 1961.

Politica "perfecta." Trans. William of Moerbeke, ca. 1265. In Aristotle, *Opera Omnia*, ed. F. Susemihl. Leipzig, 1907.

Maistre Nicole Oresme, Le Livre des Politiques d'Aristote. Trans. Nicole Oresme, ca. 1370. Text ed. A. D. Menut, in *Transactions of the American Philosophical Society* (Philadelphia), n.s., 60, pt. 6 (1970).

Aristotelis Ethica, Politica, Œconomica, Leonardo Bruni interprete. Trans. Leonardo Bruni, ca. 1438 for the *Politics*. Argentinae [Strasbourg], 1475.

La Philosofia natural del Arisotel, es asaber Ethicas, Polithicas, y Economicas, en romance. Spanish translation from Bruni's Latin by Don Carlos de Viana de Navarra. Saragossa, 1509.

Los ochos libros de Republica des Filosopho Aristotels, traduzidos originalemente de lengue Griega en Castellano. Trans. Simon Abril. Saragossa, 1534.

Gli Otto libri della Republica, che chiamono Politica del Aristotile, nuovamente tradotti di greco in vulgare italiano per Antonio Brucioli. Trans. Antonio Brucioli. 1547.

Trattato dei Governi di Aristotile. Tradotto di greco in lingua vulgare fiorentina da Bernado Segni. Trans. Bernardo Segni. Florence, 1549.

Petri Victorii Commentarii in VIII Libros Aristotelis de optime Statu Civitatis. Trans. Pietro Vettori. Florence, 1552.

Les Politiques d'Aristote, esquelles est monstrée la science de gouverner le genre humain en toutes espèces d'estats publics, traduictes de grec en françois . . . par Loys le Roy, dit Regius. Trans. Loys Le Roy. Paris, 1568.

Aristoteles, Politiques or discourses of Governement. Translated out of Greeke into French, with Expositions taken out of the best Authours, specially out of Aristotle himself, and out of Plato, conferred together where occasion of matter treated by them both offer itselfe. An anonymous translation from Le Roy's French. London, 1598.

A Treatise on Government, translated from the Greek of Aristotle by William Ellis. London, 1778.

La Politique d'Aristote ou la science des gouvernemens. Ouvrage traduit du Grec, avec des notes historiques et critiques. Trans. Champagne. Paris, 1797.

Aristoteles politik und fragment der Œconomik. Trans. J. G. Schlosser. Lübeck and Leipzig, 1798.

Politique d'Aristote. Trans. Charles Millou. Paris: Artaud, 1803.

La Politique. Trans. M. Thurot. Paris: Didot, 1824.

Politique d'Aristote. Trans. Jules Barthélemy Saint-Hilaire. Paris, 1837.

Aristoteles Politik. Trans. Jacob Bernays. Berlin: Verlag von Wilhelm Hetz, 1872.

Politica. Trans. V. Costanzi. Bari: Laterza, 1918.

La Politica. Trans. Esévanez. Paris: Garnier Hermanos, 1923.

The Politics of Aristotle. Trans. Ernest Barker. Oxford: Oxford University Press, 1946.

La Politique. Trans. Jean Aubonnet. 5 vols. Paris: Les Belles Lettres, 1960–89.

La Politique. Trans. Jean Tricot. 2 vols. Paris: Vrin, 1962.

The Politics. Trans. Carnes Lord. Chicago: University of Chicago Press, 1984.

Les Politiques. Trans. Pierre Pellegrin. Paris: Flammarion, 1990.

Arnauld, Antoine. *Œuvres.* 38 vols. Lausanne, 1775–83.

Aron, Raymond. *Démocratie et totalitarisme.* Paris: Gallimard, 1965.

Arquillière, H. F. *L'Augustinisme politique. Essai sur la formation des théories politiques du Moyen-Age.* Paris: Vrin, 1933.

Augustine. *Concerning the City of God Against the Pagans.* Trans. Henry Bettenson. London: Penguin Books, 1972.

—. *De Civitate Dei.* Ed. B. Dombart and A. Kalb. 4th ed. For the "Bibliotheca Taubneriana," Leipzig, 1928–29. Reprinted in the *Bibliothèque augustinienne*, vols. 33–37 (Paris: Desclée de Brouwer, 1959).

—. *De Genesi ad litteram.* In *Patrologia Latina*, vol. 34.

—. *Epistolae.* In *Patrologia Latina*, vol. 33.

—. *The Essential Augustine.* Ed. Vernon J. Bourke. Indianapolis: Hackett, 1964.

Bacon, Roger. *Opus majus.* 1267. London: G. Bowyer, 1733.

Badie, Bertrand. *Les deux Etats. Pouvoir et société en Occident et en terre d'Islam.* Paris: Fayard, 1986.

Badie, Bertrand, and Pierre Birnbaum. *The Sociology of the State.* Trans. Arthur Goldhammer. Chicago: University of Chicago Press, 1983.

Barclay, William. *De potestate papae.* 1609.

—. *De regno et regali potestate, adversus Buchananum, Brutum, Boucherium et reliquos monarchomachos libri sex.* 1600.

—. *Traicté de la puissance du pape scavoir s'il a quelque droit, empire ou domination sur les rois et princes séculiers.* Pont-à-Mousson, 1611. Translated into English under the title *Of the Authority of the Pope, whether and how far forth he has power and authority over Temporal Kings and Princes* (London, 1611).

Baron, Hans. *The Crisis of the Early Italian Renaissance: Civic Humanism and Republican Liberty in an Age of Classicism and Tyranny.* Rev. ed. Princeton: Princeton University Press, 1966.

—. *From Petrarch to Leonardo Bruni.* Chicago: University of Chicago Press, 1968.

—. *Humanistic and Political Literature in Florence and Venice at the Beginning of the Quattrocento.* Cambridge: Harvard University Press, 1955.

Barrès, Maurice. *Une enquête aux pays du Levant.* Vol. 1. Paris: Plon, 1923.

Barret-Kriegel, Blandine. *Les Chemins de l'Etat.* Paris: Calmann-Levy, 1986.

———. *L'Etat et les esclaves.* Paris: Payot, 1990.

Baruzi, Jean. *Leibniz et l'organisation religieuse de la terre, d'après des documents inédits.* Paris: Alcan, 1907. Reprint. Darmstadt: Scientia Verlag Aalen, 1975.

Baudelaire, Charles. *Les Paradis artificiels.* 1860. In *Œuvres complètes*, vol. 1. Bibliothèque de la Pléiade. Paris: Gallimard, 1975. Translated into English by Ellen Fox under the title *Artificial Paradise* (New York: Herder & Herder, 1971).

Baxandall, Michael. *The Limewood Sculptors of Renaissance Germany, 1475–1525.* New Haven: Yale University Press, 1980.

Bayle, Pierre. *Dictionnaire historique et critique.* 1697.

Bec, Christian, Ivan Cloulas, Bertrand Jestz, and Alberto Tenenti. *L'Italie de la Rénaissance. Un monde en mutation (1378–1494).* Paris: Fayard, 1990.

Bedouelle, Guy, and Bernard Roussel, eds. *Le Temps des Réformes et la Bible.* Vol. 5 of *Bible de tous les temps.* Paris: Beauchesne, 1989.

Bellarmin, Robert. *Tractatus de potestate summi pontificis in rebus temporalibus, adversus Gulimun Barclay.* Rome, 1610. Translated into English by G. A. Moore under the title *Power of the Pope in Temporal Affairs, against William Barclay* (Chevy Chase, Md.: The Country Dollar Press, 1950).

Bellenden, J. *Livy's History of Rome.* 1533.

Benveniste, Emile. *Le vocabulaire des institutions indo-européennes.* Vol. 2, *Pouvoir, droit, religion.* Paris: Editions de Minuit, 1969.

Bergère, Marie-Claire, Lucien Bianco, and Jürgen Domes, eds. *La Chine au 20ème siècle.* 2 vols. Vol. 2, *De 1949 à aujourd'hui.* Paris: Fayard, 1989.

Bernard of Clairvaux, Saint. Letter 256. In *Patrologia Latina*, vol. 182.

Bèze, Théodore de. *Confession de la foi chrétienne.* 1560.

———. *Du Droit des Magistrats sur leurs sujets.* Magdebourg, 1574.

Bialostocki, Jan. "La *Mélancolie Paysanne* d'Albrecht Dürer." *Gazette des Beaux-Arts.* 1956.

Bianchi, Serge. *Dictionnaire des usages socio-politiques 1770–1815.* Vol. 1. Paris: Klincksieck, 1985.

Black, Antony. *Guilds and Civil Society in European Political Thought from the Twelfth Century to the Present.* London: Methuen, 1984.

———. *Political Thought in Europe,1250–1450.* Cambridge: Cambridge University Press, 1992.

Bloch, Ernst. *Thomas Münzer, Theologe der Revolution.* Munich: Kurt Wolff Verlag, 1921.

Bobbio, Norberto. *Gramsci e la concezione della società civile.* Milan: Feltrinelli, 1976.

———. "Società civile." In *Dizionario di Politica*, ed. Norberto Bobbio, Nicola

Matteucci, and Gianfranco Pasquino, pp. 1061–65. Milan: TEA I Dizionari UTET, 1990.

——. "Sulla nozione di societa civile." *De homine.* Rome, 1968.

Bodin, Jean. *De republica.* Paris, 1562, and Frankfurt, 1586.

——. *La République.* 1576.

Boespflug, François. "Les images de Dieu dans l'art occidental." In *Annuaire de l'Ecole des Hautes Etudes en Sciences sociales.* Paris: EHESS, 1990.

Boileau, Nicolas. *Epître XII.* 1698.

Bonald, Louis de. *Théorie du pouvoir politique et religieux dans la société civile.* 1796.

Boniface VIII. *Unam sanctam.* 1302. Papal bull.

——. Letter of May 13, 1300, to the German princes. In *Monumenta Germaniae Historica. Constitutiones et acta publica,* vol. 4, pt. 1, pp. 80–81. Ed. J. Schwalm. Hanover and Leipzig, 1906.

Bossuet, Jacques Bénigne. *Avertissement sur les écrits suivants et sur un nouveau livre de Mgr l'Archevêque de Cambrai imprimé à Bruxelles.* 1697. In *Œuvres Complètes* [Bar-le-Duc], vol. 10.

——. *Correspondance.* 9 vols. Vol. 6. Collection des Grands Ecrivains de France. Paris: Hachette, 1909–15.

——. *Instruction sur les états d'oraison.* 1697. In Bar-le-Duc, vol. 9.

——. *Œuvres Complètes* [Bar-le-Duc]. 12 vols. Ed. Prêtres de l'Immaculée conception. Bar-le-Duc, 1862–63.

——. *Œuvres complètes* [Lechat]. 31 vols. Ed. F. Lechat. Paris: Louis Vivès, 1862–66.

——. *Oraison funèbre de Henriette de France.* 1669.

——. *Oraison funèbre du Père Bourgoing.* 1662.

——. *Oraisons funèbres.* Ed. Jacques Truchet. Paris: Garnier, 1961.

——. *La Politique tirée des Propres paroles de l'Ecriture sainte.* 1688. Translated into English by Patrick Riley under the title *Politics Drawn from the Very Words of Holy Scripture,* ed. Riley (Cambridge: Cambridge University Press, 1990).

——. *Quakerism A-la-Mode: or a History of Quietism, particularly that of the Lord Archi-bishop of Cambray and Madame Guyone.* London, 1698.

——. *Relation sur le quiétisme.* 1697. In Bar-le-Duc, vol. 10.

——. *Remarques sur la Réponse de Mgr. l'archevêque de Cambrai à l'écrit de Mgr. l'évêque de Meaux intitulé "Relation sur le quiétisme."* 1698. In Bar-le-Duc, vol. 10.

——. *Sommaire de la doctrine des Maximes des Saints.* 1698. In Bar-le-Duc, vol. 10.

——. *Tradition des nouveaux mystiques.* 1697. In Lechat, vol. 19.

——. *Variations des Eglises protestantes.* 1686. In Bar-le-Duc, vol. 4.

Bottomore, Tom. *Sociology: A Guide to Problems and Literature*. 3d ed. London: Allen & Unwin, 1987.

Bourdieu, Pierre. "L'Opinion publique n'existe pas." *Les Temps modernes* 29, no. 318 (Jan. 1973). Republished with revisions in *Questions de sociologie* (Paris: Editions de Minuit, 1988) and translated into English by Richard Nice under the title "Public Opinion Does Not Exist," in *Sociology in Question* (London: Sage Publications, 1993).

——. *Sociologie de l'Algérie*. Paris: Presses Universitaires de France, 1958.

Bremond, Abbé Henri. *Histoire littéraire du sentiment religieux en France*. 11 vols. 1916-36.

Brown, Peter. *Augustine of Hippo*. London: Faber & Faber, 1967.

Brueys, David Augustin de. *Histoire du fanatisme de notre temps*. 1696 and 1702.

——. *Traité de l'obéissance des Chrétiens aux puissances temporelles*. Preface by Esprit Fléchier. 1710.

Buridan, Jean. *Quaestiones super decem libros Ethicorum Aristotelis ad Nicomachum*. Paris, 1513.

——. *Quaestiones super octo libros Politicorum Aristotelis*. Ca. 1350. Paris, 1513.

Burke, Edmund. *Reflections on the Revolution in France*. 1797.

Burlamaqui, Jacques. *Principes du droit naturel*. 1748.

Burley, Walter [Walter De Bourles]. *Gualterus Burleaus. Expositio cum quaestionibus super octo libros Politicorum*. 1338-39. Paris: Bibliothèque Mazarine. Latin MS 3496.

——. *Gualterus Burleaus. Expositio et quaestiones in I–X Ethicorum Aristotelis*. 1333-45. Paris: Bibliothèque Nationale. Latin MS 6459.

Burns, James H. *Medieval Political Thought, c. 350–c. 1450*. Cambridge: Cambridge University Press, 1988.

Calvin, John. *Advertissement contre l'astrologie qu'on appelle judiciaire et d'autre curiositez qui règnent aujourd'huy au monde*. 1549. In *Corpus Reformatorum [CR]*, vol. 7. Translated into English under the title *An Admonicion against Astrology iudiciall and other curiosities, that raigne now in the world* (London, 1561). Unpaginated.

——. *Brève Instruction pour armer tous bons fidèles contre les erreurs de la secte commune des Anabaptistes*. 1545. In *CR*, vol. 7. Translated into English under the title *A Short Instruction for to arme all Good Christian people agaynst the pestiferous errours of the common secte of Anabaptists* (London, 1549).

——. *Contre la secte phantastique et furieuse des Libertins qui se nomment spirituelz*. 1547. In *CR*, vol. 7.

——. *Corpus Reformatorum [CR]. Ioannis Calvini Opera quae supersunt omnia*. 59 vols. Ed. G. Baum, E. Cunitz, and E. Reuss. Brunswick and Berlin, 1863-1900.

—. *Institutio Religionis Christianiae.* Latin editions of 1536, 1557, and 1561. In *CR*, vols. 1 and 2. (Translations follow in chronological order.)

Institution de la Religion chrétienne. French edition of 1546. 4 vols. Ed. Jacques Pannier. Paris: Les Belles-Lettres, 1946.

Institution de la Religion Chrestienne. Calvin's French translation from the Latin, 1554. In *CR*, vol. 2.

The Institution of Christian Religion. Translated from the Latin by T. Norton. London, 1562.

Institutes of the Christian Religion. Translated from the 1559 French edition by John Allen. 1813. 2 vols. Philadelphia: Presbyterian Board of Publication, 1930.

"On Civil Government." Bk. 4, chap. 20, of *Institutio Religionis Christianiae.* Trans. Harro Höpfl. In *Luther and Calvin on Secular Authority*, ed. Höpfl. Cambridge: Cambridge University Press, 1991.

—. *Le Livre des Pseaumes. Commentaire sur les Pseaumes.* 1558. In *CR*, vol. 13.

—. *Petit Traicté de la saincte Cène de Nostre Seigneur Jesus Christ.* 1541. In *CR*, vol. 5. Translated into English under the title *A Treatise concerning the most sacred Sacrament of the Body and Blood of our Savior Christ* (London, 1549).

—. Preface to *Somme de théologie.* In the second edition of the French translation of Melanchthon's *Loci communes theologici*, 1551. In *CR*, vol. 9.

—. *Pro Farello adversus Petri Caroli Calumnias.* 1545. In *CR*, vol. 7.

—. *Traité des reliques (Advertissement tres utile du grand profit qui reviendroit à la chrestienté, s'il se faisoit inventoire de tous les corps saintz, et reliques, qui sont tant en Italie, qu'en France, Allemoigne, Hespaigne, et autre Royaumes et pays).* 1543. In *CR*, vol. 6. First translated into English in 1561 under the title *An Admonition showing the advantages which Christendom might Derive from An Inventory of Relics.* For a later translation see *Calvin's Tracts and Treatises*, vol. 1, trans. Henry Beveridge (1844; reprint, Grand Rapids, Mich.: William. B. Eerdmans, 1958).

The Cambridge History of the Bible. Vol. 3, *The West From the Reformation to the Present Day*. Ed. S. L. Greenslade. Cambridge: Cambridge University Press, 1963.

Cannac, Yves. *Le Juste pouvoir. Essai sur les deux chemins de la démocratie.* Paris: Pluriel, J. C. Lattès, 1983.

Cargill Thompson, W.D.J. *The Political Thought of Martin Luther.* Brighton: Harvester Press, 1984.

Carlen, Claudia, ed. *The Papal Encyclicals: 1740–1981.* Vol. 1, *1740–1878*, and Vol. 2, *1878–1903*. Raleigh, N.C.: The Pieran Press, 1981.

Cavalier, Jean. *Mémoires sur la Guerre des Camisards.* 1708. Translated into French from an English translation of the lost French original by Frank Puaux. Paris: Payot, 1973.

Cavallera, Ferdinand. "La doctrine d'Origène sur les rapports du christianisme et de la société civile." *Bulletin de littérature écclésiastique*, 1937.

Chamley, Paul. *Economie politique et philosophie chez Steuart et Hegel*. Paris: Dalloz, 1963.

Chastel, André. *The Sack of Rome, 1527*. Princeton: Princeton University Press, 1983.

Cicero. *De oratore*.

——. *De republica*.

——. *De divinatione*.

——. *De officiis*. See Melanchthon's preface to this text, *Praefatio in officia Ciceronis*.

Civil Society: Democratic Transformation in the Arab World. Cairo: Ibn Khaldun Center. Periodical.

Codurc, Philippe. *Traicté de l'obéissance des chrestiens envers leurs magistrats et princes souverains*. 1645. Includes a partial translation of Luther's *Secular Authority*.

Cohen, Jean L. *Class and Civil Society: The Limits of Marxian Critical Theory*. Amherst: University of Massachusetts Press, 1982.

Cohen, Jean L., and Andrew Arato. *Civil Society and Political Theory*. Cambridge: MIT Press, 1992.

Cohn, Norman. *The Pursuit of the Millennium: A History of Popular Religious and Social Movements in Europe from the Eleventh to the Sixteenth Century*. London: Secker & Warburg, 1957.

Colas, Dominique. "Les avatars de la société civile." *Libération*, July 16, 1988.

——. "Civil Society: From Utopia to Management, from Marxism to Anti-Marxism." *Nations, Identities, Cultures*, ed. V. Y. Mudimbe. Special issue of the *South Atlantic Quarterly* 94, no. 4 (Fall 1995): 1009-23.

——. "La Grammaire politique de l'Occident." Foreword to *Xénophon-Aristote: Constitutions de Sparte et d'Athènes et de Sparte*. Paris: Gallimard, 1996.

——. *Lénine et le léninisme*. Collection "Que sais-je?" 2391. Paris: Presses Universitaires de France, 1987.

——. "Lénine, la politique et l'hystérie." *Critique* 32, nos. 349-50 (June–July 1976): 684-702.

——. *Le léninisme. Philosophie et sociologie politiques du léninisme*. Paris: Presses Universitaires de France, 1982.

——. "Société civile." In *Cinquante idées qui ébranlent le monde. Dictionnaire de la glasnost*, ed. Marc Ferro and Youri Affanasiev, pp. 351-55. Paris: Payot, 1989.

——. *Textes constitutionnels soviétiques*. Collection "Que sais-je?" 2364. Paris: Presses Universitaires de France, 1986.

Colliot-Thélène, Catherine. "Les origines de la théorie du *Machstaat*." *Philosophie* 20 (Fall 1988).

Conway, Sir William Martin. *The Literary Remains of Albrecht Dürer*. Cambridge: Cambridge University Press, 1889.

Cooper, Thomas. *An Admonition to the People of England*. 1580.

Cranz, Frederick Edward. *A Bibliography of Aristotle Editions, 1501–1600*. 2d rev. ed. Baden-Baden: Koerner, 1984.

Cristin, Olivier. "Iconographie de l'iconoclasme. A propos de la mutilation du portail de la cathédrale de Bourges." *Actes de la Recherche en Sciences sociales* (Nov. 1988).

Dante Alighieri. *Monarchia*. 1328. Ed. Pier Giorgio Ricci. Verona: Arnoldo Mondadori, 1965.

David-Ménard, Monique. *La Folie dans la raison pure. Kant lecteur de Swedenborg*. Paris: Vrin, 1990.

Debray, Régis. *A demain De Gaulle*. Paris: Gallimard, 1990.

Derathé, Robert. *Jean-Jacques Rousseau et la science politique de son temps*. Paris: Vrin, 1950.

Derrida, Jacques. *Glas*. Paris: Galilée, 1974. Translated into English by John P. Leavey, Jr. and Richard Rand (Lincoln: University of Nebraska Press, 1990).

——. *Politiques de l'amitié*. Paris: Galilée, 1995.

Descombes, Vincent. "Pour elle un Français doit mourir." *Critique* 336 (1977).

Devailly, Guy, ed. *Le diocèse de Bourges*. Paris: Letouzey et Ané, 1973.

Deyon, Solange, and Alain Lottin. *Les Casseurs de l'été 1566. L'iconoclasme dans le Nord*. Lille and Westhoek: Presses Universitaires de Lille/Westhoek, 1986.

Dickey, Laurence. *Hegel, Religion, Economics, and the Politics of Spirit, 1770–1807*. Cambridge: Cambridge University Press, 1987.

Dictionnaire théologique portatif. Paris, 1756.

Diderot, Denis, and Jean Le Rond d'Alembert. *Encyclopédie, ou dictionnaire raisonné des sciences, des arts, et des métiers*. 1751-72. S.v. "Société" (vol. 15) and "Fanatisme" (vol. 6).

Doughty, Charles M. *Travels in Arabia Deserta*. 2 vols. 3d ed. with foreword by T. E. Lawrence. 1936. Reprint. New York: Dover Publications, 1979.

Duby, Georges. *The Three Orders: Feudal Society Imagined*. Trans. Arthur Goldhammer. Chicago: University of Chicago Press, 1980. Originally published as *Les Trois ordres ou l'imaginaire du féodalisme* (Paris: N. R. F., Gallimard, 1978).

Dumézil, Georges. *Archaic Roman Religion*. Trans. Ph. Krapp. Foreword by Mircea Eliade. Chicago: University of Chicago Press, 1970.

——. *The Destiny of the Warrior*. Trans. Alf Hiltebeitel. Chicago: University of Chicago Press, 1970.

——. *L'idéologie des trois fonctions dans les épopées des peuples indo-européens.* 5th ed. Paris: Gallimard, 1986.

Dupuy, Pierre. *Histoire du différend d'entre le pape Boniface VIII et Philippes le Bel, roy de France.* Paris, 1655.

Dürer, Albrecht. *Diary of His Journey to the Netherlands.* Greenwich, Conn.: New York Graphic Society, 1971.

——. *Unterweisung der Messung mit dem Zirckel und Richtscheyt in Linien ebnen und gantzen Corporem.* Nuremberg, 1525. Translated into Latin under the title *Albertus Durerus nurembergensis pictor huius aetatis celeberrimus versus ex Germanica lingua in Latinam* (Paris, 1535). Translated into English by Walter L. Strauss under the title *The Painters' Manual: A Manual of Measurement of Lines, Areas, and Solids by Means of Compass and Ruler* (New York: Abaris, 1977).

Durkheim, Emile. *"L'Allemagne au-dessus de tout." La mentalité germanique et la guerre.* Paris: Armand Colin, 1915. Translated into English by J. S. under the title *"Germany above All": German Mentality and War* (Paris: Armand Colin, 1915).

Eisenstadt, S., and S. Rokkan. *Building States and Nations.* 2 vols. Beverly Hills, Calif.: Sage Publications, 1973.

Elster, Jon. *Leibniz et la formation de l'esprit capitaliste.* Paris: Aubier, 1975.

Engels, Friedrich. "Afterword to *On Social Relations with Russia.*" 1894. In *Collected Works of Marx and Engels*, vol. 27.

——. "Introduction to the German edition of Marx's *The Civil War in France.*" 1891. In Marx and Lenin, *The Civil War in France: The Paris Commune.* New York: International Publishers, 1993.

——. *The Peasant War in Germany.* 1850. In *Collected Works of Marx and Engels*, vol. 10.

Enthusiastik Imposters no divinely inspired prophets. London, 1707.

Erard, Zoé, and Georges M. Zygier, eds. *La Pologne, une société en dissidence.* Paris: Maspero, 1978. Texts translated from Polish.

Erichson, Alfredus. *Bibliographica Calviniana.* 1900. Nieuwkoop: B. De Graaf, 1979.

Erikson, Erik H. *Young Man Luther.* New York: Norton, 1958.

Evans-Pritchard, E. E. *The Nuer.* Oxford: Clarendon Press, 1950.

Fauré, Christine, ed. *Les Déclarations des droits de l'homme de 1789.* Paris: Payot, 1988.

Febvre, Lucien. *Martin Luther, a Destiny.* Trans. Robert Tapley. London: J. M. Dent, 1930. Originally published as *Martin Luther, un destin* (Paris: Presses Universitaires de France, 1928).

Fenchel, Rheinhard, and Hans-Willi Weiss. "Staat, Partei, Gewerkschaft." *Links* (Nov. 1980).

Fénelon, François de Salignac de La Mothe. *The Archibishop of Cambray's dissertation on Pure Love with an Account of the Life and Writings of the Lady [Mme Guyon] for whose sake the Archibishop was banished from Court. And the grievous Persecutions she suffered in France for the Religion.* London: 1735.

——. *Explication des maximes des saints sur la vie intérieure.* 1697. In *Œuvres* 1: 999-1095. Translated into English under the title *The Maxims of the Saints explained, concerning the interior life* (1785).

——. *Œuvres.* Vol. 1. Ed. Jean Le Brun. Bibliothèque de la Pléiade. Paris: Gallimard, 1983.

——. *Réponse de Monseigneur l'archevêque de Cambrai à l'écrit de Monseigneur l'évêque de Meaux intitulé "Relation sur le quiétisme."* 1698.

Ferguson, Adam. *An Essay on the History of Civil Society.* 1773. Reprint of the 4th revised edition. Farnborough Hants, U.K.: Gregg International Publishers, 1969. Translated into German under the title *Versuch über die Geschichte der bürgerlichen Gesellschaft* (Leipzig, 1768). Translated into French under the title *Essai sur l'histoire de la société civile* (Paris, 1783).

Fichte, Johann Gottlieb. *Beitrag zur Berichtigung der Urteile des Publikums über die französische Revolution* (Considerations destined to rectify public judgment on the French Revolution). 1793.

Fish, Steven M. *Democracy from Scratch; Opposition and Regime in the New Russian Revolution.* Princeton: Princeton University Press, 1995.

Fléchier, Esprit. *Lettres choisies avec une relation des fanatiques du Vivarez, et des réflexions sur les différens caractères des hommes.* 1715.

Fliche, Augustin. *La Réforme grégorienne et la reconquête chrétienne (1057-1123).* Vol. 8 of *Histoire de l'Eglise depuis les origines jusqu'à nos jours.* Paris: Bloud et Gay, 1946.

Flodr, Miroslav. *Incunabula classicorum.* Amsterdam: A. M. Hakkert, 1973.

Foucault, Michel. *Surveiller et punir. Naissance de la prison.* Paris: Gallimard, 1975. Translated by Alan Sheridan under the title *Discipline and Punish: The Birth of the Prison* (New York: Vintage, 1995).

——. *Dits et écrits.* 4 vols. Paris: Gallimard, 1994.

——. "Entretien avec Michel Foucault." 1980. In *Dits et écrits*, 3: 41-95.

——. *Histoire de la folie à l'âge classique.* Paris: Plon, 1961.

——. "Médecins, juges et sorciers au XVIIe siècle." In *Médécins de France*, n. 200 (1st trimester 1969), pp. 121-28. Reprinted in *Dits et écrits*, 1: 753-66.

——. "Naissance de la biopolitique." 1979. In *Dits et écrits*, 3: 818-25.

——. "La Phobie d'Etat." *Libération*, Jun. 30-Jul. 1, 1984, p. 21. Excerpts from a lecture given Jan. 31, 1979.

——. "Un système fini face à une demande infinie." In *Dits et écrits*, 4: 367-83.

Fremantle, Anne, ed. *The Papal Encyclicals in Their Historical Context*. New York: G. P. Putnam, 1956.

Freud, Sigmund. "Draft H.–Paranoïa." 1895. In *The Standard Edition of the Complete Psychological Works of Sigmund Freud*, ed. James Strachey. Vol. 1, 1886–99. London: The Hogarth Press, 1966.

—. *Psychoanalytic Notes Upon an Autobiographical Account of a Case of Paranoia*. 1911. In *Three Case Histories*, ed. Philip Reiff. New York: Collier Books. 1972.

—. *Reflections upon War and Death*. 1915. In *Character and Culture*, ed. Philip Rieff, trans. E. Colburn Mayne. New York: Collier Books, 1963.

Friedrich, Carl J., ed. *Totalitarianism*. Cambridge: Harvard University Press, 1954.

Gardet, Louis. *La Cité musulmane. Vie sociale et politique*. 4th ed. Paris: Vrin, 1976 .

Garin, Eugenio. *Educazione umanistica in Italia*. 1949. Bari: Laterza, 1975.

—. *L'Umanesimo italiano*. 1947. Bari: Laterza, 1990.

Garreton, Manuel Antonio. *Reconstruir la politica: Transicion y consolidacion democratica in Chile*. Santiago: Editorial Andante, 1987.

Garrisson, Jeanne. *L'Edit de Nantes et sa révocation. L'histoire d'une intolérance*. Paris: Editions du Seuil, 1985.

Gaule, John. *Sapienta justificata*. 1657.

Gautier, Théophile. *Le Club des Hachichins*. Reprinted in Baudelaire, *Les Paradis artificiels*, ed. Claude Pichois (Paris: Gallimard, Folio, 1972).

Gazette de France (Théophraste Renaudot's) 15. 1671.

Geertz, Clifford, ed. *Old Societies and New States: The Quest for Modernity in Asia and Africa*. New York: Free Press of Glencoe, 1963.

Gellner, Ernest. *Conditions of Liberty: Civil Society and Its Rivals*. London: Allen Lane, Penguin Press, 1994.

—. "Islam and Marxism: Some Comparisons." *International Affairs* 67 (Jan. 1991): 1-6.

—. *Nations and Nationalism*. Ithaca: Cornell University Press, 1983.

—. *Saints of the Atlas*. Chicago: University of Chicago Press, 1969.

Genet, Jean Philippe, and Jean-Yves Tilliette, eds. *Droit et théologie dans la Science Politique de l'Etat moderne*. Rome: Bibliothèque de l'Ecole française de Rome, 1990.

The German Peasants' War: A History in Documents. Ed. and trans. Tom Scott and Bob Scribner. Atlantic Highlands, N.J.: Humanities Press International, 1991.

Giddens, Anthony. *The Nation-State and Violence*. Berkeley: University of California Press, 1987.

Giles of Rome (Aegidius Romae). *Aegidii Romani Opera Omnia*. Francesco del Punta and Gianfranco Fiorarenti, gen. eds. Vol. 1 (1987), vol. 2 (1988), vol. 3 (1993). Florence: Leo S. Olschki, 1987- .

—. *De ecclesiastica potestate*. 1301. Ed. R. Scholz. Weimar, 1929. Translated into English by Arthur P. Monahan under the title *On Ecclesiastical Power* (Lewiston, N.Y.: E. Mellen Press, 1990).

—. *De regimine principum*. 1278. Paris: Bibliothèque Nationale. Latin MS 16123. Part 2 of this work includes a commentary on Aristotle's *Politics*. (Last printed edition of the Latin original was in Rome, 1608; translations follow in chronological order.)

> *Li livres du Gouvernement des princes*. Trans. Henri de Gauchy, 1282. Ed. S. M. Moleanaer from the Kerr manuscript. New York: Macmillan, 1899. The only extant printed edition of a French translation.
>
> *Reggimento del Principe*. 1288. Paris: Bibliothèque Nationale. Italian MS 233.
>
> *Gouvernement des princes*. 1330. Trans. Guillaume de Bellesvoies. Paris: Bibliothèque de l'Arsenal. MS 2690.
>
> *Gouvernement des princes*. 1444. Paris: Bibliothèque de l'Arsenal. MS 5062.
>
> *Regiment del princeps*. Barcelona, 1480. In Catalan.
>
> *Regimiento de los principes*. Trans. Bernardo de Osma for the Infant Pedro, son of Don Alfonso, king of Castile, Toledo, and Léon. Séville, 1494.

—. *De renuntiatione papae*. Ed. John R. Eastman. Lewiston, N.Y.: E. Mellen Press, 1992.

Gilson, Etienne. *Les Métamorphoses de la Cité de Dieu*. Paris: Vrin; Louvain: Publications Universitaires, 1952.

Giner, Salvador. "Civil Society and Its Future." In *Civil Society: Theory, History, Comparison*, ed. John Hall. Cambridge: Polity Press, 1995.

Gombrich, Ernest H. *Aby Warburg: An Intellectual Biography*. London: The Warburg Institute, 1970.

Grabar, André. *L'Iconoclasme byzantin*. Paris: Flammarion, 1984.

Gramsci, Antonio. "Appunti et note sparse per un gruppo di saggi sulla storia degli intellettuali e della cultura in Italia." Notebook 12, 1932. In *Quaderui del carcere*, ed. Valentino Geratana, 3: 1511-51. Turin: Giulio Einaudi Editore, 1975. In English see "The Formation of the Intellectuals," in *Selections from the Prison Notebooks*, trans. Quentin Hoare and Geoffroy Nowell Smith (London: Lawrence & Wishart, 1971).

Grannou, André. "Institutions, appareils d'Etat et société civile." *Les Temps modernes* 19, no. 318 (Jan. 1973).

Greenblatt, Stephen J. "Murdering Peasants." In *Learning to Curse: Essays in Early Modern Culture*, pp. 99-130. London: Routledge, 1990.

Grégoire, Pierre [Petrus Gregorius Tholosano]. *De republica*. Pont-à-Mousson, 1596.

Gurvitch, Georges. *Traité de Sociologie*. 2 vols. Paris: Presses Universitaires de France, 1958.

Hall, John. A., ed. *Civil Society: Theory, History, Comparison*. Cambridge: Polity Press, 1995.

Haller, Karl Ludwig von. *Restauration der Staatswissenschaft oder Theorie des natürlich-geselligen Zustands der Chimäre des künstlichbürgerlichen entgegengesetzt*. Winterthur, 1816-25. Translated into French by Haller under the title *Restauration de la science politique ou Théorie de l'Etat social naturel et opposée à la fiction d'un état civil factice*, 3 vols. (Paris, 1824-1830).

Hammer, Josef von. *Die Geschichte der Assassinen aus morgenländischen Quellen*. Stuttgart and Tubingen, 1818. Translated into French by J. Hellert and P. A. de La Nourais under the title *Histoire de l'ordre des Assassins* (Paulin, 1833).

Hancock, Ralph C. *Calvin and the Foundations of Modern Politics*. Ithaca: Cornell University Press, 1989.

Hecquet, Philippe. *Le Naturalisme des convulsions dans les maladies de l'épidemie convulsionnaire*. 1733. In three parts, each paginated independently.

Hegel, G. W. F. *Elements of the Philosophy of Right*. 1820. Ed. Allen W. Wood. Trans. H. B. Nisbet. Cambridge: Cambridge University Press, 1991.

——. *Enzyklopädie der philosophischen Wissenschaften* (Encyclopedia of the philosophical sciences). 1817.

——. *Lectures on the History of Philosophy*. 3 vols. Trans. Elizabeth Haldane. London: Kegan Paul, Trench, Trübner, 1892-96.

——. *The Phenomenology of Mind*. Trans. J. B. Baillie. Rev. 2d ed. London: George Allen & Unwin; New York: Macmillan, 1931.

——. *The Philosophy of History*. Trans. J. Sibree. Intro. C. J. Friedrich. New York: Dover, 1956.

——. *La Société civile bourgeoise*. Compilation of excerpts from texts either by Hegel or his students. Edited and translated into French by J. P. Lefebvre. Paris: François Maspero, 1975.

——. *Vorlesungen über die Geschichte der Philosophie*. Ed. J. Hoffmeister. In *Hegels Sämtliche Werke*, vol. 15a. Leipzig, 1940.

Henry IV, Holy Roman Emperor (1050-1106). Encyclical letter of April 1076. In *Monumenta Germaniae Historica. Constitutiones et acta publica*, vol. 1, ed. L. Weiland. Hanover, 1893.

Hildebert du Mans (Hildebertus Marbodus). Letter 7. In *Patrologia Latina*, vol. 171.

Hill, Christopher. *The World Turned Upside Down*. London: Maurice Temple Smith, 1972.

Hissette, Roland. *Enquête sur les 219 articles condamnés à Paris le 7 mars 1277*. Louvain: Publication Universitaires; Paris: Vander-Oyez, 1977.

Histoire des ouvrages des savans. Oct., Nov., Dec. 1698. Rotterdam: Reinier Leers.

Hobbes, Thomas. *De cive*. 1642. Translated into French by S. Sorbière under the title *Elémens philosophiques du citoyen, traicté politique où les fondemens de la société civile sont descouverts* (Amsterdam, 1649; translation checked by Hobbes), and into English under the title *The Citizen* (1651).

——. *Leviathan*. 1651.

——. *Man and Citizen* (*De Homine* and *De Cive*). Ed. Bernard Gert. Indianapolis: Hackett, 1991.

Hotman, François. *Brutum Fulmen papae Sixti V*. 1586. Translated into French under the title *Protestation et défense pour le roy de Navarre Henri IV* (1587).

——. *Franco-Gallia*. 1573.

——. *P. Sixti V Fulmen Brutum in Henricum serenis*. 1603.

Hume, David. *Essays, Moral and Political*. 2 vols. Edinburgh, 1741-42.

Huntington, Samuel. *Political Order in a Changing Society*. New Haven: Yale University Press, 1968.

——. *The Soldier and the State: The Theory and Politics of Civil-Military Relations*. Cambridge: Harvard University Press, 1957.

Ingerflom, Claudio Sergio. *Le Citoyen impossible*. Paris: Payot, 1988.

Jacobi, Friedrich Heinrich. *Ueber die Lehre des Spinoza*. In *Briefen an den Herrn Moses Mendelssohn*. 1785.

Jameson, Fredric. *The Seeds of Time*. New York: Columbia University Press, 1994.

John Paul II. *Centesimus annus. Encyclical Letter of the Supreme Pontiff John Paul II on the hundredth anniversary of "Rerum novarum."* N.p.: Saint Paul Publications, 1991.

——. *Evangelum vitae*. 1995.

John XXIII. *Peace on Earth. On establishing universal peace in truth, justice, charity and liberty. Encyclical Letter*. London: London Catholic Truth Society, 1963.

Jourdain, Amable. *Recherches critiques sur l'âge et l'origine des traductions latines d'Aristote. Nouvelle édition revue et augmentée par Charles Jourdain*. Paris: Joubert, 1843.

Kant, Immanuel. *Anthropologie du point de vue pragmatique*. Trans. into French by Michel Foucault. Paris: Vrin, 1954.

——. *Anthropology from a Pragmatic Point of View*. 1798. Trans. Victor Lyle Dowdell. London: Southern Illinois University Press, 1978.

——. *Conjectures on the Beginning of Human History*. 1786.

——. *The Contest of Faculties*. 1798.

——. *Critique de la faculté de juger*. Trans. A. Philonenko. Paris: Vrin, 1965.

——. *The Critique of Judgement*. 1790. Trans. James Creed Meredith. 1928. Reprint. Oxford: Clarendon Press, 1991.

——. *The Critique of Pure Reason*. 1781. Trans. Max Müller. London: Macmillan, 1907.

——. *Dreams of a Spirit-Seer*. 1767.

——. *Idea for a Universal History with a Cosmopolitan Purpose*. 1784.

——. *Kants Gesammelte Schriften (Akademieausgabe)*. Berlin, 1910- .

——. *Kant: Political Writings*. Ed. Hans Reiss. Trans. H. B. Nisbet. Cambridge: Cambridge University Press, 1991.

——. *Metaphysics of Morals*. 1797. Trans. Mary Gregor. Cambridge: Cambridge University Press, 1991.

——. *Perpetual Peace: A Philosophical Sketch*. 1795.

——. *Theory and Practice. On the Common Saying: "This may be true in theory, but it does not apply in practice."* 1793.

——. *What Is Orientation in Thinking?* 1796.

Kantorowicz, Ernst Hartwig. *Frederick the Second, 1194-1250*. Trans. E. O. Lorimer. London: Constable, 1931; New York: Frederick Ungar, 1957.

Karady, Victor. "A l'Est la grande transformation." *Actes de la Recherche en sciences sociales* 85 (Nov. 1990): 2.

Karlstadt, Andreas. *De Coelibatu Monachatu et viduitate*. 1521

——. *Von abtuhung der Bilder*. Wittenberg, 1522.

Keane, John. "Despotism and Democracy." In *Civil Society and the State: New European Perspectives*, ed. John Keane, pp. 35-71. London: Verso, 1988.

Kedourie, Elie. *Hegel, Marx: Introductory Lectures*. London: Blackwell, 1995.

Kleist, Heinrich von. *Michael Kohlhaas*. 1810.

Klibansky, Raymond, Erwin Panofsky, and Fritz Saxl. *Saturn and Melancholy: Studies of Natural Philosophy, Religion and Art*. London: Thomas Nelson & Son, 1964.

Knox, R. A. *Enthusiasm: A Chapter in the History of Religion, with Special Reference to the Seventeenth and Eighteenth Centuries*. Oxford: Clarendon Press, 1950.

Kolakowski, Leszek. *Chrétiens sans Eglise. La conscience religieuse et le lien confessionnel au XVIIe siècle*. Trans. from Polish. Paris: Gallimard, 1969.

——. *Main Currents of Marxism*. 3 vols. Oxford: Oxford University Press, 1978.

——. "The Myth of Human Self-Identity: Unity of Civil and Political Society in Socialist Thought." In *The Socialist Idea: A Reappraisal*, ed. Stuart Hampshire and Leszek Kolakowski. London: Weindenfeld & Nicolson, 1974.

Kretzmann, Norman, Anthony Kenny, and Jan Pinborg, eds. *The Cambridge History of Later Medieval Philosophy*. Cambridge: Cambridge University Press, 1982.

Kumar, Krishan. "Civil Society." In *Twentieth-Century Social Thought*, ed. William Outhwaite, Tom Bottomore, Ernest Gellner, Robert Nisbet, and Alain Touraine, pp. 75-77. London: Blackwell, 1993.

La Bruyère, Jean de. *Dialogues posthumes sur le quiétisme*. Collection des Grands Ecrivains de France, vol. 2. Paris: Hachette, 1865.

Lacan, Jacques. "R. S. I." (Réel-Symbolique-Imaginaire), in *Ornicar?* 5 (Winter 1975-76): 17-66.

——. *Télévision*. Paris: Edition du Seuil, 1974.

Lacroix, Bernard. "Ordre politique et ordre social." In *Traité de science politique*, ed. M. Grawitz and Jean Leca, vol. 1, pp. 469-565. Paris: Presses Universitaires de France, 1985.

Lagarde, G. de, *La naissance de l'esprit laïque au déclin du Moyen Age*. 6 vols. Paris: Béatrice; Louvain: Neuwelaerts, 1958.

Lamennais, Félicité Robert de. *De la religion considérée dans ses rapports avec l'ordre politique et civil*. 1830.

Lamoignon de Bâville, Nicolas de. Letters. In *Histoire générale de Languedoc*, ed. Cl. Devic and J. Vaisette, vol. 14. Toulouse: Privat, 1936.

——. *Mémoires pour servir à l'histoire de Languedoc*. 1734.

Lancelot, Alain. Interview in *L'Express*, Oct. 21-27, 1988.

Landry, B. *L'idée de chrétienté chez les scolastiques du XIIIè siècle*. Paris: Alcan, 1929.

Lebey de Batilly, Denis. *Traicté de l'origine des anciens Assasins porte-couteaux, avec quelques exemples de leurs attentats et homicides ès personnes d'aucuns roys, princes et seigneurs de la chrestienté*. Lyon, 1603.

Le Bras, Gabriel. *Institutions ecclésiastiques de la Chrétienté médiévale*. 2 vols. Vol. 12 of *Histoire de l'Eglise depuis les origines jusqu'à nos jours*. Paris: Bloud et Gay, 1964-65.

Le Brun, Jacques. *La Spiritualité de Bossuet*. Paris: Klincksieck, 1972.

Lecler, Joseph. *Histoire de la tolérance au siècle de la Réforme*. 2 vols. Paris: Aubier, 1955.

Lefort, Claude. *L'invention démocratique. Les limites de la domination totalitaire*. Paris: Fayard, 1980.

Leibniz, Gottfried Wilhelm. *Allgemeiner politischer und historischer Briefwechsel*, vol. 4, 1684-1687. In *Sämtliche Schriften und Briefe I*. Berlin: Akademie-Verlag, 1950.

——. *Caesarinus Fürstenerius (De Suprematu Principium Germaniae)*. 1677.

——. *Confessio philosophi*. 1675. Ed. Yvon Belaval. Paris: Vrin, 1961.

—. *Discourse on Metaphysics*; *Correspondance with Arnauld*; *Monadology*. Trans. George Montgomery. 1902. Reprint. La Salle, Ill.: Open Court Publishing Company, 1989.

—. *Divisio Societatum*. In *Leibniz's Deutsche Schriften*, ed. G. E. Guhrauer, vol. 2. Berlin, 1838. Published in English translation in *Leibniz: Political Writings*.

—. *Essais de Théodicée. Sur la bonté de Dieu, la liberté de l'homme et l'origine du mal*. 1710. Ed. J. Jalabert. Paris: Aubier, 1962.

—. *Fragments philosophiques*. Vol. 4. Ed. Victor Cousin. 5th ed. Paris, 1866.

—. *Leibniz: Political Writings*. Ed. and trans. Patrick Riley. Cambridge: Cambridge University Press, 1989.

—. Letters to the Palatine Princess. In *Lettres de la Princesse Palatine* (appendix). Ed. Olivier Amiel. Paris: Mercure de France, 1985.

—. *Lettres de Leibniz à Arnauld*. Ed. Geneviève Lewis. Paris: Presses Universitaires de France, 1952.

—. *Mars Christianissimus*. 1683. In *Sämtliche Schriften und Briefe IV: Politische Schriften*, vol. 2. Berlin: Akademie Verlag, 1963. Originally written in French. The English translation can be found in *Leibniz: Political Writings*, pp. 121-45.

—. *New Essays on Human Understanding*. Published posthumously in 1795. Trans. Peter Remnant and Jonathan Bennett. Cambridge: Cambridge University Press, 1981. Originally written in French under the title *Nouveauz essais sur l'entendement humain*.

—. *Œuvres*. Ed. A. Foucher de Careil. 7 vols. Paris, 1859-75.

—. *Opera Omnia*. Ed. Louis Dutens. 6 vols. Geneva, 1768.

—. *Die philosophischen Schriften*. 7 vols. Ed. C. I. Gerhardt. Berlin, 1875-90.

—. "Sur Isaac Papin." In *Textes inédits*, 2: 577-79.

—. *Textes inédits*. 2 vols. Ed. Gaston Grua. Paris: Presses Universitaires de France, 1948.

—. *La tolérance des religions. Lettres de M. Leibniz et réponses de M. Pélissier*. Paris, 1692.

—. "Trois dialogues mystiques inédits." In Jean Baruzi, *Revue de Métaphysique et de Morale* (Jan. 1905).

Lenin, Vladimir Illich. *Can The Bolsheviks Retain State Power?* In *Collected Works* [*CW*], vol. 26.

—. *Collected Works* [*CW*]. 47 vols. Moscow: Foreign Languages Publishing House, 1960-63, and Progress Publishers, 1964-80.

—. *Declaration of Rights of the Working and Exploited People*. In *CW*, vol. 26.

—. *How to Organize Competition*. In *CW*, vol. 26.

——. *Polnoe sobranie sochinenii.* 55 vols. Moscow: Marxist-Leninist Institute, 1958–65.

——. *The State and Revolution: The Marxists' Theory of the State and the Tasks of the Proletariat in the Revolution.* In *CW,* vol. 25.

——. Summary of Marx's *Holy Family.* In *Polnoe sobranie sochinenii,* vol. 29.

Leo XIII. *Allocutiones, epistolae, constitutiones,* vol. 7 (1897–1900). Bruges: Desclée de Brouwer, 1906.

——. *Au milieu des consolations.* Sept. 23, 1900. Letter to the Cardinal Archbishop of Paris.

——. Encyclicals in *The Papal Encyclicals,* ed. Claudia Carlen, vol. 2.

Diuturnum. 1881. On the origin of civil power.

Humanum genus. 1884. On the sect of Freemasons.

Immortale Dei. 1885.

Libertas praestantissimum. 1888.

Rerum novarum. 1891.

Tametsi futura prospicientibus. 1900. On Jesus Christ the Redeemer.

——. *Lettre à M. le Président de la République française pour revendiquer les droits des catholiques.* May 12, 1883.

Le Roy Ladurie, Emmanuel. *Les Paysans du Languedoc.* The Hague: Mouton, 1966. Translated into English by John Day under the title *The Peasants of Languedoc* (Urbana, Ill.: Urbana University Press, 1974).

Le Roy, Loys [Regius]. *Considérations sur l'histoire françoise et l'universelle de ce temps.* 1567.

——. *De l'Origine, antiquité, progrès, excellence, et utilité de l'art politique.* 1567.

——. *Des Troubles et différents advenans entre les hommes par la diversité des religions.* 1567.

——. *Exhortation aux François.* 1570.

——. *Traité d'Aristote touchant les changemens, ruines, et conservations des estats publics.* 1570. Translation into French of book 5 of Aristotle's *Politics.*

Lévi-Strauss, Claude. "Introduction à l'œuvre de Marcel Mauss." In *Marcel Mauss. Sociologie et anthropologie,* 3d ed. Paris: Presses Universitaires de France, 1966. Translated into English by Felicity Baker and published separately under the title *Introduction to the Work of Marcel Mauss* (London: Routledge & Kegan Paul, 1987).

Lewis, Bernard. *The Assassins: A Radical Sect in Islam.* New York: Basic Books, 1968.

——. "State and Society Under Islam." *Wilson Quarterly* 13, no. 4 (Fall 1989): 39–53.

Lochak, Danièle. "La société civile: du concept au gadget." In *La Société civile.* Paris: Presses Universitaires de France, 1986. Papers from a 1986 colloquium on civil society.

Locke, John. *An Essay Concerning Human Understanding*. 1689. Ed. A. D. Woozley. New York: New American Library, 1974.

—. *An Essay Concerning Toleration*. 1667. In *John Locke, Scritti Editi e Inediti Sulla Toleranza*, ed. Carlo Augusto Viano. Turin: Taylor, 1961.

—. *A Letter Concerning Toleration*. 1689. Ed. James H. Tully. Indianapolis: Hackett, 1983.

—. *Two Treatises on Government*. 1689. London: Dent, Everyman's Library, 1924.

Loraux, Nicole. *The Children of Athena: Athenian Ideas about Citizenship and the Division Between the Sexes*. Trans. Caroline Levine. Princeton: Princeton University Press, 1993. Originally published as *Les Enfants d'Athéna. Idées athéniennes sur la citoyenneté et la division des sexes* (Paris: Maspero, 1981).

Louvreleuil, Jean-Baptiste. *Le fanatisme renouvelé*. 4 vols. Avignon, 1704-6.

Lovy, René-Jacques. *Luther*. Paris: Presses Universitaires de France, 1964.

Lukes, Steven. *Durkheim, His Life and Work*. Stanford: Stanford University Press, 1985.

Lustiger, Jean-Marie, cardinal and archbishop of Paris. Interview in *Le Monde*, Oct. 5, 1988.

Luther, Martin. *Admonition to Peace, A Reply to the Twelve Articles of the Peasants in Swabia*. 1522. In *Luther's Works* [*LW*], vol. 46.

—. *Against the Robbing and Murdering Hordes of Peasants*. 1525. In *LW*, vol. 46.

—. *The Bondage of the Will* (*De servo arbitrio*). 1526. In *LW*, vol. 33.

—. *Confession Concerning Christ's Supper*. 1528. In *LW*, vol. 37.

—. *D. Martin Luthers Werke. Weimarer Ausgabe* [*WA*]. Weimar: H. Böhlau, 1883- .

—. *A Sermon on Keeping Children in School*. 1530. In *LW*, vol. 46.

—. *Eight Sermons at Wittenberg*. 1522. In *LW*, vol. 51. The Invocavit sermons.

—. *The Freedom of a Christian*. 1520. In *LW*, vol. 31.

—. *Letter to the Christians at Strassburg in Opposition to the Fanatic Spirit*. 1524. In *LW*, vol. 40.

—. *Letter to the Princes of Saxony Concerning the Rebellious Spirit*. 1524. In *LW*, vol. 40.

—. *Letters*. In *LW*, vols. 48 (1507-March 1522) and 49 (April 1522-1530).

—. *Luther at the Diet of Worms*. 1521. In *LW*, vol. 32.

—. *Luther's Works* [*LW*]. 55 vols. Ed. Jaroslav Pelikan (vols. 1-30) and Helmut T. Lehmann (vols. 31-55). Philadelphia: Muhlenberg Press. 1955- .

—. *Martin Luther. Studienausgabe*. Vol. 2. Ed. Hans-Ulrich Delius. Berlin: Evangelische Verlagsanstalt, 1982.

—. *Of the Jews and Their Lies*. 1543. In *LW*, vol. 47.

——. *On Secular Authority: How Far Does the Obedience Owed to It Extend?* Trans. Harro Höpfl. In *Luther and Calvin on Secular Authority*, ed. Höpfl. Cambridge: Cambridge University Press, 1991.

——. *An Open Letter on the Harsh Book Against the Peasants.* 1525. In *LW*, vol. 46.

——. *The Sacrament of the Body and Blood of Christ. Against the Fanatics.* 1526. In *LW*, vol. 36.

——. *A Sincere Admonition to All Christians to Guard Against Insurrection or Rebellion.* 1522. In *LW*, vol. 45.

——. *Temporal Authority, to What Extent It Should Be Obeyed.* 1523. In *LW*, vol. 45.

——. *That these words of Christ, "This is my body," etc. still stand firm against the Fanatics.* 1527. In *LW*, vol. 37.

——. *Tractatus de libertate christiana* (Freedom of a Christian). 1520. In *Studienausgabe*, vol. 2.

——. *Von Abendmahl Christi, Bekenntnis.* 1528. In *WA*, vol. 26.

——. *Whether One May Flee from a Deadly Plague.* 1527. In *LW*, vol. 43.

Lyotard, Jean-François. *La Condition postmoderne.* Paris: Editions de Minuit, 1989.

——. *L'Enthousiasme. La Critique kantienne de l'histoire.* Paris: Galilée, 1986.

——. *Instructions païennes.* Paris: Editions Galilée, 1977. Translated under the title "Lessons in Paganism," in *The Lyotard Reader*, ed. Andrew Benjamin (Oxford: Blackwell, 1989).

Maimbourg, Louis. *Histoire du calvinisme.* 1686.

——. *Histoire du luthéranisme.* 1686.

Malia, Martin. *The Soviet Tragedy: A History of Socialism in Russia, 1917–1991.* New York: Free Press, 1994.

Mandeville, Bernard de. *The Fable of the Bees, or Private vices, publick benefits.* London, 1714.

——. [Another edition.] *The Fable of the Bees, or Private vices, publick benefits. Containing several discourses, that demonstrate that human frailties may be turned to the advantage of the Civil Society.* London, 1714. Translated into French under the title *La fable des abeilles où les fripons devenus honnêtes gens, avec les commentaires où l'on prouve que les vices des particuliers tendent à l'avantage du public* (Paris: 1740).

Manen, Henri, and Philippe Joutard. *Une foi enracinée, la Pervenche: La résistance exemplaire d'une paroisse protestante ardéchoise (1685–1820).* Valence: Presses des Imprimeries Réunies, 1972.

Mariana, Juan de. *De rege et regis institutione.* 1599.

Marrou, Henri-Irénée. *Saint Augustine and His Influence Through the Ages.* Trans. P. Hepburne-Scott. New York: Harper Torch Books, 1957. Originally published as *Saint Augustin et l'Augustinisme* (Paris: Editions du Seuil, 1955).

Marx, Karl. "Bastiat und Carey." 1851. In *Ökonomische Manuskripte, 1857–58*, vol. 1 of *"Das Kapital" und Vorarbeiten*, which is pt. 1 of *Marx Engels Gesamtausgabe* (Berlin: Marx Engels Verlag, 1975–).

—. *Capital*. Vol. 1. Trans. Ben Fowkes. London: Penguin Books, 1990.

—. *Le Capital, critique de l'économie politique*. 8 vols. Paris: Editions sociales, 1950.

—. *The Civil War in France*. 1871. For the first version of the original, *Der Bürgerkrieg in Frankreich*, see *Marx Engels Werke*, vol. 17.

—. *Contribution to the Critique of Hegel's "Philosophy of Law."* 1843. In *Collected Works* [*CW*], vol. 3. Unpublished in Marx's lifetime.

—. *A Contribution to the Critique of Political Economy*. 1859. The translation in *Marx-Engels Reader* is not complete.

—. *Critique of the Gotha Program*. 1875.

—. *Drafts of the Letter to Vera Zasulich*. Feb.-Mar. 1881. In *CW*, vol. 24. The original texts, in French, are in *Œuvres* 2: 1557-73.

—. *Eighteenth Brumaire of Louis Bonaparte*. 1852. The translation in *Marx-Engels Reader* is not complete.

—. *General Introduction to the Critique of Political Economy*. 1857.

—. *Karl Marx: Early Writings*. Trans. Rodney Livingstone and Gregor Benton. New York: Vintage, 1975.

—. *Letter to Vera Zasulich*. March 8, 1881. In *CW*, vol. 46.

—. *Marx: Early Political Writings*. Ed. and trans. Joseph O'Malley. Cambridge University Press, 1994.

—. *Misère de la Philosophie*. 1847. In *Œuvres*, vol. 1. The French original.

—. *Notes on Bakunin's Book "Statehood and Anarchy."* In *CW*, vol. 24.

—. *Œuvres*. 3 vols. Ed. Maximilien Rubel. Bibliothèque de La Pléiade. Paris: Gallimard, 1963, 1968, 1982.

—. *On the Jewish Question*. 1843. In *CW*, vol. 3. Complete in *Marx-Engels Reader*.

—. "Theses on Feuerbach." Both Marx's original and Engels's version are in *Marx Engels Werke*, vol. 3 (Marx, pp. 5-7; Engels, pp. 533-35). For the English translation see *The Marx-Engels Reader*, pp. 107-9.

—. *Zur Kritik der Hegelschen Rechtsphilosophie, Einleitung*. 1843. In *Marx Engels Werke*, vol. 1. Translated in *The Marx-Engels Reader* under the title *Contribution to the Critique of Hegel's "Philosophy of Right": Introduction*.

Marx, Karl, and Friedrich Engels. *Collected Works* [*CW*]. Ed. M. Dobbs, E. J. Hobsbawm, J. S. Allen, D. F. Stuik, et al. London: Lawrence & Wishart, 1975-94.

—. *Die deutsche Ideologie*. 1845-46. In *Marx Engels Gesamtausgabe* [*MEGA*], vol. 5.

—. *The German Ideology. Part I*. Trans. S. Ryazanskaya. In *Marx-Engels Reader*.

——. *The Holy Family: A Critique of Critical Criticism.* 1845.

——. *L'Idéologie allemande, première partie, Feuerbach.* French trans. R. Cartelle. Paris: Editions sociales, 1953.

——. *L'Idéologie allemande, première partie, Feuerbach.* French trans. R. Cartelle and G. Badia. Paris: Editions sociales, 1966.

——. *L'Idéologie allemande.* Presented and annotated by G. Badia. Translated into French by H. Auger, G. Badia, J. Baudrillard, and R. Cartelle. Paris: Editions sociales, 1968.

——. *Manifest der Kommunistischen Partei.* 1848. In *MEGA*, vol. 6.

——. *Marx Engels Gesamtausgabe [MEGA].* 12 vols. Frankfurt-am-Main, Berlin, and Moscow: Marx-Engels Verlag, Marx-Engels Institute, 1927-35.

——. *The Marx-Engels Reader.* Ed. Robert C. Tucker. New York: Norton, 1972.

——. *Marx Engels Werke.* 41 vols. Berlin: Dietz Verlag, 1956-68.

Massignon, Louis. *La Passion d'al-Hallaj.* Paris: Geuthner, 1922.

Maultrot, G.-N., and C. Mey. *Apologie de tous les jugemens rendus par les tribunaux séculiers en France contre le schisme.* Vol. 1. N.p., 1752.

Mauss, Marcel. *La Nation et l'internationalisme.* In *Œuvres*, vol. 3. Paris: Editions de Minuit, 1969.

Maxwell, A.B.P. *Sacro-sancta regnum, or the Sacred and Royal Prerogative of Christian Kings.* 1644.

Meinsma, Kœnraad Œge. *Spinoza et son cercle.* Translated from Dutch to French by S. Roosenburg. Paris: Vrin, 1983.

Melanchthon, Philipp. *Adversus anabaptistas iudicium.* 1528. In *Corpus Reformatorum [CR]*, vol. 16.

——. *Commentarii in aliquot Politicos libros Aristotelis Philippi Melanchthoni.* 1529. In *CR*, vol. 16.

——. *Contra anabaptismus.* 1536.

——. *Corpus Reformatorum [CR].* Philippi Melanchthonis Opera quae supersunt omnia [*CR*]. 28 vols. Ed. C. G. Bretschneider and H. E. Bindseil. Halle and Brunswick, 1834-60.

——. *De Philosophie oratio.* 1536.

——. *Ethicae doctrinae elementarum libri duo.* 1550.

——. *Glaube und Bildung. Texte zum christlichen Humanismus.* Stuttgart: Philipp Reclam, 1988. In Latin and German.

——. *In Ethica Aristotelis commentarius.* Paris, 1529.

——. *Loci communes rerum theologicarum seu hypotyposes theologicae.* 1521.

——. *Loci communes theologici, jam postremo recogniti et aucti.* Basel, 1545.

——. *Loci praecipui theologici.* 1559.

——. *Melanchthon on Christian Doctrine.* Translated from the 1555 German version of *Loci communes* and edited by L. Manschreck. New York: Oxford University Press, 1965.

—. *A Melanchthon Reader*. Translated from the German by Ralph Keen. New York: Peter Lang, 1988.

—. *Philosophia Moralis Epitomes*. 1538. In *CR*, vol. 16.

—. *Praefatio in officia Ciceronis*. 1530.

—. *La Somme de théologie*. 1546. Translation of *Loci communes theologici* (Basel, 1545).

—. *La Somme de théologie ou lieux communs reveuz et augmentez de nouveau*. Translation of *Loci communes theologici* (Basel, 1545). Preface by Calvin. Geneva, 1551.

—. *Werke*. 6 vols. Gütersloh: C. Bertelsmann Verlag, 1951–56.

Melber von Gerolzhoffen, John. *Vocabularius predicantium*. Strasbourg, 1486. Latin-German dictionary.

Mémoires pour servir à la vie de Nicolas de Catinat, Maréchal de France. Paris, 1775.

Merle, Marcel. "Sociologie comparée du pouvoir dans l'Eglise et dans la société civile." In *Revue de droit canonique* 23 (Mar.-Dec. 1973).

Michelet, Jules. *Histoire de France. Le Moyen Age*. 1870. Paris: Robert Laffont, Bouquins, 1981.

—. *Histoire de France. Renaissance et Réforme*. 1855. Paris: Robert Laffont, Bouquins, 1982.

Miliband, Ralph. *Marxism and Politics*. Oxford: Oxford University Press, 1979.

Miller, Robert F. *The Developments of Civil Society in Communist Systems*. North Sydney: Allen & Unwin, 1992.

Minc, Alain. Interview in *L'Express*, Apr. 14, 1989.

Molinos, Miguel de. *Guia espiritual que desembaraza al alma y la conduce por el camino interior para alcanzar la perfecta contemplacion y el rico tesoro de la paz interior*. Rome, 1675.

Molnar, Miklos. *La démocratie se lève à l'Est. Société civile et communisme en Europe de l'Est: Pologne et Hongrie*. Paris: Presses Universitaires de France, 1990.

Montaigne, Michel de. *The Complete Essays*. Trans. M. A. Screech. London: Penguin Books, 1991.

—. *Essais*. 1580. Ed. Albert Thibaudet. Bibliothèque de la Pléiade. Paris: Gallimard. 1950.

Montesquieu, Charles de Secondat, baron de la Brède et de. *L'Esprit des lois*. In *Œuvres complètes*, vol. 2. Bibliothèque de la Plèiade. Paris: Gallimard, 1951.

Moore, W. G. *La Réforme allemande et la littérature française: Recherche sur la notoriété de Luther en France*. Strasbourg: Faculté des Lettres de l'Université de Strasbourg, 1932.

Moreau, Pierre-François. "La notion d'*imperium* dans le *Traité Politique.*" In *Proceedings of the First Italian International Congress on Spinoza*, ed. Emilia Giancotti. Naples: Bibliopolis, 1985.

Moreau de Tours, J. *Du Hachisch.* 1845. Ed. Dr. Claude Olievenstein. Geneva: Slatkine Reprints, 1980.

Müntzer, Thomas. *Sermon Before the Princes.* July 13, 1524. In *Spiritual and Anabaptist Writers*, ed. G. H. Williams and A. G. Merga. Philadelphia: Westminster Press, 1957.

Naert, Emillienne. *Leibniz et la querelle du pur amour.* Paris: Vrin, 1959.

La Nécessité de donner un prompt et puissant secours aux protestants des Cévennes. London, 1703.

Neiderman, Cary, and Kate Forhan, eds. *Medieval Political Theory, A Reader: The Quest for the Body Politic, 1100–1400.* London: Routledge, 1993.

New Catholic Encyclopedia. 15 vols. New York: McGraw-Hill, 1967.

Nietzsche, Friedrich. *Human, All Too Human: A Book for Free Spirits.* 1888. Trans. R. J. Hollingdale. Cambridge: Cambridge University Press, 1986.

——. *Thus Spoke Zarathustra.* 1883–92. Trans. R. J. Hollingdale. London: Penguin Books, 1969.

Niqueux, Michel, ed. *Vocabulaire de la perestroïka.* Paris: Editions Universitaires, 1990.

Oberman, Heiko A. *Luther: Man Between God and the Devil.* Trans. Eileen Walliser-Schwarzbart. New Haven: Yale University Press, 1989.

Pacaut, Marcel. *La théocratie. L'Eglise et le pouvoir au Moyen Age.* Paris: Desclée de Brouwer, 1989.

Panofsky, Erwin. *The Life and Art of Albrecht Dürer.* 2 vols. Princeton: Princeton University Press, 1943.

Patrologia Latina (Patrologiae cursus completus—series latina). 223 vols. Ed. Abbé Jacques-Paul Migne. Paris, 1844–64.

Pelczynski, Z. A. "Solidarity and the 'Rebirth of Civil Society' in Poland, 1976–81." In *Civil Society and the State: New European Perspectives*, ed. John Keane. London: Verso, 1988.

——, ed. *The State and Civil Society: Studies in Hegel's Political Philosophy.* Cambridge: Cambridge University Press, 1984.

Penn, William. *An Account of W. Penns Traevels in Holland and Germany Anno MDCLXXVII for the Service of the Gospel of Christ.* 1677.

——. *The Christian Quaker and his divine testimony vindicated by Scripture, reason, and authorities, against the injurious attempts lately made to render him odiously inconsistent with Christianity and Civil Society. In two parts. The first by William Penn. The second by G. Whitehead.* London, 1674.

Pepys, Samuel. *Diary.* 1659–69. Ed. John Warrington. 3 vols. New York: Dutton, 1966.

Peter of Auvergne. See Thomas Aquinas.

Pius IX. *Quanta cura. Encyclical of Pope Pius IX condemning current errors.* Dec. 8, 1864. In *The Papal Encyclicals*, ed. Claudia Carlen, vol. 1.

——. *The Syllabus of the principal errors of our time which are censured in the Consistorial Allocutions, Encyclical and other Apostolic Letters of our most Holy Lord, Pope Pius IX.* 1864. (See Ann Fremantle, ed., *The Papal Encyclicals in Their Historical Context.*)

Plato. *The Statesman.* Trans. G. P. Skemp. London: Routledge & Kegan Paul, 1952.

Pocock, J.G.A. *The Machiavellian Moment: Florentine Political Thought and the Atlantic Republican Tradition.* Princeton: Princeton University Press, 1975.

Poliakov, Léon. *History of Anti-Semitism.* Trans. Richard Howard. New York: Schocken Books, 1974.

Pollock, Frederick. *Spinoza, His Life and Philosophy.* London: Duckworth, 1912.

Potter, George Richard. *Zwingli.* Cambridge: Cambridge University Press, 1976.

Pufendorf, Samuel. *De jure naturae et gentium.* 1672

——. *De officio hominis et civilis juxta legem naturalem.* 1673. Translated into French by Jean Barbeyrac under the title *Les devoirs de l'homme et du citoyen, tels qu'ils sont prescrits pas la Loi Naturelle.* (The fourth edition [1707] contains the "Judgement by Leibniz.") Translated into English under the title *The Whole Duty of Man according to the Law of Nature* (1735).

——. *On the Nature and Qualification of Religion, in Reference to Civil Society.* 1698.

Quelquejeu, Bernard. "K. Marx a-t-il constitué une théorie du pouvoir d'Etat?" In three parts in *Revue des sciences philosophiques et théologiques*, vols. 1–3. Paris: Vrin, 1979.

Rabelais, François. *Le Cinquiesme et dernier livre des faicts et dicts héroïques du bon Pantagruel.* 1562.

——. *Gargantua and Pantagruel. The Five Books.* Trans. Jacques LeClercq. New York: Heritage Press, 1936.

——. *Œuvres complètes.* Ed. Jacques Boulenger. Bibliothèque de la Pléiade. Paris: Gallimard, 1955.

——. *Œuvres complètes.* Ed. Ch. Marty-Laveaux. Paris: Lemerre, 1873.

——. *Le Tiers livre des faicts et dicts héroïques du bon Pantagruel.* 1546.

Richer, Edmond. *Tractatus de Potestates summi pontificis in rebus temporalibus.* Rome, 1610.

——. *De ecclesiastica et politica potestate libellus.* 1611. Translated into English under the title *A treatise of Ecclesiastical and Politike power shewing the church is a Monarchicall governement, ordained to a supernaturall and spiritual end tempered withe an aristocratical order (which is the best of all and most confortable to nature) by the great pastor of souls Jesus Christ* (1612).

Riedel, Manfred. "Hegels 'bürgerliche Gesellshaft' und das Problem ihres geschichtlichen Ursprungs." *Archiv für Rechts und Sozialphilosophie* 48 (1962): 539-66.

Rittersporn, Gabor T. "L'Etat en lutte contre lui-même." *Libre* 4 (1978): 3-38.

Rivière, J. *Le problème de l'Eglise et de l'Etat au temps de Philippe le Bel.* Paris: Emile Champion, 1926.

Rodinson, Maxime. *Marxism and the Muslim World.* Trans. M. Pallis. London: Zed Press, 1979.

——. Preface to *Les Assassins. Terrorisme et politique dans l'Islam médiéval.* Brussels: Editions Complexe, 1984. French translation of Bernard Lewis, *The Assassins.*

Robin Hood and the Stranger. In *Robin Hood: a Collection of all Ancient Poems, Songs, and Ballads now Existent Relative to that Celebrated Outlaw,* ed. Joseph Ritson. 1795.

Rosanvallon, Pierre. *Le libéralisme économique. Histoire de l'idée de marché.* Paris: Editions du Seuil, 1989. First published in 1979 under the title *Le Capitalisme utopique.*

Rose, Guillaume. *De justa reipublicae christianae in reges impios authoritate, justissimaque catholicorum ad Henricum Navarreum et quemcunque haereticum a regno Galliae repellendum confederatione.* Paris, 1590.

Rousseau, Jean-Jacques. *The Basic Political Writings.* Trans. Donald A. Cress. Intro. Peter Gay. Indianapolis: Hackett, 1987. Includes *Discourse on the Origin of Inequality, Discourse on Political Economy,* and *On the Social Contract, or Principles of Political Right.*

——. *Discours sur l'Economie politique.* 1755.

——. *Discours sur l'origine et les fondements de l'inégalité entre les hommes.* 1754.

——. *Du Contrat social ou, principes du droit politique.* 1762

——. *Du Contrat social.* 1760. The Geneva Manuscript. In *Œuvres complètes,* 3: 281-346.

——. *Emile, ou de l'éducation.* 1762. Trans. M. Nugent under the title *Emilius, or an Essay on Education,* 2 vols. (1763).

——. *Fragments politiques.* 1762. In *Œuvres complètes,* 3: 473-560.

——. *Lettres écrites de la montagne.* 1764.

——. *Œuvres complètes.* 3 vols. Vol. 3. Ed. Robert Dérathé, François Bouchardy, Jean Starobinski, et al. Bibliothèque de la Pléiade. Paris: Gallimard, 1964.

Rupnik, Jacques. "Dissent in Poland, 1968-78: The End of Revisionism and the Rebirth of the Civil Society." In *Opposition in Eastern Europe*, ed. R. Tökes. London: Macmillan for St. Antony's College, Oxford, 1979.

Sainctes, Claude de. *Discours sur le saccagement des églises catholiques par les hérétiques anciens et nouveaux calvinistes*. Verdun, 1562.

Saint-Simon, Louis de Rouvroy, duc de. *Mémoires*. Ed. de Boislisle. Collection des Grands Ecrivains de France. Paris: Hachette, 1879-1930.

Salamé, Ghassan. "Raison du régime et raison d'Etat." *Libération*, Jan. 16, 1991.

Sartre, Jean-Paul. "Elections piège à cons." *Les Temps modernes* 29, no. 318 (Jan. 1973). Translated into English by Paul Auster and Lydia Davis under the title "Elections: A Trap for Fools," in *Sartre in the Seventies: Interviews and Essays* (London: André Deutsch, 1978).

Schmitt, Carl. *The Concept of the Political*. Trans. George Schwab. New Brunswick, N.J.: Rutgers University Press, 1976. Originally published as *Der Begriff des Politischen*, 2d ed. (Munich: Duncker & Humblot, 1932).

Schwartz, Hillel. *The French Prophets: The History of a Millenarian Group in Eighteenth-Century England*. Berkeley: University of California Press, 1980.

Scribner, Bob. *For the Sake of Simple Folk: Popular Propaganda for the German Reformation*. Cambridge: Cambridge University Press, 1981.

—. *Popular Culture and Popular Movements in Reformation Germany*. London: Hambledon Press, 1987.

Semper idem: Or a Parallel betwixt the Ancient and Modern Fanatiks. London, 1661.

Senellart, Michel. *Les arts de gouverner. Du regimen médiéval au concept de gouvernement*. Paris: Editions du Seuil, 1995.

Senko, Wladyslaw. *Repertorium commentariorum Medii Aevi in Aristotelem Lationorum quae in bibliothecis publicis Parisiis asservantur*. 2 vols. Warsaw: Akademia Theologii Katolickiej, 1982.

Shaftesbury, Anthony Ashley Cooper, earl of. *A Letter Concerning Enthusiasm to my Lord XXX*. 1708. In *Characteristics of Men, Manners, Opinions, Times, etc.*, ed. John M. Robertson. Indianapolis: Bobbs-Merrill, 1964.

Sharlet, Robert. *The Soviet Constitutional Crisis: From De-Stalinization to Disintegration*. Armonk, N.Y.: M. E. Sharpe, 1992.

Shils, Edward. *Center and Periphery: Essays in Macrosociology*. Chicago: University of Chicago Press, 1975.

—. *Political Development in the New States*. The Hague: Mouton, 1960.

Showstack Sasson, Anne. "Civil Society." In *A Dictionary of Marxist Thought*, ed. Tom Bottomore, pp. 72-74. London: Blackwell Reference, 1991.

Solzhenitsyn, Aleksander. Interviewed by David Aikman for *Time*, July 24, 1989, pp. 55-58.

Spinoza, Baruch. *The Correspondence of Spinoza.* Trans. and ed. A. Wolf. London: Frank Cass, 1966.

——. *Ethica.* 1677. Trans. and ed. Edwin Curley under the title *Ethics.* In *A Spinoza Reader: The Ethics and Other Works* (Princeton: Princeton University Press, 1994).

——. *Œuvres complètes.* French translations by or reviewed by Roland Caillois, Madeleine Francès, and Robert Misrahi. Bibliothèque de la Pléiade. Paris: Gallimard, 1954.

——. *Opera.* Ed. J. Van Vloten and J. P. Land. 4 vols. The Hague: Martin Nijhoff, 1914.

——. *Tractatus politicus.* 1677. Translated into English by R.H.M. Elwes under the title *Political Treatise.* In *Chief Works of Benedict de Spinoza,* 2 vols. (London: George Brill & Sons, 1883–84).

——. *Tractatus théologico-politicus.* 1670. Trans. Samuel Shirley under the title *Theological-Political Treatise* (Leiden: E. J. Brill, 1989).

de Staël, Germaine. *De l'Allemagne.* 1810.

Stalin, Joseph V. "Dizzy with Success: Concerning Questions of the Collective-farm Movement." 1930. In *Works,* vol. 12, pp. 197–205 (Moscow: Foreign Languages Publishing House, 1955).

Stouppe, Jean-Baptiste. *La Religion des Hollandais.* 1673.

Strauss, Leo. *Spinoza's Critique of Religion.* Trans. E. M. Sinclair. New York: Shocken Books, 1965.

Sue, Eugène. *Jean Cavalier ou les fanatiques des Cévennes.* 1840.

Swift, Jonathan. *A Discourse concerning the Mechanical Operation of the Spirit.* 1720.

——. *Gulliver's Travels.* 1726.

——. *A Voyage to Lilliput/Voyage à Lilliput.* Paris: Gallimard Folio, 1990. Bilingual edition of Book 1 of *Gulliver's Travels.*

——. *The Writings of Jonathan Swift.* Ed. Robert A. Greenberg and William B. Piper. New York: Norton, 1973.

Taylor, Charles. *Philosophical Arguments.* Cambridge: Harvard University Press, 1995.

Le Théâtre sacré des Cévennes, ou Récit de Diverses merveilles nouvellement opérées dans cette partie de la Province des Cévennes. Ed. Maximilien Misson. London, 1707. Reprint. Brignon: Les Presses du Languedoc, 1978.

Thomas Aquinas. *In decem libros Ethicorum Arisotelis expositio.* 1269. Ed. Raymundi Spiazzi. Rome: Marietti, 1964.

——. *In octo libros Politicorum Aristotelis expositio.* 1269–72. Ed. Raymundi Spiazzi. Rome: Marietti, 1966. Commentary on books 1–3 of Aristotle's *Politics*; the commentary on books 4–8 (1274–90) is by Peter of Auvergne.

——. *Summa Theologiae.* 1259–74.

Thomas Müntzer: Historische-biographische Austellung des Museums für Deutsche Geschichte. East Berlin: Museum für Deutsche Geschichte, 1989.

Tobon, William Ramirez. *Estado, violencia y democracia: ensayos.* Bogota: Tercer Mundo, 1990.

Tocqueville, Alexandre de. *De la démocratie en Amérique.* 1835.

Trotsky, Leon. *Stalin: An Appraisal of the Man and His Influence.* 1941. 2 vols. Trans. and ed. Charles Malamuth. London: Panther, 1969.

Vauban, Sébastien le Prestre de. *Projet d'une dixme royale.* 1707. Ed. Jean-François Pernot. Saint-Léger-Vauban: Association des amis de la Maison Vauban, 1988.

Vindiciae contra Tyrannos. Edinburgh, 1579. Attributed to Théodore de Bèze; probably written by Philippe de Mornay. Translated into French under the title *De la Puissance légitime du prince sur le peuple et du peuple sur le prince* (1581). Reprint of translation. Geneva: Droz, 1979.

Voltaire [François Arouet]. *Dictionnaire philosophique.* 1764-74. Trans. William Fleming under the title *A Philosophical Dictionary.* In vol. 5, pt. 1, of *The Works of Voltaire. A Comtemporary Version*, 22 vols. (New York: Dingwall Rock, 1927).

——. "Du Protestantisme de la guerre des Cévennes." In the annex to *Essai sur les mœurs et l'esprit des nations.* 1763. Ed. René Pomeau. 2 vols. Paris: Garnier, 1953.

——. *The History of the Misfortunes of John Calas, a victim to fanaticism.* London. 1775.

——. *Mahomet ou le fanatisme.* 1742. Translated into English by Robert L. Myers under the title *Mahomet the Prophet, or Fanaticism* (New York: Frederick Ungar, 1964).

——. *Le siécle de Louis XIV.* 1751. Translated into English under the title *The Age of Lewis XIV*, 2 vols. (London, 1752).

——. *Traité sur la tolérance.* 1762.

Waetzoldt, Wilhelm. *Dürer and His Time.* Trans. R. H. Boothroyd. London: Phaidon Press, 1950.

Warburg, Aby. "Dürer und die Italienische Antike." 1905. In *Gesammelte Schriften*, vol. 2. Leipzig and Berlin, 1932.

——. "Heidnischantike Weissagung in Wort und Bild zu Luthers Zeiten." 1919. In *Gesammelte Schriften*, vol. 2. Leipzig and Berlin, 1932.

Weber, Max. *Economy and Society.* Ed. G. Ross and Claus Wittich. Berkeley: University of California Press, 1978.

——. *Politik als Beruf.* 1919. Berlin: Duncker & Humblot, 1991. Translated into English under the title *The Profession and Vocation of Politics.* In *Weber: Political Writings*, ed. Peter Lassman and Ronald Speirs (Cambridge: Cambridge University Press, 1994).

——. *The Protestant Ethic and the Spirit of Capitalism.* Intro. Anthony Giddens. Trans. Talcott Parsons. Gloucester, Mass.: Peter Smith, 1988.

Wesley, John. *The Journal of the Reverend John Wesley.* 8 vols. Vol. 2, ed. Nehemiah Curnock. London: Robert Culley, 1909.

William of Tyre, Archbishop. *Historia rerum in partibus transmarinis gestarum.* 1169–84. In *Patrologia Latina*, vol. 201.

Wirth, Jean. "La Réforme luthérienne et l'art." In *Luther, Mythe et réalité*, ed. Michèle Mat and Jacques Max. Brussels: Editions de l'Université de Bruxelles, 1984.

——. *Luther. Etudes d'histoire religieuse.* Geneva: Droz, 1981.

Wittkower, Rudolf, and Margot Wittkower. *Born Under Saturn. Character and Conduct of Artists: A Documented History from Antiquity to the French Revolution.* London: Weidenfeld & Nicolson, 1963.

Yates, Frances Amelia. *Occult Philosophy in the Elizabethan Age.* London: Routledge & Kegan Paul, 1979.

Zac, Sylvain. *Spinoza en Allemagne: Mendelssohn, Lessing et Jacobi.* Paris: Méridiens Klincksieck, 1989.

Zwingli, Huldrych. *An Exposition of the Christian Faith.* 1531. In *Writings.* Trans. H. Wayne Pipkin. Vol. 1. Pittsburgh Theological Monographs. Allison Park, Pa.: Pickwick Publications, 1984.

——. *Ein Göttliche Vermahnung an die Eidgenossen zu Schwyz* (Exhortation from God to the confederates of Switzerland). 1522.

——. *Eine treue und ernstliche Vermahnung an die Eidgenossen* (A loyal and earnest exhortation to the confederates). 1534.

——. *Short Christian Instruction.* 1523. In *Writings*, vol. 2.

Index

In this index an "f" after a number indicates a separate reference on the next page, and an "ff" indicates separate references on the next two pages. A continuous discussion over two or more pages is indicated by a span of page numbers, e.g., "57-59." *Passim* is used for a cluster of references in close but not consecutive sequence.

Library of Congress Cataloging-in-Publication Data

Colas, Dominique.
    [Glaive et le fléau. English]
    Civil society and fanaticism : conjoined histories / Dominique
Colas ; translated from the French by Amy Jacobs.
      p.   cm. – (Mestizo spaces = Espaces métissés)
    Includes bibliographical references and index.
    ISBN 0-8047-2734-1 (cloth : alk. paper). –
ISBN 0-8047-2736-8 (paper : alk. paper)
    1. Civil society. 2. Fanaticism. I. Title. II. Series: Mestizo
spaces.
JC336.C8313 1997
306.2–dc21   96-50098
                                           CIP

Original printing 1997
Last figure below indicates year of this printing:
06 05 04 03 02 01 00 99 98 97